ECONOMICS

FIFTH EDITION

AS LEVEL

ALAIN ANDERTON

Credits

Original cover design by Susan and Andrew Allen, fifth edition by Tim Button

Cover drawing by Pete Turner, provided by Getty images

Cartoons by Brick

Graphics by Kevin O'Brien and Caroline Waring-Collins

Photography by Andrew Allen and Dave Gray

Edited by Dave Gray

Proofreading by Mike Kidson, Heather Doyle, Sue Oliver

British Library Cataloguing in Publication Data.

A catalogue record for this book is available from the British Library.

ISBN 978 1 4058 9234 6

Pearson Education, Edinburgh Gate, Harlow, Essex, CM20 2JE
Contribution © Alain Anderton
Published 1991 (reprinted 3 times)
Second edition 1995 (reprinted 4 times)
Third edition 2000 (reprinted 4 times)
Fourth edition 2006 (reprinted twice)
Fifth edition 2008
10 9 8

Typesetting by Caroline Waring-Collins (Waring Collins Limited), Ormskirk, L39 2YT.
Printed and bound in Great Britain by Ashford Colour Press Ltd.

Contents

Mioo Economic .

Basic concepts and techniques

1 The basic economic problem 2
2 The function of an economy 10
3 Economic data 17
4 Positive and normative economics 24

Markets

5 The demand curve ✓ *study (✓)* 30
6 The supply curve 39
7 Price determination 45
8 Interrelationships between markets 53
9 Price elasticity of demand ✓ 59
10 Elasticities 66
11 Normal, inferior and Giffen goods ✓ 72
12 Indirect taxes and subsidies ✓ 78

Efficiency and market failure

13 Markets and resource allocation 84
14 Economic efficiency and market failure 90
15 Externalities 96
16 Public and merit goods 106
17 Market stabilisation 112
18 Government failure 122

For Friday

Macro Economics

The national economy

19 National economic performance 129
20 The circular flow of income 135
21 Consumption and saving 143
22 Investment 151
23 Government spending, exports and imports 158
24 Aggregate demand 161
25 Aggregate supply 169
26 Equilibrium output 177
27 Economic growth 185
28 Economic growth and welfare 195
29 The economics of happiness 202
30 Unemployment 209
31 Inflation 217
32 The balance of payments 224
33 Fiscal policy 231
34 Supply side policies 238
35 Monetary policy *not coming* 246
36 Exchange rate policy 253
37 Free market and mixed economies 258

38 Effective study 266
39 Assessment 270

Index 275

Essay will be from " MACROECONOMICS"

Preface

Teachers and students of economics are critical groups of people. Constantly dissatisfied with the materials that they use, they face the problems of limited resources, a wide variety of needs and a constantly changing world. This book is intended to go some way to resolving this example of the basic economic problem.

The book has a number of distinctive features.

Comprehensive The book contains sufficient material to satisfy the demands of students taking a wide range of examinations including AS Level and Higher Grade economics.

Flexible unit structure The material is organised not into chapters but into shorter units. This reflects the organisation of a number of GCSE textbooks, and therefore students should be familiar with this style of presentation. The unit structure also allows the teacher greater freedom to devise a course. Economics teachers have a long tradition of using their main textbooks in a different order to that in which they are presented. So whilst there is a logical order to the book, it has been written on the assumption that teachers and students will piece the units together to suit their own teaching and learning needs. Cross referencing has been used on occasions. This approach also means that it is relatively easy to use the book for a growing number of courses which encompass part of an AS Level specification, such as professional courses with an economics input. To allow flexibility in course construction **Economics (Fifth Edition)** is also available. It is a complete coursebook for AS/A Level, Higher Grade, IB, Higher Education and profeessional courses.

Accessibility The book has been written in a clear and logical style which should make it accessible to all readers. Each unit is divided into short, easily manageable sections. Diagrams contain concise explanations which summarise or support the text.

A workbook The text is interspersed with a large number of questions. These are relatively short for the most part, and, whilst some could be used for extended writing work, most require relatively simple answers. They have been included to help teachers and students assess whether learning and understanding has taken place by providing immediate application of content and skills to given situations. I hope that many will be used as a basis for class discussion as well as being answered in written form. **Economics Teachers' Guide (Fifth Edition)** provides suggested answers to questions that appear in the book.

Applied economics as well as economic theory Many economics courses require teachers and students to have a book covering economic theory **and** an applied economic text. In this book, a systematic approach to applied economics has been included alongside economic theory. Each unit has an applied economics section and some units deal only with applied economics. It should be noted that many of the questions also contain applied economics material, and where sufficiently significant, this has been referred to in the index.

Use of data Modern technology has allowed much of the book to proceed from manuscript to book in a very short period. This has meant that we have been able to use statistics which were available in 2007. Many statistical series therefore go up to 2006/2007, although some were only available for earlier years. At the same time, experience has shown that too many current stories quickly date a book. Materials have therefore been chosen, particularly for the macroeconomic section of the book, from throughout the post-war era, with particular emphasis on the turbulent times of the 1970s and 1980s, as well as the 1990s and 2000s. This approach will help candidates to answer questions which require knowledge of what has happened 'in recent years' or 'over the past decade'.

Study skills and assessment The last two units of this book provide guidance on effective study and the methods of assessment used in economics.

Key terms Many units contain a key terms section. Each section defines new concepts, which appear in capitals in the text of the unit. Taken together, they provide a comprehensive dictionary of economics

Presentation Great care has been taken with how this book is presented. It is hoped that the layout of the book, the use of colour and the use of diagrams will make learning economics a rewarding experience.

Online support MyEconSpace.co.uk is an online support resource for teachers and students using **Economics (Fifth Edition)**. It includes an online student book, an accurate graphing tool, questions from the student book that can be answered and marked online, links to key websites providing access to latest economic data and a regular updated news section. .

Alain Anderton

Acknowledgements

The author and publishers wish to thank the following for permission to reproduce photographs and copyright material. Other copyright material is acknowledged at source.

Shutterstock pp 25(t,b), 89, 95, 116, 122, 126, 127, 128, 132, 141, 157, 158 (l,r), 160, 168, 175, 183, 184, 196(t), 205, 206, 208, 259, 265, Corel pp 3(t), 21, Digital Vision pp 2, 3(b), 7, 16(b), 67(t), 87, 92, Image100 156, Photodisc pp 9, 29, 65, 96(bc,br), 110, 120, 244, 264, Rex Features pp 12, 107, 112, 151, Stockbyte p 175, Stockdisc p 143, Topfoto pp 96(bl), 178.

Office for National Statistics material is Crown Copyright, reproduced with the permission of the Controller of Her Majesty's Stationery Office.

Every effort has been made to locate the copyright owners of material used in this book. Any omissions brought to the notice of the publisher are regretted and will be credited in subsequent printings.

Thanks
I have many thanks to make. Brian Ellis has provided invaluable comments on the fifth edition. Susan Gardner managed the project expertly and provided essential support. Mike Kidson, Sue Oliver and Heather Doyle carried out the unenviable task of proof reading the fifth edition and Waring Collins Limited designed the book with their usual flair and skill. Dave Gray has been a superb editor and, as always, has been an enormous pleasure to work with. Not least, I would like to thank my wife who has performed a variety of tasks, in particular putting up with the stresses and strains of the production of such a large volume. All mistakes in the book, however, remain my own responsibility.

Finally, I would like to thank all those who read this book. It is an enormous privilege to be able to explore the world of economics with you. Your comments are always welcome, whether critical or otherwise. I hope you find the subject as exciting, stimulating and rewarding as I have always found it.

Alain Anderton

Summary

1. Nearly all resources are scarce.
2. Human wants are infinite.
3. Scarce resources and infinite wants give rise to the basic economic problem - resources have to be allocated between competing uses.
4. Allocation involves choice and each choice has an opportunity cost.
5. The production possibility frontier (PPF) shows the maximum potential output of an economy.
6. Production at a point inside the PPF indicates an inefficient use of resources.
7. Growth in the economy will shift the PPF outwards.

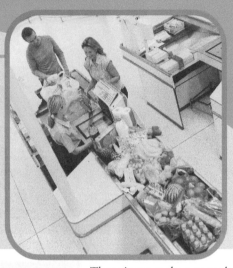

Scarcity

It is often said that we live in a global village. The world's resources are finite; there are only limited amounts of land, water, oil, food and other resources on this planet. Economists therefore say that resources are SCARCE.

Scarcity means that economic agents, such as individuals, firms, governments and international agencies, can only obtain a limited amount of resources at any moment in time. For instance, a family has to live on a fixed budget; it cannot have everything it wants. A firm might want to build a new factory but not have the resources to be able to do so. A government might wish to build new hospitals or devote more resources to its foreign aid programme but not have the finance to make this possible. Resources which are scarce are called ECONOMIC GOODS.

Not all resources are scarce. There is more than enough air on this planet for everyone to be able to breathe as much as they want. Resources which are not scarce are called FREE GOODS. In the past many goods such as food, water and shelter have been free, but as the population of the planet has expanded and as production has increased, so the number of free goods has diminished. Recently, for instance, clean beaches in many parts of the UK have ceased to be a free good to society. Pollution has forced water companies and seaside local authorities to spend resources cleaning up their local environment. With the destruction of the world's rain forests and increasing atmospheric pollution, the air we breathe may no longer remain a free good. Factories may have to purify the air they take from the atmosphere, for instance. This air would then become an economic good.

Infinite wants

People have a limited number of NEEDS which must be satisfied if they are to survive as human beings. Some are material needs, such as food, liquid, heat, shelter and clothing. Others are psychological and emotional needs such as self-esteem and being loved. People's needs are finite. However, no one would choose to live at the level of basic human needs if they could enjoy a higher standard of living.

This is because human WANTS are unlimited. It doesn't matter whether the person is a farmer in Africa, a mystic in India, a manager in the UK or the richest individual in the world, there is always something which he or she wants more of. This can include more food, a bigger house, a longer holiday, a cleaner environment, more love, more friendship, better relationships, more self-esteem, greater fairness or justice, peace, or more time to listen to music, meditate or cultivate the arts.

The basic economic problem

Resources are scarce but wants are infinite. It is this which gives rise to the BASIC ECONOMIC PROBLEM and which forces economic agents to make choices. They have to allocate their scarce resources between competing uses.

Economics is the study of this allocation of resources - the choices that are made by economic agents. Every CHOICE involves a range of alternatives. For instance, should the

Question 1

Time was when people used to take their car out for a Sunday afternoon 'spin'. The novelty of owning a car and the freedom of the road made driving a pleasant leisure pursuit. Today, with 34 million cars registered in the UK, a Sunday afternoon tour could easily turn into a nightmare traffic jam.

Of course, many journeys are trouble free. Traffic is so light that cars do not slow each other down. But most rush hour journeys today occur along congested roads where each extra car on the road adds to the journey time of every other car. When London introduced a £5 a day 'congestion charge', a fee for cars to use roads in central London, the amount of traffic dropped by 17 per cent. This was enough to reduce journey times considerably.

Traffic congestion also greatly increases the amount of pollution created by cars. Our ecosystem can cope with low levels of emissions, but, as cities like Paris and Athens have discovered, high levels of traffic combined with the right weather conditions can lead to sharp increases in pollution levels. The car pollutes the environment anyway because cars emit greenhouse gases. One quarter of CO_2 emissions in the UK come from road transport.

Source: adapted from *Transport Statistics for Great Britain 2007*, Department for Transport; Office for National Statistics.

Explain whether roads are, in any sense, a 'free good' from an economic viewpoint.

Draw up a list of minimum human needs for a teenager living in the UK today. How might this list differ from the needs of a teenager living in Bangladesh or sub-Saharan Africa?

government spend £10 billion in tax revenues on nuclear weapons, better schools or greater care for the elderly? Will you choose to become an accountant, an engineer or a vicar?

These choices can be graded in terms of the benefits to be gained from each alternative. One choice will be the 'best' one and a rational economic agent will take that alternative. But all the other choices will then have to be given up. The benefit lost from the next best alternative is called the OPPORTUNITY COST of the choice. For instance, economics may have been your third choice at 'A' level. Your fourth choice, one which you didn't take up, might have been history. Then the opportunity cost of studying economics at 'A' level is studying

Over the past 10 years, university students have come under increasing financial pressure. For the previous 40 years, the government paid for all student tuition fees. It also gave a grant to students to cover their living expenses, although this grant was means tested according to the income of parents. In the 1990s, the government froze student grants and introduced a system of subsidised student loans to allow students to make up for the falling real value of the grants. In 1998, students for the first time were charged for part of their tuition fees. The amount they had to pay each year was set at £1 000. In 1999, maintenance grants were replaced completely by loans. In 2006, students began to pay £3 000 a year toward tuition fees. The cost of going to university had risen to average over £7 000 a year to the student.

What might be the opportunity cost of the £7 000 in fees and maintenance:
(a) to parents if they pay them on behalf of their sons or daughters;
(b) to students if they have to borrow the money to pay them?

history at 'A' level. Alternatively, you might have enough money to buy just one of your two favourite magazines - *totalDVD* or *DVD Monthly*. If you choose to buy *totalDVD*, then its opportunity cost is the benefit which would have been gained from consuming *DVD Monthly*.

Free goods have no opportunity cost. No resources need be sacrificed when someone, say, breathes air or swims in the sea.

Production possibility frontiers

Over a period of time, resources are scarce and therefore only a finite amount can be produced. For example, an economy might have enough resources at its disposal to be able to produce 30 units of manufactured goods and 30 units of non-manufactured. If it were now to produce more manufactured goods, it would have to give up some of its production of non-manufactured items. This is because the production of a manufactured item has an opportunity cost - in this case the production of non-manufactured. The more manufactured that are produced, the less non-manufactured can be produced.

This can be shown in Figure 1. The curved line is called the PRODUCTION POSSIBILITY FRONTIER (PPF) - other names for it include PRODUCTION POSSIBILITY CURVE or BOUNDARY, and TRANSFORMATION CURVE. The PPF shows the different combinations of economic goods which an economy is able to produce if all resources in the economy are fully and efficiently employed. The economy therefore could be:

- at the point C on its PPF, producing 30 units of manufactured goods and 30 units of non-manufactured;
- at the point D, producing 35 units of manufactured goods and 20 units of non-manufactured;
- at the point A, devoting all of its resources to the production of non-manufactured goods;
- at the points B or E or anywhere else along the line.

The production possibility frontier illustrates clearly the principle of opportunity cost. Assume that the economy is producing at the point C in Figure 1 and it is desired to move to the point D. This means that the output

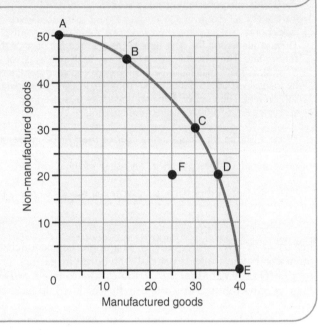

of manufactured goods will increase from 30 to 35 units.
However, the opportunity cost of that (i.e. what has to be given
up because of that choice) is the lost output of non-
manufactured, falling from 30 to 20 units. The opportunity
cost at C of increasing manufacturing production by 5 units is
10 units of non-manufactured.

Another way of expressing this is to use the concept of the
MARGIN. In economics, the margin is a point of possible

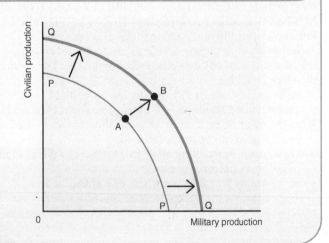

change. At the point C in Figure 1, the economy could produce
more manufactured goods, but at the cost of giving up non-
manufactured goods. For example, the marginal cost of 5 more
units of manufactured goods would be 10 fewer units of non-
manufactured goods. This is shown by the movement from C to
D along the boundary.

The production possibility frontier for an economy is drawn
on the assumption that all resources in the economy are fully
and efficiently employed. If there are unemployed workers or
idle factories, or if production is inefficiently organised, then
the economy cannot be producing on its PPF. It will produce
within the boundary. In Figure 1 the economy could produce
anywhere along the line AE. However, because there is
unemployment in the economy, production is at point F.

The economy cannot be at any point outside its existing
PPF because the PPF, by definition, shows the maximum
production level of the economy. However, it might be able to
move to the right of its PPF in the future if there is **economic
growth**. An increase in the productive potential of an economy
is shown by a shift outwards of the PPF. In Figure 2 economic
growth pushes the PPF from PP to QQ, allowing the economy
to increase its maximum level of production, say, from A to B.
Growth in the economy can happen if:
● the quantity of resources available for production increases;
  for instance there might be an increase in the number of
  workers in the economy, or new factories and offices might
  be built;
● there is an increase in the quality of resources; education will
  make workers more productive whilst technical progress will
  allow machines and production processes to produce more
  with the same amount of resources.
Production possibility frontiers can shift inwards as well as
outwards. The productive potential of an economy can fall. For
example, war can destroy economic infrastructure. A rapid fall
in the number of workers in a population can reduce potential
output. Some environmentalists predict that global warming
will devastate world agriculture and this will have a knock-on
effect on all production. Global warming could therefore lead
to a shift inwards of the world's PPF.

The production possibility frontiers in Figures 1 and 2 have
been drawn concave to the origin (bowing outwards) rather
than as straight lines or as convex lines. This is because it has
been assumed that not all resources in the economy are as
productive in one use compared to another.

Take, for instance, the production of wheat in the UK.
Comparatively little wheat is grown in Wales because the soil
and the climate are less suited to wheat production than in an
area like East Anglia. Let us start from a position where no
wheat is grown at all in the UK. Some farmers then decide to
grow wheat. If production in the economy is to be maximised
it should be grown on the land which is most suited to wheat
production (i.e. where its opportunity cost is lowest). This will
be in an area of the country like East Anglia. As wheat
production expands, land has to be used which is less
productive because land is a finite resource. More and more
marginal land, such as that found in Wales, is used and output
per acre falls. The land could have been used for another form
of production, for instance sheep rearing. The more wheat is
grown, the less is the output per acre and therefore the greater
the cost in terms of sheep production.

In Figure 3 only sheep and wheat are produced in the
economy. If no wheat is produced the economy could produce
0C of sheep. If there is one unit of wheat production only 0B

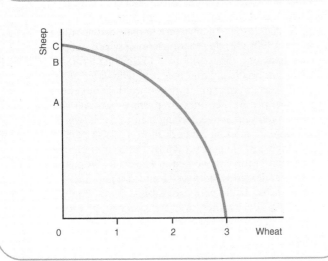

Figure 3 *Opportunity costs*
The production possibility frontier is concave, showing that the opportunity cost of production rises as more of a good is produced.

of sheep can be produced. Therefore the opportunity cost of the first unit of wheat is BC of sheep. The second unit of wheat has a much higher opportunity cost - AB. But if the economy produces wheat only, then the opportunity cost of the third unit of wheat rises to 0A of sheep.

The PPF by itself gives no indication of which combination of goods will be produced in an economy. All it shows is the combination of goods which an economy could produce if output were maximised from a given fixed amount of resources. It shows a range of possibilities and much of economics is

Question 4

Draw a production possibility frontier. The vertical axis shows the production of public sector goods and the horizontal axis shows production of private sector goods. The economy is currently producing at point A on the frontier where 50% of all production is devoted to public sector goods and 50% to private sector goods.

(a) Mark the following points on your drawing.
  (i) Point A.
  (ii) Point B which shows production following the election of a government which increases government spending on both education and the National Health Service.
  (iii) Point C where unemployment is present in the economy.
  (iv) Point D where the government takes over production of all goods and services in the economy.
(b) Draw another diagram putting on it the original production possibility frontier you drew for (a), labelling it AA.
  (i) Draw a new production possibility frontier on the diagram, labelling it PP, which shows the position after a devastating war has hit the economy.
  (ii) Draw another PPF labelling it QQ which shows an increase in productivity in the economy such that output from the same amount of resources increases by 50 per cent in the public sector but twice that amount in the private sector.

concerned with explaining why an economy, ranging from a household economy to the international economy, chooses to produce at one point either on or within its PPF rather than another.

Key terms

Basic economic problem - resources have to be allocated between competing uses because wants are infinite whilst resources are scarce.
Choice - economic choices involve the alternative uses of scarce resources.
Economic goods - goods which are scarce because their use has an opportunity cost.
Free goods - goods which are unlimited in supply and which therefore have no opportunity cost.
Margin - a point of possible change.
Needs - the minimum which is necessary for a person to survive as a human being.

Opportunity cost - the benefits forgone of the next best alternative.
Production possibility frontier (also known as the production possibility curve or the production possibility boundary or the transformation curve) - a curve which shows the maximum potential level of output of one good given a level of output for all other goods in the economy.
Scarce resources - resources which are limited in supply so that choices have to be made about their use.
Wants - desires for the consumption of goods and services.

Applied economics

Work and Leisure

Paid work

Time is a scarce resource. There are only 24 hours in a day and 365 days in a year. Average life expectancy for a UK male born in 2006 was 76.8 and 81.2 for a female. So people have to make choices about how to allocate their time.

One fundamental choice is how to divide time between work and leisure. Work can be narrowly defined as paid work. Statistics suggest that men are in paid employment for less time over their whole life than before. The position for women is more complicated.

- Table 1 shows that there has been a small reduction in the average number of paid hours worked per week over the past 20 years.
- Holiday entitlements have shortened the working year. All full time workers are now entitled to 4 weeks paid holiday each year which includes bank holidays. In 1970, the average was only 2 weeks.
- Men are working fewer years over their lifetime. Figure 4 shows how economic activity rates have changed since 1971. The economic activity rate in Figure 4 is the percentage of the population (men aged 16-64 and women aged 16-59) in work or seeking work (i.e. officially unemployed). Over time,

Table 1 Average weekly hours of full-time employees

	1986	2006
Males	41.8	38.9
Females	37.3	34.0

Source: adapted from *Annual Abstract of Statistics*, Office for National Statistics.

Figure 4 Employment rates: by sex

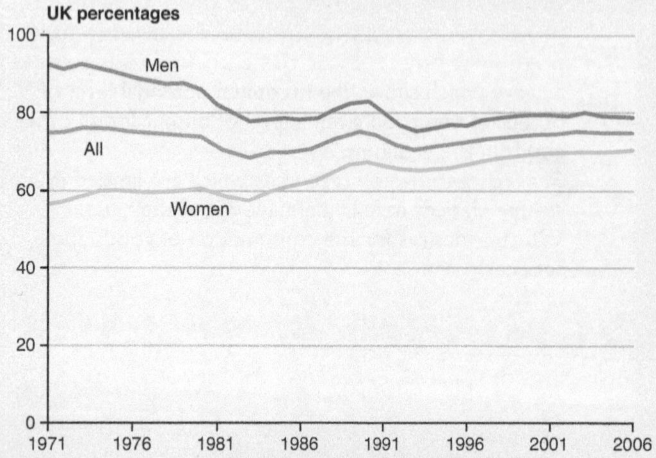

Source: adapted from *Social Trends, 2007*, Office for National Statistics.

more males are choosing to stay longer in education. There has also been a smaller fall in activity rates for men aged 25-64. The increase in male activity rates in the 1990s was due to job creation which pulled men back into the workforce. In the long term, many are predicting that men will retire later. This is partly because they are in better health than before. But also pension schemes are pushing back the official retirement age, forcing men to work longer.

- Women are tending to work more years in paid employment. This is shown by the continuing rise in activity rates for women in Figure 4. Women are better educated than in 1971 and can get much better jobs. Child care provision is continuing to improve. For women over 50, like men, pension ages are being pushed back.

The motivators for paid work

People work for a variety of motives, including the satisfaction of doing a job and enjoying being part of a team. However, the primary motivator is pay. When workers retire, they might choose to undertake voluntary work, or do jobs about the house which previously they would have paid someone else to do, but rarely will they will put the time or the energy into these activities that they put into their previous paid job. Over time, the opportunity cost of not working has been rising because wages have been rising. Since 1945, earnings have roughly been doubling every 30 years in real terms (i.e. after inflation has been taken into account). Workers today can buy far more goods and services than their parents or grandparents at a similar age. If a 40 year old doesn't work today, he or she will have to forego the purchase of far more goods and services than, say, 30 years ago. This is arguably the most important reason why more and more women are choosing to stay in work rather than give up work to stay at home to bring up their families.

For those taking early retirement, the opportunity cost of leisure time is typically far less than for other workers. When they retire, they receive a pension. Hence, the money foregone is only the difference between what they would have earned and their pension. Tax, national insurance contributions and work related payments like pension contributions or costs of commuting to work all help to reduce the monetary value of a wage. Hence, many workers taking early retirement find that their new retirement income is not that much below their old take home pay. The benefits of the extra leisure time they can gain by retiring far outweigh the losses in terms of the goods and services they could buy had they stayed in work.

Early retirement, however, is likely to become less common in the future. With rising life expectancies, employers are finding it more expensive to provide pensions for workers. The public sector is reacting by trying to force up retirement ages and make it more difficult for workers to retire early. Private sector employers are tending to close down their existing pension schemes and replace them with far less generous schemes where workers have to save more to get the same pension. The result is that the opportunity cost of retiring early is likely to rise substantially. Workers will react by staying on in work longer.

Non-paid work

Paid work is not the only type of work undertaken by individuals. People also have to work at home, cooking, cleaning, maintaining equipment and property and looking after others, particularly children, the sick and the elderly. Table 2 shows that women tend to spend nearly twice as much time on housework and childcare as men. They also spend less time on leisure activities than men. However, men tend to spend more time on employment and study. The traditional stereotype of the man coming home from work and expecting the house to be clean, the children fetched from school and the meal on the table is to some extent still true, even though more and more women are going out to work.

Leisure

Individuals spend their leisure time in a variety of ways. Table 3 shows participation rates in the main home-based leisure activities and how they have changed over time. The most popular leisure activity is watching television. Nearly everybody had watched some television in the four weeks prior to being interviewed for the survey. Equally, seeing friends or relatives is a highly popular activity. Table 3 shows that there are gender differences between leisure activities. Men are far more likely to do DIY and gardening, whilst women are more likely to do dressmaking, needlework and knitting. This time series shows that participation rates in most leisure activities have been rising over time. A greater proportion of the population, for example, read books, did DIY or did some gardening at the end of the twentieth century than they did in the 1970s. This greater variety of leisure activities has probably come about for a variety of reasons: increased incomes, allowing people to afford to engage in particular activities such as listening to CDs; better education, giving people access to activities such as reading; and

Seeing friends is a highly popular pastime.

Table 2 Adults aged 16+, time spent on main activities by sex, 2005

	Hours and minutes per day	
	Males	Females
Sleep	8.04	8.18
Resting	0.43	0.48
Personal care	0.40	0.48
Eating and drinking	1.25	1.19
Leisure		
Watching TV/DVD and listening to radio/music	2.50	2.25
Social life and entertainment/culture	1.22	1.32
Hobbies and games	0.37	0.23
Sport	0.13	0.07
Reading	0.23	0.26
All leisure	5.25	4.53
Employment and study	3.45	2.26
Housework	1.41	3.00
Childcare	0.15	0.32
Voluntary work and meetings	0.15	0.20
Travel	1.32	1.22
Other	0.13	0.15

Source: adapted from www.statistics.gov.uk

Table 3 Participation in home-based leisure activities: by sex

Great Britain				Percentages
	1977	1986	1996	2002
Males				
Watching TV	97	98	99	99
Visiting/entertaining				
friends or relations	89	92	95	-
Listening to recorded music	64	69	79	83
Reading books	52	52	58	58
DIY	51	54	58	-
Gardening	49	47	52	-
Dressmaking/needlework/knitting	2	3	3	-
Females				
Watching TV	97	98	99	99
Visiting/entertaining				
friends or relations	93	95	97	-
Listening to recorded music	60	65	77	83
Reading books	57	64	71	72
DIY	22	27	30	-
Gardening	35	39	45	-
Dressmaking/needlework/knitting	51	48	37	-

Source: adapted from *Social Trends, General Household Survey,* Office for National Statistics.

less time spent at work giving more time for DIY or gardening.

Individuals have to allocate their scarce resources of time and money between different leisure pursuits. Children tend to be time rich but financially poor. 45 year olds tend to be the reverse: time poor but financially better off. Old age pensioners are time rich but less financially well off than when they were working. Their health may also preclude them from activities such as taking part in sport. These constraints could be represented on a production

possibility frontier. For instance, a diagram could be drawn showing the trade off between home based leisure pursuits and leisure activities away from the home. The more time spent in the pub means that less time is available to watch television at home or do gardening. Equally, a production possibility diagram could be used to illustrate the trade-off between work and leisure. The more time spent at work, the less leisure time is available. Ultimately, choices have to be made between work and leisure and individuals have to assume responsibility for the choices they make.

DataQuestion — Production possibility frontiers

The break up of Eastern Europe

When communism in Eastern Europe and the former Soviet Union was replaced by more democratic systems of government at the end of the 1980s, there was a move away from state control of the economy towards a market-led economy. Before, the state had often decided which factories were to produce what products, and would issue instructions about who was to buy the resulting output. In the new market-led system, factories had to find buyers for their products. The result was that many factories closed down. Consumers began buying foreign made goods, or found their incomes drastically slashed as they were made redundant from closing enterprises. Factories making goods for the defence industry were particularly badly affected as governments cut their spending on defence. Some attempted to transfer their skills to making civilian goods, but it often proved impossible to make the jump from the manufacture of fighter jets to the manufacture of washing machines. The total incomes and output of countries such as Russia and Georgia were actually lower in 2006 than they were in 1990. These countries have faced enormous problems in making the transition. Others, such as Hungary, have been more successful and have seen a rise in their total incomes and output.

Table 4 National income, selected countries in Eastern Europe and the former Soviet Union, 2006 as a % of 1990

	%
Albania	64.6
Belarus	39.6
Bulgaria	9.8
Croatia	11.0
Georgia	- 41.9
Hungary	38.7
Romania	19.2
Russian Federation	- 3.4
Serbia	- 28.2

Source: adapted from United Nations, unstats.un.org.

Former Yugoslavia

The collapse of communism in Eastern Europe was a mixed blessing for some. In Yugoslavia, it led to the break-up of the federation of states which formed the country. Serbia, which considered itself the most important part of the federation, strongly resisted the process. In 1992, it fought a war with Croatia and over-ran parts of that country which had majority Serb populations. Serbia then helped fuel a civil war in Bosnia-Herzegovina. In 1999, Serbian forces were accused of attempting to ethnically cleanse the majority Albanian population from its province of Kosovo. This resulted in intervention by US and European troops. Serbia saw its economy shrink as infrastructure, such as houses and factories, was destroyed in fighting. Embargoes by the USA and the EU on trade with Serbia disrupted exports and imports. It was only from 2000 when peace was restored in the region that Serbia's economy began to grow again. Even then, as Table 5 shows, Serbia paid a heavy price for its aggression towards its neighbours. Croatia, which also engaged in war, was less badly affected because it had stopped fighting by the mid-1990s, allowing its economy to begin growing again.

Source: adapted from www.state.gov; www.washingtonpost.com.

Table 5 Croatia and Serbia, national income, 2006 as a % of 1990

	%
Croatia	+ 11.0
Serbia	- 28.2

Source: adapted from United Nations, *Economic Survey of Europe.*

China

Since the mid-1970s, China has been growing dramatically. Currently, it is growing by nearly 10 per cent per annum. This means that output is doubling roughly every seven years. It is not difficult to understand why the Chinese economy has been so successful. By the mid-1970s, it already had a relatively well educated workforce. compared to other poor developing countries. However, its economy was otherwise inefficient and backward. From the mid-1970s, there was a gradual easing of Communist control of the economy which allowed ordinary Chinese people to set up their own businesses in a more free market style economy. Exports began to be encouraged. This linked China to the global economy. Finally, there was a considerable flow of investment money and technological know-how into China. Foreign investors were keen to take advantage of cheap labour and found the lure of what is likely to become the world's largest economy irresistible.

Table 6 *China, average annual growth in real national income, 1971-2006*

				Percentage
	1971-1980	1981-1990	1991-2000	2001-2006
National income	6.3	9.4	10.5	9.7

Source: adapted from unstats.un.org.

Of all the world's regions, Africa has had the most disappointing economic performance over the past few decades. Sub-Saharan Africa in particular has performed poorly. As Table 7 shows, average annual growth in national income was only 1.8 per cent in the 1980s and 2.4 per cent in the 1990s. This was below other regions of the world. It was also not enough to prevent average incomes falling. This is because population growth was higher than growth in national income.

Table 7 *Sub-Saharan Africa: average annual real growth in national income and national income per head*

			Percentage
	1980-89	1990-99	2000-04
National income	1.8	2.4	4.0
National income per head	-1.1	-0.2	1.6

Source: adapted from World Bank, *African Development Indicators 2006*

A number of factors account for these statistics. Economic management was often poor and governments were corrupt. Disastrous borrowing in the late 1970s and 1980s left many countries with foreign debts they couldn't afford to repay. There was a failure to invest in everything from education to health care to roads. Too few businesses were set up. The aids epidemic has also hit incomes because it has hit at people in the prime of their lives when they could be most productive.

Since the start of the new millennium, growth figures have improved. However, Africa needs much higher growth rates to raise its peoples out of poverty. At the moment, with India growing at around 6 per cent per annum and China at 10 per cent, the gulf between Sub-Saharan Africa and the rest of the world is increasing.

1. What is a production possibility frontier for an economy?
2. Explain why a production possibility frontier might shift inwards or outwards. Illustrate your answer with examples from the data.
3. A peace group has put forward a proposal that the UK should halve its spending on defence, including giving up its nuclear capability. Using production possibility frontiers, evaluate the possible economic implications of this proposal.

2 The function of an economy

Summary

1. An economy is a social organisation through which decisions about what, how and for whom to produce are made.
2. The factors of production – land, labour, capital and entrepreneurship – are combined together to create goods and services for consumption.
3. Specialisation and the division of labour give rise to large gains in productivity.
4. The economy is divided into three sectors, primary, secondary and tertiary.
5. Markets exist for buyers and sellers to exchange goods and services using barter or money.
6. The main actors in the economy, consumers, firms and government, have different objectives. Consumers, for instance, wish to maximise their welfare whilst firms might wish to maximise profit.

What is an economy?

Economic resources are scarce whilst human wants are infinite. An economy is a system which attempts to solve this basic economic problem. There are many different levels and types of economy. There is the household economy, the local economy, the national economy and the international economy. There are free market economies which attempt to solve the economic problem with the minimum intervention of government and command economies where the state makes most resource allocation decisions. Although these economies are different, they all face the same problem.

Economists distinguish three parts to the economic problem.

- **What** is to be produced? An economy can choose the mix of goods to produce. For instance, what proportion of total output should be spent on defence? What proportion should be spent on protecting the environment? What proportion should be invested for the future? What proportion should be manufactured goods and what proportion services?
- **How** is production to be organised? For instance, are DVD players to be made in the UK, Japan or Taiwan? Should car bodies be made out of steel or fibreglass? Would it better to automate a production line or carry on using unskilled workers?
- **For whom** is production to take place? What proportion of output should go to workers? How much should pensioners get? What should be the balance between incomes in the UK and those in Bangladesh?

An economic system needs to provide answers to all these questions.

Economic resources

Economists commonly distinguish three types of resources available for use in the production process. They call these resources the FACTORS OF PRODUCTION.

LAND is not only land itself but all natural resources below the earth, on the earth, in the atmosphere and in the sea. Everything from gold deposits to rainwater and natural forests are examples of land.

NON-RENEWABLE RESOURCES, such as coal, oil, gold and copper, are land resources which once used will never be replaced. If we use them today, they are not available for use by our children or our children's children. RENEWABLE RESOURCES, on the other hand, can be used and replaced. Examples are fish stocks, forests, or water.

SUSTAINABLE RESOURCES are a particular type of renewable resource. Sustainable resources are ones which can be exploited economically and which will not diminish or run out. A forest is a renewable resource. However, it is only a sustainable resource if it survives over time despite economic activities such as commercial logging or farming. It ceases to be a sustainable resource if it is cleared to make way for a motorway. NON-SUSTAINABLE RESOURCES are resources which are diminishing over time due to economic exploitation. Oil is a non-sustainable resource because it cannot be replaced.

Question 1

Consider your household economy.

(a) What is produced by your household (e.g. cooking services, cleaning services, accommodation, products outside the home)?

(b) How is production organised (e.g. who does the cooking, what equipment is used, when is the cooking done)?

(c) For whom does production take place (e.g. for mother, for father)?

(d) Do you think your household economy should be organised in a different way? Justify your answer.

LABOUR is the workforce of an economy - everybody from housepersons to doctors, vicars and cabinet ministers. Not all workers are the same. Each worker has a unique set of inherent characteristics including intelligence, manual dexterity and emotional stability. But workers are also the products of education and training. The value of a worker is called his or her HUMAN CAPITAL. Education and training will increase the value of that human capital, enabling the worker to be more productive.

CAPITAL is the manufactured stock of tools, machines, factories, offices, roads and other resources which is used in the production of goods and services. Capital is of two types. WORKING or CIRCULATING CAPITAL is stocks of raw materials, semi-manufactured and finished goods which are waiting to be sold. These stocks circulate through the production process till they are finally sold to a consumer. FIXED CAPITAL is the stock of factories, offices, plant and machinery. Fixed capital is fixed in the sense that it will not be transformed into a final product as working capital will. It is used to transform working capital into finished products.

Sometimes a fourth factor of production is distinguished. This is ENTREPRENEURSHIP. Entrepreneurs are individuals who:
- organise production - organise land, labour and capital in the production of goods and services;
- take risks - with their own money and the financial capital of others, they buy factors of production to produce goods and services in the hope that they will be able to make a profit but in the knowledge that at worst they could lose all their money and go bankrupt.

Entrepreneurs are typically the owners of small and medium sized businesses who run those businesses on a day to day basis. However, **managers** in companies can also be entrepreneurial if they both organise resources and take risks on behalf of their company.

Specialisation

When he was alone on his desert island, Robinson Crusoe found that he had to perform all economic tasks by himself. When Man Friday came along he quickly abandoned this mode of production and specialised. SPECIALISATION is the production of a limited range of goods by an individual or firm or country in co-operation with others so that together a complete range of goods is produced.

Specialisation can occur between nations. For instance, a country like Honduras produces bananas and trades those for cars produced in the United States. **Globalisation** is currently intensifying this process of specialisation between nations. Specialisation can also occur within economies. Regional economies specialise. In the UK, Stoke-on-Trent specialises in pottery whilst London specialises in financial services.

Specialisation by individuals is called THE DIVISION OF LABOUR. Adam Smith, in a passage in his famous book *An Enquiry into the Nature and Causes of the Wealth of Nations* (1776), described the division of labour amongst pin workers. He wrote:

A workman not educated to this business ... could scarce ... make one pin in a day, and certainly could not make twenty. But in the way in which this business is now carried on, ... it is divided into a number of branches ... One man draws out the wire, another straightens it, a third cuts it, a fourth points, a fifth grinds it at the top for receiving the head; to make the head requires two or three distinct operations; to put it on is a peculiar business, to whiten the pins is another; it is even a trade by itself to put them into the paper.

He pointed out that one worker might be able to make 20 pins a day if he were to complete all the processes himself. But ten workers together specialising in a variety of tasks could, he estimated, make 48 000 pins.

This enormous increase in PRODUCTIVITY (output per unit of input employed) arises from both increases in LABOUR PRODUCTIVITY (output per worker) and CAPITAL PRODUCTIVITY (output per unit of capital employed).
- Specialisation enables workers to gain skills in a narrow range of tasks. These skills enable individual workers to be far more productive than if they were jacks-of-all-trades. In a modern economy a person could not possibly hope to be able to take on every job which society requires.
- The division of labour makes it cost-effective to provide workers with specialist tools. For instance, it would not be profitable to provide every farm worker with a tractor. But it is possible to provide a group of workers with a tractor which they can then share.
- Time is saved because a worker is not constantly changing tasks, moving around from place to place and using different machinery and tools.
- Workers can specialise in those tasks to which they are best suited.

The division of labour has its limits. If jobs are divided up too much, the work can become tedious and monotonous. Workers feel alienated from their work. This will result in poorer quality of work and less output per person. Workers will do everything possible to avoid work - going to the toilet, lingering over breaks and reporting sick for instance. The size of the market too will limit the division of labour. A shop owner in a village might want to specialise in selling health foods but finds that in order to survive she has to sell other products as well.

Over-specialisation also has its disadvantages. For example, the north of England, Wales, Scotland and Northern Ireland suffered high unemployment in the 1960s, 1970s and 1980s as their traditional heavy industry, such as coal mining and shipbuilding, declined and was not replaced by enough new service sector jobs. Another problem with specialisation is that a breakdown in part of the chain of production can cause chaos within the system. Eighteen Toyota production plants in Japan were brought to a halt for two weeks in 1997 when the factory of the sole supplier of brake parts to Toyota in Japan was destroyed in a fire. Toyota had to work round the clock with new suppliers to get production going again. Equally, London businesses can be crippled by an Underground strike or a bus strike.

Sectors of the economy

Economies are structured into three main sectors. In the PRIMARY SECTOR of the economy, raw materials are extracted and food is grown. Examples of primary sector industries are agriculture, forestry, fishing, oil extraction and mining. In the SECONDARY or MANUFACTURING SECTOR, raw materials are transformed into goods. Examples of secondary sector industries are motor manufacturing, food processing, furniture making and steel production. The TERTIARY or SERVICE SECTOR produces services such as transport, sport and leisure, distribution,

Question 2

(a) Explain, with the help of the photograph, what is meant by 'specialisation'.
(b) What might be some of the (i) advantages to firms and (ii) disadvantages to workers of the division of labour shown in the photograph?

financial services, education and health.

Most firms tend to operate in just one of these sectors, specialising in producing raw materials, manufactured goods or services. Some very large firms, such as BP, operate across all three sectors, from the extraction of oil to its refining and sale to the public through petrol stations.

Money and exchange

Specialisation has enabled people to enjoy a standard of living which would be impossible to achieve through self-sufficiency. Specialisation, however, necessitates exchange. Workers can only specialise in refuse collecting, for instance, if they know that they will be able to exchange their services for other goods and services such as food, housing and transport.

Exchange for most of history has meant **barter** - swapping one good for another. However, barter has many disadvantages and it would be impossible to run a modern sophisticated economy using barter as a means or **medium of exchange**. It was the development of **money** that enabled trade and specialisation to transform economies into what we know today. Money is anything which is widely accepted as payment for goods received, services performed, or repayment of past debt. In a modern economy, it ranges from notes and coins to money in bank accounts and deposits in building society accounts.

Markets

Markets play a fundamental role in almost all economies today. Markets are where buyers and sellers meet. For economists, markets are not just street markets. Buying and selling can take place in newspapers and magazines, through mail order or over the telephone in financial deals in the City of London, or on industrial estates as well as in high street shopping centres. A MARKET is any convenient set of arrangements by which buyers and sellers communicate to exchange goods and services.

Economists group buyers and sellers together. For

instance, there is an international market for oil where large companies and governments buy and sell oil. There are also national markets for oil. Not every company or government involved in the buying and selling of oil in the UK, say, will be involved in the US or the Malaysian oil markets. There are also regional and local markets for oil. In your area there will be a small number of petrol filling stations (sellers of petrol) where you (the buyers) are able to buy petrol. All these markets are inter-linked but they are also separate. A worldwide increase in the price of oil may or may not filter down to an increase in the price of petrol at the pumps in your local area. Equally, petrol prices in your area may increase when prices at a national and international level remain constant.

How buyers and sellers are grouped together and therefore how markets are defined depends upon what is being studied. We could study the tyre industry or we could consider the market for cars and car components which includes part but not all of the tyre industry. Alternatively, we might want to analyse the market for rubber, which would necessitate a study of rubber purchased by tyre producers.

Many Western economists argue that specialisation, exchange and the market lie at the heart of today's economic prosperity in the industrial world. Whilst it is likely that the market system is a powerful engine of prosperity, we shall see that it does not always lead to the most efficient allocation of resources.

Question 3

Table 2 Shops selling grocery items in Burscough	
	Number
Small independent grocers	2
Convenience store grocers	1
Supermarket grocers	1

Burscough is a town in Lancashire which has shops selling grocery items such as fresh vegetables, dairy products or tinned food.

(a) Who might be the buyers and sellers in the local Burscough market for grocery products?
(b) What is the relationship between this market and the market for (i) meat and (ii) petrol?

The objectives of economic actors

There are four main types of economic actors in a market economy - consumers, workers, firms and governments. It is important to understand what are the economic objectives of each of these sets of actors.

Consumers In economics, consumers are assumed to want to maximise their own ECONOMIC WELFARE, sometimes referred to as UTILITY or **satisfaction**. They are faced with the problem of scarcity. They don't have enough income to be able to purchase all the goods or services that they would like. So they have to allocate their resources to achieve their objective. To do this, they consider the utility to be gained from consuming an extra unit of a product with its opportunity cost. If there is 30p to be spent, would it best be spent on a Mars Bar, a newspaper or a gift to a charity? If you could afford it, would you prefer to move to a larger but more expensive house, or spend the money on going out more to restaurants, or take more holidays abroad? Decisions are made at the **margin**. This means that consumers don't look at their overall spending every time they want to spend an extra 30p. They just consider the alternatives of that decision to spend 30p and what will give them the highest utility with that 30p.

Sometimes it is argued that economics portrays consumers as being purely selfish. This isn't true. Consumers do spend money on giving to charity. Parents spend money on their children when the money could be spent on themselves. Seventeen year old students buy presents for other people. What this shows, according to economists, is that the utility gained from giving money away or spending it on others can be higher than from spending it on oneself. However, individuals are more likely to spend money on those in their immediate family than others. This shows that the utility to be gained from paying for a holiday for your child is usually higher than paying for a holiday for a disabled person you do not know.

Workers Workers are assumed in economics to want to maximise their own welfare at work. Evidence suggests that the most important factor in determining welfare is the level of pay. So workers are assumed to want to maximise their earnings in a job. However, other factors are also important. Payment can come in the form of fringe benefits, like company cars. Satisfaction at work is also very important. Many workers could earn more elsewhere but choose to stay in their present employment because they enjoy the job and the workplace.

Firms The objectives of firms are often mixed. However, in the UK and the USA, the usual assumption is that firms are in business to maximise their PROFITS. This is because firms are owned by private individuals who want to maximise their return on ownership. This is usually achieved if the firm is making the highest level of profit possible. In Japan and continental Europe, there is much more of a tradition that the owners of firms are just one of the STAKEHOLDERS in a business. Workers, consumers and the local community should also have some say in how a business is run. Making profit would then only be one objective amongst many for firms.

Governments Governments have traditionally been assumed to want to maximise the welfare of the citizens of their country or locality. They act in the best interests of all. This can be very difficult because it is often not immediately obvious what are the costs and benefits of a decision. Nor is there often a consensus about what value to put on the gains and losses of different groups. For instance, in the 1990s the UK government brought the motorway building programme to a virtual halt following the growing feeling that motorways were destroying the environment and were therefore an economic 'bad' rather than a 'good'. However, many, particularly in industry, would argue that the environmental costs of new motorway building are vastly exaggerated and that the benefits of faster journey times more than outweigh any environmental costs.

Governments which act in the best interests of their citizens face a difficult task. However, it can also be argued that governments don't act to maximise the welfare of society. Governments are run by individuals and it could be that they act in their own interest. Certain Third World countries have immense economic problems because their governments are not impartial, but are run for the monetary benefit of the few that can extort bribes from citizens. There is equally a long tradition of 'pork barrel politics'. This is where politicians try to stay in power by giving benefits to those groups who are important at election times. In the UK, it is expected that MPs (Members of Parliament) will fight for the interests of their constituents even if this clearly does not lead to an overall increase in welfare for the country as a whole.

So governments may have a variety of motives when making decisions. In an ideal world, governments should act impartially to maximise the welfare of society. In practice they may fall short of this.

Question 4

In April 2005, just weeks before a General Election, MG Rover, the last remaining UK owned mass car manufacturer, announced that it was going into receivership. The Labour government immediately announced a £150 million aid package. This included up to £50 million for training workers made redundant at MG Rover and its suppliers, over £40 million to cover redundancy payments and protective awards for Longbridge workers, £24 million to establish a loan fund to help otherwise viable businesses affected by MG Rover's collapse and £41.6 million for MG Rover suppliers who were left being owed large sums of money for products delivered but not paid for.

It could be argued that the aid package smacked of favouritism and 'election year politics'. MG Rover's main plant at Longbridge in Birmingham, where most of the company's 5 000 workers were employed, was in an area with several marginal constituencies. A swing to the Conservatives of just a few per cent of the voters would have turned those constituencies from being Labour held to Conservative held.

Many commentators pointed out that very few of the hundreds of thousands of workers made redundant each year across the UK received such generous help.

On the other hand, trade unions representing workers at Longbridge argued that the package was too small. There were calls for the government to provide a generous aid package to any buyer for MG Rover which would guarantee the safeguarding of its 5 000 jobs. It was pointed out that it was not just the MG Rover jobs which were at stake. It was also all the jobs at suppliers which would disappear if production ceased at Longbridge.

Source: adapted from www.manifest.co.uk.

(a) Suggest what might have been the motives of the UK government in offering a £150 million aid package for MG Rover.
(b) What might have motivated trade unions to call for government aid to help keep the Longbridge plant open?

Key terms

Capital productivity - output per unit of capital employed.

Division of labour - specialisation by workers.

Factors of production - the inputs to the production process: land, which is all natural resources; labour, which is the workforce; capital, which is the stock of manufactured resources used in the production of goods and services; entrepreneurs, individuals who seek out profitable opportunities for production and take risks in attempting to exploit these.

Fixed capital - economic resources such as factories and hospitals which are used to transform working capital into goods and services.

Human capital - the value of the productive potential of an individual or group of workers. It is made up of the skills, talents, education and training of an individual or group and represents the value of future earnings and production.

Labour productivity - output per worker.

Market - any convenient set of arrangements by which buyers and sellers communicate to exchange goods and services.

Non-renewable resources - resources, such as coal or oil, which once exploited cannot be replaced.

Non-sustainable resource - resource which is being economically exploited in such a way that it is being reduced over time.

Primary sector - extractive and agricultural industries.

Productivity - output per unit of input employed.

Profits - the reward to the owners of a business. It is the difference between a firm's revenues and its costs.

Renewable resources - resources, such as fish stocks or forests, which can be exploited over and over again because they have the potential to renew themselves.

Secondary sector - production of goods, mainly manufactured.

Specialisation - a system of organisation where economic units such as households or nations are not self-sufficient but concentrate on producing certain goods and services and trading the surplus with others.

Stakeholders - groups of people which have an interest in a firm, such as shareholders, customers, suppliers, workers, the local community in which it operates and government.

Sustainable resource - renewable resource which is being economically exploited in such a way that it will not diminish or run out.

Tertiary sector - production of services.

Utility - the satisfaction derived from consuming a good.

Welfare - the well being of an economic agent or group of economic agents.

Working or circulating capital - resources which are in the production system waiting to be transformed into goods or other materials before being finally sold to the consumer.

Applied economics

Sport and Leisure

Different markets

The sport and leisure market is made up of many different markets. For instance, there is a market for travel and tourism, a market for football, a television entertainment market and a restaurant market. Some of these markets overlap. A Japanese visitor to the UK might eat in a restaurant in London and so the tourism and the 'eating out' markets overlap. Some markets are closely linked. Pubs near a football stadium are likely to benefit from increased trade on the day of matches.

Figure 1 gives data for one segment of this market, the market for visitor attractions, such as historic houses, theme parks and museums. The figures given are for attractions like museums such as the National Gallery, Historic properties such as the Tower of London and steam railways such as the Severn Valley Railway. The data show that the most popular type of visitor attraction in 2006 was museums and art galleries. This was closely followed by historic properties. These two types of visitor attraction accounted for approximately 50 per cent of the market by visitor numbers.

Economic resources

Each market uses land, labour and capital to produce services. For instance, a visit to a National Trust property utilises land as a factor. There is likely to be a house built on land and the gardens too use land as their basic resource. Labour is needed for the upkeep of the property and to provide services to the visitor, including volunteers on the door and in the tea shop. Buildings on the property represent capital.

There are many examples of entrepreneurs in the market. Andrew Lloyd Webber, for instance, is an entrepreneur putting on musical shows for the mass market. Rich owners of football clubs are entrepreneurs too.

Objectives of participants in the market

In a market there are buyers and sellers. The objectives of consumers are to maximise their welfare or utility when buying sport and leisure services. They consider whether they will get more satisfaction per pound spent from going to a pub or going to a nightclub, for instance. They have to choose between spending on sport and leisure services and all other goods and services, like clothes or consumer durables. They also have to choose between different sport and leisure services.

There is a number of different types of suppliers to the market. First there are firms whose aim is to maximise profit. For example, Table 2 shows that 29 per cent of tourist attractions in the UK were either privately owned by an individual or group of individuals, or by a company with shareholders. Their aim is likely to be to make a profit from that attraction. Alton Towers, Blackpool Pleasure Beach, Chessington World of Adventures or Legoland at Windsor are not charities, but run for profit for the benefit of their owners.

Second, however, as Table 2 shows, there are many examples of charities and trusts in the market, making up 31 per cent of visitor attractions. The largest is the National Trust. Charities and trusts do not necessarily have the same objectives, but few are likely to have profit maximisation as their principal objective. The National Trust has as its primary aim to 'preserve places of historic interest and natural beauty permanently for the nation to enjoy'. Financially, it must break even over time to survive. However, it is unlikely to see maximising profits or revenues as its priority. For instance, there are restrictions on the number of visitors to some properties that it owns because more visitors would lead to unacceptable levels of wear and tear.

Third, government is a major provider of services. If English Heritage, Historic Scotland and Cadw are included as part of government, Table 2 shows that 34 per cent of visitor attractions in the UK are owned by different government bodies. They include the British Museum, the Tower of London and London Zoo. The management of these tourist attractions want to maximise resources available to them, particularly by securing larger grants from government. However, government itself is often interested in minimising spending on such bodies because of conflicting objectives. Government may prefer to spend more money on the National Health Service than on museums. The arts and sport have tended to be subsidised by government. Concerning the arts, there is a belief that 'culture' is important to the health of the nation. Hence, the Royal Opera House is heavily subsidised, whilst an Andrew Lloyd Webber production like The Phantom of the Opera receives no subsidy. Some would argue that there is no difference between a Mozart opera like The Marriage of Figaro and The Phantom of the Opera. Indeed, The Phantom of the Opera might be a better case for subsidy because more foreign tourists are likely to see it than a Royal Opera House production. Tourism brings money into the country and creates prosperity.

The same arguments apply to sport. There is an argument that everyone should have access to sporting facilities. Traditionally, local authorities have subsidised swimming pools, leisure centres and sports facilities. Sometimes government is swayed by lobbying from a particular part of the country for spending on the arts or leisure. Local MPs fight for grants for new theatres or recreational facilities. So government is likely to be motivated by a variety of factors when deciding on spending on sport and leisure.

Table 2 UK distribution of attractions by ownership type, 2002

Ownership	Attraction	Visits
Sample	3,295	284.8m
	%	%
Government	5	17
English Heritage/Historic Scotland/Cadw	7	4
Local Authority	22	23
Privately owned	27	26
Public company/plc	2	3
The National Trust/National Trust for Scotland	10	6
Other trust/charity	21	14
Educational institution	2	1
Religious body	3	5
Other	2	1
UK	100	100

Source: adapted from UK Research Liaison Group, www.staruk.org.uk.

Figure 1 English tourist attractions: number of visitors, 2006

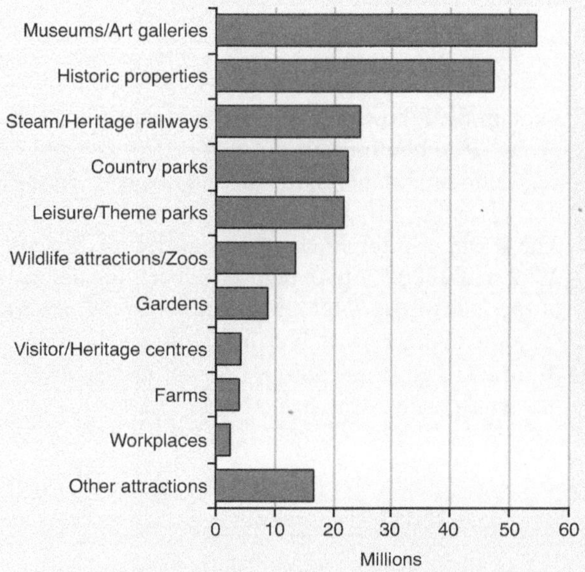

Source: adapted from VisitBritain, *Annual Visits to Visitor Attractions Survey 2006.*

DataQuestion

The oil industry

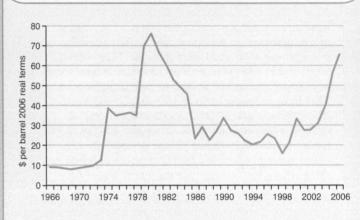

Figure 2 Brent crude oil price 1966-2006

Source: adapted from UK Offshore Operators Association, *Activity Survey 2006*.

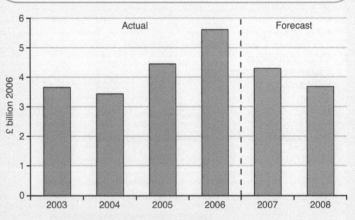

Figure 3 Capital investment in oil and gas, UK continental shelf, £ billion at 2006 prices

Source: adapted from UK Offshore Operators Association, *Activity Survey 2006*.

Chancellor announces rise in the tax levied on North Sea oil producers following record crude prices.

Motorists switch to smaller, more fuel efficient cars as petrol prices stay high.

Workers on oil rigs pressing for large pay increases.

North Sea oil producers cut back their spending on investment in exploration and new equipment because of higher costs and taxes

1. Explain the following economic concepts in the context of the UK oil industry:
   (a) economic resources; (b) specialisation; (c) money and exchange; (d) markets.
2. The world price of oil changed significantly between 2002 and 2006. What might have been the objectives of the following groups when faced with these changes:
   (a) oil companies with North Sea oil installations;
   (b) the UK government; (c) UK motorists;
   (d) workers on North Sea oil rigs?

Summary

1. Economic data are collected not only to verify or refute economic models but to provide a basis for economic decision making.
2. Data may be expressed at nominal (or current) prices or at real (or constant) prices. Data expressed in real terms take into account the effects of inflation.
3. Indices are used to simplify statistics and to express averages.
4. Data can be presented in a variety of forms such as tables or graphs.
5. All data should be interpreted with care given that data can be selected and presented in a wide variety of ways.

The collection and reliability of data

Economists collect data for two main reasons.

- The scientific method requires that theories be tested. Data may be used to refute or support a theory. For instance, an economist might gather data to support or refute the hypothesis that 'Cuts in the marginal rate of income will increase the incentive to work', or that 'An increase in the real value of unemployment benefit will lead to an increase in the number of people unemployed'.

- Economists are often required to provide support for particular policies. Without economic data it is often difficult, if not impossible, to make policy recommendations. For instance, in his Budget each year the Chancellor of the Exchequer has to make a statement to the House of Commons outlining the state of the economy and the economic outlook for the next 12 months. Without a clear knowledge of where the economy is at the moment it is impossible to forecast how it might change in the future and to recommend policy changes to steer the economy in a more desirable direction.

Collecting economic data is usually very difficult and sometimes impossible. Some macro-economic data - such as the balance of payments figures or the value of national income - are collected from a wide variety of sources. The figures for the balance of payments on current account are compiled from returns made by every exporter and importer on every item exported and imported. Not surprisingly the information is inaccurate. Some exporters and importers will conceal transactions to avoid tax. Others will not want to be bothered with the paper work.

Other macroeconomic data such as the Consumer Price Index (used to measure inflation) or the Labour Force Survey (used to measure employment and unemployment) are based on surveys. Surveys are only reliable if there is accurate sampling and measuring and are rarely as accurate as a complete count.

Some macro-economic data are very reliable statistically but do not necessarily provide a good measure of the relevant economic variable. In the UK, the Claimant Count is calculated each month at benefit offices throughout the country. It is extremely accurate but no economist would argue that the figure produced is an accurate measure of unemployment. There is general agreement that some people who claim benefit for being unemployed are not unemployed and conversely there are many unemployed people who are not claiming benefit.

In micro-economics use is again made of survey data, with the limitations that this implies. Economists also make use of more

In November 1998, the Office for National Statistics (ONS) suspended publication of one of the most important economic series it compiles. The average earnings index was found to be giving inaccurate information. The average earnings index is a measure of how much earnings in the whole of the UK are rising. It is calculated monthly by taking data from thousands of returns from businesses. They report on whether or not they have given any pay rises during the previous month and if so, by how much.

Problems arose because of different ways of calculating the average. In October 1998, the ONS launched a new series for average earnings which used a different way of calculating the average than before. But as Figure 1 shows, this revised series gave very different figures from the original series used before. It also didn't fit in very well with what other economic indicators were showing at the time.

A government enquiry found that the revised series was based on inadequate statistical methods which gave too much importance to large changes in earnings by small businesses. In March 1999, a new series was published which followed more closely the old series.

(a) The three lines in Figure 1 should show the same data: the percentage change in average earnings. Give ONE time period when the original series showed an upward movement in earnings when the revised series showed a downward movement.

(b) Why do the three sets of statistics differ in their estimate of changes in average earnings?

(c) Explain TWO reasons why it is important for economic statistics, like growth in average earnings, to be measured accurately.

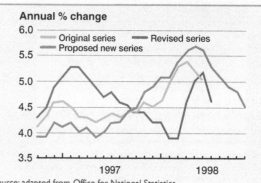

Figure 1 Estimates of growth in average earnings, October 1996 to November 1998

Source: adapted from Office for National Statistics.

experimental data, gathering evidence for case studies. For instance, an economist might want to look at the impact of different pricing policies on entry to sports centres. He or she might study a small number of sports centres in a local area. The evidence gathered would be unlikely decisively to refute or support a general hypothesis such as 'Cheap entry increases sports centre use'. But it would be possible to conclude that the evidence **tended** to support or refute the hypothesis.

In economics it is difficult to gather accurate data and, for that reason, academic economists mostly qualify their conclusions.

Real and nominal values

There are many different **measures** in use today such as tonnes, litres, kilograms and kilometres. Often, we want to be able to compare these different measures. For instance, an industrialist might wish to compare oil measured in litres, and coal measured in kilograms. One way of doing this is to convert oil and coal into therms using gross calorific values. In economics, by far the most important measure used is the value of an item measured in **monetary terms,** such as pounds sterling, US dollars or euros. One problem in using money as a measure is that inflation (the general change in prices in an economy) erodes the purchasing power of money.

For instance, in 1948 the value of output of the UK economy (measured by gross domestic product at market prices) was £12.0 billion. 58 years later, in 2006, it was £1 299.6 billion. It would seem that output had increased about 108 times - an enormous increase. In fact, output increased by only a fraction of that amount. This is because most of the measured increase was an increase not in output but in prices. Prices over the period rose about 25 times. Stripping the inflation element out of the increase leaves us with an increase in output of 4.2 times.

Values unadjusted for inflation are called NOMINAL VALUES. These values are expressed AT CURRENT PRICES (i.e. at the level of prices existing during the time period being measured).

If data are adjusted for inflation, then they are said to be at REAL VALUES or at CONSTANT PRICES. To do this in practice involves taking one period of time as the BASE PERIOD. Data are then adjusted assuming that prices were the same throughout as in the base period.

For instance, a basket of goods costs £100 in year 1 and £200 in year 10. Prices have therefore doubled. If you had £1 000 to spend in year 10, then that would have been equivalent to £500 at year 1 prices because both amounts would have bought 5 baskets of goods. On the other hand, if you had £1 000 to spend in year 1, that would be equivalent to £2 000 in year 10

prices because both would have bought you 10 baskets of goods.

Taking another example, the real value of UK output in 1948 at 1948 prices was the same as its nominal value (i.e. £12 billion). The real value of output in 2006 at 1948 prices was £50.9 billion. It is much lower than the nominal 2006 value because prices were much higher in 2006.

On the other hand, at 2006 prices, the real value of output in 1948 was £306.2 billion, much higher than the nominal value because prices in 2006 were much higher than in 1948. Further examples are given in Table 1.

UK government statistics expressed in real terms are adjusted to prices three or four years previously. In 2007, figures were expressed at 2003 or 2004 prices.

Question 2

Table 2 *Components of final demand at current prices*

	2003=100	£ billion		
	Index of prices	Households' expenditure	Government expenditure	Fixed investment
2003	100.0	697	233	187
2004	102.4	733	251	202
2005	105.5	761	269	212
2006	108.4	795	287	235

Source: adapted from *Monthly Digest of Statistics,* Office for National Statistics.

Using a calculator or a spreadsheet, work out for the period 2003-2006 (a) at constant 2003 prices and (b) at constant 2006 prices the values of:
(i) households' expenditure;
(ii) government expenditure;
(iii) fixed investment.
Present your calculation in the form of two tables, one for 2003 prices and the other for 2006 prices.

Indices

It is often more important in economics to compare values than to know absolute values. For instance, we might want to compare the real value of output in the economy in 1996 and 2006. Knowing that the real value of output (GDP at market prices at 2003 prices) in 2004 was £913.8 billion and in 2006 was £1 209.3 billion is helpful, but the very large numbers make it difficult to see at a glance what, for instance, was the approximate percentage increase. Equally, many series of statistics are averages. The Retail Price Index (the measure of the cost of living) is calculated by working out what it would cost to buy a typical cross-section or 'basket' of goods. Comparing say £458.92 in one month with £475.13 the next is not easy.

So, many series are converted into INDEX NUMBER form. One time period is chosen as the base period and the rest of the statistics in the series are compared to the value in that base period. The value in the base period is usually 100. The figure 100 is chosen because it is easy to work with mathematically.

Table 1 *Nominal and real values*

Nominal value	Inflation between year 1 and 2	Real values Value at year 1 prices	Value at year 2 prices
Example 1 £100 in year 1	10%	£100	£110
Example 2 £500 in year 1	50%	£500	£750
Example 3 £200 in year 2	20%	£166.66	£200
Example 4 £400 in year 2	5%	£380.95	£400

Note: £100 at year 1 prices is worth £100 x 1.1 (i.e. 1+10%) in year 2 prices.
£200 at year 2 prices is worth £200 ÷ 1.2 in year 1 prices.

Table 3 *Converting a series into index number form*

	Consumption			
Year	£ millions	Index number if base year is:		
		year 1	year 2	year 3
1	500	100.0	83.3	62.5
2	600	120.0	100.0	75.0
3	800	160.0	133.3	100.0

Note: The index number for consumption in year 2, if year 1 is the base year, is
(600 ÷ 500) × 100.

Taking the example of output again, if 1948 were taken as the base year, then the value of real output in 1948 would be 100, and the value of real output in 2006 would be 423.4. Alternatively if 2006 were taken as the base year, the value of output would be 100 in 2006 and 23.6 in 1948. Or with 2003 as the base year, the value of output in 1948 would be 25.5 whilst in 2006 it would be 108.1. Further examples are given in Table 3.

The interpretation of data

Data can be presented in many forms and be used both to inform and mislead the reader. To illustrate these points, consider inflation figures for the UK economy. Inflation is the general rise in prices in an economy. If there has been 2 per cent inflation over the past year, it means that prices on average have increased by 2 per cent. One way in which inflation figures can be presented is in **tabular form** as in Table 5.

The data could also be presented in **graphical form** as in Figure 2 (a). Graphs must be interpreted with some care. Figure 2 (b) gives a far more pessimistic view of inflation between 2004 and 2006 than Figure 2 (a) at first glance.

Question 3

Table 4 *Consumers' expenditure*

			£ billion
	Food and drink	Transport	Restaurants and hotels
2003	63.2	104.6	78.9
2004	65.5	109.2	83.6
2005	67.5	112.9	88.9
2006	70.9	116.4	92.0

Source: adapted from *Monthly Digest of Statistics*, Office for National Statistics.

Using a calculator or a spreadsheet, convert each category of expenditure into index number form using as the base year:
(a) 2003 and (b) 2006.
Present your calculations in the form of two tables, one for each base year.

Table 5 *UK inflation (CPI)*

Year	Inflation %
1990	7.0
1991	7.5
1992	4.2
1993	2.5
1994	2.0
1995	2.6
1996	2.5
1997	1.8
1998	1.6
1999	1.3
2000	0.8
2001	1.2
2002	1.3
2003	1.4
2004	1.3
2005	2.1
2006	2.3

Source: adapted from www.statistics.gov.uk.

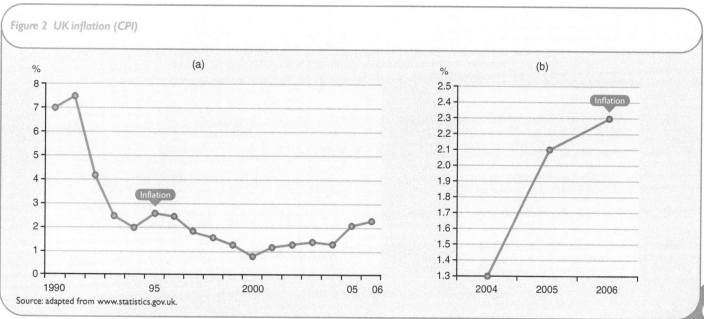

Figure 2 UK inflation (CPI)

(a)

(b)

Source: adapted from www.statistics.gov.uk.

Question 4

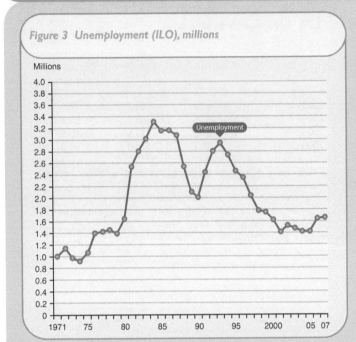

Figure 3 Unemployment (ILO), millions

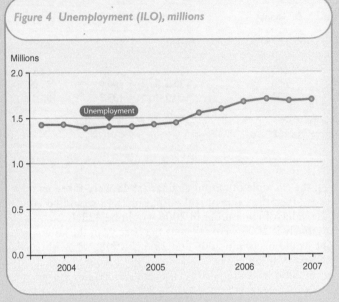

Figure 4 Unemployment (ILO), millions

Source: adapted from *Monthly Digest of Statistics*, Office for National Statistics.

Consider each graph in turn.
(a) What does each show?
(b) Explain why each seems to give a different picture of unemployment in the UK.

One reason is that Figure 2 (b) is taken out of the context of its surrounding years. Figure 2 (a) would suggest that inflation between 2004 and 2006 was relatively low for the whole period shown. Figure 2 (b) suggests the opposite, a dramatic increase in inflation. Another reason why Figure 2 (b) suggests a dramatic increase in inflation is because the line is drawn very steeply. This has been achieved through the scales used on the axes. The vertical axis in Figure 2 (b) only covers 1.3 to 2.5 per cent. In Figure 2 (a), in contrast, the vertical axis starts at zero and rises to 8 per cent over the same drawn height. The gradient of the line in Figure 2 (b) could have been even steeper if the length of the horizontal time axis had been drawn shorter.

Graphs are sometimes constructed using log scales for the vertical axis. This has the effect of gradually compressing values on the vertical axis as they increase. The vertical distance between 0 and 1, for instance, is larger per unit than between 999 and 1 000.

Data can also be expressed in **verbal form**. Figure 2 shows that inflation rose between 1990 and 1991, and then broadly fell to a low of 0.8 per cent in 2000 before fluctuating in the 1.2 to 1.4 per cent range between 2001 and 2004. Inflation then rose to 2.3 per cent by 2006. When expressing data in verbal form, it can become very tedious to describe each individual change. For instance, it would be inappropriate to say 'Inflation in 1990 was 7 per cent. Then it rose to 7.5 per cent in 1991 before falling to 4.2 per cent in 1992. Then in 1993 it fell again to 2.5 per cent and again in 1994 to 2.0 per cent'. When expressing data in verbal form, it is important to pick out the main trends and perhaps give a few key figures to illustrate these trends.

Key terms

Base period - the period, such as a year or a month, with which all other values in a series are compared.
Index number - an indicator showing the relative value of one number to another from a base of 100. It is often used to present an average of a number of statistics.

Nominal values - values unadjusted for the effects of inflation (i.e. values **at current prices**).
Real values - values adjusted for inflation (i.e. values at **constant prices**).

Applied economics

Tourism

Spending on tourism

Tourism is a major industry in the UK. Is it growing in size? There is a number of ways in which growth can be measured. Table 6 shows how total spending on tourism has grown between 1989 and 2005. It divides tourists into three categories - UK tourists who take a holiday within the country, foreign tourists who come to the UK and UK tourists who take holidays abroad. The figures in Table 6 are expressed at current prices. This means that inflation is not taken into account. If there had been very high inflation over the period 1989-2005, the volume of tourism could have declined given the data in Table 6. In fact, consumer prices over the 16 year period rose 67 per cent. So real growth in spending is anything which is above that 67 per cent rise.

Table 6 Spending on tourism at current prices, £ million

	£ millions at current prices		
	Spending on holidays by UK citizens in the UK	Spending in the UK by foreign visitors	Spending on foreign holidays by UK residents
1989	17 071[1]	6 945	9 357
1995	20 072	11 763	15 386
2005	22 667	14 248	32 154

1. Estimated

Source: adapted from *Annual Abstract of Statistics*, Office for National Statistics.

Table 7 shows the figures in Table 6 expressed at constant 2001 prices, i.e. after the inflation element has been stripped out and adjusted to the level of prices in 2001. Taking 2001 as the reference year for prices means that the 1989 and 1995 data at current prices increase as numbers when they become data at constant prices, whilst the 2005 numbers fall.

Table 8 shows the figures in Table 7 in index number form. This has the advantage that it is much easier to

Table 7 Spending on tourism at constant 2001 prices, £ million

	£ millions at constant 2001 prices		
	Spending on holidays by UK citizens in the UK	Spending in the UK by foreign visitors	Spending on foreign holidays by UK residents
1989	25 677	10 446	14 047
1995	23 332	13 674	17 885
2005	25 118	15 789	35 632

Source: adapted from *Annual Abstract of Statistics*, Office for National Statistics.

see which of the three areas of tourism has grown more quickly. At a glance, it can be seen that spending on holidays by UK citizens in the UK fell by 2.1 per cent in real terms over the period 1989 to 2005. In contrast, spending on foreign holidays by UK citizens grew by 153.7 per cent. Foreign visitors to the UK spent 51.1 per cent more. Because these are index numbers, it is not possible to say how important is the 51.1 per cent rise in spending by foreign visitors to the total domestic tourist industry. For instance, if foreign tourists accounted for just 1 per cent of total spending, a 51.1 per cent rise would have almost no impact on tourism. This illustrates one of the disadvantages of using index numbers. To assess the relative impact of the increase in foreign tourists, we have to look back to Table 7. Total spending on tourism in the UK by UK citizens and by foreigners at constant 2001 prices rose from £36.1 billion to £40.9 billion, a 13.2 per cent increase, over the period 1989 to 2005. A 13.2 per cent change over 16 years is not particularly large. The data show that spending by UK citizens has broadly been unchanged over the period. The increase comes entirely from increased spending by overseas visitors.

Employment in tourism

Tables 8 and 9 show that employment in tourist industries grew by 6.6 per cent between 2000 and 2004. Tourism is a major employer in the UK

Table 8 Spending on tourism at constant 2001 prices, 1989 = 100

			1989 = 100
	Spending on holidays by UK citizens in the UK	Spending in the UK by foreign visitors	Spending on foreign holidays by UK residents
1989	100.0	100.0	100.0
1995	90.7	130.9	127.3
2005	97.9	151.1	253.7

Source: adapted from *Annual Abstract of Statistics*, Office for National Statistics.

accounting for 5 per cent of all employment. In some regions of the UK such as the South West of England, it is an even more important provider of jobs.

Table 9 shows that the largest tourism employer is restaurants, bars and canteens, accounting for 43.5 per cent of employment in tourist industries. When Table 9 is converted into index number form in Table 10, this cannot be seen from the data. The largest number in Table 10 for 2004, which is 113.0 for Recreation services, shows the largest increase in employment from 2000.

Trips and prices

Data for UK domestic tourism, trips made by British citizens within Great Britain, reveal some very interesting aspects of tourism. Table 11 shows that the number of trips made increased by 29.1 million between 1989 and 2005. Each trip, though, was shorter. In 1989, the average number of nights spent was 4.0 but in 2005 had fallen to 3.2. Spending per trip at constant prices fell by 1.1 per cent. This compares to the 50.9 per cent increase in real household consumption expenditure over the same period.

Table 11 therefore shows that between 1989 and 2005, people went on more holidays in Britain, but they were shorter and spending on holidays per trip failed to keep up with increases in household spending on all other goods and services. Part of the reason for these trends is that 'short breaks' have now become far more popular. More people are now taking a weekend holiday, for instance. These will be less expensive than longer holidays. The fall in spending per trip could also be an indication that the price of holidays has fallen relative to all other prices in the economy. Since 1989, there has been considerable expansion of chains of budget hotels such as Travel Inn or Travel Lodge. These have exercised downward pressure on the cost of hotel and other accommodation.

Table 9 Employment in tourism, UK

	Hotels and other tourist accommodation	Restaurants, bars and canteens	Transport	Travel agents, tour operators	Recreation services	Rest of the economy	Total employment
							Thousands
2000	230.0	556.1	132.2	135.2	73.2	205.2	1 331.9
2002	222.0	586.8	133.4	138.8	78.4	208.2	1 367.4
2004	229.6	618.2	131.5	146.8	82.7	211.1	1 419.9

Source: adapted from *Annual Abstract of Statistics*, Office for National Statistics.

Table 10 Employment in tourism, UK, 2000=100

	Hotels and other tourist accommodation	Restaurants, bars and canteens	Transport	Travel agents, tour operators	Recreation services	Rest of the economy	Total employment
							2000=100
2000	100.0	100.0	100.0	100.0	100.0	100.0	100.0
2002	96.5	105.5	100.9	102.7	107.1	101.5	102.7
2004	99.8	111.2	99.5	108.6	113.0	102.9	106.6

Source: adapted from *Annual Abstract of Statistics*, Office for National Statistics.

Table 11 UK domestic tourism

	Number of trips, millions	Number of nights spent, millions	Average nights spent	Average expenditure per trip at current prices (£)	Average expenditure per trip trip at constant 2001 prices (£)
1989	109.6	443.2	4.0	99.1	149.1
1995	121.0	526.0	3.6	135.8	157.9
2005	138.7	442.3	3.2	163.4	147.5

Source: adapted from *Annual Abstract of Statistics*, Office for National Statistics.

DataQuestion — Cinema data

Table 12 *Cinema exhibitor statistics, UK[1]*

	Number of sites	Number of screens	Number of admissions, millions	at current prices			at constant 2001 prices		
				Gross box office takings, £ millions	Revenue per admission, £	Revenue per screen, £ 000	Gross box office takings, £ millions	Revenue per admission, £	Revenue per screen, £ 000
1987	492	1 035	66.8	123.8	1.85	118.7	210.6	3.15	201.9
1995	728	2 003	114.6	354.2	3.09	176.8	411.7	3.59	205.5
2006	783	3 569	156.6	762.1	4.87	213.5	677.8	4.34	189.9

Source: adapted from *Annual Abstract of Statistics*, Office for National Statistics.

Table 13 *Cinema exhibitor statistics, UK[1]*

1987=100

	Number of sites	Number of screens	Number of admissions	at current prices			at constant 2001 prices		
				Gross box office takings	Revenue per admission	Revenue per screen	Gross box office takings	Revenue per admission	Revenue per screen
1987	100.0	100.0	100.0	100.0	100.0	100.0	100.0	100.0	100.0
1995	148.0	193.5	171.6	286.1	167.0	148.9	195.5	114.0	101.8
2006	159.1	344.8	234.4	615.6	263.2	179.9	321.8	137.8	94.1

Source: adapted from *Annual Abstract of Statistics*, Office for National Statistics.
1. 1987 data are Great Britain. 1995 and 2006 data are UK.

1. Describe the main trends in cinema admissions shown in the data.
2. Explain the advantages and disadvantages of using index numbers to present data. Illustrate your answer from the data.
3. 'Revenues per admission and the number of screens cannot carry on rising.' (a) To what extent does this data support this statement for the period 1987-2006? (b) Discuss whether it is likely to be true in the future.

4 Positive and normative economics

Summary

1. Positive economics deals with statements of 'fact' which can either be refuted or supported. Normative economics deals with value judgments, often in the context of policy recommendations.
2. Economics is generally classified as a social science.
3. It uses the scientific method as the basis of its investigation.
4. Economics is the study of how groups of individuals make decisions about the allocation of scarce resources.
5. Economists build models and theories to explain economic interactions.
6. Models and theories are simplifications of reality.
7. Models can be distinguished according to whether they are static or dynamic, equilibrium or disequilibrium, or partial or general.

Positive and normative economics

Economics is concerned with two types of investigation. POSITIVE ECONOMICS is the scientific or objective study of the subject. It is concerned with finding out how economies and markets actually work. POSITIVE STATEMENTS are statements about economics which can be proven to be true or false. They can be supported or refuted by evidence. For example, the statement 'The UK economy is currently operating on its production possibility boundary' is a positive statement. Economists can search for evidence as to whether there are unemployed resources or not. If there are large numbers of unemployed workers, then the statement is refuted. If unemployment is very low, and we know that all market economies need some unemployment for the efficient workings of labour markets as people move between jobs, then the statement would be supported. Statements about the future can be positive statements too. For example, 'The service sector will grow by 30 per cent in size over the next five years' is a positive statement. Economists will have to wait five years for the proof to support or refute the statement to be available. However, it is still a statement which is capable of being proved or disproved.

NORMATIVE ECONOMICS is concerned with value judgements. It deals with the study of and presentation of policy prescriptions about economics. NORMATIVE STATEMENTS are statements which cannot be supported or refuted. Ultimately, they are opinions about how economies and markets should work. For example, 'The government should increase the state pension', or 'Manufacturing companies should invest more' are normative statements.

Economists tend to be interested in both positive and normative economics. They want to find out how economies work. But they also want to influence policy debates. Normative economics also typically contains positive economics within it. Take the normative statement 'The government should increase the state pension'. Economists putting forward this value judgement are likely to back up their opinion with positive evidence. They might state that 'The average pensioner has a disposable income of 40 per cent of the average worker'; and 'The average pensioner only goes on holiday once every four years'. These are positive statements because they are capable of proof or disproof. They are used to build up an argument which supports the final opinion that state pensions should be raised.

Normative statements tend to contain words like 'should' and 'ought'. However, sometimes positive statements also contain these words. 'Inflation should be brought down' is a normative statement because it is not capable of refutation. 'Inflation should reach 5 per cent by the end of the year' is a positive statement. At the end of the year, if inflation has reached 5 per cent, then the statement will have been proven to be correct.

The scientific method

There are many sciences covering a wide field of knowledge. What links them all is a particular method of work or enquiry called the SCIENTIFIC METHOD. The scientific method at its most basic is relatively easy to understand. A scientist:
- postulates a THEORY - the scientist puts forward a hypothesis which is capable of refutation (e.g. the earth travels round the sun, the earth is flat, a light body will fall at the same speed as a heavy body);
- gathers evidence to either support the theory or refute it - astronomical observation gives evidence to support the theory that the earth travels round the sun; on the other hand, data refutes the idea that the earth is flat; gathering evidence may be done through **controlled experiments**;
- accepts, modifies or refutes the theory - the earth does travel round the sun; a light body will fall at the same speed as a heavy body although it will only do so under certain conditions; the earth is not flat.

Theories which gain universal acceptance are often called LAWS. Hence we have the law of gravity, Boyle's law, and in economics the laws of demand and supply.

Economics - the science

Some sciences, such as physics or chemistry, are sometimes called 'hard sciences'. This term doesn't refer to the fact that physics is more difficult than a science such as biology! It refers to the fact that it is relatively easy to apply the scientific method to the study of these subjects. In physics much of the work can take place in laboratories. Observations can be made with some degree of certainty. Control groups can be established. It then becomes relatively easy to accept or refute a particular hypothesis.

This is all much more difficult in social sciences such as economics, sociology, politics and anthropology. In economics,

Question 1

London's business leaders are hoping that one of Gordon Brown's first acts as prime minister will be to fund the Crossrail scheme, a new railway linking Heathrow, the City and Canary Wharf. Estimated to cost £16 billion, Crossrail is not cheap. Why does the City think Crossrail is so important? Mostly, because it will link Heathrow airport to the City of London. Currently, rail travellers to the City from Heathrow have to get off at London Paddington and catch a slow tube train. In comparison with other major cities, such as Paris or Amsterdam, the service is poor and slow. It places the City at a major competitive disadvantage with other financial centres.

The City of London is vital to the success of the UK economy. The UK government should give this support to an industry which is a major contributor to the wealth of the country.

Source: adapted from the *Financial Times*, 22.6.2007.

Explain which are the positive statements and which are the normative statements in this passage.

it is often not possible to set up experiments to test hypotheses. It is often not possible to establish control groups or to conduct experiments in environments which enable one factor to be varied whilst other factors are kept constant. The economist has to gather data in the ordinary everyday world where many variables are changing over any given time period. It then becomes difficult to decide whether the evidence supports or refutes particular hypotheses.

Economists sometimes come to very different conclusions when considering a particular set of data as their interpretations may vary. For example, an unemployment rate of 6 per cent in Scotland compared to a national average of 3 per cent may indicate a failure of government policy to help this area. Others may conclude that policy had been a success as unemployment may have been far greater without the use of policy.

It is sometimes argued that economics cannot be a science because it studies human behaviour and human behaviour cannot be reduced to scientific laws. There is an element of truth in this. It is very difficult to understand and predict the behaviour of individuals. However, nearly all economics is based on the study of the behaviour of groups of individuals. The behaviour of groups is often far more predictable than that of individuals. Moreover, we tend to judge a science on its ability to establish laws which are certain and unequivocal. But even in a hard science such as physics, it has become established that some laws can only be stated in terms of probabilities. In economics, much analysis is couched in terms of 'it is likely that' or 'this may possibly happen'. Economists use this type of language because they know they have insufficient data to make firm predictions. In part it is because other variables may change at the same time, altering the course of events. However, it is also used because economists know that human behaviour, whilst broadly predictable, is not predictable to the last £1 spent or to the nearest 1 penny of income.

Theories and models

The terms 'theory' and MODEL are often used interchangeably. There is no exact distinction to be made between the two. However, an economic theory is generally expressed in looser terms than a model. For instance, 'consumption is dependent upon income' might be an economic theory. '$C_t = 567 + 0.852Y_t$' where 567 is a constant, C_t is current consumption and Y_t current income would be an economic model. Theories can often be expressed in words. But economic models, because they require greater precision in their specification, are often expressed in mathematical terms.

The purpose of modelling

Why are theories and models so useful in a science? The universe is a complex place. There is an infinite number of interactions happening at any moment in time. Somehow we all have to make sense of what is going on. For instance, we assume that if we put our hand into a flame, we will get burnt. If we see a large hole in the ground in front of us we assume that we will fall into it if we carry on going in that direction.

One of the reasons why we construct theories or models is because we want to know why something is as it is. Some people are fascinated by questions such as 'Why do we fall downwards and not upwards?' or 'Why can birds fly?'. More importantly we use theories and models all the time in deciding how to act. We keep away from fires to prevent getting burnt. We avoid holes in the ground because we don't want to take a tumble.

Simplification

One criticism made of economics is that economic theories and models are 'unrealistic'. This is true, but it is equally true of Newton's law of gravity, Einstein's Theory of Relativity or any theory or model. This is because any theory or model has to be a simplification of reality if it is to be useful. Imagine, for instance, using a map which described an area perfectly. To do this it would need to be a full scale reproduction of the entire area which would give no practical advantage. Alternatively, drop a feather and a cannon ball from the top of the leaning tower of Pisa. You will find that both don't descend at the same speed, as one law in physics would predict, because that law assumes that factors such as air resistance and friction don't exist.

If a model is to be useful it has to be simple. The extent of simplification depends upon its use. If you wanted to go from London to Tokyo by air, it wouldn't be very helpful to have maps which were on the scale of your local A to Z. On the other hand, if you wanted to visit a friend in a nearby town it wouldn't be very helpful to have a map of the world with you. The local A to Z is very much more detailed (i.e. closer to reality) than a world map but this does not necessarily make it more useful or make it a 'better' model.

Simplification implies that some factors have been included in the model and some have been omitted. It could even be the case that some factors have been distorted to emphasise particular points in a model. For instance, on a road map of the UK, the cartographer will almost certainly not have attempted to name every small hamlet or to show the geological formation of the area. On the other hand, he or she will have marked in roads and motorways which will appear several miles wide according to the scale of the map.

Types of model

Equilibrium and disequilibrium models Equilibrium is a central feature of all the models studied in this book. In economics, EQUILIBRIUM can be described as a point when expectations are being realised and where no plans are being frustrated. For instance, in the model of demand and supply, equilibrium price is achieved when the planned quantity that buyers wish to purchase is equal to the planned quantity that sellers wish to sell. Equilibrium models are models where it is predicted that the market or economy will return to an equilibrium point. Disequilibrium models are ones where there is no tendency to return to the equilibrium point. Disequilibrium models are more complex than equilibrium models and tend to be expressed using complex mathematical language.

Static and dynamic models A DYNAMIC model is one which

contains time as one of its variables. A STATIC model is one which contains no time element within the model. Nearly all the models explained in this book are static models. They tend to be simpler and easier to use. Dynamic models tend to be complex. They are more suited, for example, to computer modelling.

General and partial models A GENERAL MODEL is one which contains a larger number of variables. For instance, a model which includes all markets in the economy would be a general model. A PARTIAL MODEL is one which contains relatively few variables. A model of the oil market or of the demand for labour would be a partial model. A partial model will be one in which most variables are assumed to be in the category of CETERIS PARIBUS. Ceteris paribus is Latin for 'all other things being equal' or 'all other things remaining the same'. It is a very powerful simplifying devise which enables economists to explain clearly how an economy or market market works. For instance, in neo-classical price theory, we assume that income and tastes remain the same when drawing a demand curve.

Equilibrium and disequilibrium models

As stated above, equilibrium is a central feature of all the models studied in this book. All static models are equilibrium models because they deal with equilibrium positions.

An equilibrium position may be stable. If there is a movement away from equilibrium for some reason, there will be an in-built tendency for equilibrium to be restored. If the equilibrium point is unstable, there will be no tendency to move towards an equilibrium point once disequilibrium has been established.

It is easy to make the incorrect assumption that the market (or whatever is being studied) will always return to an equilibrium position; or that the equilibrium point is somehow the optimal or most desirable position. Neither is necessarily true even if economists tend to believe that knowing where is the equilibrium point is helpful in explaining economic events and in making policy recommendations.

Macroeconomics and microeconomics

A macroeconomic model is one which models the economy as a whole. It deals with economic relationships at the level of all participants in the economy. A micro-economic model, on the other hand, deals with the economic behaviour of individuals or groups within society. For instance, the study of the spending decisions of individual consumers or consumers within a particular market such as the market for cars (demand theory) would be micro-economics. The study of consumption patterns for the whole economy (the consumption function) would be an example of macro-economics. The study of the determination of wage rates (wage theory) would be micro-economics. The study of the overall level of wages in the economy (part of national income accounting) would be macro-economics.

Key terms

Ceteris paribus - the assumption that all other variables within the model remain constant whilst one change is being considered.

Equilibrium - the point where what is expected or planned is equal to what is realised or actually happens.

Law - a theory or model which has been verified by empirical evidence.

Normative economics - the study and presentation of policy prescriptions involving value judgements about the way in which scarce resources are allocated.

Normative statement - a statement which cannot be supported or refuted because it is a value judgment.

Partial and general models - a partial model is one with few variables whilst a general model has many.

Positive economics - the scientific or objective study of the allocation of resources.

Positive statement - a statement which can be supported or refuted by evidence.

Static and dynamic models - a static model is one where time is not a variable. In a dynamic model, time is a variable explicit in the model.

The scientific method - a method which subjects theories or hypotheses to falsification by empirical evidence.

Theory or model - a hypothesis which is capable of refutation by empirical evidence.

Applied economics

Positive and normative economics

The *Financial Times*, in a editorial dated 10.9.2007, wrote about 'How government can sustain UK manufacturing success'. The editorial covered why manufacturing industry was currently successful and how best the government can support manufacturing industry in the future.

It starts off with a normative statement, an opinion: 'Rumours of the death of UK manufacturing have been greatly exaggerated.' It then supports this opinion with a number of positive statements, or facts, about UK manufacturing such as 'surveys report bulging order books' and 'productivity growth has outstripped the rest of the economy'.

The article goes on with a number of positive statements about how manufacturing has remained competitive. For example, it states that 'what remains in Britain is often the high-value-added production that cannot easily be shipped overseas; and they 'make complex and innovative products that are hard to copy'.'

The article then turns to the role of government. It

argues that government can support manufacturing industry. It makes two value judgements about government buying policies of equipment such as aircraft, and about innovation: 'while government procurement contracts should not favour British manufacturers merely because of their nationality, they could do more to favour innovation.' It then makes another normative statement: 'The biggest contribution the government could make would be to sort out the lamentable state of UK state secondary education and skills training.' It supports this value judgement with a number of positive statements such as 'skills shortages have been filled recently by engineers from eastern Europe.'

The editorial concludes by making the positive statements that 'The manufacturers that have survived the shakeout have devised successful strategies for remaining competitive in the global economy. But they also know that continuing success depends on raising the pace of innovation and further developing the skills of the workforce.'

DataQuestion — The Common Agricultural Policy (CAP)

CAP

In 2005, there were difficult negotiations about the EU budget between member countries. The British Prime Minister, Tony Blair, wanted to reopen a deal made in 2002 about the Common Agricultural Policy which set CAP budgets to 2014. He, in turn, came under intense pressure to give up the 'British Rebate', an annual refund to the UK first negotiated in the 1980s to compensate the UK for its low level of subsidies from the CAP budget. The ten, mainly Eastern European, countries which joined in the EU in 2004 wanted a larger slice of EU spending than proposed. France and Ireland, both major beneficiaries of CAP subsidies, strongly defended the deal made in 2002.

Two contributions to this debate follow, one from Bertie Ahern, the Irish Prime Minister who was against further CAP reform, the other from Tony Blair's Press Spokesperson, who argued for CAP reform.

We must stand by the Common Agricultural Policy

In an article written for the *Financial Times*, Bertie Ahern, the Irish Prime Minister, argued for maintaining the CAP deal made in 2002. His comments included the following.

The defeat of the European Union's proposed constitution in the French and Dutch referendums has led to a renewed debate on the way forward for Europe. As part of this debate, the Common Agricultural Policy has in recent months been the subject of much criticism, with repeated calls for further reform.

2003 saw a radical reform of CAP, decoupling 'subsidies' from production. This reform is in its first year of implementation. It would be both unfair and unwise to ask farmers to accept another radical reform now. Farmers, like other business people, need a reasonable degree of stability in the policy environment in which they operate. However, there is more at stake. To try to overturn an agreement reached unanimously by the European Council as recently as October 2002 would be to send the wrong signal to Europe's people. The public needs to see a Europe that stands by its agreements.

There are other issues too. Reform would mean that European agricultural production would fall rapidly. The food supply gap would be filled by imports from, for example, South America and Australia, which can produce at prices below European levels. Europe's food supplies could, once again, become vulnerable. Reform would also result in serious damage to the social and economic fabric of rural areas across Europe. As for the scale of subsidies, the Organisation for Economic Co-operation and Development (OECD) has estimated that transfers to agriculture from both consumers and taxpayers amount to $103bn (£58bn) in the EU and $92bn (£52bn) in the USA, or 1.32 per cent of GDP for the EU and 0.92 per cent for the US. There is therefore broad comparability of support.

Calls for radical CAP reform are misplaced and outdated; they are based on a misunderstanding of the role of the CAP in European society and the world economy. They are also based on a false premise about the relative cost of the CAP.

Source: adapted from the *Financial Times*, 26.9.2005.

Briefing from the Prime Minister's Official Spokesperson on the Common Agricultural Policy

Our policy all along has been to get rid of subsidies for crops because we believe that this was a distorted way in which to support the rural economy. Therefore what we have always argued for was a managed process of change in which you maintained sustainable livelihoods in the countryside but didn't do so at the expense of distorting world trade. That was why we always argued for fundamental reform of CAP and we recognised that there had been some progress in that direction but we are arguing for more.

We are still in a situation where some 80 per cent of the existing budget is directed towards the original 15 member states, and that does not allow the spending to be prioritised towards providing the infrastructure support that accession countries need. Therefore we still have a distorted system.

There should be a policy of managed change which would include more efficient farming and viable, sustainable rural communities. You cannot have a situation where we go into another decade with 40 per cent of the EU budget being spent on 5 per cent of the population.

Source: adapted from The Office of the Prime Minister, www.number-10.gov.uk/output/page7762.asp.

1. Explain the difference between positive and normative statements. Give at least six examples from the views of Bertie Ahern and Tony Blair.
2. Evaluate the case for and against reform of the CAP using the arguments put forward in the data.

Summary

1. Demand for a good is the quantity of goods or services that will be bought over a period of time at any given price.
2. Demand for a good will rise or fall if there are changes in factors such as incomes, the price of other goods, tastes, and the size of the population.
3. A change in price is shown by a movement along the demand curve.
4. A change in any other variable affecting demand, such as income, is shown by a shift in the demand curve.
5. The market demand curve can be derived by horizontally summing all the individual demand curves in the market.

Demand

A market exists wherever there are buyers and sellers of a particular good. Buyers **demand** goods from the market whilst sellers **supply** goods to the market.

DEMAND has a particular meaning in economics. Demand is the quantity of goods or services that will be bought at any given price over a period of time. For instance, approximately 2 million new cars are bought each year in the UK today at an average price of, say, £8 000. Economists would say that the annual demand for cars at £8 000 would be 2 million units.

ceteris paribus: with other conditions remaining the same.

Demand and price

If everything else were to remain the same (this is known as the **ceteris paribus** condition), what would happen to the quantity demanded of a product as its price changed? If the average price of a car were to fall from £8 000 to £4 000, then it is not difficult to guess that the quantity demanded of cars would rise. On the other hand, if the average price were £35 000 very few cars would be sold.

This is shown in Table 1. As the price of cars rises then, ceteris paribus, the quantity of cars demanded will fall. Another way of expressing this is shown in Figure 1. Price is on the vertical axis and quantity demanded over time is on the horizontal axis. The curve is downward sloping showing that as price falls, quantity demanded rises. This DEMAND CURVE shows the quantity that is demanded at any given price. When price changes there is said to be a **movement along** the curve. For instance, there is a movement along the curve from the point A to the point B, a fall of 1 million cars a year, when the price of cars rises from £8 000 to £16 000. There is an **extension of demand** when the quantity demanded rises. There is a **contraction of demand** when the quantity demanded falls.

It is important to remember that the demand curve shows

Table 1 The demand schedule for cars

Price (£)	Demand (million per year)
4 000	4.0
8 000	2.0
16 000	1.0
40 000	0.4

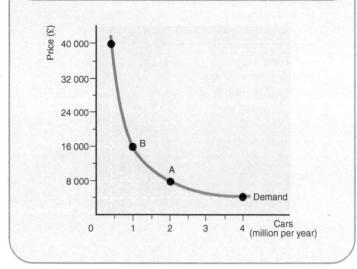

Figure 1 The demand curve
The demand curve is downward sloping, showing that the lower the price, the higher will be the quantity demanded of a good. In this example, only 0.4 million cars per year are demanded at a price of £40 000 each, but a reduction in price to £4 000 increases quantity demanded to 4 million units per year.

EFFECTIVE DEMAND. It shows how much would be bought (i.e. how much consumers can afford to buy and would buy) at any given price and not how much buyers would like to buy if they had unlimited resources.

Economists have found that the inverse relationship between price and quantity demanded - that as price rises, the quantity demanded falls - is true of nearly all goods. In the unit 'Normal, inferior and Giffin goods', we shall consider the few examples of goods which might have upward sloping demand curves.

Demand and income

Price is not the only factor which determines the level of demand for a good. Another important factor is income. Demand for a normal good rises when income rises. For instance, a rise in income leads consumers to buy more cars. A few goods, known as inferior goods, fall in demand when incomes rise.

The effect of a rise in income on demand is shown in Figure 2. Buyers are purchasing 0A of clothes at a price of 0E. Incomes rise and buyers react by purchasing more clothes at the same

Question 1

Stagecoach operates both bus and train services. It charges different prices to different passengers for the same journeys depending, for instance, on when they travel, their age, whether they are making a single or return journey or whether they have a season ticket. Using a demand curve diagram, explain what happens when:
(a) children are charged half price for a bus journey instead of being charged full price;
(b) senior citizens are given a free bus pass paid for by the local authority rather than having to pay the full fare;
(c) Stagecoach increases its prices on a route by 5 per cent;
(d) passengers can get a 60 per cent reduction by buying a day return if they travel after 9.30 compared to having to pay the full fare.

Figure 2 A change in income

An increase in income will raise demand for a normal good. At a price of 0E, for instance, demand will rise from 0A to 0B. Similarly, at all other prices, an increase in income will result in a level of demand to the right of the existing demand curve. So the demand curve will shift from D_1 to D_2. A fall in income will result in less being demanded at any given price. Hence the demand curve will shift to the left, from D_1 to D_3.

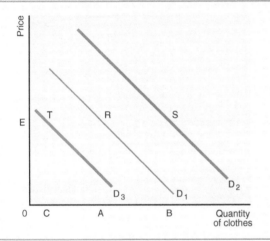

price. At the higher level of income they buy, say, 0B of clothes. A new demand curve now exists passing through the point S. It will be to the right of the original demand curve because at any given price more will be demanded at the new higher level of income.

Economists say that a rise in income will lead to an **increase in demand** for a normal good such as clothes. An increase in demand is shown by a SHIFT IN THE DEMAND CURVE. (Note that an **increase in quantity demanded** would refer to a change in quantity demanded resulting from a change in price and would be shown by a movement along the curve.) In Figure 2, the original demand curve D_1 shifts to the right to its new position D_2. Similarly, a fall in income will lead to a **fall in demand** for a normal good. This is shown by a **shift** to the left of the demand curve from D_1 to D_3. For instance, at a price of 0E, demand will fall from 0A to 0C.

Two points need to be made. First, the demand curves in Figure 2 have been drawn as straight lines. These demand curves drawn show a hypothetical (or imaginary) position. They are drawn straight purely for convenience and do not imply that actual demand curves for real products are straight. Second, the

shifts in the demand curves are drawn as parallel shifts. Again this is done for convenience and neatness but it is most unlikely that a rise or fall in income for an actual product would produce a precisely parallel shift in its demand curve.

Question 2

Table 2

Quantity demanded (million tyres)	Price(£)
10	20
20	16
30	12
40	8
50	4

Table 2 shows the demand curve facing a tyre manufacturer.
(a) Draw a demand curve for tyres from the above data.
(b) An increase in income results in an increase in quantity demanded of tyres of: (i) 5 million; (ii) 10 million; (iii) 15 million; (iv) 25 million. For each of these, draw a new demand curve on your diagram.
(c) Draw a demand curve for tyres which would show the effect of a fall in incomes on the original demand for tyres.
(d) Draw a demand curve for tyres which would show that no products were demanded when their price was £8.

The price of other goods

Another important factor which influences the demand for a good is the price of other goods. For instance, in the great drought of 1976 in the UK, the price of potatoes soared. Consumers reacted by buying fewer potatoes and replacing them in their diet by eating more bread, pasta and rice.

This can be shown on a demand diagram. The demand curve for pasta in Figure 3 is D_1. A rise in the price of potatoes leads

Figure 3 A rise in the price of other goods

A rise in the price of potatoes will lead to a rise in the demand for substitute goods. So the demand for pasta will increase, shown by a shift to the right in the demand curve for pasta from D_1 to D_2.

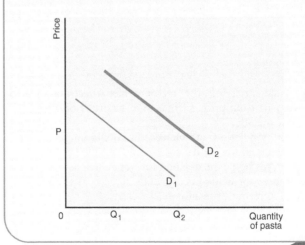

to a rise in the demand for pasta. This means that at any given price a greater quantity of pasta will be demanded. The new demand curve D₂ will therefore be to the right of the original demand curve.

Not all changes in prices will affect the demand for a particular good. A rise in the price of tennis balls is unlikely to have much impact on the demand for carrots, for instance. Changes in the price of other goods as well may have either a positive or negative impact on demand for a good. A rise in the price of tennis rackets is likely to reduce the demand for tennis balls as some buyers decide that tennis is too expensive a sport. On the other hand, the demand for cinema places, alcoholic drink or whatever other form of entertainment consumers choose to buy instead of tennis equipment, will increase.

Question 3

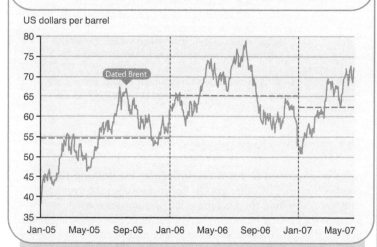

Figure 4 Brent crude oil price, $ per barrel, 2005-2007

Between 2005 and 2007, the price of Brent crude oil rose from $38 a barrel and peaked at $79 a barrel. The price of oil was predicted to remain high for the foreseeable future because of growing demand for oil from emerging countries such as China. Explain, using diagrams, what effect you would expect this to have on the demand in the UK for:
(a) oil-fired central heating systems;
(b) luxury cars with high-mileage petrol consumption;
(c) rail travel;
(d) ice-cream;
(e) air travel.

Other factors

There is a wide variety of other factors which affect the demand for a good apart from price, income and the prices of other goods. These include:
- changes in population - an increase in population is likely to increase demand for goods;
- changes in fashion - the demand for items such as wigs or flared trousers or white kitchen units changes as these items go in or out of fashion;
  - changes in legislation - the demand for seat belts, anti-pollution equipment or places in residential

homes has been affected in the past by changes in government legislation;
- advertising - a very powerful influence on consumer demand which seeks to influence consumer choice.

Question 4

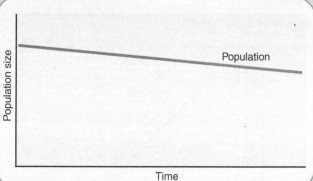

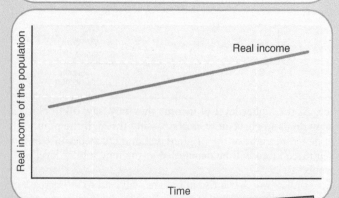

(a) Explain the likely effect on demand for Activia of each of the four factors shown in the data. Use a separate demand diagram for each factor to illustrate your answer.

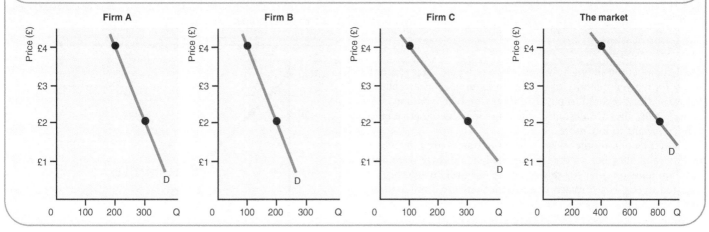

Figure 5 Individual and market demand curves
The market demand curve can be derived from the individual demand curves by adding up individual demand at each single price. In this example, for instance, the market demand at a price of £2 is calculated by adding the demand of firms A, B and C at this price.

A summary

It is possible to express demand in the form of a **functional** relationship. The quantity demanded of good N (Q_n) varies according to (i.e. is a function of) the price of good N (P_n), income (Y), the price of all other goods ($P_1, ... P_{n-1}$) and all other factors (T). Mathematically, this is:

$$Q_n = f [P_n, Y, (P_1, ... P_{n-1}), T]$$

At this stage, this mathematical form of expressing the determinants of demand is a convenient shorthand but little else. The major tools for dealing with demand at this level are either the written word or graphs. At a far more advanced level, the algebraic formula for demand is often the most powerful and useful tool in analysing demand.

Individual and market demand curves

So far, it has been assumed that demand refers to demand for a product in a whole market (i.e. MARKET DEMAND).

Question 5

$$Q = 20 - \frac{1}{2} P$$

where Q is the monthly quantity demanded of compact discs (CDs) in millions and P is their price.
(a) Draw the demand curve given by this equation between CD prices of £1 and £20.
(b) A new format results in a fall in demand of CDs of 5 million per month at any given price. (i) What is the new formula for quantity demanded of CDs?
(ii) Plot the new demand curve on your diagram.
(c) A rise in consumer incomes results in consumers being less price sensitive than before when buying CDs. As a result, instead of monthly demand falling by half a million when price is increased by £1, monthly demand now falls only by 400 000. Assume that the original equation for demand is as in part (a) of this question. (i) What is the new formula for quantity demanded of CDs? (ii) Plot the new demand curve on your diagram.

However, it is possible to construct individual demand curves and derive market demand curves from them. An INDIVIDUAL DEMAND CURVE is the demand curve of an individual buyer. This could be a consumer, a firm or a government.

The determinants of demand for an individual are no different from those of the market as a whole. When price rises, there is a fall in the quantity demanded of the product; when income rises, assuming that the product is a normal good, demand will increase, etc.

Figure 5 shows a situation where there are three and only three buyers in a market, firms A, B and C. At a price of £2, firm A will buy 300 units, firm B 200 units and firm C 300 units. So the total market demand at a price of £2 is 300 + 200 + 300 or 800 units. At a price of £4, total market demand will be 200 + 100 + 100 or 400 units. Similarly, all the other points

Question 6

Table 3

Price (£)	Quantity demanded of good Y (000 units)		
	Firm A	Firm B	Firm C
100	500	250	750
200	400	230	700
300	300	210	650
400	200	190	600
500	100	170	550

There are only three buyers of good Y, firms A, B and C.
(a) Draw the individual demand curves for each firm.
(b) Draw the market demand curve for good Y.
(c) A fourth business, firm D, enters the market. It will buy 500 at any price between £100 and £500. Show the effect of this by drawing a new market demand curve for good Y.
(d) Firm B goes out of business. Draw the new market demand curve with firms A, C and D buying in the market.

on the market demand curve can be derived by summing the individual demand curves. This is known as **horizontal summing** because the figures on the horizontal axis of the individual demand curves are added up to put on the market demand curve. But the figures on the vertical axis of both individual and market demand curves remain the same.

Consumer surplus

The demand curve shows how much buyers would be prepared to pay for a given quantity of goods. In Figure 6, for instance, they would be prepared to pay 10p if they bought 1 million items. At 8p, they would buy 2 million items. As the price falls, so buyers want to buy more.

This can be put another way. The more buyers are offered, the less value they put on the last one bought. If there were only 1 million units on offer for sale in Figure 6, buyers would be prepared to pay 10p for each one. But if there are 3 million for sale, they will only pay 6p. The demand curve, therefore, shows the value to the buyer of each item bought. The first unit bought is worth almost 12p to a buyer. The one millionth unit is worth 10p. The four millionth unit would be worth 4p.

The difference between the value to buyers and what they actually pay is called CONSUMER SURPLUS. Assume in Figure 6 that the price paid is 6p. The buyers who would have paid 10p for the millionth unit have gained a consumer surplus of 4p (10p - 6p). Those who would have paid 8p for the 2 millionth unit would gain 2p. So the total consumer surplus at a price of 6p is the shaded triangular area in Figure 6.

Adam Smith, writing in the 18th century, was puzzled why consumers paid high prices for goods such as diamonds which were unnecessary to human existence, whilst the price of necessities such as water was very low. Figure 6 explains this **paradox of value**. If there are few goods available to buy, as with diamonds, then consumers are prepared to pay a high price for them. If goods are plentiful, then consumers are only prepared to pay a low price. This doesn't mean to say that they don't place a high value on necessities when they are in short supply. In famine times, diamonds can be traded for small amounts of food. If diamonds were as common as water, buyers would not be prepared to pay much for the last diamond bought. Consumers enjoy large amounts of consumer surplus

on water because the price is low and large amounts are bought. Far less consumer surplus is enjoyed by consumers on diamonds because far fewer diamonds are bought.

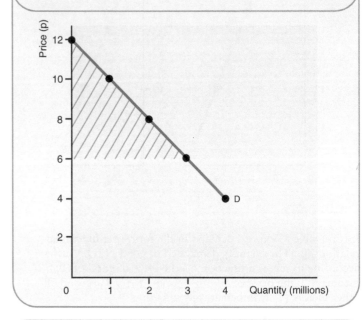

Figure 6 Consumer surplus
The demand curve shows the price that the buyer would be prepared to pay for each unit. Except on the last unit purchased, the price that the buyer is prepared to pay is above the market price that is paid. The difference between these two values is the consumer surplus. It is represented by the shaded area under the demand curve.

Question 7

Demand for a good is zero at £200. It then rises to 50 million units at £100 and 75 million at £50.
(a) Draw the demand curve for prices between 0 and £200.
(b) Shade the area of consumer surplus at a price of £60.
(c) Is consumer surplus larger or smaller at a price of £40 compared to £60? Explain your answer.

Key terms

Consumer surplus - the difference between how much buyers are prepared to pay for a good and what they actually pay.
Demand curve - the line on a price-quantity diagram which shows the level of effective demand at any given price.
Demand or effective demand - the quantity purchased of a good at any given price, given that other determinants of demand remain unchanged.

Individual demand curve - the demand curve for an individual consumer, firm or other economic unit.
Market demand curve - the sum of all individual demand curves.
Shift in the demand curve - a movement of the whole demand curve to the right or left of the original caused by a change in any variable affecting demand except price.

Applied economics

The demand for housing

Housing tenure

The housing market is not a single market because there are different forms of tenure in the market.

Owner-occupied housing Figure 7 shows that most homes today are owner-occupied. This means that they are owned by at least one of the people who live in the house.

Rented from local authorities The single largest group of landlords in the UK are local councils. Since the 1980s, their importance has declined as local authority housing has been sold off.

Rented from housing associations Housing associations are organisations set up to provide housing for rent. They have no shareholders and are not in business to make a profit. Their aim is to serve the needs of their customers. Much of their funding for building new houses comes from the government in the form of grants. Housing associations have grown in importance since the 1980s because the government has increasingly channelled grants for house building in the rented sector away from local authorities and towards housing associations.

Rented from private landlords Private landlords are in business to make a profit from renting property. The 1988 Housing Act (amended in 1996) revitalised the private renting sector. It allowed for new 'assured tenancies' where landlords could charge whatever rent they wished. For the first time in decades, landlords could charge the rent that the market would bear instead of having it capped, typically at a rent far below the market price. Landlords could also end tenancy agreements with an individual. This meant they could reclaim their property if they wanted to get rid of a difficult tenant, move back into the property or sell it without have a sitting tenant in place. The result has been an increase in the number of private properties for rent and a considerable improvement in the quality of housing for rent. In a competitive market where landlords are charging market rents, tenants can shop around not just for the cheapest rent but also for the best quality property at the price. Figure 7 shows that there was a slow rise in privately rented accommodation in the 1990s. However, this rise accelerated and between 2002 and 2006 approximately 100 000 'buy-to-let' properties were added to the rented sector each year. Individuals were buying properties with the intention of renting them out to earn a profit and to make capital gains when selling properties. Buy-to-let between 2002 and 2006 accounted for on average half of the increase in all dwellings in the UK.

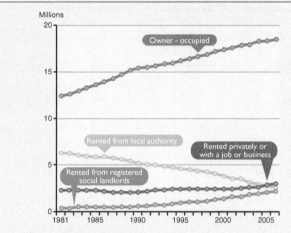

Figure 7 *Stock of dwellings by tenure, United Kingdom*

Source: adapted from www.odpm.gov.uk.

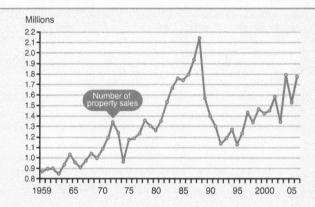

Figure 8 *Number of property sales: England and Wales (millions)*

Source: adapted from *Economic Trends*, Office for National Statistics.

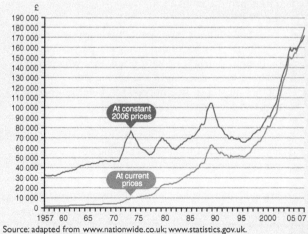

Figure 9 *Average UK house prices, £ at constant 2006 prices*

Source: adapted from www.nationwide.co.uk; www.statistics.gov.uk.

Factors affecting the demand for housing

There are many factors which determine the demand or quantity demanded of housing.

The price of owner-occupied housing Economic theory suggests that the higher the price, the less will be demanded of a good. In the owner-occupied market, rising house prices should lead to less demand and vice versa. However, Figures 8 and 9 show no evidence of this. In fact, rising house prices in the 1980s were associated with rising sales, whilst falling prices in the first half of the 1990s saw falling house sales. Equally, the house price boom which started in the mid-1990s has also been associated with rising numbers of property sales.

One explanation is that the price of a house is arguably the wrong price to consider when looking at the demand for homes. Most houses are bought with a **mortgage**. This is a loan used to buy property. When potential buyers look at the price of the transaction, they tend to look at the value of the monthly repayments on the mortgage rather than the actual house price. In the short term, the value of monthly repayments is more influenced by interest rates than house prices. If interest rates rise, mortgage repayments rise and vice versa. Comparing Figure 7, the number of property sales, with Figure 10, the level of interest rates, very large changes in interest rates do seem to have an impact on property sales. However, relatively small changes in interest rates seem to have little impact. Since 2000, for example, there seems to be little correlation between the small changes in interest rates seen and property sales.

Subsidies too can affect the monthly payments on a mortgage. In the 1970s and 1980s, the government subsidised borrowing to buy a house through giving tax relief on the interest paid on mortgages. This effectively reduced the monthly repayment cost of the mortgage. Starting in 1987, the value of mortgage tax relief was progressively reduced by the government and was finally abolished in 1999. This increased the cost of borrowing to buy a house and was one factor which dampened the demand for owner-occupied housing in the 1990s.

Even so, not all houses are purchased using a mortgage. Higher priced houses in particular tend to be bought outright or with mortgages which only account for a fraction of the buying price. So other factors must also be important in determining the demand for owner-occupied housing.

Incomes Real incomes (incomes after inflation has been taken into account) have been rising at an average of 2.5 per cent over the past 40 years in the UK. Figure 11 shows how the average real personal disposable income (income after income tax and National Insurance contributions have been deducted) of households has changed since 1971. Rising income has led to a rising

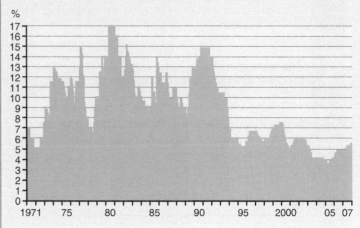

Figure 10 Interest rates: the base rate set by the Bank of England

Source: adapted from Bank of England website.

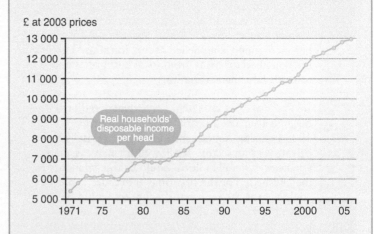

Figure 11 Real households' disposable income per head at 2003 prices

Source: adapted from *Economics Trends*, Office for National Statistics.

Table 4 Population and number of households: UK

		Millions
	Population	Number of households
1961	52.8	16.3
1971	55.9	18.6
1981	56.4	20.2
1991	57.8	22.4
2001	59.1	23.8
2006	60.5	24.2

Source: adapted from *Social Trends*, Office for National Statistics; *Monthly Digest of Statistics*, Office for National Statistics.

demand for housing. When growth in income slowed or fell, as in the early 1980s and early 1990s, this was associated with slowdowns or falls in housing prices. In the early 2000s, moderate growth in average household income undoubtedly contributed to the housing boom.

The increase in owner-occupation compared to renting is also probably due to rising income. Households in the UK prefer to own their own homes rather than renting them. Rising incomes makes home ownership more affordable to more people. Equally, though, the growth in buy-to-let from the 1990s onwards has also increased demand for housing and contributed to rising house prices.

Population trends Population trends have also been important in increasing the demand for housing. As Table 4 shows, the population of the UK is growing over time. However, the number of households is growing at a much faster rate. A household is defined as a group of people living together in a dwelling. Households have been getting smaller over time. More people are living longer and pensioners tend to live on their own. Divorce rates have increased whilst there are more one parent families than before. Fewer young people want to live at home with their parents once they have left school. So the number of dwellings needed to accommodate households has been rising and is predicted to carry on rising to 2050.

Other factors Other factors may affect the demand for housing apart from prices, income and population trends. One factor which influenced house buying in the 1970s and 1980s, and from the late 1990s onwards, was speculation. Because house prices rose consistently during the 1950s and 1960s, many saw housing more as an investment rather than as a place to live. In the property booms of the early 1970s and late 1980s, higher house prices were encouraging people to buy houses in the hope that their value would go up even further. The 1990s saw far less speculative activity because house price increases remained relatively subdued, but speculation again took off from the late 1990s as house prices soared.

The end of the housing boom in the late 1980s saw a reverse effect to this. Millions of households in the early 1990s were caught in a **negative equity** trap. They bought houses at the top of the property boom in 1988

and 1989, borrowing almost all the money needed for the purchase. House prices fell in the early 1990s. This meant that many owed more money on their mortgage than their house was worth. Hence they had 'negative equity'. This discouraged people from buying houses because it was feared that house prices might fall even further, leading to equity losses. Moreover, due to very high interest rates and high unemployment, many fell behind with their mortgage payments and eventually saw their houses repossessed by their lenders. This experience discouraged households from overborrowing throughout much of the rest of the 1990s.

In the rented housing market, important legal changes led to changes in demand. In 1980, the government gave tenants of council houses the right to buy their homes at very low prices. Over the next two decades, more than one and half million council houses were sold to their tenants. So this legal change led to a rise in demand for owner-occupied housing.

Another important legal change was the passing of the 1988 Housing Act. This gave landlords the right to set their own rents. Previously, rents had been controlled by law and in practice were very low. In theory, higher rents should have led to a fall in demand for rented accommodation. However, two other factors more than outweighed this effect. First, property rented under the 1988 Housing Act arrangements tended to be much better quality than under rent controls. Second, rising prices for houses forced some people into the rented sector because they couldn't afford to buy.

The relative importance of different factors

In the long term, rising incomes and an increasing number of households are pushing up the demand for

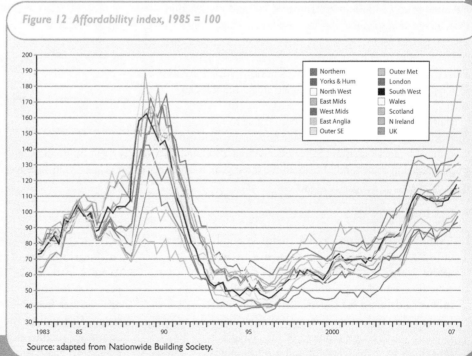

Figure 12 Affordability index, 1985 = 100

Northern	Outer Met
Yorks & Hum	London
North West	South West
East Mids	Wales
West Mids	Scotland
East Anglia	N Ireland
Outer SE	UK

Source: adapted from Nationwide Building Society.

both owner-occupied and rented housing in the UK. In the short term, other factors have had a significant impact on the demand for housing, including property speculation, changes in the law, the ending of mortgage tax relief and changes in interest rates.

One measure which attempts to combine a variety of factors is the First time Buyer Nationwide Affordability Index shown in Figure 12. The Nationwide Building Society calculates the index based on first time home buyers. Average mortgage payments depend on the size of the mortgage, and therefore for new house purchases the price of housing, and the rate of interest paid on the mortgage. If house prices fall, interest rates fall, or take home pay rises, then houses become more affordable and the index goes down. If house prices rise, interest

rates rise, or take home pay falls, then houses become less affordable and the index rises.

Figure 12 shows that houses were least affordable at the end of the 1980s due to a combination of relatively high prices and high interest rates. Figure 12 also shows that affordability deteriorated sharply from 2002. Despite low interest rates and rising incomes, the size of mortgages increased rapidly because house prices were rising sharply. What the index cannot indicate, however, is at what level houses would become unaffordable to first time buyers. In the late 1980s, a high affordability index was associated with a housing slump. The same would happen today if the affordability index reached too high a level.

DataQuestion   Independent Schools

The number of school age children might be falling, but the numbers going to private schools are rising. Figures from the Independent Schools Council show an increase of 0.7 per cent in 2006. This is despite rising school fees. Average school fees were up 5.9 per cent this year. The average termly fee for a private day school is £ 2 930, a 6.4 per cent rise, and £6 990 for boarders, an increase of 5.6 per cent.

The increase in student numbers comes after private schools sharply raised spending on advertising and a more professional marketing effort. A survey to be published later this summer will show the average school's marketing budget has risen from £33 966 in 2001 to £59 330 in 2006. Within that, advertising spending has increased on average from £9 500 to £19 600.

The number of affluent, time-poor parents is rising too. Hilary Moriarty, from the Boarding Schools Association, says: 'Time-poor parents value all that independent schools can offer.'

Many private schools have also been trying to make themselves more affordable to poorer families by increasing the amount of financial assistance they offer. About £300 million a year is spent on financial assistance, with almost a third of pupils receiving some kind of help. In the latest year, the number of pupils receiving such help rose by 3.4 per cent to 158 807.

Source: adapted from the *Financial Times*, 4.5.2007.

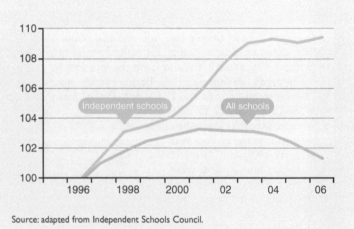

Figure 13 Change in pupil numbers at independent schools, Number of pupils (index, 1996=100)

Source: adapted from Independent Schools Council.

1. Using Figure 13, compare the trends in pupil numbers in independent schools with those in all schools in recent years.
2. The data describes a number of factors which might influence demand for independent school places. Using a demand curve diagram for each example, explain the effect on demand of the changes in (a) school fees; (b) school population numbers;

(c) marketing and advertising; (d) numbers of 'affluent, time-poor parents'; (e) financial assistance.
3 Average incomes are rising by around 4.0 per cent per year, but for the top 10 per cent of income earners, this rise has been higher. School fees too have been rising. Using diagrams, discuss whether the amount of consumer surplus derived by parents from independent education has been rising over the past ten years.

Summary

1. A rise in price leads to a rise in quantity supplied, shown by a movement along the supply curve.
2. A change in supply can be caused by factors such as a change in costs of production, technology and the price of other goods. This results in a shift in the supply curve.
3. The market supply curve in a perfectly competitive market is the sum of each firm's individual supply curves.

Supply

In any market there are buyers and sellers. Buyers **demand** goods whilst sellers **supply** goods. SUPPLY in economics is defined as the quantity of goods that sellers are prepared to sell at any given price over a period of time. For instance, in 2006 UK farmers sold 5.1 million tonnes of potatoes at an average price of £129 per tonne, so economists would say that the supply of potatoes at £129 per tonne over the 12 month period was 5.1 million tonnes.

Supply and price

If the price of a good increases, how will producers react? Assuming that no other factors have changed, they are likely to expand production to take advantage of the higher prices and the higher profits that they can now make. In general, quantity supplied will rise (there will be an **extension of supply**) if the price of the good also rises, all other things being equal.

This can be shown on a diagram using a **supply curve**. A supply curve shows the quantity that will be supplied over a period of time at any given price. Consider Figure 1 which shows the supply curve for wheat. Wheat is priced at £110 per tonne. At this price only the most efficient farmers grow wheat. They supply 110 million tonnes per year. However, if the price of wheat rose to £140 per tonne, farmers already growing wheat might increase their acreage of wheat, whilst other non-wheat growing farmers might start to grow wheat. Farmers would do this because at a price of £140 per tonne it is possible to make a profit on production even if costs are higher than at a production level of 110 million units.

A fall in price will lead to a **fall in quantity supplied**, or **contraction of supply**, shown by a **movement along** the supply curve. At a lower price, some firms will cut back on relatively unprofitable production whilst others will stop producing altogether. Some of the latter firms may even go bankrupt, unable to cover their costs of production from the price received.

An upward sloping supply curve assumes that:
- firms are motivated to produce by profit - so this model does not apply, for instance, to much of what is produced by government;
- the cost of producing a unit increases as output increases (a situation known as rising marginal cost) - this is not always

Figure 1 The supply curve

The supply curve is upward sloping, showing that firms increase production of a good as its price increases. This is because a higher price enables firms to make profit on the increased output whereas at the lower price they would have made a loss on it. Here, an increase in the price of wheat from £110 to £140 per tonne increases quantity supplied from 110 million tonnes to 150 million tonnes per year.

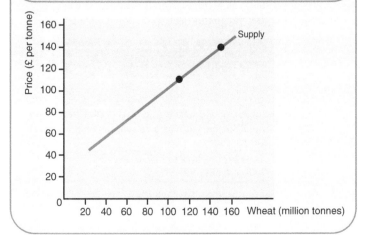

Question 1

Table 1

Price (£)	Quantity supplied (million units per year)
5	5
10	8
15	11
20	14
25	17

(a) Draw a supply curve from the above data.
(b) Draw new supply curves assuming that quantity supplied at any given price:
   (i) increased by 10 units; (ii) increased by 50 per cent; (iii) fell by 5 units; (iv) halved.

true but it is likely that the prices of factors of production to the firm will increase as firms bid for more land, labour and capital to increase their output, thus pushing up costs.

Costs of production

The supply curve is drawn on the assumption that the general costs of production in the economy remain constant (part of the **ceteris paribus** condition). If other things change, then the supply curve will shift. If the costs of production increase at any given level of output, firms will attempt to pass on these increases in the form of higher prices. If they cannot charge higher prices then profits will fall and firms will produce less of the good or might even stop producing it altogether. A rise in the costs of production will therefore lead to a decrease in supply.

This can be seen in Figure 3. The original supply curve is S_1. A rise in the costs of production means that at any given level of output firms will charge higher prices. At an output level of 0A, firms will increase their prices from 0B to 0C. This increase in prices will be true for all points on the supply curve. So the supply curve will **shift** upwards and to the left to S_2 in Figure 3. There will have been a **fall in supply**. (Note that a fall in **quantity supplied** refers to a change in quantity supplied due to a change in price and would be shown by a movement along the supply curve.) Conversely a fall in the costs of production will lead to an increase in supply of a good. This is shown by a shift to the right in the supply curve.

Technology

Another factor which affects supply of a particular good is the state of technology. The supply curve is drawn on the

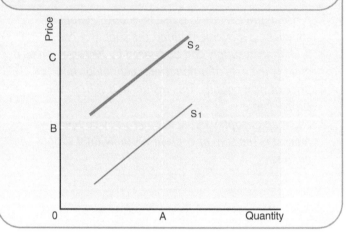

Figure 3 A rise in the costs of production
A rise in the costs of production for a firm will push its supply curve upwards and to the left, from S_1 to S_2. For any given quantity supplied, firms will now want a higher price to compensate them for the increase in their costs.

assumption that the state of technology remains unchanged. If new technology is introduced to the production process it should lead to a fall in the costs of production. This greater **productive efficiency** will encourage firms to produce more at the same price or produce the same amount at a lower price or some combination of the two. The supply curve will shift downwards and to the right. It would be unusual for firms to replace more efficient technology with less efficient technology. However, this can occur at times of war or natural disasters. If new technical equipment is destroyed, firms may have to fall back on less efficient means of production, reducing supply at any given price, resulting in a shift in the supply curve to the left.

The prices of other goods

Changes in the prices of some goods can affect the supply of a particular good. For instance, if the price of beef increases substantially there will be an increase in the quantity of beef supplied. More cows will be reared and slaughtered. As a result there will be an increase in the supply of hides for leather. At the same price, the quantity of leather supplied to the market will increase. An increase in the price of beef therefore leads to an increase in the supply of leather. On the other hand, an increase in cattle rearing is likely to be at the expense of production of wheat or sheep farming. So an increase in beef production is likely to lead to a fall in the supply of other agricultural products as farmers switch production to take advantage of higher profits in beef.

Question 2

Figure 2 Average percentage change in earnings over the previous 12 months

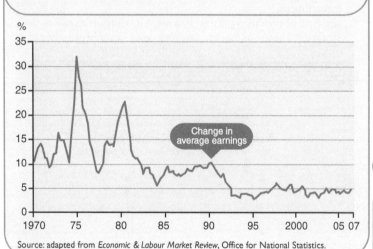

Source: adapted from *Economic & Labour Market Review*, Office for National Statistics.

(a) Explain how a change in earnings can shift the supply curve of a product to the left.
(b) Discuss in which years the supply curves for goods made in the UK are likely to have shifted (i) furthest and (ii) least far to the left according to the data.

Question 3

Explain, using supply curves, why it cost £10 000 in 1970 for a machine that could do the same as a calculator which cost £100 in 1975 and £5 today.

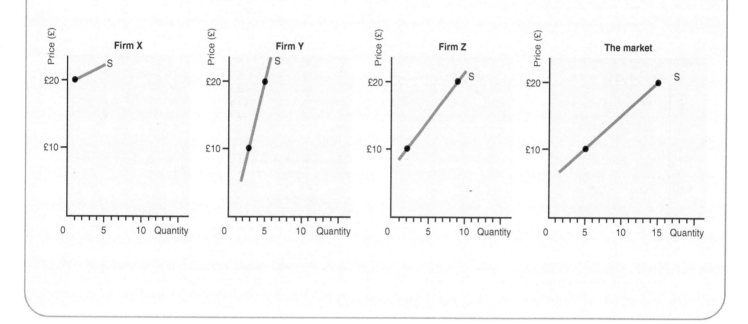

Figure 4 Individual and market supply curves
The market supply curve is calculated by summing the individual supply curves of producers in the market. Here the market supply at £20, for instance, is calculated by adding the supply of each individual firm at a price of £20.

Other factors

A number of other factors affect supply. These include:
• the goals of sellers - if for some reason there is a change in the profit levels which a seller expects to receive as a reward for production, then there will be a change in supply; for instance, if an industry such as the book retailing industry went from one made up of many small sellers more interested in selling books than making a profit to one where the industry was dominated by a few large profit-seeking companies, then supply would fall;
• government legislation - anti-pollution controls which raise the costs of production, the abolition of legal barriers to setting up business in an industry, or tax changes, are some examples of how government can change the level of supply

in an industry;
• expectations of future events - if firms expect future prices to be much higher, they may restrict supplies and stockpile goods; if they expect disruptions to their future production because of a strike they may stockpile raw materials, paying for them with borrowed money, thus increasing their costs and reducing supply;
• the weather - in agricultural markets, the weather plays a crucial role in determining supply, bad weather reducing supply, good weather producing bumper yields;
• producer cartels - in some markets, producing firms or producing countries band together, usually to restrict supply; this allows them to raise prices and increase their profits or revenues; the best known cartel today is OPEC which restricts the supply of oil onto world markets.

Question 4

Explain, using diagrams, how you would expect supply of the following goods to be affected by the events stated, all other things being equal.

(a) Wheat. A drought in Romania reduced its wheat harvest by 46 per cent in 2007.
(b) Beef. Embrapa, a Brazilian agricultural research body, developed new strains of grass that allowed Brazilian cattle ranches to feed more cattle per hectare of grazing land.
(c) Houses. The government published a white paper in 2007 which wants to see an easing of planning permission restrictions on land in the South East of England.

Individual and market supply curves

The MARKET SUPPLY CURVE can be derived from the INDIVIDUAL SUPPLY CURVES of sellers in the market (this assumes that supply is not affected by changes in the demand curve as would happen under monopoly or oligopoly). Consider Figure 4. For the sake of simplicity we will assume that there are only three sellers in the market. At a price of £10 per unit, Firm X is unwilling to supply any goods. Firm Y supplies 3 units whilst Firm Z supplies 2 units. So the market supply at a price of £10 is 5 units. At a price of £20, Firm X will supply 1 unit, Firm Y 5 units and Firm Z 9 units. So the market supply at a price of £20 is 15 units. The rest of the market supply curve can be derived by **horizontally summing** the level of output at all other price levels.

Figure 5 Producer surplus

The supply curve shows how much will be supplied at any given price. Except on the last unit supplied, the supplier receives more for the good than the lowest price at which it is prepared to supply. This difference between the market price and lowest price at which a firm is prepared to supply is producer surplus. Total producer surplus is shown by the shaded area above the supply curve.

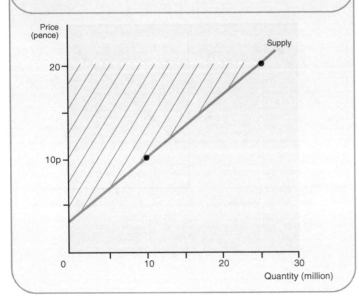

Question 5

Table 2

Quantity supplied (million units)			Price (£)
Firms in area A	Firms in area B	Firms in area C	
10	2	0	1
12	5	3	2
14	8	6	3
16	11	9	4
18	14	12	5

Firms in areas A, B and C are the sole suppliers in the market and the market is perfectly competitive.

(a) Draw the market supply curve.
(b) What is supply at a price of (i) £1 and (ii) £3.50?
(c) One firm in area A decides to increase production by 5 units at every given price. Draw the new market supply curve on your diagram.
(d) Explain what would happen to the market supply curve if new technology in the industry led to greater productive efficiency amongst individual firms.

Producer surplus

The supply curve shows how much will be supplied at any given price. In Figure 5, firms will supply 10 million units at 10p whereas they will supply 25 million units at 20p. Assume that the price that firms receive is actually 20p. Some firms will then receive more than the lowest price at which they are prepared to supply. For instance, one firm was prepared to supply the 10 millionth unit at 10p. The firm receives 20p, which is 10p more. This 10p is PRODUCER SURPLUS. It is the difference between the market price which the firm receives and the price at which it is prepared to supply. The total amount of producer surplus earned by firms is shown by the area between the supply curve and horizontal line at the market price. It is the sum of the producer surplus earned at each level of output.

Key terms

Individual supply curve - the supply curve of an individual producer.
Market supply curve - the supply curve of all producers within the market. In a perfectly competitive market it can be calculated by summing the supply curves of individual producers.

Producer surplus - the difference between the market price which firms receive and the price at which they are prepared to supply.
Supply - the quantity of goods that suppliers are willing to sell at any given price over a period of time.

Applied economics

The supply of new housing

New housing

There is a number of different markets within the housing market, each of which has its own supply. One way of subdividing the housing market is into the market for new dwellings and the market for second hand dwellings. Approximately 90 per cent of house sales are of existing dwellings. The remaining 10 per cent is of new dwellings.

Figure 6 shows that new dwellings are of two types. Most new dwellings are sold privately, either to owner-occupier buyers or as buy-to-let properties. In 2005/06, 210 000 new properties were sold in this way. The other source of new dwellings is 'Social Landlords'. In practice, this means housing associations. They mainly rent out properties to those for whom owner occupation might be unsuitable. This includes those on below average incomes or the elderly. Social landlords receive most of their funding for new houses from the government. So the supply of new social housing is dependent on the political priorities of governments rather than market forces. Note that local authorities which supply council housing effectively no longer build new houses. Although they own and rent out a large stock of houses, they play no part in the new housing market.

Factors affecting the supply of new private housing

Economic theory would suggest that the supply of new private housing would be affected by a variety of factors including price, costs and government legislation.

Price A rise in the price of new housing should lead to a rise in quantity supplied. Figure 7 shows that the rapid rise in prices since 2000 has lead to a significant rise in private housing. However, the response has been relatively weak. In the 1990s, there was little correlation between the two variables. Over the period 2000-2006,

the 74 per cent price rise led to a 26 per cent rise in supply of new dwellings. This would suggest that other factors are important in determining the supply of new housing.

Costs Costs of new housing have risen over time. Figure 9 shows that the price of land for building has risen substantially over time. Wages of workers in the construction industry have risen too. Other costs, such as costs of building materials have also risen. Rises in costs will have shifted the supply curve for new housing to the left.

Government regulation House building companies often argue that they would build more houses if only government regulations were relaxed. All new houses need planning permission. The vast majority of the land in the UK which is not already built on is not available for building. A whole variety of restrictions such as Green Belt regulations and limited access to National Parks prevent any sort of development outside urban areas. Even within built up areas, there is a very limited amount of land available for new house building. Getting planning permission for this land takes years. Initial applications are usually refused because planners feel that the development is inappropriate. The planning regime therefore ensures that house builders cannot respond quickly to large changes in house prices. If the planning regime were relaxed, this would push the supply curve for new housing to the right, allowing more houses to be built at the same price.

Technology Some argue that the supply of housing could increase if UK house builders adopted new technology in their construction techniques. In the UK, the typical dwelling is still built using bricks and mortar. On the Continent and in the USA, many houses are built using pre-fabricated techniques where much of the dwelling is built off site and then assembled on site. These techniques, it is argued, would produce lower cost

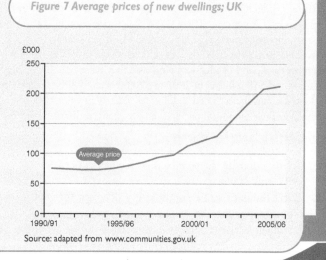

Figure 6 Annual completions of new houses

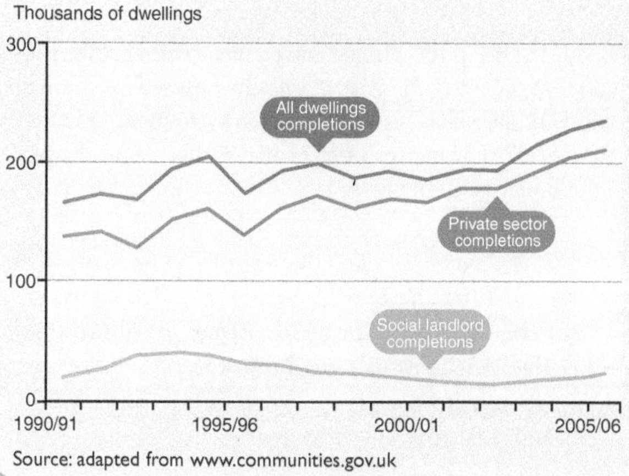

Thousands of dwellings

All dwellings completions
Private sector completions
Social landlord completions

Source: adapted from www.communities.gov.uk

Figure 7 Average prices of new dwellings; UK

£000

Average price

Source: adapted from www.communities.gov.uk

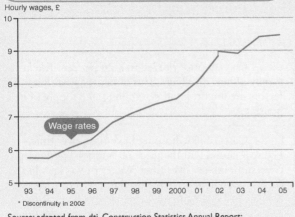

Figure 8 *New house building costs: average hourly earnings of bricklayers and masons. £ per hour*

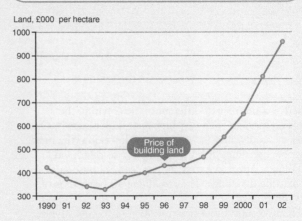

Figure 9 *Average price of building land, £000 per hectare*

houses, pushing the supply curve to the right.

The supply of new housing is a major political issue in the UK. The environmental and rural lobbies argue that almost all new housing must be built within existing urban areas to prevent the 'concreting over' of Britain. Planning regulations effectively ensure that this is what actually occurs. The result is that the lack of supply

forces building land prices up and increases the cost of new homes. The only way to increase supply substantially would be to ease planning restrictions, building in what is now countryside. This is unlikely to occur in the immediate future given the strength of the environmental and rural lobbies.

DataQuestion — Coffee

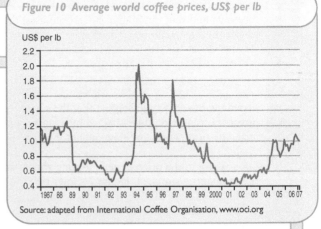

Figure 10 *Average world coffee prices, US$ per lb*

Commodity prices have soared over the past few years but coffee has not shared in this bonanza for producers. In fact, coffee prices have never recovered from the collapse of the coffee cartel in 1989.

Before 1989, a number of countries agreed to limit sales and production of coffee on world markets. In 1989, this arrangement collapsed. To make the cartel work, individual countries had withheld stocks of unsold coffee. Over the next few years, these stocks were sold off in addition to normal annual production. This caused a glut of coffee in world markets.

Prices rebounded when Brazil, one of the world's largest coffee producers, was hit by frost in 1994. Severe frost can seriously damage coffee bushes and reduce their yield. Frost hit Brazil again in 1995. There followed a period of four or five years of good prices. This provided the incentive for many coffee producers to increase their production of coffee. For example, Vietnam went from being an insignificant grower of coffee to the world's second largest producer.

Rising production eventually outstripped demand for coffee. In 2000, supply grew by 3.5 per cent when world demand for coffee only increased by 1.5 per cent. There was a sharp correction in coffee prices. Coffee growers were quick to react. Brazil's coffee production, for example, fell from a peak of 55 billion bags per year to 30 million.

By 2005 prices began to rise again. Production, however, has not increased. Higher prices should have given coffee growers an incentive to expand production. However, they have been hit by higher costs, particularly the cost of oil which increased dramatically from around $10 a barrel in 2002 to $70 a barrel in 2007. Higher prices in US dollars has also not necessarily resulted in higher prices in domestic currencies. The US dollar fell sharply in value between 2005 and 2007. For many coffee growers, this meant the price they received in their own local currency barely changed despite sharp rises in the dollar price of coffee.

Source: adapted from www.ico.org/news.asp.

1. Briefly describe the trends in coffee prices between 1987 and 2006.
2. Using the data and a supply curve diagram for each example, explain the impact on the world supply of coffee of: (a) severe frosts in important coffee growing regions; (b) changes in costs for coffee growers; (c) changes in the price of coffee; (d) dumping of coffee stocks onto world markets.
3. Discuss whether severe frosts in Vietnam would benefit all coffee producers.

Summary

1. The equilibrium or market clearing price is set where demand equals supply.
2. Changes in demand and supply will lead to new equilibrium prices being set.
3. A change in demand will lead to a shift in the demand curve, a movement along the supply curve and a new equilibrium price.
4. A change in supply will lead to a shift in the supply curve, a movement along the demand curve and a new equilibrium price.
5. Markets do not necessarily tend towards the equilibrium price.
6. The equilibrium price is not necessarily the price which will lead to the greatest economic efficiency or the greatest equity.

Equilibrium price

Buyers and sellers come together in a market. A price (sometimes called the **market price**) is struck and goods or services are exchanged. Consider Table 1. It shows the demand and supply schedule for a good at prices between £2 and £10.

Table 1

Price (£)	Quantity demanded (million units per month)	Quantity supplied (million units per month)
2	12	2
4	9	4
6	6	6
8	3	8
10	0	10

Figure 1 Equilibrium

At £6, the quantity demanded is equal to the quantity supplied. The market is said to be in equilibrium at this price.

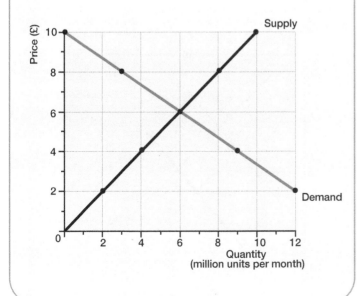

- If the price is £2, demand will be 12 million units but only 2 million units will be supplied. Demand is greater than supply and there is therefore EXCESS DEMAND (i.e. too much demand in relation to supply) in the market. There will be a **shortage** of products on the market. Some buyers will be lucky and they will snap up the 2 million units being sold. But there will be a 10 million unit shortfall in supply for the rest of the unlucky buyers in the market. For instance, it is not possible to buy some luxury cars without being on a waiting list for several years because current demand is too great.
- If the price is £10, buyers will not buy any goods. Sellers on the other hand will wish to supply 10 million units. Supply is greater than demand and therefore there will be EXCESS SUPPLY. There will be a glut or surplus of products on the market. 10 million units will remain unsold. A sale in a shop is often evidence of excess supply in the past. Firms tried to sell the goods at a higher price and failed.
- There is only one price where demand equals supply. This is at a price of £6 where demand and supply are both 6 million units. This price is known as the EQUILIBRIUM PRICE. This is the only price where the planned demand of buyers equals the planned supply of sellers in the market. It is also known as the MARKET-CLEARING price because all the products supplied to the market are bought or cleared from the market, but no buyer is left frustrated in his or her wishes to buy goods.

An alternative way of expressing the data in Table 1 is shown in Figure 1. The equilibrium price is where demand equals supply. This happens where the two curves cross, at a price of £6 and a quantity of 6 million units. If the price is above £6, supply will be greater than demand and therefore excess supply will exist. If the price is below £6, demand is greater than supply and therefore there will be excess demand.

Changes in demand and supply

It was explained in the previous two units that a change in price would lead to a change in quantity demanded or supplied, shown by a movement along the demand or supply curve. A change in any other variable, such as income or the costs of production, would lead to:

Question 1

Table 2

Price (£)	Quantity demanded (million units)	Quantity supplied (million units)
30	20	70
20	50	50
10	80	30

(a) Plot the demand and supply curves shown in Table 2 on a diagram.
(b) What is the equilibrium price?
(c) In what price range is there (i) excess demand and (ii) excess supply?
(d) Will there be a glut or a shortage in the market if the price is: (i) £10; (ii) £40; (iii) £22; (iv) £18; (v) £20?

● an **increase** or **decrease** in demand or supply and therefore
● a **shift** in the demand or supply curve.
Demand and supply diagrams provide a powerful and simple tool for analysing the effects of changes in demand and supply on equilibrium price and quantity.

Consider the effect of a rise in consumer incomes. This will lead to an increase in the demand for a normal good. In Figure 2(a) this will push the demand curve from D_1 to D_2. As can be seen from the diagram, the equilibrium price rises from P_1 to P_2. The quantity bought and sold in equilibrium rises from Q_1 to Q_2. The model of demand and supply predicts that an increase in incomes, all other things being equal (the **ceteris paribus** condition) will lead to an increase both in the price of the product and in the quantity sold. Note that the increase in income **shifts** the demand curve and this then leads to a **movement along** the supply curve.

Figure 2(b) shows the market for televisions in the early 2000s. In the early 2000s, many manufacturers introduced flat screen, slimline televisions. As a result, there was a boom in sales of these televisions and a slump in sales of older, more bulky sets. In economic terms the demand for older, bulky sets

Figure 2 *Shifts in the demand and supply curves*
Shifts in the demand or supply curves for a product will change the equilibrium price and the equilibrium quantity bought and sold.

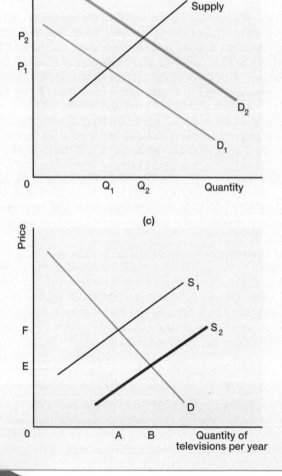

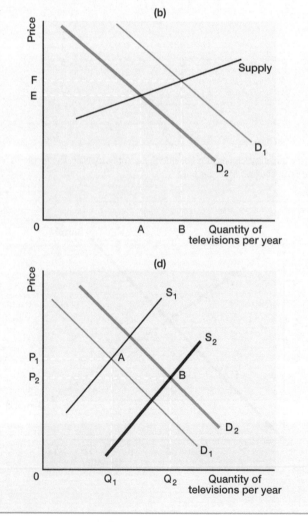

Question 2

During the 1970s the price of metals such as nickel was historically high. This prompted nickel producers to invest in new production facilities which came on stream during the late 1970s and early 1980s. But the world economy went into deep recession during the early 1980s, prompting a collapse in the world price of nickel. Producers reacted by closing facilities. Between 1980 and 1986, the industry lost about 32 500 tonnes of annual capacity compared with an annual demand of between 400 000 and 500 000 tonnes.

The world economy started to recover from 1982 but it wasn't until 1987 that a sharp increase in demand from Japanese stainless steel producers, one of the major buyers in the industry, made prices rise. In the last quarter of 1987, nickel could be bought for $1.87 per lb. By March 1988, it had soared to over $9 per lb. This price proved unsustainable. Both the US and UK economies began to go into recession in 1989 and nickel prices fell to below $3 per lb by the end of 1989.

The invasion of Kuwait by Iraq in 1990 and the subsequent large military involvement of the USA and other countries in defeating Iraq led to a rise in most metal prices. The markets feared a long drawn out war with a possible increase in demand from armaments manufacturers and a possible fall in supply if any nickel producing countries decided to side with Iraq and suspend nickel sales onto the world market. However, the swift defeat of Iraq led to a sharp fall back in price. Recession in Europe and Japan produced further falls in price between 1991 and 1993 despite the beginning of recovery in the US economy, with the price falling below $2 per lb in the last quarter of 1993. The price would have been even lower but for cutbacks in output by major nickel producers over the period.

1994 saw a sharp rise in demand as all the major industrialised countries showed economic growth. By the start of 1995, nickel prices had risen to over $3 per lb. The next major price movement occurred in 1997. An increase in productive capacity led to oversupply and falling prices. However, at the end of the year, this was compounded by the start of the Asian crisis. Several countries in East Asia, including South Korea and Thailand, experienced a financial

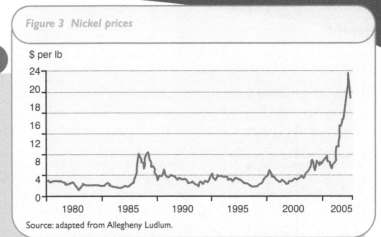

Figure 3 Nickel prices

$ per lb

Source: adapted from Allegheny Ludlum.

crisis which led to a sharp fall in domestic production. Demand for nickel from the Far East fell sharply, going below $2 per lb at the end of 1998 before recovering in price as East Asian economies bounced back in 1999 and 2000, reaching a high of nearly $5 per lb.

Fears of a recession in the world economy in 2000 and 2001 then led to a fall in the price of nickel back down to nearly $2 per lb at the end of 2002. However, growing demand from the Far East, particularly China, led to a surge in commodity prices from 2003, returning prices to levels not seen since the late 1980s.

Using demand and supply diagrams, explain why the price of nickel changed when:
(a) new production facilities came on stream in the late 1970s;
(b) there was a world recession in the early 1980s;
(c) the industry closed capacity during the early 1980s;
(d) Japanese stainless steel producers increased purchases in 1987;
(e) Iraq invaded Kuwait in 1990;
(f) all the major industrialised countries showed economic growth in 1994;
(g) the 1998 Asian crisis occurred;
(h) China, a country with the world's largest population, experienced fast economic growth between 2003 and 2007.

fell. This is shown by a shift to the left in the demand curve. The equilibrium level of sales in Figure 2(b) falls from 0B to 0A whilst equilibrium price falls from 0F to 0E. Note again that a shift in the demand curve leads to a movement along the supply curve.

Prices of many models of television set tended to fall in the 1970s and 1980s. The main reason for this was an increase in productive efficiency due to the introduction of new technology, enabling costs of production to fall. A fall in costs of production is shown by the shift to the right in the supply curve in Figure 2(c). At any given quantity of output, firms will be prepared to supply more television sets to the market. The result is an increase in quantity bought and sold from 0A to 0B and a fall in price from 0F to 0E. Note that there is a shift in the supply curve which leads to a movement along the demand curve.

So far we have assumed that only one variable changes and that all other variables remain constant. However, in the real world, it is likely that several factors affecting demand and supply will change at the same time. Demand and supply diagrams can be used to some extent to analyse several changes. For instance, in the 2000s the demand for flat screen and high definition television sets increased due to rising real incomes. At the same time, supply increased too because of an increase in

productive efficiency. Overall, the price of television sets fell slightly. This is shown in Figure 2(d). Both the demand and supply curves shift to the right. This will lead to an increase in quantity bought and sold. In theory, depending upon the extent of the shifts in the two curves, there could be an increase in price, a fall in price or no change in the price. Figure 2(d) shows the middle of these three possibilities.

Do markets clear?

It is very easy to assume that the equilibrium price is either the current market price or the price towards which the market moves. Neither is correct. The market price could be at any level. There could be excess demand or excess supply at any point in time.

Nor will market prices necessarily tend to change to equilibrium prices over time. One of the most important controversies in economics today is the extent to which markets tend towards market-clearing prices.

The argument put forward by neo-classical free market economists is that markets do tend to clear. Let us take the example of the coffee market. In this market, there are many producers (farmers, manufacturers, wholesalers and

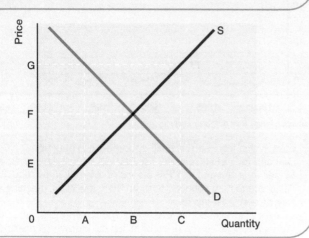

Figure 4 *The operation of market forces in the coffee market*
Market pressure will tend to force down coffee prices when there is excess supply, such as at price OG, but force up coffee prices when there is excess demand, such as at price OE.

retailers) that are motivated by the desire to make as large a profit as possible. When there is excess demand for coffee (demand is greater than supply), coffee producers will be able to increase their prices and therefore their profits and still sell all they produce. If there is excess supply (supply is greater than demand), some coffee will remain unsold. Producers then have a choice. Either they can offer coffee for sale at the existing price and risk not selling it or they can lower their price to the level where they will sell everything offered. If all producers choose not to lower their prices, there is likely to be even greater pressure to reduce prices in the future because there will be unsold stocks of coffee overhanging the market. Therefore when there is excess demand, prices will be driven upwards whilst prices will fall if there is excess supply.

This can be shown diagrammatically. In Figure 4, there is excess demand at a price of 0E. Buyers want to purchase AC more of coffee than is being supplied. Shops, manufacturers and coffee growers will be able to increase their prices and their production and still sell everything they produce. If they wish to sell all their output, they can increase their prices to a maximum

Question 3

Aggressive discounts have pulled in large numbers of shoppers to retailers' winter sales. December 27, the day on which many big retailers started their sales, was the busiest sales shopping day for four years and busier than any shopping day in the run-up to Christmas.

The slow start to the Christmas season had left retailers with a lot of unsold stock, prompting heavy discounting in clothing and some other categories. Despite disappointing sales before Christmas, the big retailers had avoided the temptation to bring their sales forward to before Christmas. If they can off-load their unsold stock in the post-Christmas sales season, the decision not to bring forward their sales will have helped keep their profits up.

Source: adapted from the *Financial Times*, 2.1.2007.

(a) Using a supply and demand diagram, explain why there was excess supply of goods in the shops in the run up to Christmas 2006.
(b) Using another diagram, explain how retailers acted after Christmas 2006 to restore equilibrium to the market.

of 0F and their output to a maximum 0B, the market-clearing prices and production levels. This they will do because at higher prices and production levels they will be able to make more profit. If there is excess supply, coffee producers will be left with unsold stocks. At a price of 0G, output left unsold will be AC. Producers in a free market cannot afford to build up stocks forever. Some producers will lower prices and the rest will be forced to follow. Production and prices will go on falling until equilibrium output and price is reached. This is usually referred to as a **stable equilibrium** position.

These pressures which force the market towards an equilibrium point are often called FREE MARKET FORCES. However, critics of the market mechanism argue that free market forces can lead away from the equilibrium point in many cases. In other markets, it is argued that market forces are too weak to restore equilibrium. Many Keynesian economists cite the labour market as an example of this. In other markets, there are many forces such as government legislation, trade unions and multi-national monopolies which more than negate the power of the market.

Consumer and producer surplus

Consumer and producer surplus can be shown on a demand and supply diagram. In Figure 5, the equilibrium price is 0J. Consumer surplus, the difference between how much buyers are prepared to pay for a good and what they actually pay, is the area JHG. Producer surplus, the difference between the market price which firms receive and the price at which they are prepared to supply, is shown by the area JGF.

The amounts of consumer and producer surplus will change if either demand or supply change. For example, in Figure 6, demand increases, shown by a shift to the right in the demand curve. For suppliers, an increase in demand results in higher equilibrium output and higher prices. Suppliers will experience an increase in producer surplus. For consumers, the increase in demand shows that they are prepared to pay a higher price for the same quantity bought. They place a greater value on the good. So their consumer surplus also increases. This can be seen by the increase in the shaded areas in Figure 6.

Points to note

Equilibrium is a very powerful concept in economics but it is essential to remember that the equilibrium price is unlikely to be the most desirable price or 'right' price in the market. The most desirable price in the market will depend upon how one defines 'desirable'. It may be, for instance, the one which leads to the greatest economic efficiency, or it may be the one which leads to greatest equity. Alternatively it may be the one which best supports the defence of the country.

Demand can also equal supply without there being equilibrium. At any point in time, what is actually bought must equal what is actually sold. There can be no sellers without buyers. So actual demand (more often referred to as **realised** or **ex post** demand in economics) must always equal actual (or realised or ex post) supply. Equilibrium occurs at a price where there is no tendency to change. Price will not change if, at the current price, the quantity that consumers wish to buy (called **planned** or **desired** or **ex ante** demand) is equal to the quantity that suppliers wish to sell (called planned or desired or ex ante supply).

Therefore only in equilibrium will planned demand equal planned supply.

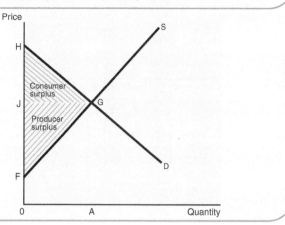

Figure 5 *Consumer and producer surplus*
Consumer surplus is the shaded area JGH, showing how much more consumers are prepared to pay for buying a total of 0A goods. Producer surplus is FGJ, showing how less they would have been prepared to accept in revenue for supplying 0B than they actually received.

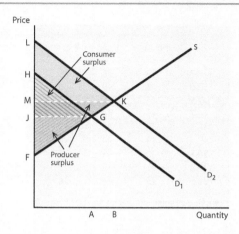

Figure 6 *Changing consumer and producer surplus*
A rise in demand from D_1 to D_2 increases consumer surplus from JGH to MKL and producer surplus from FGJ to FKM.

Key terms

Equilibrium price - the price at which there is no tendency to change because planned (or desired or ex ante) purchases (i.e. demand) are equal to planned sales (i.e. supply).
Excess demand - where demand is greater than supply.
Excess supply - where supply is greater than demand.

Free market forces - forces in free markets which act to reduce prices when there is excess supply and raise prices when there is excess demand.
Market clearing price - the price at which there is neither excess demand nor excess supply but where everything offered for sale is purchased.

Applied economics

Demand and supply in the passenger transport market

The quantity demanded and supplied of passenger transport in the UK over the past 50 years has almost quadrupled, as Figure 7 shows. Almost all of this growth is accounted for by a rise in the demand for car

Table 3 *Disposable income and household expenditure on passenger transport*

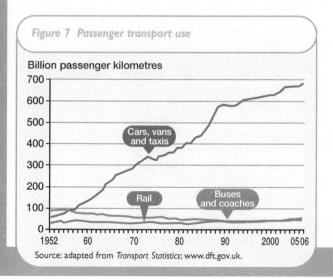

Figure 7 *Passenger transport use*

Billion passenger kilometres

Source: adapted from *Transport Statistics*; www.dft.gov.uk.

	Personal households' disposable income per head, £, at 2001 prices	Household expenditure on transport, £, average per week at 2001 prices	Household expenditure on transport as a percentage of total household expenditure %	Motoring expenditure as a percentage of all household expenditure on transport %
1965	4 640	30.90	9.7	74.5
1970	5 084	36.29	10.2	77.2
1975	5 873	37.78	13.8	80.2
1980	6 611	40.55	14.6	81.2
1985	7 147	44.25	15.2	84.4
1990	9 015	54.99	16.2	84.5
1995	9 978	50.16	15.1	85.7
2000	11 120	62.79	19.9	85.2
2004	12 094	65.52	16.9	85.2

1. Figures for expenditure for 1995 are 1994/5, for 2000 are 1999/2000 and for 2006 are 2005/6.
Source: adapted from *Economic Trends Annual Supplement*, Office for National Statistics; Department for the Environment, Transport and the Regions, *Transport Statistics*.

Table 4 Car ownership

	Number of private cars licensed, millions	Households with regular use of car(s) %			
		no car	I car	2 cars	3 or more
1965	7.7	59	36	5	-
1970	10.0	48	45	6	I
1975	12.5	44	45	10	I
1980	14.7	41	44	13	2
1985	16.5	38	45	15	3
1990	19.7	33	44	19	4
1995	20.5	30	45	21	4
2000	23.2	27	45	23	5
2005	26.5	25	44	26	5

Source: Department for the Environment, Transport and the Regions, *Transport Statistics*.

Table 5 National rail statistics

	National rail, passenger journeys (million)	National rail passenger kilometres (billion)
1946	1 266	47.0
1960	1 037	34.7
1985/86	686	30.4
1990/91	809	33.2
1995/96	761	30.0
2000/01	957	38.2
2006/07	1 164	46.5

Source: Department for the Environment, Transport and the Regions, *Transport Statistics*.

Table 6 Bus and coach travel

	Number of kilometres travelled by passengers on buses and coaches (bn)	Number of buses and coaches on UK roads (000)	Number of kilometres travelled by buses and coaches (bn)	Index of prices (1995=100) bus and coach fares	Index of all prices (RPI) 1995=100
1965	67	-	3.9	5.7	10.0
1970	60	-	3.6	8.0	12.4
1975	60	76.9	3.2	15.3	22.9
1980	52	69.9	3.5	36.5	44.9
1985	49	67.9	3.3	52.8	63.5
1990	46	71.9	4.1	73.8	84.6
1995	43	75.7	4.1	100.0	100.0
2000	47	79.2	4.2	119.6	114.2
2006	50	51.6	4.1	140.9	132.8

Source: adapted from Department for the Environment, *Transport and the Regions, Transport Statistics*.

Table 7 Passenger transport: consumer price indices (1995=100)

	Motor vehicles Total	of which net purchase	Rail	Bus and coach	All transport	All consumer expenditure (RPI)
1965	9.4	11.6	6.7	5.7	9.1	10.0
1970	12.0	13.6	8.5	8.0	11.7	12.4
1975	22.6	23.8	17.4	15.3	22.0	22.9
1980	47.1	55.4	39.6	36.5	45.8	44.9
1985	65.1	70.8	50.7	52.8	62.7	63.5
1990	79.4	87.8	72.3	73.8	84.6	84.6
1995	100.0	100.0	100.0	100.0	100.0	100.0
2000	119.0	94.7	116.5	119.6	114.2	114.2
2006	122.6	79.5	141.4	140.9	142.2	132.8

Source: adapted from *Economic Trends Annual Supplement*, Office for National Statistics; Department for the Environment, Transport and the Regions, *Transport Statistics*.

travel. Rail travel (national rail plus the London Underground plus light rail systems) has grown by around 60 per cent since the mid-1990s, having been broadly constant over the previous 40 years. Bus and coach travel declined until the early 1980s when it broadly stabilised. Air travel has grown significantly from 0.2 billion passenger kilometres in 1952 to 9.9 billion passenger kilometres in 2006, but today only accounts for approximately 1 per cent of the total passenger miles travelled in the UK.

Demand and income

The main reason for the growth in demand for passenger transport has been rising incomes. As Table 3 shows, real personal households' disposable income (the average income per household after income tax and inflation has been accounted for) has grown more than 2.5 times between 1965 and 2006. Consumers have tended to spend a relatively high proportion of increases in income on transport. As a result, spending on transport as a proportion of household expenditure has risen from 9.7 per cent in 1965 to 16.9 per cent in 2006. Spending on car transport has risen faster than spending on other types of passenger transport. In 1965, there were 7.7 million cars on the road as Table 4 shows. 41 per cent of households had the use of at least one car whilst spending on cars and their running costs accounted for three quarters of total household spending on transport. By 2006, there were 26.5 million cars on

the roads. 75 per cent of households had use of at least one car and spending on motor transport accounted for 85.2 per cent of total transport spending.

Rising income seems to have had little effect on overall rail travel. Between 1945 and 1985, the number of passenger journeys fell on the national rail network as shown in Table 5. Between the mid-1980s and mid-1990s, the number of journeys made was roughly constant. Since then, the number of journeys and distances travelled has increased by more than a half. There is a number of possible reasons for this. One is that road congestion has become so bad that some motorists have abandoned their cars for the train. Another reason is the rail privatisation that took place in the mid-1990s. Before, the railways were owned by the government which tended to limit investment in the railways. When overcrowding became a problem on a particular line (i.e. there was excess demand), the response tended to be to put up prices. With privatisation, private rail companies such as Virgin have introduced much more sophisticated pricing policies. Such policies include reducing fares when this attracts more passengers onto the railways and raises the total revenue of the train companies. Investment on the railways has also increased, making rail travel more attractive. In the long term, privatisation has led to an increase in the supply of rail services.

As for bus and coach travel, Table 6 shows that the long term trend has been for bus and coach travel to fall. In 1952, 92 billion passenger kilometres were travelled. By 2004, this had fallen by approximately 50 per cent. With rising incomes over the period, it could be argued that passengers have deserted buses and coaches for cars.

Bus and coach travel would then be an inferior good. However, Table 6 shows that there has been a slight upturn in bus and coach travel since the late 1990s. This perhaps reflects improved services offered by bus and coach services, or increased congestion on the roads which have led to some motorists abandoning their cars for public transport. However, the increase, at 9 per cent, over the period 1995 to 2006 is relatively small.

Demand and prices

The average price of transport has risen broadly in line with the average increase in all prices in the economy, as can be seen from Table 7. However, Table 7 shows that the price of travelling by rail, bus and coach rose substantially faster than that of travelling by car in the 1980s and 1990s. The price of bus travel continued to increase above the rate of general inflation in the early 2000s. This broad trend can be explained mainly by a reduction in subsidies to bus and rail travel and the need for bus and rail companies to adopt a more commercial, profit-orientated approach to their operations. Bus and rail also suffered greater price competition from the car. In 2006, it was relatively cheaper to travel by car than by bus or train compared to 1965 or 1995. It is not surprising that demand for car travel has outstripped demand for bus or rail travel over the period.

For the past 15 years, the government's response to growing congestion on Britain's roads has been to talk about increasing the cost of motoring. Between 1993 and 2000, the government increased the tax on petrol above the rate of inflation in an attempt to discourage car use on both congestion and environmental grounds. The government was forced to abandon this policy when an alliance of farmers and truck drivers brought the country almost to a halt for a few days in protest against rising fuel prices. The congestion charge in London is another example of government using the price mechanism to reduce demand.

However, pricing motorists off the roads is a highly unpopular policy. Partly this is because the demand for motor transport is fairly unresponsive to increases in price (i.e. demand is fairly **inelastic**. It needs very substantial increases in price to discourage potential motorists from either owning a car or making fewer journeys. For many journeys, there is no suitable alternative to car transport. For many other journeys, public transport takes longer, is far less convenient and is more expensive. Table 7 shows that the cost of motoring actually went down compared to the increase in all prices in the economy over the period 1995 to 2004 despite increases in tax. Market forces are positively

encouraging consumers to own cars and run them.

Other factors affecting the demand for transport

Demand for transport has grown for a number of other reasons apart from rising income. The population of the UK has increased. In 1951, it was 52.7 million; in 1971 it had increased to 55.9 million and in 2005 it was 60.1 million. Population-led increases in demand are set to continue with an estimated UK figure of 71.1 million by 2031.

Planning policies have led to a greater separation of housing and places of work. In Victorian England, workers tended to live within walking distance of their work. Planning regulations over the past 50 years, though, have created distinct zones within urban areas and, as a result, most people are no longer within walking distance of their place of work.

Improvements in infrastructure and advances in technology have created their own demands. Building a new motorway or bypass reduces journey times and encourages people to live further away from their place of work. Faster roads or rail links also encourage greater leisure travel. Equally, improvements in car design have made motoring more reliable and comfortable. One reason why railways failed to attract more passengers in the second half of the twentieth century was that there was not a similar increase in quality of service. For instance, the shortest journey time from London to Birmingham was longer in 1999 than it was in 1979 and rolling stock had barely improved. Privatisation of the UK's railways in the mid-1990s, however, has led to increased investment in new rolling stock and shorter journey times. Since 2000, this has led to some increase in passenger numbers.

The supply of transport

There is no 'supply curve' for transport in general or for parts of the transport industry. For instance, there is no supply curve for motor vehicle transport because no single firm or industry provides this service. There are, though, supply curves for some of the components of the service such as petrol or servicing of cars. Nor is there a supply curve for rail travel. Until 1995, the rail industry was operated by a single company, British Rail, which was a monopoly (i.e. only) supplier and there is no supply curve under monopoly. Since 1995, the industry has been privatised but the key companies in the industry, such as Railtrack or Virgin, are still monopolies in their areas of service.

However, it could been argued that there has been a supply curve for bus and coach travel since 1980 (for coaches) and 1985 (for buses) when the industry was **deregulated**. Before deregulation, the government issued licences, and in general only one licence was offered on a route, establishing monopolies. After deregulation, any firm could set up and offer regular bus services in the UK. Table 6 shows that there was an increase in the number of buses on the roads during the 1980s and 1990s, travelling more kilometres. This was despite a fall in the number of kilometres travelled by passengers. The demand curve for bus transport has therefore probably been shifting to the left as more people switch to cars. The supply curve, however, has shifted to the right with new companies coming into the market and existing companies expanding their services. Opposing this rightward shift has been a fall in government subsidies to bus companies, which, all other things being equal, would have shifted the supply curve to the left.

Price determination

The supply and demand model cannot be used in industries where there is no supply curve in the market. In the rail industry, for instance, prices are fixed by the rail companies influenced by the actions of the rail regulator. In the bus industry, where arguably there is a supply curve, fares have risen by more than the general rate of inflation since the 1980s. As Table 7 shows, fares between 1980 and 2006 rose nearly four fold whilst prices in general only increased nearly three fold. Falls in demand for bus travel due to increased demand for car travel, and an increase in supply as evidenced by the increased number of bus companies and buses, should have led to a relative fall in bus fares. Instead they rose, almost certainly due to the cuts in government subsidies during the period.

DataQuestion

Copper

Figure 8 Copper price

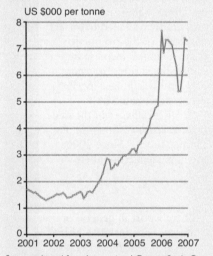

US $000 per tonne

Source: adapted from International Copper Study Group, http://www.icsg.org

Figure 9 Copper: world refined production and consumption

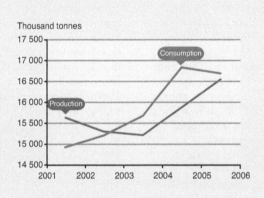

Thousand tonnes

Source: adapted from International Copper Study Group, http://www.icsg.org

Figure 10 Chinese imports of copper

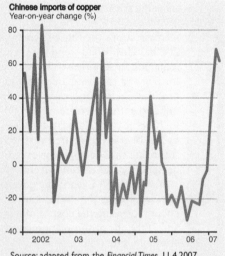

Chinese imports of copper
Year-on-year change (%)

Source: adapted from the *Financial Times*, 11.4.2007.

Mine executives and industry analysts, meeting for a copper conference in Santiago recently, expressed confidence that copper prices would remain high. In particular, China's demand is likely to continue to rise due to intensive demand for copper in construction. With stocks of copper low, any significant increase in world demand will put upward pressure on prices.

High prices are making marginally profitable mining projects more feasible. New mines, or extensions to existing mines are more likely to get the go-ahead if prices remain at their current levels. However, recent expansion of world production has led to severe cost inflation in the industry. A shortage of speciality engineering services and a scarcity of mining professionals and technicians have helped push up investment costs by 40 per cent. Labour costs in the industry over the past couple of years have risen by 20 or 30 per cent it is estimated.

Source: adapted from the *Financial Times*, 11.4.2007.

1. Using Figure 9, state how much refined copper was (a) demanded and (b) supplied by world users in 2001.
2. Using Figure 8 and Figure 9, suggest why the price of copper rose between 2002 and 2006.
3. Using Figure 10 and the data in the passage, explain how demand and supply trends in 2007 and 2008 for copper are likely to affect its price. Use demand and supply diagrams to illustrate your answer.

IB 2.1
OCR 3.1, 3.4 Tr

Summary

1. Some goods are complements, in joint demand.
2. Other goods are substitutes for each other, in competitive demand.
3. Derived demand occurs when one good is demanded because it is needed for the production of other goods or services.
4. Composite demand and joint supply are two other ways in which markets are linked.

Partial and general models

A model of price determination was outlined in the previous unit. It was explained that the price of a good was determined by the forces of demand and supply. This is an example of a **partial model**. A partial model is an explanation of reality which has relatively few variables. However, a more **general model** or wider model of the market system can be constructed which shows how events in one market can lead to changes in other markets. In this unit we will consider how some markets are interrelated.

Complements

Some goods, known as COMPLEMENTS, are in JOINT DEMAND. This means that, in demanding one good, a consumer will also be likely to demand another good. Examples of complements are:

- tennis rackets and tennis balls;
- washing machines and soap powder;
- strawberries and cream;
- DVD disks and DVD recorders.

Economic theory suggests that a rise in the quantity demanded of one complement will lead to an increase in the demand for another, resulting in an increase in the price and quantity bought of the other complement. For instance, an increase in the quantity demanded of strawberries will lead to an increase in

demand for cream, pushing up the price of cream.

This can be shown on a demand and supply diagram. Assume that new technology reduces the cost of production of washing machines. This leads to an increase in supply of washing machines shown by a shift to the right of the supply curve in Figure 1 (a). As a result there is a fall in price and a rise in the quantity demanded of washing machines, shown by a movement along the demand curve. This in turn will increase the demand for automatic soap powder, shown by a shift to the right in the demand curve in Figure 1 (b). This leads to a rise in the quantity purchased of automatic soap powder and also an increase in its price.

Substitutes

A SUBSTITUTE is a good which can be replaced by another good. If two goods are substitutes for each other, they are said to be in COMPETITIVE DEMAND. Examples of substitutes are:

- beef and pork;
- Coca-cola and Pepsi-cola;
- fountain pens and biros;
- gas and oil (in the long term but not particularly in the short term).

Economic theory predicts that a rise in the price of one good will lead to an increase in demand and a rise in price of a substitute good.

Figure 2 shows a rise in the price of beef, due to a fall in its supply. This leads to a fall in the quantity demanded of beef as

Figure 1 Complements

An increase in supply and the consequent fall in price of washing machines will lead to a rise in the quantity of washing machines and a rise in demand (shown by a shift in the demand curve) for a complementary good such as automatic washing powder.

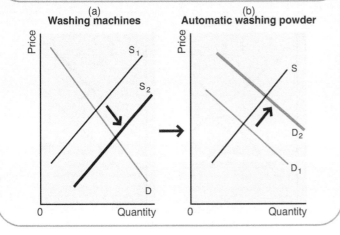

Figure 2 Substitutes

A fall in the supply of beef leading to a rise in its price will lead to a fall in the quantity demanded of beef and an increase in the demand for a substitute product such as pork.

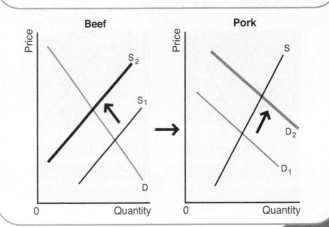

the price of beef rises. In turn, there will be an increase in the demand for pork as consumers substitute pork for beef. The demand for pork will increase, shown by a shift to the right in the demand curve for pork. This leads to a rise in the price of pork and a rise in quantity purchased.

Many substitute goods are not clearly linked. For instance, a rise in the price of foreign holidays will lead some consumers to abandon taking a foreign holiday. They may substitute a UK holiday for it, but they may also decide to buy new curtains or a new carpet for their house, or buy a larger car than they had originally planned.

Question 1

(a) It could be argued that the following pairs of products are both complements **and** substitutes. Explain why.
  (i) Electricity and gas.
  (ii) Tea and milk.
  (iii) Bus journeys and train journeys.
  (iv) Chocolate bars and crisps.
(b) (i) For each pair of products, explain whether you think they are more likely to be complements or substitutes.
  (ii) Show on a demand and supply diagram the effect on the price of the first product of a rise in price of the second product.

Derived demand

Many goods are demanded only because they are needed for the production of other goods. The demand for these goods is said to be a DERIVED DEMAND.

For instance, the demand for steel is derived in part from the demand for cars and ships. The demand for flour is derived in part from the demand for cakes and bread. The demand for sugar is in part derived from demand for some beverages, confectionery and chocolate.

Figure 3 shows an increase in the demand for cars. This leads to an increase in quantity bought and sold. Car manufacturers will increase their demand for steel, shown by a rightward shift of the demand curve for steel. The price of steel will then increase as will the quantity bought and sold. Economic theory therefore predicts that an increase in demand for a good will

lead to an increase in price and quantity purchased of goods which are in derived demand from it.

Question 2

Milk sales have been in decline for 30 years, but one of the latest food fads has helped reverse the trend. About 35 million more litres of liquid milk were sold to consumers last year than the year before. This is not a big increase on 4.45 billion litres sold in the year to April 2004, but it represents welcome news for Britain's dairy farmers.

Liz Broadbent, director of market development at the Milk Development Council (MDC), said: 'The rise is down to an increase in the frequency of buying milk rather than people buying more during each shopping trip. The indications are that the extra milk is being used mainly in porridge, tea and coffee.'

Porridge consumption rose by 25 per cent last winter, according to TNS, which carried out market research for the MDC. Consumption of tea and coffee also improved by 17 per cent and 8 per cent respectively. According to Tesco, which saw its sales of porridge increased markedly over the year, an important factor in increased sales of porridge was the fashionability of the Glycemic or GI diet. This diet encouraged dieters to maintain their blood sugar at a steady level by having a healthy breakfast.

Gwyn Jones, chairman of the National Farmers' Union dairy board, said that the increase in milk consumption 'is certainly a welcome development, even if it's only by a small amount. Eventually it ought to mean more money for farmers but there are lots of ifs and buts.'

Source: adapted from the *Financial Times* 20.5.2005.

(a) 'Milk is in derived demand from porridge.' Explain this statement.
(b) Analyse, with the help of diagrams, the effect of the change in demand for porridge on the demand for milk.
(c) Why might there be 'lots of ifs and buts' about whether the price of milk will go up due to the increase in demand for porridge?

Composite demand

A good is said to be in COMPOSITE DEMAND when it is demanded for two or more distinct uses. For instance, milk may be used for yoghurt, for cheese making, for butter or for

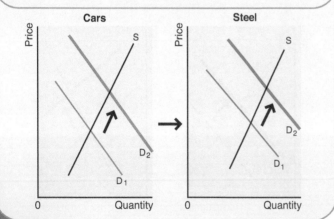

Figure 3 Derived demand

An increase in the demand for cars will lead to an increase in demand for steel. Steel is said to be in derived demand from cars.

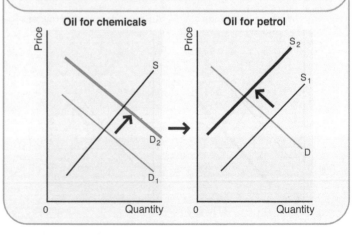

Figure 4 Composite demand

An increase in the demand for oil from chemical producers will result in a fall in the supply of oil to the petrol market because oil is in composite demand.

drinking. Land may be demanded for residential, industrial or commercial use. Steel is demanded for car manufacturing and for shipbuilding.

Economic theory predicts that an increase in demand for one composite good will lead to a fall in supply for another. Figure 4 shows that an increase in the demand by the chemical industry for oil will push the demand curve to the right, increasing both the quantity sold and the price of oil. With an upward sloping supply for oil as a whole, an increase in supply of oil to the chemical industry will reduce the supply of oil for petrol. This is shown by a shift upwards in the supply curve in Figure 4. The price of oil for petrol will rise and the quantity demanded will fall.

Economic theory therefore predicts that an increase in demand for a good will lead to a rise in price and a fall in quantity demanded for a good with which it is in composite demand.

Joint supply

A good is in JOINT SUPPLY with another good when one good is supplied for two different purposes. For instance, cows are supplied for both beef and leather. An oil well may give both oil and gas.

Economic theory suggests that an increase in demand for one good in joint supply will lead to an increase in its price. This leads to an increase in the quantity supplied. The supply of the other good therefore increases, leading to a fall in its price. Figure 5 shows that an increase in demand for beef leads to an increase in both price and quantity bought and sold of beef. More beef production will lead, as a by-product, to greater

Question 3

At the start of 2000, most customers could withdraw cash from a cash machine free of charge. Since then there has been a dramatic expansion of new cash machines which charge customers a fee for withdrawing cash, typically £1.50 for any withdrawal. Fee-charging cash machines only handle an estimated 3 per cent of all transactions with most customers getting their money from cash machines inside or outside banks where there is no charge. However, fee-charging machines tend to be situated away from banks in locations like convenience stores, pubs, petrol stations and shopping centres and are becoming increasingly popular with customers.

Many fee-charging cash machines also have a facility for playing advertisements. So a cash machine can generate revenues and profits for its owners not just by charging customers for cash withdrawals but also by selling advertising space to companies.

Source: adapted from the *Financial Times*, 15.11.2004.

A cash machine can give two products: cash for bank customers and advertising. With the help of diagrams and the concept of joint supply, explain what impact an increase in demand by bank customers for withdrawals from fee-charging cash machines might have on the price of advertising space.

supply of leather. This is shown by a shift to the right in the supply curve for leather. The price of leather will then fall and quantity demanded, bought and sold will increase.

Key terms

Competitive demand - when two or more goods are substitutes for each other.
Complement - a good which is purchased with other goods to satisfy a want.
Composite demand - when a good is demanded for two or more distinct uses.
Derived demand - when the demand for one good is the result of or derived from the demand for another good.

Joint demand - when two or more complements are bought together.
Joint supply - when two or more goods are produced together, so that a change in supply of one good will necessarily change the supply of the other goods with which it is in joint supply.
Substitute - a good which can be replaced by another to satisfy a want.

Figure 5 *Joint supply*
An increase in the demand for beef, which leads to more beef being produced, results in an increase in the supply of leather. Beef and leather are said to be in joint supply.

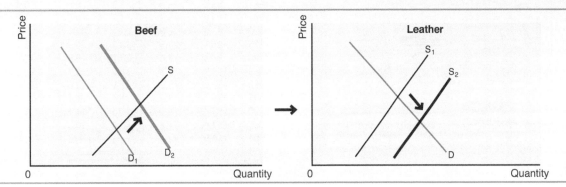

Applied economics

Commercial transport

Derived demand

Commercial transport, the transporting of goods in the UK from factory to shop for instance, is a derived demand. It is ultimately derived from the purchase of consumer goods and services. The movement of coal from a coal pit to an electricity power station is part of the long chain of production in the eventual consumption of, say, a packet of cornflakes.

Demand for commercial transport

Demand for commercial transport has grown over time as consumer incomes have risen and more goods and services have been consumed. Table 1 shows, however, that the growth in tonnage of goods moved has been relatively small since the 1960s. Much of this is due to the fact that goods have got lighter and less bulky. Far more plastic and far less metal are used today, for instance. So whilst more consumer goods are purchased, the total weight and volume have only increased a little. In contrast, Table 2 shows that there has been a significant growth over the same period in the number of tonne kilometres travelled. Each tonne is travelling a longer distance today than 40 years ago. This is the result of greater specialisation between regions and firms. In turn, this has been encouraged by the growth of the motorway network in the UK, which has allowed much faster journey times.

Substitutes

Different modes of transport are substitutes for each other. Both Tables 1 and 2 and Figure 6 indicate that there has been a switch away from rail transport to other modes, particularly road transport. In the early 1950s, railways carried slightly more freight than the

roads. By the 1960s, rail had already lost much of its market share to road haulage. However, since rail privatisation in 1995, there has been a significant increase in rail freight. Pipeline traffic has increased, mainly due to growth of gas consumption and North Sea oil production. The sudden increase in the share of water transport between 1976 and 1985 was entirely due to the growth of the North Sea oil industry.

Complements

The privatisation of British Rail led to an increase in the amount of rail freight carried. The private freight companies have proved more flexible than British Rail and have been able to drive down costs and win orders. However, the future of rail transport lies mainly as a complement to road transport. Lorries and vans will take goods to railway collection depots. The goods will then be transported by rail before being taken away again by lorry. Loading and unloading from one mode of transport to another is relatively expensive.

Table 1 Goods: total transported in millions of tonnes, Great Britain

	Road	Rail	Water: coastwise oil	Water: other	Pipelines	Total
1961	1 295	249	57		6	1 607
1965	1 634	239	64		27	1 964
1970	1 610	209	58		39	1 916
1975	1 602	176	48		52	1 878
1980	1 383	154	54	83	83	1 757
1985	1 452	122	50	92	89	1 805
1990	1 749	152	44	108	121	2 163
1995	1 701	101	47	98	168	2 115
2000	1 693	96	40	97	151	2 077
2005	1 868	108	42	91	168	2 277
2006	1 936	108	na	na	159	2 336

Source: adapted from Department for the Environment, Transport and the Regions, *Transport Statistics.*

Table 2 Goods: distance transported, total tonne kilometres (billions), Great Britain

	Road	Rail	Water: coastwise oil	Water: other	Pipelines	Total
1961	85.6	16.4	3.2	0.6	0.4	106.2
1965	108.0	15.8	3.7	0.6	1.8	129.8
1970	85.0	26.8	23.2	0.01	3.0	138.1
1975	95.3	23.5	18.3	0.1	5.9	143.1
1980	92.4	17.6	38.2	15.9	10.1	174.2
1985	103.2	15.3	38.9	18.7	11.2	187.3
1990	136.3	15.8	32.1	23.6	11.0	218.8
1995	149.6	13.3	31.4	11.1	11.1	226.6
2000	159.4	18.1	26	41.4	11.4	256.3
2005	163.4	21.7	30.3	30.6	10.8	256.8
2006	166.9	22.1	na	na	10.8	259.8

Source: adapted from Department for the Environment, Transport and the Regions, *Transport Statistics.*

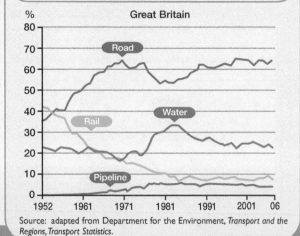

Figure 6 Domestic commercial transport: proportion of goods moved (billion tonne kilometres) by different modes of transport

Source: adapted from Department for the Environment, *Transport and the Regions, Transport Statistics.*

Therefore rail transport has proved to be economic mainly when journeys of over 300-400 miles are made by rail or when a dedicated rail link can take goods door to door, for instance from a pit head to a power station. The number of dedicated rail links could decrease in the immediate future if the electricity industry burns more gas and imported coal and less domestic coal. The Channel Tunnel should have given a significant boost to rail freight. It is ideally suited, for example, for the transport of goods such as new cars being taken from manufacturing plants to dealers in other countries. However, inefficiencies in the rail system in the UK and even more so in Europe have meant that services using the Tunnel have been too unreliable and too slow to attract much extra traffic. Rail freight in general can only grow in future if journey times become faster and services are more reliable.

Composite demand

Roads are in composite demand with commercial transport and passenger transport. At present, there is no systematic pricing mechanism for the road system. Most roads are free from congestion at all times of day. A minority of roads suffer from congestion at certain times of the day. This is a problem of scarce resources. Some potential road users react by either not travelling or travelling by an alternative mode of transport. Commuters in the London area, for instance, may choose to travel by rail, underground or bus because the opportunity cost of travelling by car is too high. Some commuters arrive earlier or later to their place of work to avoid the rush hour. Other road users accept that their road journey times will be longer in the rush hour than at other times of the day.

The more cars on the road, the greater the potential for congestion and longer journey times for freight transport. Road pricing could help the freight industry if car users were discouraged from travelling. Road pricing is when cars and lorries are charged for the use of a road, as for instance with the London congestion charge or the toll on the M6 toll motorway. However, any road pricing system is likely to place charges on lorries as well as cars. Journey times for lorries might be reduced, lowering costs, but road tolls will increase freight costs. The experience of the M6 toll motorway shows the trade off between cost and time. Lorries have avoided using the toll motorway, opened in 2004, because of what they say are too high charges. Instead, most hauliers prefer to use the M6 through Birmingham, which is free, but they risk getting held up by congestion. For these hauliers, the cost of the toll motorway is greater than that of the possible loss of time through congestion of using the free motorway. Overall, British hauliers are estimated to lose up to £20 billion a year through congestion in increased journey times. Reducing journey times through applying tolls on all congested roads would reduce these costs but hauliers would inevitably have to pay tolls too, meaning that their gain would be far less than the £20 billion.

Imposing tolls on road freight transport could act as an incentive for firms to switch some freight from road to rail. Indeed, some environmentalists have argued that revenues from road tolls should be used to subsidise rail freight to create a large shift from road to rail.

DataQuestion

Land usage

The cost of planning restrictions

Planning restrictions have increased the price of housing land. The price of farming land, for instance, is often one-thirtieth or one-fortieth of what it is when housebuilding is allowed. Hence, there are plenty of farmers willing to sell their land for residential use. A 1994 study commissioned by the Department for the Environment, however, pointed out that this is a misleading comparison because the cost of preparing farming land for housing or industrial purposes is high. Instead, it estimated the opportunity cost of housing land by looking at prices of housing land in Barnsley, where at the time there was no shortage of housing land available for sale. The cost of planning restrictions could then be calculated. For instance, in Reigate, prime commuter country in Surrey in the South of England, land prices were 3.6 times their opportunity cost. In Beverley in Yorkshire, the ratio was 2.2.

Nimbyism

A 'Nimby' is someone who says 'not in my backyard'. The word came into fashion in the 1980s to describe people who were all in favour of better facilities, better roads, more housing and more places of work to reduce unemployment so long as none of this happened in their local area.

It has often been justified by high-sounding references to preserving rural England, maintaining local amenities and protecting areas of natural beauty. Every new bypass or road upgrade seems to run through a patch of land which is the habitat of some rare species of plant or animal. However, in practice, the vast majority of Nimbys are motivated solely by the losses that they might incur if development went ahead. For instance, building a new housing estate next door is unlikely to help the property prices of existing houses in the area.

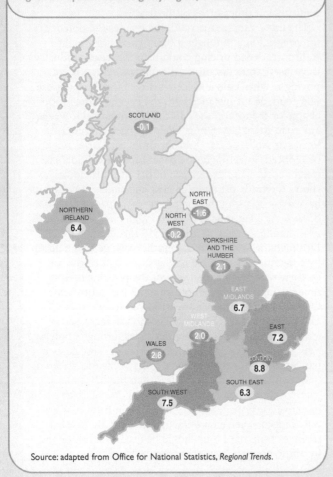

Figure 7 Population change by region, 1991-2004

Source: adapted from Office for National Statistics, *Regional Trends*.

Table 3 Changing population and number of households, Great Britain

	1971	1981	1991	2001	2006	2021 projected
Population	55.4	54.9	55.8	57.4	60.5	64.7
Number of households	18.6	20.2	22.4	23.8	24.2	28.0

Source: adapted from *Social Trends*, Office for National Statistics; *Regional Trends*, Office for National Statistics.

Greenbelt policies

Britain's greenbelts were established after the Second World War. They were intended to throw a cordon around urban areas to prevent their spread into the countryside. Within the greenbelt, planning restrictions are very strict about development. No new housing or industrial development is permitted. Greenbelt policies have severely restricted the supply of new land for housing and industry in the UK and contributed to the relatively high price of land in urban areas. This increases the costs of living for urban dwellers, the vast majority of people in the UK. Not only are house prices and rents much higher than they would otherwise be but the cost of services from supermarkets to cinemas is much higher. This is because high land prices paid by industry have to be paid for in the form of higher prices by consumers.

Households

The number of households in the UK is growing at a much faster rate than the slow growth in the overall population. The growth is coming partly from changes in society. The increase in divorce has created many one-person households and rising incomes mean that more young single people now have the choice between living at home with their parents or getting their own accommodation. Growth is also coming from demographic changes. There is an increasing number of elderly people who are living longer and living alone. The number of households with two parents and several children is declining.

New land for housing

New land for building houses comes from a variety of sources. 'Windfall sites' are those which come from homeowners selling part of their garden for development, or housebuilders buying a large old house, knocking it down and replacing it with a small estate of smaller houses. Another source is 'brownfield sites'. These are sites which have already been used for commercial or other urban purposes but now have a higher value as housing land. Third, and most controversially, new land can be found by small scale easing of greenbelt and other restrictions, usually amounting to just a few tens of acres in a specific locality.

1. Explain the following.
   (a) The demand for land is a derived demand.
   (b) Land is in composite demand.
   (c) Land is sometimes in joint supply.
   (d) Land is sometimes in joint demand with buildings.
2. Explain the economic relationships in the UK between land use and:
   (a) a growing population;
   (b) a shifting population geographically;
   (c) increasing affluence.
3. Do you think greenbelt regulations should be loosened to allow more house building in the UK? In your answer, consider the costs and benefits of such a change in policy. This will include an analysis of the effects on the price of houses, industrial property and agricultural land.

9 Price elasticity of demand

Summary

1. Elasticity is a measure of the extent to which quantity responds to a change in a variable which affects it, such as price or income.
2. Price elasticity of demand measures the proportionate response of quantity demanded to a proportionate change in price.
3. Price elasticity of demand varies from zero, or infinitely inelastic, to infinitely elastic.
4. The value of price elasticity of demand is mainly determined by the availability of substitutes and by time.

The meaning of demand elasticity

The quantity demanded of a good is affected by changes in the price of the good, changes in price of other goods, changes in income and changes in other relevant factors. Elasticity is a measure of just how much the quantity demanded will be affected by a change in price or income etc.

Assume that the price of gas increases by 1 per cent. If quantity demanded consequently falls by 20 per cent, then there is a very large drop in quantity demanded in comparison to the change in price. The price elasticity of gas would be said to be very high. If quantity demanded falls by 0.01 per cent, then the change in quantity demanded is relatively insignificant compared to the large change in price and the price elasticity of gas would be said to be low.

Different elasticities of demand measure the proportionate response of quantity demanded to a proportionate change in the variables which affect demand. So price elasticity of demand measures the responsiveness of quantity demanded to changes in the price of the good. Income elasticity measures the responsiveness of quantity demanded to changes in consumer incomes. Cross elasticity measures the responsiveness of quantity demanded to changes in the price of another good. Economists could also measure population elasticity, tastes elasticity or elasticity for any other variable which might affect quantity demanded, although these measures are rarely calculated.

Price elasticity of demand

Economists choose to measure responsiveness in terms of proportionate or percentage changes. So PRICE ELASTICITY OF DEMAND - the responsiveness of changes in quantity demanded to changes in price - is calculated by using the formula:

$$\frac{\text{percentage change in quantity demanded}}{\text{percentage change in price}}$$

Sometimes, price elasticity of demand is called OWN PRICE ELASTICITY OF DEMAND to distinguish it from cross price elasticity of demand.

Table 1 shows a number of calculations of price elasticity. For instance, if an increase in price of 10 per cent leads to a fall in quantity demanded of 20 per cent, then the price elasticity of demand is 2. If an increase in price of 50 per cent leads to a fall

in quantity demanded of 25 per cent then price elasticity of demand is ½.

Elasticity is sometimes difficult to understand at first. It is essential to memorise the formulae for elasticity. Only then can they be used with ease and an appreciation gained of their significance.

Table 1

Percentage change in quantity demanded	Percentage change in price	Elasticity
20	10	2
25	50	0.5
28	7	4
3	9	0.333

Question 1

Table 2

	Percentage change in quantity demanded	Percentage change in price
(a)	10	5
(b)	60	20
(c)	4	8
(d)	1	9
(e)	5	7
(f)	8	11

Calculate the price elasticity of demand from the data in Table 2.

Alternative formulae

Data to calculate price elasticities are often not presented in the form of percentage changes. These have to be worked out. Calculating the percentage change is relatively easy. For instance, if a consumer has 10 apples and buys another 5, the percentage change in the total number of apples is of course 50 per cent. This answer is worked out by dividing the change in the number of apples she has (i.e. 5) by the original number of apples she possessed (i.e. 10) and multiplying by 100 to get a percentage figure. So the formula is:

$$\text{percentage change} = \frac{\text{absolute change}}{\text{original value}} \times 100\%$$

Price elasticity of demand is measured by dividing the percentage change in quantity demanded by the percentage change in price. Therefore an alternative way of expressing this is $\Delta Q/Q \times 100$ (the percentage change in quantity demanded Q) divided by $\Delta P/P \times 100$ (the percentage change in price P). The 100s cancel each other out, leaving a formula of:

$$\frac{\Delta Q}{Q} \div \frac{\Delta P}{P} \quad \text{or} \quad \frac{\Delta Q}{Q} \times \frac{P}{\Delta P}$$

This is mathematically equivalent to:

$$\frac{P}{Q} \times \frac{\Delta Q}{\Delta P}$$

Examples of calculations of elasticity using the above two formulae are given in Figure 1.

Question 2

Table 3

	Original values		New values	
	Quantity demanded	Price (£)	Quantity demanded	Price (£)
(a)	100	5	120	3
(b)	20	8	25	7
(c)	12	3	16	0
(d)	150	12	200	10
(e)	45	6	45	8
(f)	32	24	40	2

Calculate the price elasticity of demand for the data in Table 3.

Elastic and inelastic demand

Different values of price elasticity of demand are given special names.
- Demand is price ELASTIC if the value of elasticity is greater than one. If demand for a good is price elastic then a percentage change in price will bring about an even larger percentage change in quantity demanded. For instance, if a 10 per cent rise in the price of tomatoes leads to a 20 per cent fall in the quantity demanded of tomatoes, then price elasticity is 20 ÷ 10 or 2. Therefore the demand for tomatoes is elastic. Demand is said to be **infinitely elastic** if the value of elasticity is infinity (i.e. a fall in price would lead to an infinite increase in quantity demanded whilst a rise in price would lead to the quantity demanded becoming zero).

Figure 1 Calculations of elasticity of demand

Example 1
Quantity demanded originally is 100 at a price of £2. There is a rise in price to £3 resulting in a fall in demand to 75. Therefore the change in quantity demanded is 25 and the change in price is £1.
The price elasticity of demand is:

$$\frac{\Delta Q}{Q} \div \frac{\Delta P}{P} \quad = \quad \frac{25}{100} \div \frac{1}{2} = \frac{1}{2}$$

Example 2
Quantity demanded originally is 20 units at a price of £5 000. There is a fall in price to £4 000 resulting in a rise in demand to 32 units.
Therefore the change in quantity demanded is 12 units resulting from the change in price of £1 000.
The price elasticity of demand is:

$$\frac{P}{Q} \times \frac{\Delta Q}{\Delta P} \quad = \quad \frac{5\,000}{20} \times \frac{12}{1\,000} = 3$$

- Demand is price INELASTIC if the value of elasticity is less than one. If demand for a good is price inelastic then a percentage change in price will bring about a smaller percentage change in quantity demanded. For instance, if a 10 per cent rise in the price of tube fares on London Underground resulted in a 1 per cent fall in journeys made, then price elasticity is 1 ÷ 10 or 0.1. Therefore the demand for tube travel is inelastic. Demand is said to be **infinitely inelastic** if the value of elasticity is zero (i.e. a change in price would have no effect on quantity demanded).
- Demand is of UNITARY ELASTICITY if the value of elasticity is exactly 1. This means that a percentage change in price will lead to an exact and opposite change in quantity demanded. For instance, a good would have unitary elasticity if a 10 per cent rise in price led to a 10 per cent fall in quantity demanded. (It will be shown in unit 10 that total revenue will remain constant at all quantities demanded if elasticity of demand is unity.)

This terminology is summarised in Table 4.

Question 3

Explain whether you think that the following goods would be elastic or inelastic in demand if their price increased by 10 per cent whilst all other factors remained constant: (a) petrol; (b) fresh tomatoes; (c) holidays offered by a major tour operator; (d) a Ford car; (e) a Mars Bar; (f) *GQ* magazine.

Graphical representations

Figure 2 shows a straight line graph. It is a common mistake to conclude that elasticity of a straight line demand curve is constant all along its length. In fact nearly all straight line demand curves vary in elasticity along the line.
- At the point A, price elasticity of demand is infinity. Here

Table 4 Elasticity: summary of key terms

	Verbal description of response to a change in price	Numerical measure of elasticity	Change in total outlay as price rises[1]
Perfectly inelastic	Quantity demanded does not change at all as price changes	Zero	Increases
Inelastic	Quantity demanded changes by a smaller percentage than does price	Between 0 and 1	Increases
Unitary elasticity	Quantity demanded changes by exactly the same percentage as does price	1	Constant
Elastic	Quantity demanded changes by a larger percentage than does price	Between 1 and infinity	Decreases
Perfectly elastic	Buyers are prepared to purchase all they can obtain at some given price but none at all at a higher price	Infinity	Decreases to zero

1. This is explained in unit 10.

quantity demanded is zero. Putting Q = 0 into the formula for elasticity:

$$\frac{\Delta Q}{Q} \div \frac{\Delta P}{P}$$

we see that zero is divided into ΔQ. Mathematically there is an infinite number of zeros in any number.
● At the point C, price elasticity of demand is zero. Here price is zero. Putting P = 0 into the formula for elasticity, we see that P is divided into ΔP giving an answer of infinity. Infinity is then divided into the fraction ΔQ ÷ Q. Infinity is so large that the answer will approximate to zero.

Figure 2 Price elasticity along a straight demand curve
Price elasticity varies along the length of a straight demand curve, moving from infinity, where it cuts the price axis, to half way along the line, to zero where it cuts the quantity axis.

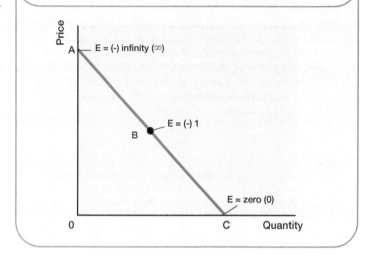

● At the point B exactly half way along the line, price elasticity of demand is 1.
  It is worth noting that the elasticity of demand at a point can be measured by dividing the distance from the point to the quantity axis by the distance from the point to the price axis, BC ÷ AB. In Figure 2, B is half way along the line AC and so BC = AB and the elasticity at the point B is 1.
  Two straight line demand curves discussed earlier do not have the same elasticity all along their length.
  Figure 3(a) shows a demand curve which is perfectly inelastic. Whatever the price, the same quantity will be demanded.
  Figure 3(b) shows a perfectly elastic demand curve. Any amount can be demanded at one price or below it whilst nothing will be demanded at a higher price.
  Figure 3(c) shows a demand curve with unitary elasticity. Mathematically it is a rectangular hyperbola. This means that any percentage change in price is offset by an equal and opposite

Figure 3 Perfectly elastic and inelastic demand curves and unitary elasticity
A vertical demand curve (a) is perfectly inelastic, whilst a horizontal demand curve (b) is perfectly elastic. A curve with unitary elasticity (c) is a rectangular hyperbola with the formula PQ = k where P is price, Q is quantity demanded and k is a constant value.

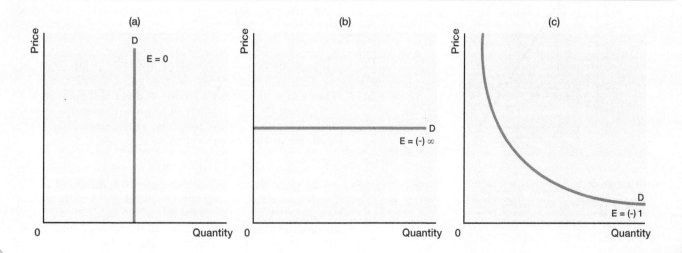

change in quantity demanded.

Another common mistake is to assume that steep demand curves are always inelastic and demand curves which have a shallow slope are always elastic. In Figure 4, two demand curves are drawn. In Figure 4(a), the demand curve has a very shallow slope. The part that is drawn is indeed elastic but this is only because it is just the top half of the curve which is drawn. If the whole curve were drawn, the bottom half would be inelastic even though the gradient of the curve is shallow. Similarly, in Figure 4(b), the demand curve has a very steep slope. The part that is shown is indeed price inelastic but this is only because it is the bottom half of the line. The top half of the steep line would be elastic.

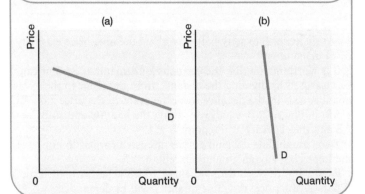

Figure 4 Slopes of straight line demand curves
Figure 4(a) shows an elastic demand curve but it is only elastic because it is the top half of the curve, not because it has a shallow gradient. Similarly, Figure 4(b) shows an inelastic demand curve but it is only inelastic because it is the bottom half of the curve, not because it has a steep gradient.

Question 4

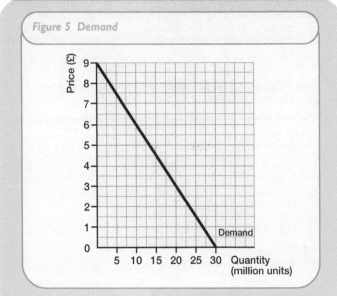

Figure 5 Demand

Consider Figure 5.
(a) Between what prices is demand (i) elastic and
(ii) inelastic?
(b) At what price is demand (i) perfectly inelastic,
(ii) perfectly elastic and (iii) equal to 1?

Two technical points

So far we have written of price elasticity of demand as always being a positive number. In fact any downward sloping demand curve always has a negative elasticity. This is because a rise in one variable (price or quantity) is always matched by a fall in the other variable. A rise is positive but a fall is negative and a positive number divided by a negative one (or vice versa) is always negative. However, economists find it convenient to omit the minus sign in price elasticity of demand because it is easier to deal in positive numbers whilst accepting that the value is really negative.

A second point relates to the fact that elasticities over the same price range can differ. For example, at a price of £2, demand for a good is 20 units. At a price of £3, demand is 18 units. Price elasticity of demand for a rise in price from £2 to £3 is:

$$\frac{P}{Q} \times \frac{\Delta Q}{\Delta P} = \frac{2}{20} \times \frac{2}{1} = \frac{1}{5}$$

However, price elasticity of demand for a fall in price from £3 to £2 is:

$$\frac{P}{Q} \times \frac{\Delta Q}{\Delta P} = \frac{3}{18} \times \frac{2}{1} = \frac{1}{3}$$

The price elasticity for a rise in price is therefore less than for a fall in price over the same range. This is not necessarily a problem so long as one is aware of it. One way of resolving this is to average out price and quantity. In the formulae, P becomes not the original price but the average price (i.e. the original price plus the new price divided by 2) and Q becomes the average quantity demanded (i.e. the original quantity demanded plus the new quantity demanded divided by 2). In the above example, the average price is £(2 + 3) ÷ 2 or £2.50. The average quantity demanded is (20 + 18) ÷ 2 or 19. Price elasticity of demand is then:

$$\frac{P}{Q} \times \frac{\Delta Q}{\Delta P} = \frac{2.5}{19} \times \frac{2}{1} = \frac{5}{19}$$

As you would expect, this value is in between the two price elasticities of ⅕ and ⅓.

The determinants of price elasticity of demand

The exact value of price elasticity of demand for a good is determined by a wide variety of factors. Economists, however, argue that two factors in particular can be singled out: the availability of substitutes and time.

The availability of substitutes The better the substitutes for a product, the higher the price elasticity of demand will tend to be. For instance, salt has few good substitutes. When the price of salt increases, the demand for salt will change little and therefore the price elasticity of salt is low. On the other hand, spaghetti has many good substitutes, from other types of pasta, to rice, potatoes, bread, and other foods. A rise in the price of spaghetti, all other food prices remaining constant, is likely to have a significant effect on the demand for spaghetti. Hence the elasticity of demand for spaghetti is likely to be higher than that for salt.

Width of market definition The more widely the product is defined, the fewer substitutes it is likely to have. Spaghetti has many substitutes, but food in general has none. Therefore the elasticity of demand for spaghetti is likely to be higher than that for food. Similarly the elasticity of demand for boiled sweets is likely to be higher than for confectionery in general. A 5 per cent increase in the price of boiled sweets, all other prices remaining constant, is likely to lead to a much larger fall in demand for boiled sweets than a 5 per cent increase in the price of all confectionery.

Time The longer the period of time, the more price elastic is the demand for a product. For instance, in 1973/74 when the price of oil quadrupled the demand for oil was initially little affected. In the short term the demand for oil was price inelastic. This is hardly surprising. People still needed to travel to work in cars and heat their houses whilst industry still needed to operate. Oil had few good substitutes. Motorists couldn't put gas into their petrol tanks whilst businesses could not change oil-fired systems to run on gas, electricity or coal. However, in the longer term motorists were able to, and did, buy cars which were more fuel efficient. Oil-fired central heating systems were replaced by gas and electric systems. Businesses converted or did not replace oil-fired equipment. The demand for oil fell from what it would otherwise have been. Taking the ten year period to 1985, and given the changes in other variables which affected demand for oil, estimates suggest that the demand for oil was slightly elastic. It is argued that in the short term, buyers are often locked into spending patterns through habit, lack of information or because of durable goods that have already been purchased. In the longer term, they have the time and opportunity to change those patterns.

It is sometimes argued that **necessities** have lower price elasticities than **luxuries**. Necessities by definition have to be bought whatever their price in order to stay alive. So an increase in the price of necessities will barely reduce the quantity demanded. Luxuries on the other hand are by definition goods which are not essential to existence. A rise in the price of luxuries should therefore produce a proportionately large fall in demand. There is no evidence, however, to suggest that this is true. Food, arguably a necessity, does not seem to have a lower elasticity than holidays or large cars, both arguably luxuries. Part of the reason for this is that it is very difficult to define necessities and luxuries empirically. Some food is a necessity but a significant proportion of what we eat is unnecessary for survival. It is not possible to distinguish between what food is consumed out of necessity and what is a luxury.

It is also sometimes argued that goods which form a relatively low proportion of total expenditure have lower elasticities than those which form a more significant proportion. A large car manufacturer, for instance, would continue to buy the same number of paper clips even if the price of paper clips doubled because it is not worth its while to bother changing to an alternative. On the other hand, its demand for steel would be far more price elastic. There is no evidence to suggest that this is true. Examples given in textbooks, such as salt and matches, have low price elasticities because they have few good substitutes. In the case of paper clips, manufacturers of paper clips would long ago have raised prices substantially if they believed that price had little impact on the demand for their product.

Key terms

Elastic demand - where the price elasticity of demand is greater than 1. The responsiveness of demand is proportionally greater than the change in price. Demand is infinitely elastic if price elasticity of demand is infinity.
Inelastic demand - where the price elasticity of demand is less than 1. The responsiveness of demand is proportionally less than the change in price. Demand is infinitely inelastic if price elasticity of demand is zero.

Price elasticity of demand or own elasticity of demand - the proportionate response of changes in quantity demanded to a proportionate change in price, measured by the formula:

$$\frac{P}{Q} \times \frac{\Delta Q}{\Delta P}$$

Unitary elasticity - where the value of price elasticity of demand is 1. The responsiveness of demand is proportionally equal to the change in price.

Applied economics

Price elasticity of demand for oil

The price of oil

Oil is a key world commodity. In the 1950s and 1960s, the price of oil was relatively stable at around $2 a barrel. Since 1970, however, the price of oil has proved volatile and the actual or nominal price has increased dramatically as can be seen in Figure 6. There have been four major oil price spikes in that period.

- Between 1972 and 1975, the price of oil increased from $2 a barrel to $11 a barrel. High world growth during that period increased demand for all commodities and led to a boom in commodity prices. In the case of oil, the Yom Kippur War in 1973 between Israel and Egypt led Arab countries to threaten to cut off oil supplies to the West for selling arms to Israel. OPEC, the Organisation of the Petroleum Exporting Countries, played a key role during the crisis. Set up in 1960, it had had little impact on world oil markets up to that point. However, its response to the war was to enforce a set of limits or quotas on production of member states. By restricting supply at a time of growing demand, it led to a large rise in the price of oil. Once the political crisis was over, OPEC members continued to impose quotas to maintain high prices which were to their economic advantage.
- Another political crisis, the 1978 revolution in Iran which led to an Islamic fundamentalist government coming to power, led to the next oil price rise. The revolution severely disrupted oil production in Iran and Iran was a major supplier of oil to world markets. Between 1978 and 1980, oil prices rose from $13 a barrel to $36 a barrel.
- In the 1980s, oil prices fell from their 1980 peak. In 1990, however, this fall was reversed when the USA and its allies fought the first Gulf War against Iraq. Again it was the threat of interruption of supplies of oil which led to the price increase.
- The rise in the price of oil from the early 2000s was caused by rising world demand, particularly from the fast growing Chinese economy. By 2004-2005, OPEC countries were producing at full capacity. An inability to increase supply substantially further pushed up the price of oil.

Price elasticity of demand for oil

Economic theory would suggest that a rise in the price of oil would lead to a fall in quantity demanded. Looking at Figure 7, it can be seen that the sharp rise in the price of oil from $2 a barrel to $36 a barrel between 1972 and 1980 was associated with a sharp decline in the UK consumption of oil from 106 million tonnes in 1973 to a low of 68.6 million tonnes in 1983. An 850

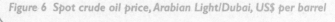

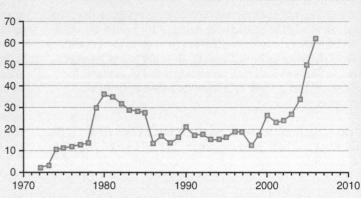

Figure 6 Spot crude oil price, Arabian Light/Dubai, US$ per barrel

Source: adapted from *BP Statistical Review of World Energy*.

per cent rise in the price of oil was associated with a 55 per cent fall in demand. Other factors affecting the UK demand for oil were changing over this ten year period. Incomes rose, for example, and more fuel efficient technology was developed. However, these figures would suggest that the demand for oil at the time was price inelastic.

Figure 7 shows that the UK demand for oil since 1990 has remained fairly stable at between 75 and 79 million tonnes per year. Other factors that affected demand over the period including rising incomes. However, the large rises in oil prices since 2000 seem to have had little impact on quantity demanded, again suggesting a very low price elasticity of demand for oil.

Figure 8 shows estimates of the price elasticity of demand for oil between different regions of the world. Demand is price inelastic in every instance. The UK is part of OECD Europe. This estimate puts price elasticity of demand for oil at -0.3.

Short term and long term price elasticities

In the short term, demand for oil is likely to be highly price inelastic. Consumers of oil have little choice but to buy oil to run their cars, trains or heating systems. In the longer term, demand for oil is likely to be less inelastic. This is partly because consumers can substitute oil for other forms of energy such as gas and coal. It is also because of energy saving measures which make it economical, for example, to install insulation in lofts or develop more fuel-efficient cars.

OPEC and some of its member countries like Saudi Arabia are aware that too high a price for oil could result in a long term decline in demand for oil despite rising world incomes. A large scale switch from petrol driven vehicles to ones powered by hydrogen, for example, could bring the price of oil down to below $10 a barrel. This would have a significant impact on economies such as Saudi Arabia which are highly dependent on oil revenues for their prosperity. It is in the interests of these countries to have an oil price which is as high as possible but is not so high that in encourages the long term development of technologies which considerably reduce the demand for oil.

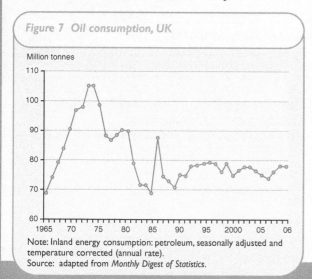

Figure 7 Oil consumption, UK

Note: Inland energy consumption: petroleum, seasonally adjusted and temperature corrected (annual rate).
Source: adapted from *Monthly Digest of Statistics*.

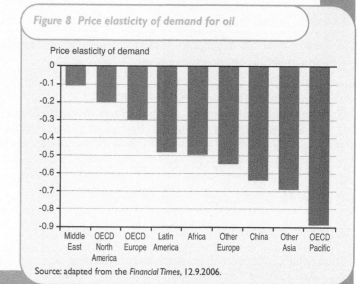

Figure 8 Price elasticity of demand for oil

Source: adapted from the *Financial Times*, 12.9.2006.

DataQuestion

Food prices

Sharply higher wheat prices will mean another increase in bread prices in the next few weeks, Premier Food, owner of the Hovis brand, said yesterday. Given price increases by other bread manufacturers, this could mean a 10 per cent increase in the price of a standard loaf.

Source: adapted from the *Financial Times*, 10.7.2007.

Consumer groups in Italy have asked consumers to boycott eating pasta for a day. They are protesting about recent rises in the price of pasta of around 20 per cent. Pasta manufacturers have been forced to increase prices by soaring wheat prices. Durum flour, the main ingredient for Italian pasta, has risen from €0.26 per kg to €0.45 per kg just in the last two months.

Source: adapted from newsvote.bbc.co.uk, 13.9.2007.

Consumers are likely to be hit by price rises for meat and dairy products as the Far East competes with the West for stocks. The Chinese, for example, have developed a taste for yoghurt, cheese and milk. Wholesale milk prices have risen from about 17p a litre to almost 25p a litre in recent months. This could push the price of a pint of milk in the shops up 10 per cent.

Source: adapted from *The Times*, 29.8.2007.

Table 5 Estimates of price elasticities of demand for selected foods

	Price elasticity
Bread	-0.40
Milk and cream	-0.36
Cereal and cereal products other than bread e.g. pasta	-0.94

Source: adapted from National Food Survey 2000, Defra.

1 Assume that the price elasticities for Hovis bread, a pint of milk and Italian pasta are those given in Table 5. Calculate the effect on demand for those products given the price rises mentioned in the data.
2 Define inelastic demand and suggest why milk and bread have such low price elasticities of demand.
3 Table 5 shows that the price elasticity of demand for all cereal and cereal products other than bread is -0.94. Discuss whether the price elasticity of demand for pasta is likely to be higher or lower than this.

10 Elasticities

Summary

1. Income elasticity of demand measures the proportionate response of quantity demanded to a proportionate change in income.
2. Cross elasticity of demand measures the proportionate response of quantity demanded of one good to a proportionate change in price of another good.
3. Price elasticity of supply measures the proportionate response of quantity supplied to a proportionate change in price.
4. The value of elasticity of supply is determined by the availability of substitutes and by time factors.
5. The price elasticity of demand for a good will determine whether a change in the price of a good results in a change in expenditure on the good.

Income elasticity of demand

The demand for a good will change if there is a change in consumers' incomes. INCOME ELASTICITY OF DEMAND is a measure of that change. If the demand for housing increased by 20 per cent when incomes increased by 5 per cent, then the income elasticity of demand would be said to be positive and relatively high. If the demand for food were unchanged when income rose, then income elasticity would be zero. A fall in demand for a good when income rises gives a negative value to income elasticity of demand.

The formula for measuring income elasticity of demand is:

$$\frac{\text{percentage change in quantity demanded}}{\text{percentage change in income}}$$

So the numerical value of income elasticity of a 20 per cent rise in demand for housing when incomes rise by 5 per cent is +20/+5 or +4. The number is positive because both the 20 per cent and the 5 per cent are positive. On the other hand, a rise in income of 10 per cent which led to a fall in quantity demanded of a product of 5 per cent would have an income elasticity of -5/+10 or -½. The minus sign in -5 shows the fall in quantity demanded of the product. Examples of items with a high income elasticity of demand are holidays and recreational activities, whereas washing up liquid tends to have a low income elasticity of demand.

Just as with price elasticity, it is sometimes easier to use alternative formulae to calculate income elasticity of demand. The above formula is equivalent to:

$$\frac{\Delta Q}{Q} \div \frac{\Delta Y}{Y}$$

where is change, Q is quantity demanded and Y is income. Rearranging the formula gives another two alternatives:

$$\frac{Y}{Q} \times \frac{\Delta Q}{\Delta Y} \quad \text{or} \quad \frac{\Delta Q}{Q} \times \frac{Y}{\Delta Y}$$

Examples of the calculation of income elasticity of

Table 1 Calculation of income elasticity of demand

Original quantity demanded	New quantity demanded	Original income (£)	New income (£)	$\frac{\Delta Q}{Q} \div \frac{\Delta Y}{Y}$		Numerical value
20	25	16	18	5/20 ÷ 2/16		+2
100	200	20	25	100/100 ÷ 5/20		+4
50	40	25	30	-10/50 ÷ 5/25		-1
60	60	80	75	0/60 ÷ -5/80		0
60	40	27	30	-20/60 ÷ 3/27		-3

demand are given in Table 1. Some economists use the terms 'elastic' and 'inelastic' with reference to income elasticity. Demand is income inelastic if it lies between +1 and -1. If income elasticity of demand is greater than +1 or less than -1, then it is elastic.

Question 1

Table 2

	Original		New		£
	Quantity demanded	Income	Quantity demanded	Income	
(a)	100	10	120	14	
(b)	15	6	20	7	
(c)	50	25	40	35	
(d)	12	100	15	125	
(e)	200	10	250	11	
(f)	25	20	30	18	

Calculate the income elasticity of demand from the data in Table 2.

Cross elasticity of demand

The quantity demanded of a particular good varies according to the price of other goods. In unit 9 it was argued that a rise in price of a good such as beef would increase the quantity demanded of a substitute such as pork. On the other hand, a rise in price of a good such as cheese would lead to a fall in the quantity demanded of a complement such as macaroni. CROSS ELASTICITY or CROSS PRICE ELASTICITY OF DEMAND measures the proportionate response of the quantity demanded of one good to the proportionate change in the price of another. For instance, it is a measure of the extent to which demand for pork increases when the price of beef goes up; or the extent to which the demand for macaroni falls when the price of cheese increases.

The formula for measuring cross elasticity of demand for good X is:

$$\frac{\text{percentage change in quantity demanded of good X}}{\text{percentage change in price of another good Y}}$$

Two goods which are substitutes will have a positive cross elasticity. An increase (positive) in the price of one good, such as gas, leads to an increase (positive) in the quantity demanded of a substitute such as electricity. Two goods which are complements will have a negative cross elasticity. An increase (positive) in the price of one good such as sand leads to a fall (negative) in demand of a complement such as cement. The cross elasticity of two goods which have little relationship to each other would be zero. For instance, a rise in the price of cars of 10 per cent is likely to have no effect (i.e. 0 per cent change) on the demand for Tipp-Ex.

As with price and income elasticity, it is sometimes more convenient to use alternative formulae for cross elasticity of demand. These are:

$$\text{Cross elasticity of good X} = \frac{\Delta Q_X}{Q_X} \div \frac{\Delta P_Y}{P_Y}$$

$$\text{or} \qquad \frac{P_Y}{Q_X} \times \frac{\Delta Q_X}{\Delta P_Y}$$

Some economists use the terms 'elastic' and 'inelastic' with reference to cross elasticity. Demand is cross elastic if it lies between +1 and -1. If cross elasticity of demand is greater than +1 or less than -1, then it is elastic.

Question 2

Explain what estimated value you would put on the cross elasticity of demand of: (a) gas for electricity; (b) tennis shorts for tennis rackets; (c) luxury cars for petrol; (d) paper for socks; (e) CDs for MP3 downloads; (f) Sainsbury's own brand baked beans for Tesco's own brand baked beans; (g) Virgin Cola for Coca-Cola.

Price elasticity of supply

Price elasticity of demand measures the responsiveness of changes in quantity demanded to changes in price. Equally, the responsiveness of quantity supplied to changes in price can also be measured - this is called PRICE ELASTICITY OF SUPPLY. The formula for measuring the price elasticity of supply is:

$$\frac{\text{percentage change in quantity supplied}}{\text{percentage change in price}}$$

This is equivalent to:

$$\frac{\Delta Q}{Q} \div \frac{\Delta P}{P}$$

$$\text{or} \qquad \frac{P}{Q} \times \frac{\Delta Q}{\Delta P}$$

where Q is quantity supplied and P is price.

The supply curve is upward sloping (i.e. an increase in price leads to an increase in quantity supplied and vice versa). Therefore price elasticity of supply will be positive because the top and bottom of the formula will be either both positive or both negative.

As with price elasticity of demand, different ranges of elasticity are given different names. Price elasticity of supply is:

- **perfectly inelastic** (zero) if there is no response in supply to a change in price;
- **inelastic** (between zero and one) if there is a less than proportionate response in supply to a change in price;
- **unitary** (one) if the percentage change in quantity supplied equals the percentage change in price;
- **elastic** (between one and infinity) if there is a more than proportionate response in supply to a change in price;
- **perfectly elastic** (infinite) if producers are prepared to supply any amount at a given price.

These various elasticities are shown in Figure 1.

It should be noted that any straight line supply curve passing through the origin has an elasticity of supply equal to 1. This is best understood if we take the formula:

$$\frac{P}{Q} \times \frac{\Delta Q}{\Delta P}$$

$\Delta Q / \Delta P$ is the inverse of (i.e. 1 divided by) the slope of the line, whilst P/Q, assuming that the line passes through the origin, is the slope of the line. The two multiplied together must always equal 1.

Determinants of elasticity of supply

As with price elasticity of demand, there are two factors which determine supply elasticity across a wide range of products.

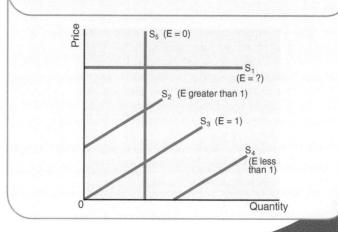

Figure 1 Elasticity of supply
The elasticity of supply of a straight line supply curve varies depending upon the gradient of the line and whether it passes through the origin.

Question 3

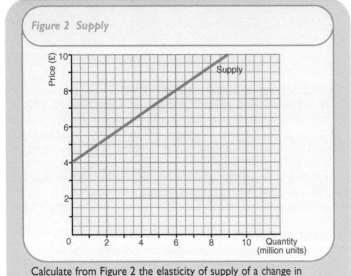

Figure 2 Supply

Calculate from Figure 2 the elasticity of supply of a change in price from: (a) £4 to £6; (b) £6 to £8; (c) £8 to £10; (d) £9 to £7; (e) £7 to £5.

Availability of substitutes Substitutes here are not consumer substitutes but producer substitutes. These are goods which a producer can easily produce as alternatives. For instance, one model of a car is a good producer substitute for another model in the same range because the car manufacturer can easily switch resources on its production line. On the other hand, carrots are not substitutes for cars. The farmer cannot easily switch from the production of carrots to the production of cars. If a product has many substitutes then producers can quickly and easily alter the pattern of production if its price rises or falls. Hence its elasticity will be relatively high. However, if a product has few or no substitutes, then producers will find it difficult to respond flexibly to variations in price. If there is a fall in price, a producer may have no alternative but either to carry on producing much the same quantity as before or withdrawing from the market. Price elasticity of supply is therefore low.

Time The shorter the time period, the more difficult producers find it to switch from making one product to another. So in the short term, supply is likely to be more price inelastic than in the long term. There is a number of reasons why this is the case.
- Some items take a long time to make. For example, if there is a crop failure of a product like hazelnuts, it will take until the next growing season to increase supply again whatever price the market sets for hazelnuts in the short term.
- If there is no spare capacity to make more of a product, it will be difficult to increase supply very much even if prices rise sharply. The more spare capacity, the less constraint this places on increasing supply in response to price rises.
- With some products, it is easy and relatively cheap to hold stocks to supply the market when they are demanded. With others, it is impossible to hold stocks. For example, large stocks of wheat are kept around the world which can be released if prices rise, so keeping price elasticity of supply relatively high. However, it is impossible in most cases to store electricity. So when there is a sharp rise in price of electricity in a free market, there is unlikely to be much response in terms of extra supply in the short term if

the system is working at full capacity. The longer the time period, the easier it is for the market to build up appropriate stocks or to build excess capacity if stocks are not possible. So price elasticity of supply is higher in the longer term.
- Price elasticity of supply will be higher the easier it is for a firm to switch production from one product to another or for firms to enter the market to make the product.

Price elasticity of demand and total expenditure

Price elasticity of demand and changes in total expenditure on a product are linked. Total expenditure can be calculated by multiplying price and quantity:

Total expenditure = quantity purchased x price

For instance, if you bought 5 apples at 10 pence each, your total expenditure would be 50 pence. If the price of apples went up, you might spend more, less, or the same on apples depending upon your price elasticity of demand for apples. Assume that the price of apples went up 40 per cent to 14p each. You might react by buying fewer apples. If you now buy 4 apples (i.e. a fall in demand of 20 per cent), the price elasticity of demand is 20 ÷ 40 or 0.5. Your expenditure on apples will also rise (from 50 pence to 56 pence). If you buy two apples (i.e. a fall in quantity demanded of 60 per cent), your elasticity of demand is 60 ÷ 40 or 1.5 and your expenditure on apples will fall (from 50 pence to 28 pence).

These relationships are what should be expected. If the percentage change in price is larger than the percentage change in quantity demanded (i.e. elasticity is less than 1, or inelastic), then expenditure will rise when prices rise. If the percentage change in price is smaller than the percentage change in quantity demanded (i.e. elasticity is greater than 1 or elastic), then spending will fall as prices rise. If the percentage change in price is the same as the change in quantity demanded (i.e. elasticity is unity), expenditure will remain unchanged because the percentage rise in price will be equal and opposite to the percentage fall in demand.

Key terms

Cross or cross-price elasticity of demand - a measure of the responsiveness of quantity demanded of one good to a change in price of another good. It is measured by dividing the percentage change in quantity demanded of one good by the percentage change in price of the other good.
Income elasticity of demand - a measure of the responsiveness of quantity demanded to a change in income. It is measured by dividing the percentage change in quantity demanded by the percentage change in income.
Price elasticity of supply - a measure of the responsiveness of quantity supplied to a change in price. It is measured by dividing the percentage change in quantity supplied by the percentage change in price.

Question 4

(a) Suggest reasons why the demand for some foods in Table 3 is more price elastic than the demand for others.

(b) An increase in the price of which foods would be most likely to lead to
(i) the greatest and
(ii) the least change in household expenditure? Explain your answer.

	Price elasticity
Milk and cream	-0.36
of which	
Liquid wholemilk and skimmed milks	-0.17
Cheese	-0.35
Carcass meat	-0.69
Other meat and meat products	-0.52
Fresh fish	-0.80
Processed and shellfish	-0.17
Prepared fish	0.00
Frozen fish	-0.32
Eggs	-0.28
Fats	-0.75
Sugar and preserves	-0.79
Fresh potatoes	-0.12
Fresh green vegetables	-0.66
Other fresh vegetables	-0.33
Processed vegetables	-0.60
of which	
Frozen peas	-0.68
Frozen convenience potato products	-0.58
Fresh fruit	-0.29
of which	
Bananas	-0.32
Other fruit and fruit products	-0.81
of which	
Fruit juices	-0.55
Bread	-0.40
Other cereal and cereal products	-0.94
of which	
Cakes and pastries	-0.56
Frozen convenience cereal foods	-0.69
Beverages	-0.37

Source: adapted from *National Food Survey 2000*, Defra.

Applied economics

Cross elasticities of demand for food

Many foods are substitutes for each other. Eggs are a substitute for fish; fish is a substitute for meat. Economic theory would suggest that these goods would therefore have a positive cross elasticity of demand. An increase in the price of one good would lead to an increase in demand of the substitute good, whilst a fall in price of one good would lead to a fall in demand of another.

The National Food Survey 2000 gives some evidence for this. Table 4 shows estimates of the cross elasticity of demand for three foods: carcass meat, fresh fish and eggs. In orange, going across diagonally, are the own-price elasticities of demand for each good. For example, the price elasticity of demand for carcass meat is - 0.69 (i.e. it is price inelastic). In black, reading across the rows, are the figures for cross elasticity of demand for a product with respect to the price of another. For example, the cross elasticity of demand of carcass meat with respect to the price of

fresh fish is + 0.15. The cross elasticity of demand of eggs with respect to the price of fresh fish is + 0.16.

These cross elasticities are relatively low suggesting, for example, that eggs are only a weak substitute for fresh fish or carcass meat. So a 10 per cent rise in the price of fresh fish, leading to a 8 per cent fall in demand for fresh fish (because the price elasticity of demand for fresh fish is - 0.8), is associated with only a 1.6 per cent rise in demand for eggs (because the cross price elasticity of eggs with respect to the price of fresh fish is + 0.16). Equally, a 10 per cent rise in the price of fresh fish is associated with only a 1.5 per cent rise in demand for carcass meat.

When cross elasticities are negative, it shows that goods might be complements to each other. Table 5 would suggest that milk and cream, eggs and fats are all complements. For example, the ingredients for pancakes, and some cakes include milk, eggs and fats. The National Food Survey estimates suggest that a

Table 4 *Estimates of price and cross elasticity of demand for carcass meat, fresh fish and eggs, 1988-2000*

	Elasticity with respect to the price of		
	Carcass meat	Fresh fish	Eggs
Carcass meat	-0.69	+0.15	+0.15
Fresh fish	+0.02	-0.8	+0.14
Eggs	+0.02	+0.16	-0.28

Source: adapted from HMSO, *Household Food Consumption and Expenditure.*

Table 5 *Estimates of price and cross elasticity of demand for milk and cream, eggs and fats, 1988-2000*

	Elasticity with respect to the price of		
	Milk and cream	Eggs	Fats
Milk and cream	-0.36	-0.40	-0.20
Eggs	-0.05	-0.28	-0.10
Fats	-0.04	-0.19	-0.75

Source: adapted from HMSO, *Household Food Consumption and Expenditure.*

10 per cent rise in the price of eggs leads to a 4 per cent fall in the quantity demanded of milk and cream. Interestingly, a 10 per cent rise in the price of milk and cream only leads to a fall of 0.4 per cent in the quantity demanded of eggs. As with the data on substitutes, the

Table 6 *Estimates of price and cross elasticity of demand for eggs, non-fresh fruit and fruit products, and meat and meat products other than carcass meat, 1988-2000*

	Elasticity with respect to the price of		
	Eggs	Non-fresh fruit and fruit products	Meat and meat products other than carcass meat
Eggs	-0.28	0.00	0.00
Non-fresh fruit and fruit products	0.00	-0.81	-0.01
Meat and meat products other than carcass meat	+0.03	-0.04	-0.52

Source: adapted from HMSO, *Household Food Consumption and Expenditure.*

National Food Survey estimates suggest that where foods are compliments, they tend to be fairly weak compliments with numbers fairly near zero.

Where changes in the price of one good have no effect on the quantity demanded of another good, the cross elasticity of demand is zero. Table 6, which shows data from the National Food Survey, would suggest that changes in the price of eggs, non-fresh fruit and fruit products, and meat and meat products other than carcass meat have little impact on demand for each other.

DataQuestion — Clothing, footwear and transport

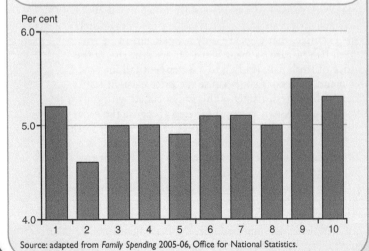

Figure 3 Expenditure on clothing and footwear as a percentage of total expenditure by gross income decile group, 2005-2006

Source: adapted from *Family Spending* 2005-06, Office for National Statistics.

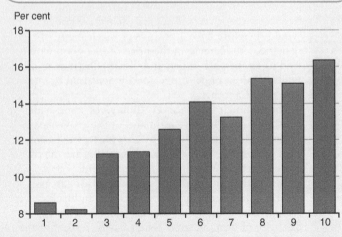

Figure 4 Expenditure on transport as a percentage of total expenditure by gross income decile group, 2005-2006

Source: adapted from *Family Spending* 2005-06, Office for National Statistics.

Decile groups

A population can be split into ten equal groups. These are called decile groups. In Table 8 the groups are households, which are split according to their gross income. So the first decile group is the tenth of households which have the lowest income. The fifth decile group is the tenth of households between 40 and 50 per cent of the total, whilst the tenth decile group is made up of the highest 10 per cent of households by gross income. In Table 8 data for the other 7 decile groups is available but is not printed here in order to simplify the data.

Table 7 Clothing and footwear and transport as a percentage of total household expenditure, real household disposable income 1980 to 2005-2006

	Clothing and footwear %	Transport %	Real household disposable income 1980=100
1980	8.1	14.6	100.0
1992	6.0	15.8	141.2
2005-06	5.1	13.9	200.0

Source: adapted from *Family Spending 2005-06*, Office for National Statistics.

Table 8 Weekly household expenditure, £, on clothing and footwear and transport by gross income decile group 2005-2006

	Average weekly expenditure, £		
	First decile	Fifth decile	Tenth decile
Men's outer garments	1.10	3.00	10.70
Men's under garments	0.10	0.20	0.80
Women's outer garments	3.20	6.00	21.50
Women's under garments	0.50	1.10	2.20
Boys' outer garments (5-15)	0.40	0.40	1.30
Girls' outer garments (5-15)	0.30	0.80	1.60
Infants' outer garments (under 5)	0.30	0.60	1.00
Children's under garments (under 16)	0.10	0.30	0.50
Accessories	0.30	0.50	2.00
Haberdashery and clothing hire	0.00	0.20	0.60
Dry cleaners, laundry and dyeing	0.10	0.10	1.10
Footwear	1.70	4.10	9.00
Total clothing and footwear	**8.00**	**17.30**	**52.00**
Purchase of vehicles	4.10	14.80	71.80
Petrol, diesel and other motor oils	3.70	15.00	38.20
Other motoring costs	1.90	9.00	23.80
Rail and tube fares	0.40	1.00	8.20
Bus and coach fares	0.90	1.40	1.70
Combined fares	0.50	0.30	3.60
Other travel and transport	1.70	3.40	14.80
Total transport	**13.20**	**44.80**	**161.90**
Total household expenditure on all goods and services	**153.60**	**356.70**	**989.70**
Total household income £	**0-134**	**364-472**	**1 224+**

Source: adapted from *Family Spending 2005-06*, Office for National Statistics.

Measuring income elasticity of demand

Income elasticity of demand is measured by dividing the percentage change in quantity demanded of a good or a basket of goods by the percentage change in income of consumers. Quantity demanded is a physical number, like 100 washing machines or 1 000 shirts. However, when data for quantity is not available, a good proxy variable is expenditure. This is quantity times price. If prices remain the same as expenditure changes, then the percentage change in quantity will be the same as the percentage change in expenditure.

1. Describe how spending on clothing and footwear and on transport (a) varies with income and (b) has changed over time.
2. Using the data, explain whether 'clothing and footwear' is likely to have a higher income elasticity of demand than transport.
3. Using Table 8, explain which components of clothing and footwear and transport are likely to have the highest income elasticities.
4. Using the data in Table 8 and the concept of income elasticity of demand, discuss whether bus and coach transport has a future in the UK.

Normal, inferior and Giffen goods

Summary

1. An increase in income will lead to an increase in demand for normal goods but a fall in demand for inferior goods.
2. Normal goods have a positive income elasticity whilst inferior goods have a negative elasticity.
3. A Giffen good is one where a rise in price leads to a rise in quantity demanded. This occurs because the positive substitution effect of the price change is outweighed by the negative income effect.
4. Upward sloping demand curves may occur if the good is a Giffen good, if it has snob or speculative appeal or if consumers judge quality by the price of a product.

Normal and inferior goods

The pattern of demand is likely to change when income changes. It would be reasonable to assume that consumers will increase their demand for most goods when their income increases. Goods for which this is the case are called NORMAL GOODS.

However, an increase in income will result in a fall in demand for other goods. These goods are called INFERIOR GOODS. There will be a fall in demand because consumers will react to an increase in their income by purchasing products which are perceived to be of better quality. Commonly quoted examples of inferior goods are:

*   bread - consumers switch from this cheap, filling food to more expensive meat or convenience foods as their incomes increase;
*   margarine - consumers switch from margarine to butter, although this has become less true recently with greater health awareness;
*   bus transport - consumers switch from buses to their own cars when they can afford to buy their own car.

A good can be both a normal and an inferior good depending upon the level of income. Bread may be a normal good for people on low incomes (i.e. they buy more bread when their income increases). But it may be an inferior good for higher income earners.

Normal and inferior goods are shown on Figure 1. D_1 is the demand curve for a normal good. It is upward sloping because demand increases as income increases. D_2 is the demand curve for an inferior good. It is downward sloping, showing that demand falls as income increases. D_3 is the demand curve for a good which is normal at low levels of income, but is inferior at higher levels of income.

Question 1

Table 1   Estimated household food consumption in Great Britain

| | Grammes per person per week | | | | |
	1985	1990	1995	2000	2005/6
Sugar	238	171	136	105	94
Chicken	196	226	237	253	224
Bananas	80	125	176	206	225
Bread	878	797	756	720	701
Pickles and sauces	61	67	80	107	125
Butter	80	46	36	39	38

Source: adapted from *Annual Abstract of Statistics*, Office for National Statistics.

Household incomes rose between each of the years 1985, 1990, 1995, 2000 and 2005/6. Assuming that all other factors remained constant, which of the goods shown in Table 1 are normal goods and which are inferior goods?

Inferior goods and income elasticity

Inferior goods can be distinguished from normal goods by their income elasticity of demand. The formula for measuring income elasticity is:

$$\frac{\text{percentage change in quantity demanded}}{\text{percentage change in income}}$$

A normal good will always have a positive income elasticity because quantity demanded and income either both increase

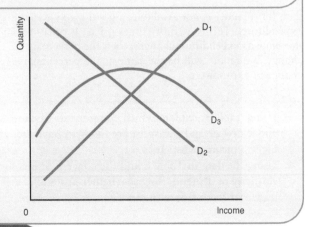

Figure 1   Normal and inferior goods
On the quantity-income diagram, a normal good such as D_1 has an upward sloping curve, whilst an inferior good such as D_2 has a downward sloping curve. D_3 shows a good which is normal at low levels of income but is inferior at higher levels of income.

(giving a plus divided by a plus) or both decrease (giving a minus divided by a minus). An inferior good, however, will always have a negative elasticity because the signs on the top and bottom of the formula will always be opposite (a plus divided by a minus or a minus divided by a plus giving a minus answer in both cases).

For instance, if the demand for bread falls by 2 per cent when incomes rise by 10 per cent then it is an inferior good. Its income elasticity is -2/+10 or -0.2.

Giffen goods   certain situations (India)

A GIFFEN GOOD is a special sort of inferior good. Alfred Marshall (1842-1924), an eminent economist and author of a best selling textbook of his day, claimed that another eminent economist, Sir Robert Giffen (1837-1910), had observed that the consumption of bread increased as its price increased. The argument was that bread was a staple food for low income consumers. A rise in its price would not deter people from buying as much as before. But 'poor' people would now have so little extra money to spend on meat or other luxury foods that they would abandon their demand for these and instead buy more bread to fill up their stomachs. The result was that a rise in the price of bread led to a rise in the demand for bread. Another way of explaining this phenomenon is to use the concepts of INCOME and SUBSTITUTION effects. When a good changes in price, the quantity demanded will be changed by the sum of the substitution effect and the income effect.

- **Substitution effect**. If the price of a good rises, consumers will buy less of that good and more of others because it is now relatively more expensive than other goods. If the price of a good falls, consumers will buy more of that good and less of others. These changes in quantity demanded solely due to the relative change in prices are known as the substitution effect of a price change.
- **Income effect**. If the price of a good rises, the real income of consumers will fall. They will not be able to buy the same basket of goods and services as before. Consumers can react to this fall in real income in one of two ways. If the good is a normal good, they will buy less of the good. If the good is an inferior good, they will buy more of the good. These changes in quantity demanded caused by a change in real income are known as the income effect of the price change.

For a normal good the substitution effect and the income effect both work in the same direction. A rise in price leads to a fall in quantity demanded because the relative price of the good has risen. It also leads to a fall in quantity demanded because consumers' real incomes have now fallen. So a rise in price will always lead to a fall in quantity demanded, and vice versa.

For an inferior good, the substitution effect and income effect work in opposite directions. A rise in price leads to a fall in quantity demanded because the relative price of the good has risen. But it leads to a rise in quantity demanded because consumers' real incomes have fallen. However, the substitution effect outweighs the income effect because overall it is still true for an inferior good that a rise in price leads to an overall fall in quantity demanded.

A Giffen good is a special type of inferior good. A rise in price leads to a fall in quantity demanded because of the substitution effect but a rise in quantity demanded because of the income effect. However, the income effect outweighs the substitution effect, leading to rises in quantity demanded. For instance, if a 10p rise in the price of a standard loaf leads to a 4 per cent fall in

the demand for bread because of the substitution effect, but a 10 per cent rise in demand because of the income effect, then the net effect will be a 6 per cent rise in the demand for bread.

The relationship between normal, inferior and Giffen goods and their income and substitution effects is summarised in Table 2.

Giffen goods are an economic curiosity. In theory they could exist, but no economist has ever found an example of such a good in practice. There is no evidence even that Sir Robert Giffen ever claimed that bread had an upward sloping demand curve - it crept into textbooks via Alfred Marshall and has remained there ever since!

Table 2 Substitution and income effects on quantity demanded of a rise in price for normal, inferior and Giffen goods

Type of good	Effect on quantity demanded of a rise in price		
	Substitution effect	Income effect	Total effect
Normal good	Fall	Fall	Fall
Inferior good	Fall	Rise	Fall because substitution effect > income effect
Giffen good	Fall	Rise	Rise because substitution effect < income effect

Question 2

Table 3

Good	Change in price (pence per unit)	Change in quantity demanded as a result of	
		income effect	substitution effect
Bacon	+10	+5%	-8%
Bus rides	+15	+7%	-5%
Jeans	-100	+1%	+5%
Baked beans	-2	-1%	+4%
Compact discs	-150	+4%	+3%

An economist claims that she has observed the effects detailed in Table 3 resulting solely from a change in price of a product. Which of these products are normal goods, which are inferior and which are Giffen goods?

Necessities and luxuries

Some economists distinguish between **necessities** (or **basic goods**) and **luxuries** (or **superior goods**). They state that necessities have an income elasticity of less than +1 whilst luxury goods have an income elasticity of greater than +1. The problem with this distinction is that many products which have an income elasticity of less than +1 would hardly be classified as 'necessities' by most consumers. In

Table 4, for example, all the foods have an income elasticity of less than +1 and would therefore all be classified as necessities. Yet should a fruit juice be just as much a necessity as tea, milk or meat? Whilst it can be useful to discuss necessities and luxuries in theory, putting a precise value on these in terms of income elasticity of demand may not be particularly helpful.

Upward sloping demand curves

Demand curves are usually downward sloping. However, there are possible reasons why the demand curve for some goods may be upward sloping.

Giffen goods Giffen goods, a type of inferior good, have been discussed above.

Goods with snob appeal Some goods, sometimes called **Veblen goods**, are bought mainly because they confer status on the buyer. Examples might be diamonds, fur coats or large cars. The argument is that these goods are demanded because few people can afford to buy them because their price is high. If large numbers of people could afford to buy them, then the demand (the quantity buyers would buy) would be low. This might be true for some individual consumers, but economists have not found any proof that it is true for markets as a whole. Whilst some might buy diamonds only because they are expensive, the majority of consumers would buy more diamonds if their price fell because they like diamonds. So there must be some doubt as to whether snob appeal does give rise to upward sloping demand curves.

Speculative goods Throughout most of 1987, stock markets worldwide boomed. Share prices were at an all time high and the demand for shares was high too. But in October 1987 share prices slumped on average between 20 and 30 per cent. Overnight the demand for shares fell. This could be taken as evidence of an upward sloping demand curve. The higher the price of shares, the higher the demand because buyers associate high share prices with large speculative gains in the future. However, most economists would argue that what is being seen is a shift in the demand curve. The demand curve is drawn on the assumption that expectations of future gain are constant. When share prices or the price of any speculative good fall, buyers revise their expectations downwards. At any given share price they are willing to buy fewer shares, which pushes the demand curve backwards to the left.

Quality goods Some consumers judge quality by price. They automatically assume that a higher priced good must be of better quality than a similar lower priced good. Hence, the higher the price the greater the quantity demanded. As with snob appeal goods, this may be true for some individuals but there is no evidence to suggest that this is true for consumers as a whole. There have been examples where goods that have been re-packaged, heavily advertised and increased in price have increased their sales. But this is an example of a shift to the right in the demand curve caused by advertising and repackaging rather than of an upward sloping demand curve.

In conclusion, it can be seen that there are various reasons why in theory demand curves might be upward sloping. But few, if any, such goods have been found in reality. The downward sloping demand curve seems to be true of nearly all goods.

Question 3

Figure 2 Number of Stock market transactions, FTSE all share price index (1962 = 100)

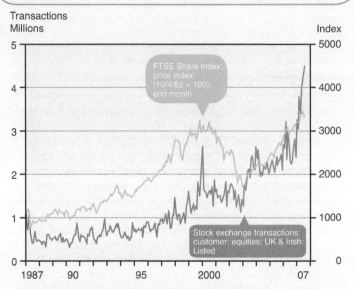

Source: adapted from *Financial Statistics*, Office for National Statistics.

In October 1987, prices on the London Stock Market crashed by around 25 per cent. The result was a sharp fall in the number of shares bought and sold. Similarly, in 2000, prices of 'dotcom' shares (shares in companies related to the Internet), having created a boom in share prices, fell sharply. By September 2002, the FTSE All Share Price Index stood at 1802 compared to 3242 in December 1999 at the height of the dotcom bubble. Equally, the number of shares traded per month fell from a high of 2.6 million in March 2000 to a low of 1.1 million in December 2002.

To what extent does the data support the existence of an upward sloping demand curve for shares?

Key terms

Giffen good - a special type of inferior good where demand increases when price increases.
Income effect - the impact on quantity demanded of a change in price due to a change in consumers' real income which results from this change in price.
Inferior good - a good where demand falls when income increases (i.e. it has a negative income elasticity of demand).
Normal good - a good where demand increases when income increases (i.e. it has a positive income elasticity of demand).
Substitution effect - the impact on quantity demanded due to a change in price, assuming that consumers' real incomes stay the same (i.e. the impact of a change in price excluding the income effect).

Applied economics

Income elasticities and inferior goods

Table 4 gives estimates of the income elasticity of demand for certain foods in the UK. The estimates have been calculated using data from the National Food Survey (which from 2001 was amalgamated with the Family Expenditure Survey to become the Expenditure and Food Survey) conducted by Defra (Department for the Environment, Food and Rural Affairs) and ONS (Office for National Statistics, the UK government statistical service).

The calculations pool data for the three year period 1998-2000. Sophisticated statistical techniques were used to take account of factors such as regional spending patterns and household size. The estimates are based on how food expenditure varies between households on different incomes.

Food itself, according to the data, has an income elasticity of demand of + 0.20. Hence, a 10 per cent increase in incomes leads to a 2 per cent increase in the quantity demanded of all foods. Incomes in the UK are growing at around 2.5 per cent per year on average. Growth in demand for food is increasing, therefore, at just one fifth of that amount, at around 0.5 per cent per year on average. An income elasticity of +0.20 also means that spending on food is declining as a proportion of total household expenditure over time.

Most categories of food have a positive income elasticity of demand and are therefore normal goods. For example, cheese has an income elasticity of +0.23, fish +0.27 and fresh fruit +0.30. Some foods, however, are inferior goods with negative income elasticities. In Table 4, these are liquid wholemilk, eggs, margarine, apples and tea. There is a variety of reasons why these particular foods have negative income elasticities.

- Some reflect growing awareness of what constitutes a healthy diet. So liquid wholemilk and margarine with their typically high fat content show a fall in demand as incomes increase. Higher income households tend to be more aware of health issues related to diet. They also have higher incomes to be able to afford to buy acceptable substitutes if these are more expensive.
- Some reflect changing tastes. Tea drinking is declining in the UK as consumers drink more coffee. Because coffee is more expensive than tea, this shift is arguably happening at a faster rate amongst higher income groups. Hence tea has a negative income elasticity of demand. Equally, -0.02 is so small that, according to the National Food Survey report, it is 'not statistically different from zero', i.e. the evidence would suggest that tea is on the borderline between

being a normal and an inferior good.
- Others are more difficult to explain. Healthy eating campaigns should be encouraging consumers to eat apples and yet, according to the data, apples are an inferior good with an income elasticity of -0.07. Perhaps as incomes increase, households are switching from apples to other fruit such as oranges and bananas, both of which have positive income elasticities.

The item with the highest income elasticity of demand in Table 4 is fruit juices with an income elasticity of +0.45. Fruit juices tend to be purchased more by high income households than low income households. The high cost of fruit juices and their perceived health benefits might account for this.

Table 4 Estimated income elasticities of food products

	Income elasticity
Milk and cream	0.05
of which	
Liquid wholemilk	-0.17
Cheese	0.23
Carcass meat	0.20
Fish	0.27
Eggs	-0.01
Fats	0.08
of which	
Butter	0.20
Margarine	-0.37
Sugar and preserves	0.00
Fresh potatoes	0.09
Fresh green vegetables	0.27
Fresh fruit	0.30
of which	
Apples	-0.07
Oranges	0.23
Bananas	0.12
Fruit juices	0.45
Bread	0.12
Cakes and biscuits	0.13
Beverages	0.10
of which	
Tea	-0.02
Coffee	0.16
All foods	0.20

Source: *National Food Survey 2000*, Defra.

DataQuestion

Tourism

Figure 3 Real household disposable income per head at 2003 prices, £

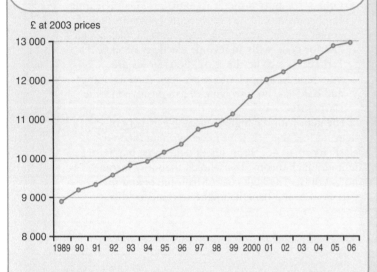

£ at 2003 prices

Source: adapted from *Economic and Labour Market Review*, Office for National Statistics.

Figure 4 Domestic and international tourism by UK residents: number of trips taken in the UK and overseas by UK residents[1]

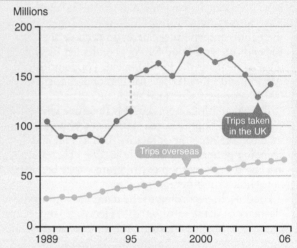

Millions

Trips taken in the UK

Trips overseas

1 Figures include business trips as well as holidays.
2 In 1995, there was a change in the way that domestic trips were calculated which led to an increase in the number of trips being recorded of 26.8 million trips.

Source: adapted from *Annual Abstract of Statistics*, Office for National Statistics.

Figure 5 Holidays abroad[1] by destination, percentages

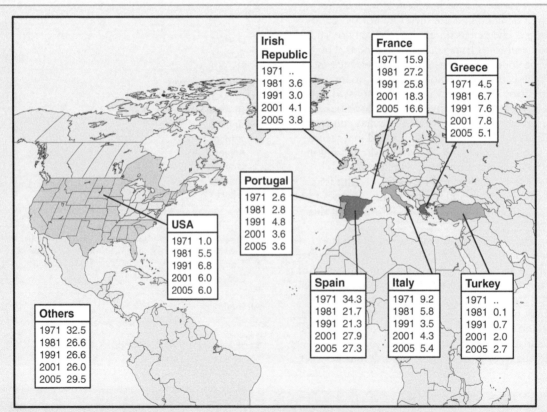

Irish Republic

1971	..
1981	3.6
1991	3.0
2001	4.1
2005	3.8

France

1971	15.9
1981	27.2
1991	25.8
2001	18.3
2005	16.6

Greece

1971	4.5
1981	6.7
1991	7.6
2001	7.8
2005	5.1

Portugal

1971	2.6
1981	2.8
1991	4.8
2001	3.6
2005	3.6

USA

1971	1.0
1981	5.5
1991	6.8
2001	6.0
2005	6.0

Spain

1971	34.3
1981	21.7
1991	21.3
2001	27.9
2005	27.3

Italy

1971	9.2
1981	5.8
1991	3.5
2001	4.3
2005	5.4

Turkey

1971	..
1981	0.1
1991	0.7
2001	2.0
2005	2.7

Others

1971	32.5
1981	26.6
1991	26.6
2001	26.0
2005	29.5

Source: adapted from *Social Trends*, Office for National Statistics.

1. Holidays of four nights or more taken by British residents; percentages

Table 5 Visits to the most popular tourist attractions

Great Britain

Millions

	1981	1991	2006		1981	1991	2006
Museums and galleries				**Historic houses**			
British Museum	2.6	5.1	4.8	**and monuments**			
National Gallery	2.7	4.3	4.6	Edinburgh Castle	0.8	1.0	1.2
Natural History Museum	3.7	1.6	3.8	Tower of London	2.1	1.9	2.1
Tate Gallery	0.9	1.8	4.6	Stonehenge	0.5	0.6	0.9
Theme parks				**Wildlife parks and zoos**			
Blackpool Pleasure Beach	7.5	6.5	5.7	London Zoo	1.1	1.1	0.9
Pleasure Beach, Great Yarmouth	..	2.5	1.4	Chester Zoo	..	0.9	1.2
				Knowsley Safari Park	..	0.3	0.5

Source: adapted from *Social Trends*, Office for National Statistics; *Visitor Attraction Trends England 2006*, VisitBritain.

Table 6 Holiday taking: by social grade

Great Britain

Percentages[1]

	Holidays in Britain	Holidays abroad	No holiday
AB	44	59	18
C1	37	47	31
C2	38	32	38
DE	28	20	57

1. Percentage of people in each social grade taking holidays in each location. Percentages do not sum to 100 because some people take holidays in Britain and abroad.

AB = higher/middle management, administration and professional; C1 = junior management, supervisory or clerical; C2 = skilled manual; DE = semi and unskilled, lowest paid or unemployed.

Source: adapted from *Social Trends*, Office for National Statistics.

Figure 6 Domestic holidays[1] taken by United Kingdom residents: by destination, 2005

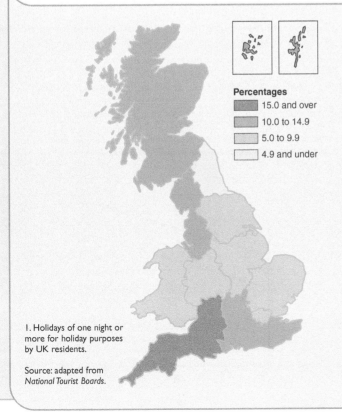

Percentages
- 15.0 and over
- 10.0 to 14.9
- 5.0 to 9.9
- 4.9 and under

1. Holidays of one night or more for holiday purposes by UK residents.

Source: adapted from *National Tourist Boards*.

1. Describe the main trends in tourism shown in the data.
2. 'A visit to Stonehenge could be classified as a normal good.' Explain what this means.
3. What evidence is there in the data that some tourist destinations and attractions are inferior goods?
4. Firms associated with tourism in the Great Yarmouth area are concerned that they are losing out in the expansion of tourism in the UK and abroad. (a) Suggest THREE reasons why a tourist might prefer to go to places such as Scotland, Cornwall, Spain or Florida rather than Great Yarmouth. (b) Discuss THREE strategies which stakeholders in the tourist industry in the Great Yarmouth area could adopt to make the income elasticity of demand more favourable to themselves.

Summary

1. Indirect taxes can be either ad valorem taxes or specific taxes.
2. The imposition of an indirect tax is likely to lead to a rise in the unit price of a good which is less than the unit value of the tax.
3. The incidence of indirect taxation is likely to fall on both consumer and producer.
4. The incidence of tax will fall wholly on the consumer if demand is perfectly inelastic or supply is perfectly elastic.
5. The incidence of tax will fall wholly on the producer if demand is perfectly elastic or supply is perfectly inelastic.

Indirect taxes and subsidies

An indirect tax is a tax on expenditure. The two major indirect taxes in the UK are VAT and excise duties.

VAT is an example of an AD VALOREM tax. The tax levied increases in proportion to the value of the tax base. In the case of VAT, the tax base is the price of the good. Most goods in the UK carry a 17.5 per cent VAT charge. Excise duties on the other hand are an example of a SPECIFIC or UNIT tax. The amount of tax levied does not change with the value of the goods but with the amount or volume of the goods purchased. So the excise duty on a bottle of wine is the same whether the bottle costs £5 or £500, but the VAT is 100 times more on the latter compared to the former. The main excise duties in the UK are on alcohol, tobacco and petrol. They should not be confused with customs duties which are levied on imports.

A SUBSIDY is a grant given by government to encourage the production or consumption of a particular good or service.

Subsidies, for instance, may be given on essential items such as housing or bread. Alternatively they may be given to firms that employ disadvantaged workers such as the long term unemployed or people with disabilities. Thay may also be given to firms manufacturing domestically produced goods to help them be more competitive than imported goods.

The incidence of tax

Price theory can be used to analyse the impact of the imposition of an indirect tax on a good. Assume that a specific tax of £1 per bottle is imposed upon wine. This has the effect of reducing supply. Sellers of wine will now want to charge £1 extra per bottle sold. In Figure 1, this is shown by a vertical shift of £1 in the supply curve at every level of output. However many bottles are produced, sellers will want to charge £1 more per bottle and therefore there is a parallel shift upwards and to the left of the whole supply curve from S_1 to S_2.

The old equilibrium price was £3.30, at which price 60 million bottles were bought and sold. The introduction of the £1 tax

Question 1

The price of a litre of unleaded petrol at the pumps is made up as follows:

	pence
Petrol cost before tax	28.6
Excise duty	53.7
	82.3
VAT @ 17.5%	14.4
Price at the pumps	96.7

Calculate the new price of petrol if:
(a) an increase in the cost of crude oil pushed up the cost of petrol before tax from 28.6p to 32.3p;
(b) the government increased excise duty from 53.7 to 58.2p;
(c) VAT was reduced from 17.5 per cent to 15 per cent;
(d) the government removed both excise duties and VAT on petrol and instead introduced a subsidy of 2p a litre.
(For each part, assume that the price at the pumps is initially 96.7p.)

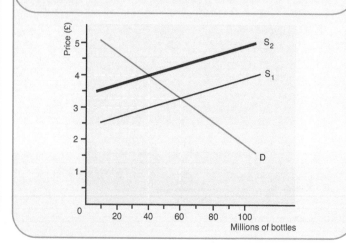

Figure 1 The incidence of a specific tax
The imposition of an indirect tax of £1 per unit on wine will push up the supply curve from S_1 to S_2. The vertical distance between the two supply curves at any given output is £1. As a consequence equilibrium price will rise from £3.30 to £4.00. The consumer therefore pays an extra 70p per bottle of wine. The other 30p of the tax is paid by the producer because the price it receives per bottle before tax falls from £3.30 to £3.00.

will raise price and reduce quantity demanded. The new equilibrium price is £4, at which price quantity demanded falls to 40 million bottles.

This result might seem surprising. The imposition of a £1 per bottle tax has only raised the price of a bottle by 70p and not the full £1 of the tax. This is because the INCIDENCE OF TAX is unlikely to fall totally on consumers. The incidence of tax measures the burden of tax upon the taxpayer. In this case the consumer has paid 70p of the tax. Therefore the other 30p which the government receives must have been paid by producers.

Question 2

Table 1

Price (£)	Quantity demanded	Quantity supplied
4	16	4
6	12	6
8	8	8
10	4	10
12	0	12

(a) Draw the demand and supply curves from the data in Table 1.
(b) What is the equilibrium quantity demanded and supplied?

The government now imposes a specific tax of £3 per unit.
(c) Show the effect of this on the diagram.
(d) What is the new equilibrium quantity demanded and supplied?
(e) What is the new equilibrium price?
(f) What is the incidence of tax per unit on (i) the consumer and (ii) the producer?
(g) What is (i) the tax per unit and (ii) total government revenue from the tax?
(h) By how much will the before tax revenue of producers change?

Tax revenues

Using Figure 1 we can also show the change in total expenditure before and after imposition of the tax as well as the amount of tax revenue gained by the government. The government will receive total tax revenue of £1 x 40 million (the tax per unit x the quantity sold); hence tax revenues will be £40 million. Consumers will pay 70p x 40 million of this, whilst producers will pay 30p x 40 million. Consumers will therefore pay £28 million of tax whilst producers will pay £12 million. Total spending on wine will fall from £198 million (£3.30 x 60 million) to £160 million (£4 x 40 million). Revenues received by producers will fall from £198 million (£3.30 x 60 million) to £120 million (£3 x 40 million).

Ad valorem taxes

The above analysis can be extended to deal with ad valorem taxes. The imposition of an ad valorem tax will lead to an upwards shift in the supply curve. However, the higher the price, the greater will be the amount of the tax. Hence the shift will

look as in Figure 2. Consumers will pay FG tax per unit whilst the incidence of tax on producers per unit will be HG.

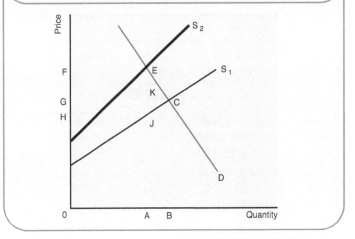

Figure 2 The incidence of an ad valorem tax
The imposition of an ad valorem tax will push the supply curve upwards from S_1 to S_2. The following gives the key facts about the change:
(a) original equilibrium price and quantity, OG and OB;
(b) new equilibrium price and quantity, OF and OA;
(c) incidence of tax per unit on consumers, GF;
(d) incidence of tax per unit on producers, HG;
(e) tax per unit in equilibrium, HF;
(f) total tax paid by consumers, GKEF;
(g) total tax paid by producers, GHJK;
(h) total tax revenue of government, FHJE;
(i) change in producers' revenue, OBCG - OAJH;
(j) change in consumers' expenditure, OBCG - OAEF.

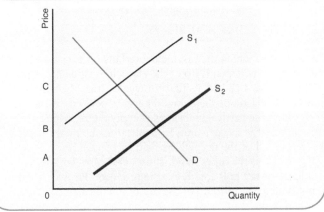

Figure 3 The effect of a subsidy on price
A subsidy of AC per unit will push the supply curve down from S_1 to S_2. The price to the consumer will fall by BC (i.e. less than the value of the subsidy per unit given).

Subsidies

A subsidy on a good will lead to an increase in supply, shifting the supply curve downwards and to the right. This is shown in Figure 3. It should be noted that a subsidy of AC will not lead to a fall in price of AC. Part of the subsidy, AB, will be appropriated by producers because of the higher unit cost of production of higher levels of output (shown by the upward sloping supply curve). Prices to consumers will only fall by BC.

Question 3

The Prime Minister's Strategy Unit has suggested that taxing unhealthy foods might be part of a wider strategy to combat rising levels of obesity. In a paper, *Personal Responsibility and Changing Behaviour*, it says: 'There might even be potential to consider fiscal measures - a 'fatty food tax' - applied to food not people - or different VAT treatment for food with poor nutritional standards. This would be a signal to producers as well as consumers and serve more broadly as a signal to society that nutritional content in food is important.'

Currently, VAT is levied at the full rate of 17.5 per cent on many foods most associated with obesity, such as crisps, fizzy drinks and ice cream. But a burger bought in a supermarket, like most foods, has no VAT on it. In contrast, burgers sold in fast food restaurants carry 17.5 per cent VAT.

Tom Marshall, a public health specialist who recently studied the possible effects of a fat tax, believes that adding VAT to foods high in saturated fats - such as full-fat milk, hard cheeses, butter, buns and biscuits - could have a major impact on health. If VAT were extended to the principal sources of dietary saturated fat, while exempting goods such as orange juice and low-fat yoghurt, consumers would be more likely to buy the cheaper, low-fat alternatives.

Source: adapted from *The Times*, 19.2.2004.

(a) Explain, using a diagram, what would happen to the supply of hard cheeses if they became subject to VAT at 17.5 per cent.
(b) Analyse whether the price of hard cheeses would go up by 17.5 per cent if VAT were imposed at this rate. Use a diagram to illustrate your analysis.
(c) Why might the imposition of VAT on hard cheeses have an impact on the demand for orange juice?
(d) 'A positive impact on health of the imposition of VAT would be most likely if demand for fatty foods were price elastic.' Using a diagram, explain this statement.

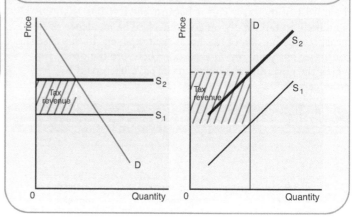

Figure 4 Where the incidence of tax falls wholly on the consumer
If supply is perfectly elastic or demand perfectly inelastic, then it can be seen from the graphs that the incidence of tax will fall wholly on consumers.

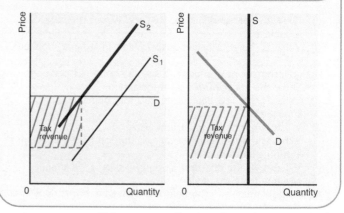

Figure 5 Where the incidence of tax falls wholly on the producer
If supply is perfectly inelastic or demand perfectly elastic, then it can be seen from the graphs that the incidence of tax will fall wholly on producers.

Taxes, subsidies and elasticity

The extent to which the tax incidence falls on consumers rather than producers depends upon the elasticities of demand and supply. Figure 4 shows a situation where either the supply curve is perfectly elastic or the demand curve is perfectly inelastic. In both cases, the vertical shift in the supply curve, which shows the value of the tax per unit, is identical to the final price rise. Therefore, all of the tax will be paid by consumers.

Figure 5, on the other hand, shows two cases where the incidence of tax falls totally on the producer. Producers will find it impossible to shift any of the tax onto consumers if the demand curve is perfectly elastic. Consumers are not prepared to buy at any higher price than the existing price. If the supply curve is perfectly inelastic, then the supply curve after imposition of the tax will be the same as the one before. Equilibrium price will therefore remain the same and producers will have to bear the full burden of the tax.

Generalising from these extreme situations, we can conclude that the more elastic the demand curve or the more inelastic the supply curve, the greater will be the incidence of tax on producers and the less will be the incidence of tax on consumers. So far as the government is concerned,

taxation revenue will be greater, all other things being equal, the more inelastic the demand for the product taxed. For instance, if demand were perfectly elastic, the imposition of an indirect tax would lead to quantity demanded falling to zero and tax revenue

Question 4

Table 2

	Price elasticity of demand
Food	- 0.52
Durables	- 0.89
Fuel and light	- 0.47
Services	- 1.02

Source: John Muellbauer, 'Testing the Barten Model of Household Composition Effects and the Cost of Children', *Economic Journal*.

The government wishes to raise VAT on selected goods, all these goods and services being zero-rated at present. Which categories of goods does the data suggest would yield (a) the most and (b) the least revenues? (Assume that at present the average price and the quantity demanded of goods in each category is identical.) Explain your reasoning carefully.

being zero. At the opposite extreme, if demand were perfectly inelastic, consumers would buy the same quantity after imposition of the tax as before. Hence revenue will be equal to the tax per unit times the quantity demanded before imposition. If the price elasticity of demand lies between these two extremes, the imposition of a tax will lead to a fall in quantity demanded. The higher the elasticity, the larger will be the fall in quantity demanded and hence the lower will be the tax revenue received by government. Hence, it is no coincidence that in the UK excise duties are placed on alcohol, tobacco and petrol, all of which are relatively price inelastic.

The same analysis can be applied to subsidies. In general, subsidies tend to be given where the policy objective is to reduce the price of the good. The largest fall in price will occur when either demand is highly inelastic or supply is highly elastic. If demand is very elastic or supply very inelastic, there will be very little, if any change, in price following the granting of a subsidy.

This is because producers will not pass on the subsidy to consumers. They will absorb the subsidy, which will allow them to increase their profits.

Key terms

Ad valorem tax - tax levied as a percentage of the value of the good.
Incidence of tax - the tax burden on the taxpayer.
Specific or unit tax - tax levied on volume.
Subsidy - a grant given which lowers the price of a good, usually designed to encourage production or consumption of a good.

Applied economics

Taxes, subsidies, congestion and the environment

The demand for transport keeps growing as Figure 6 shows. However, this growing demand is concentrated on motor transport. Other modes of transport, such as bus and rail, are today relatively insignificant. The increase in demand for motor transport poses two problems. One is that it is causing ever increasing congestion on the roads. The other is that it is causing a variety of environmental problems. The government, through taxes and subsidies, can tackle both problems but, as with so many complex economic issues, there are no easy and painless solutions.

Road congestion

Britain's roads are becoming ever more congested. In 1950, there were fewer than 2 million cars. Today, there are over 27 million. The Department for Transport projects that this will rise to 30 million by 2015 and 40 million by 2025. The demand for road space is therefore growing over time. The supply of road space in terms of the number of kilometres of road or the number of lanes on roads is hardly changing. Hence, key roads regularly become congested at certain times of day or certain days of the week. Figure 7 shows how average traffic speeds in London have declined over time as a result of this increasing congestion.

The overall cost of motoring is one factor which limits the demand for road space. The fixed costs of owning a car, in terms of purchase, insurance, licensing and servicing, deter those on lower incomes from owning a car. However, the decision for a car owner about whether to use a particular road is determined by the cost of fuel, the variable cost of motoring.

Raising taxes on motoring, such as raising taxes on petrol and diesel prices, is one way in which the government can price motorists off the road. However,

this is a very crude way of doing this because it gives no incentive for motorists to switch their journey times to when roads are less congested. It also hits motorists, particularly in rural areas, who rarely face any congestion.

Reducing congestion through raising taxes on fuel is also likely to be politically impossible. In 2000, the country was brought to a halt by a relatively small group of protesters from the farming and road haulage lobby who wanted the government to reduce the price of petrol through cutting taxes. Because the demand for motoring is relatively inelastic, there would have to be very large rises in tax on fuel to have an impact on congestion. Petrol would have to be, say, £5 a litre compared to £1 today, to force enough cars off the road at peak times to reduce congestion. Such prices would hit all motorists, not just those whose journeys create congestion in the first place.

Economists therefore favour taxing congestion directly. A start has already been made with the London Congestion Charge, where motorists have to pay £8 a day to enter central London. This has been highly effective at reducing congestion in central London and raising journey speeds. More broadly, the government has plans to introduce congestion charging across the whole country, currently by 2014. The hope is that all vehicles can be tracked via satellite and be charged when they travel in any zone where there is congestion. It might be politically acceptable to introduce such a charge if the revenues raised were used to reduce the tax on fuel. However, the technology is still unproven. It would also have to give significant benefits to motorists in terms of shorter journey times in congested areas.

In central London, the introduction of the Congestion Charge was accompanied by higher spending on, and subsidies for, public transport. In particular, bus services were expanded to offer an alternative to those who no longer wanted to bring their cars into Central London. Using part of the revenues from congestion charging throughout the country could prove less effective, however. For example, where cars were priced off the motorway system, it might be difficult to offer satisfactory public transport alternatives. Equally, it would raise the overall cost of motoring since the cash raised from the congestion charges was not being recycled into lower fuel taxes or reduced vehicle licence fees. This might prove politically unpopular.

The environment

Motor vehicles are environmentally damaging. Roads eat into the countryside. Scarce natural resources are used up in the making and running of vehicles. There is noise pollution in the vicinity of roads. Engines run on carbon fuels and emit greenhouse gasses which contribute to global warming. Diesel engines emit particulates which can cause cancer.

One solution to reducing the damage done to the environment is simply to reduce the number and length of journeys made. Raising taxes on fuel would therefore be a good way of achieving this. In its April 1993 Budget, the government committed itself to such a rise in taxes on petrol by 3 per cent per year in real terms for the foreseeable future, a figure which it increased to 5 per cent in its December 1993 Budget. It justified this by pointing out that petrol was cheaper in real terms in 1993 than it had been in the early 1980s. It was this policy which fuel protesters succeeded in getting the government to abandon in 2000. The vast majority of motorists put lower taxes on fuel ahead of any environmental concerns.

Another solution to at least some of the environmental problems associated with motoring is to modify vehicles themselves. Vehicles are slowly becoming more fuel efficient. Diesel engines emit fewer greenhouse gases than petrol cars. If everyone drove around in diesel powered minis, there would be considerable environmental gains. Figure 8 shows that over the period 1976 to 2006, there were some modest gains in efficiency. Distance travelled by all types of road vehicle increased 108 per cent whilst fuel consumption only increased by 70 per cent. The data also suggest that efficiency gains are increasing over time. Between 1997 and 2003, for example, distance travelled increased by 12 per cent but fuel consumption only increased by 3 per cent.

However, making incremental improvements in the efficiency of oil driven engines is unlikely to prevent the motor car from causing more damage to the environment in the future. This is because the number of motor cars worldwide will increase 5, 10 or 20 fold over the next few decades as developing economies such as China and India develop to the point where most households can afford at least one car. The only solution to this is to change the engine which powers the motor car. Electric cars driven by batteries or engines fuelled by hydrogen

have been developed but both have so many drawbacks today that they are not being widely adopted. However, in 10 or 20 years' time, circumstances may have changed and the petrol driven car with its damaging effects on the environment may have largely disappeared. It could be that the market mechanism will bring about this change. More likely, governments will intervene and through a combination of policies such as government regulations, taxes and subsidies, we will see fewer environmentally damaging vehicles on the roads.

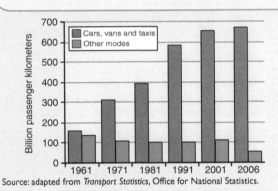

Figure 6 Passenger journeys by mode of transport

Source: adapted from *Transport Statistics*, Office for National Statistics.

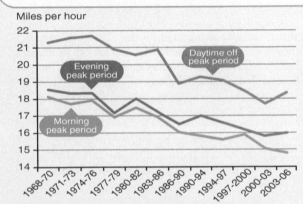

Figure 7 Average traffic speeds in London, 1968-2006

Source: adapted from *Transport Statistics*, Office for National Statistics.

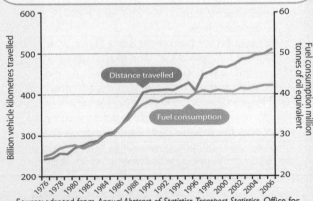

Figure 8 Distance travelled and fuel consumption: all transport UK

Source: adapted from *Annual Abstract of Statistics, Transport Statistics*, Office for National Statistics.

DataQuestion

SUVs

SUVs

SUVs, sports utility vehicles, are sometimes also called 'off-roaders'. They differ from ordinary cars in that they are taller, placing the driver in a higher position than other car drivers. They have 4x4 transmissions, meaning that power is directly taken to all four wheels rather than just two wheels on an ordinary car. This gives them much better grip for travelling across rough terrain such as fields or dirt tracks - hence the name 'off-roader'. They are designed to give the handling of a traditional work vehicle or utility vehicle like a farm Land Rover with the comfort of a modern car. According to a survey by YouGov, almost two thirds of the population want special taxes on sports utility vehicles. Londoners were even more strongly in favour of restrictions on 4x4s. Ken Livingstone, mayor of London, has described SUV drivers as 'complete idiots'.

Source: adapted from the *Financial Times*, 2.9.2004.

Demand for and supply of SUVs

Demand for SUVs has seen strong growth. In the past 10 years, sales have doubled with 76 000 sold in 2006 alone. They now account for 7.5 per cent of all new cars sold in the UK. Motor manufacturers have responded by developing new SUV models and all the major sellers in the UK market now have an SUV on offer. There is an added incentive for motor manufacturers in that the profit margins on SUVs are higher than on the average car. Customers seem to be less price sensitive, viewing their SUVs as luxuries for which they are prepared to pay extra.

Table 3 SUV price ranges, new, September 2007

Nissan X-trail	£17 637 - £22 999
Toyota Rav 4	£16 995 - £24 881
Mitsubishi Shogun	£21 716 - £33 269
Land Rover Discovery	£24 566 - £40 374
Suzuki Grand Vitara	£10 394 - £14 381

Source: adapted from www.smmt.co.uk, January 2007, www.broadspeed.com.

The Chelsea tractor

SUVs are sometimes known as 'Chelsea tractors'. They are used by the well heeled of one of the richest boroughs in London to do such exciting things as go to the local supermarket or pick up the children from school. They certainly would never be let out into the open countryside - that is just the fantasy which helps sell the car.

So what is the attraction for buyers? Women say they feel safer driving an SUV because they are higher up and so get better vision. They are also a tremendous status symbol. They are a very large and prominent display of wealth and social standing. Not merely can you afford to buy it, but you can also afford the high running costs of the vehicle. A YouGov Survey found that a fifth of SUV owners bought them for 'pose value'. However, in the same survey, half of the respondents who didn't own an SUV believed that 'pose value' was the main reason for owners buying them.

Source: adapted from the *Financial Times*, 2.9.2004.

Vehicle Excise Duty

The Prime Minister has been re-examining the case for penalising drivers of gas-guzzling cars. He is investigating whether to raise the highest rate of Vehicle Excise Duty on the most polluting vehicles, which would include many SUVs. Vehicle Excise Duty is a specific, flat rate, tax on the purchase of every new car.

Source: adapted from the *Financial Times*, 17.3.2007.

Fuel consumption

SUVs tend to have very poor fuel consumption. Some petrol versions do as little as 13.4 miles to the gallon in a city and 25mpg on a motorway. The environmental lobby argues that few drivers of off-roaders ever need the 4x4 capability, but the extra weight of the complex system makes the vehicles less fuel-efficient. 'It is bound to be less efficient because it has the aerodynamics of a brick and the extra weight of a four-wheel-drive drivetrain' said John Wormaid, partner at Autopolis, the consultants.

Source: adapted from the *Financial Times*, 2.9.2004.

1. Outline TWO reasons why the government might want to raise the level of Vehicle Excise Duty on SUVs. (Vehicle Excise Duty is a specific tax on the purchase of new cars.)

2. Using a demand and supply diagram, explain how the price and quantity bought of SUVs might be affected by an increase in Vehicle Excise Duty.

3. Discuss just how high the tax would need to be to bring about a significant reduction in purchases of SUVs by those who would never use their vehicles off-road.

Summary

1. The market is a mechanism for the allocation of resources.
2. In a free market, consumers, producers and owners of the factors of production interact, each seeking to maximise their returns.
3. Prices have three main functions in allocating resources. These are the rationing, signalling and incentive functions.
4. If firms cannot make enough profit from the production of a good, the resources they use will be reallocated to more profitable uses.

The role of the market

Adam Smith, in his book *An Enquiry into the Nature and Causes of the Wealth of Nations*, attacked the economic system of his day. It was a system founded upon protectionism, economic restrictions and numerous legal barriers. He presented a powerful case for a free market system in which the 'invisible hand' of the market would allocate resources to everyone's advantage. There are three main types of actor or agent in the market system. Consumers and producers interact in the **goods markets** of the economy. Producers and the owners of the factors of production (land, labour and capital) interact in the **factor markets** of the economy.

The main actors in the market

The consumer In a pure free market system it is the consumer who is all powerful. Consumers are free to spend their money however they want and the market offers a wide choice of products. It is assumed that consumers will allocate their scarce resources so as to maximise their welfare, satisfaction or utility.

The firm In a pure free market, firms are servants of the consumer. They are motivated by making as high a profit as possible. This means maximising the difference between revenues and costs.
- **Revenues**. If they fail to produce goods which consumers wish to buy, they won't be able to sell them. Consumers will buy from companies which produce the goods they want. Successful companies will have high revenues; unsuccessful ones will have low or zero revenues.
- **Costs**. If firms fail to minimise costs, then they will fail to make a profit. Other more efficient firms will be able to take their market away from them by selling at a lower price.

The price of failure - making insufficient profit to retain resources and prevent factor owners from allocating their resources in more profitable ways - will be the exit of the firm from its industry. On the other hand, in the long run firms cannot make higher than average levels of profit. If they did, new competitors would enter the industry attracted by the high profits, driving down prices and profits and increasing output.

Owners of the factors of production Owners of land, labour and capital - rentiers, workers and capitalists - are motivated by the desire to maximise their returns. Landowners wish to rent their land at the highest possible price.

Workers wish to hire themselves out at the highest possible wage, all other things being equal. Capitalists wish to receive the highest rate of return on capital. These owners will search in the market place for the highest possible reward and only when they have found it will they offer their factor for employment. Firms, on the other hand, will be seeking to minimise cost. They will only be prepared to pay the owner the value of the factor in the production process.

'In a free market, consumers have no choice about what they can buy. Firms simply impose their wishes on the consumer.' Use the photograph to explain why this is incorrect.

The function of prices in the market

In a market, there are buyers who demand goods and sellers who supply goods. The interactions of demand and supply fix the price at which exchange takes place. Price has three important functions in a market.

Rationing Consumer wants are infinite, but we live in a world of scarce resources. Somehow, those scarce resources need to be allocated between competing uses. One function of price in a market is to allocate and ration those resources. The demand curve for a good shows the relationship between the price and the value that buyers place on purchasing that good. Movements up and down the demand curve show the rationing function in action. If the price of a good is very high because supply is limited, relatively few goods will bought. Limited supply will be rationed to those buyers prepared to pay a high enough price. If the price of the same good is relatively low because supply is plentiful, then more goods will be bought. The low price ensures that high numbers of goods will be bought, reflecting the **relative** lack of scarcity of the good.

Signalling The price of a good is a key piece of information to both buyers and sellers in the market. Prices come about because of the transactions of buyers and sellers. They reflect market conditions and therefore act as a signal to those in the market. Decisions about buying and selling are based on those signals.

Incentive Prices act as an incentive for buyers and sellers. Low prices encourage buyers to purchase more goods. For consumers, this is because the amount of satisfaction or utility gained per pound spent increases relative to other goods. Higher prices discourage buying because consumers get fewer goods per pound spent. On the supply side, higher prices encourage suppliers to sell more to the market. Firms may have to take on more workers and invest in new capital equipment to achieve this. Low prices discourage production. A prolonged fall in prices may drive some firms out of the market because it is no longer profitable for them to supply.

To illustrate how these functions help allocate resources, consider two examples.

Example 1 Assume that the demand for fur coats falls because of lobbying from animal welfare groups. The demand curve for fur coats therefore shifts to the left. At the old price, more is supplied than is now demanded, i.e. there is excess supply. The equilibrium price will then fall. The lower price is a **signal** to manufacturers of fur coats that market conditions have changed for the worse. The lower price reduces **incentives** for fur coat manufacturers. Lower prices indicate that their profits will fall. Hence, they will make fewer fur coats. The new price **rations** the fur coats for sale amongst potential buyers. The new downward sloping demand curve shows that if prices were lower, buyers would wish to purchase more fur coats. If prices were higher, they would buy fewer coats. The new equilibrium price is the only price at which the number of fur coats available for sale (shown by the supply curve) is exactly equal to the number of fur coats that buyers which to purchase.

Example 2 Assume that the supply of oil falls. The supply curve for oil therefore shifts to the left. At the old equilibrium price, there is excess demand. The equilibrium price will then

rise, with less oil being supplied and demanded. The higher price is a **signal** to consumers that market conditions have changed. The higher price also reduces the incentive for buyers to purchase oil. For example, some motorists will switch from using their cars to travelling by bus. Some owners of oil-fired central heating systems will switch to electric or gas central heating systems. The new price **rations** oil amongst buyers. There is now less oil available at any given price. So there is a movement up the demand curve for oil. Some consumers of oil will be priced out of the market altogether. Others will cut back on their purchases of oil.

Question 3

Samsung Electronics, the South Korean manufacturer, has come from nowhere to become a global force in products such as memory chips, flat panel displays and mobile phones. Last week, the company held an unusual news conference dedicated to its new MP3 players, declaring it would increase its share of the mini hard disk-drive music player market from just 7.7 per cent now to become the world's top producer, unseating Apple which controls 70 per cent, by 2007.

Apple's iPod has proved an unexpected and spectacular success. Easy to use and with a 'cool', 'must have' image amongst its young buyers, it has transformed the fortunes of Apple. The company quadrupled its first quarter profits this year compared to last year's figures on the back of sales of the iPod.

Samsung hopes young people will be lured to its multi-functional MP3 players with a built-in voice recorder, camera and radio tuners, which will allow users to play electronic games, watch music videos and movies and take digital photographs. Technologically, the company has a strong advantage over Apple because it is the world's largest producer of flash memory chips, a key component of MP3 players. Samsung's global brand power and sales network are also expected to help it increase market share in the US. This year, the company plans to spend $40 million on marketing for its MP3 players.

Analysts warn, though, that Samsung's strategy may not work, as many consumers still prefer simple products with user-friendly interfaces, which is the strength of iPod. 'Cool' is also very difficult to capture in a copycat product. Yet it is the 'cool' factor which allows products such as Nike shoes and BMW cars to be sold at higher prices than competing products and generates large profits for their owners.

Source: adapted from the *Financial Times*, 30.3.2005.

Explain, using Samsung as an example, the role of profit in allocating resources.

Maximising behaviour

In the market mechanism, everyone is assumed to be motivated by self interest. Consumers are motivated by the desire to maximise their welfare or utility. Producers wish to maximise profits. Workers, rentiers and capitalists seek to maximise the returns from the factor that they own. This maximising behaviour determines the way in which resources are allocated.

Consumers, for instance, will spend to maximise their satisfaction or utility. They cast spending 'votes' between different products and different firms. If consumer tastes change so that they want more ice cream and fewer hot dogs, then they will spend more on ice cream and less on hot dogs. Ice cream manufacturers will collect more money from the sale of ice cream which they will use to expand production. Manufacturers of hot dogs will be forced to lay off staff, buy fewer raw materials and in the long term shut factories.

Profit and not revenue is the signal to firms to change levels of production. When consumers demand more ice cream, firms will expand production only if it is profitable to do so. Hot dog manufacturers will shut down manufacturing plant only if these resources could be used at higher profit levels elsewhere. In a free market, changes in consumer demand are met by changes in patterns of production by firms because of their desire to maximise profit.

Judging the market

Markets are one way of allocating resources. There are alternatives. For instance, the government could allocate resources as it does with defence, education or the police. Economists are interested in knowing how to judge whether markets are the best way of allocating resources. There are two main ways in which they do this.

First, they consider whether markets are **efficient** ways of allocating resources. By this, we mean whether firms produce at lowest cost and are responsive to the needs of consumers as in the ice cream and hot dog example above. Second, they consider issues of **equity**. Efficiency takes income distribution for granted. However, is income and wealth in society distributed in an acceptable way?

If resources are allocated inefficiently and inequitably, then there may be a case for governments to intervene, either by altering conditions in the market or by removing production from the market mechanism altogether. The next few units consider these complex issues.

Applied economics

Motor cars

The history of the UK motor car industry in recent decades is a good example of how markets allocate resources. In the 1950s and 1960s, the British market was insulated to a great extent from foreign competition. The British motorist bought cars made in British factories, even if some of these factories were owned by foreign companies such as Ford. It was largely a sellers' market, with demand constrained by the ability of consumers to obtain credit for the purchase of cars.

However, the car industry suffered two major weaknesses at the time. First, it failed to address problems of quality. In a sellers' market, firms had little incentive to manufacture world beating cars. Second, there was underinvestment by the industry. This was perhaps not surprising given the poor profitability of some companies. For instance, the original Mini car, first produced in 1959, failed to make a profit in its first five years of production because its price was set too low. Poor profitability led to resources being reallocated in the market. There was widespread rationalisation. Companies were taken over and car plants closed. However, the necessary investment in new production processes and facilities lagged behind the UK's main overseas competitors.

These weaknesses hit the British motor industry hard

in the 1970s and 1980s. As Figure 2 shows, imports soared, whilst exports declined. Domestic production fell from a peak of 1.9 million cars per year in 1972 to 0.9 million by 1984. What happened was that UK consumers increasingly wanted to buy foreign cars because they were better built, more reliable and, in the case of Japanese cars, more keenly priced. Lower prices for Japanese cars signalled to the market that resources should be reallocated. Foreign customers turned away from British cars too, reducing exports to a third of their 1960s levels. As British car manufacturers made losses, they responded to this market signal by closing factories, laying off workers and reducing orders for components. The reduction in demand for British made cars resulted in a fall in demand for the factors of production used to manufacture those cars.

The mid-1980s was a turning point for British motor manufacturing. Arguably the most important factor in forcing change was the arrival of Japanese manufacturers in the UK. Honda established a working partnership with the then UK owned Rover and also built an engine plant in Swindon. Nissan built a new car plant in the North East of England, followed by Toyota which set up in Derby.

This extra competition in the market forced US and

European car manufacturers in the UK market to change the way in which they designed and built cars. They adopted Japanese production methods such as just-in-time deliveries of components to factories. Workers were given far greater skills. New investment and new models were given to car plants which could show that they had high levels of productivity. British factories in particular were given a choice. Either they adopted new ways of working or they would be starved of investment and eventually closed. If British factories could not be profitable and supply the right goods, the market would force them to shut down.

Market forces also played a part in the decision by the Japanese to come to the UK. In the first half of the 1980s, the government of Margaret Thatcher pursued **supply side policies** which attracted foreign investment. Trade union power was curbed. Taxes on company profits were cut. Higher rates of tax paid by company executives were slashed. Finally, taxes paid by employers on their workers fell. The poor performance of the UK economy in the 1960s and 1970s relative to other European countries also meant that wages in the UK were now often lower than in Germany or France. Low taxes and low wages acted as powerful incentives for the Japanese and other foreign countries to set up in the UK.

In the 1990s, as Figures 1 and 2 show, the UK car industry made a substantial recovery. Domestic production increased from 1.3 million cars in 1990 to 1.8 million cars in 1999, an increase of nearly 40 per cent. Over the same period, exports rose 73 per cent whilst imports only rose 49 per cent. The market was signalling that UK car plants could be as competitive as, if not more competitive than, foreign car plants. The market was also providing an incentive for car manufacturing firms to invest in their UK car plants because they could be as profitable as, if not more profitable than, car plants abroad.

The highly competitive nature of the car industry if anything intensified in the 2000s. For example, countries in Eastern Europe which joined the EU in 2004, with their low wage labour force and low taxes, saw significant investment by multinationals. As a result, a boom in car sales in the UK, rising from 2.3 million cars a year in 2000 to 2.6 million cars a year in 2004, was supplied entirely by imports rather than an increase in domestic production. Another example of the fierce nature of competition in the market was the collapse in 2004 of Rover, the UK's only remaining UK-owned mass car manufacturer.

Despite this competition, the long term future of the UK car industry looks secure. UK car plants, for the most part, are competitive. Nissan's car plant in Sunderland has the highest labour productivity in Europe and is also Nissan's most productive plant worldwide. This shows that British car plants can be world class units if managed effectively and if their owners continue to invest in them.

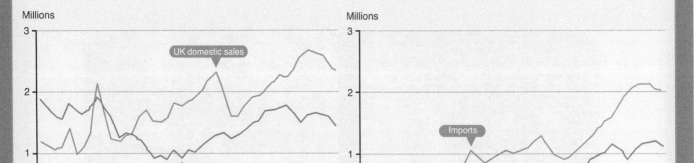

Figure 1 *Annual production and sales of cars, UK (millions)*

Figure 2 *Annual exports and imports of cars, UK (millions)*

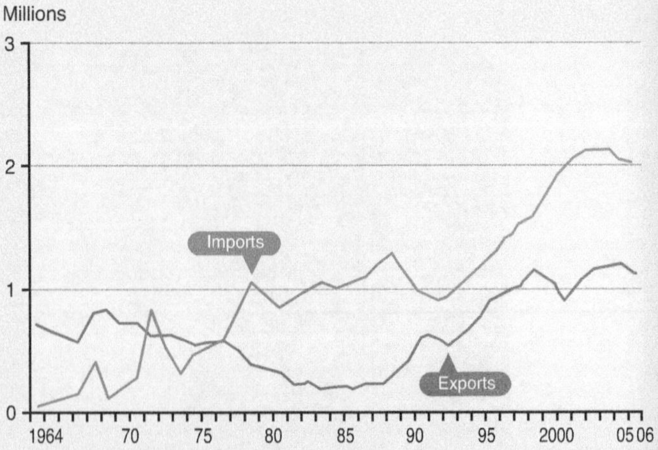

Source: adapted from *Economic & Labour Market Review*, Office for National Statistics.

Source: adapted from *Economic & Labour Market Review*, Office for National Statistics.

DataQuestion

Biofuels

Figure 3 Index of oil and biofuel prices (January 2006 = 100)

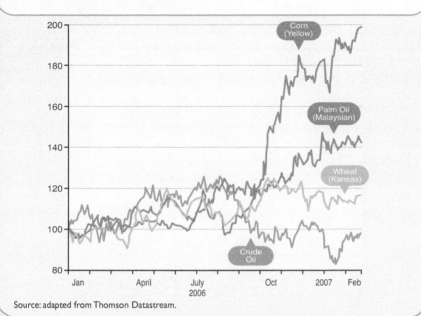

Source: adapted from Thomson Datastream.

European Union energy ministers this week agreed to set a legal requirement that, by 2020, 10 per cent of petrol and diesel used in vehicles will have to come from biofuels. Biofuels are fuels made from renewable biological materials such as corn, sugar cane, wheat and palm oil. Already, most petrol sold in the UK contains around 2 per cent ethanol made from Brazilian sugar cane. The UK government has itself said that petrol and diesel sold at the pump must contain 5 per cent biofuel by 2010.

Source: adapted from the *Financial Times*, 23.2.2007.

High prices are being felt around the world.

- Growing US demand for crop-based ethanol has pushed prices of yellow corn to a 10-year high. This in turn has lifted prices of white corn used to make tortilla flat bread, a staple food in Mexico. There have been protests on the street in Mexico about rising corn and tortilla prices.
- Farmland from Iowa to Argentina is rising faster in price than apartments in Manhattan and London for the first time in 30 years. Demand for corn used in ethanol increased the value of farm land 16 per cent in Indiana and 35 per cent in Idaho in 2006.
- US farmers plan to plant 8.4 million or 11 per cent less acres of soyabeans in 2007 compared to 2006 whilst the acreage devoted to corn will rise by 12.1 million acres or 7 per cent compared to 2006. The amount of land given over to cotton production will also fall as farmers switch to corn production. The US Department of Agriculture estimates that US demand for ethanol made from corn in 2007 will be 15 per cent more than in 2006.
- The Spanish engineering company Abengoa has

threatened to half production at its biggest bioethanol plant. The facility uses wheat, and wheat prices have risen 50 per cent this year, making production unprofitable.

Source: adapted from the *Financial Times*, 23.2.2007, 4.4.2007 and 29.6.2007.

1. Compare the changes in the price of the commodities shown in Figure 3.
2. Explain how the rationing, signalling and incentive functions are acting to allocate resources in the markets for different biofuels and related markets.
3. 'Governments forcing oil companies to include biofuels in their products will lead to much higher food prices for all and starvation for some.' Discuss whether the EU should have a 10 per cent biofuels target by 2020.

14 Economic efficiency and market failure

Summary

1. Static efficiency refers to efficiency at a point in time. Dynamic efficiency concerns how resources are allocated over time so as to promote technical progress and economic growth.
2. Productive efficiency exists when production is achieved at lowest cost.
3. Allocative efficiency is concerned with whether resources are used to produce the goods and services that consumers wish to buy.
4. All points on an economy's production possibility frontier are both productively and allocatively efficient.
5. Free markets tend to lead to efficiency.
6. Market failure occurs when markets do not function efficiently. Sources of market failure include lack of competition in a market, externalities, missing markets, information failure, factor immobility and inequality.

Efficiency

The market mechanism allocates resources, but how well does it do this? One way of judging this is to consider how **efficiently** it resolves the three fundamental questions in economics of how, what and for whom production should take place. Efficiency is concerned with how well resources, such as time, talents or materials, are used to produce an end result. In economic terms, it is concerned with the relationship between scarce inputs and outputs. There are a number of different forms of efficiency which need to be considered.

Static vs dynamic efficiency

STATIC EFFICIENCY exists at a point in time. An example of static efficiency would be whether a firm could produce 1 million cars a year more cheaply by using more labour and less capital. Another example would be whether a country could produce more if it cut its unemployment rate. Productive and allocative efficiency (discussed below) are static concepts of efficiency. Economists use them to discuss whether more could be produced now if resources were allocated in a different way. These concepts can be used, for instance, to discuss whether industries dominated by a monopoly producer might produce at lower cost if competition were introduced into the industry or whether a firm should be allowed to pollute the environment.

DYNAMIC EFFICIENCY is concerned with how resources are allocated **over a period of time**. For instance, would there be greater efficiency if a firm distributed less profit over time to its shareholders and used the money to finance more investment? Would there be greater efficiency in the economy if more resources were devoted to investment rather than consumption over time? Would an industry invest more and create more new products over time if it were a monopoly than if there were perfect competition?

Productive efficiency

PRODUCTIVE EFFICIENCY exists when production is achieved at lowest cost. There is productive inefficiency when the cost of production is above the minimum possible given the state of knowledge. For

instance, a firm which produces 1 million units at a cost of £10 000 would be productively inefficient if it could have produced that output at a cost of £8 000.

Productive efficiency will only exist if there is TECHNICAL EFFICIENCY. Technical efficiency exists if a given quantity of output is produced with the minimum number of inputs (or alternatively, if the maximum output is produced with a given number of units). For instance, if a firm produces 1 000 units of

Question 1

Table 1

| Output | Minimum input levels | Units |
	Labour	Capital
10	4	1
20	8	2
30	11	3
40	14	4
50	16	5

(a) Firm A uses 21 units of labour and 6 units of capital to produce 60 units of output. A competing firm uses 19 units of labour and 6 units of capital to produce the same output. Explain whether Firm A is more technically efficient than the competing firm.

(b) Firm B uses 24 units of labour and 7 units of capital to produce 70 units of output. Firm B pays £10 000 to employ these factors. A competing firm employs the same number of factors to produce the same level of output but only pays £8 000 for them. Explain whether Firm B is more productively efficient.

(c) Now look at Table 1. From the table, which of the following combinations are: (i) technically efficient and (ii) productively efficient if the minimum cost of a unit of labour is £100 and of a unit of capital is £500?
(1) 8 units of labour and 2 units of capital to produce 20 units of output at a cost of £1 800. (2) 15 units of labour and 4 units of capital to produce an output of 40 units at a cost of £3 500. (3) 4 units of labour and 1 unit of capital to produce 10 units of output at a cost of £1 000.

output using 10 workers when it could have used 9 workers, then it would be technically inefficient. However, not all technically efficient outputs are productively efficient. For instance, it might be possible to produce 1 000 units of output using 9 workers. But it might be cheaper to buy a machine and employ only 2 workers.

Equally, Firm A might be using a machine and two workers to produce a given output. However, if it is paying £100 000 a year for this, whilst a competing business is paying only £80 000 a year for the same factor inputs, then Firm A is productively inefficient.

Allocative efficiency

ALLOCATIVE or ECONOMIC EFFICIENCY is concerned with whether resources are used to produce the goods and services that consumers wish to buy. For instance, if a consumer wants to buy a pair of shoes, are the shoes available in the shops? If a consumer wants schooling for her child, is education available?

There are many examples of where allocative efficiency is not present. In the Second World War, a system of rationing in the UK limited what consumers could buy. They were not free to buy more food and less clothing because both food and clothing could only be bought using coupons issued by the government. In the Soviet Union (now Russia), there were constant chronic shortages of consumer goods. What was available was often distributed via queuing mechanisms. Consumers did not have the power to choose between shoes and food because shoes might be unavailable in the shops at the time.

Allocative efficiency occurs when no-one could be made better off without making someone else worse off. In the Second World War, for instance, some people would have preferred to buy more clothes and consume less food. Others wanted more food and fewer clothes. Allocative efficiency would have been greater if people had been allowed to trade their clothes coupons for food coupons because both groups would have gained.

Efficiency and the production possibility frontier

The various concepts of efficiency can be illustrated using a **production possibility frontier** or **PPF**. A production possibility frontier shows combinations of goods which could be produced if all resources were fully used (i.e. the economy were at full employment).

There is productive efficiency in an economy only if it is operating on the PPF. To understand why, consider an economy where all industries except the shoe industry are productively efficient. This means that the shoe industry is not operating at lowest cost and is using more resources than is necessary for its current level of output (i.e. it is technically inefficient). If the shoe industry became technically efficient, it could produce more shoes without reducing the output of the rest of the economy. Once the shoe industry is productively efficient, all industries are productively efficient and output cannot be increased in one industry without reducing it in another industry. However, this is true about any point on the PPF. In Figure 1, the economy is initially at B, within the PPF. The shoe industry is productively inefficient because YZ more shoes could be produced without affecting the output, 0X, of the rest of the economy. At A, the shoe industry cannot produce any more shoes without taking away resources from other industries and causing their output to fall. Hence the shoe industry must be productively efficient at A.

All points on the PPF are productively efficient because at any point, production must be taking place using the least amount of resources. All points are also allocatively efficient. Points to the right of the PPF are not obtainable. If production takes place within the PPF, it is possible to gain both more shoes and more of all other goods which can be distributed to consumers. So consumers don't have to give up shoes in order to get more of all other goods. On the frontier, a trade-off has to be made. So at any point on the frontier, a movement to another point would involve giving up one good for another. It is not possible to say which point is the most socially desirable because we would need information about social preferences to make this judgment.

Question 2

In some areas of the country, some state schools are over-subscribed. This means that there are more children wanting to come to the school than there are places available. In such circumstances schools have to choose their children according to admission rules. Typically, these are based on catchment areas. Children who live close to the school get in. Those who live further away do not. This might not be the most efficient way of allocating places. Some economists have advocated giving each child in the country a voucher worth £x which is handed over to their school and then cashed in to pay for the expenses of running the school. Oversubscribed schools could charge fees over and above the value of the voucher. The size of the fee would be fixed to limit the number of entrants to the school to the number of places offered. Just as in, say, the market for second hand cars, if some cars are more popular than others then car sellers can charge higher prices, so would be the case in the education market. Resources will thus be efficiently allocated.

(a) Why might it be argued that there is allocative inefficiency in areas where some schools are oversubscribed?
(b) What might be the advantages and disadvantages to introducing a voucher and fee system in education?

Figure I Efficiency and the production possibility frontier
At B, the economy is productively inefficient because more shoes could be produced without affecting the amount of all other goods available. All points on the PPF are productively efficient and allocatively efficient.

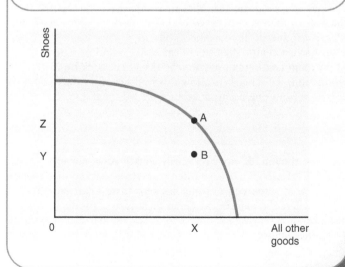

Question 3

Privatisation (the transfer of ownerships of assets from the government to the private sector) in the UK in the 1980s and 1990s led to a considerable reduction in the number of workers employed in the industries that were privatised. In electricity, gas, the railways and water, fewer workers were employed after privatisation to produce the same amount of goods and services. In the case of coal, the output of coal and the number of miners employed declined substantially after privatisation as coal mines found that demand for UK coal fell. The main customer for coal, the electricity industry, switched to gas fired power stations and also increased its imports of cheaper foreign coal.

(a) Using a production possibility diagram, explain the effect of privatisation on productive efficiency in the UK.
(b) Using a production possibility diagram and labelling the axes 'coal' and 'all other goods', explain how privatisation coincided with a change in allocative efficiency.

The market and economic efficiency

Markets often lead to an efficient allocation of resources. In a market where there are many buyers and sellers, competition forces producers to produce at lowest cost. If they fail to do so, buyers will purchase their goods from lower cost firms. So competitive markets tend to lead to productive efficiency. Markets also tend towards allocative efficiency. Customers are able to cast their spending 'votes' in the market. This determines what is produced. If consumers want to buy more shoes and fewer garden chairs, then shoe firms will expand production, whilst manufacturers of garden chairs will cut back on their production. Free markets allow this transfer of productive resources from one use to another.

Market failure

Markets, though, do not necessarily lead to economic efficiency. MARKET FAILURE occurs when markets lead to an inefficient allocation of resources. In some markets, there is **partial market failure** where the market exists but there is over production or underproduction of goods. In other cases, there is **complete market failure** where markets fail to lead to any production of good or services. A missing market is then said to exist.

Lack of competition in a market Economic efficiency is likely to be present in a market where there are many buyers and sellers. However, in many markets, there are either only a few buyers or a fewer sellers. In the rail transport industry, for instance, most travellers have no choice about which company to use on a particular journey. In the water industry, households are forced to buy their water from one company. In the UK soap powder market, two firms dominate sales. In the defence industry, the UK government is the only UK buyer of goods. Trade unions would like to be in a position where only union members work in a place of work. Where there is **imperfect competition**, there is likely to be market failure. Firms which dominate their markets, for instance, will attempt to charge high prices in order to make greater profit. However, they can only do this by restricting supply to the market, denying customers the ability to buy as much as they would have done if the market had been competitive. This leads to allocative inefficiency. Trade unions can push up costs to firms if they are successful in getting higher wages for their members than the market rate. This leads to productive inefficiency.

Externalities Prices and profits should be accurate signals, allowing markets to allocate resources efficiently. In reality, market prices and profits can be misleading because they may not reflect the true prices and profits to society of economic activities. These differences are known as the externalities of an economic activity. For instance, in Brazil it makes commercial sense to cut down the rain forest to create grazing land for cattle sold to the West as meat for hamburgers. However, this could lead to economic catastrophe in the long term because of global warming. The market is putting out the wrong signals, leading to a misallocation of resources.

Missing markets The market, for a variety of reasons, may fail to provide certain goods and services. Some goods such as defence (called **public goods**) will not be provided by the market. Other goods, called **merit goods**, will be underprovided. Health care and education are two examples of merit goods. Part of the reason for underprovision is that the market mechanism can be poor at dealing with risk and providing information to agents in the market.

Information failure In an efficient market, both buyers and sellers have good knowledge of the product. Sometimes, though, information is imperfect. For example, a consumer buying a soft drink is likely to have tried out a variety of drinks before. The drink being bought is likely to be something the consumer likes and so the consumer has good information about the product. However, what about the purchase of a washing machine which the consumer might only make every 8 years? In this case, the consumer might have imperfect information and make the wrong choice. Other examples relate to the problem of ASYMMETRIC INFORMATION. This is when either the buyer or seller has more information than the other party. One example is private dentists. If a dentist recommends a treatment when the patient is not in any pain, how does the patient know that the treatment is really in his best interest? Could it be that the dentist is recommending far more work than is necessary and is more interested in gaining a fee than treating the patient properly? Another common example given is second hand cars. Some cars are 'lemons', constantly breaking down and requiring large repair bills. Other cars of the same make and model are very reliable. The owner of the car for sale knows whether the car is a 'lemon' or not. However, the buyer does not have this information. Should the buyer offer a high price for the car on the assumption it isn't a 'lemon' or should he offer a low price assuming it will have problems?

Factor immobility Factors of production (land, labour and capital) may be immobile. This means that they are difficult to transfer from one use to another. For instance, a train once built is only useful as a train. It cannot be changed into a car or a plane. As for labour, workers can be immobile. A coal miner made redundant might have few skills to offer in other types of work. So he or she may find it difficult to get a job. An unemployed worker in a high unemployment area might be unable or not be willing to move to a job in a low unemployment area. For instance, it may be impossible to find housing at an affordable rent or price in the low unemployment area, or the worker might not want to leave family and friends in the local area. The greater the immobility of factors, the more time it will take for markets to clear when there is a shock to the economic system. Factor immobility was one of the reasons why the North of England, Wales, Scotland and Northern Ireland suffered above average unemployment rates during the 1960s, 1970s and 1980s. Traditional heavy primary and manufacturing industries were concentrated in these areas. As they declined, workers were made redundant. However, new industry with new capital was not created in sufficient volume to compensate for the decline of old industries. Unemployed workers found it hard, if not impossible, to get jobs. Neither were sufficient workers prepared to leave these regions to find employment in low unemployment areas of the UK.

Inequality Market failure is not just caused by economic inefficiency. It can also be caused by **inequality** in the economy. In a market economy, the ability of individuals to consume goods depends upon the income of the household in which they live. Household income comes from a variety of sources.

- Wages are paid to those who work outside the household. In the labour market, different wages are paid to different workers depending on factors such as education, training, skill and location.
- Interest, rent and dividends are earned from the wealth of the

household. Wealth may include money in bank and building society accounts, stocks and shares, and property.
- Private pensions are another type of unearned income. Private pensions represent income from a pension fund which can be valued and is a form of wealth.
- Other income includes state benefits such as unemployment benefit, child benefit and state pensions.

The market mechanism may lead to a distribution of income which is undesirable or unacceptable. For instance, income levels may be so low that a household is unable to afford basic **necessities** such as food, shelter or clothing. If healthcare is only provided by the private sector, a household may not be able to afford medical care. The state may then need to intervene, either to provide income in the form of benefits, or goods and services such as healthcare to increase consumption levels.

Key terms

Allocative or economic efficiency - occurs when resources are distributed in such a way that no consumers could be made better off without other consumers becoming worse off.
Dynamic efficiency - occurs when resources are allocated efficiently over time.
Market failure - where resources are inefficiently allocated due to imperfections in the working of the market mechanism.
Productive efficiency - is achieved when production is achieved at lowest cost.
Static efficiency - occurs when resources are allocated efficiently at a point in time.
Technical efficiency - is achieved when a given quantity of output is produced with the minimum number of inputs.

Applied economics

The Common Agricultural Policy (CAP)

When the European Union (EU), formerly the European Community, was first formed there was a commitment to free trade between member countries. This found its first major expression in 1962 in the Common Agricultural Policy, a Community-wide policy which aimed to harmonise the agricultural policies of the original six member countries. One of the implicit aims of the CAP was to increase efficiency in the market for agricultural products. To what extent has this been achieved?

Productive efficiency has certainly increased. Table 2

shows that the number of small, relatively inefficient, farms has declined over time whilst the number of large farms over 50 hectares with lower overall costs has increased. There has been a substantial fall in employment in the agricultural sector as Table 3 shows. At the same time, due to more intensive farming methods, more use of fertilisers and machinery and higher yielding crop and animal strains, output has risen.

However, European agriculture is not fully productively efficient. There are still far too many small farmers producing on marginal land, such as in Wales or the French Alps. In 2005, considering the 27 EU member countries that had joined by 2006, the average size of a farm ranged from 1.2 hectares in Malta, to 21.1 hectares in Bulgaria, 27.9 hectares in Belgium, 52.1 hectares in France and 81.3 hectares in the UK. Small farms are unable to exploit the economies of scale enjoyed by large farms and consequently their costs of production are much higher.

However, it could be argued that the difference in productivity between farms in Europe is not as important an issue as the difference in the cost of production between the EU and the rest of the world. World prices for many agricultural commodities, such as wheat or butter, have been considerably below those maintained by the complex system of tariffs, quotas and intervention prices in the EU.

Consumers lose out because of these high domestic prices. Their loss can be calculated by multiplying the amount they purchase by the difference between domestic and world farm gate prices.

However, farmers worldwide also tend to be supported by the taxpayer. Figure 2 shows the extent of the subsidies paid to farmers throughout the world. In the EU, for instance, farmers in 2005 received in subsidies an average 32 per cent of the market value of what they produced.

The agricultural market is not just productively inefficient. It is arguably allocatively inefficient. The fact that taxpayers throughout the developed world are having to subsidise farmers means that the marginal cost of production far exceeds the price consumers are prepared to pay. Allocative efficiency could therefore be increased by shifting resources out of agriculture into other industries.

Over the past 20 years, there has been an increasing awareness of the costs of the CAP and other agricultural support systems. In the latest Doha round of trade talks, many Third World countries along with agricultural exporting countries such as Australia and New Zealand were fighting to get trade in agricultural products liberalised. In practice, this means both the EU and the USA dismantling their support regimes for

agriculture. In the EU, there is strong resistance to a reduction in subsidies to farmers from certain countries, particularly those which benefit the most from the CAP, such as France.

The abolition of the CAP would produce losers as well as gainers. Land prices would plummet because prices for produce would fall substantially. Marginal farmers too would lose because their land would not be productive enough to support them in business. The experience of New Zealand, which almost abolished farm subsidies in the 1980s, suggests, however, that farm profits would remain roughly constant. There would be lower prices and fewer state handouts. However, equally, the costs of production, particularly rents on farms, would fall too leaving most farmers on good farming land with broadly similar incomes.

Table 3 Employment in agriculture, hunting, forestry and fishing

					Millions
	1970	1980	1990	2000	2003
Greece	1.3	1.0	0.9	0.7	0.6
Spain	3.7	2.2	1.5	1.0	0.9
France	2.8	1.8	1.4	1.0	1.0
Germany	2.3	1.4	1.1	1.0	0.9
UK	-	0.6	0.6	0.4	0.3
EU12	-	11.9	8.9	6.4	6.1
EU15	-	12.7	9.5	7.2	6.8
EU25	-	-	-	11.2	10.4

Source: European Commission, *The Agricultural Situation in the European Union 1997*; European Commission, *Agricultural Statistics Pocketbook*.

Table 2 Number of holdings by size, millions

	Total	0-5ha	5-20ha	20-50ha	50+ha
EUR-10					
1970	7.67	4.26	2.36	0.85	0.20
1987	5.00	2.32	1.53	0.78	0.37
EUR-12					
1987	6.92	3.40	2.10	0.95	0.47
1993	7.23	4.23	1.68	0.78	0.53
2000	5.18	2.65	1.33	0.64	0.56
EU-27					
2005	7.82	3.92	2.41	0.81	0.68

Note: ha is the abbreviation for hectares
Source: adapted from European Commission, *European Economy, EC Agricultural Policy for the 21st Century*, Number 4, 1994; European Commission, *The Agricultural Situation in the European Union 1997*; European Commission, *Agricultural Statistics Pocketbook*.

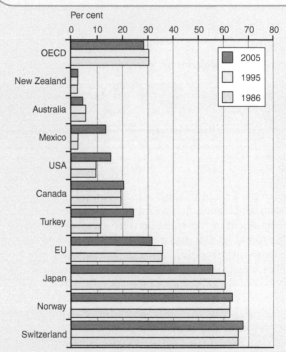

Figure 2 Farming subsidies: producer subsidies as a percentage of total farm incomes[1]

1 Farm incomes = market value of farm production + producer subsidies.
Source: adapted from www.oecd.org.

DataQuestion

Market failure

Tesco, the UKs largest supermarket chain, has been accused of trying to sabotage the opening of a new small store in the market town of Ludlow in Shropshire. Harry Tuffins is a small chain of four stores in the Welsh borders and Wales. Days before the opening of the new store, Tesco leafleted every house within a ten mile radius with two vouchers worth £10 off on £30 of shopping at the local Tesco. One voucher was valid for the the two weeks before Harry Tuffin's opening dates and the other covered the two weeks immediately after. The Association of Convenience Stores, the body representing small stores, has reported the matter to the Competition Commission, the government body which deals with unfair competition.

Source: adapted from *The Sunday Times*, 21.1.2007.

Yixing in China is a prosperous city of one million people. Incomes are high as the population works in more than 1 000 factories producing textiles and chemicals. However, there is a price to pay. Most of the factories are located on the local river where it is easy to transport raw materials but also untreated waste is dumped into the river. The river feeds Lake Tai, China's third-largest freshwater lake. On the lake is sited the industrial city of Wuxi. This summer, pollution in the lake became so bad that the water authorities in Wuxi were forced to cut off supplies to households in Wuxi. They were without tap drinking water for weeks. Local campaigners have claimed that the pollution is damaging both people's health and the environment.

Source: adapted from news.bbc.co.uk 18.9.2007.

The 5 million people who live in former coalmining communities have poorer standards of health, education and employment than the rest of the population, according to a report published yesterday. Average household incomes are £50 a week lower than regional averages and more than 250 000 people in coalfields are claiming incapacity benefit. 22 per cent of coalfield residents have some form of long-term illness. The proportion of 16 year olds getting five or more A-C grades at GCSE is 7 to 10 percentage points below the national average and more than half of adults have no or low-level qualifications. Unemployment is well above the national average. These communities were devastated by the closure of most of the UK's coal mining industry following the miners' strike in 1984-85. Around 250 000 jobs were lost directly and many more indirectly from the closures.

Source: adapted from the *Financial Times*, 23.3.2007.

More and more older people are working beyond the retirement age. Since 1992, the number of people above pensionable age in work has risen by 400 000 to 1.2 million, two thirds of them women. They are doing this because they realise they can't afford to live off their retirement income. The government has warned workers that they must save more for their old age, especially since life expectancy continues to rise. However, many are choosing to ignore the government warnings. Young workers in particular are failing to save, choosing instead to either take on large mortgages or spend their money to support their lifestyle.

Source: adapted from the *Financial Times*, 19.7.2007.

Burkina Faso is a land-locked country in Western Africa. With an income per head of just $516, it is one of world's poorer nations. Despite a decade of relatively high economic growth, malnutrition is still common in the countryside. Poverty sits alongside new Grecian-style villas in the capital, Ouagadougou. The increasingly wealthy political and trading classes are able to afford flashy cars and a Western life style.

Source: adapted from the *Financial Times*, 18.9.2007.

1. 'Efficiency is concerned with how well resources, such as time, talents or materials, are used to produce an end result. Market failure occurs where resources are inefficiently allocated due to imperfections in the working of the market mechanism.' Explain how market failure occurs in each of the examples given in the data.

15 Externalities

IB 2.4
OCR 3.1, 3.4 Tr

Summary

1. Externalities are created when social costs and benefits differ from private costs and benefits.
2. The greater the externality, the greater the likelihood of market failure.
3. Market failure occurs when marginal social cost and marginal social benefit are not equal at the actual level of output. There will be a welfare loss at this level of output shown by the 'welfare triangle' on a marginal social and private cost and benefit diagram.
4. Governments can use regulation, the extension of property rights, taxation and permits to reduce the market failure caused by externalities.

Private and social costs and benefits

A chemical plant may dump waste into a river in order to minimise its costs. Further down the river, a water company has to treat the water to remove dangerous chemicals before supplying drinking water to its customers. Its customers have to pay higher prices because of the pollution.

This is a classic example of EXTERNALITIES or SPILLOVER EFFECTS. Externalities arise when private costs and benefits are different from social costs and benefits. A PRIVATE COST is the cost of an activity to an individual economic unit, such as a consumer or a firm. For instance, a chemical company will have to pay for workers, raw materials and plant and machinery when it produces chemicals. A SOCIAL COST is the cost of an activity not just to the individual economic unit which creates the cost, but to the rest of society as well. It therefore includes all private costs, but may also include other costs. The chemical manufacturer may make little or no payment for the pollution it generates. The difference between private cost and social cost is the externality or spillover effect. If social cost is greater than private cost, then a NEGATIVE EXTERNALITY or EXTERNAL COST is said to exist.

However, not all externalities are negative. A company may put up a building which is not just functional but also beautiful.

The value of the pleasure which the building gives to society over its lifetime (the SOCIAL BENEFIT) may well far exceed the benefit of the building received by the company (the PRIVATE BENEFIT). Hence, if social benefit is greater than private benefit, a POSITIVE EXTERNALITY or EXTERNAL BENEFIT is said to exist.

This is often the case with health care provision (an example of a merit good). Although one individual will benefit from inoculation against illness, the social benefit resulting from the reduced risk of other members of society contracting the illness will be even greater. Positive externalities could also result from education and training. An individual may benefit in the form of a better job and a higher salary but society may gain even more from the benefits of a better trained workforce.

Activities where social benefit exceeds private benefit are often inadequately provided by a market system. In many cases this results in either state provision or a government subsidy to encourage private provision.

Market failure

The price mechanism allocates resources. Prices and profits are the signals which determine this allocation. However, a misallocation of resources will occur if market prices and profits

Question 1

(a) Why might each of the examples in the photographs give rise to positive and negative externalities?

do not accurately reflect the costs and benefits to society of economic activities.

For instance, in the case of the chemical plant, the price of chemicals does not accurately reflect their true cost to society. The private cost of production to the manufacturer is lower than the social cost to society as a whole. Because the price of chemicals is lower than that which reflects social cost, the quantity demanded of chemicals and therefore consumption of chemicals will be greater than if the full social cost were charged. On the other hand, if the water company is pricing water to consumers, it will have to charge higher prices to consumers than would have been the case without the chemical pollution. Demand for water and consumption of water will therefore be less than it would otherwise have been without the externality.

The greater the externality, the greater the market failure and the less market prices and profits provide accurate signals for the optimal allocation of resources.

Marginal costs and benefits

The difference between social costs and social benefits changes as the level of output changes. This can be shown using **marginal analysis**. The margin is a possible point of change. So the marginal cost of production is the extra cost of producing an extra unit of output. The marginal benefit is the benefit received from consuming an extra unit of output.

The marginal cost of production is likely to change as output increases. In Figure 1, it is shown as at first falling and then rising. Marginal costs fall at first because producing more can lead to greater efficiencies. However, then they start to rise.This could be because a firm is having to pay higher prices to obtain more factors of production: to employ more workers it might have to pay higher wages, for example. Or production might be less efficient if a firm is operating beyond its optimum capacity of production.

In contrast, the marginal benefit of consumption of a product falls as consumption increases. Each extra unit of consumption brings less benefit to the consumer. The marginal benefit curve is the same as the demand curve. This is because the demand curve too shows that the value of the benefit put on the consumption of the product by a buyer.

Assume that the marginal cost curve and marginal benefit curves in Figure 1 are the costs and benefits to society. Then welfare would be maximised at a quantity level of 0A and a price of 0B. What if production and consumption are not at 0A?

● If quantity produced and consumed were greater than 0A, the extra cost of production would be greater than the extra benefit from consumption. Welfare would be improved by reducing production and consumption. So this would lead to an inefficient allocation of resources.
● If quantity produced and consumed were less than 0A, then the marginal benefit of production would be greater than the marginal cost of production. Welfare could be increased if production and consumption were increased.

Note that when this diagram is usually drawn, only the upward sloping part of the marginal cost curve is shown as in Figure 2. This is because it is assumed that the marginal benefit curve will cut the marginal cost curve when marginal cost is increasing.

Welfare losses

In many markets, social costs and private costs differ. So too do social benefits and private benefits. Figure 2 shows a situation where there are PRODUCTION EXTERNALITIES or EXTERNALITIES IN PRODUCTION. Production externalities occur when the social cost of production is greater than the private cost of production.

Figure 2 shows that at every level of output, the MARGINAL SOCIAL COST of production is higher than the MARGINAL PRIVATE COST. So the marginal social cost curve, the MSC curve, is higher and to the left of the marginal private cost curve, the MPC curve. It is assumed here that the marginal social benefit (MSB) and marginal private benefit (MPB) are the same. So the demand curve is also the MSB and MSC curves.

The market equilibrium is where the marginal private cost equals the marginal private benefit. This is at an output level of 0B and a price of 0E. If the price were higher than 0E,

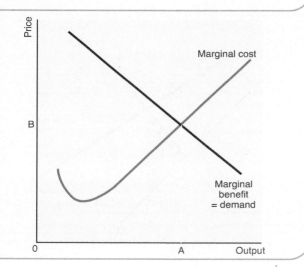

Figure 1 The optimal level of production and consumption
Welfare is maximised when the marginal cost of product equals the marginal benefit of consumption.This is at the output level 0A and a marginal price or cost of 0B.

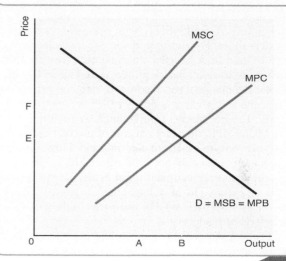

Figure 2 Free market and optimal levels of production
In a free market, production will take place at 0B where MPC = MPB. However, the socially optimal level of production is 0A where marginal social cost and marginal social benefit are the same.

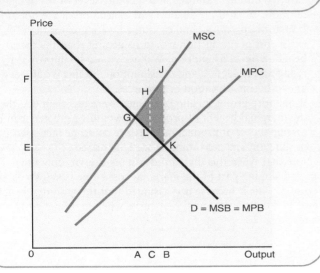

Figure 3 *Welfare loss triangle from production externalities*
If production takes place at the free market level of output of 0B, then there will be a deadweight loss of welfare to society of GJK.

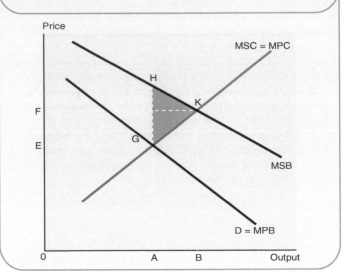

Figure 4 *Welfare loss triangle from positive consumption externalities*
If production takes place at the free market level of output of 0B, then there will be a deadweight loss of welfare to society of GHK.

consumers would buy less than 0B because the demand curve shows the value or utility placed by consumers on the product. If the price were lower than 0E, producers would not be prepared to supply 0B because they would make a loss on the last or marginal units produced.

However, the socially optimum level of production is lower than 0B. It is 0A where marginal social cost equals marginal social benefit (MSC = MSB). The price of 0F is higher than the free market price of 0E. This reflects the fact that the free market price does not include the production externality generated by the good.

If production and consumption takes place at 0B, then there is a welfare loss to society. The loss is the difference between the marginal social cost and the marginal private benefit shown in Figure 3. On the last unit produced, the 0Bth unit, this is JK. On the 0Cth unit, the welfare loss is HL. So the total welfare loss is the sum of the vertical distances between the MSC curve and MSB curve between the output levels of 0A and 0B. This is the triangle GJK, sometimes called the **welfare loss triangle** or the **deadweight loss triangle**.

The same analysis can be applied to when there are CONSUMPTION EXTERNALITIES or EXTERNALITIES IN CONSUMPTION. Figure 4 shows a situation where the MARGINAL SOCIAL BENEFIT is greater than the MARGINAL PRIVATE BENEFIT. This means that there are positive externalities. For example, if some individuals pay to go to the gym to keep fit, it benefits others because they are less likely later in life to suffer health problems. In Figure 4, it is assumed that the marginal social cost and marginal private cost is the same, and so the curve is simply called the marginal cost (MC) curve. The free market equilibrium is at an output level of 0A where MC = MPB, the marginal cost of production is equal to the marginal private benefit of consumption. However, the socially optimum level of output is 0B where MC = MSB, the marginal cost equals the marginal social benefit. If the output were at 0B, an extra GHK of welfare could be gained. There is therefore a loss of welfare of GHK compared to the socially optimal level of production.

Figure 5 shows a situation where there is a negative externality in consumption. An example would be

parents smoking at home and forcing children to smoke through passive smoking. The free market equilibrium is at 0A where MC = MPB. The socially optimal level of production and consumption is 0B. The welfare loss due to passive smoking is GHK.

Government policy

The government has a wide range of policies that it could use to bring about an efficient allocation of resources where externalities exist.

Regulation Regulation is a method which is widely used in the UK and throughout the world to control externalities. The government could lay down maximum pollution levels or might even ban pollution creating activities altogether. For instance, in the UK, the Environmental Protection Act 1989 laid down minimum environmental standards for emissions from over 3 500

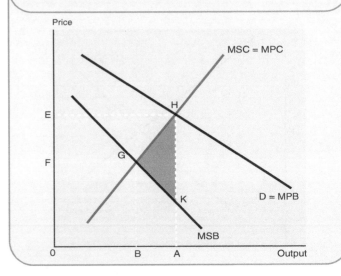

Figure 5 *Welfare loss triangle from negative consumption externalities*
If production takes place at the free market level of output of 0B, then there will be a deadweight loss of welfare to society of GHK.

Question 2

Small to medium sized businesses are responsible for 80 per cent of environmental crimes. Yet, according to a report by the House of Commons environmental audit committee, almost all offences fail to be detected or prosecuted by the relevant legal authorities. For example, since 2001 when businesses have had to pay to use waste tips, fly-tipping has increased by 40 per cent. This is the illegal dumping of waste by the roadside, or on waste land. The cost of dealing with fly-tipping is estimated at between £100 million and £150 million per year.

Fly-posting is another major problem, but local authorities will soon be able to recover the cost of removing fly-posting and graffiti from offending companies under the provisions of the Clean Neighbourhoods and Environment Bill. Fly-posting has been regularly used by clubs and concert promoters wishing to advertise particular events. The local area is deluged with posters strapped to lamp posts but not taken down afterwards. Local authorities then have to pay their workers to remove the posters.

The House of Commons Report said that 'unless there is a real threat of being detected, the offender will continue to offend'. The Department for Environment, Food and Rural Affairs believes that, even when prosecutions do reach the court, many companies receive unreasonably small fines for polluting.

Source: adapted from the *Financial Times*, 9.2.2005.

(a) Explain how fly-tipping creates an externality.
(b) From an economic viewpoint, why do lack of detection and small fines for environmental crimes limit the effectiveness of regulation as a way of dealing with environmental problems?
(c) Explain why matching fines to the environmental damage caused might be a better way of dealing with environmental crimes than simply levying fixed penalties.

factories involved in chemical processes, waste incineration and oil refining. There are limits on harmful emissions from car exhausts. Cars that do not meet these standards fail their MOT tests. Forty years before these MOT regulations came into force, the government banned the burning of ordinary coal in urban areas.

Regulation is easy to understand and relatively cheap to enforce. However, it is a rather crude policy. First, it is often difficult for government to fix the right level of regulation to ensure efficiency. Regulations might be too lax or too tight. The correct level would be where the economic benefit arising from a reduction in externality equalled the economic cost imposed by the regulation. For instance, if firms had to spend £30 million fitting anti-pollution devices to plant and machinery, but the fall in pollution was only worth £20 million, then the regulation would have been too tight. If the fall in pollution was worth £40 million, it implies that it would be worth industry spending even more on anti-pollution measures to further reduce pollution and thus further increase the £40 million worth of benefits.

Moreover, regulations tend not to discriminate between different costs of reducing externalities. For instance, two firms might have to reduce pollution emissions by the same amount. Firm A could reduce its emissions at a cost of £3 million whilst it might cost Firm B £10 million to do the same. However, Firm A could double the reduction in its pollution levels at a cost of £7 million. Regulations which set equal limits for all firms will mean that the cost to society of reducing pollution in this case is £13 million (£3 million for Firm A and £10 million for Firm B). However, it would be cheaper for society if the reduction could be achieved by Firm A alone at a cost of £7 million.

Extending property rights If a chemical company lorry destroyed your home, you would expect the chemical company to pay compensation. If the chemical company polluted the atmosphere so that the trees in your garden died, it would be unlikely that you would gain compensation, particularly if the chemical plant were in the UK and the dead trees were in Germany.

Externalities often arise because property rights are not fully allocated. Nobody owns the atmosphere or the oceans, for instance. An alternative to regulation is for government to extend property rights. It can give water companies the right to charge companies which dump waste into rivers or the sea. It can give workers the right to sue for compensation if they have suffered injury as a result of working for a company. It can give local residents the right to claim compensation if pollution levels are more than a certain amount.

Extending property rights is a way of **internalising the externality** - eliminating the externality by bringing it back into the framework of the market mechanism. Fifty years ago, asbestos was not seen as a dangerous material. Today, asbestos companies around the world are having to pay compensation to workers suffering from asbestosis. They have also had to tighten up considerably on safety in the workplace where asbestos is used. Workers have been given property rights which enable them to sue asbestos companies for compensation.

One advantage of extending property rights is that the government does not have to assess the cost of pollution. It is generally assumed that property owners will have a far better knowledge of the value of property than the government. There should also be a direct transfer of resources from those who create pollution to those who suffer. With regulation, in contrast, the losers are not compensated whilst polluters are free to pollute up to the limit despite the fact that the pollution is imposing costs on society.

Question 3

The death of the drinks can is now a distinct possibility in environmentally conscious Germany. Since January, a new refundable deposit of between 25 and 50 cents has been levied on most recyclable cans and bottles. The deposit in effect doubles the retail price of the drinks. Consumers can get their deposit back by returning the empty can to the retailer who sold them the can. However, this is so much trouble for most consumers (and impossible if bought from most vending machines) that sales of drinks in cans have slumped. Can manufacturers estimate that sales of cans in Germany fell by about 50 per cent in the first half of this year.

The new measures have been introduced not just to encourage recycling of cans but also to encourage consumers to move more towards using refillable bottles. Refillable bottles are used in the UK by door step milk delivery companies where empty milk bottles are returned to the dairy to be reused. The deposit, though, was too successful this year. In June, both Coca-Cola and the German Brewers' League ran out of refillable bottles and launched advertising campaigns to stop buyers hoarding them or throwing them away.

Source: adapted from the *Financial Times*, 9.7.2003.

(a) Why might cans and bottles create an externality?
(b) The German scheme is an example of extending property rights. Explain why.
(c) How will the scheme reduce externalities?

There are problems though. One is that a government may not have the ability to extend property rights. This occurs, for instance, when the cause of the externality arises in another country. How do Western governments prevent countries like Brazil from logging huge areas of forest, leading to global warming, which imposes costs on them? One way around this is to pay the agents causing the externality to stop their economic activity. So Western countries could pay countries like Brazil not to log their forests.

Another problem is that extending property rights can be very difficult in many cases. Asbestos companies, for instance, will not pay claims to asbestos workers unless it can definitely be proved that their medical condition was caused by working with asbestos. The compensation process can take years, and many ex-workers die before their cases are settled. They receive no compensation and the asbestos company has not had to include payment in its costs. This would tend to lead to a continuing overproduction of asbestos.

A final problem is that it is often very difficult even for the owners of property rights to assess the value of those rights. For instance, one homeowner might put a far higher value on trees in his or her garden than another homeowner. If a cable company lays cable in the road, cutting the roots of trees in front gardens, should the homeowner who places a high value on trees be compensated more than the homeowner who is fairly indifferent when trees die? What happens if the homeowner wanted to get rid of the trees anyway?

Taxes Another solution, much favoured by economists, is the use of taxes. The government needs to assess the cost to society of a particular negative externality. It then sets tax rates on those externalities equal to the value of the externality. This increases costs to customers by shifting the supply curve to the left. The result is a fall in demand and output and thus fewer externalities are created.

For example, the government might put a tax on petrol for cars because emissions from cars contribute to global warming. The tax should be set at the level where the tax revenues equal the cost to society of the emissions. This **internalises** the externality, as explained above, making the polluter pay the cost of pollution.

Taxes, like extending property rights, have the advantage that they allow the market mechanism to decide how resources should best be allocated. Those creating the highest levels of negative externalities have a greater incentive to reduce those externalities than those creating fewer externalities.

However, it is often very difficult for government to place a monetary value on negative externalities and therefore decide what should be the optimal tax rate. With global warming, for instance, there is considerable disagreement about its likely economic impact. Some environmentalists would argue that the potential economic costs are so large that cars should be virtually priced off the roads. At the opposite extreme, some argue that global warming, if it occurs at all, will bring net economic benefits. For instance, slightly higher temperatures will increase the amount of food that can be produced and make it easier to feed the world's growing population. There is therefore no need for taxes on petrol designed to reduce emissions.

Where positive externalities occur, governments should offer subsidies. It can be argued, for instance, that parks, libraries, art galleries, concert halls and opera houses create positive externalities. Therefore they should be subsidised. As with taxes and negative externalities, the level of subsidy should equal the positive externality created.

Permits A variation on regulating negative externalities through direct controls is the idea of issuing permits. Assume that the government wishes to control emissions of sulphur into the atmosphere. It issues permits to pollute, the total of which equals the maximum amount of sulphur it wishes to see emitted over a period of time like a year. The government then allocates permits to individual firms or other polluters. This could be done, for instance, on the basis of current levels of emissions by firms or on output of goods giving rise to sulphur emissions in production. The permits are then tradable for money between polluters. Firms which succeed in reducing their sulphur levels below their permit levels can sell their permits to other producers who are exceeding their limits.

The main advantage of permits over simple regulation is that costs in the industry and therefore to society should be lower than with regulation. Each firm in the industry will consider whether it is possible to reduce emissions and at what cost. Assume that Firm A, with just enough permits to meet its emissions, can reduce emissions by 500 tonnes at a cost of £10 million. Firm B is a high polluter and needs 500 tonnes worth of permits to meet regulations. It calculates that it would need to spend £25 million to cut emissions by this amount.

If there was simple regulation, the anti-pollution costs to the industry, and therefore to society, would be £25 million. Firm B would have to conform to its pollution limit whilst there would be no incentive for Firm A to cut pollution.

With permits, Firm A could sell 500 tonnes of permits to Firm B. The cost to society of then reducing pollution would only be £10 million, the cost that Firm A would incur, and not

Question 4

Smoking is widely accepted to be a killer. But so too is passive smoking, the taking in of smoke fumes in a room when another person is smoking. A leaked Report from the Scientific Committee on Tobacco and Health indicated that second-hand smoke increased the risk of heart disease by an estimated 25 per cent.

The UK is about to implement the 2003 European Union Tobacco Advertising and Sponsorship Directive which orders member states to outlaw advertising in the press and other forms of media by 2005. The UK has chosen to allow tobacco companies to advertise at the point of sale so long as posters are no larger than a single A5 sheet.

The tobacco industry has long argued that advertising doesn't attract new users or increase the quantity of cigarette smoking. Instead, it shifts customer preferences between brands. It is arguing the implementation of the new ban on advertising will not hurt them. However, there is evidence that overall sales do decline with increases in taxes on tobacco. In Germany, the government over the past 18 months has increased taxes on tobacco, raising the price of a packet of cigarettes from €3.00 to €3.80 (£2.00 to £2.63). Volumes of cigarettes sold have decreased 13 per cent over the period, and are expected to fall further.

Source: adapted from the *Financial Times*, 19.10.2004.

(a) Explain why cigarette smoking causes externalities.
(b) Discuss whether the market failure caused by the sale of cigarettes is best tackled by bans on advertising **or** rising taxes. Use demand and supply diagrams and the concept of price elasticity of demand in the analysis to your answer.

Question 5

Industry reacted with fury yesterday when the government announced plans to further reduce emissions of greenhouse gases. Under the Kyoto Protocol, signed in 1997, the UK agreed to reduce emissions by 12.5 per cent from their 1990 levels. But government ministers yesterday announced a two-stage plan to cut emissions by 20 per cent from 1990 levels by 2010.

The burden will fall disproportionately on a few heavy industries, such as electricity generation, oil refining, and steel, cement, glass and paper production, which currently account for half of the UK's CO_2 emissions. These industries will have to cut their emissions quite dramatically under a new EU-wide emissions trading scheme starting in 2005. Transport and domestic emissions will not be covered. Individual industrial sites will be allocated a set number of 'emission permits'. For each tonne of CO_2 they produce over their allocation, they will have to buy extra permits from those sites which have produced less CO_2 than they are allowed to.

Business organisations warned that the effect of the scheme would be to increase electricity prices and force production offshore to countries that did not recognise the Kyoto Protocol.

Source: adapted from *The Independent*, 20.1.2004.

(a) Explain what is meant by an 'emission permit'.
(b) How can a system of tradable permits lead to a more efficient way of reducing pollution than simple regulation?
(c) Discuss whether UK producers are being put under an unfair competitive disadvantage because of the Kyoto Protocol.

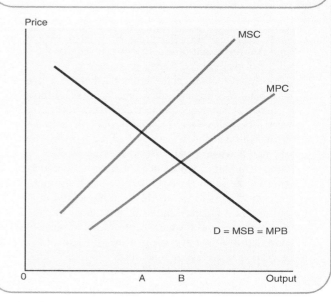

Figure 6 *Effects of different policies*
Regulation and pollution permits attempt to fix output levels at 0A, the socially optimal point of production and consumption. Extending property rights and taxes attempt to do the same thing by shifting the MPC curve upwards so that it becomes equal to to the MSC curve.

£25 million as with regulation. It might cost Firm B more than £10 million to buy the permits. It would be prepared to spend anything up to £25 million to acquire them. Say Firm A drove a hard bargain and sold the permits to Firm B for £22 million. Society would save £15 million (£25 million - £10 million), distributed between a paper profit of £12 million for Firm A and a fall in costs from what otherwise would have been the case for Firm B of £3 million.

Using diagrams to illustrate government policy

These different policies can be illustrated on a marginal social cost and benefit diagram. In Figure 6, it is assumed that externalities arise in production and so the marginal social cost is higher than the marginal private cost. The socially optimal level of production is 0A but the free market level of production is 0B.

- **Regulation** attempts to fix output at 0A. In the case of emissions, this is typically done by controlling the level of emissions. With a given state of technology, this then determines the socially optimal output level.
- **Extending property rights** attempts to make the marginal social cost curve and marginal private cost identical by shifting the MPC curve upwards. This is done by changing the externality into a private cost of production.
- **Taxation** again attempts to make the marginal social cost curve and marginal private cost the same. The tax should be levied in such a way that the marginal tax plus the MPC equals the MSC at output 0A.
- **Pollution permits** act like regulations. In theory, permits to pollute should be given so that production is limited to 0A.

Key terms

Consumption externalities or external benefits in consumption - when the social costs of consumption are different from the private costs of consumption.
Externality or spillover effect - the difference between social costs and benefits and private costs and benefits. If net social cost (social cost minus social benefit) is greater than net private cost (private cost minus private benefit), then a negative externality or external cost exists. If net social benefit is greater than net private benefit, a positive externality or external benefit exists.

Marginal social and private costs and benefits - the social and private costs and benefits of the last unit either produced or consumed.
Private cost and benefit - the cost or benefit of an activity to an individual economic unit such as a consumer or a firm.
Production externalities or externalities in production - when the social costs of production differ from the private costs of production.
Social cost and benefit - the cost or benefit of an activity to society as a whole.

Applied economics

Global warming

The environmental problem

During the 1980s, there was a growing awareness that levels of greenhouse gases in the atmosphere were rising and that this might pose a serious problem for the future of the planet. Global warming, a rise in world temperatures, comes about because greenhouse gases act as a blanket, trapping heat within the earth's atmosphere.

A rise of a few degrees in world temperatures sounds very little. However, it would be enough to cause major shifts in the desert zones of the world. Many of the major wheat producing areas, such as the American plains, would become deserts. Old deserts, such as the Sahara, would become fertile in time. The transition costs to the world economy would be substantial. Figure 7 shows by how much world temperatures and those in Central England have deviated from the average of 1961-1990 since 1772. It is clear that average temperatures rose during the twentieth century compared to the nineteenth century. It is also clear that average temperatures since 1990 have been rising compared to the historical average. Four of the five warmest years since 1772 in Central England have been since 1990.

A second problem associated with global warming is rising sea levels. Higher world temperatures would lead to some melting of the polar icecaps, releasing large volumes of water in the oceans. With a 3 degree centigrade rise in world temperatures, there could be an increase in sea levels of 30cm. This would be enough to flood areas such as the east coast of England, the Bangladesh delta and the Maldive Islands. Sea defences and dykes could and probably would be built, but the cost to the world economy would be considerable. Figure 8 shows sea level rises that have already taken place at selected sites around the UK between 1850 and 2006.

Sources of greenhouse gas emissions

Figure 9 shows that around 80 per cent of greenhouse gas emissions come from carbon dioxide. Almost all the rest is split roughly equally between methane and nitrous oxide.

In terms of who creates these emissions, roughly 90 per cent of carbon dioxide emissions are split equally between the transport, industry and domestic sectors. Petrol and diesel fuels account for almost all transport CO_2 emissions. Industry uses power generated by burning gas, coal and oil, as well as a variety of industrial processes which in themselves release CO_2 into the atmosphere. Equally, homes use gas, electricity and oil for heating and other uses. Agriculture creates roughly half the methane and nitrous oxide emissions. Nitrous oxide comes from fertilisers that farmers put onto the

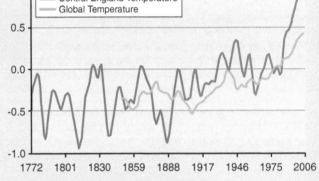

Figure 7 *Average surface temperature, world and Central England, 1772-2006*

Difference between actual temperature and 1961 -1990 average, degrees Centigrade

Source: adapted from Defra, *Environment in your pocket.*

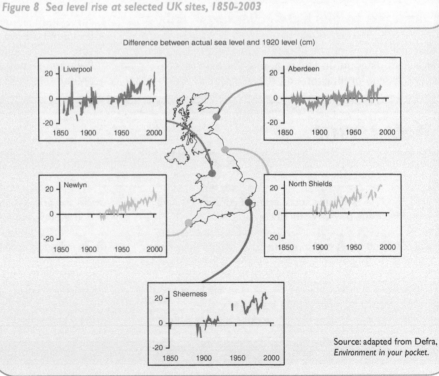

Figure 8 *Sea level rise at selected UK sites, 1850-2003*

Difference between actual sea level and 1920 level (cm)

Source: adapted from Defra, *Environment in your pocket.*

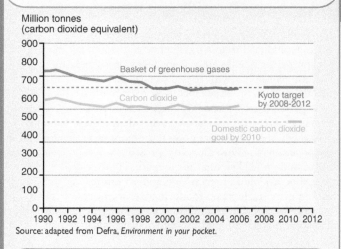

Figure 9 *UK emissions of greenhouse gases, 1990-2006*

Million tonnes
(carbon dioxide equivalent)

Basket of greenhouse gases

Carbon dioxide

Kyoto target by 2008-2012

Domestic carbon dioxide goal by 2010

Source: adapted from Defra, *Environment in your pocket*.

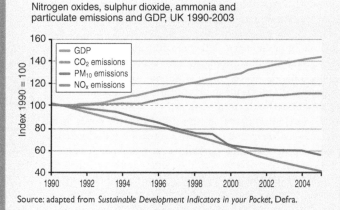

Figure 10 *Road transport emissions and Gross Domestic Product, 1990-2005*

Nitrogen oxides, sulphur dioxide, ammonia and particulate emissions and GDP, UK 1990-2003

Index 1990 = 100

GDP
CO_2 emissions
PM_{10} emissions
NO_x emissions

Source: adapted from *Sustainable Development Indicators in your Pocket*, Defra.

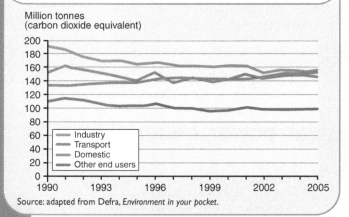

Figure 11 *Carbon dioxide emissions, by end users: 1970-2005*

Million tonnes
(carbon dioxide equivalent)

Industry
Transport
Domestic
Other end users

Source: adapted from Defra, *Environment in your pocket*.

land, whilst methane comes from sheep and cattle.

Reducing greenhouse gas emissions

It is easy to assume that there is a direct link between growth in the economy and pollution: the higher the income of a country, for example, the higher its pollution levels. However, the evidence does not bear this out. Figure 10 shows how road transport CO_2 emissions have risen far less than the increase in real income (GDP) over the period. Whilst the number of miles travelled by passenger cars increased 18 per cent, CO_2 emissions only went up 6 per cent and nitrous oxides and particulate emissions fell. There are two main reasons why higher growth may lead to less rather than more pollutions. First, as in the case of road vehicles, the technology becomes less polluting. Advances in technology mean that emissions per mile travelled has fallen. Also, most of the growth in spending has been on low pollution services anyway. Manufacturing and primary sector industries, which are big polluters, have shrunk in size.

Second, government has been implementing policies to reduce the amount of pollution. Some of these policies have come about because of agreed action on an international scale. For example, the Montreal Protocol signed in 1987 committed 93 countries, including the major industrialised nations of the world, to phasing out the use of CFCs which were destroying the earth's ozone layer. The Rio Summit of 1992, which was followed by the Kyoto Protocol of 1997, led to industrialised nations, excluding the USA, agreeing to reducing greenhouse gas emissions to 12.5 per cent less than their 1990 levels.

Figure 11 shows how greenhouse gas emissions by end user have changed since 1970. Carbon emissions of the electricity generation industry have been divided up according to who consumes the electricity. Figure 11 shows that industry has been the most successful end user in reducing carbon emissions. Reduction in domestic emissions have come almost entirely from less carbon polluting forms of electricity generation. Transport in the 1990s and early 2000s saw a small increase in carbon emissions. 'Other users' is mainly agriculture, which has made a small but not particularly significant contribution to reductions in carbon emissions.

UK policies

In signing the 1997 Kyoto Protocol, the UK government agreed to reduce its greenhouse gas emissions to 12.5 per cent less than their 1990 levels by 2010. In 2004, it went further, announcing that it would reduce emissions to 20 per cent less than their 1990 levels by 2010. The government has adopted a piecemeal approach to ensuring that it meets its greenhouse gas emission targets.

One major source of greenhouse gas emissions is industry, including the power generation industry. In 2005 the government, in conjunction with other EU countries, introduced an emissions trading scheme. Existing industrial users were given carbon permits for each site they operated. If the company created more carbon than its total permits allowed, it would have to buy permits on the open market from other companies which created less carbon than their total permits allowed. Over time, companies will be given fewer permits, giving them an incentive to reduce their carbon emissions.

Industrial users include electricity generation companies. In the 1980s and 1990s, major reductions in carbon emissions were achieved by the shrinkage of the coal industry and a shift towards more carbon efficient electricity power stations powered by gas. However, the government now faces a dilemma because of nuclear power. In 2005, around 20 per cent of UK electricity was generated by nuclear power stations. These, however, are nearing the end of their operational life. They could be replaced by building new nuclear power stations, but this would be vigorously opposed by the environmental lobby on safety grounds. Equally, they could be replaced by 'renewable' energy sources such as wind power. However, renewable energy sources are still relatively expensive. There are environmental concerns about building large numbers of 'wind farms' which 'spoil' the landscape where they are situated. Finally, there are doubts about whether renewables can provide energy security at all times of the year given that there are times when the wind doesn't blow or the sun doesn't shine and so no electricity is generated. The third alternative is to build more gas or coal fired stations, but this would lead to a significant increase in greenhouse gas emissions which would make achieving the Kyoto targets impossible.

Transport, too, poses problems for government policy. Increasing numbers of road journeys have led carbon emissions from transport to increase over time. In 1993, the Chancellor announced that the duty on fuel would be increased by 3 per cent per year above the rate of inflation to curb growth in journeys. In 1998, this was increased to 6 per cent. However, this policy was effectively abandoned in 2000 when a blockade of oil refineries by a mix of farmers and road hauliers angry at high fuel prices brought the country almost to a

standstill. It is also doubtful whether higher petrol prices would lead to much reduction in the number of car journeys made because fuel is highly price inelastic. Government policy with regard to road transport is now mainly targeted at reducing congestion rather than fuel emissions. Road transport is likely to add to carbon emissions over the next decade rather than reduce them.

Growth in air transport poses even more problems for the government. With air traffic growing at 3-5 per cent per annum, it is likely that the aviation industry will contribute to higher carbon emissions in future. As with road transport, the main focus of government policy is concentrated on how to accommodate the growth of air transport rather than curbing it to achieve lower carbon emissions over time.

The government has a large number of small scale initiatives to curb carbon emissions by households. These range from encouraging householders to lag their lofts, to getting householders to turn down their central heating and getting builders to build new houses which are more energy efficient. Agriculture is also a major contributor to greenhouse gas emissions. Through encouraging 'greener', less intensive, farming methods, the government is hoping to have some impact on emissions. However, the government does not expect significant reductions in greenhouse gas emissions from either households or agriculture.

Most environmental groups argue that the government is unlikely to achieve its Kyoto Protocol targets by 2010. With households and agriculture only making at best very small contributions to the target, and with emissions from transport likely to grow, it is industry including power generation that will have to make the reduction needed. This would be very challenging at the best of times. However, if nuclear power is replaced, mainly by gas or coal fired power stations, it will be impossible. The choice about how to generate electricity over the next 20 years will probably be key to whether greenhouse gas emissions rise or fall in the UK.

DataQuestion   Nuclear power generation

In recent decades, around one fifth of electricity in the UK has been generated from nuclear power stations. However, the last nuclear power station to be built was completed in 1995. Over the next 30 years, all the UK's existing nuclear power stations will close because of age. In its 2007 Energy White Paper, the government stated that it was in favour of building new nuclear power stations for two reasons.
- Nuclear power was a relatively cheap form of generating electricity given that it produced very little greenhouse gases. Using other forms of energy generation would lead to higher

prices being paid by UK electricity consumers.
- The UK needed to have a range of energy resources to ensure security of supplies. For example, the amount of electricity generated from many renewables like wind power depended on the weather. Gas supplies might be imported from abroad and those supplies could be cut off if there were an international dispute.

However, many, including environmental groups, oppose any resumption of building of nuclear stations.

Source: adapted from dti, 'The role of nuclear power in a low carbon UK economy', May 2007.

In the 2007 Energy White Paper the government published estimates of how much carbon in grams different forms of electricity generation emitted per kilowatt of energy produced. The range of estimate is shown by the horizontal distance on each block in Figure 12. The estimate is over the lifecyle of the plant. Coal and natural gas produce most of their carbon emissions when burning fuel. Wind and nuclear energy create carbon emissions when windmills and nuclear plants are manufactured, built and then taken down or decommissioned.

Figure 12 *Relative carbon emissions of generating technologies*

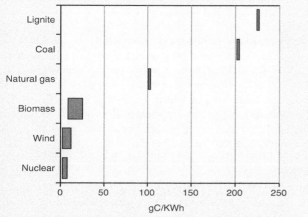

Source: adapted from dti, 'The role of nuclear power in a low carbon UK economy', May 2007.

In its 2007 Energy White Paper, the government estimated the relative cost of generating 1 megawatt of electricity at the prices of energy in November 2006. For coal and gas, it added a carbon tax of €25 per tonne of CO_2 emitted. The bars in Figure 13 show the range of prices from different plants, with a central estimate given in red for nuclear and renewable energy. For coal and gas, the red bar shows the cost of generation and the green bar the cost of the carbon tax.

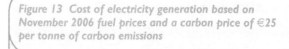

Figure 13 *Cost of electricity generation based on November 2006 fuel prices and a carbon price of €25 per tonne of carbon emissions*

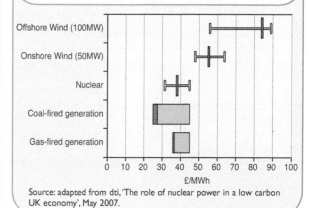

Source: adapted from dti, 'The role of nuclear power in a low carbon UK economy', May 2007.

Environmental pressure groups attacked the 2007 Energy White Paper as misguided. They were particularly critical of the government's proposals to build new nuclear power stations.

- They pointed out that whilst nuclear power provided 20 per cent of the UK's electricity, it only provided around 4 per cent of the nation's total energy.
- Nuclear power stations have a history of being more costly to build than predicted.
- The technology is inherently unsafe. If a nuclear power plant went into meltdown, as in Chernobyl in Russia in 1986, it would have devastating consequences for the local and international environment.
- The full cost of decommissioning nuclear plants is unclear but it is large. At the moment, there is no strategy for what to do with the UK's most radioactive waste which will still be dangerous in 1000 years time.

The government has totally underestimated the cost of clean up.
- There is a danger that radioactive material from nuclear power plants will fall into the hands of terrorists.
- The proposed sites for new nuclear power stations in the UK are all on the coast and could be flooded if sea levels rise significantly due to global warming.
- Although the cost of renewable energies is higher now than for gas and coal, further development will bring the cost down substantially. The true cost of gas, coal and nuclear energies are considerably underestimated. The real cost of CO_2 emissions from coal and gas plants, for example, is much higher than the current carbon levy or tax.

Source: with information from Greenpeace, the 2007 Energy White Paper - Media briefing; Friends of the Earth, Press release: Energy White Paper reaction.

1. Using examples from the data, what might be included in (a) the private cost and (b) the social cost of generating electricity from nuclear power stations?
2. Using a diagram, explain why environmental groups like Greenpeace might suggest that the current taxes on carbon emissions from coal and gas fired electricity power stations are too low.
3. An environmental pressure group suggests that motorists should be forced to cut the number of miles they travel by 20 per cent. This would be achieved by considerably increasing the tax on petrol, trebling its price. At the same time, the number of air flights into and out of the UK should be frozen. Discuss whether these measures would be a better solution to solve the UK's energy problems than building nuclear power stations. In your answer, compare the social and private costs and benefits of the proposals.

Summary

1. There will inevitably be market failure in a pure free market economy because it will fail to provide public goods.
2. Public goods must be provided by the state because of the free rider problem.
3. Merit goods are goods which are underprovided by the market mechanism, for instance because there are significant positive externalities in consumption.
4. Governments can intervene to ensure provision of public and merit goods through direct provision, subsidies or regulation.

Markets and market failure

Markets may lead to an efficient allocation of resources. However, there are some goods and services which economists recognise are unlikely to be best produced in free markets. These may include defence, the judiciary and the criminal justice system, the police service, roads, the fire service and education. More controversially, some believe that the free market is poor at producing health care and housing for the less well off. There are different reasons why there might be market failure in the production of these goods.

Public goods

Nearly all goods are PRIVATE GOODS (not to be confused with goods produced in the private sector of the economy). A private good is one where consumption by one person results in the good not being available for consumption by another. For instance, if you eat a bowl of muesli, then your friend can't eat it; if a firm builds a plant on a piece of land, that land is not available for use by local farmers.

A few goods, however, are PUBLIC GOODS or PURE PUBLIC GOODS. These are goods which possess two characteristics:

- **non-rivalry** - consumption of the good by one person does not reduce the amount available for consumption by another person; sometimes this is also known as **non-diminishability** or **non-exhaustibility**;
- **non-excludability** - once provided, no person can be excluded from benefiting (or indeed suffering in the case of a public good like pollution).

There are relatively few examples of pure public goods, although many goods contain a public good element. Clean air is a public good. If you breathe clean air, it does not diminish the ability of others to breathe clean air. Moreover, others cannot prevent you from breathing clean air. Defence is another example. An increase in the population of the UK does not lead to a reduction in the defence protection accorded to the existing population. A person in Manchester cannot be excluded from benefiting even if she were to object to current defence policy, prefer to see all defence abolished, and refuse to pay to finance defence.

Goods which can be argued to be public goods are:

- defence;
- the judiciary and prison service;
- the police service;
- street lighting.

Many other goods, such as education and health, contain a small public good element.

The free rider problem

If the provision of public goods were left to the market mechanism, there would be market failure. This is because of the FREE RIDER problem. A public good is one where it is impossible to prevent people from receiving the benefits of the good once it has been provided. So there is very little incentive for people to pay for consumption of the good. A free rider is someone who receives the benefit but allows others to pay for it. For instance, citizens receive benefits from defence expenditure. But individual citizens could increase their economic welfare by not paying for it.

In a free market, national defence is unlikely to be provided. A firm attempting to provide defence services would have difficulty charging for the product since it could not be sold to benefit individual citizens. The result would be that no one would pay for defence and therefore the market would not provide it. The only way around this problem is for the state to provide defence and force everyone to contribute to its cost through taxation.

In practice, there are often ways in which providers of public

Question 1

Explain why lamp posts might be classed as a public good.

goods can exclude consumers from benefiting from the public good. The problem of free riding can to some extent be solved for these NON-PURE or QUASI-PUBLIC GOODS. For example, motorists can be made to pay a toll for using a road. Television viewers can be forced to buy subscriptions because reception is encoded. Ships entering a port can be forced to pay taxes for the upkeep of local lighthouses. However, quasi-public goods possess the second characteristic of pure public goods. They are non-rival. So for most roads, for example, one motorist travelling along the road does not exclude another motorist from travelling along the same road. When goods are non-rival, it is unlikely that the free market mechanism will provide enough of the good. How many country roads would private firms provide if they were tolled? The answer is very few because the tolls collected would not cover the building and maintenance of the road. Hence, there is a very strong case for government providing this quasi-public good.

Merit and demerit goods

Even the most fervent advocates of free market economics agree that public goods are an example of market failure and that the government should provide these public goods. However, more controversial are merit and demerit goods.

A MERIT GOOD is one which is underprovided by the market mechanism (i.e. one which some people think should be provided in greater quantities). One reason for underprovision is that individuals lack perfect **information** and find it difficult to make rational decisions when costs occur today but the benefits received only come in, say, thirty years time. Another reason is because there are significant **positive externalities** present.

Health, education and insurance are the main merit goods provided today by government in the UK. Health and insurance are two examples where consumers find it difficult to make rational choices because of time. If left totally to market forces, the evidence suggests that individuals would not give themselves sufficient health cover or cover against sickness, unemployment and old age. Young people tend to be healthy and in work. Many find it difficult to appreciate that one day they will be ill and out of work. However, the cost of health care and pensions is so great that young people can only afford them if they save for the future. If they don't, they find when they are older that they do not have sufficient resources to pay for medical services, or the insurance needed to cover them against loss of earnings due to illness or retirement. Therefore it makes sense for the state to intervene and to force young people in particular to make provision against sickness, unemployment and old age.

In the case of education, the main beneficiary (the child or student) is unlikely to be the person paying for the education. Therefore there could be a conflict of interest. It could be in the interest of the parents to pay as little as possible for the child's education but in the interest of the child to receive as high quality an education as possible. Others in society also have an interest. Children who, for instance, cannot read or write are an economic liability in the UK today. They are more likely than not to have to receive support from others rather than contribute to the nation's welfare. This is an example of a **principal agent problem** where those benefiting or losing from a decision are not the same as those making the decision and where the objectives of, and outcomes for, the two groups are different. There are many other examples of goods with a merit good element. Lack of industrial training, for instance, is seen as a major problem in the UK. Individual firms have an incentive not to train workers,

not only because it is so costly but also because their trained workers can then be poached by competitors. Rather, they go into the market place and recruit workers who have been trained at other firms' expense. This is an example again of the free rider problem. It is partly countered by the government providing funding for organisations which provide training in local areas.

A DEMERIT GOOD is one which is overprovided by the market mechanism. The clearest examples of demerit goods are drugs - everything from hard drugs such as heroin to alcohol and tobacco. Consumption of these goods produces large negative **externalities**. Crime increases, health costs rise, valuable human economic resources are destroyed, and friends and relatives suffer distress. Moreover, individuals themselves suffer and are unable to stop consuming because drugs are addictive. Therefore it can be argued that consumers of drugs are not the best judges of their own interests.

Governments intervene to correct this market failure. They have three main weapons at their disposal: they can ban consumption as with hard drugs; they can use the price system to reduce demand by placing taxes on drugs; or they can try to persuade consumers to stop using drugs, for instance through advertising campaigns.

Equity

It would be extremely improbable that a free market system would lead to a distribution of resources which every individual would see as equitable. It is therefore argued by some economists that the state has a duty to reallocate resources.

Question 2

Suggest reasons why education might be considered a merit good.

Cost of school places to rise

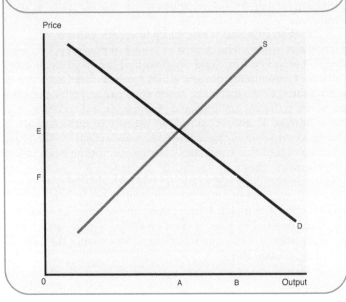

Figure 1 Market failure.
Assume the good is a public or merit good. In a free market, OA would be produced and consumed. However, to prevent market failure, assume that this should be OB. The free market therefore produces and consumes AB too little.

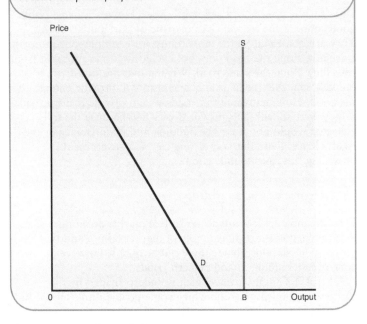

Figure 2 Direct provision.
Assume this is the market for defence. To prevent market failure, OB should be produced. However, there is no price on the demand curve at which OB would be demanded. The government must therefore step in and provide OB, whatever the price of defence.

In the UK today, for instance, there is some consensus that British citizens should not die for lack of food, or be refused urgent medical treatment for lack of money.

In the UK, over 30 per cent of all public spending is devoted to social security payments. Some of these payments come from the National Insurance fund and therefore could be seen as merit goods. However, benefits such as family credit are an explicit attempt to redistribute income to those in need. It could also be argued that the free provision of services such as health and education leads to a more equitable distribution of resources.

Government intervention

Markets are likely to underprovide public and merit goods. This leads to **inefficiency** because consumers are not able to spend their money in a way which will maximise their utility (their welfare or satisfaction). For instance, households in a city would be prepared to pay a few pounds a year to have street lighting throughout the city. However, because of the free rider problem, they are reluctant to make any contribution either because they hope everyone else will pay or because they don't want to make large payments because few others are paying. It then makes sense for government to force everyone to pay through a system of taxes.

Merit goods are more controversial, partly because they contain a private good element. The main beneficiaries of health care and education, for instance, are patients and students. Governments can attempt to increase the provision of merit goods in a variety of ways.

Direct provision Governments can supply public and merit goods directly to consumers free of charge. In the UK, primary school education, visits to the doctor and roads are provided in this way. The government may choose to produce the good or service itself, as with primary school education, or it may buy in the services of firms in the private sector. General practitioners, for instance, work for themselves and

the government buys their services.

Subsidised provision The government may pay for part of the good or service (a **subsidy**) but expect consumers to pay the rest. Prescriptions or dental care are subsidised in this way in the UK.

Regulation The government may leave provision to the private sector but force consumers to purchase a merit good or producers to provide a merit good. For instance, motorists are forced to buy car insurance by law. There is an ongoing debate in industrialised countries about whether workers should be forced to pay into private pensions. Motorway service stations are forced to provide toilet facilities free of charge to motorists whether or not they purchase anything.

These different types of intervention can be seen using demand and supply curves. In Figure 1, the demand and supply curve for a public or merit good is shown. The market equilibrium output is 0A. However, assume that this level of output is too low to

Question 3

There is a variety of ways in which the government could ensure that all households have access to dental services.
(a) It could provide the service directly, making it free to all users, and raise the required finance through taxes.
(b) It could subsidise some dental treatment considered to be essential, but not subsidise other treatment. This is the present system in the UK.
(c) It could make it a legal obligation that all households take out dental insurance to cover the cost of essential dental treatment.

Discuss the relative merits of each of these options.

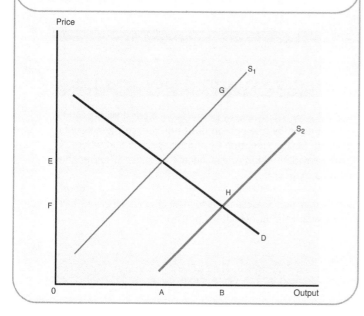

Figure 3 *Subsidies*
Assume this shows the market for a merit good. A subsidy which shifts the free market supply curve from S_1 to S_2 can lead to market failure being eliminated with output rising to 0B.

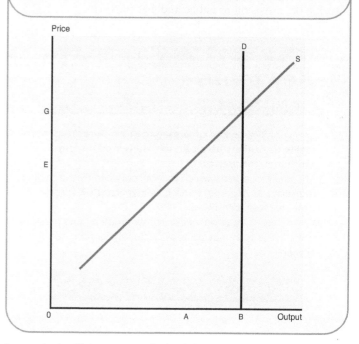

Figure 4 *Regulation*
Forcing motorists to buy car insurance means that the demand curve for motor insurance becomes vertical at the socially optimal output level of 0B.

ensure that welfare is maximised. Market failure would only be eliminated if output were higher at 0B.

- Direct provision of the good by government simply sees the government supplying 0B. This could be illustrated by drawing a vertical supply curve at 0B. Whatever the price of the good, the government will supply 0B. In Figure 2, a good like defence is shown. The government supplied 0B free of charge. The position of the demand curve shows that there is no price at which citizens would buy 0B of defence in a free market.
- Subsidising provision shifts the supply curve downwards so that it cuts the demand curve at output 0B. This is shown in Figure 3. The subsidy shifts the supply curve downwards from S_1 to S_2. The fall in price from 0E to 0F increases quantity demanded from 0A, where there was market failure, to the socially optimal level 0B. The level of subsidy per unit is GH.
- Regulation can work in a number of different ways but regulations serve to increase output from 0A to 0B in Figure 1. Take the example of car insurance. Whatever the price of car insurance, motorists have to buy it to drive their cars legally. So the demand curve for car insurance is perfectly inelastic, shown by the vertical demand curve in Figure 4. Equilibrium output is therefore at 0B where there is market failure. The price of motor insurance is, however, higher than it would have been if there had been no regulation at output 0A.

Advantages and disadvantages of different methods

There is a number of advantages and disadvantages to each of these solutions. The advantage of direct provision is that the government directly controls the supply of goods and services. It determines the number of hospital beds in the system because it provides them. It decides how many soldiers there are because it pays them directly. However, direct provision has disadvantages.

It may be inefficient, particularly if the government produces the good itself. Employees of the state, whether providing the good or buying it in, may have no incentive to cut costs to a minimum. It may also be inefficient because the wrong mix of goods is produced, especially if the goods are provided free of charge to taxpayers. The government may provide too many soldiers and too few hospital beds, for instance. Markets, in contrast, give consumers the opportunity to buy those goods which give the greatest satisfaction. In a market, if producers supplied too many soldiers, they would be left unsold. Firms would then move resources out of the production of defence and into the production of a good which consumers were prepared to buy.

Subsidies are a way of working through the market mechanism to increase the consumption of a good. So subsidising dental care, for instance, increases the amount of dental care provided, hopefully to a level which maximises economic welfare. Subsidies can also help those on low incomes to afford to buy goods. One problem with subsidies is that decisions about the level of subsidies can become 'captured' by producers. Subsidies then become too large to maximise welfare. For instance, it can be argued that farmers in Europe have to some extent 'captured' the Common Agricultural Policy. Instead of government ministers deciding what level of farm subsidy will maximise economic welfare, they bow to the pressure of the farming lobby. Farming subsidies then become far too large. The resultant welfare gains to farmers are far less than the welfare loss to consumers and taxpayers.

Regulation has the advantage that it requires little or no taxpayers' money to provide the good. Consumers are also likely to be able to shop around in the free market for a product which gives them good value, ensuring productive and allocative efficiency. However, regulations can impose heavy costs on the poor in society. How many poor families, for instance, could afford to pay for private health care insurance if it was a requirement for them to do so? Regulations can also be ignored. Not all motorists have insurance, for instance. If parents had a legal obligation to pay for their children to go to school, some parents would defy the law and not give their children an education. The more likely citizens are to evade regulations, the less efficient they are as a way of ensuring the provision of public and merit goods.

All these solutions also suffer from the valuation problem.

With public and merit goods, it is difficult, if not impossible, in practice to say what exactly is the socially optimal level of output for a good. If an exact value cannot be put on production and consumption of public and merit goods, then it becomes difficult to know exactly what level of output is required.

Key terms

Free rider - a person or organisation which receives benefits that others have paid for without making any contribution themselves.
Merit good - a good which is underprovided by the market mechanism. A **demerit good** is one which is overprovided by the market mechanism.
Private good - a good where consumption by one person results in the good not being available for consumption by another.

Public good or pure public good - a good where consumption by one person does not reduce the amount available for consumption by another person and where once provided, all individuals benefit or suffer whether they wish to or not.
Quasi-public good or non-pure public good - a good which may not possess perfectly the characteristics of being non-excludable but which is non-rival.

Applied economics

Lighthouses

Public goods are goods which possess the two properties of non-excludability (once provided, it is impossible to prevent others from benefiting) and non-rivalry (benefit by one does not diminish the amount by which others can benefit). Lighthouses possess both these characteristics. Once the lighthouse is working, it is impossible to prevent any ship in the area benefiting. The fact that one ship sees the lighthouse doesn't prevent other ships from seeing it as well.

Economists from Adam Smith onwards have argued that public goods need to be provided by the public sector because there is no economic incentive for the private sector to provide them. Non-excludability would mean that there would be large numbers of free-riders - individuals or firms which benefited but did not pay. For instance, how could ships be made to pay for lighthouses?

In the UK, government doesn't provide lighthouses. They are provided by Trinity House, a private corporation. However, the government has given it the right to build lighthouses. In return, the government allows it to charge each ship which visits a British port a 'light charge'. This is collected by Revenue and Customs, part of the government. Trinity House has to submit its budget to both the government and representatives of the shipping industry each year, where it has to justify the scale of its charges. So in this case, whilst the government doesn't provide the

public good, it is involved at every stage and crucially in forcing ships to pay charges for the upkeep of lighthouses.

It is in fact difficult to think of any public good for which the government doesn't provide or regulate its private provision. However, the example of lighthouses shows that a public good is not necessarily one directly provided by the government.

DataQuestion

Television

Watching television is one of the nation's favourite occupations. Almost all households have a television and on average we watch 3.8 hours per day. When television first became widely available in the UK in the 1950s, television watchers needed three things: a television set and an aerial both of which could be bought from shops, and a television licence. The licence was a tax on households owning a television, the proceeds of which were used to run the British Broadcasting Corporation, the BBC. When terrestrial commercial television in the form of ITV came on the market in 1955, television viewers didn't pay for the service. It was funded through the sale of advertisements on the channel.

Source: adapted from www.which.co.uk.

Sending out unscrambled television signals means that anyone with an aerial and a television set can receive television broadcasts, whether they have paid their licence fee or not. However, there are two other models of broadcasting in the UK where consumers are forced to pay. One is cable television. In 2007, 3.4 million households subscribed to cable. If the customer doesn't pay the subscription, their cable signal can be cut off. The other is Sky satellite television. Sky, a broadcasting company, sells equipment and cards to receive a signal. Cards are issued annually and are only sent to subscribers who pay a fee. In 2007, over 8 million households had Sky subscriptions.

Source: adapted from www.ofcom.org.uk.

Many regard the BBC as the world's best broadcaster. Partly this is because of the quality of much of its output. In commercial television, there is an incentive to produce the cheapest programmes which will appeal to a mass audience. Games shows, soaps and sitcoms are ideal formats for this. High quality programming which does not appeal to a mass audience is marginalised. Because the BBC does not have to chase ratings all the time, and because its funding does not come from advertising, it can afford to produce a wide range of material to appeal to a variety of tastes. The BBC is also world renowned for its impartiality in news and current affairs. It is independent of government and so it is not forced to churn out political propaganda. Equally, because it is not dependent on advertisers, it can tackle issues which might either offend commercial interests or lower ratings for programmes. Lastly, the BBC offers a broad range of channels from those on television to radio to the Internet.

The BBC, however, is constantly under attack from commercial broadcasters who would like to see the BBC liquidated. Commercial broadcasters would then be able to take the BBC's current audience and either charge them to view and listen, or use them as targets for advertising. Almost inevitably, the quality of broadcasting in the UK would slump to the levels seen in countries such as France, Italy and the USA.

Source: adapted from *The Guardian*, 1.4.2004.

In the 1990s and 2000s, Sky Television aggressively bid for the exclusive rights to broadcast major sporting events. One of the main reasons why it became so successful was its purchase of the broadcasting rights to Premier League football in 1992. This gave it a core subscriber base of young males who could no longer watch live Premier League matches on free-to-air BBC or ITV channels. There was concern that Sky would buy up the rights to sporting events from the football FIFA World Cup to the Olympics to the Rugby World Cup final. In 1996, the government acted by passing the Broadcasting Act. This created a list of 'Category A' sporting events which had to be broadcast on free-to-air channels. To the disappointment of many, the list did not include English test cricket matches, the golf Ryder Cup, and non-finals matches in Wimbledon tennis and the Rugby World Cup.

Source: with information from www.ofcom.org.uk.

Does quality matter in broadcasting? Does it matter whether someone is watching a critically acclaimed adaptation of a Jane Austen novel like *Pride and Prejudice* or a badly made American sitcom? Does it matter whether viewers are watching half an hour of in-depth quality news reporting or whether they only have access to three minute roundups of news sandwiched in between adverts and games shows? Some say that it doesn't matter. If you want to watch a game show rather than a wild life documentary, then it is your choice. Others argue that broadcasting has a vital role in informing and challenging viewers. Do we want to be a nation of ignorant couch potatoes or do we want to be aware, living, informed and cultured individuals?

1. Explain what is meant by a 'public good' using television broadcasting as an example.
2. It could also be argued that (a) television broadcasting is a quasi-public good and that (b) quality broadcasting is a merit good. Suggest why this might be the case.
3. Discuss whether 'liquidating the BBC', closing it down and distributing its rights to air waves to commercial broadcasters would result in market failure.

17 Market stabilisation

Summary

1. The price of a good may be too high, too low or fluctuate too greatly to bring about an efficient allocation of resources.
2. Governments may impose maximum or minimum prices to regulate a market.
3. Maximum prices can create shortages and black markets.
4. Minimum prices can lead to excess supply and tend to be maintained only at the expense of the taxpayer.
5. Prices of commodities and agricultural products tend to fluctuate more widely than the prices of manufactured goods and services.
6. Buffer stock schemes attempt to even out fluctuations in price by buying produce when prices are low and selling when prices are high.

Prices and market failure

The market mechanism establishes equilibrium prices for each good or service in the economy. However, this price or the way in which it has been set may not lead to an efficient allocation of resources. The price may fluctuate too greatly in the short term, or it may be too high or too low.

Large fluctuations in price In some markets, particularly agricultural and commodity markets, there can be large fluctuations in price over a short space of time. Prices act as signals and incentives to producers. Large fluctuations in price mean that these signals can give a very confusing picture to producers and result in over or under production in the short term, and over or under investment in the longer term. This in turn can lead to a less than optimal allocation of resources.

Too high a price The price of a good may be too high. It may be an essential item, such as bread, rice or housing, which poor households are unable to afford to buy in sufficient amounts. The government may judge these items as **merit goods**, or it may want to reduce inequalities in society and hence want to reduce their prices. Alternatively, there could be significant positive **externalities** in consumption. Too high a market price would lead to a less than optimal level of demand for the good.

Too low a price The free market price of goods like cigarettes may be too low because their consumption gives rise to significant negative externalities. Alternatively, the government may judge that too low a price is having a negative economic impact on producers. For instance, it may judge that farmers' incomes need to be raised because otherwise they would leave the land and there would be rural depopulation.

Governments can intervene in markets and change prices. For instance, they can impose indirect taxes or give subsidies. They can set maximum or minimum prices or they can establish buffer stock schemes to stabilise prices.

Prices and revenues

Governments can have other motives for market intervention other than to correct market failure. Sometimes, they intervene in markets in order to change prices for their own benefit or the benefit of their own citizens. For example, OPEC, the Organisation of the Petroleum Exporting Countries, is a group of countries which attempts to maximise its long term revenues from the sale of oil. In doing so, it switches income from oil consumers, particularly in rich industrialised countries, to the countries of its own members. In theory, this should raise the living standards of their citizens at the expense of citizens living in countries which purchase the oil. It also tends to enrich ruling elites in member OPEC countries.

Maximum prices

The government can fix a maximum price for a good in a market. In Figure 1, the free market price is P_1 and Q_1 is bought and sold. Assume that this is the market for rented accommodation. At a price of P_1 the poorest in society are unable to afford to rent houses and there is therefore a problem of homelessness. The government intervenes by fixing a maximum price for accommodation of P_2. In the very short term, this may well seem to alleviate the problem. Landlords will continue to offer Q_1 of housing whilst the poorest in society will be more able to afford the new lower cost housing. However, in the longer term, economic theory predicts that new problems will arise. At a price of P_2, demand will be higher than at P_1, whilst supply will be lower. There will in fact be an excess demand of Q_2Q_3. At the lower price, consumers will demand more housing. On the other hand, landlords will reduce their supply, for instance by selling off their properties for owner occupation, not buying new properties to rent out, or living in their own properties instead of renting them out.

Permanent rent controls will thus reduce the supply of privately rented accommodation to the market whilst increasing its demand. The market may react in a number of ways. In a law abiding society, queues or waiting lists may develop. It may be a matter of luck rather than money whether one is able to get

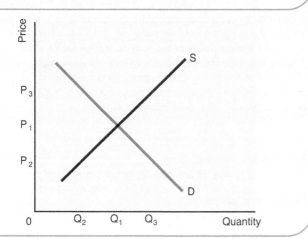

Figure 1 Maximum prices

OP_1 is the free market price. If the government sets a maximum price of OP_2 in the market, demand will increase to OQ_3 whilst supply will fall to OQ_2. The result will be excess demand in the market of Q_2Q_3.

rented accommodation. The state may devise systems to allocate rented accommodation on the basis of greatest need. Landlords may develop a variety of ways in which they can get round the price controls. A black market may develop, illegal and uncontrolled, where rents are fixed at, or greater than, the free market price of P_1. Economic theory therefore predicts that

Question 1

In the 1960s, the government introduced a system of maximum rents for privately rented properties in the UK. Typically, these 'registered' rents were below the free market rent. In the late 1980s, the government reversed its policy by introducing a new type of private tenancy agreement, assured tenancies, which allowed private landlords to set whatever rent they wished. By 2006, there were very few rented properties left with registered rent contracts.

Table 1 Number of privately rented properties, UK

	Number of properties rented privately or with a job or busines
	millions
1961	5.0
1971	3.7
1981	2.4
1991	2.2
2001	2.5
2006	3.0

Source: adapted from *Housing Statistics*, Office for National Statistics.

(a) What happened to the stock of privately rented properties between 1961 and 1991?
(b) Using a demand and supply diagram, explain why the introduction of registered rents in the 1960s might have caused (i) a fall in the supply of rented property and (ii) excess demand for private rented property.
(c) Using a demand and supply diagram, explain why the introduction of assured tenancies led to a change in the quantity demanded for and supply of privately rented housing.

maximum prices may benefit some consumers - those able to obtain the goods which are controlled in price - but will disadvantage those who are prepared to pay a higher price for the good but are unable to obtain it because of a shortage of supply.

If the maximum price were set at P_3, there would be no effect on the market. P_1, the free market price, is below the maximum price and therefore nothing will happen following the introduction of maximum price controls.

Minimum prices

Minimum prices are usually set to help producers increase their incomes. Consider Figure 2, which shows the market for wheat. The free market price is P_1. The government decides that this is too low a price for farmers to receive and sets a minimum price of P_2. As a result, farmers will now grow Q_1Q_3 more wheat. Consumers will react to the new higher prices by reducing their demand by Q_1Q_2. Total excess supply of Q_2Q_3 will result.

This poses a problem for the government. With maximum prices, the government did not need to intervene when excess demand appeared. The excess demand could remain in the market forever if need be. However, this is not true of excess supply. If consumers only buy Q_2 of wheat then farmers can only sell Q_2 of wheat. Q_2Q_3 will remain unbought. Unless the government takes action, there will be strong pressure for farmers to sell this at below the minimum price. Average prices will fall until the market is cleared. The resulting price structure is likely to be very complex, some wheat being sold at the official minimum price of P_2 whilst the rest is sold at a variety of prices, the lowest of which is likely to be below the free market clearing price of P_1. Government action will have been frustrated.

So an effective minimum price structure must be accompanied by other measures. There are two main ways of dealing with this problem. The first is for the government to buy up the wheat that consumers refuse to buy (i.e. buy up the excess supply Q_2Q_3). This in turn creates problems because the government has to do something with the wheat it buys. This has been the classic problem with the Common Agricultural Policy in the European Union. A variety of solutions, such as selling wheat

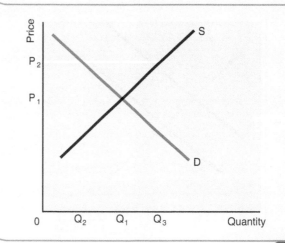

Figure 2 Minimum prices

OP_1 is the free market price. If the government sets a minimum price of OP_3 in the market, supply will increase to OQ_3 whilst demand will fall to OQ_2. The result will be excess supply in the market of Q_2Q_3.

Question 2

A bumper cereals harvest across Eastern Europe has forced the European Commission to intervene, buying up and moving large amounts of surplus stocks to prevent a European-wide fall in prices. EU cereal stocks are now at their highest for a decade after EU countries produced 290 million tons in 2004, an increase of one quarter compared to 2003. The main problem has been an increase of 40 per cent in production from the ten new member states in Eastern Europe. For example, Hungarian farmers increased their production by 89 per cent whilst farmers in the Czech Republic increased their harvest by 54 per cent.

Storage is now a major problem with the EU already committed to buying up 13.5 million tons as intervention stocks. There simply isn't enough storage capacity in the new Eastern European member states to store all this grain. The Hungarian Ministry of Agriculture has requested the use of storage facilities in Belgium and Germany to help solve its storage crisis.

To reduce intervention stocks, the EU has begun offering export subsidies for the first time since 2003. Last week, it increased the payment to farmers for each ton of grain they sold for export to €10. In addition, it has offered to subsidise the transport of some grain from landlocked Eastern European countries to the nearest ports for export.

Source: adapted from www.nutraingredients.com and www.farmersjournal.

(a) Using demand and supply diagrams, explain (i) why 'EU cereal stocks are now at their highest for a decade'; (ii) how giving subsidies for grain exports can reduce EU cereal stocks.
(b) How did EU grain farmers benefit and EU taxpayers lose out from the bumper grain harvest of 2004?

mountains to Third World countries at rock bottom prices, selling it back to farmers to feed to animals, or offering it at reduced prices to those in need in the EU, or simply destroying the produce, has been adopted. All have one drawback - they cost the taxpayer money because the price paid to farmers is

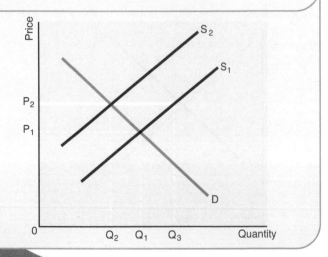

Figure 3 Achieving minimum prices through reducing supply
OP₁ is the free market price. If a government or organisation wishes to set a minimum price of OP₂, it may be able to force producers to reduce their supply, shifting the supply curve to the left from S₁ to S₂.

inevitably higher than the price received from the sale of the surplus.

The second solution to the problem of excess supply is to restrict production. Governments can either force, or pay, farmers to reduce the size of their herds or leave part of their land uncultivated. This has the effect of shifting the supply curve to the left, from S_1 to S_2 in Figure 3. To achieve a minimum price of P_2, supply has to be reduced by Q_2Q_3. Reducing output to achieve higher prices is the way in which OPEC, the Organisation for the Petroleum Exporting Countries, operates. At regular meetings, it sets quotas (maximum limits) on production for its members which are below what these countries would otherwise supply.

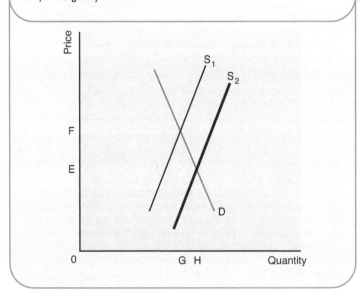

Figure 4 The effect of an increase in supply on price
If demand and supply are both relatively inelastic, then a small increase in supply from S₁ to S₂ will lead to a large fall in price of FE. Incomes will therefore be greatly reduced.

Buffer stock schemes

The free market price of **primary products** (commodities such as gold and tin, and agricultural products such as wheat and beef) tends to fluctuate much more than the price of either manufactured goods or services. This is mainly due to supply side influences. The demand for canned tomatoes or fresh tomatoes is likely to remain broadly constant over a twelve month period. However, the supply of these two products will differ. Canned tomatoes can be stored. Therefore the supply too will remain broadly the same over a twelve month period. However, the supply of fresh tomatoes varies greatly. In the summer months, supply is plentiful and the price of tomatoes is therefore low. In winter, supply is low and prices are high.

On a year to year basis, the supply of raw agricultural commodities can vary greatly according to crop yields. A bumper crop will depress prices whilst crop failure will lead to high prices. Bumper crops can be disastrous for farmers. In Figure 4, if the demand for a product is price inelastic, a large fall in price is needed to sell a little extra produce. This will greatly reduce farmers' revenues.

Equally, a poor crop can be disastrous for individual farmers. Although farm income overall will be higher than average, only

Figure 5 *The effect of a fall in demand on price*
If demand and supply are both relatively inelastic, then a small fall in demand from D_1 to D_2 will lead to a large fall in price of FE.

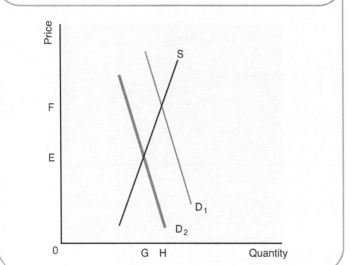

farmers who have crops to sell will benefit. Farmers whose crops have been mostly or completely destroyed will receive little or no income.

Manufactured goods and services also contain greater value added than primary products. The cost of a can of tomatoes is made up not only of the cost of tomatoes themselves but also of the canning process and the can. If fresh tomatoes only account for 20 per cent of the cost of a can of tomatoes, then a doubling in the price of fresh tomatoes will only increase the price of a can by just over 7 per cent.

Demand side influences can, however, also be a source of price fluctuations for commodities. In manufacturing and services,

producers devote much effort and money to stabilising demand through branding, advertising and other marketing techniques. However, Zambian copper is little different from Chilean copper. Buyers are free to buy from the cheapest source so demand fluctuates more greatly. In the short term, supply is relatively inelastic. Countries have invested in mines, oil wells and other commodity producing plant and need, often for foreign exchange purposes, to maximise output and sales. Small changes in demand, as shown in Figure 5, can produce large changes in price. Any slowdown in the world economy is likely to have a larger impact on commodities than on manufactured goods. Manufacturers may react to a small fall in their sales by cutting their stock levels and perhaps delaying the buying of stock by a few months. This results in a large, if temporary, fall in the price of raw materials. Whilst the slowdown persists, prices are likely to remain low. The converse is also true - in a boom, commodity prices go up far faster than those of manufactured goods or services.

Demand and supply influences combine to bring about large fluctuations in the price of commodities. Governments and other bodies have often reacted to this situation by intervening in the market place. One way to do this is to set up a BUFFER STOCK SCHEME which combines elements of both minimum and maximum pricing. In theory it is designed to even out price fluctuations for producers. An intervention price is set, shown as P_1 in Figure 6. If the free market price is the same as the intervention price, as in Figure 6(a), then the scheme doesn't need to intervene in the market. If the free market price is below the intervention price, as in Figure 6(b), then the buffer stock agency buys up enough supply to restore prices to the minimum price. In Figure 6(b), it increases demand by buying up Q_2Q_3. In contrast, if the free market price is above the intervention price, as in Figure 6(c), it can sell stocks it has accumulated. In Figure 6(c) it increases supply by selling Q_2Q_3, forcing the price down to the intervention level. In effect, the buffer stock shifts the demand curve for the product to the right when free market prices are below the intervention price, and shifts the supply

Figure 6 *Buffer stock interventions*
In (a), the free market price of P_1 is the same as the intervention price set by the buffer stock scheme and so it does not need to intervene in the market. In (b), the free market price, P_2, is below the intervention price and so it has to buy up Q_2Q_3 to bring prices back up to P_1. In (c), the free market price, P_3, is above the intervention price. So the buffer stock scheme can sell up to Q_2Q_3 from its stocks without bringing prices down below the intervention level.

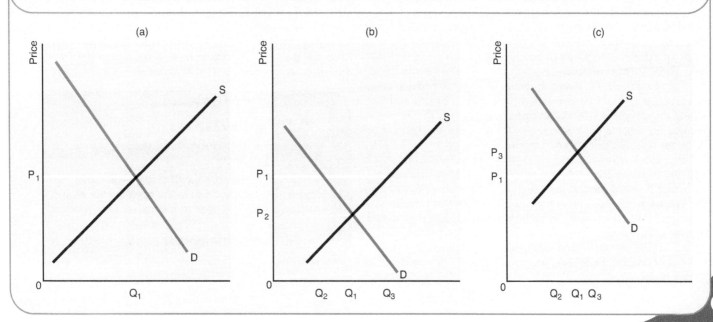

Question 3

The world tin industry has commodity agreements going back to 1921. The International Tin Council (ITC) came into being in 1956. It was able to support the price of tin during periods of low prices by buying tin for its buffer stockpile and selling tin when prices were high. During the 1970s, its stockpile of tin was not sufficiently large to prevent serious price rises in the commodity. However, the world recession of 1981-82 hit world tin consumption. The ITC was able to avoid sharp declines in tin prices by buying in the open market. However, it was only able to afford the cost of its increasing stockpile by extensive borrowing from banks and metal trading firms. In late 1985, it reached its credit limits and its supporters, such as the UK, refused to extend further credit. The International Tin Council was disbanded and its stocks sold off over a four year period. Prices did not recover their early 1980 levels until 2004 when sharp increases in demand from the booming countries of East Asia, particularly China, fuelled a commodity price boom.

Source: adapted from
http://minerals.er.usgs.gov/minerals/pubs/commodity/tin/.

(a) Explain, using a demand and supply diagram, how the International Tin Council (ITC) affected the price of tin in the market.
(b) According to the data, how well did the ITC succeed in fixing prices in the 1970s and 1980s?
(c) Explain why the price of tin was low in the 1990s compared to the late 1970s and early 1980s.

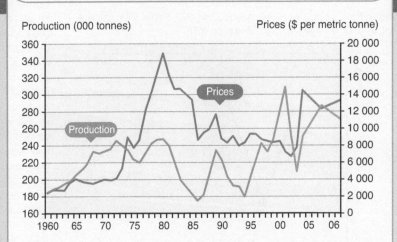

Figure 7 Prices and world production of tin

Source: adapted from *Historical Statistics for Mineral Commodities in the United States, Metal prices in the United States through 1998,* United States Geological Survey

curve to the right when free market prices are above the intervention price.

Buffer stock schemes are not common. One major reason for this is that a considerable amount of capital is needed to set them up. Money is required to buy produce when prices are too low. There are also the costs of administration and storage of produce purchased. However, in theory, the overall running costs of the scheme should be low. Indeed, with skilful buying and selling the scheme may make an operational profit. This is because the scheme buys produce at or below the intervention price but sells at a price above the intervention price.

Buffer stock schemes also have a mixed record of success. Pressure to set up these schemes tends to come from producers who have a vested interest in setting the intervention price above the average market price. If they succeed in doing this, their revenues in the short term are likely to be larger than they would otherwise have been. However, the buffer stock scheme will have been buying more produce than it sold. Eventually it will run out of money, the scheme will collapse, and prices will

plummet because the accumulated stocks will be sold to pay the debts of the scheme. The glut of produce on the market will result in producers receiving below average prices for some time to come. Successful buffer stock schemes are those which correctly guess the average price and resist attempts by producers to set the intervention price above it.

Key terms

Buffer stock scheme - a scheme whereby an organisation buys and sells in the open market so as to maintain a minimum price in the market for a product.

Applied economics

The Common Agricultural Policy (CAP)

One of the most important steps taken by the European Union (formerly the European Community) in its early years was to create the Common Agricultural Policy in 1958. Article 39 of the Treaty of Rome cites five objectives of agricultural policy:
- to increase agricultural productivity;
- to ensure a fair standard of living for farmers;
- to stabilise markets;
- to guarantee availability of supplies;
- to ensure fair prices for consumers.

It was hoped that the CAP would achieve this through regulation of the agricultural industry in the Union. For many products, an intervention price was established. Farmers could then choose to sell their produce on the open market or to the EU at this minimum fixed price. The EU guaranteed to buy up any amount at the intervention price. Farmers were protected from overseas competition through a complex system of tariffs (taxes on imported goods) and quotas (physical limits on the amount that could be imported). Tariffs and quotas effectively raised the price of imported agricultural produce to EU consumers. With high enough tariffs and quotas, agricultural produce from outside the EU could be kept out, allowing EU farmers to sell their own produce into their domestic markets at much higher prices than they would otherwise have been able to do.

CAP proved to be far more favourable to farmers than to consumers. The farming community in the EU became very good at lobbying their individual governments to vote for high intervention prices at the annual price fixing negotiations in Brussels. Consumers lost out in two ways. First, they had to pay directly for food which was much higher in price than it would otherwise have been if it had been bought on world markets. Second, as taxpayers, they had to pay for the heavy costs of running the CAP.

In theory, the CAP should have been fairly inexpensive to run. If there was a glut of produce on the market in one season, the EU would buy some of it at the intervention price and store it. The next season, when there was perhaps a shortage, the EU could take the produce out of storage and sell it. Prices would not fluctuate by as much as under a market system and the sale of produce would ensure that the major cost of the system would be administration and storage.

In practice, the cost of the CAP rose year after year. High intervention prices led to increased production, as economic theory would predict. Supply then began to outstrip demand. Instead of selling produce taken into storage to European consumers at a later date, mountains and lakes of produce developed, as shown in Figure 8. This produce then had to be sold, often at a fraction of the cost of production, to the former USSR, Third World countries, and to EU farmers for

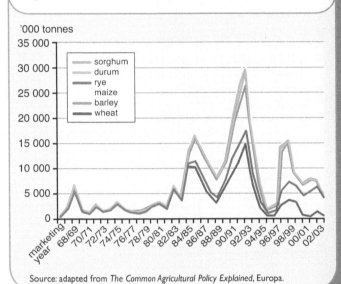

Figure 8 EU intervention stocks, cereal crops

'000 tonnes

Source: adapted from *The Common Agricultural Policy Explained*, Europa.

use as animal feed. Some was even destroyed.

EU reform

Reform of CAP has been a long standing issue. As early as 1968, the Mansholt Plan recommended that farm size should increase to enable farmers to enjoy economies of scale and thus be better able to provide food at world market prices. By the early 1980s, political pressure was building to limit the growth of the CAP budget. In 1984, a quota system (see below) was introduced for milk production to limit production and therefore subsidies to dairy farmers. In 1988, a ceiling was introduced on the CAP budget.

However, the first fundamental changes to CAP were the MacSharry reforms of 1992. Ray MacSharry was the European Commissioner for Agriculture at the time. There were two major ways in which agriculture was affected. One was through a set-aside scheme (see below) where farmers received payments for leaving ground uncultivated rather than growing crops on it. The second was limiting the amount of financial support to selected crops and animals and replacing them by direct grants to farmers for a variety of schemes not linked to production. Giving grants to farmers which are not linked to their production levels is known as **decoupling**.

In 2003, EU farm ministers agreed on a more radical scheme to decouple farm subsidies. Between 2005 and 2012, it was agreed that EU member states would change their farm subsidy regime to eliminate most production subsidies and replace them with direct grants to farmers. The total EU agricultural budget was fixed up to 2012 and included changes needed to accommodate new Eastern European entrants to the European Union.

Economic effects of different schemes

Agricultural policy in the EU distorts free markets in a variety of ways.

External trade barriers Putting tariffs (i.e. taxes) on agricultural produce entering the EU keeps out cheap food produced outside the EU. EU farmers benefit because the market price inside the EU is higher as a result. EU consumers lose out because they have to pay higher prices for their food. There are many types of trade barrier other than tariffs. The EU, for example, has been accused of using safety and welfare standards to keep imports out of the EU area.

Intervention prices Intervention prices were minimum prices set for some (but not all) agriculture products in the EU. They were effectively minimum prices which were often above the free market price. They raised farmers' incomes. Consumers paid not just higher prices for those agricultural products but also taxes to buy up surplus produce which would then have to be disposed of in some way at less than the buying price.

Quotas Quotas on milk production were introduced in 1984. Each member country of the EU was given a milk quota, a maximum amount of milk that could be produced. This was then divided up between farmers, originally depending on how much milk they produced before quotas were introduced. Quotas were transferable. A farmer owning a quota could sell all or part it to another farmer. Quotas were set at levels

Table 2 EU farm support

	Yearly average 1986-88	2005
	EU15	EU25
Transfers from consumers (€ millions)	82 142	47 159
Transfers from taxpayers (€ millions)	25 747	74 467
Budget revenues (€ millions)	1 517	533
Total support estimate (€ millions)	106 372	121 093
EU population (million)	363	456
Total support cost per head (€)	293	266
Total support estimate as percentage of GDP	2.82	1.10

Source: adapted from *Agricultural policies in OECD countries: monitoring and evaluation 2005*, OECD.

which would reduce the production of milk. In terms of demand and supply, quotas shifted the supply curve of milk to the left, reducing the equilibrium level of production but raising the equilibrium price compared to the free market price. This benefited farmers but consumers had to pay higher prices for their milk and milk-based products. The quota system was cheap to run for the EU taxpayer because dairy farmers did not receive subsidies for production of milk.

Set-aside Set-aside was introduced in 1992 for cereal farmers. They were paid for setting aside (i.e. not using) a certain proportion of their land. The land set aside had to be rotated from year to year to prevent farmers simply setting aside their least productive land. By reducing the amount of land available for production, the supply of cereals is reduced, thus raising their price. Farmers received a payment from the EU for each acre set-aside. Hence, not only did EU consumers pay higher prices for cereals than they would otherwise, but EU taxpayers had to pay a direct subsidy to farmers.

Decoupling Decoupling subsidies from production in theory should reduce, if not eliminate, production distortions. Farmers will receive a grant according to the number of acres they own, not how much they produce. Prices for agricultural products will be set by the forces of demand and supply in a free market. Consumers will therefore not pay higher prices for agricultural products as they would, say, with a system of intervention prices, set aside or quotas. In a rational world, marginal farmers who find it difficult to make a reasonable profit from agricultural activities will simply not produce. Instead, they will do nothing and collect their subsidy on their acreage. In practice, farmers are likely to be less rational. With a basic income given by the subsidy, they will be prepared to work for lower returns than they would otherwise. Hence, production is likely to be higher than if there were no subsidies at all.

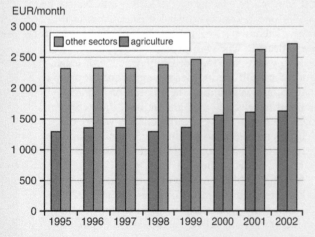

Figure 9 Farm incomes - development of average gross monthly wages in the economy and gross monthly agricultural income

Source: adapted from *The Common Agricultural Policy Explained*, Europa.

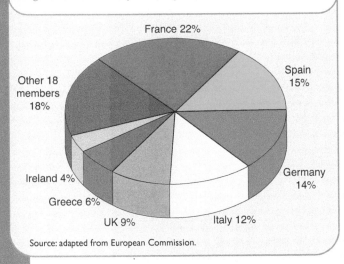

Figure 10 Main beneficiaries of CAP 2004

France 22%

Spain 15%

Other 18 members 18%

Germany 14%

Ireland 4%

Greece 6%

UK 9%

Italy 12%

Source: adapted from European Commission.

Advantages and disadvantages of the Common Agricultural Policy

The Common Agricultural Policy is highly controversial. It can be judged in a variety of ways.

Maintaining farmers' incomes One key argument for the CAP is that it transfers income from the richer non-farming community to the poorer farming community. Figure 9 shows that farm incomes on average are below those in the non-farm sector. However, there are no other industries in the EU where income transfers are made on an industrial basis. Average wages in the EU tourist industry, for example, are below those in all other industries but there is no call to subsidise the whole of the tourist industry as a result. Critics would argue that application of the general system of taxes and welfare benefits to the poorer workers in farming would be a fairer way of dealing with rural poverty than the CAP. They also point out that 80 per cent of total spending on the CAP goes to 20 per cent of the EU's largest farmers and agricultural corporations. In the UK, the largest beneficiary of the CAP was the sugar company Tate and Lyle which received £127 million in subsidies.

Cost The cost of the CAP to EU citizens has been substantial. In the past, they have not only had to pay for subsidies to the farming community through their taxes, but they have also had to pay higher prices for the food they buy because it was available at lower prices on world markets. Table 2 gives a breakdown of the cost of that support, comparing the yearly average for 1986-88 and 2005 for the EU 15 and then EU 25 countries. What it shows is that the balance of support has shifted. In 1986-88, by far the largest cost of farm support was from consumers having to pay higher prices for the food they purchased. By 2005, the reverse was true with the taxpayer picking

up most of the bill. In 2005, the cost of the CAP per head in the EU was €265, roughly equivalent to £175. A family of four people living in the UK was therefore subsidising EU farming by roughly £700 per year.

The EU budget In the 1970s, expenditure on the CAP was over 70 per cent of the EU budget. By 2005, this was approximately 50 per cent. Supporters of the CAP argue that agriculture is a key industry within the EU. Critics would point out that agriculture now accounts for only 2 per cent of EU GDP. Agriculture is of little importance to the EU economy. The opportunity cost of spending so much of the EU budget on agriculture is considerable. It would be better spent on areas such as regional assistance.

Government failure Support for reform of the CAP varies between countries across the EU. The countries which are most resistant to change tend to be those countries which most benefit from the CAP. Figure 10 shows that France is the single largest beneficiary from the CAP. For both Ireland and Greece, although they receive relatively small percentages of the total, the CAP is especially important. On average, countries receive CAP support of around 0.5 per cent of GDP. For Ireland and Greece, this is three times as large at 1.5 per cent of GDP. Critics of the CAP argue that the support of countries like France for the CAP has little to do with economic efficiency or the economic welfare of the EU. They support the CAP and resist change simply because they are the major beneficiaries of the policy.

Self sufficiency Supporters of the CAP point out that it has created a Europe which is broadly self sufficient in food. In times when a country was at war, food self sufficiency was a strategic objective. However, critics point out that in no other commodity does the EU attempt to be self sufficient. There are no objectives, for example, for the EU to be self sufficient in the production of television sets, microchips, clothes or foreign holidays. In an era of globalisation, self sufficiency in food could be argued to be an outdated goal.

Food quality and animal welfare Supporters of the CAP argue that EU farmers provide high quality food with minimum guaranteed levels of animal welfare. By implication, some food that is imported to the EU is below acceptable standards and comes from unacceptable farming practices. Critics would argue that the quality of food produced in the EU is on average no better than that produced elsewhere in the world. To be sold in the EU, imported food has to conform to certain standards anyway. Some animal rearing practices outside the EU do not conform to EU standards. However, the EU can and does impose a wide variety of conditions upon meat imported to the EU and has the power to prohibit imports if there are good reasons to do so under its trading obligations with the World Trade Organisation (WTO).

The environment Supporters of the CAP argue that it is a key factor in supporting the rural environment. Farmers look after the countryside, ensuring that it is protected for future generations. Critics of the CAP point out that the agricultural sector is a major polluter of the environment. Animals are the major source of methane gas, a key contributor to global warming. Farmers, through the use of fertilisers and pesticides, pollute the environment.

In southern European countries, their overuse of scarce water resources for irrigation is causing major problems to the environment. Little of the rural environment, anyway, is 'natural' in any sense. It has been created over thousands of years by farmers to suit the needs of production.

Supporting the rural economy Supporters of the CAP argue that it is needed to maintain an appropriate economic environment in rural areas. Without the CAP, some rural areas would become completely depopulated because there would be no jobs or income in the area. Other areas would suffer considerable depopulation as residents left to find jobs in towns and cities. There would be pressure on the urban environment which would have to expand to accommodate these migrants. Critics of the CAP argue that urban dwellers have no duty to support financially those living in the countryside: the countryside should not be seen as a charity. There is no benefit overall to having a thriving rural economy in a locality as opposed to seeing it completely depopulated. Urban areas have been expanding to take in people from rural areas for centuries. If towns and cities created large costs for their inhabitants, people would not have migrated to them from rural areas in the first place.

Impact on poorer countries in the world Supporters of the CAP argue that the EU is a major importer of food from countries round the world, including poorer developing countries. The EU has helped millions of poor farmers establish markets for their products. Critics accuse the EU of damaging farming markets round the globe. First, through its system of protection for its farmers, the EU has denied access to farmers outside the EU to EU markets. Second, the EU has dumped large amounts of food onto world markets at low prices to get rid of the surpluses that its farming regime has created. This has hurt non-EU farmers because it has denied them the opportunity to sell into those markets. Critics of the EU argue that the CAP has increased world poverty over the past fifty years.

CAP is already being radically reformed Supporters of CAP point to the radical reforms which have already been implemented and will be implemented over the next ten years. They argue that any further quickening of pace of reform will have serious consequences for the farming sector and the rural economy. Critics argue that the pace of reform is too slow and that the reforms are too timid. They point out that there are some areas of the CAP, such as the dairy sector, wine, fruit and vegetables, where there are no current plans for reform. Export subsidies and tariffs on imported food remain too high. Agriculture remains a major source of inefficiency within the EU even with the current reform programme.

DataQuestion

Rubber

The International Natural Rubber Organisation (INRO) is to break up following the withdrawal of two of the world's largest rubber producers, Thailand and Malaysia. The buffer stock scheme, set up in 1980, buys up rubber when prices fall and sells when prices rise. Members include the six leading rubber producing countries as well as the biggest consuming countries such as the US, Japan and China.

Thailand and Malaysia have become dissatisfied with the low price of rubber in world markets in recent years. They have accused INRO of failing to intervene to stop the price of rubber falling. For instance, at the start of 1998, rubber was 230 Malaysian cents a kilo. By 1999, this had fallen to 150 cents. They also accuse INRO of pursuing policies which favour member countries with low volumes of production and failing to pay sufficient attention to the interests of the three countries which account for nearly three-quarters of world production. Thailand, for instance, paid around 40 per cent of the total yearly contributions which financed INRO, but was only responsible for 30 per cent of output.

Source: adapted from the *Financial Times*, 6.10.1999

In August 2002, Malaysia, Indonesia and Thailand, the world's three largest producers of natural rubber, controlling around two thirds of world production, set up the International Rubber Consortium (IRCo). The Consortium was established to co-ordinate production and exports of the three countries. In April 2004, IRCo was officially registered with a capital of US$225 million. Its objectives are to achieve a long term price trend that is stabilised, sustainable and remunerative to farmers, and to maintain a supply-demand balance to ensure adequate supply of natural rubber in the market at fair prices.

Source: adapted from International Rubber Consortium, www.irco.biz

The collapse of the International Natural Rubber Organisation could have spelt disaster for rubber prices as stocks built up were offloaded onto the market. As it was, growing demand allowed prices to remain relatively stable, although prices fell to an all time low at the end of 2001. Since then, growing demand, especially from the booming economies of East Asia and particularly China, has driven up prices. Without this increased demand, rubber prices could easily have collapsed.

Figure 11 World natural rubber production and consumption

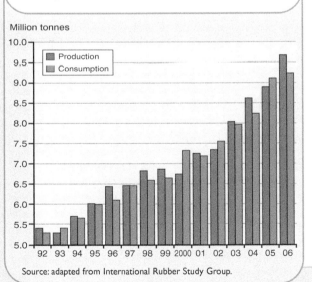

Source: adapted from International Rubber Study Group.

Figure 12 Rubber prices

Source: adapted from Singapore Commodity Exchange.

1. Explain, using INRO as an example, what is meant by a buffer stock scheme.
2. Why had INRO built up stocks of rubber by 1999?

3. To what extent could IRCo be seen as having been responsible for substantially increasing the price of rubber from 2001?

Summary

1. Government failure can be caused by inadequate information, conflicting objectives, administrative costs and creation of market distortions.
2. Public choice theory suggests that governments may not always act to maximise the welfare of society because politicians may act to maximise their own welfare.

Reasons for government failure

Markets can fail. They may underprovide public and merit goods. They may lead to externalities in production and consumption. There may be wild fluctuations in price which harm both producers and consumers. One response is for governments to intervene to correct these market failures. However, if markets can fail, so too can government. GOVERNMENT FAILURE occurs when it intervenes in the market but this intervention leads to a loss of economic welfare rather than a gain. There is a number of reasons why government failure may occur.

Inadequate information Governments, like any economic agents, rarely possess complete information on which to base a decision. In some cases, the information available is positively misleading. It is not surprising, then, that governments may make the wrong policy response to a problem. For instance, governments have to make decisions about whether to fund a selective school system or a comprehensive school system. In Germany, the school system is selective. In the USA, it is comprehensive. In the UK, it is mainly comprehensive, but a significant minority of local authorities fund selective schools. The issue is important because education is a key determinant of the long term competitiveness of the UK. It also affects every child. However, the evidence about which is the most effective form of education is conflicting. In the 1960s and 1970s, the UK government supported the change from a mainly selective system to a mainly comprehensive system. In the 1980s and 1990s, the Conservative government favoured selective schools. In the 2000s the Labour government was pushing for a variety of provision and specialist schools.

Conflicting objectives Governments often face conflicting objectives. For instance, they may want to cut taxes but increase spending on defence. Every decision made by the government has an opportunity cost. Sometimes, a decision is made where the welfare gain from the alternative foregone would have been even higher. In the case of education, assume that those receiving a selective education in grammar schools receive a better education than if they were in a comprehensive school. In contrast, assume that those who fail to get into a selective school achieve less than if they were in a comprehensive school. There is now a conflict of objectives about which system to implement. Are the needs of those who would be selected for grammar schools more important than those of the rest of the school population, or vice versa? Governments may make the wrong policy decision when there are such conflicts of objective, choosing the option which gives lower economic welfare rather than higher economic welfare. They may do this because of lack of information, or they may deliberately choose this option because they wish to reward their supporters in the electorate who voted for them.

Question 1

In 1861, Mrs Beeton, then the authority on cookery and household management and the Victorian equivalent of Delia Smith, wrote that her readers should always make their own vinegar. This was because shop bought vinegar of the day tended to consist of diluted sulphuric acid.

Today, food manufacturers and retailers are so strictly controlled by government regulations that this could not happen. Some argue, though, that such regulations are excessive. Government red tape restricts the opening and running of new businesses. Consumers have to pay higher prices for their food because it costs firms money to conform to government regulations. For instance, in 1999, the costs of production to UK pig farmers went up because they could no longer rear pigs in stalls. Animal welfare activists would like to see battery hen production stopped and all chickens reared in free range conditions, but why shouldn't consumers have the choice about whether or not they buy cheaper battery produced eggs and chickens?

(a) Explain why markets fail according to the data.
(b) Discuss whether, in the examples given in the data, government intervention leads to market failure.

Administrative costs Sometimes, the administrative cost of correcting market failure is so large that it outweighs the welfare benefit from the correction of market failure. For instance, the government may put into place a scheme to help the unemployed back into work. During a year, 100 000 pass through the scheme. Of those, 50 000 would have found jobs anyway but simply use the scheme because it is advantageous for them or their employer to do so. 10 000 find a job who would otherwise not have done so. 40 000 remain unemployed. It may cost £3 000 per person per year on the scheme, giving a total cost of £300 million. This means that the cost per worker who would otherwise not have got a job is
£300 million ÷ 10 000 or £30 000 per worker. This is an enormous cost for the benefit likely to be gained by the 10 000 workers. Indeed, they almost certainly would have preferred to have been given the £30 000 rather than gain a job. Another example would be the payment of welfare benefits. If it costs £1 to pay out a £3 benefit, is this likely to improve economic welfare?

Market distortions In some cases, government intervention to correct one market failure leads to the creation of far more serious market failures. One example is government intervention in agricultural markets such as the Common Agricultural Policy. Here, governments offer farmers financial support, partly to raise farm incomes which can be low and second to even out fluctuations in income from year to year arising from changes in the size of crops. However, financial support typically leads to increases in the supply of food which may not be matched by increases in demand. The result is an over-supply of farm produce. Countries may choose to dump this over-supply on world markets at low prices. This leads to lower farm incomes for world farmers outside the European Union, destroying the markets for their produce. Higher farm incomes in Europe may be gained at the expense of lower farm incomes in Egypt or New Zealand. Agricultural markets within the EU may also be distorted. For instance, the price of beef is artificially high in the EU because of CAP support but pig prices receive no subsidy. The result is that EU consumers buy less beef and more pork than they would otherwise do if there were no government intervention. Another market distortion may occur with respect to the environment. The CAP encourages over-production of food. Marginal land is brought into production when it might otherwise be left wild. Too much pesticide and fertiliser may be used to raise yields because CAP offers too high prices to farmers. Lower prices might lead to less intensive modes of production and less destruction to wildlife.

There are many examples of market distortions in the labour market. For instance, the government may want to raise income levels for the poor by setting a high minimum wage. However, this may be so high that employers shed low paid workers, putting out of work large numbers of people whom the government wanted to protect. Similarly, the government may raise unemployment benefit to help the unemployed. However, this may discourage them from looking for work since more are now better off on the dole than working. This increases the numbers of unemployed.

Public choice theory

It is generally assumed that governments act in a way which they believe will maximise economic welfare. They may not succeed in this because of lack of information, conflicting objectives, etc.

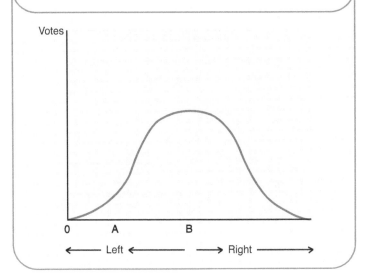

Figure 1 Voting behaviour of electors.
Politicians will tend to maximise their votes by moving to the centre ground in politics.

However, PUBLIC CHOICE THEORY suggests that governments may not attempt to maximise economic welfare at all.

Public choice theory analyses how and why public spending and taxation decisions are made. 'Consumers' or 'customers' are voters in the system. They vote for politicians and political parties who are the 'producers' in the system. Producers make decisions about how public money should be spent, about taxes and about laws. The decisions have to be 'sold' by politicians to voters.

The voters want to maximise the net benefits they get from the state. For instance, all other things being equal, voters would like the state to provide large quantities of goods and services but with minimal levels of taxation.

Politicians want to maximise their welfare too. In the simplest models, politicians are assumed to want to maximise their votes, so that they can get into power and remain in power. In more complicated models, more sophisticated assumptions can be made, such as that politicians want to get posts in government, or use their political connections to maximise their own earnings.

If politicians want to maximise their votes, then the most obvious thing to do is to appeal to the centre ground. Consider Figure 1 which shows a normal distribution of votes. A right wing politician is facing a left wing politician who has pitched his policies so that they will attract votes to the left of 0A. The obvious stance to take is for the right wing politician to pitch his policies just to the right of B, as near as possible to the middle ground whilst remaining to the right of the political spectrum. On the other hand, if the left wing politician were rational, he too would move to the centre ground to try and maximise his vote.

In practice, democracies tend to throw up governments which do veer towards the centre. It is for this reason that governments like those of Margaret Thatcher's in the 1980s were so unusual. Due to Britain's first past the post voting system, a UK party can get a majority in Parliament with as little as 40 per cent of the votes cast. With a 75 per cent turnout on polling day (i.e. 25 per cent of eligible voters don't vote), this means that a British government only has to gain the vote of 30 per cent of all voters. Not surprisingly, this sometimes allows a right

Question 2

Table 1 Shares of disposable income

Percentages

| | Quintile groups of individuals | | | | |
	Bottom fifth	Next fifth	Middle fifth	Next fifth	Top fifth
Year 0	10	14	18	23	35
Year 5	8	12	17	23	36
Year 10	6	11	17	23	43

A right wing political party enjoys the support mainly of above average income voters. It faces a left wing party which gains a majority of its votes from below average income supporters. The electoral system is such that a party only needs 40 per cent of the vote to secure a majority in Parliament, whilst a 45 per cent vote would give it a massive majority. On average, 75 per cent of the electorate vote, but the higher the income of the individual, the more likely they are to turn out to vote. The top 20 per cent of income earners have a turnout rate of 90 per cent.

The right wing party wins an election in year 0 committed to 'increasing incentives for individuals to earn money and create wealth for the nation'. It wins two further elections in year 5 and year 10.

(a) (i) Would Table 1 suggest that the nation's welfare has been maximised?
(ii) What additional information would you need to support your conclusion?
(b) Explain why the party can win elections when the relative income position of most individuals is worsening over time.

wing party which itself has voted in a right wing leader to gain office. The same would of course be true for a left wing party in the UK which had a left wing leader.

In much of economic theory, there is a hidden assumption that governments act so as to maximise the welfare of society as a whole. Public choice theory can help explain why governments often fail to do this.

Local interests Assume that an MP has a large textile mill in her constituency which employs 1 000 workers. The company owning the mill lobbies the MP to support the imposition of higher tariffs (taxes on imports) on textiles, arguing that the mill will have to close unless foreign competition is reduced. Economic theory would probably suggest that the mill should be allowed to close and the resources released be used to produce something which the UK is better at producing. However, the MP may be frightened that losing 1 000 jobs could mean losing 1 000 votes. Therefore, she could well put pressure on the government to impose higher tariffs even if she knows that the nation's welfare would be lessened as a result.

Favouring minorities Assume that a political party can get elected with considerably less than 50 per cent of the votes, because of the nature of the voting system and because not all voters turn out on polling day. In UK national elections, as argued above, a party could get a majority with the support of just 30 per cent of voters. In a local election, where the turnout is often only 30-50 per cent, a party can get a majority with far less. Assume that those who do vote tend to possess similar characteristics. For instance, in the UK, middle class voters are more likely to vote than working class voters. In a local election, voters from one ethnic group may be far more likely to vote than voters from another ethnic group. In these situations, it is clear that politicians wishing to maximise their share of the vote will want to appeal to a minority, not the majority, because it is the minority who cast votes. A government might, for instance, introduce government spending and tax changes which leave 30 per cent of the population better off and 70 per cent worse off. This would be rational behaviour if the 30 per cent of the population better off tended to vote for that party in a first past the post system with a 75 per cent turnout. However, it is arguable as to whether the nation's

welfare would be maximised as a result.

Conflicting personal interests Politicians, parties and governments may be prone to corruption. Assume that politicians are not just interested in winning votes and retaining power, but also in gaining personal economic wealth. There may then be a conflict of interest between maximising the nation's welfare and maximising the welfare of the individual politician. Assume, for instance, that a Third World political leader can remain in power by giving massive bribes to electors at election time. Between elections, he accepts bribes from electors for granting political favours. In the process, the country fails to develop because decisions are made on the basis of maximising the wealth of the individual politician rather than that of the country. The individual politician is far better off as a rich head of a poor country than as a leader who has lost power in a fast growing country.

Short-termism In the UK, there has to be a general election at least every five years. Assume that a government wants a high growth, low inflation economy. Unfortunately, the current state of the economy at the time is one of high inflation and low growth. If the government pursues anti-inflationary policies, these will need to be long term policies if they are to be successful. However, they are also likely to push up unemployment and lead to a tough tax and low government spending regime. A government coming up to re-election has two choices. It can cut taxes, increase public spending, and cut interest rates to stimulate spending and make voters 'feel good', or it can pursue austere policies which might keep the economy on course but leave voters feeling they are not particularly well off. Assume that the austere policies are the ones which will maximise welfare in the long term, but would mean the government losing the election. It is obvious that the government will go for the reflationary policies if that means it can win the election, even though it knows this will damage welfare.

Regulatory capture Governments are responsible for regulating many areas, such as monopolies or the environment. 'Regulatory capture' means that groups such as monopolists earning abnormal profit or polluters damaging the environment can strongly influence the way they are being regulated to their own advantage. Take, for instance, a utility which is about to be privatised. The board of the utility will want to make sure that it is as easy as possible after privatisation for it to make high profits to satisfy its shareholders and maximise the pay of members of the board. It will lobby hard to have as weak powers as possible given to the regulatory body which will supervise it after privatisation. National welfare would probably be maximised if the regulatory body were given strong powers to keep consumer prices as low as possible.

However, in the short term, the government is far more likely to be wanting to maximise its own short term electoral advantage from having a successful sale of the shares and by allowing small investors (probably its own voters) to make quick gains on the share price. This requires weak regulation. Once the company has been privatised, it will want to dominate the regulator. It will do this by supplying only the information which is favourable to its case. For instance, it will tend to underestimate revenues and overestimate costs in order to make it seem that future profits will be low. The regulator, with little evidence apart from that supplied by the utility, will constantly make decisions which are in the utility's interest.

Evidence from the UK since 1984, when the first regulator was appointed, suggests that the individual appointed to head the regulatory team can be crucial in determining whether or not the regulatory body is captured. A regulator who wants to minimise confrontation with a utility (i.e. have a quiet life) will allow him- or herself to be captured.

In economic theory, it is often assumed that market failure should be corrected by government. If a monopolist is exploiting the consumer, then the government should regulate or abolish the monopoly. If a polluter is damaging the environment, then the government should act to limit the actions of those responsible. Public choice theory suggests that government may fail to act in these cases because politicians are more interested in maximising their own rewards (such as votes to stay in power) than in maximising the nation's welfare. Indeed, in some cases, politicians maximising their own rewards may lead to an even greater loss of economic welfare than if market failure had been left unregulated. At one extreme, some economists argue that governments should intervene as little as possible in the economy because their interventions are likely to be more damaging than the problems they are trying to solve. On the other hand, it is argued that politicians are not all out to maximise their own self-interest. Some politicians do act in the public interest even when this does not accord with their own self-interest. A left wing MP, for instance, who votes for higher income tax rates on higher income earners is likely to pay more in tax as a result. This doesn't mean to say that he or she won't vote in favour. The more a political system can encourage its politicians to act in the public interest, the more it will accord with the traditional view that government acts as an impartial actor in the economic system, intervening to maximise national welfare.

Key terms

Government failure - occurs when government intervention leads to a net welfare loss compared to the free market solution.

Public choice theory - theories about how and why public spending and taxation decisions are made.

Applied economics

Government failure and environmental policy

Governments round the world are facing increasing pressure to implement measures which will help solve environmental problems. A wide variety of policies is in use. However, in many circumstances, it could be argued that they create more problems than they solve. The result is government failure rather than a solution to market failure.

Landfill taxes

The UK Landfill Tax was first introduced in 1996. It was designed to solve a market failure. Households and firms were disposing of rubbish to landfill sites but were not paying the full social cost of the disposal. For example, taking material to landfill creates CO_2 emissions from lorries. Local residents next to landfill sites suffer noise and other types of pollution. New landfill sites destroy the environment on which they are situated. Leakages from landfill sites can also cause environmental problems. Materials which could have been recycled at low cost were simply being thrown away. In theory, a landfill tax extends property rights and internalises the externality. Because households and firms now have to pay the full social cost of

is no difference made between landfill targets in London where land is scarce and Northumbria where population densities are much lower. Second, there are conflicting objectives. 'Green taxes' have political impact and help governments get elected into office. It could be that higher green taxes are a way of winning votes.

Carbon offsetting

Carbon offsetting occurs when an economic agent creates carbon emissions in one activity and then reduces them, or offsets them, in another. One example is air flights. It is now standard practice for airlines to ask passengers booking a flight whether they would like to pay extra to offset the carbon emissions they will create. The money is used to fund schemes such as planting trees which reduce CO_2 or developing renewable energy which saves on emissions from coal and gas fired power stations.

At the moment, governments have played little part in carbon offsetting schemes. These are private contracts between individual economic agents. However, there are reservations about how effective carbon offsetting is. It is difficult, for a start, to get exact offsets. The same trees planted in different locations, for example, will have different growth rates and will react differently to the soil in which they are planted. This affects the amount of CO_2 which they will store. More problematic is that not all the money given for carbon offsets is being spent efficiently. Some projects are started but are not completed for a variety of reasons. High administration costs and even fraud were found by the *Financial Times* when it reported on such schemes in 2007.

It is likely that at some point in the future the government will step in to regulate carbon offsetting schemes to correct the market failure currently being generated. However, this could in turn lead to government failure. For example, the cost of regulating schemes might be larger than the benefits gained from greater efficiency and transparency of existing schemes. Regulation might deter some carbon offsetting schemes from going ahead.

Carbon emissions trading

Carbon emissions trading schemes are a form of tradeable pollution permits. Currently, the most developed scheme is the European Union Emission Trading Scheme. The scheme began in 2005 when the EU issued firms with allowances for the amount of carbon they can emit. The total amount of allowances

disposal, they reduce the amount of waste being sent to landfill tips. Either they find ways of cutting down the amount of waste they create, or they recycle their waste.

For the purposes of the UK Landfill Tax, waste is classified into two types. Inactive waste is mainly materials used in building which cannot be recycled. Examples are concrete and soil excavated from foundations. Active waste is all other waste which includes household waste and building waste such as wood, piping and plastics. Active waste is waste which is capable of being recycled or disposed of in another way such as incineration. When first introduced in 1996, the tax on disposal of active waste at landfill sites was £7 a tonne. For inactive waste, this was £2 per tonne. By 2007/8, this had risen to £24 per tonne for active waste but inactive waste was still £2 per tonne. By 2010/11, the government have announced it will be £48 per tonne for active waste and £2.50 per tonne for inactive waste.

It can be argued that the Landfill Tax has been a great success. It has altered behaviour. In 1997-1998, the quantity of waste deposited at landfill sites was 96 million tonnes. By 2005/06, this had fallen to 72 million tonnes, a fall of 25 per cent. It is also clear that households and firms were not paying the full social cost of landfill before 1996.

However, it is also likely that the Landfill Tax has created government failure. First, the UK government has little precise information about the social costs and benefits of landfill disposal and its alternatives. It is unclear as to what is the socially optimal level of landfill use. For example, recent evidence suggests that local communities protest much more vigorously about the opening of an incineration plant for waste than a new landfill site. Their perception is that the pollution created by an incineration plant is much greater than that created by a landfill site. UK government targets for waste disposal are in practice set by the EU. There

represents the maximum amount of carbon emissions that can be emitted throughout the EU. This maximum amount is related to the EU's commitments under treaties such as the Kyoto agreement. Firms which do not use up all their allowances can then trade them for cash with other firms. In theory, this is a cheaper way to reduce carbon emissions than through regulation because it provides incentives for firms to reduce their carbon emissions in the most cost-effective way.

However, the scheme has been criticised. The scheme only covers half of the EU carbon emissions, targeting large carbon emitters such as power stations and heavy industry. These industries feel that they have been unfairly penalised and put under a competitive disadvantage. Economic theory suggests that if only some firms are taxed, there is sometimes a misallocation of resources which outweighs the misallocation present in the first place. Another criticism was that the 2005-2007 scheme was too lax and did little to curb emissions. Too lax a scheme could mean that the costs of compliance and administration outweigh any benefits. The scheme also distributed carbon allowances to existing polluters according to how much carbon they were emitting at the start of the scheme - so called 'grandfathering'. Arguably, this was done mainly for political reasons because of lobbying from firms that would be affected. However, greater economic efficiency could probably have been achieved if the carbon permits had been auctioned to the highest bidder. This is an example of government failure.

Renewable energy certificates

Renewable energy certificates can be seen as a negative carbon emission trading scheme. Instead of firms having to acquire carbon certificates to emit carbon, firms which generate renewable energy are given renewable energy certificates. They can then sell these to firms generating carbon and which need carbon certificates. In the UK, the government has created the Renewable Obligations Scheme where renewable energy certificates can legally offset the need for UK firms to buy carbon permits from the European Union Emission Trading Scheme. However, critics argue that the scheme has been relatively ineffective at encouraging anything other than wind power and even then incentives within the scheme have been weak.

Renewable energy itself is highly controversial. Critics argue that renewable energies can create as many if not more negative externalities as they create positive externalities. Few local communities want any wind turbines located in their area because of their visual impact on the landscape and alleged problems with noise. Bio-fuels, where fuel is manufactured from corn for example, perpetuates ecologically damaging intensive farming methods. It can also send the price of basic foodstuffs rocketing as the experience of 2007 has shown. At worst, this could cause starvation in Third World countries amongst the poor who can no longer afford to pay the high prices. The proposed barrage across the estuary of the river Severn, which could generate 5-7 per cent of the UK's electricity, has been opposed by environmentalists because it will destroy rare wildlife habitats. Excessive use of renewable energy resulting from government incentives could itself lead to government failure.

DataQuestion   Bio-fuels and US pork-barrel politics

The world is rushing towards its end. Global warming, according to the gloomiest predictions, will raise temperatures so much that most life on this planet will disappear within the next 100 years. However, there is a solution and it comes from a farm near you. Farmers will grow crops such as corn or sugar cane. This will absorb CO_2 from the atmosphere. The crop can then be converted into bio-fuel and, mixed with conventional petrol or diesel, can be used to power vehicles. Bio-fuels will then be carbon neutral rather than emitting CO_2 as with the burning of oil.

In the United States, bio-fuels are already big business. In 2007, one quarter of the country's corn crop is set to be converted into ethanol which will then be mixed with conventional petrol and diesel products. There are already 116 ethanol plants with 79 under construction and 200 more planned. The major oil company ConocoPhillips in partnership with Tyson Foods wants to expand the industry by processing animal fats from the food group's herds and flocks and blending it with conventional fuel.

However, all this is only coming about because of subsidies. The US government is already paying $8.4 billion per year in subsidies for corn and ethanol production, which equates to 79 cents per litre. Petrol blended with ethanol has reduced tax of 5.3 cents per gallon. Then the oil industry gets a subsidy of 51 cents per gallon for blending the ethanol with petrol. This makes US ethanol a very expensive source of renewable energy. This is especially so when you take into account the fact that Brazilian ethanol, made from much more efficient sugar cane, is being kept out of US markets by a 51 cents a gallon tax on imports.

Devoting so much land to growing bio-fuels is not supported even by environmentalists. They point out that growing bio-fuel crops leads to soil acidification, high use of fertilisers and pesticides and bio-diversity loss. The rapid expansion of bio-fuels has also led to sharp increases in the prices of many agricultural products. Corn, for example, is used as a major feedstock for animals. So meat prices are likely to rise.

Ethanol plant.

Devoting extra land to corn means less wheat is produced, pushing up the price of bread. It is the poor, particularly in the Third World, who will suffer most from rising prices.

To understand why all this is happening, you need to consider traditional American pork-barrel politics. The farming lobby and the oil lobby have always had enormous influence in Washington. Farm subsidies, which go mainly to large agri-businesses rather than small farmers, remain substantial. Bio-fuels are just the latest, very profitable, way for these lobbies to milk the US taxpayer. Then there is the location of the states most involved in growing bio-fuel crops. One leading state is Iowa. This just happens to be one of the key states which votes early on to select the presidential candidates for each party. No presidential candidate who wants to get his party's nomination for president can afford to upset the voters of Iowa. The state gets a disproportionate amount of its income from agriculture. So no presidential candidate can afford to be less than enthusiastic about bio-fuels.

Source: adapted from the *Financial Times*, 20.7.2007; OECD, *Biofuels: is the cure worse than the Disease?*, 2007; EA2020, *Peak Soil: why biofuels are not sustainable and a threat to America's national security*.

1. **Explain how increasing the output of bio-fuels could (a) help solve the problem of market failure in the market for fuels or (b) create an example of government failure.**

2. **Using public choice theory, explain why there might be an overproduction of bio-fuels in the USA.**

Summary

1. Macroeconomics is concerned with the economy as a whole whilst microeconomics is the study of individual markets within the economy.
2. National economic performance can be measured in a number of different ways. Four key macroeconomic variables are the economic growth rate, unemployment, inflation and the current account balance.

Microeconomics and macroeconomics

MICROECONOMICS is the study of individual markets within an economy. For instance, microeconomics is concerned with individual markets for goods or the market for labour. Housing, transport, sport and leisure are all mainly microeconomic topics because they concern the study of individual markets.

In contrast, MACROECONOMICS is concerned with the study of the economy as a whole. For instance, macroeconomics considers the total quantity produced of goods and services in an economy. The price level of the whole economy is studied. Total levels of employment and unemployment are examined. Housing becomes a macroeconomic issue when, for instance, rises in house prices significantly affect the average level of all prices in the economy.

National economic performance

One of the reasons why macroeconomics is useful is because it tells us something about the performance of an economy. In particular, it allows economists to compare the economy today with the past. Is the economy doing better or worse than it was, say, ten years ago? It also allows economists to compare different economies. Is the Japanese economy doing better than the US economy? How does the UK compare with the average in Europe?

An economy is a system which attempts to resolve the basic economic problem of scarce resources in a world of infinite wants. An economic system is a mechanism for deciding what is to be produced, how production is to take place and who is to receive the benefit of that production. When judging the performance of an economy, one of the criteria is to consider how much is being produced. The more that is produced, the better is usually considered the economic performance. Another criterion is whether resources are being fully utilised. If there are high levels of unemployment, for instance, the economy cannot be producing at its potential level of output. Unemployment also brings poverty to those out of work and therefore affects the living standards of individuals. The rate at which prices rise is important too. High rates of price rises disrupt the workings of an economy. A national economy must also live within its means. So over a long period of time, the value of what it buys from other economies must roughly equal what it sells. In this, it is no different from a household which cannot forever overspend and accumulate debts.

Economic growth

One of the key measures of national economic performance is the rate of change of output. This is known as economic growth. If an economy grows by 2.5 per cent per annum, output will double roughly every 30 years. If it grows by 7 per cent per annum, output will approximately double every 10 years. At growth rates of 10 per cent per annum, output will double every 7 years.

There is a standard definition of output based on a United Nations measure which is used by countries around the world to calculate their output. Using a standard definition allows output to be compared between countries and over time. This measure of output is called **gross domestic product** or **GDP**. So growth of 3 per cent in GDP in one year means that the output of the economy has increased by 3 per cent over a 12 month period.

Economic growth is generally considered to be desirable because individuals prefer to consume more rather than fewer goods and services. This is based on the assumption that wants are infinite. Higher economic growth is therefore better than lower economic growth. Periods when the economy fails to grow at all, or output shrinks as in a RECESSION or DEPRESSION, are periods when the economy is performing poorly. The depression years of the 1930s in Europe and the

Question 1

Table 1 Economic growth rates

	1961-73	1974-1979	1980-1989	1990-1999	2000-2007
				Average yearly changes, %	
United States	3.9	2.5	2.5	3.0	2.6
Japan	9.6	3.6	4.0	1.7	1.8
Germany	4.3	2.4	2.0	2.2	1.6
France	5.4	2.8	2.3	1.7	2.0
Italy	5.3	3.7	2.4	1.5	1.4
Mexico	6.6	6.1	2.0	3.0	3.0
United Kingdom	3.1	1.5	2.4	2.1	2.7

Source: adapted from OECD, Historical Statistics, Economic Outlook.

(a) Which country had the highest average yearly growth rate between (i) 1961 and 1973; (ii) 1974 and 1979; (iii) 1980 and 1989; (iv) 1990 and 1999; (v) 2000 and 2007?
(b) 'Mexico enjoyed a better economic performance than Germany over the period 1961 to 2007'. Does the evidence support this statement?
(c) In 1961, the UK enjoyed one of the highest living standards in Europe. By the mid-1990s, as measured by GDP, it lagged behind countries such as France and Germany. By 2007, the UK had caught up again with its main European competitors. Explain how the data show this story of the UK's poor relative economic performance over the period 1961 to the mid-1990s and its subsequent improvement.

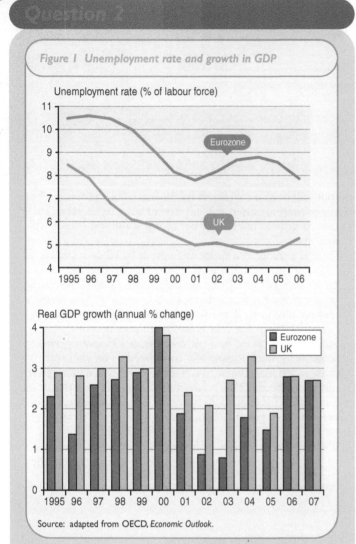

Figure 1 Unemployment rate and growth in GDP

Unemployment rate (% of labour force)

Real GDP growth (annual % change)

Source: adapted from OECD, *Economic Outlook*.

In 2007, the Eurozone was made up of 13 European countries, including France and Germany. 12 of these countries were the founder members of the 1999 European Monetary Union which led to the creation of a single European currency. The UK decided not to join and in 2007 was still not a member.
(a) Compare the economic performance of the UK with countries in the Eurozone.
(b) Suggest why the UK's unemployment record between 1995 and 2007 was better than that for the Eurozone.

Americas, for instance, were years when poverty increased and unemployment brought misery to millions of households.

Unemployment

Unemployment is a major problem in society because it represents a waste of scarce resources. Output could be higher if the unemployed were in work. It also leads to poverty for those who are out of work. So high unemployment is an indicator of poor national economic performance. Conversely, low unemployment is an indicator of good national economic performance.

Economic growth and unemployment tend to be linked. Fast growing economies tend to have low unemployment. This is because more workers are needed to produce more goods and services. Low levels of economic growth tend to be associated with rising levels of unemployment.

Over time, technological change allows an economy to produce more with fewer workers. If there is little or no economic growth, workers are made redundant through technological progress but fail to find new jobs in expanding industries. If growth is negative and the economy goes into recession, firms will lay off workers and unemployment will rise.

Fast economic growth, then, will tend to lead to net job creation. More jobs will be created than are lost through the changing structure of the economy. So another way of judging the performance of an economy is to consider its rate of job creation.

Inflation

Inflation is the rate of change of average prices in an economy. Low inflation is generally considered to be better than high inflation. This is because inflation has a number of adverse effects. For instance, rising prices mean that the value of what savings can buy falls. If a person had £50 in savings and the price of DVDs went up from £10 to £25, then they would be worse off because their savings could only now buy 2 DVDs compared to 5 before. Another problem with inflation is that it disrupts knowledge of prices in a market. If there is very high inflation, with prices changing by the month, consumers often don't know what is a reasonable price for an item when they come to buy it.

Today, inflation of a few per cent is considered to be acceptable. When inflation starts to climb through the 5 per cent barrier, economists begin to worry that inflation is too high. Inflation was a major problem for many countries including the UK in the 1970s and 1980s. In the UK, inflation reached 24.1 per cent in 1975, for instance. However, these levels of inflation are nothing compared to the **hyperinflation** experienced by countries such as Argentina and Brazil in the 1980s. Prices were increasing by up to 1 000 per cent per year.

The current balance

A household must pay its way in the world. If it spends more than it earns and takes on debt, then at some point in the future it must repay that debt. Failure to repay debt can lead to seizure of assets by bailiffs and the household being barred from future borrowing. The same is true of a national economy. A nation's spending on foreign goods and services is called **imports**. It earns money to pay for those imports by selling goods and services, known as **exports**, to foreigners. If imports are greater than exports then this must be financed, either through borrowing or running down savings held abroad. The economic performance of a country is sound if, over a period of time, its exports are either greater than or approximately equal to its imports. However, if its imports are significantly greater than exports, then it could face difficulties.

Where exports of goods and services are greater than imports, there is said to be a **current account surplus**. Where imports exceed exports, there is a current account deficit. Deficits become a problem when foreign banks and other lenders refuse to lend any more money. A 'credit crunch' like this occurred, for instance, in Mexico in 1982 and Thailand in 1998. Countries have to respond to restore confidence. This is likely to involve cutting domestic spending, which leads to less demand for imports. Cutting domestic spending, though, also leads to reduced economic growth and rising unemployment. So the current account position of a country is an important indicator of performance.

In July 2005, four terrorists planted bombs on London's underground and buses, killing 52 people and injuring many more. London is a major tourist destination and inevitably there was a wave of cancellations for London hotels in the aftermath of the bomb.

The World Travel and Tourism Council (WTTC) made an immediate impact assessment of the likely effects of the bombings on UK tourism. It predicted that in 2005 there would be nearly 600 000 fewer visitors to the UK, down from 31 million visitors. The contribution of travel and tourism to UK GDP would fall by £927 million, a 2 per cent fall in this contribution. UK Tourism contributes £185 billion to GDP and represents 4 per cent of the total. It directly and indirectly creates 2.8 million jobs.

The WTTC's conclusion was that the effects of the bombings on UK tourism would continue to be felt through to 2007. Jean-Claude Baumgarten, President of the WTTC, said the day after the bombings: 'This assumes that UK authorities undertake at least similarly strong measures of reassurance and encouragement to regain and rebuild visitor confidence and that no further events take place in the meantime.'

Source: adapted from www.wttc.org.

What impact might the 2005 London bombings have had on the performance of the UK economy (a) in the short term; (b) in the long term?

Government objectives

Governments attempt to manipulate the economy so as to improve its economic performance. Different economies perform in different ways. So what is possible for the UK economy might be very different from what is possible for the Chinese economy or the Russian economy. However, typically, governments have four main macroeconomic objectives.

- Economic growth should be as high as possible. The UK economy has grown at approximately 2.5 per cent per annum over the past 50 years. This has been fairly typical of western European economies and the USA too. So the UK government currently has an unofficial objective of seeing the economy grow at 2.5 per cent and would like to be able to increase this to 3.0 per cent. In China, with growth rates averaging 10 per cent per annum over the past thirty years, the Chinese government aims to achieve yearly growth rates of up to 10 per cent.
- Unemployment should be as low as possible. It is impossible to have zero unemployment in a market economy because there are always workers moving between jobs. They might have a new job to go to but it hasn't yet started, or they might be looking for a new job. The UK government has no official target for UK unemployment. However, it would like to see unemployment continue to fall from its present levels. In the 1950s and 1960s, UK unemployment was between 250 000 and 500 000 and the typical unemployment rate was 1.5 per cent. In 2007, the workforce was much larger but unemployment rates were higher at around 3 per cent. What's more, this does not include

several million people of working age who were long term sick. So the UK government would like to see further falls in unemployment.

- Inflation should be low but not necessarily zero. Inflation is the only indicator of macroeconomic performance for which there is an official target in the UK. The central target in 2007 was 2 per cent.
- The balance of payments on current balance should broadly balance over time. Exports and imports for an economy like the UK are very large. So annual deficits or surpluses of even tens of billions of pounds can be relatively unimportant. However, history shows that large sustained deficits on the current account can lead to economic crises. So governments might have to intervene if the current account is threatening the rest of the economy.

Governments also have other major objectives apart from those to do with economic growth, unemployment, inflation and the balance of payments on current account. One objective relates to the **distribution of income**. Some governments attempt to make the distribution of income more equal. So the Labour government elected in 1997 had this commitment. Other governments, such as the Conservative government of Margaret Thatcher in the 1980s, are committed to making the distribution of income less equal.

Another objective of most governments today is to reduce damage to the **environment**. There is no simple measure of the impact of economy activity on the environment. So a wide variety of measures have to be used from tonnes of waste sent to landfill sites to CO_2 emissions into the atmosphere. Governments do not aim to eliminate pollution and environmental damage since this would be impossible. However, they set targets and impose limits on different environmental outcomes of economic activity.

In this, my 11th budget, my report to the country is of rising employment and rising investment; continued low inflation and low interest and mortgage rates; and this is a Budget to expand prosperity and fairness for Britain's families - and it is built on the foundation of the longest period of economic stability and sustained growth in our country's history. I can report the British economy is today growing faster than all the other G7 economies - growth stronger this year than the euro area, stronger than Japan and stronger even than America. Our forecast and the consensus of independent forecasts agree that looking ahead to 2008 and 2009 inflation will also be on target. Mr Deputy Speaker, six months ago when we published the Stern report on climate change, we set a framework for environmental action combining a call to personal and social responsibility, with European and international co-operation. Since then we have secured support for a strengthened European carbon trade scheme on the road to a global scheme.

Source: excerpts from *The Budget Speech*, March 2007.

(a) Name **four** economic objectives mentioned in the 2007 Budget Speech.
(b) What evidence was there in the speech that the UK was succeeding in meeting its growth and inflation objectives but failing in its environmental objectives?

Trade-offs

Governments cannot necessarily achieve all their objectives at any single point in time. There are frequently trade-offs that have to be made. For example, in the short term, lower unemployment might only be achievable if there is higher inflation. This is known as the Phillips curve relationship. The reason why is that lower unemployment is typically associated with fast economic growth. Fast economic growth tends to put upward pressure on prices. Equally, fast economic growth for the UK economy is often associated with a worsening balance of payments on current account. This is because UK consumers buy more imported goods with their high incomes. However, in countries like China or Japan, faster economic growth is often caused by booms in export sales which in turn lead to current account surpluses. Trade-offs will be explored in much more detail in many of the macroeconomic units of this book.

Applied economics

A tale of four economies

The USA, Germany, Japan and the UK are four of the largest economies in the world. They form part of the G7 group (the other three being France, Italy and Canada) which meets regularly to discuss common economic problems. For much of the post-war period, Japan and Germany were seen as highly successful. They had high economic growth, low inflation, low unemployment and a persistent current account surplus. The USA was less successful mainly because its growth rate seemed low in comparison with Japan and much of continental Europe. As for the UK, it seemed to have a disappointing economic performance with slow growth and persistent inflation and balance of payment problems.

The 1990s, though, saw a reversal of fortunes as Figures 2 to 5 show. Japan's growth rate at the start of the decade was not untypical of what it had achieved during the previous four decades. However, it became bogged down in a series of recessions interspersed with short periods of positive economic growth. Over the period 1991-2006, it only averaged economic growth of 1.3 per cent per annum, compared to the 4-10 per cent range of its 'economic miracle' years of the 1950s to 1980s. Inflation reflected depressed demand. In 1995, prices fell and this was followed by six years of price stability or falls between 1999 and 2006. In the 1990s, unemployment remained low, but by the end of the decade was beginning to rise as years of low economic growth resulted in a shake out of jobs from Japanese industry. By 2006, unemployment was double what it

had been in 1991.

The period 1991-2006 was difficult for Germany too. Part of its problems arose from the cost of reunification of East Germany with West Germany in 1990. East Germany had been a **command economy** within the Soviet sphere of influence since 1945. By 1990, East Germany was a relatively inefficient economy where output per head was far below that of its highly successful western neighbour. Reunification resulted in a transfer of resources from West Germany to East Germany. Despite this, the East German economy remained a drag on the performance of the German economy as a whole. Growth for the reunited German economy was relatively slow after 1991. By the late 1990s, the failure of the German economy to pick up after reunification began to be blamed on its 'social' economic model which it shared with low growth countries, such as France and Italy. 'Social Europe' was growing slowly because it lacked flexibility

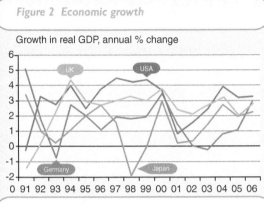

Figure 2 *Economic growth*

Growth in real GDP, annual % change

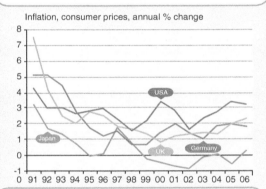

Figure 3 *Inflation*

Inflation, consumer prices, annual % change

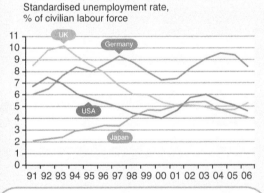

Figure 4 *Unemployment*

Standardised unemployment rate, % of civilian labour force

Figure 5 *The current balance as a percentage of GDP*

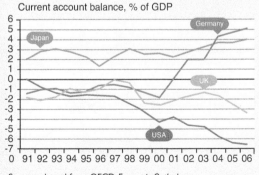

Current account balance, % of GDP

Source: adapted from OECD, *Economic Outlook*.

in its markets. Government red tape, high taxes on labour, difficulties in sacking workers and other **supply side** constraints were discouraging firms from investing and taking on workers. The result was low growth and high unemployment. By 2006, German unemployment was still 40 per cent higher than its 1991 level. Inflation, which rose at the start of the 1990s following reunification, fell back quickly to below 2 per cent, partly a reflection of low economic growth and lack of demand.

The story for the USA and the UK was the reverse for that of Germany and Japan. Both the USA and the UK, after decades of relatively low economic growth, saw their position transformed into relatively high economic growth countries. Between 1960 and 1990, the US's long term growth rate had been around 2.5 per cent per year. However, from 1992, economic growth averaged over 3 per cent. Strong economic growth was also combined with subdued inflation.

In the UK, after a deep recession in the early 1990s, the economy bounced back and enjoyed average growth of 2.9 per cent between 1993 and 2006. This compared to a 2.6 per cent average for the period 1950-1990 and 2.3 per cent for 1970-1990. Unemployment nearly halved between its peak in 1993 and 2006 whilst inflation also fell.

The performance of the four economies on the current account of the balance of payments can be interpreted in two ways. One is to argue that the persistent current account deficits of the UK and the USA will drag down future growth of these economies. If the deficits have been financed through borrowing to pay for current spending, the money will one day have to be repaid with interest. Just as heavy borrowing now by a household means lower consumption in the future when the debt has to be repaid, so it could be with both the UK and the USA. On this argument, Japan, which has run a persistent surplus, will benefit in the future. On the other hand, if the current account deficits have been caused by inflows of investment capital, where foreigners are investing in UK and US businesses, then the economies of the UK and the USA have been strengthened, not weakened over the period. If, for example, Japan is using part of its current account surplus to invest in new car plants in the UK, the British economy is likely to benefit in the long term. Economists are divided about whether the current account deficits and surpluses the UK, USA, Germany and Japan have had, and will have an effect on economic performance.

It could be argued that the performance of the UK and the US economies has barely changed since the 1970s and 1980s. An increase in the average economic growth rate of around half a percent looks fairly insignificant. However, it should be taken in the context of the fall in the long term growth rate of countries like Germany and Japan. In the 1970s and 1980s, Japan and Germany were growing at up to twice the rate of the UK and the USA. Since 1991, the growth rates of Japan and Germany have been half that of the UK and the USA. This turnaround has been used to argue that the 'Anglo-Saxon economic model' associated with free markets and globalisation is superior to the 'social economic model' of countries like Germany associated with more controlled markets and protectionism. By 2006, the UK's economic performance looked extremely good compared to that of Germany. The USA was outperforming its long term economic rival, Japan. The only worrying feature of the performance of the UK and the USA was their persistent current account deficits.

DataQuestion Ireland and The Czech Republic

Ireland

Ireland joined the European Union at the same time as the UK in 1973. When it joined, it was one of the poorer EU members and consequently attracted a considerable amount of EU regional aid as well as benefiting from agricultural subsidies from the EU Common Agricultural Policy (CAP).

Successive Irish governments pursued two sets of policies which were, arguably, to prove crucial in its economic success. One was to spend generously on education so that by the 1990s, the workforce of Ireland was as richly endowed with human capital as its economic rivals. The other was, for example through grants and tax breaks, to attract foreign companies to set up in Ireland. Not only did these directly and indirectly create jobs, but they encouraged Irish companies to come up to world class standards.

With many low wage countries in Central and Eastern Europe having joined the EU in 2004, and possibly more to come over the next ten years, Ireland faced the same problem as other Western European EU members: can they compete successfully or will they see jobs drain away to the East? For Ireland, is this the end of its economic boom time and will its growth rate fall to the Western European average of little more than 2 per cent per annum?

The Czech Republic

Until 1990, the Czech Republic was a command economy and part of the Eastern Bloc. Relatively poor by Western standards, its trade was orientated towards other Eastern Bloc countries such as Poland, East Germany and the Soviet Union.

From 1990, it began a transition to democracy and a free market economy. Much of the industry owned by the state was privatised (i.e. sold off to the private sector). Trade was re-orientated towards Western Europe. However, the transition was painful. Inefficient firms closed down. Other enterprises had to scale back their production. Increases in GDP in some sectors of the economy were offset by decreases in other sectors. Czech consumers and producers showed a preference for imported goods over Czech-made products. In 2004, the Czech Republic joined the European Union. It looked to the success of economies such as Ireland and Portugal following their accession to the European Union as a model for its own future development.

1. Compare the economic performance of the Czech Republic and Ireland over the period 1994 to 2006.
2. What problems may the Czech Republic and Ireland face in the future and how might these problems impact on the future economic performance of these two countries?

Economic indicators

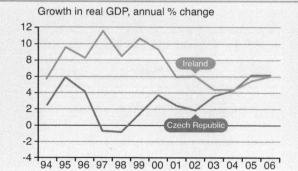

Figure 6 *Economic growth*

Growth in real GDP, annual % change

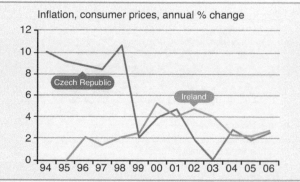

Figure 7 *Inflation*

Inflation, consumer prices, annual % change

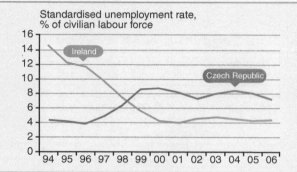

Figure 8 *Unemployment*

Standardised unemployment rate, % of civilian labour force

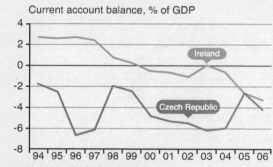

Figure 9 *The current balance as a percentage of GDP*

Current account balance, % of GDP

Source: adapted from OECD, *Economic Outlook*.

Summary

1. National income can be measured in three ways: as national output, national expenditure or national income.
2. The most commonly used measure of national income is Gross Domestic Product (GDP). Other measures include Gross National Product (GNP) and Net National Product (NNP). All these measures can be at market prices or factor cost.
3. National income statistics are used by academics to formulate and test hypotheses. They are used by policy makers to formulate economic policy both on a microeconomic and macroeconomic level. They are often used as a proxy measure for the standards of living and to compare living standards between countries and within a country over time.
4. National income statistics can be inaccurate because of statistical errors, the existence of the black economy, of non-traded sectors, and difficulties with valuing public sector output.
5. Problems occur when comparing national income over time because of inflation, the accuracy and presentation of statistics, changes in population, the quality of goods and services and changes in income distribution.
6. Further problems occur when comparing national income between countries. In particular, an exchange rate has to be constructed which accurately reflects different purchasing power parities.

Income, output and expenditure

Macroeconomics is concerned with the economy as a whole. A key macroeconomic variable is the level of total output in an economy, often called NATIONAL INCOME. There are three ways in which national income can be calculated. To understand why, consider a very simple model of the economy where there is no foreign trade (a CLOSED ECONOMY as opposed to an OPEN ECONOMY where there is foreign trade) and no government. In this economy, there are only households and firms which spend all their income and revenues.

● Households own the WEALTH of the nation. They own the stock of land, labour and capital used to produce goods and services. They supply these factors to firms in return for rents, wages, interest and profits - the rewards to the factor of production. They then use this money to buy goods and services.
● Firms produce goods and services. They hire factors of production from households and use these to produce goods and services for sale back to households.

The flow from households to firms is shown in Figure 1. The flow of money around the economy is shown in colour. Households receive payments for hiring their land, labour and capital. They spend all that money on the goods and services produced by firms (consumption). An alternative way of putting this is to express these money payments in real terms, taking into account changes in prices. The real flow of products and factor services is shown in black. Households supply land, labour and capital in return for goods and services. The CIRCULAR FLOW OF INCOME MODEL can be used to show that there are three ways of measuring the level of economic activity.

National output (O) This is the value of the flow of goods and services from firms to households. It is the black line on the right of the diagram.

National expenditure (E) This is the value of spending by households on goods and services. It is the red line on the right of the diagram.

National income (Y) This is the value of income paid by firms to households in return for land, labour and capital. It is the blue line on the left of the diagram.

So income, expenditure and output are three ways of measuring the same flow. To show that they must be identical and not just equal, we use the '≡' sign.

$$O \equiv E \equiv Y$$

Injections and withdrawals

The simple circular flow of income model in Figure 1 can be made more realistic by adding injections and withdrawals. An INJECTION into the circular flow is spending

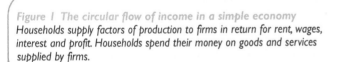

Figure I The circular flow of income in a simple economy
Households supply factors of production to firms in return for rent, wages, interest and profit. Households spend their money on goods and services supplied by firms.

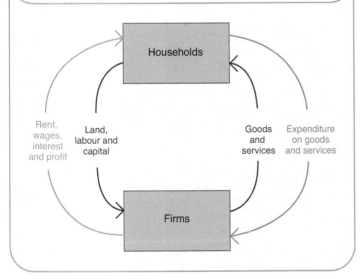

Table 1

	£bn
Rent	5
Wages	75
Interest and profit	20

The figures in Table 1 represent the only income payments received by households. There are no savings, investment, government expenditure and taxes or foreign trade in the economy.

(a) Draw a circular flow of income diagram. Label it at the appropriate place with the value of: (i) income, (ii) output and (iii) expenditure.

(b) How would your answer be different if wages were £100 billion?

which does not come from households. There are three injections.

- Investment is spending by firms on new capital equipment like factories, offices and machinery. It is also spending on stocks (or inventories) of goods which are used in the production process.
- Government spending is spending by central and local government as well as other government agencies.
- Exports is spending by foreigners on goods and services made in the UK.

A WITHDRAWAL or LEAKAGE from the circular flow is spending which does not flow back from households to firms. There are three withdrawals which correspond to the three injections.

- Saving by households is money which is not spent by households. Equally, firms do not spend all of their money

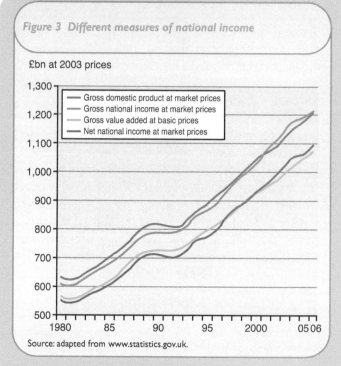

Figure 3 Different measures of national income

£bn at 2003 prices

- Gross domestic product at market prices
- Gross national income at market prices
- Gross value added at basic prices
- Net national income at market prices

Source: adapted from www.statistics.gov.uk.

(a) Briefly explain the difference between each measure of national income shown on the graph.

(b) 'Changes in GDP at market prices broadly reflect changes in other measures of national income over time.' To what extent do the data support this?

on wages and profits but may save some of it.

- Taxes paid to the government take money from both households and firms.
- Imports from abroad are bought both by households and firms. The money paid in taxes then does not flow back round the circular flow.

A circular flow diagram which includes injections and withdrawals is shown in Figure 2.

In equilibrium, when there is no tendency to change, injections must equal withdrawals. When this happens output, expenditure and income flowing round the circular flow remain the same. When injections are greater than withdrawals, national income will rise to reflect the greater spending. Equally, when withdrawals are less than injections, spending will fall. For example, a rise in investment will increase spending in the economy. A rise in saving will reduce spending.

Measures of national income

Economies are not as simple as that shown in Figure 1. Calculating national income in practice involves a complex system of accounts. The standard used in most countries today is based on the System of National Accounts (SNA) first published in 1953 by the United Nations. This system of accounts has subsequently been developed and modified. The system currently in use in the UK is based on the European System of Accounts last modified in 1995 (ESA 1995).

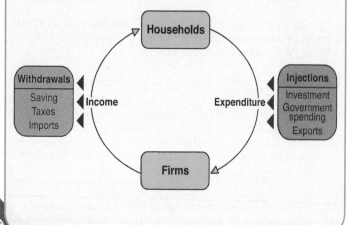

Figure 2 Injections and withdrawals and the circular flow
Investment, government spending and exports are injections into the circular flow. They raise spending. Saving, taxes and imports are withdrawals and reduce spending.

The key measure of national income used in the UK is GROSS DOMESTIC PRODUCT (GDP). This is at market prices, which means it is a measure of national income that includes the value of **indirect taxes** (taxes on expenditure) like VAT. Indirect taxes are not part of the output of the economy, so this measure inflates the actual value of national income. GDP also includes the value of exports and imports and is therefore a more complex measure of national income than in the simple circular flow model described earlier. There are other measures of national income.

Gross value added (GVA) at basic cost This is GDP minus indirect taxes plus subsidies on goods. Indirect taxes minus subsidies is called the basic price adjustment.

Gross national income (GNP) at market prices GROSS NATIONAL INCOME (GNP) is GDP plus income earned abroad on investments and other assets owned overseas minus income paid to foreigners on their investments in the UK.

Net national income at market prices Each year, the existing capital stock or physical wealth of the country depreciates in value because of use. This is like depreciation on a car as it gets older. If individuals run down their savings to finance spending, their actual income must be their spending minus how much they have used from their savings. Similarly with a country, its true value of income is gross (i.e. before depreciation has been taken into account) national income minus depreciation. This is net national income.

GDP at market prices is the main headline figure used for national income because the data to calculate it is most quickly available. When comparing over time and between countries, movements in GDP at market prices are broadly similar to movements in other measures of national income. So it is a good guide to what is happening in the economy and can be used to judge the performance of the economy.

Transfer payments

Not all types of income are included in the final calculation of national income. Some incomes are received without there being any corresponding output in the economy. For instance:
- the government pays National Insurance and social security benefits to individuals, but the recipients produce nothing in return;
- students receive student grants from government, but again produce nothing which can be sold;
- children receive pocket money and allowances from their parents;
- an individual selling a second hand car receives money, but no new car is created.

These incomes, called TRANSFER PAYMENTS, are excluded from final calculations of national income. For instance, government spending in national income is public expenditure **minus** spending on benefits and grants.

Why is national income measured?

National income is a measure of the output, expenditure and income of an economy. National income statistics provide not only figures for these totals but also a breakdown of the totals. They are used in a number of different ways.
- Academic economists use them to test hypotheses and build models of the economy. This increases our understanding of how an economy works.
- Government, firms and economists use the figures to forecast changes in the economy. These forecasts are then used to plan for the future. Government may attempt to direct the economy, making changes in its spending or its taxes at budget time. Groups such as trade unions or the CBI will make their own recommendations about what policies they think the government should pursue.
- They are used to make comparisons over time and between countries. For instance, national income statistics can be used to compare the income of the UK in 1950 and 2007, or they can be used to compare France's income with UK income. Of particular importance when making comparisons over time is the rate of change of national income (i.e. the rate of economic growth).
- They are used to make judgements about economic welfare. Growth in national income, for instance, is usually equated with a rise in living standards.

The accuracy of national income statistics

National income statistics are inaccurate for a number of reasons.

Statistical inaccuracies National income statistics are calculated from millions of different returns to the government. Inevitably mistakes are made: returns

Question 3

Figure 4 Gross national income per capita 2006, US$ at PPPs

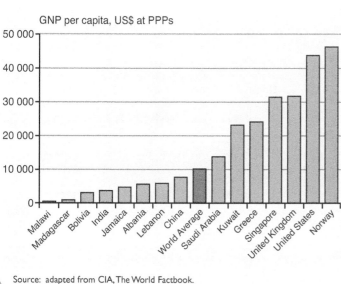

GNP per capita, US$ at PPPs

Source: adapted from CIA, The World Factbook.

(a) What statistics do governments need to collect in order to be able to calculate GNP per capita?
(b) How might (i) an economist and (ii) a government use these statistics?

The national economy **Unit 20**

Question 4

Researchers from the University of Cyprus have estimated the size of the hidden economy in the UK to be at least 10.6 per cent of GDP. They looked at the incomes of the self-employed and compared them to their expenditure using the Family Expenditure Survey compiled by the Office for National Statistics (FES). They compared this with the incomes and expenditure of employed workers such as civil servants who were unlikely to have any hidden income. They estimated that households where the head of the household was a blue collar worker and self-employed reported only 46 per cent of their income to the tax authorities. Households whose self-employed head was in a white-collar occupation on average reported only 61 per cent of their income. Given that reported self-employment income is around 12.3 per cent of GDP, this means that self-employment related black economy activities in the UK amount to 10.6 per cent of GDP.

Workers who are employed may also have undeclared part-time jobs which would increase the size of the black economy. Their ability to avoid tax, however, is limited because their employers deduct their tax from their pay packet through the PAYE (Pay As You Earn) scheme. In 2004, there were 3.6 million self-employed workers and 24.6 million employees.

Source: adapted from 'Estimates of the black economy based on consumer demand approaches', P.Lyssiotou, P.Pashardes and T.Stengos, *Economic Journal*, July 2004 and *Monthly Digest of Statistics*, Office for National Statistics.

(a) Explain why there is an incentive for workers to work in the 'hidden economy'.
(b) UK tax authorities estimate that painters and decorators, cleaners, taxi drivers and gardeners tend to evade tax. Suggest why these workers, rather than teachers or civil servants, are more likely to work in the 'hidden economy'.
(c) The UK government is currently aiming to create a more flexible workforce, with a greater proportion of part-time, casual and self-employed workers. What are the implications of this for the size of the hidden economy?

are inaccurate or simply not completed. The statistics are constantly being revised in the light of fresh evidence. Although revisions tend to become smaller over time, national income statistics are still being revised decades after first publication.

The hidden economy Taxes such as VAT, income tax and National Insurance contributions, and government regulations such as health and safety laws, impose a burden on workers and businesses. Some are tempted to evade taxes and they are then said to work in the BLACK, HIDDEN OR INFORMAL ECONOMY. In the building industry, for instance, it is common for workers to be self-employed and to under-declare or not declare their income at all to the tax authorities. Transactions in the black economy are in the form of cash. Cheques, credit cards, etc. could all be traced by the tax authorities. Tax evasion is the dominant motive for working in the hidden economy but a few also claim welfare benefits to which they are not entitled. The size of the hidden economy is difficult to estimate, but in the UK estimates have varied from 7 to 15 per cent of GDP (i.e. national income statistics underestimate the true size of national income by at least 7 per cent).

Home produced services In the poorest developing countries in the world, GNP per person is valued at less than £100 per year. It would be impossible to survive on this

amount if this were the true value of output in the economy. However, a large part of the production of the agricultural sector is not traded and therefore does not appear in national income statistics. People are engaged in subsistence agriculture, consuming what they produce. Hence the value of national output is in reality much higher. In the UK, the output of the services of housewives and househusbands is equally not recorded. Nor is the large number of DIY jobs completed each year. The more DIY activity, the greater will be the under-recording of national output by national income statistics.

The public sector Valuing the output of much of the public sector is difficult because it is not bought and sold. This problem is circumvented by valuing non-marketed output at its cost of production. For instance, the value of the output of a state school is the cost of running the school. This method of valuation can yield some surprising results. Assume that through more efficient staffing the number of nurses on a hospital ward is reduced from 10 to 8 and the service is improved. National income accounts will still show a fall in output (measured by a drop in the two nurses' incomes). In general, increased productivity in the public sector is shown by a fall in the value of output. It looks as though less is being produced when in fact output remains unchanged.

Comparing national income over time

Comparing the national income of the UK today with national income in the past presents problems.

Prices Prices have tended to increase over time. So an increase in national income over the period does not necessarily indicate that there has been an increase in the number of goods and services produced in the economy. Only if the rate of increase of national income measured in money terms (the nominal rate of

Question 5

Table 2 GDP, prices and population

	Nominal GDP at market prices (£bn)	Index of Retail Prices (2006 = 100)	Population (millions)
1948	12.0	4.0	48.7
1958	23.1	6.2	51.7
1968	43.5	8.4	55.2
1978	168.1	25.2	56.2
1988	470.7	54.0	56.9
1998	865.7	82.2	58.5
2006	1 300.0	100.0	60.6

Source: adapted from *Economic & Labour Market Review*, *Monthly Digest of Statistics*, *Annual Abstract of Statistics*, Office for National Statistics.

(a) For each year, calculate the value of: (i) nominal GDP per head of the population; (ii) real GDP per head of the population at 2006 prices.
(b) To what extent is it possible to judge from the data whether living standards increased over the period 1948-2006?

138

economic growth) has been greater than the increase in prices (the inflation rate) can there be said to have been an increase in output. So when comparing over time, it is essential to consider real and not **nominal** changes in income.

The accuracy and presentation of statistics National income statistics are inaccurate and therefore it is impossible to give a precise figure for the change in income over time. Moreover, the change in real income over time will also be affected by the inflation rate. The inevitable errors made in the calculation of the inflation rate compound the problems of inaccuracy. The method of calculating national income and the rate of inflation can also change over time. It is important to attempt to eliminate the effect of changes in definitions.

Changes in population National income statistics are often used to compare living standards over time. If they are to be used in this way, it is essential to compare national income per capita (i.e. per person). For instance, if the population doubles whilst national income quadruples, people are likely to be nearer twice as well off than four times.

Quality of goods and services The quality of goods may improve over time due to advances in technology but they may also fall in price. For instance, cars today are far better than cars 80 years ago and yet are far cheaper. National income would show this fall in price by a fall in national income, wrongly implying that living standards had fallen. On the other hand, pay in the public sector tends to increase at about 2 per cent per annum faster than the increase in inflation. This is because pay across the economy tends to increase in line with the rate of economic growth rather than the rate of inflation. Increased pay would be reflected in both higher nominal and real national income but there may well be no extra goods or services being produced.

Defence and related expenditures The GDP of the UK was higher during the Second World War than in the 1930s, but much of GDP between 1940 and 1945 was devoted to defence expenditure. It would be difficult to argue that people enjoyed a higher standard of living during the war years than in the pre-war years. So the proportion of national income devoted to defence, or for instance to the police, must be taken into account when considering the standard of living of the population.

Consumption and investment It is possible to increase standards of living today by reducing investment and increasing consumption. However, reducing investment is likely to reduce standards of living from what they might otherwise have been in the future. As with defence, the proportion of national income being devoted to investment will affect the standard of living of the population both now and in the future.

Externalities National income statistics take no account of **externalities** produced by the economy. National income statistics may show that national income has doubled roughly every 25 years since 1945. However, if the value of externalities has more than doubled over that time period, then the rate of growth of the standard of living has less than doubled.

Income distribution When comparing national income over time, it is important to remember that an increased national income for the economy as a whole may not mean that individuals have seen their income increase. Income distribution is likely to change over time, which may or may not lead to a more desirable state of affairs.

Comparing national income between countries

Comparing national income between economies is fraught with difficulties too. Income distributions may be different. Populations will be different and therefore it is important to compare per capita income figures. National income accounts will have varying degrees of inaccuracy, caused, for instance, by different sizes of the informal economy in each country. National income accounting conventions will differ.

There is also the problem of what rate of exchange to use when comparing one country's national income with anothers'. The day to day market exchange rate can bear little relation to relative prices in different countries. So prices in some countries, like Switzerland or West Germany, can be much higher at official exchange rates than in France or Italy. Therefore if national income statistics are to be used to compare living standards between countries it is important to use an exchange rate which compares the cost of living in each country. These exchange rates are known as PURCHASING POWER PARITIES. For instance, if a typical basket of goods costs 2 Euros in France and £1 in the UK, then national income should be converted at an exchange rate of 2 Euros to the £1, even if the market exchange rate gives a very different figure.

Even this is not accurate enough. In some countries, consumers have to purchase goods which in others are free. For instance, Sweden spends a greater proportion of its national income than Italy on fuel for heating because of its colder climate. However, this extra expenditure does not give the Swedes a higher standard of living. Again, countries are different geographically and one country might have higher transport costs per unit of output than another because of congestion or having to transport goods long distances. In practice, it is almost impossible to adjust national income figures for these sorts of differences.

Income and wealth

National income tends to be correlated with national wealth. Wealth is a **stock** of assets which produce a **flow** of income over time. Countries with high levels of wealth, which includes both human wealth and non-human wealth, tend to produce higher levels of income than countries with low levels of wealth. The wealthiest nation in the world, the USA, also has the highest national income. A poor country like Tanzania with relatively little wealth also has a low national income. Wealth can be mismanaged and used poorly. So there is not a perfect correlation between wealth and income.

Key terms

Circular flow of income - a model of the economy which shows the flow of goods, services and factors and their payments around the economy.

Closed economy - an economy where there is no foreign trade.

Gross domestic product (GDP) and gross national product (GNP) - measures of national income which exclude and include respectively net income from investments abroad, but do not include an allowance for depreciation of the nation's capital stock.

Hidden, black or informal economy - economic activity where trade and exchange take place, but which goes unreported to the tax authorities and those collecting national income statistics. Workers in the hidden economy are usually motivated by the desire to evade paying taxes.

Injections - in the circular flow of income, spending which is not generated by households including investment, government spending and exports.

National income - the value of the output, expenditure or income of an economy over a period of time.

Open economy - an economy where there is trade with other countries.

Purchasing power parities - an exchange rate of one currency for another which compares how much a typical basket of goods in one country costs compared to that of another country.

Transfer payments - income for which there is no corresponding output, such as unemployment benefits or pension payments.

Wealth - a stock of assets which can be used to generate a flow of production or income. For example, physical wealth such as factories and machines is used to make goods and services.

Withdrawals or leakages - in the circular flow of income, spending by households which does not flow back to domestic firms. It includes savings, taxes and imports.

Applied economics

The UK and the USA

The UK has a lower GDP than the USA. In 2006, US GDP was $13 060 billion compared to £1300 billion for the UK. At a market exchange rate of $1.8429 to the pound, this meant that the US economy produced 5.5 times as much output as that of the UK.

Crude national income statistics like these have a story to tell when making inter-country comparisons but they are only a small part of the story. For a start, populations may be vastly different. The population of the USA at 301.2 million is five times the size of that of the UK. A better comparison might therefore be GDP per capita. US GDP per capita in 2006 was $43 800 (or £23 800 at market exchange rates) compared to $39 400 (or £21 380 at market exchange rates) for the UK. So the USA produces more than the UK per person. The USA also has a lower cost of living. So the gap between the two countries is larger when compared using purchasing power parity exchange rates. At PPP rates expressed in US dollars, US GDP per capita is $43 800 but UK GDP per capita is only $31 800. Measured at purchasing power rates, the average US citizen has an income which is 38 per cent higher than that of the average UK citizen.

In making comparisons about living standards, national income is only one among many factors to be taken into account. One other factor is the distribution of income. Table 3 shows that income in the UK is slightly more evenly distributed than in the USA. In the UK, the poorest 20 per cent enjoyed 6.1 per cent of the

national cake compared to 5.4 per cent in the USA. At the other end of the income scale, the top 20 per cent in the UK received 44 per cent of the national cake compared to 45.8 per cent in the USA.

Another group of factors which are important relates to how national income is distributed between different types of expenditure. In 2006, spending by the state accounted for 45.1 per cent of GDP compared to 36.4 per cent in the USA. One reason for this is spending on healthcare. In the UK, healthcare is mostly provided by the state. In the USA, healthcare is mostly provided by the private sector. In the UK, there is universal access to free health care. In the USA, only the retired and those on low incomes have access to free health care, accounting for around 27 per cent of the population. Approximately 57 per cent of the population are covered by health insurance schemes through their employer. 16 per cent of the population, or 47 million people, are uninsured and have to fund all medical bills themselves. Despite the fact that 16 per cent of the population are not covered, the USA has the world's highest spending on health care as a proportion of GDP. In 2006, it was 15.2 per cent compared to 8.0 per cent for the UK. Despite spending almost twice as much on healthcare as the UK, the USA performs worse on a variety of medical statistics than the UK. For example, life expectancy is 77.5 years in the USA but 79.5 years in the UK. Infant mortality rates are 6 per thousand in the USA but only 5 per thousand in the UK.

Healthcare is one reason why public spending differs between the UK and the USA. In general, welfare spending is lower in the USA as a proportion of GDP. Individuals are expected to be less dependent on the state. One area where government spending is higher in the USA than the UK is defence. In 2005, defence expenditure was 4.1 per cent of GDP in the USA compared to 2.6 per cent in the UK. In terms of quality of life, there are differences of opinion about whether higher defence spending in the USA is increasing quality of life compared to the UK or reducing it.

There is a wide range of other quality of life measures that could be taken into consideration, as Table 4 shows. The UK has a high population density with most of its population crammed into urban centres with limited space. The USA has a low population density. Houses and housing plots tend to be much larger in the USA. Equally the cost of housing tends to be lower. Crime rates are higher in the USA. The homicide rate is nearly three times as high in the USA as in the UK.

Overall, the USA is a good place to live for those who have a good job and a good income. The safety net for the poor is weaker than in the UK. So low income workers, the unemployed and the retired may be better off in the UK.

Table 3 *Income distribution*

| | Percentage share of income | | | | |
	Lowest 20%	Next 20%	Middle 20%	Next 20%	Highest 20%
USA (2000)	5.4	10.7	15.7	22.4	45.8
UK (1999)	6.1	11.4	16.0	22.5	44.0

Source: adapted from World Bank, *World Development Indicators*.

Table 4 *Standard of living measures, 2006*

	Average life expectancy	Infant mortality rates	Defence spending	Population density	Homicide rate	Carbon dioxide emissions per capita
	years	per thousand	% of GDP	People per sq km 2005	Per 100 000 inhabitants	metric tonnes
USA	77.5	6	4.1	32	5.9	20.2
UK	79.5	5	2.3	249	2.0	9.2

Source: adapted from World Bank, *World Development Report*; en.wikipedia.org

DataQuestion — Living standards

Table 5 National income and population indicators 2005

	PPP estimates of gross national income per capita ($)	Population millions	Gross national income ($million)	Gross national income per capita ($)	Population, % of population aged 0-14
Tanzania	730	38	12.7	340	43
Kenya	1 170	34	18.0	530	43
Pakistan	2 350	156	107.3	690	38
Indonesia	3 720	221	282.2	1 280	28
China	6 600	1 305	2 263.8	1 740	21
Colombia	7 420	46	104.5	2 290	31
Russian Federation	10 640	143	639.1	4 460	15
Czech Republic	20 140	10	109.2	10 710	15
New Zealand	23 030	4	106.7	25 960	21
UK	32 690	60	2 263.7	37 600	18
USA	41 950	296	12 969.6	43 740	21

Table 6 Health indicators

	Life expectancy at birth, years, 2005	Under-five mortality rate, per thousand of the population 2005	Prevalence of child malnutrition, % of children under 5 underweight 2005	Access to safe water, % of population 2000	Access to sanitation facilities, % of urban population 2000
Tanzania	46.3	122.0	21.8	58	53
Kenya	49.0	120.0	21.2	57	47
Pakistan	64.9	99.0	-	89	89
Indonesia	67.8	28.0	24.6	76	71
China	70.3	27.0	10.0	76	66
Colombia	72.8	21.4	7.0	92	96
Russian Federation	65.5	17.5	-	96	93
Czech Republic	75.0	5.0	0.0	100	99
New Zealand	79.6	6.0	0.0	100	100
UK	78.9	6.0	0.0	100	100
USA	77.0	7.0	0.0	100	100

Table 7 Education

	Adult illiteracy, % of people aged 15 and older, 2000-04	School enrolment, % gross, 2005 (Primary)	School enrolment, % gross, 2005 (Secondary)	Primary completion rate, total (% of relevant age group)	Ratio of girls to boys in primary and secondary education, %
Tanzania	31	110.5	-	71.6	-
Kenya	26	112.2	48.8	95.0	95.8
Pakistan	50	87.3	26.9	63.2	75.4
Indonesia	10	117.3	63.1	101.1	97.2
China	9	112.8	74.3	-	99.4
Columbia	7	112.0	78.1	96.9	103.6
Russian Federation	1	128.7	91.9	-	98.9
Czech Republic	-	101.2	95.8	102.3	100.5
New Zealand	-	102.2	122.7	-	104.1
UK	-	106.7	105.1	100.0	101.5
USA	-	99.0	94.7	100.0	100.3

Table 8 Selected indicators

	Paved roads, % of total, 2000	Fixed line and mobile phone subscribers (per 1 000 people), 2005	Internet users (per 1 000 people), 2005	Electric power consumption (kwh per capita), 2000	High-technology exports (% of manufactured 2005	Military expenditure (% of GDP), 2005 exports),
Tanzania	-	8.4	1.2	58.5	1.2	1.0
Kenya	12.1	142.9	32.4	111.9	3.9	1.4
Pakistan	56.0	115.9	67.4	373.5	1.6	3.3
Indonesia	57.1	270.6	72.5	400.4	16.3	0.9
China	82.5	570.2	85.1	992.7	30.6	2.0
Colombia	-	657.0	105.4	803.7	4.9	3.7
Russian Federation	-	1 118.7	152.3	5 208.8	8.1	3.7
Czech Republic	100.0	1 465.0	269.5	5 693.7	8.1	1.8
New Zealand	62.8	1 283.0	671.9	8 911.8	14.2	1.0
UK	100.0	1 615.5	473.5	6 031.0	28.0	2.6
USA	-	1 070.0	439.4	13 667.4	31.8	4.1

Source: adapted from World Bank, *World Development Report*; World Bank, *Country Profiles*.

1. You have been asked to write an article for a magazine of no more than 1 000 words. The editor wants you to compare the standard of living of 11 countries using national income statistics. Using the data provided, in your article: (a) make such a comparison; (b) discuss the limitations of using national income statistics to compare living standards between countries, giving examples of how different economic indicators might provide an additional or perhaps even better basis for making a comparison.

Summary

1. Consumption can be divided into spending on durable goods and non-durable goods.
2. The consumption function shows the relationship between consumption and its determinants, the main one being income.
3. Increases in wealth will lead to an increase in consumption.
4. Expected inflation tends to lead to a rise in saving and a fall in consumption. The effect of households attempting to restore the real value of their stock of savings more than outweighs the effect of households bringing forward their purchases of goods.
5. The rate of interest and the availability of credit particularly affect the consumption of durable goods.
6. A change in the structure of the population will affect both consumption and saving. The greater the proportion of adults aged 35-60 in the population, the higher is likely to be the level of saving.
7. Keynesians hypothesise that consumption is a stable function of current disposable income in the short run.
8. The life cycle hypothesis and the permanent income hypothesis both emphasise that consumption is a stable function of income only in the very long run. In the short run, other factors such as the rate of interest and wealth can have a significant impact upon consumption and savings.

Defining consumption and saving

CONSUMPTION in economics is spending on consumer goods and services over a period of time. Examples are spending on chocolate, hire of videos or buying a car. Consumption can be broken down into a number of different categories. One way of classifying consumption is to distinguish between spending on **goods** and spending on **services**. Another way is to distinguish between spending on DURABLE GOODS and NON-DURABLE GOODS. Durable goods are goods which, although bought at a point in time, continue to provide a stream of services over a period of time. A car, for instance, should last at least 6 years. A television set might last 10 years. Non-durable goods are goods and services which are used up immediately or over a short period of time, like an ice-cream or a packet of soap powder.

SAVING is what is not spent out of income. For instance, if a worker takes home £1 000 in her wage packet at the end of the month, but only spends £900, then £100 must have been saved. The saving might take the form of increasing the stock of cash, or an increase in money in a bank or building society account, or it might take the form of stocks or shares. Income in this case is DISPOSABLE INCOME, income including state benefits such as child benefit and interest on, say, building society shares, but after deductions of income tax and National Insurance contributions.

Consumption and income

There is a number of factors which determine how much a household consumes. The relationship between consumption and these factors is called the CONSUMPTION FUNCTION. The most important determinant of consumption is disposable income. Other factors, discussed in sections below, are far less important but can bring about small but significant changes in the relationship between consumption and income.

Assume that one year a household has an income of £1 000 per month. The next year, due to salary increases, this rises to £1 200 per month. Economic theory predicts that the consumption of the household will rise.

How much it will rise can be measured by the MARGINAL PROPENSITY TO CONSUME (MPC), the proportion of a change in income that is spent:

$$\text{MPC} = \frac{\text{Change in consumption}}{\text{Change in income}} = \frac{\Delta C}{\Delta Y}$$

where Y is income, C is consumption and Δ is 'change in'. If the £200 rise in income leads to a £150 rise in consumption, then the marginal propensity to consume would be 0.75 (£150 ÷ £200).

For the economy as a whole, the marginal propensity to consume is likely to be positive (i.e. greater than zero) but less than 1. Any rise in income will lead to more spending but also some saving too. For individuals, the marginal propensity to consume could be more than 1 if money was borrowed to finance spending higher than income.

The AVERAGE PROPENSITY TO CONSUME (or APC) measures the average amount spent on consumption out of total income. For instance, if total disposable income in an economy were £100 billion and consumption were £90 billion, then the average propensity to consume would be 0.9. The formula for the APC is:

$$\text{APC} = \frac{\text{Consumption}}{\text{Income}} = \frac{C}{Y}$$

Question 1

Table 1 *Real consumption and household disposable income*

		£bn at 2003 prices
	Consumption	Disposable income
1965	260.6	268.8
1966	265.2	275.0
1975	328.8	347.6
1976	330.2	346.3
1985	402.2	425.5
1986	427.8	443.1
1995	541.1	588.5
1996	561.8	602.4
2005	760.2	775.1
2006	776.0	783.6

Source: adapted from *Economic & Labour Market Trends*, Office for National Statistics.

(a) Using the data, explain the relationship between consumption and disposable income.
(b) (i) Calculate the MPC and the APC for 1966, 1976, 1986, 1996 and 2006.
  (ii) What happened to saving during these years?

Question 2

The number of mortgages being approved fell to its lowest level for more than nine years in November, sending out a strong signal that house prices are set for further falls. The number of loans is an important indicator for consumer spending. Most economists regard a slowdown in consumer spending as a risk to the UK economy over the next year.

Higher house prices lead directly to more consumer spending because people feel wealthier. But Ben Broadbent at Goldman Sachs, the investment bank, argues that consumer spending is more likely to be affected by a slowdown in house turnover than a decline in house prices. He said: 'When you move house, you have to buy a lot of stuff, such as carpets, curtains and fridges. There is already a trend towards slower retail sales and we expect data over the next weeks that will include the Christmas period to reflect this more strongly.'

Consumer spending is also linked to mortgage equity release, when housebuyers take out a larger mortgage than they need to buy a house and then spend the difference. Equally, existing homeowners may remortgage their house, taking on a bigger mortgage and spending the balance. Mortgage equity withdrawal totalled £12.4bn between July and September, down from £13.0bn in the previous quarter.

Source: adapted from the *Financial Times*, 5.1.2005.

Explain three ways in which the housing market can affect consumption levels.

In a rich industrialised economy, the APC is likely to be less than 1 because consumers will also save part of their earnings.

Wealth

The wealth of a household is made up of two parts. **Physical wealth** is made up of items such as houses, cars and furniture. **Monetary wealth** is comprised of items such as cash, money in the bank and building societies, stocks and shares, assurance policies and pension rights.

If the wealth of a household increases, consumption will increase. This is known as the WEALTH EFFECT. There are two important ways in which the wealth of households can change over a short time period.
- A change in the price of houses. If the real price of houses increases considerably over a period of time, as happened in the UK from the mid-1990s to 2007, then households feel able to increase their spending. They do this mainly by borrowing more money secured against the value of their house.
- A change in the value of stocks and shares. Households react to an increase in the real value of a household's portfolio of securities by selling part of the portfolio and spending the proceeds. The value of stocks and shares is determined by many factors. One of these is the rate of interest. If the rate of interest falls, then the value of stocks will rise. So consumption should be stimulated through the wealth effect by a fall in the rate of interest.

Inflation

Inflation, a rise in the general level of prices, has two effects on consumption. First, if households expect prices to be higher in the future they will be tempted to bring forward their purchases. For instance, if households know that the price of cars will go up by 10 per cent the next month, they will attempt to buy their cars now. So expectations of inflation increase consumption and reduce saving.

However, this can be outweighed by the effect of inflation on wealth. Rising inflation tends to erode the real value of money wealth. Households react to this by attempting to restore the real value of their wealth (i.e. they save more). This reduces consumption.

Overall, rising inflation in the UK tends to reduce consumption. The negative effect on consumption caused by the erosion of real wealth more than offsets the positive effect on consumption caused by the bringing forward of purchases.

The rate of interest

Households rarely finance expenditure on **non-durables** such as food or entertainment by borrowing money. However, much of the money to buy **durables** such as cars, furniture, kitchen equipment and hi-fi equipment comes from credit finance. An increase in the rate of interest increases the monthly repayments on these goods. This means that, effectively, the price of the goods has increased. Households react to this by reducing their demand for durables and thus cutting their consumption.

Many households also have borrowed money to buy their houses. Increased interest rates lead to increased mortgage repayments. Again, this will directly cut spending on other items and perhaps, more importantly, discourage households from borrowing more money to finance purchases of consumer durables.

It has already been explained above that a rise in the rate of interest reduces the value of stocks on stock markets and thus reduces the value of household wealth. This in turn leads to a fall in consumption.

Question 3

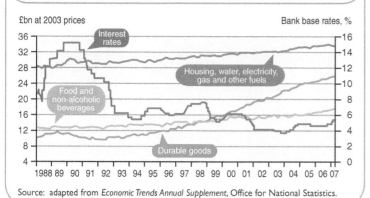

Figure 1 *Interest rates and selected categories of consumption expenditure*

£bn at 2003 prices   Bank base rates, %

Source: adapted from *Economic Trends Annual Supplement*, Office for National Statistics.

(a) Describe the trends shown in Figure 1.
(b) Explain, using examples from the data, the extent to which interest rates affect consumption.

The availability of credit

The rate of interest determines the price of credit. However, the price of credit is not the only determinant of how much households borrow. Governments in the past have often imposed restrictions on the availability of credit. For instance, they have imposed maximum repayment periods and minimum deposits. Before the deregulation of the mortgage market in the early 1980s in the UK, building societies rationed mortgages. They often operated queueing systems and imposed restrictive limits on the sums that could be borrowed. When these restrictions are abolished, households increase their level of debt and spend the proceeds. Making credit more widely available will increase consumption.

Expectations

Expectations of increases in prices tend to make households bring forward their purchases and thus increase consumption. Expectations of large increases in real incomes will also tend to encourage households to increase spending now by borrowing more. So when the economy is booming, autonomous consumption tends to increase. On the other hand, if households expect economic conditions to become harsher, they will reduce their consumption now. For instance, they might expect an increase in unemployment rates, a rise in taxes or a fall in real wages.

The composition of households

Young people and old people tend to spend a higher proportion of their income than those in middle age. Young people tend to spend all their income and move into debt to finance the setting up of their homes and the bringing up of children. In middle age, the cost of homemaking declines as a proportion of income. With more income available, households often choose to build up their stock of savings in preparation for retirement. When they retire, they will run down their stock of savings to

supplement their pensions. So if there is a change in the age composition of households in the economy, there could well be a change in consumption and savings. The more young and old the households, the greater will tend to be the level of consumption.

The determinants of saving

Factors which affect consumption also by definition must affect saving (remember, saving is defined as that part of disposable income which is not consumed). The SAVINGS FUNCTION therefore links income, wealth, inflation, the rate of interest, expectations and the age profile of the population with the level of saving. However, because a typical AVERAGE PROPENSITY TO SAVE (the APS - the ratio of total saving to total income calculated by Saving ÷ Income) is 0.05 to 0.2 in Western European countries, income is far less important in determining saving than it is in determining consumption. Factors other than income are therefore relatively more important. This explains why, in the UK, for instance, the APS has varied from 0.12 to 0.04 between the 1980s and mid-2000s. The MARGINAL PROPENSITY TO SAVE (the proportion that is saved out of a change in income calculated by Change in saving ÷ Change in income) is equally unstable for these reasons.

Question 4

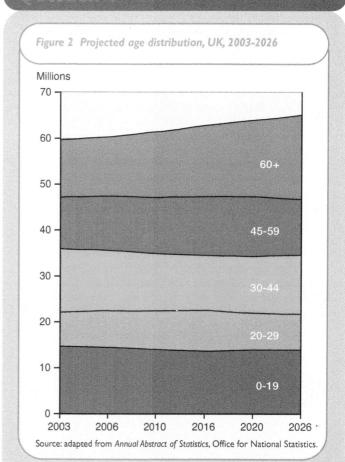

Figure 2 *Projected age distribution, UK, 2003-2026*

Millions

Source: adapted from *Annual Abstract of Statistics*, Office for National Statistics.

What effects do you think that the changing structure of the population to 2026 is likely to have on consumption and saving?

Confusion sometimes arises between 'saving' and 'savings'. Saving is a **flow** concept which takes place over a period of time. Saving is added to a **stock** of savings fixed at a point in time. A household's stock of savings is the accumulation of past savings. For instance, you might have £100 in the bank. This is your stock of savings. You might then get a job over Christmas and save £20 from that. Your saving over Christmas is £20. Your stock of savings before Christmas was £100 but afterwards it was £120. The savings function explains the relationship between the flow of savings and its determinants. It attempts to explain why you saved £20 over Christmas. It does not explain why you have £100 in the bank already.

The Keynesian consumption function

John Maynard Keynes was one of the greatest economists working in the first half of the twentieth century. He was the founder of modern macroeconomics, the subject of much of the rest of this book. It was he who first popularised the idea that consumption was linked to income. 'Keynesian' means that an idea is linked to an idea first put forward by Keynes. Keynesian economists are economists who work within the framework first established by Keynes.

The Keynesian consumption function lays stress upon the relationship between planned current consumption and current disposable income. Other factors, particularly the availability of credit, can have an important impact upon expenditure on consumer durables. However, in the short term at least, income is the most significant factor determining the level of consumption. Changes in wealth and changes in the rate of interest (the two can be interrelated as argued above) have little impact upon short term consumption. This means that the consumption function is relatively stable. It is not subject to frequent large scale shifts.

Keynes was worried that increasing prosperity would lead to a stagnant economy. As households became better off, they would spend less and less of their increases in income. Eventually their demand for consumer goods would be completely satiated and without increases in spending, there could be no more increases in income.

The evidence of the past 70 years has proved Keynes wrong. There does not seem to be any indication that households are reducing their MPCs as income increases. However, this view has also led Keynesians to argue that higher income earners have a lower MPC (and therefore save a higher proportion of their income) than low income earners. Therefore, redistributing income from the poor to the rich will lower total consumption. The reverse, taking from the rich to give to the poor, will increase total consumption. However, as we shall now see, this too seems to be contradicted not only by the evidence but also by alternative theories of the consumption function.

The life cycle hypothesis

Franco Modigliani and Albert Ando suggested that current consumption is not based upon current income. Rather, households form a view about their likely income over the whole of their lifetimes and base their current spending decisions upon that. For instance, professional workers at the start of their careers in their early 20s may earn as much as manual workers of the same age. But the APC of professional workers is likely to be higher. This is because professional workers expect to earn more in the future and are prepared to

borrow more now to finance consumption. A professional worker will expect, for instance, to buy rather than rent a house. The mortgage she takes out is likely to be at the top end of what banks or building societies will lend. The manual worker, on the other hand, knowing that his earnings are unlikely to increase substantially in the future, will be more cautious. He may be deterred from buying his own home and, if he does, will take out a small rather than large mortgage.

During middle age, households tend to be net savers. They are paying off loans accumulated when they were younger and saving for retirement. During retirement they spend more than they earn, running down their savings.

The permanent income hypothesis

Developed by Milton Friedman, this in many ways develops the insights of the life cycle hypothesis. Friedman argued that households base their spending decisions not on current income but on their PERMANENT INCOME. Broadly speaking, permanent income is average income over a lifetime. Average income over a lifetime can be influenced by a number of factors.

- An increase in wealth will increase the ability of households to spend money (i.e. it will increase their permanent income). Hence a rise in wealth will increase actual consumption over a lifetime.
- An increase in interest rates tends to lower both stock and share prices. This leads to a fall in wealth, a fall in permanent income and a fall in current consumption.
- An increase in interest rates also leads to future incomes being less valuable. One way of explaining this is to remember that a sum of money available in the future is worth less than the same sum available today. Another way is to consider borrowing. If interest rates rise, households will need either to earn more money or cut back on their spending in the future to pay back their loans. Therefore, the real value of their future income (i.e. their permanent income) falls if interest rates rise.
- Unexpected rises in wages will lead to an increase in permanent income.

Friedman argued that the long run APC from permanent income was 1. Households spend all their income over their lifetimes (indeed, Friedman defined permanent income as the income a household could spend without changing its wealth over a lifetime). Hence, the long run APC and the MPC are stable.

In the short run, however, wealth and interest rates change. Measured income also changes and much of this change is unexpected. Income which households receive but did not expect to earn is called transitory income. Initially, transitory income will be saved, as households decide what to do with the money. Then it is incorporated into permanent income. The MPC of the household will depend upon the nature of the extra income. If the extra income is, for instance, a permanent pay rise, the household is likely to spend most of the money. If, however, it is a temporary rise in income, like a £10 000 win on the lottery, most of it will be saved and then gradually spent over a much longer period of time. Because the proportion of transitory income to current income changes from month to month, the propensity to consume from current income will vary too. So in the short run, the APC and the MPC are not constant. This contradicts the Keynesian hypothesis that current consumption is a stable function of current income.

Key terms

Average propensity to consume - the proportion of total income spent. It is calculated by C ÷ Y.
Average propensity to save - the proportion of a total income which is saved. It is calculated by S ÷ Y.
Consumption - total expenditure by households on goods and services over a period of time.
Consumption function - the relationship between the consumption of households and the factors which determine it.
Disposable income - household income over a period of time including state benefits, less direct taxes.
Durable goods - goods which are consumed over a long period of time, such as a television set or a car.
Marginal propensity to consume - the proportion of a change in income which is spent. It is calculated by ΔC ÷ ΔY.

Marginal propensity to save - the proportion of a change in income which is saved. It is calculated by ΔS ÷ ΔY.
Non-durable goods - goods which are consumed almost immediately like an ice-cream or a packet of washing powder.
Permanent income - the income a household could spend over its lifetime without reducing the value of its assets. This approximates to the average income of a household over its lifetime.
Savings function - the relationship between the saving of households and the factors which determine it.
Saving (personal) - the portion of households' disposable income which is not spent over a period of time.
Wealth effect - the change in consumption following a change in wealth.

Applied economics

Consumption in the UK

The composition of consumption expenditure

Total real consumption roughly trebled between 1964 and 2007. However, as Figure 3 shows, there were significant differences in the rate of growth of the components of expenditure. Real spending on food and non-alcoholic drinks, for instance, only increased by approximately 60 per cent whilst spending on communication, which includes mobile phones, increased 12 fold. Real expenditure on alcoholic drink and tobacco remained constant whilst spending on restaurants and hotels increased 150 per cent. These changes partly reflect a number of different factors. As incomes increase, how consumers choose to spend the extra they earn differs from how they spend their existing income. So they choose not to spend very much extra on food, but quite a lot more on recreation and culture, which is reflected in the different income elasticities of demand for products. Some products, such as mobile phones, were not available in 1965. Increased spending reflects a desire to buy into these new technologies. Some changes also reflect changes prices. The price of clothing and footwear has fallen considerably over the past 30 years with globalisation of production. This has arguably led to a significant rise in total spending on clothing and footwear.

Consumption and income

Keynesian theory suggests that income is a major determinant of consumption. The evidence in Figure 4 would tend to support this theory. Over the period 1955 to 2006, real households' disposable income rose 4.1

times whilst real consumers' expenditure increased by 3.8 times. Keynesian theory would also suggest that the average propensity to consume declines as incomes rise over time. Figure 5 would tend not to support this. The average APC in the 1960s was 0.94. It fell slightly in the 1970s and 1980s, stabilised in the 1990s but then rose again between 2000-2006. Note that in Figure 6 income used to calculate the APC is defined as households' disposable income **plus** an adjustment for the net equity of households in pension funds. It is the accounting convention used by the Office for National Statistics (ONS). This produces a slightly lower value of the APC than if only households' disposable income were included. There is considerable fluctuation of the APC, however, around these long term averages. For instance, there was a sharp rise in the APC between 1986 and 1988 during the Lawson boom, and between 1997 and 2004 in the prolonged upswing experienced at the time, whilst the APC fell to less than 0.9 in the two major recessions of 1980-82 and 1990-92. This would suggest that other factors can be important in determining consumption apart from income.

Other determinants of consumption

Economists in the 1960s and early 1970s were fairly confident that the relationship between consumption and income was highly stable. However, from the mid-1970s a number of key variables which can affect consumption were subject to large changes and this had a small but significant effect on the average propensity to consume.

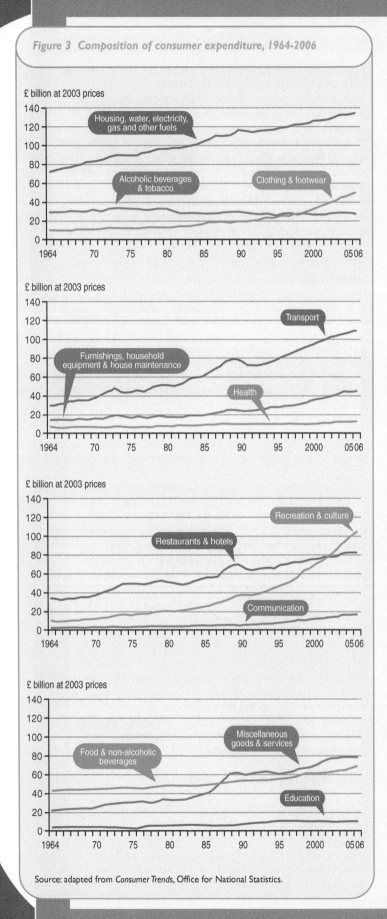

Figure 3 Composition of consumer expenditure, 1964-2006

Source: adapted from *Consumer Trends*, Office for National Statistics.

Wealth A sharp appreciation in household wealth was a key feature of most of the 1980s. Figure 6 shows that share prices rose considerably between 1980 and 1987. This increase in stock market values was a key element in persuading households to increase their spending in 1986 and 1987. In October 1987, on 'Black Monday', world stock markets crashed and 25 per cent of the value of shares on the London Stock Exchange was wiped out. This helped knock consumer confidence and the subsequent poor performance of share prices was one factor which reduced the average propensity to consume in the late 1980s and early 1990s. Equally, UK stock markets put in a strong performance in the second half of the 1990s, fuelled towards the end by sharp rises in shares of companies related to the Internet. This contributed to strong growth in consumer spending whilst the fall in share prices following the bursting of the 'dot-com' bubble helped subdue consumer spending. The revival in share prices from 2003 also helped buoy up consumer demand.

Many households do not own shares but the majority own their home. Again, in the mid-1980s the boom in house prices shown in Figure 7 was a major determinant of increased consumer spending during the Lawson boom. Equally, the fall in house prices in the early 1990s

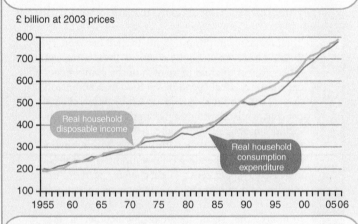

Figure 4 Consumption and disposable income, 1955-2006

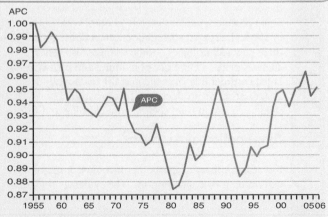

Figure 5 The average propensity to consume (APC)

Source: adapted from *Economic & Labour Market Review*, Office for National Statistics.

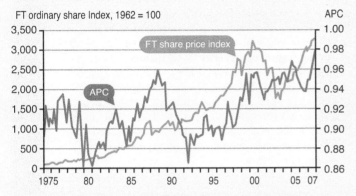

Figure 6 *London Stock Market prices (FT Ordinary Share Index, 1962=100) and the average propensity to consume*

Source: adapted from Office for National Statistics, *Economic & Labour Market Review*, *Financial Statistics*.

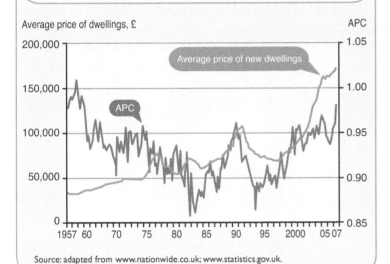

Figure 7 *Average house prices, £ at 2006 prices, and the average propensity to consume*

Source: adapted from www.nationwide.co.uk; www.statistics.gov.uk.

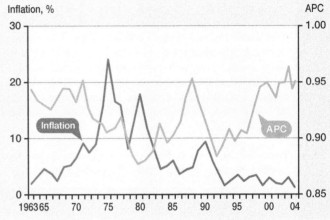

Figure 8 *Inflation (RPI, % change year on year) and the average propensity to consume*

Source: adapted from *Economic & Labour Market Review*, Office for National Statistics.

relatively low interest rates helped fuel a consumer spending boom. The raising of bank base rates to 15 per cent in 1988 and the period of high interest rates which followed was the key factor which helped reduce growth in consumer spending and pushed the economy into recession. The reduction of interest rates from 1992 onwards then helped the recovery during the rest of the 1990s. The changes in the rate of interest between 1995 and 2004 were relatively small compared to the changes in the 1980s. A rise in interest rates of 2 per cent does not have the same impact as a rise in interest rates of, say, 8 per cent seen during the 1980s. Therefore, the rises and falls in interest rates from 1995 onwards had an impact on consumer spending but these were relatively small. Certainly, they were not large enough to bring about reductions in total consumer spending.

Interest rates affect consumption in a number of ways. Higher interest rates makes borrowing more expensive and in particular hits spending on consumer durables. It also makes it more expensive to buy a house using a mortgage. The rise in interest rates in the late 1980s

played an important role in dampening consumption. The stagnation in house prices which followed until 1996 helped break growth in consumer spending. Then, with the subsequent boom in house prices there was strong growth in consumer spending.

Inflation Periods of high inflation tend to be marked by a falling APC and vice versa. Following the rise in inflation during the late 1980s, consumers reacted by increasing their savings and reducing the average propensity to consume. They wanted to rebuild the real value of their wealth. Equally, the low inflation of the mid-1990s to 2007 contributed to a rise in spending out of income. The relationship between inflation and consumption is shown in Figure 8.

The rate of interest The rate of interest has a significant impact on spending, particularly on items typically bought on credit such as consumer durables. Figure 9 shows that during the Lawson boom of 1986-88,

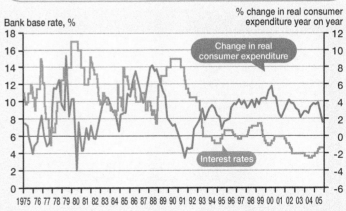

Figure 9 *Interest rates and the change in real consumer expenditure*

Source: adapted from Office for National Statistics, *Economic & Labour Market Review*.

helped bring about a crash in the housing market, with house prices falling after 1989 in many areas of the country. This affected consumer confidence and reduced willingness to take on further debt. For most of the 1990s, consumers remained cautious about borrowing despite low interest rates. However, the late 1990s saw a sharp growth in spending as consumers became more confident that interest rates would not be driven sharply higher. The early 2000s saw a considerable increase in consumer debt, both to buy houses and finance purchase of goods.

Expectations Expectations can be a crucial determinant of consumption. In the 1980s, the Lawson boom was fuelled by expectations that the economy would grow at fast rates for the foreseeable future. There was much talk at the time about Britain's 'economic miracle'. Unfortunately, the boom was unsustainable. In the subsequent recession, consumers became very pessimistic about the future, particularly since unemployment climbed from 1.5 million in 1989 to 3 million in 1993. In the subsequent recovery, consumers remained cautious about taking on large amounts of new debt, fearing that a recession would recur. It was only in the late 1990s that consumer confidence was restored and this helped increase the rate of growth of consumer spending until 2004.

DataQuestion — The determinants of saving

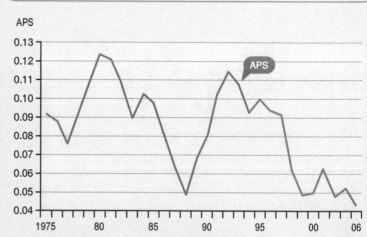

Figure 10 *The average propensity to save (APS), 1975-2006*

Source: adapted from *Economic & Labour Market Review*, Office for National Statistics.

You have been asked to write a report for a bank on the determinants of saving in the economy. Use the data here and in the Applied Economics section to construct your report.

Briefly outline trends in saving and the APS since 1975.
Briefly outline the main factors which affect saving in the economy.
Produce a case study of the period 1975 to 2006 to illustrate your discussion.

22 Investment

Summary

1. Investment is the purchase of capital goods which are then used to create other goods and services. This differs from saving, which is the creation of financial obligations.
2. Marginal efficiency of capital theory suggests that investment is inversely related to the price of capital - the rate of interest.
3. Factors which shift the MEC or investment demand schedule include changes in the cost of capital goods, technological change, and changes in expectations or animal spirits.
4. The accelerator theory suggests that investment varies with the rate of change in income.
5. The past and current profitability of industry too may be more important than future rates of return on capital in determining current investment.

A definition of investment

Economists use the word INVESTMENT in a very precise way. Investment is the addition to the **capital stock** of the economy - factories, machines, offices and stocks of materials, used to produce other goods and services.

In everyday language, 'investment' and 'saving' are often used to mean the same thing. For instance, we talk about 'investing in the building society' or 'investing in shares'. For an economist, these two would be examples of saving. For an economist, investment only takes place if real products are created. To give two more examples:

● putting money into a bank account would be saving; the bank buying a computer to handle your account would be investment;

● buying shares in a new company would be saving; buying new machinery to set up a company would be investment.

A distinction can be made between **gross** and **net** investment. The value of the capital stock depreciates over time as it wears out and is used up. This is called **depreciation** or **capital consumption**. Gross investment measures investment before depreciation, whilst net investment is gross investment less the value of depreciation. Depreciation in recent years in the UK has accounted for about three-quarters of gross investment. So only about one-quarter of gross investment represents an addition to the capital stock of the economy.

Another distinction made is between investment in **physical capital** and in **human capital**. Investment in human capital is investment in the education and training of workers. Investment in physical capital is investment in factories etc.

Investment is made both by the public sector and the private sector. Public sector investment is constrained by complex political considerations. In the rest of this unit, we will consider the determinants of private sector investment in physical capital.

Marginal efficiency of capital theory

Firms invest in order to make a profit. The profitability of investment projects varies. Some will make a high **rate of return**, some will yield a low rate of return and others will result in losses for the company. The rate of return on an investment project is also known as the MARGINAL EFFICIENCY OF CAPITAL (MEC).

At any point in time in the economy as whole, there exists a large number of possible individual investment projects. Table 1 shows an economy where there are £4bn of investment projects with an MEC of 20 per cent and above, £8bn with an MEC of 15 per cent and above and so on.

How much of this investment takes place will depend upon the rate of interest in the economy. If the rate of interest is 20 per cent, then firms having to borrow money will make a loss if they undertake any project with an MEC of less than 20 per cent. Hence, planned investment will be £4bn. If, on the other hand,

Using the photograph, showing the interior of a UK bank, give examples of: (a) past investment in physical capital; (b) past investment in human capital; (c) saving; (d) capital consumption.

Table 1 Planned investment and the marginal rate of return on capital

Marginal rate of return on capital (% per year)	Planned investment (£bn per year)
20	4
15	8
10	12
5	16

Figure 1 The planned investment schedule

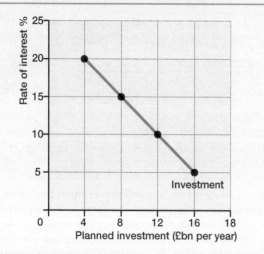

Figure 1 The planned investment schedule
A fall in the rate of interest will make more investment projects profitable. Planned investment will rise if the rate of interest falls.

In our explanation above, the rate of interest was assumed to be the rate of interest at which firms have to borrow money. However, most investment by firms in the UK is financed from RETAINED PROFIT. This is profit which is not used to pay dividends to shareholders or taxes to the government, but is kept back by the firm for its own use. This does not alter the relationship between the rate of interest and investment. Firms which keep back profits have a choice about what to do with the money. They can either invest it or save it. The higher the rate of interest on savings, such as placing the money on loan with banks or other financial institutions, the more attractive saving the money becomes and the less attractive becomes investment. Put another way, the higher the rate of interest, the higher the **opportunity cost** of investment and hence the lower will be the amount of planned investment in the economy.

Factors which shift the planned investment schedule

Cost of capital goods If the price of capital goods rises, then the expected rate of return on investment projects will fall if firms cannot pass on the increase in higher prices. So increases in the price of capital goods, all other things being equal, will reduce planned investment. This is shown by a shift to the left in the planned investment schedule in Figure 2.

Technological change Technological change will make new capital equipment more productive than previous equipment. This will raise the rate of return on investment projects, all other things being equal. Hence, technological change such as the introduction of computer aided machinery will raise the level of planned investment at any given rate of interest. This is shown by a shift to the right in the planned investment schedule.

Expectations Businesses have to form views about the future. When calculating the possible rate of return on future

Question 2

Table 2 Average cost of funds (as % of sales) of top spending companies on research and development

	Chemicals	Pharmaceuticals	Engineering	Electronics and electrical equipment
Japan	2.1%	2.8%	2.2%	1.5%
Germany	3.8%	5.1%	2.1%	2.9%
France	5.0%	n.a.	2.5%	2.8%
US	5.9%	9.5%	3.0%	4.2%
UK	5.6%	12.5%	3.1%	5.8%

Source: adapted from DTI, R&D Scoreboard.

The UK's high interest rates in the 1980s and 1990s put British industry at a severe disadvantage. It meant that fewer projects were worth taking on because the thresholds for returns were higher. Table 2 shows the cost of investment funds measured as a percentage of sales revenues for firms in different industries. In all these industries, the UK had the highest or nearly the highest cost of funds.

Source: adapted from the *Financial Times*.

(a) Explain, using a diagram, why high interest rates may have put British industry at a disadvantage in investment.
(b) During the 1990s and 2000s, UK interest rates have been above those in the rest of the EU. What are the possible implications for UK investment if Britain were to join the euro?

Figure 2 Shifts in planned investment

An increase in the cost of planned capital will reduce the rate of return on investment projects. Therefore at any given rate of interest, planned investment will fall. This is shown by a shift to the left in the planned investment schedule. Changes in technology which make capital more productive raise the level of planned investment, shown by a shift to the right of the schedule.

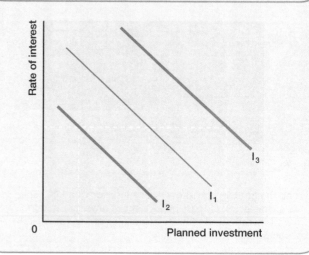

the rate of interest is 5 per cent, then all investment projects with an MEC of 5 per cent or more will be profitable. Hence, planned investment will be £16bn. So the conclusion of marginal efficiency of capital theory is that planned investment in the economy will rise if the rate of interest falls. This relationship, using the figures from Table 1, is shown in Figure 1.

Assume that I_1 in Figure 2 shows the planned investment schedule for the UK. Is it more likely to shift to I_2 or I_3 if: (a) there is a rise in the real prices of commercial property; (b) the government announces a billion pound programme to encourage the use of computers in industry; (c) the economy grew much faster than expected last year and forecasts show this set to continue; (d) the price of computers and computer aided tools falls; (e) prices on the New York Stock Exchange crash?

investment, they have to make assumptions about future costs and future revenues. If managers become more pessimistic about the future, they will expect the rate of return on investment projects to fall and hence planned investment will be reduced. If, on the other hand, they become more optimistic their expectations of the rates of return on investment projects will tend to rise. Hence planned investment will rise and this will be shown by a shift to the right in the investment schedule. Keynes called the expectations of businessmen their 'animal spirits'. He believed that expectations were crucial in determining changes in investment, and that these expectations could change suddenly.

Government policy Government can play a crucial role in stimulating private sector investment. This will be discussed in more detail in the unit on supply-side policies.

The accelerator theory

The ACCELERATOR THEORY of investment suggests that the level of planned investment varies with the rate of change of income or output rather than with the rate of interest. To see why this might be the case, consider Table 3.

Table 3

Year	Annual output £m	Number of machines required	Investment in machines
1	10	10	0
2	10	10	0
3	12	12	2
4	15	15	3
5	15	15	0
6	14	14	0

A firm producing toys needs one machine to produce £1m of output per year. The machines last 20 years and for the purpose of this example we will assume that none of the firm's machines need replacing over the time period being considered (so we are considering net and not gross investment). Initially in year 1 the firm has £10m worth of orders. It already has 10 machines and therefore no investment takes place. In year 2, orders remain unchanged and so again the firm has no need to invest. However, in year 3 orders increase to £12m. The firm now

needs to invest in another two machines if it is to fulfil orders. Orders increase to £15m in year 4. The firm needs to purchase another 3 machines to increase its capital stock to 15 machines. In year 5, orders remain unchanged at £15m and so investment returns to zero. In year 6, orders decline to £14m. The firm has too much capital stock and therefore does not invest.

In this example investment takes place when there is a change in real spending in the economy. If there is no change in spending, then there is no investment. What is more, the changes in spending lead to much bigger changes in investment. For instance, the increase in spending of 25 per cent in year 4 (from £12m to £15m) resulted in an increase in investment of 50 per cent (from 2 machines to 3 machines). In reality, it should be remembered that about 75 per cent of gross investment is replacement investment which is far less likely than net investment to be affected by changes in income. Even so, the accelerator theory predicts that investment spending in the economy is likely to be more volatile than spending as a whole.

The simplest form of the accelerator theory can be expressed as:

$$I_t = a (Y_t - Y_{t-1})$$

where I_t is investment in time period t, $Y_t - Y_{t-1}$ is the change in real income during year t and a is the accelerator coefficient or CAPITAL-OUTPUT RATIO. The capital-output ratio is the amount of capital needed in the economy to produce a given quantity of goods. So if £10 of capital is needed to produce £2 of goods, then the capital-output ratio is 5. The theory therefore predicts that changes in the level of investment are related to past changes in income.

This accelerator model is very simplistic. There is a number of factors which limit the predictive power of the model.

- The model assumes that the capital-output ratio is constant over time. However, it can change. In the long term, new technology can make capital more productive. In the shorter term, the capital-output ratio is likely to be higher in a recession when there is excess capacity than in a boom.
- Expectations may vary. Businesses may choose not to satisfy extra demand if they believe that the demand will be short lived. There is little point in undertaking new investment if the extra orders will have disappeared within six months. On the other hand, businesses may anticipate higher output. Despite constant income, they may believe that a boom is imminent and invest to be ahead of their rivals.
- Time lags involved are likely to be extremely complicated. Changes in investment are likely to respond to changes in income over several time periods and not just one.
- Firms may have excess capacity (i.e. they can produce more with current levels of capital than they are at present doing). If there is an increase in income, firms will respond not by investing but by bringing back into use capital which has been mothballed or by utilising fully equipment which had been underutilised.
- The capital goods industry will be unable to satisfy a surge in demand. Some investment will therefore either be cancelled or delayed.

Despite these qualifications, evidence suggests that net investment is to some extent linked to past changes in income. However, the link is relatively weak and therefore other influences must be at work to determine investment.

Profits

About 70 per cent of industrial and commercial investment in the UK is financed from retained profit. Some economists argue that many firms do not consider the opportunity cost of investment. They retain profit but rarely consider that it might be better used saved in financial assets. They automatically assume that the money will be spent on investment related to the activities of the firm. The rate of interest is then much less important in determining investment. Investment becomes crucially dependent upon two factors.

- The amount of retained profit available. So the poor investment record of companies in the UK compared to many competitors overseas over the past 50 years may be due to the fact that UK companies pay out a larger

percentage of their profits in dividends to their owners. This leaves less for investment.

- The availability of suitable investment projects. If firms do not have suitable investment projects to hand, they will bank the cash or pay it out to shareholders in dividends. New technology or new products can act as a spur to investment on this view.

Question 4

$$I_t = 2 (Y_t - Y_{t-1})$$

(a) In year 0 income was £100m. In subsequent years, it grew by 5 per cent per annum. Calculate the level of investment in years 1 to 5.
(b) Compare what would happen to investment in each year if income grew instead by (i) 10 per cent and (ii) 2.5 per cent.

Key terms

Accelerator theory - the theory that the level of planned investment is related to past changes in income.
Capital-output ratio - the ratio between the amount of capital needed to produce a given quantity of goods and the level of output.
Investment - the addition to the capital stock of the economy.
Marginal efficiency of capital - the rate of return on the last unit of capital employed.
Retained profit - profit kept back by a firm for its own use which is not distributed to shareholders or used to pay taxation.

Applied economics

Investment in the UK

The composition of investment

Gross investment is called **gross fixed capital formation (GFCF)** in UK official statistics. Figure 3 shows the composition of investment in 1979 and 2006. Significant changes in this composition are apparent from the data.

- In real terms, investment in housing has risen from £33.0 bn to £45.7 bn. However, as a percentage of total investment, it has fallen one third, from 34 per cent to 21 per cent. Within these totals, there has been a significant fall in public sector housing (mainly council housing), but a rise in private sector housing investment.
- Investment in 'other machinery and equipment' has more than trebled compared to an approximate doubling in real GDP. This investment ranges from milking machines to machine lathes to computers and desks.
- Investment in 'other new buildings and structures', has more than doubled, outpacing the percentage growth in real GDP. This includes new factories and offices.
- Investment in transport equipment has barely changed in real terms, but as a proportion of total investment has nearly halved. This is investment in ships

and aircraft.

Table 4 shows how the composition of investment has changed by industry. 1989 was an exceptional year for investment. The Lawson boom of 1986-88 had left many firms short of capacity. They had therefore sharply increased their spending on investment. Many firms came to regret this because the economy then went into a deep recession, between 1989 and 1992, leaving them with excess capacity. Even by 1996, four years into the recovery, investment was 15 per cent below its 1989 peak. Firms were reluctant to invest either because they had continued spare capacity or they feared that the economy would fail to recover. The prolonged period of economic growth of the late 1990s and early 2000s, however, saw investment increase and by 2004 was 11 per cent above its 1989 level.

The pattern of investment spending to some extent reflects trends in output between sectors of the economy. Primary industries, including agriculture and mining, have seen their share of output decline between 1989 and 2004. As a consequence, investment in these industries has been relatively static or fallen. Manufacturing output has increased only by a few per cent but real investment in manufacturing has halved. Investment by the

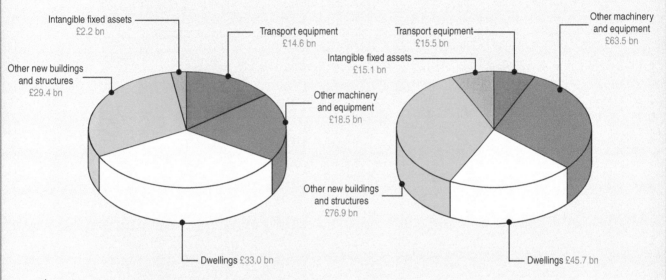

Figure 3 *Gross domestic fixed capital formation by type of asset, 1979 and 2006 (£ billion at 2003 prices)*

1979
Total investment £97.7 bn (at 2003 prices)
GDP at market prices £644.4bn

2006
Total investment £216.7 bn (at 2003 prices)
GDP at market prices £1 209.3 bn

Intangible fixed assets
£2.2 bn

Transport equipment
£14.6 bn

Other new buildings
and structures
£29.4 bn

Other machinery
and equipment
£18.5 bn

Dwellings £33.0 bn

Transport equipment
£15.5 bn

Intangible fixed assets
£15.1 bn

Other machinery
and equipment
£63.5 bn

Other new buildings
and structures
£76.9 bn

Dwellings £45.7 bn

Source: adapted from *Economic Trends Annual Supplement*, *Monthly Digest of Statistics*, Office for National Statistics.

construction industry has increased by 76 per cent, reflecting particularly an increase in construction of retail and office space. The 63 per cent increase in education, health and social work, investment mainly in new buildings and equipment reflects growing spending in public services, particularly after the election of the Labour government in 1997.

The determinants of investment

Economic theory suggests that there may be several determinants of private sector investment. The accelerator theory suggests that investment is a function of changes in income. The growth of the economy, measured for example by past changes in income, might be the crucial factor. Neo-classical theory argues that the rate of interest is the most important determinant, whilst other theories point to the current level of profits as significant.

The evidence tends to support the ideas that the level of investment is determined by a number of variables. In Table 5 there is some weak correlation between investment and changes in income, profits and the rate of interest. However, these variables tend to move together throughout the business or trade cycle and so changes in investment may in themselves affect the three variables in the data.

Table 4 *GDP and gross capital formation by industry*

	£ billion, at 2003 prices			% change
	1989	1996	2004	1989-2004
GDP at market prices	813.0	914.3	1 154.3	42.0
Total gross fixed capital formation	182.6	156.0	201.8	10.5
of which				
Construction	2.7	1.1	4.7	76.0
Education, health & social work	6.2	6.7	10.1	62.9
Transport, storage & communication	16.0	16.5	22.6	41.1
Investment in dwellings etc.	43.0	32.2	49.7	15.5
Other services	8.9	7.9	10.6	18.9
Public administration & defence	10.5	10.0	13.0	24.3
Distribution, hotels & catering	17.8	15.7	17.8	0.5
Business services & finance	33.5	24.5	31.6	-5.8
Electricity, gas & water supply	5.9	5.4	5.2	-12.6
Agriculture, hunting, forestry and fishing	3.0	3.3	2.6	-15.5
Mining & quarrying	7.7	4.9	4.2	-44.6
Manufacturing	23.6	21.8	11.1	-52.9

Source: adapted from *United Kingdom National Accounts* (Blue Book), Office for National Statistics.

Table 5 Determinants of investment

	£ billion, at 2003 prices			Per cent
	Private sector investment	Annual change in GDP	Company profits	Interest rate[1]
1987	55.5	33.2	179.9	9.7
1988	67.6	37.9	187.9	10.1
1989	75.8	17.4	191.4	13.8
1990	75.8	6.3	181.0	14.8
1991	69.7	-11.2	166.3	11.7
1992	67.1	1.7	169.8	9.6
1993	64.6	18.3	185.8	6.0
1994	67.8	35.7	208.3	5.5
1995	73.1	25.4	214.5	6.7
1996	80.7	24.8	227.3	6.0
1997	88.8	28.4	232.2	6.6
1998	106.0	31.6	232.7	7.2
1999	110.3	29.6	231.1	5.3
2000	115.2	38.1	231.1	6.0
2001	117.0	24.7	225.6	5.1
2002	118.3	21.9	243.1	4.0
2003	117.2	30.1	257.6	3.7
2004	119.9	36.4	273.3	4.4
2005	123.5	21.2	269.1	4.7
2006	132.8	33.4	281.0	4.6

1. London clearing banks, base rate: annual average.

Source: adapted from *Economic & Labour Market Review; Monthly Digest of Statistics*, Office for National Statistics.

DataQuestion

Investment

Figure 4 Investment by and output of manufacturing industry, and GDP, quarterly (£ billion at 2003 prices)

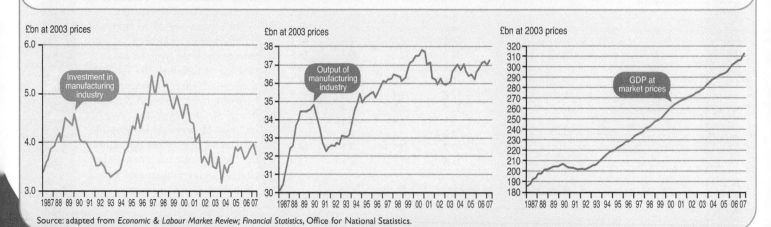

Source: adapted from *Economic & Labour Market Review; Financial Statistics*, Office for National Statistics.

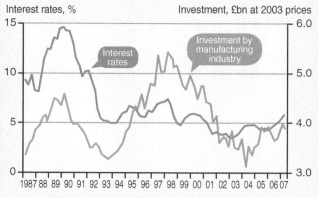

Figure 5 Short term interest rates[1] and investment by manufacturing industry, quarterly

Interest rates, %   Investment, £bn at 2003 prices

[1] Average quarterly Treasury bill rate
Source: adapted from *Economic Trends Annual Supplement, Financial Statistics*, Office for National Statistics.

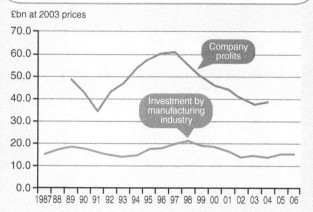

Figure 6 Profits of and investment by manufacturing industry, yearly, (£ billion at 2003 prices)

£bn at 2003 prices

Source: adapted from *National Income Blue Book, Monthly Digest of Statistics*, Office for National Statistics.

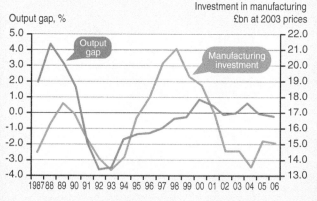

Figure 7 The UK output gap[1] and investment by manufacturing industry

Output gap, %   Investment in manufacturing £bn at 2003 prices

[1] Deviation of actual GDP from trend GDP as a percentage of trend GDP.
Source: adapted from *Monthly Digest of Statistics*, Office for National Statistics; *Economic Outlook*, OECD.

1. Briefly outline the trends in manufacturing investment between 1987 and 2007.
2. Taking each possible determinant of investment (a) explain why economic theory suggests there is a link between the two variables and (b) evaluate whether the evidence from 1987 to 2007 supports the theory.
3. A manufacturing company is reviewing its investment policies. Evaluate which macroeconomic variable is the most important variable that it should take into consideration when making an investment decision.

Summary

1. Government spending, exports and imports are an important part of total demand in the economy.
2. Government spending is influenced by factors such as the need to provide public and merit goods as well as a desire to control total spending in the economy.
3. Demand for exports and imports is influenced by factors such as their price, exchange rates, changes in the state of the world economy, and non-price factors including quality of goods.

Reasons for government spending

Government plays a crucial role in modern economies. One way in which they intervene is by spending money on a wide variety of goods and services. For example, they provide public goods such as defence and the judiciary. They also provide merit goods such as education and healthcare.

The size of government spending varies from country to country. In a modern economy, the government will fund defence, the police and judiciary, roads and education. There are then wide divergencies between economies. In a free market economy like the United States, the private sector is expected to provide goods such as health care, housing and social care. In a mixed economy, the state will provide many of these goods. Some mixed economies, like Sweden, have much higher state involvement than countries like the UK.

Much of government spending is fixed from year to year. Schools must be funded. Warships must be fuelled. Pensions must be paid. However, governments vary what they spend their money on and how much they spend from year to year. Government announcements about changes in spending are made in **budgets**.

Typically, changes in government spending reflect changing priorities about how to spend money. A government might choose to spend more on education and less on defence next year, for example. However, changes in government spending can also be made deliberately to affect total spending in the economy. Higher government spending can boost total spending and so affect variables such as unemployment and inflation.

The impact of changes in government spending on total spending in the economy depends on levels of taxation. If the government raises taxes by the same amount as a rise in its spending, then there might be little impact on total spending in the economy. On the other hand, a rise in total spending with no change in taxation will have more impact.

Government spending can be greater than government receipts such as taxation. When this happens there will be a **budget deficit**. When government spending is less than government receipts such as taxation, there will be a **budget surplus**. A rise in government spending with no change in taxation will either reduce a budget surplus or increase a budget deficit.

Question 1

Since 2001, public finances have been worsening. Government spending has grown faster than taxes. The result is that the budget has moved from a healthy surplus to a substantial deficit. The Chancellor has increased government spending to pay for much needed improvements in the health and education systems. But he hasn't raised taxes fast enough to pay for the extra doctors and nurses and the new hospitals.

At the same time, the economy has been receiving a boost. The extra spending over taxes has been adding to demand and helping to create jobs and reduce unemployment. Cutting off the spending could dampen economic activity and even put the economy into a recession.

Source: adapted from the *Financial Times*, 22.3.2007.

Figure 1 Government budget surplus and deficit

% of GDP

[Line chart showing "Total managed expenditure" and "Tax and other receipts" as % of GDP from 1996-97 to 2006-07, y-axis ranging from 36 to 42]

Source: adapted from HM Treasury.

(a) Using examples from the data, explain two reasons why a government increases its spending.
(b) Using the circular flow of income model, analyse the impact of an increase in the budget deficit on income.

Exports and imports

Exports are goods and services sold to foreigners. **Imports** are goods and services bought from foreigners. Exports are an important part of total demand in an economy like the UK. The demand for exports and imports is influenced by a number of factors.

Price Buyers make decisions partly on the price of a good. The higher the price, the lower the quantity demanded. The price itself depends upon a variety of supply factors including costs. Over the past 15 years, production of low and medium technology manufactured goods has gone from high wage economies like the UK to low wage economies like China. So imports into the UK from China have increased because UK domestic producers can no longer compete.

The exchange rate The exchange rate is the price at which one currency is sold for another. A rise in the value of the pound means that it costs foreigners more to buy pounds with their local currency. This makes exports from the UK less price competitive and hence UK exports are likely to fall. Equally, a rise in the value of the pound means that UK buyers can buy foreign currency more cheaply with pounds. So imports become more price competitive to UK buyers. A fall in the value of the pound leads to the opposite result. UK exports become more price competitive to foreign buyers. In contrast, UK buyers find that imports become less price competitive.

World and UK income When the world economy is booming, foreign income is rising fast. This provides UK exporters with an opportunity to sell more exports. When foreign markets slump, UK exports will fall because foreigners can no longer afford to buy as many goods from the UK. Sometimes there are world wide booms and recessions. At other times, individual economies go into boom or slump. In the first half of the 2000s, for example, economic growth was slow in the EU and so UK exporters found it hard to increase their exports to the rest of the EU. When the UK goes into a recession, foreign companies selling imports to the UK will find trading conditions difficult and imports may fall. In contrast, a boom in the UK economy will suck in imports from abroad as UK buyers spend their extra income.

Non-price factors Exports and imports may be bought solely on price. This is particularly true where goods are of standard quality. Copper, steel or wheat, for example, are standard commodities which tend to be traded on price. However, many products are unique in quality. They may have a unique design protected by patents. It may be a unique service, such as next day delivery. So a whole range of non-price factors affects the competitiveness of exports and imports.

Applied economics

EEF

EEF, the organisation which represents UK manufacturing companies, said that British firms were coping well with the export challenge. In a report published in 2007, *Export support: How UK firms compete abroad*, it said that most British manufacturers had increased their dependence on exports since the late 1990s. As Figure 2 shows, 90 per cent of UK manufacturing companies sell to other western European EU countries whilst 45 per cent sell goods to China.

One key reason for the success of British exporting companies has been the strong economic growth in many overseas countries. Whilst the UK enjoyed a period of above average growth from 1995 of between 2.5 and 3 per cent per annum, the USA has grown even faster. China, a key market, has been growing at nearly 10 per cent per annum.

Another reason for export success has been that UK

companies have exploited niche markets. These markets have allowed them to exploit new technologies or make small numbers of products to order. Foreign owned firms with subsidiary companies in the UK have been better at exporting from the UK than UK owned firms. Foreign

owned firms tend to be larger which in export markets can give a variety of competitive advantages such as economies of scale or greater product knowledge. Foreign owned firms also tend to more attuned to globalisation and more aware of which markets they can exploit.

However, UK manufacturers have tended to pull out of markets where they have to compete on price on mass produced or low technology items. They cannot compete with low wage cost countries such as China. Some UK companies have exploited this trend by moving such production to low cost countries and then exporting the goods worldwide. Production might be done in China but the profits are earned by the UK company.

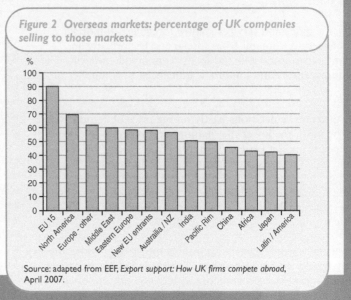

Figure 2 Overseas markets: percentage of UK companies selling to those markets

Source: adapted from EEF, *Export support: How UK firms compete abroad*, April 2007.

DataQuestion   DEK

DEK is the world's largest maker of specialist printing machines for the production of circuit boards used in the electronics industry. It has two factories, one in Weymouth in the UK and the other in China. Total production in 2006 was £100 million, with about 60 per cent of that coming from the Weymouth plant. Around 95 per cent of output from Weymouth is exported.

Part of the success of the company comes from its technology. Customers place their orders for specialist machines which come in about 150 basic variants. High levels of automation at the Weymouth plant mean that costs are only slightly higher than at its Chinese plant where wages are much lower. Automation means that wages account for only a very small part of total cost. Highly efficient production methods mean that a customer ordering a machine today can expect to receive it two weeks later from Britain via air freight.

Source: adapted from the *Financial Times*, 23.4.2007.

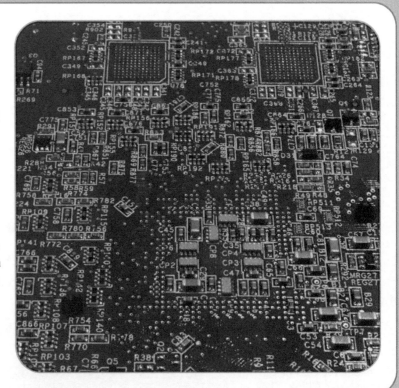

1. Explain two reasons why DEK is a successful exporter.

2. To what extent can UK exporters like DEK be successful against Chinese manufacturers in future?

Summary

1. The aggregate demand curve is downward sloping. It shows the relationship between the price level and equilibrium output in the economy.
2. A movement along the aggregate demand curve shows how equilibrium income will change if there is a change in the price level.
3. A shift in the aggregate demand curve is caused by a change in variables such as consumption and exports at any given price level.
4. The multiplier increases any impact on aggregate demand and national income of changes in an injection to the circular flow.

Aggregate demand

Demand for an individual good is defined as the quantity that is bought at any given price. In this unit, we will consider what determines AGGREGATE demand. 'Aggregate' in economics means a 'total' or 'added up' amount. AGGREGATE DEMAND is the total of all demands or expenditures in the economy at any given price.

National expenditure is one of the three ways of calculating national income, usually measured as GDP. National expenditure is made up of four components.

- **Consumption (C).** This is spending by households on goods and services.
- **Investment (I).** This is spending by firms on investment goods.
- **Government spending (G).** This includes current spending, for instance on wages and salaries. It also includes spending by government on investment goods like new roads or new schools.
- **Exports minus imports (X - M).** Foreigners spend money on goods produced in the DOMESTIC ECONOMY. Hence it is part of national expenditure. However, households, firms and governments also spend money on goods produced abroad. For instance, a UK household might buy a car produced in France, or a British firm might use components imported from the Far East in a computer which is sold to Germany. These imported goods do not form part of national output and do not contribute to national income. So, because C, I, G and X all include spending on imported goods, imports (M) must be taken away from C + I + G + X to arrive at a figure for national expenditure.

National expenditure or aggregate demand (AD) can therefore be calculated using the formula:

$$AD = C + I + G + X - M$$

The aggregate demand curve

The AGGREGATE DEMAND CURVE shows the relationship between the price level and the level of real expenditure in the economy. Figure 1 shows an aggregate demand (AD) curve. The price level is put on the vertical axis whilst real output is put on the horizontal axis.

The **price level** is the average level of prices in the economy. Governments calculate a number of different measures of the

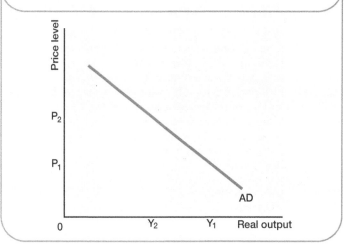

Figure 1 The aggregate demand curve

A rise in the price level will lead, via a rise in interest rates, to a fall in the equilibrium level of national income and therefore of national output. Hence the aggregate demand curve is downward sloping.

price level. In the UK, for instance, the most widely quoted measure is the **Consumer Prices Index**, figures for which are published every month and are widely reported in the news. A change in the price level is **inflation**.

Real output on the horizontal axis must equal real expenditure and real income. This is because, in the circular flow model of the economy, these are three different ways of measuring the same flow. The aggregate demand curve plots the level of expenditure where the economy would be in an equilibrium position at each price level, all other things being equal.

Demand curves are nearly always downward sloping. Why is the aggregate demand curve the same shape? One simple answer is to consider what happens to a household budget if prices rise. If a household is on a fixed income, then a rise in average prices will mean that they can buy fewer goods and services than before. The higher the price level in the economy, the less they can afford to buy. So it is with the national economy. The higher the price, the fewer goods and services will be demanded in the whole economy.

A more sophisticated explanation considers what happens to the different components of expenditure when prices rise.

Consumption Consumption expenditure is influenced by the **rate of interest** in the economy. When prices increase, consumers (and firms) need more money to buy the same number of goods and services as before. One way of getting more money is to borrow it and so the demand for borrowed funds will rise. However, if there is a fixed supply of money available for borrowing from banks and building societies, the price of borrowed funds will rise. This price is the rate of interest. A rise in interest rates leads to a fall in consumption, particularly of durable goods such as cars which are commonly bought on credit.

Another way a rise in the price level affects consumption is through the **wealth effect**. A rise in the price level leads to the real value of an individual consumer's wealth being lower. For instance, £100 000 at today's prices will be worth less in real terms in a year's time if average prices have increased 20 per cent over the 12 months. A fall in real wealth will result in a fall in consumer spending.

Investment As has just been explained, a rise in prices, all other things being equal, leads to a rise in interest rates in the economy. Investment is affected by changes in the rate of interest. The higher the rate of interest, the less profitable new investment projects become and therefore the fewer projects will be undertaken by firms. So, the higher the rate of interest, the lower will be the level of investment.

Government spending Government spending in this model of the economy is assumed to be independent of economic variables. It is exogenously determined, fixed by variables outside the model. In this case, it is assumed to be determined by the political decisions of the government of the day. Note that government spending (G) here does not include transfer payments. These are payments by the government for which there is no corresponding output in the economy, like welfare benefits or student grants.

Exports and imports A higher price level in the UK means that foreign firms will be able to compete more successfully in the UK economy. For instance, if British shoe manufacturers put up their prices by 20 per cent, whilst foreign shoe manufacturers keep their prices the same, then British shoe manufacturers will become less competitive and more foreign shoes will be imported. Equally, British shoe manufacturers will find it more difficult to export charging higher prices. So a higher UK price level, with price levels in other economies staying the same, will lead to a fall in UK exports.

Hence, aggregate demand falls as prices rise, first, because increases in interest rates reduce consumption and investment and, second, because a loss of international competitiveness at the new higher prices will reduce exports and increase imports.

Shifts in the AD curve

The aggregate demand (AD) curve shows the relationship between the price level and the equilibrium level of real income and output. A change in the price level results in a **movement along** the AD curve. Higher prices lead to falls in aggregate demand.

Shifts in the aggregate demand curve will occur if there is a change in any other relevant variable apart from the price level. When the AD curve shifts, it shows that there is a change in real output at any given price level. In Figure 2, the shift in the AD curve from AD_1 to AD_2 shows that at a price level of P, real output increases from Y_1 to Y_2. There is a number of variables which can lead to a shift of the AD curve. Some of these variables are real variables, such as changes in the willingness of consumers to spend. Others are changes in **monetary variables** such as the rate of interest.

Consumption A number of factors might increase consumption spending at any given level of prices, shifting the AD curve from AD_1 to AD_2 in Figure 2. For instance, unemployment may fall, making consumers less afraid that they will lose their jobs and more willing to borrow money to spend on consumer durables. The government might reduce interest rates, again encouraging borrowing for durables. A substantial rise in stock market prices will increase consumer wealth which in turn may lead to an increase in spending. A reduction in the relative numbers of high saving 45-60 year olds in the population will increase the **average propensity to consume** of the whole economy. New technology which creates new consumer products can lead to an increase in consumer spending as households want to buy these new products. A fall in income tax would increase consumers' disposable income, leading to a rise in consumption.

Investment One factor which would increase investment spending at any given level of prices, pushing the AD curve from AD_1 to AD_2 in Figure 2, would be an increase in business

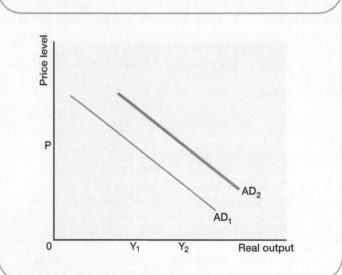

Figure 2 A shift in the aggregate demand curve
An increase in consumption, investment, government spending or net exports, given a constant price level, will lead to a shift in the aggregate demand curve from AD_1 to AD_2.

In 1975, inflation rose to a peak of 24.1 per cent. Real GDP fell in both 1974 and 1975. In 1980, inflation rose to a peak of 18.0 per cent and real GDP fell in 1980 and 1981. In 1990, inflation rose to a peak of 9.5 per cent. GDP fell in 1991 and 1992.

How might economic theory account for this?

Question 2

Explain, using a diagram, the likely effect of the following on the aggregate demand curve for the UK.

(a) The increase in real investment expenditure between 2000 and 2005.
(b) The pushing up of interest rates by the government from 7.5 per cent in May 1987 to 15 per cent in October 1989.
(c) The large cuts in taxes in the Lawson Budget of 1987.
(d) The 50 per cent per cent fall in London Stock Market prices (FTSE 100) between December 1999 and January 2003.
(e) The fall in the savings ratio from a peak of 11.7 per cent in 1992 to a low of 3.7 per cent in 2004.
(f) The increase in planned government spending on education and health care by the Labour government 2000-2007.
(g) The more than 25 per cent rise in the average value of the pound against other currencies between 1996 and 2000.

confidence - an increase in 'animal spirits' as John Maynard Keynes put it. This increase in business confidence could have come about, for instance, because the economy was going into boom. A fall in interest rates ordered by the government would lead to a rise in investment. An increase in company profitability would give firms more retained profit to use for investment. A fall in taxes on profits (corporation tax in the UK) would lead to the rate of return on investment projects rising, leading to a rise in investment.

Government spending Government spending can change automatically because of previous government spending commitments, or the government can announce changes to its

spending. A rise in government spending with no change in taxation will lead to a fall in its budget surplus or a rise in its deficit. This will increase aggregate demand, pushing the AD curve to the right from AD_1 to AD_2 in Figure 2. A fall in government spending with no change in taxation will lead to a shift to the left in the aggregate demand curve.

Exports and imports A number of factors can affect the balance between exports and imports. For example, a rise in the exchange rate is likely to lead to lower exports but higher imports. Exports minus imports will therefore fall, reducing aggregate demand. This is shown by a shift in the aggregate demand curve to the left. In contrast, an improvement in innovation and quality of UK manufactured goods is likely to lead to a rise in exports. This will increase aggregate demand and shift the aggregate demand curve to the right from AD_1 to AD_2 in Figure 2.

The multiplier

If there is an increase in, say, investment of £1, what will be the final increase in national income? John Maynard Keynes argued in his most famous book, *The General Theory of Employment, Interest and Money*, published in 1936, that national income would increase by more than £1 because of the MULTIPLIER EFFECT.

To understand why there might be a multiplier effect, consider what would happen if firms increased spending on new factories by £100m. Firms would pay contractors to build the factories. This £100m would be an increase in aggregate demand. The contractor would use the money in part to pay its workers on the project. The workers would spend the money, on everything from food to holidays. This spending would be an addition to national income. Assume that £10m is spent on food. Food manufacturers would in turn pay their workers who would spend their incomes on a variety of products, increasing national income further. John Maynard Keynes argued that this multiplier

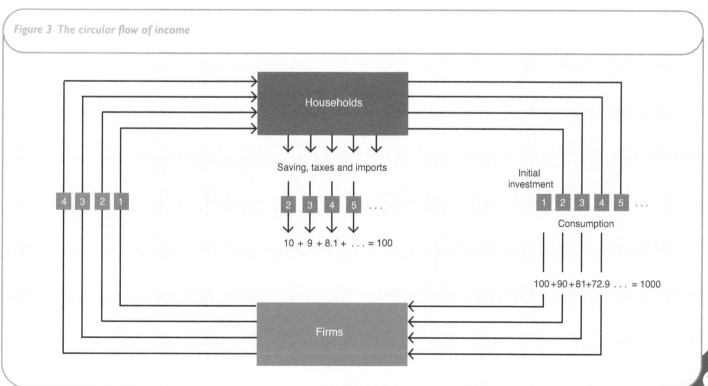

Figure 3 *The circular flow of income*

effect would increase jobs in the economy. Every job directly created by firms through extra spending would indirectly create other jobs in the economy.

This process can be shown using the **circular flow of income model**. Assume that households spend 9/10ths of their gross income. The other 1/10th is either saved or paid to the government in the form of taxes. Firms increase their spending by £100m, money which is used to build new factories. In Figure 3, this initial £100m is shown in stage 1 flowing into firms. The money then flows out again as it is distributed in the form of wages and profits back to households. Households spend the money, but remember that there are **withdrawals** of 0.1 of income because of savings and taxes. So only £90m flows back round the economy in stage 2 to firms. Then firms pay £90m back to households in wages and profits. In the third stage, £81m is spent by households with £19 million leaking out of the circular flow. This process carries on with smaller and smaller amounts being added to national income as the money flows round the economy. Eventually, the initial £100m extra government spending leads to a final increase in national income of £1 000m. In this case, the value of the MULTIPLIER is 10.

If leakages from the circular flow in Figure 3 had been larger, less of the increase in investment would have continued to flow round the economy. For instance, if leakages had been 0.8 of income, then only £20m (0.2 x £100m) would have flowed round the economy in the second stage. In the third stage, it would have been £4m (0.2 x £20m). The final increase in national income following the initial £100m increase in investment spending would have been £125m.

The multiplier model states that the higher the leakages from the circular flow, the smaller will be the increase in income which continues to flow round the economy at each stage following an initial increase in spending. Hence, the higher the leakages, the smaller the value of the multiplier. Leakages are what is not spent. So, another way of saying this is that the multiplier is smaller when the ratio of consumption to income is lower. The ratio of consumption to income at the margin is called the **marginal propensity to consume** or **MPC**. So the lower the MPC, the lower the value of the multiplier.

The multiplier effect and injections

In the example above, it was assumed that investment increased. Investment is an **injection** into the circular flow. The multiplier effect shows the impact on aggregate demand and income of a change in an injection. So if the multiplier were 2, then a £100 million increase in investment would lead to an increase in national income of £200 million.

Investment is not the only injection into the circular flow. Government spending and exports are also injections. So a rise in government spending of, say, £200 million would lead to a rise in national income of £800 million if the multiplier were 4. A fall in exports of £500 million would lead to a fall in national income of £1 500 million if the multiplier were 3.

Governments and the multiplier

Governments in the past have used changes in government spending to influence national income and macroeconomic variables such as unemployment and inflation. It would be very helpful if governments knew that an extra £1 in

government spending would produce an extra, say, £2 in national income. However, in practice, it is not so simple.

- It is difficult to measure the exact size of the multiplier. Sophisticated econometric models have to be used which describe the workings of the economy. They are not completely accurate. Equally, changes can happen in an economy which can alter the size of the multiplier from one period to the next.
- The multiplier effect is not instantaneous. A £100 increase in government spending today does not increase national income by £200 today. It takes time for the money to flow round the circular flow. So there are time lags between the increase in the government spending and the final increase in national income.
- Economists disagree about the exact size of the multiplier. However, in general it is considered to be relatively low, between 1 and 2. Increases in investment or government spending do not give very large increases in national income.

Important notes

Changes and shifts in AD Aggregate demand analysis and aggregate supply analysis are more complex than demand and supply analysis in an individual market. You may already have noticed, for instance, that a change in interest rates could lead to a movement along the aggregate demand curve or lead to a shift in the curve. Similarly, an increase in consumption could lead to a movement along or a shift in the curve. To distinguish between

---

Question 3

The small town of Bo'ness was once the centre of a booming economy. A port, situated on the Forth estuary on the east coast of Scotland, it was once only second in importance to Edinburgh's port of Leith. Today, it has fallen on hard times. Its port was closed to commercial shipping in 1958 and the town now has only 15 000 inhabitants. All that could change if a proposed £150 million development scheme goes ahead. ING Real East, a property development company, has proposed an ambitious scheme to build a marina for leisure craft, 700 harbour-front apartments and townhouses, a 100-bedroom hotel and waterside shops, restaurants, cafes and bars.

The town centre has a rich heritage of historic buildings and this year was granted outstanding conservation area status. It already houses the Scottish Rail Museum, which draws 60 000 visitors a year. Tourism is therefore important to the local economy. The proposed marina would act as a good staging post for leisure craft en route to the Falkirk Wheel, the spectacular boat lift that provides vessels cross-country passage from the west coast to the east coast via the Union Canal with the Firth and Forth Canal. The government is also keen to see development which would take some of the pressure off Edinburgh. Only 20 miles away, Scotland's capital city has virtually full employment and an overheated housing market.

Source: adapted from the *Financial Times*, 1.12.2004.

Explain how there might be a multiplier effect on income from the proposed £150 million development scheme in Bo'ness.

movements along and shifts in the curve it is important to consider what has caused the change in aggregate demand.

If the change has come about because the price level has changed, then there is a movement **along** the AD curve. For instance, a rise in the price level causes a rise in interest rates. This leads to a fall in consumption. This is shown by a movement up the curve.

If, however, interest rates or consumer spending have changed for a different reason than because prices have changed, then there will be a **shift** in the AD curve. A government putting up interest rates at a given price level would lead to a shift in the curve.

Levels and changes As with any economic analysis, it is important to distinguish between absolute changes and rates of change. For example, a fall in the level of investment will lead to a fall in aggregate demand, all other things being equal. However, a fall in the rate of change of investment, when this rate of change is positive, means that investment is still rising. If growth in investment has fallen from 5 per cent to 3 per cent, investment is still increasing. So a fall in the rate of growth of investment will lead to an increase in aggregate demand and a shift of the AD curve to the right.

Key terms

Aggregate - the sum or total.
Aggregate demand - the total of all demands or expenditures in the economy at any given price.
Aggregate demand curve - shows the relationship between the price level and equilibrium national income. As the price level rises the equilibrium level of national income falls.
Domestic economy - the economy of a single country.

Multiplier - the figure used to multiply a change in autonomous expenditure, such as investment, to find the final change in income. It is the ratio of the final change in income to the initial change in autonomous expenditure.
Multiplier effect - an increase in investment or any other autonomous expenditure will lead to an even greater increase in income.

Applied economics

Aggregate demand 1979-2007

In 1979, a new Conservative government under Margaret Thatcher was elected into office. The economy had been through very difficult times in the 1970s. Imported inflation had been a major problem and trade unions had militantly pushed up wages in an attempt to maintain the real value of their members' earnings. On coming into office, she faced rapidly rising inflation. Partly this was because of a world oil crisis where OPEC was ultimately able to increase the price of oil threefold between 1978 and 1982. Partly it was because wage inflation had taken off again.

Margaret Thatcher was strongly influenced by the relatively new and fashionable monetarist idea that inflation was solely caused by excessive increases in the money supply. If the money supply increased, this pushed up aggregate demand. Too much money, and so excess demand, chasing too few goods could only lead to increases in prices. To reduce the rate of growth of the money supply, she raised interest rates from 12 per cent in May 1979 to 17 per cent in November 1979 as Figure 4 shows. High interest rates of over 10 per cent, which were maintained for four years, depressed both

consumption and investment, reducing aggregate demand. The economy went into a major recession, with unemployment climbing from 1.3 million in 1979 to 3.1 million in 1983. As Figure 5 shows, a negative output gap of 7 per cent of GDP opened up in 1981. Aggregate demand was far below its trend level.

As interest rates fell, the economy began to recover and aggregate demand began to rise again. Part of the monetarist philosophy was that excessive growth of the money supply was usually caused by excessive government borrowing. So the government attempted to reduce government spending and even raised taxes in 1981. This limited the growth in aggregate demand from 1981 onwards.

Nevertheless, the economy was in the recovery phase of the trade cycle. Between 1983 and 1988, it grew at above its trend rate of growth of 2.5 per cent. Interest rates were still at historically high levels, averaging 10-12 per cent, but consumption and investment grew despite this. A housing boom began to develop, which further encouraged consumption.

By 1987, the government had convinced itself that

Britain was experiencing an 'economic miracle' due to its economic policies and that a 4 per cent per annum growth rate was sustainable in the long term. There was a substantial tax cutting budget in March 1987 which saw the top rate of income tax fall from 60 per cent to 40 per cent. Lower taxes led to higher disposable income and hence higher consumption. Inflation remained low, so households did not have to increase their savings levels to rebuild the real value of their wealth. The stock market also saw share prices increasing, adding to households' wealth. Unemployment fell sharply, halving from 3 million to 1.8 million between 1986 and 1989. All these factors led to increasing levels of consumer confidence. Households were more willing than before to take out loans and were less willing to save.

By 1988, the economy was operating at 5.5 per cent above its productive potential. Firms sharply increased their investment spending and planned to take advantage of the many profitable opportunities that were now available. In the meantime, importers took advantage of the UK's inability to satisfy domestic demand and a dangerously high current account deficit was recorded.

In 1988, the government realised that the economy had overheated and that inflation would increase sharply if it did not take action. So it raised interest rates and by late 1989, as Figure 4 shows, they stood at 15 per cent, double their lowest 1988 value. This led to a slowdown in consumer spending. The housing market collapsed as borrowers were less willing to take out mortgages to finance new purchases. Existing mortgage borrowers found their mortgage payments increasing sharply, reducing their ability to spend. Lower house prices lowered household wealth and severely dented consumer confidence. So too did rising unemployment, which doubled between 1989 and 1993. Firms cut back their investment spending as they found themselves with too much productive capacity, as Figure 5 shows. Government spending remained tight although there was

some increase in it after John Major became Prime Minister in 1989. As for exports, their growth remained subdued because high interest rates kept the value of the pound high. The government also made the policy mistake of taking the pound into the Exchange Rate Mechanism (ERM) of the European Monetary Union (the precursor to the euro and monetary union) at too high a level. This forced it to keep interest rates high to defend the value of the pound. Britain was forced to leave the ERM by currency speculation in September 1992. By that time, falling levels of aggregate demand meant that GDP was lower than it was in the last quarter of 1988, nearly four years earlier.

Leaving the ERM allowed the government to reduce interest rates rapidly at a time when inflation had fallen to around 2 per cent per annum. The period 1993-2007 was then characterised by above average rates of growth. 1993-1997 can be seen as the recovery from the deep recession of 1990-1992. The period 1997-2007 can be seen as a prolonged period when the economy was growing at roughly its trend rate of growth, as Figure 5 would suggest.

The drivers of aggregate demand have fluctuated over the period 1993-2007.

- Consumer spending has tended to increase at a faster rate than growth in aggregate demand overall. This has been fuelled by low interest rates and easy credit. Low interest rates have kept the cost of borrowing low to purchase consumer durables such as cars and electronic equipment. Rising house prices have also produced rising wealth which has encouraged consumer spending boom.

- Government spending growth was low between 1995 and 2000 because of political commitments to keep both government spending and taxes low. However, after 2001, the government raised its spending substantially to pay for improvement to health care and education. Taxes failed to keep pace with the growth in spending. As a result, there was a substantial boost to

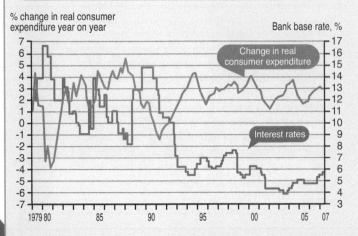

Figure 4 *Bank base rates and economic growth*

Source: adapted from *Economic & Labour Market Review*, Office for National Statistics.

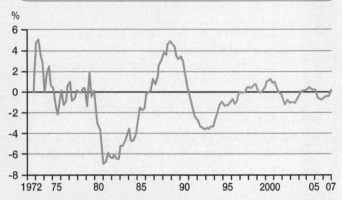

Figure 5 *The output gap[1]*

1 Deviation of actual GDP from potential GDP as a percentage of potential GDP. Positive numbers show actual GDP is above potential GDP, whilst negative numbers show actual GDP is below potential GDP.

Source: adapted from HM Treasury, *Economic Cycles*, 2005; *Budget 2007 - the economy*.

aggregate demand from government spending from 2001.

● Exports were hit by a financial crisis in Asia in 1997 and by a downturn in the US economy in 2001 made worse by the attacks on the World Trade Centre of 9/11. It could be argued that these two events were the major cause of the faltering of the UK economy in 1998

and again in 2002-2003. However, exports bounced back after 2003 as the world economy grew strongly. Imports equally grew strongly as UK consumers and firms bought goods and services from overseas. The net impact of exports minus imports after 2003 was to depress aggregate demand because imports grew more strongly than exports.

DataQuestion — Aggregate demand 2000-2007

Figure 6 *Real growth in GDP and its components, % change year on year*

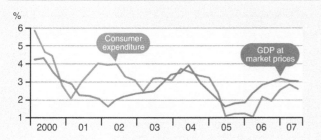
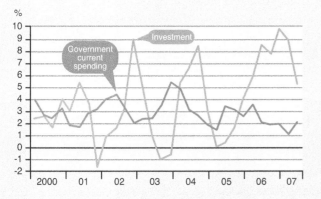
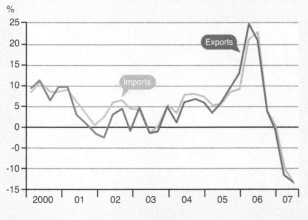

Source: adapted from *Economic & Labour Market Review*, Office for National Statistics.

Figure 7 *GDP and its components, 2nd quarter 2007*

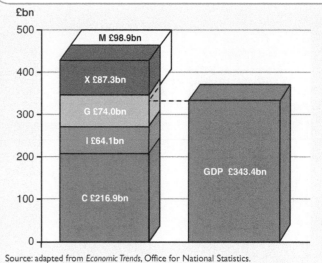

Source: adapted from *Economic Trends*, Office for National Statistics.

Figure 8 *Short term interest rates*

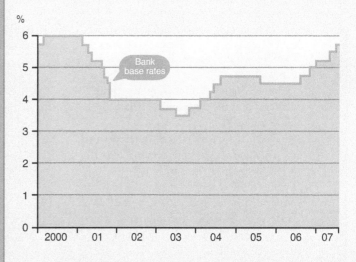

Source: adapted from *Economic & Labour Market Review*, Office for National Statistics.

Figure 9 Inflation (CPI), % change year on year

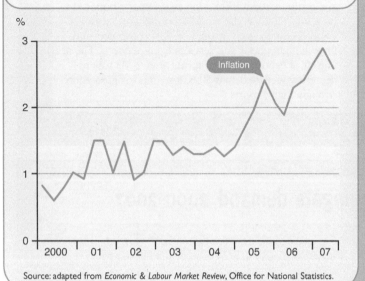

Source: adapted from *Economic & Labour Market Review*, Office for National Statistics.

Figure 10 Sterling effective exchange rate, January 2005=100

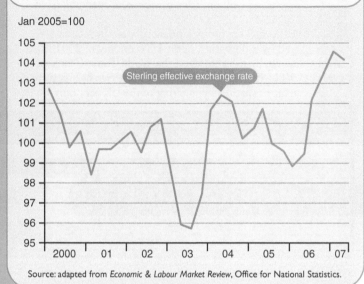

Source: adapted from *Economic & Labour Market Review*, Office for National Statistics.

Figure 11 Unemployment, ILO measure, millions

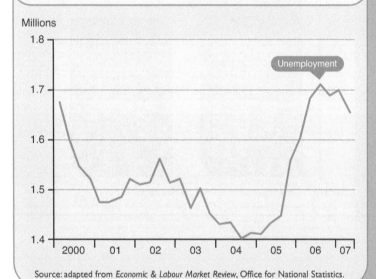

Source: adapted from *Economic & Labour Market Review*, Office for National Statistics.

Figure 12 Average house prices, % change year on year

Source: adapted from *Economic & Labour Market Review*, Office for National Statistics.

1. Explain what is meant by 'aggregate demand'.
2. Describe the trend, if any, in aggregate demand and its components between 2000 and 2007.
3. Analyse the factors which contributed to the change in aggregate demand over the period shown in the data.
4. Evaluate the extent to which the mild downturn in the UK economy in 2001-2002 was caused by the international downturn in the world economy which occurred at the time.

25 Aggregate supply

Summary

1. The aggregate supply curve shows the level of output in the whole economy at any given level of average prices.
2. In the short run, it is assumed that the prices of factors of production, such as money wage rates, are constant. Firms will supply extra output if the prices they receive increase. Hence in the short run, the aggregate supply curve is upward sloping.
3. An increase in firms' costs of production will shift the short run aggregate supply curve upwards, whilst a fall in costs will shift it downwards.
4. In the long run, it is assumed that the prices of factors of production are variable but that the productive capacity of the economy is fixed. The long run aggregate supply curve shows the productive capacity of the economy at any given price level.
5. The long run aggregate supply curve shows the productive capacity of the economy in the same way that a production possibility frontier or the trend rate of growth shows this productive capacity.
6. Shifts in the long run aggregate supply curve are caused by changes in the quantity or quality of factors of production or the efficiency of their use.
7. In the long run, it is assumed that the prices of factors of production are variable but that the productive capacity of the economy is fixed. The long run aggregate supply curve shows the productive capacity of the economy at any given price level.
8. The long run aggregate supply curve shows the productive capacity of the economy in the way that a production possibility frontier or the trend rate of growth shows this productive capacity.

The short run aggregate supply curve

In unit 6, it was argued that the supply curve for an industry was upward sloping. If the price of a product increases, firms in the industry are likely to increase their profits by producing and selling more. So the higher the price, the higher the level of output. The supply curve being talked about here is a **microeconomic** supply curve. Is the **macroeconomic** supply curve (i.e. the supply curve for the whole economy) the same?

The macroeconomic supply curve is called the AGGREGATE SUPPLY CURVE, because it is the sum of all the industry supply curves in the economy. It shows how much output firms wish to supply at each level of prices.

In the short run, the aggregate supply curve is upward sloping. The short run is defined here as the period when money wage rates and the prices of all other factor inputs in the economy are fixed. Assume that firms wish to increase their level of output. In the short run, they are unlikely to take on extra workers. Taking on extra staff is an expensive process. Sacking them if they are no longer needed is likely to be even more costly, not just in direct monetary terms but also in terms of industrial relations within the company. So firms tend to respond to increases in demand in the short run by working their existing labour force more intensively, for instance through overtime.

Firms will need to provide incentives for workers to work harder or longer hours. Overtime, for instance, may be paid at one and a half times the basic rate of pay. Whilst basic pay rates remain constant, earnings will rise and this will tend to put up both the average and marginal costs per unit of output. In many sectors of the economy, where competition is imperfect and where firms have the power to increase their prices, the rise in labour costs will lead to a rise in prices. It only needs prices to rise in some sectors of the economy for the average price level in

the economy to rise. So in the short term, an increase in output by firms is likely to lead to an increase in their costs which in turn will result in some firms raising prices. However, the increase in prices is likely to be small because, given constant prices (e.g. wage **rates**) for factor inputs, the increases in costs (e.g. wage **earnings**) are likely to be fairly small too. Therefore the short run aggregate supply curve is relatively price elastic. This is shown in Figure 1. An increase in output from Q_1 to Q_2 leads to a moderate rise in the average price level of $P_1 P_2$.

If demand falls in the short run, some firms in the economy will react by cutting their prices to try and stimulate extra orders. However, the opportunities to cut prices will be limited. Firms will be reluctant to sack workers and their overheads will remain the same, so their average cost and marginal cost will barely be altered. Again, the aggregate supply curve is relatively price elastic.

Shifts in the short run aggregate supply curve

The SHORT RUN AGGREGATE SUPPLY CURVE shows the

Question 1

Using a short run aggregate supply curve, explain the likely effect on the price level of the following, assuming that the prices of all factor inputs are fixed.
(a) In 1988, output in the UK economy boomed. Real GDP rose by 5 per cent, an increase which has yet to be repeated.
(b) In 1991, there was a recession in the UK economy and output fell. Real GDP declined by 1.5 per cent, the last time in recent economic history a fall occurred.

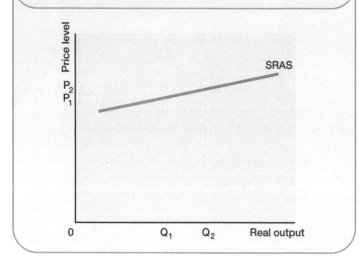

Figure 1 The short run aggregate supply curve
The slope of the SRAS line is very shallow because, whilst it is assumed that in the short run wage rates are constant, firms will face some increased costs such as overtime payments when they increase output.

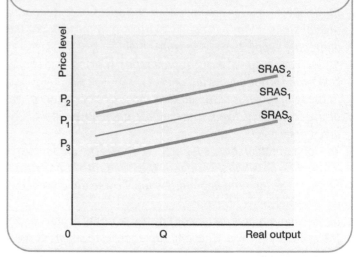

Figure 2 Shifts in the short run aggregate supply curve
The short run aggregate supply curve is drawn on the assumption that costs, in particular the wage rate, remain constant. A change in costs is shown by a shift in the curve. For instance, an increase in wage rates would push $SRAS_1$ up to $SRAS_2$ whilst a fall in wages rates would push the curve down to $SRAS_3$.

relationship between aggregate output and the average price level, assuming that money wage rates in the economy are constant. But what if wage rates do change, or some other variable which affects aggregate supply changes? Then, just as in the microeconomic theory of the supply curve, the aggregate supply curve will shift.

Wage rates An increase in wage rates will result in firms facing increased costs of production. Some firms will respond by increasing prices. So at any given level of output, a rise in wage rates will lead to a rise in the average price level. This is shown in Figure 2 by a shift in the short run aggregate supply curve from $SRAS_1$ to $SRAS_2$.

Raw material prices A general fall in the prices of raw materials may occur. Perhaps world demand for commodities falls, or perhaps the value of the pound rises, making the price of imports cheaper. A fall in the price of raw materials will lower industrial costs and will lead to some firms reducing the prices of their products. Hence there will be a shift in the short run aggregate supply curve downwards. This is shown in Figure 2 by the shift from $SRAS_1$ to $SRAS_3$.

Taxation An increase in the tax burden on industry will increase costs. Hence the short run aggregate supply schedule will be pushed upwards, for instance from $SRAS_1$ to $SRAS_2$ in Figure 2.

When there is a large change in wage rates, raw material prices or taxation, a SUPPLY SIDE SHOCK is said to occur. A supply side shock, like a doubling of the price of oil, can have a significant impact on aggregate supply, pushing the short run aggregate supply curve upwards.

The long run aggregate supply curve

In the short run, changes in wage rates or the price of raw materials have an effect on the aggregate supply curve, shifting the SRAS curve up or down. Equally, a rise in real output will lead to a movement along the SRAS curve.

In the long run, however, there is a limit to how

Using diagrams, show the likely effect of the following on the long run aggregate supply curve.
(a) Real national output in the 2nd quarter of 1992 was the same as in the fourth quarter of 1988 but average prices had increased 27 per cent over the period.
(b) In 2004-2005, the price of crude oil approximately doubled.
(c) Between 2000 and 2004, average money earnings in the UK economy rose by 16.7 per cent.

much firms can increase their supply. They run into capacity constraints. There is a limit to the amount of labour that can be hired in an economy. Capital equipment is fixed in supply. Labour productivity has been maximised. So it can be argued that in the long run, the aggregate supply curve is fixed at a given level of real output, whatever the price level. What this means is that the long run aggregate supply curve is vertical on a diagram showing the price level and real output.

Figure 3 shows such a vertical LONG RUN AGGREGATE SUPPLY CURVE or LRAS CURVE. The long run aggregate supply curve shows the productive potential of the economy. It shows how much real output can be produced over a period of time with a given level of factor inputs, such as labour and capital equipment, and a given level of efficiency in combining these factor inputs. It can be linked to three other economic concepts.
● The LRAS curve is the level of output associated with production on the production possibility frontier of an economy. In Figure 4, any point on the boundary AB is one which shows the level of real output shown by the LRAS curve.
● The LRAS curve is the level of output shown by the trend or long term average rate of growth in an economy. When output is above or below this long term trend level, an output

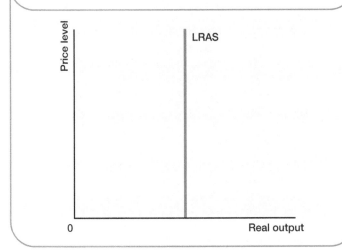

Figure 3 *The classical long run aggregate supply curve*
Classical economics assumes that in the long run wages and prices are flexible and therefore the LRAS curve is vertical. In the long run, there cannot be any unemployment because the wage rate will be in equilibrium where all workers who want a job (the supply of labour) will be offered a job (the demand for labour). So, whatever the level of prices, output will always be constant at the full employment level of income.

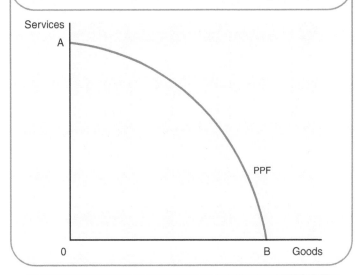

Figure 4 *A production possibility frontier*
Any point on the production possibility frontier AB shows the potential output of the economy when all resources are fully utilised. The long run aggregate supply curve also shows the potential output of the economy. At any point in time, if the economy is operating on its long run aggregate supply curve, then it will be operating at one of the points along the production possibility frontier.

gap is said to exist. In Figure 5, the economy is growing along the trend rate of growth of AB. There are short term fluctuations in actual output above and below the trend rate. This shows that actual output can be above or below that given by the long run aggregate supply curve. When actual output is above the trend rate on Figure 5 in the short run, and so to the right of the LRAS curve in Figure 3, economic forces will act to bring GDP back towards its trend rate of growth. Equally, when it is below its trend rate of growth, and so to the left of the LRAS curve in Figure 3, the same but opposite forces will bring it back to that long run position.
● The LRAS curve shows the level of FULL CAPACITY output of the economy. At full capacity, there are no underutilised resources in the economy. Production is at its long run maximum. In the short run, an economy might operate beyond full capacity, creating a positive output gap. However, this is unsustainable and the output in the economy must fall back to its full capacity levels.

Shifts in the long run aggregate supply curve

The long run aggregate supply curve is likely to shift over time. This is because the quantity and quality of economic resources changes over time, as does the way in which they are combined. These changes bring about changes in the productive potential of an economy.
Causes of shifts in the LRAS curve include:
● education and training which raises the skills of the workforce and levels of productivity (output per worker);
● investment in capital equipment which raises the stock of physical capital and hence pushes out the production possibility boundary;
● technological advances which allow new products to be made or existing products to be produced with fewer resources;
● increased world specialisation through international trade which allows production to be located in the cheapest and most efficient place in the world economy;

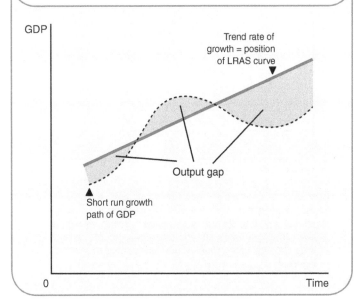

Figure 5 *The trend rate of growth for an economy*
At any point in time, the level of output shown by the long run aggregate supply is on the line of the trend rate of growth of output.

● improved work practices, such as just-in-time production which increase the productivity of both labour and capital;
● changes in government policy, such as the removal of unnecessary business regulation, which increases the efficiency of firms.
Figure 6 shows how a growth in potential output is drawn on an aggregate supply diagram. Assume that the education and skills of the workforce increase. This should lead to labour becoming more productive, in turn leading to an increase in the productive potential of the economy at full employment. The long run aggregate supply curve

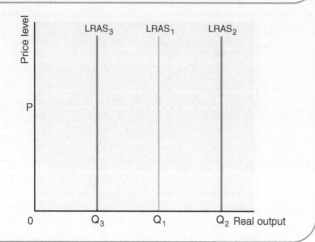

Figure 6 A shift in the long run aggregate supply curve
An increase in the productive potential in the economy pushes the long run aggregate supply curve to the right, for instance from LRAS₁ to LRAS₂. A fall in productive potential, on the other hand, is shown by a shift to the left of the curve, from LRAS₁ to LRAS₃ for instance.

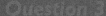

Question 3

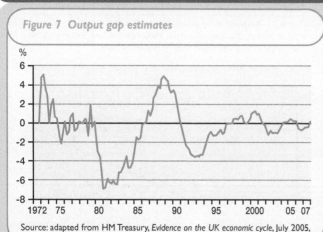

Figure 7 Output gap estimates

Source: adapted from HM Treasury, *Evidence on the UK economic cycle*, July 2005, Budget 2007 - The Economy

The output gap shows the difference between actual GDP and the long term trend level of GDP. On the diagram, the horizontal zero line shows this long term trend level of GDP.

(a) Give six years when the economy was operating on its long run aggregate supply curve, according to the data in Figure 7.
(b) GDP at constant prices rose every year between 1972 and 2004 except between 1973 and 1975, 1979 to 1983 and 1990 to 1992. Using a diagram, explain what happened to the long run aggregate supply curve between the six years given in your answer to (a).
(c) The economy experienced deep recessions between 1973 and 1975, 1979 and 1983, and 1990 to 1992. In these recessions, manufacturing suffered particularly badly, with many factories closing, never to reopen again, and some workers became deskilled, resulting in their inability ever to find another job in their working lifetime. Using a diagram, explain what might have happened to the long run aggregate supply curve for the UK economy in these years.

will then shift from $LRAS_1$ to $LRAS_2$, showing that at a given level of prices, the economy can produce more output. A fall in potential output, caused for instance by a fall in the size of the labour force, would be shown by a leftward shift in the curve, from $LRAS_1$ to $LRAS_3$.

A shift to the right in the LRAS curve shows that there has been economic growth. On a production possibility frontier (PPF) diagram, it would be represented by a movement outwards on the boundary. In Figure 5, it would be shown by a movement up along the trend rate of growth line. A shift to the left in the LRAS curve would show that the productive potential of the economy has fallen. On a PPF diagram, the boundary would shift inwards. On a trend rate of growth diagram, there would be a movement along and down the trend rate of growth line.

The classical and Keynesian long run aggregate supply curves

The vertical LRAS curve is called the **classical long run aggregate supply curve**. It is based on the classical view that markets tend to correct themselves fairly quickly when they are pushed into disequilibrium by some shock. In the long run, product markets like the markets for oil, cameras or meals out, and factor markets like the market for labour, will be in equilibrium. If all markets are in equilibrium, there can be no unemployed resources. Hence, the economy must be operating at full capacity on its production possibility boundary.

Keynesian economists, however, point out that there have been times when markets have failed to clear for long periods of time. Keynesian economics was developed out of the experience of the Great Depression of the 1930s when large scale unemployment lasted for a decade. If it had not been for the Second World War, it could be that high unemployment would have lasted for twenty or thirty years. John Maynard Keynes famously said that 'in the long run we are all dead'. There is little point in studying and drawing

Figure 8 The Keynesian long run aggregate supply curve
Traditional Keynesian economists argue that, even in the long run, unemployment may persist because wages don't necessarily fall when unemployment occurs. When there is mass unemployment, output can be increased without any increases in costs and therefore prices. As the economy nears full employment, higher output leads to higher prices. At full employment, the economy cannot produce any more whatever prices firms receive.

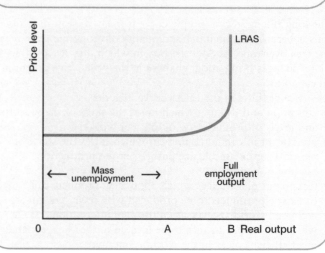

vertical long run aggregate supply curves if it takes 20-30 years to get back to the curve when the economy suffers a demand side or supply side shock.

Keynesian economists therefore suggest that the long run aggregate supply curve is the shape shown in Figure 8.

● At an output level of OB, the LRAS curve is vertical as with the classical LRAS curve. OB is the full capacity level of output of the economy. It is when the economy is on its production possibility boundary.

● At an output level below OA, the economy is in a deep and prolonged depression. There is mass unemployment. In theory, unemployment should lead to wages falling. If there is too

much supply of labour, the price of labour will fall. However, in a modern economy, there are many reasons why wages are **sticky downwards**. There might be a national minimum wage which sets a floor for wages. Trade unions might fight to maintain wage levels. High unemployment might persist in one area of the country when there is full employment in another area because of labour immobility. Firms may not want to lower wages because this could demotivate their staff and lead to lower productivity. So at output levels below OA, markets, and in particular the labour market, fail to clear. Firms can hire and fire extra workers without affecting the wage rate. Wages are stuck and there is persistent disequilibrium in the long run. Hence, there is no pressure on prices when output expands.

● At an output level between OA and OB, labour is becoming scarce enough for an increase in demand for labour to push up wages. This then leads to a higher price level. The nearer output gets to OB, the full employment level of output, the greater the effect of an increase in demand for labour on wages and therefore the price level.

Key terms

Aggregate supply curve - the relationship between the average level of prices in the economy and the level of total output.
Full capacity - the level of output where no extra production can take in the long run with existing resources. The full capacity level of output for an economy is shown by the classical long run aggregate supply curve.
Long run aggregate supply curve - the aggregate supply curve which assumes that wage rates are variable, both upward and downwards. Classical or supply side economists assume that wage rates are flexible. Keynesian economists assume that wage rates may be 'sticky downwards' and hence the economy may operate at less than full employment even in the long run.
Short run aggregate supply curve - the upward sloping aggregate supply curve which assumes that money wage rates are fixed.
Supply side shocks - factors such as changes in wage rates or commodity prices which cause the short run aggregate supply curve to shift.

Applied economics

The case of oil

As Figure 9 shows, in 1973 a barrel of oil cost $2.83. A year later the price had risen to $10.41. This price rise was possibly the most important world economic event of the 1970s. The trigger for the rise came from a war - the Yom Kippur war - when Egypt attacked Israel and was subsequently defeated. The Arab nations, to show support for Egypt, decreed that they would cut off oil supplies from any country which openly supported Israel. Because the demand for oil in the short run is highly price inelastic, any small fall in the supply of oil is enough to bring large increases in prices. After the war finished, the oil producing nations through their organisation OPEC (the Organisation for Petroleum Exporting Countries) realised that it was possible to maintain a high price for oil by limiting its supply (i.e. by operating a cartel). Since then OPEC has operated a policy of restricting the supply of oil to the market.

Oil prices rose rather more slowly between 1974 and 1978. However, between 1978 and 1982 the average price of a barrel of oil rose from $13.03 to $31.80.

Again, a political event was a major factor in triggering the price rise. The Shah of Iran, ruler of an important oil producing country, was deposed by Muslim fundamentalists led by the Ayatollah Khomeini. The revolution plunged Iran into economic chaos and the new rulers, fiercely anti-Western, showed little interest in resuming large scale exports of oil. A small disruption in oil supplies, a situation exploited by OPEC, was again enough to send oil prices spiralling.

In 1990, Iraq invaded Kuwait but was expelled in the Gulf War of 1991. This produced a short lived spike in oil prices but oil prices subsequently fell and by 1998, averaged only $12.21 a barrel. Cutting production quotas enabled OPEC to raise prices again to over $20 a barrel. However, from 2003 to 2005, another boom in oil prices occurred with oil prices at times reaching over $100 a barrel. The main cause of this boom was the relentless increase in demand for oil by fast growing Asian countries, particularly China. Underinvestment by OPEC countries in their oil production facilities over a twenty year period meant that, by 2005, the world oil industry was operating at maximum capacity. Increases in demand could only push prices up.

These three periods of sharp oil price rises all had an important effect on the short run aggregate supply curve of the UK economy. Oil price rises increase the costs of firms. So at any given level of output, firms need to charge higher prices to cover their costs. As a result, the short run aggregate supply curve shifts upwards. The oil price rises of 1973-75 and 1979-81 were a major contributor to the rises in inflation at the time shown in Figure 10. Significantly, though, the oil price increase from 2003 had very little impact on inflation. One reason was that the average amount of

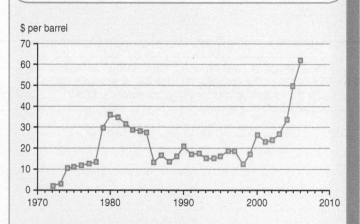

Figure 9 Price of oil

$ per barrel

Source: adapted from *BP Statistical Review of World Energy*.

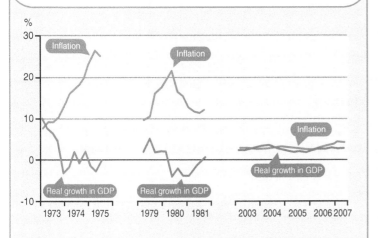

Figure 10 Economic growth and inflation (RPI), year on year, in three periods of oil shocks

Source: adapted from *Economic & Labour Market Review*, Office for National Statistics.

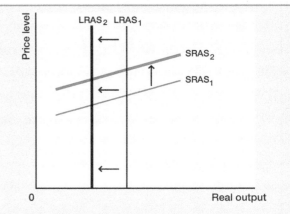

Figure 11 The effect of steep rises in oil prices on aggregate supply
A large rise in the price of oil will push the short run aggregate supply curve upwards and possibly shift the long run aggregate supply curve to the left.

Source: adapted from *Economic & Labour Market Review*, Office for National Statistics.

oil used to generate £1 of GDP was far less during this period than in 1975 or 1981. Greater energy efficiency and the decline of manufacturing industry were the main reasons for this. Another reason for the small impact of the oil price rise was that UK firms found it much more difficult to pass on price rises to their customers than in 1975 or 1981. The economic climate was more competitive and firms tended to absorb oil prices rather than pass them on.

Many economists argue that the oil price rises of 1973-75 and 1979-1981 also reduced the productive potential of the UK economy, shifting the long run aggregate supply curve to the left, as shown in Figure 11. The rise in oil prices meant that some capital equipment which was oil intensive became uneconomic to run. This equipment was mothballed and then scrapped, leading to a once-and-for-all fall in the amount of capital in the economy. Because the economy was far less oil dependent in 2003-2007, this scrapping of equipment was negligible. Firms had become reluctant to invest in equipment using oil when there were good substitutes because they were afraid of a large rise in oil prices.

DataQuestion

Aggregate supply, 1974-79

Between February 1974 and May 1979, there was a Labour government in the UK. It is often considered to have been a disastrous period for the economy. In 1975, inflation rose to a post-war peak of 24.2 per cent. Unemployment rose from half a million in 1974 to one and half million in 1977. Share prices halved in 1974. The pound fell to an all time low against the dollar in October 1976. The UK government was forced to borrow from the IMF (the International Monetary Fund) in late 1976 to shore up the value of the pound. In 1978-79, during the 'winter of discontent', the economy seemed racked by strikes as workers pressed for double digit pay rises.

However, the second half of the 1970s were difficult times for all industrialised economies. Growth rates worldwide fell as economies accommodated the supply-side shock of the first oil crisis in 1973-4. Table 1 shows that the growth in real GDP in the UK economy was above its long run trend rate of growth of 2.5 per cent per annum in three of the six years during the period;

and although the average yearly growth rate over the six years was only 1.5 per cent, if 1973, a boom year for the economy, were included, the average rate of growth would be 2.3 per cent. Investment spending in the economy remained static, with investment as a percentage of GDP slightly declining. This perhaps reflected a lack of confidence in the future of the economy. Even so, this should be contrasted with the experience of the early 1980s. Investment fell in 1980 and 1981 and did not reach its 1979 levels till 1984.

The 1970s were inflationary times throughout the world. Inflation in the UK accelerated from 7.5 per cent in 1972 to 15.9 per cent in 1974 and 24.1 per cent in 1975. However, the government adopted firm anti-inflationary policies in 1975 and inflation subsequently fell to 8.3 per cent in 1978, before rising again to 13.4 per cent in 1979 as pressure from wages and import prices, including the second round of oil price rises, worsened.

Table 1 Selected economic indicators, UK 1974-79

	Real growth in GDP	Gross investment	Inflation (RPI)	Change in import prices	Change in average earnings
	%	% of GDP	%	%	%
1974	-1.5	14.8	15.9	46.2	18.5
1975	-0.6	14.6	24.1	14.1	26.6
1976	2.8	14.4	16.6	22.3	15.9
1977	2.4	13.9	15.9	15.8	8.8
1978	3.2	13.8	8.3	3.8	13.2
1979	2.8	13.8	13.4	6.4	15.2

Source: adapted from *Economic Trends Annual Supplement*, Office for National Statistics.

1. Consider both the passage and the table carefully. Discuss, using diagrams, what happened to aggregate supply in the second half of the 1970s:
   (a) in the short run and
   (b) in the long run.

26 Equilibrium output

Summary

1. The economy is in equilibrium when aggregate demand equals aggregate supply.
2. In the short run, equilibrium occurs when aggregate demand equals short run aggregate supply.
3. In the classical model, where wages are completely flexible, the economy will be in long run equilibrium at full employment. In the Keynesian model, where wages are sticky downwards, the economy can be in long run equilibrium at less than full employment.
4. In the classical model, a rise in aggregate demand will in the short run lead to an increase in both output and prices, but in the long run the rise will generate only an increase in prices. In the Keynesian model, a rise in aggregate demand will be purely inflationary if the economy is at full employment, but will lead to an increase in output if the economy is below full employment.
5. A rise in long run aggregate supply in the classical model will both increase output and reduce prices. Keynesians would agree with this in general, but would argue that an increase in aggregate supply will have no effect on output or prices if the economy is in a slump.
6. Factors which affect aggregate demand may well affect aggregate supply and vice versa, although this may occur over different time periods. For instance, an increase in investment is likely to increase both aggregate demand and aggregate supply.

Equilibrium output in the short run

The previous two units outlined theories of aggregate demand and aggregate supply. Both Keynesian and classical economists agree that in the short run the aggregate demand curve is downward sloping whilst the aggregate supply curve is upward sloping. The equilibrium level of output in the short run occurs at the intersection of the aggregate demand and aggregate supply curves. In Figure 1, the equilibrium level of income and output is 0Q. The equilibrium price level is 0P.

An increase in aggregate demand will shift the aggregate demand curve to the right. Aggregate demand is made up of consumption, investment, government spending and export minus imports. So an increase in aggregate demand will result from an increase in one of these components. For example:
● a fall in interest rates will raise both consumption and investment;

● a fall in the exchange rate will boost exports and reduce imports;
● a lowering of income tax will raise consumption because households will now have higher disposable income.

Figure 2 shows the impact of a rise in aggregate demand on equilibrium output and the price level. The aggregate demand curve shifts from AD_1 to AD_2. Equilibrium output then rises from $0Q_1$ to $0Q_2$ whilst the price level rises from $0P_1$ to $0P_2$. A rise in aggregate demand therefore increases both real output and the price level in the short run. The opposite is also true. A fall in aggregate demand will lead both to a fall in real output and a fall in the price level.

A fall in short run aggregate supply will shift the SRAS curve upwards and to the left. A variety of factors could bring about a fall in short run aggregate supply. For example:
● wages of workers might rise;

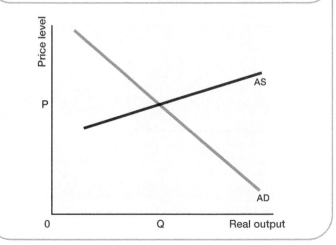

Figure I Equilibrium output
The equilibrium level of national output is set at the intersection of the aggregate demand and supply curves at 0Q. The equilibrium price level is 0P.

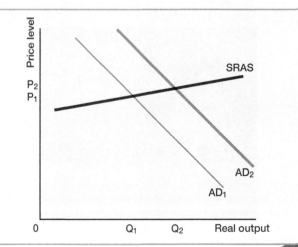

Figure 2 A rise in aggregate demand in the short run
A rise in aggregate demand, shown by the shift in the aggregate demand curve from AD_1 to AD_2, leads to a rise in both equilibrium real output from $0Q_1$ to $0Q_2$ and the price level from $0P_1$ to $0P_2$.

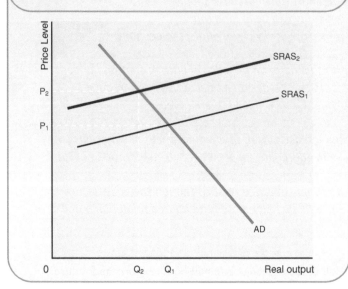

Figure 3 *A fall in aggregate supply in the short run*
A fall in short run aggregate supply, shown by the shift in the SRAS curve from SRAS₁ to SRAS₂, leads to a fall in equilibrium real output from 0Q₁ to 0Q₂ and a rise in the price level from 0P₁ to 0P₂.

- raw material prices might go up;
- taxes on goods and services might be raised by the government.

Figure 3 shows the impact of a fall in aggregate supply on equilibrium output and the price level. The SRAS curve shifts from $SRAS_1$ to $SRAS_2$. Equilibrium output then falls from $0Q_1$ to $0Q_2$. At the same time, the price level rises from $0P_1$ to $0P_2$. A fall in short run aggregate supply therefore leads to a fall in output but a rise in the price level in the short run. The opposite

Question 1

What would be the effect on equilibrium income in the short run if the workers in the photograph were (a) successful and (b) unsuccessful with their demands?

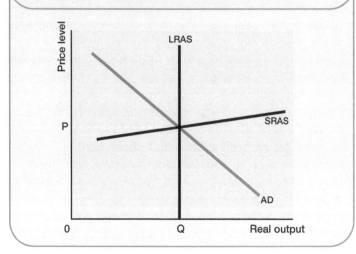

Figure 4 *Long run equilibrium in the classical model*
Long run equilibrium output is 0Q, the full employment level of output, since wages are flexible both downwards as well as upwards.

is also true. A rise in aggregate supply, shown by a downward shift to the right of the SRAS curve, will lead to a rise in equilibrium output and a fall in the price level.

Equilibrium output in the long run

In the long run, the impact of changes in aggregate demand and supply are affected by the shape of the long run aggregate supply curve. Classical economists argue that in the long run the aggregate supply curve is vertical, as shown in Figure 4. Long run equilibrium occurs where the long run aggregate supply curve (LRAS) intersects with the aggregate demand curve. Hence equilibrium output is 0Q and the equilibrium price level is 0P. Associated with the long run equilibrium price level is a short run aggregate supply curve (SRAS) which passes through the point where LRAS = AD. The long run aggregate supply curve shows the supply curve for the economy at full employment. Hence there can be no unemployment in the long run according to classical economists.

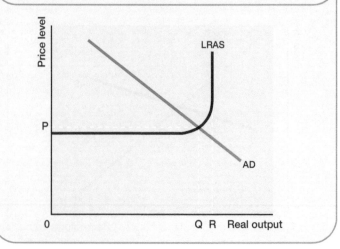

Figure 5 *Long run equilibrium in the Keynesian model*
Long run equilibrium output OQ may be below the full employment level of output OR because real wages may not fall when there is unemployment.

Keynesian economists argue that the long run aggregate supply curve is as shown in Figure 5. The economy is at full employment where the LRAS curve is vertical at output OR - a point of agreement with classical economists. However, the economy can be in equilibrium at less than full employment. In Figure 5 the equilibrium level of output is 0Q where the AD curve cuts the LRAS curve. The key point of disagreement between classical and Keynesian economists is the extent to which workers react to unemployment by accepting real wage cuts.

Classical economists argue that a rise in unemployment will lead rapidly to cuts in real wages. These cuts will increase the demand for labour and reduce its supply, returning the economy to full employment quickly and automatically. Keynesian economists, on the other hand, argue that money wages are sticky downwards. Workers will refuse to take money wage cuts and will fiercely resist cuts in their real wage. The labour market will therefore not clear except perhaps over a very long period of time, so long that it is possibly even not worth considering.

Having outlined a theory of equilibrium output, it is now possible to see what happens if either aggregate demand or aggregate supply changes.

A rise in aggregate demand

Assume that there is a rise in aggregate demand in the economy with long run aggregate supply initially remaining unchanged. For instance, there may be an increase in the wages of public sector employees paid for by an increase in the money supply, or there may be a fall in the marginal propensity to save and a rise in the marginal propensity to consume. A rise in aggregate demand will push the AD curve to the right. The classical and Keynesian models give different conclusions about the effect of this.

The classical model A rise in aggregate demand, in the classical model, will lead to a rise in the price level but no change in real output in the long run. In Figure 6, the aggregate demand curve shifts to the right from AD_1 to AD_2. This could have been

caused by a fall in interest rates, for example. The equilibrium price level rises from $0P_1$ to $0P_2$ but equilibrium real output remains the same at 0Q. In the classical model, no amount of extra demand will raise long run equilibrium output. This is because the long run aggregate supply curve shows the maximum productive capacity of the economy at that point in time.

The movement from one equilibrium point to the next can also be shown on an AD/AS diagram. Assume there is a rise in aggregate demand, which shifts the aggregate demand curve from AD_1 to AD_2. In the short run, this will result in a movement up the SRAS curve. In Figure 7, output will rise from 0L to 0M and this will be accompanied by a small rise in the price level from 0N to 0P. This will move the economy from A to B.

However, the economy is now in long run disequilibrium. The full employment level of output is 0L, shown by the position of the long run aggregate supply curve. The economy is therefore

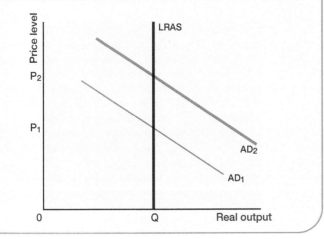

Figure 6 *A rise in aggregate demand in the classical model*
A rise in aggregate demand in the long run will shift the aggregate demand curve from AD_1 to AD_2. The equilibrium price level will rise from $0P_1$ to $0P_2$ but there will be no change in equilibrium real output..

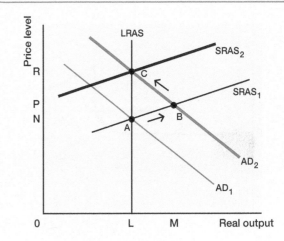

Figure 7 *The classical model in the short and long run*
A rise in aggregate demand shown by a shift to the right in the AD curve will result in a movement along the SRAS curve. Both output and prices will increase. In the long run, the SRAS curve will shift upwards with long run equilibrium being re-established at C. The rise in demand has led only to a rise in the price level.

operating at over-full employment. Firms will find it difficult to recruit labour, buy raw materials and find new offices or factory space. They will respond by bidding up wages and other costs. The short run aggregate supply curve is drawn on the assumption that wage rates and other costs remain constant. So a rise in wage rates will shift the short run aggregate supply curve upwards. Short run equilibrium output will now fall and prices will keep rising. The economy will only return to long run equilibrium when the short run aggregate supply curve has shifted upwards from SRAS$_1$ to SRAS$_2$ so that aggregate demand once again equals long run aggregate supply at C.

The conclusion of the classical model is that increases in aggregate demand will initially increase both prices and output (the movement from A to B in Figure 7). Over time prices will continue to rise but output will fall as the economy moves back towards long run equilibrium (the movement from B to C). In the long term an increase in aggregate demand will only lead to an increase in the price level (from A to C). There will be no effect on equilibrium output. So increases in aggregate demand without any change in long run aggregate supply are purely inflationary.

The Keynesian model In the Keynesian model, the long run aggregate supply curve is shaped as in Figure 8. Keynesians would agree with classical economists that an increase in aggregate demand from, say, AD$_4$ to AD$_5$ will be purely inflationary if the economy is already at full employment at 0D.

But if the economy is in deep depression, as was the case in the UK during the early 1930s, an increase in aggregate demand will lead to a rise in output without an increase in prices. The shift in aggregate demand from AD$_1$ to AD$_2$ will increase equilibrium output from 0A to 0B without raising the price level from 0P as there are unused resources available.

The third possibility is that the economy is a little below full employment, for instance at 0C in Figure 8. Then a rise in aggregate demand from AD$_3$ to AD$_4$ will increase both equilibrium output and equilibrium prices.

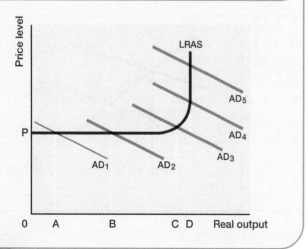

Figure 8 The Keynesian model
If the economy is already at full employment, an increase in aggregate demand in the Keynesian model creates an inflationary gap without increasing output. In a depression, an increase in aggregate demand will increase output but not prices. If the economy is slightly below full employment, an increase in aggregate demand will increase both output and prices.

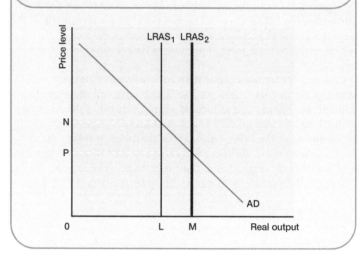

Figure 9 An increase in aggregate supply in the classical model
A shift to the right of the LRAS curve will both increase equilibrium output and reduce the price level.

In the Keynesian model, increases in aggregate demand may or may not be effective in raising equilibrium output. It depends upon whether the economy is below full employment or at full employment.

A rise in long run aggregate supply

A rise in long run aggregate supply means that the potential output of the economy has increased (i.e. there has been genuine economic growth). Rises in long run aggregate supply which are unlikely to shift the aggregate demand curve might occur if, for instance, incentives to work increased or there was a change in technology.

The classical model In the classical model, an increase in long run aggregate supply will lead to both higher output and lower prices. In Figure 9 a shift in the aggregate supply curve from LRAS$_1$ to LRAS$_2$ will increase equilibrium output from 0L to 0M. Equilibrium prices will also fall from 0N to 0P. Contrast this conclusion with what happens when aggregate demand is increased in the classical model - a rise in prices with no increase in output. It is not surprising that classical economists are so strongly in favour of **supply side policies** (this is why they are often referred to as 'supply side' economists).

The Keynesian model In the Keynesian model, shown in Figure 10, an increase in aggregate supply will both increase output and reduce prices if the economy is at full employment. With aggregate demand at AD$_1$, a shift in the aggregate supply curve from LRAS$_1$ to LRAS$_2$ increases full employment equilibrium output from Y$_E$ to Y$_F$. If the economy is at slightly less than full employment, with an aggregate demand curve of AD$_2$, then the shift to the right in the LRAS curve will still be beneficial to the economy, increasing output and reducing prices. However, Keynesians disagree with classical economists that supply side measures can be effective in a depression. If the aggregate demand curve is AD$_3$, an increase in aggregate supply has no effect on equilibrium output. It remains obstinately stuck at Y$_D$. Only an increase in aggregate demand will move the economy out of depression.

It is now possible to understand one of the most important

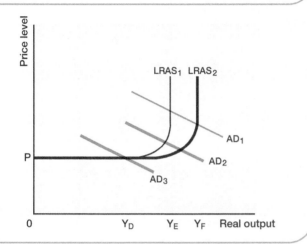

Figure 10 *An increase in aggregate supply in the Keynesian model*
The effect of an increase in long run aggregate supply depends upon the position of the aggregate demand curve. If the economy is at or near full employment, an increase will raise output and lower prices. However, if the economy is in depression at Y_D*, an increase in LRAS will have no impact on the economy.*

controversies in the history of economics. During the 1930s, classical economists argued that the only way to put the millions of unemployed during the Great Depression back to work was to adopt supply side measures - such as cutting unemployment benefits, reducing trade union power and cutting marginal tax rates and government spending. John Maynard Keynes attacked

Question 3

In June 1995, a new French government unveiled a stiff budget designed to reduce high unemployment levels by 700 000 and bring down a high budget deficit from 5.7 per cent of GDP to 5.1 per cent of GDP within the fiscal year. The measures included:
- a substantial FF19bn cut in government spending affecting all ministries apart from justice and culture, with defence bearing nearly 50 per cent of the cuts;
- a rise in corporation tax from 33.3 per cent to 36.6 per cent;
- a rise in the standard rate of VAT from 18.6 per cent to 20.6 per cent;
- a 10 per cent rise in wealth tax;
- a 40 per cent cut in employment taxes paid by firms on employment of workers at or near the minimum wage level;
- new programmes targeted particularly at youth in difficulties, offering training, apprenticeship and other policies to bring people into the workforce;
- a rise in the minimum wage by 4 per cent;
- a rise in state pensions by 0.5 per cent;
- measures to stimulate the housing market, particularly focused on lodgings for people on lower incomes.

Using diagrams, explain what effect these measures would have on aggregate supply according to:
(a) classical or supply side economists,
(b) Keynesian economists.

this orthodoxy by suggesting that the depression was caused by a lack of demand and suggesting that it was the government's responsibility to increase the level of aggregate demand. The same debate was replayed in the UK in the early 1980s. This time it was Keynesians who represented orthodoxy. They suggested that the only quick way to get the millions officially unemployed back to work was to expand aggregate demand. In the Budget of 1981, the government did precisely the opposite - it cut its projected budget deficit, reducing aggregate demand and argued that the only way to cure unemployment was to improve the supply side of the economy.

Increasing aggregate demand and supply

In microeconomics, factors which shift the demand curve do **not** shift the supply curve as well and vice versa. For instance, an increase in the costs of production shifts the supply curve but does **not** shift the demand curve for a good (although there will of course be a **movement along** the demand curve as a result). However, in macroeconomic aggregate demand and aggregate supply analysis, factors which shift one curve may well shift the other curve as well. For instance, assume that firms increase their planned investment. This will increase the level of aggregate demand. However, in the long run it will also increase the level of aggregate supply. An increase in investment will increase the capital stock of the economy. The productive potential of the economy will therefore rise. We can use aggregate demand and supply analysis to show the effects of an increase in investment.

An increase in investment in the classical model will initially shift the aggregate demand curve in Figure 11 to the right from AD_1 to AD_2. There will then be a movement along the short run aggregate supply curve from A to B. There is now long run disequilibrium. How this will be resolved depends upon the speed with which the investment is brought on stream and starts to produce goods and services. Assume that this happens fairly quickly. The long run aggregate supply curve will then shift to the right, say, from $LRAS_1$ to $LRAS_2$. Long run equilibrium will

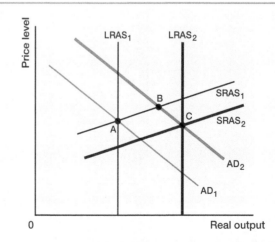

Figure 11 *An increase in investment expenditure*
An increase in investment will increase aggregate demand from AD_1 *to* AD_2*, and is likely to shift the long run aggregate supply curve from* $LRAS_1$ *to* $LRAS_2$*. The result is an increase in output and a small fall in prices.*

be restored at C. Output has increased and the price level fallen slightly. There will also be a new short run aggregate supply curve, SRAS$_2$. It is below the original short run aggregate supply curve because it is assumed that investment has reduced costs of production.

Not all investment results in increased production. For instance, fitting out a new shop which goes into receivership within a few months will increase aggregate demand but not long run aggregate supply. The long run aggregate supply curve will therefore not shift and the increased investment will only be inflationary. Equally, investment might be poorly directed. The increase in aggregate demand might be greater than the increase in long run aggregate supply. Here there will be an increase in equilibrium output but there will also be an increase in prices. The extent to which investment increases output and contributes to a lessening of inflationary pressure depends upon the extent to which it gives a high rate of return in the long run.

Using a classical model of the economy, explain the effect of the following on: (i) aggregate demand; (ii) short run aggregate supply; (iii) output and prices in the long run.
(a) A 10 per cent rise in earnings.
(b) An increase in real spending by government on education and training.
(c) An increase in the average long term real rate of interest from 3 per cent to 5 per cent.

Applied economics

Stagflation, 1974-76, 1979-1981 and 1988-1990

In a simple Keynesian model, rising inflation is associated with falling unemployment and vice versa. The experience of the 1950s and 1960s tended to support the hypothesis that there was this trade off between the two variables. However, in 1973-75, 1979-1981 and 1988-91 there were both rising inflation and rising unemployment, as shown in Figure 12. This combination of stagnation and inflation came to be called **stagflation**.

The stagflation of the first two of these periods was caused by a large rise in oil prices, an example of an external supply side shock to the economy. The rise had the effect of raising the short run aggregate supply curve from SRAS$_1$ to SRAS$_2$ in Figure 13. The economy shifted from A to B. As can be seen from the diagram, prices rose and output fell.

In the first oil crisis, inflation rose from 9.1 per cent in 1973 to 15.9 per cent in 1974 and 24.1 per cent in 1975, before falling back to 16.5 per cent in 1976. Real GDP on the other hand fell by 1.5 per cent in 1974 and 0.8 per cent in 1975, before resuming an upward path in 1976.

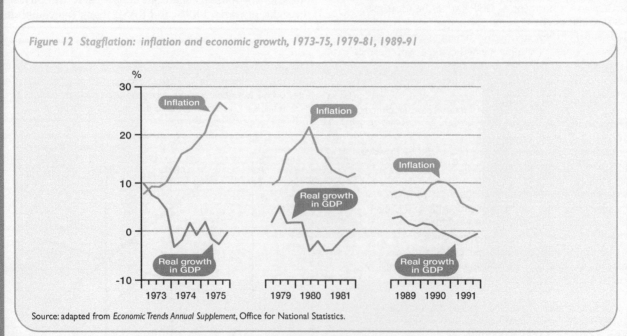

Figure 12 *Stagflation: inflation and economic growth, 1973-75, 1979-81, 1989-91*

Source: adapted from *Economic Trends Annual Supplement*, Office for National Statistics.

In the second oil crisis, inflation rose from 8.3 per cent in 1978 to 13.4 per cent in 1979 and 18.0 per cent in 1980, before falling back again in 1981. Real GDP fell by 2 per cent in 1980 and 1.2 per cent in 1981.

The classical model would suggest that, all other things being equal, the economy would fall back to A from B. Full employment would be restored at the old price level. The above figures indicate that this did not happen. This was because the aggregate demand curve shifted to the right at the same time as the short run aggregate supply curve was shifting to the left. This led to continued inflation as output rose from 1976 and again from 1982. The rise in aggregate demand in the first period was partly due to the then Labour government increasing the budget deficit, as well as increases in the money supply (the inflation was **accommodated**). Treasury estimates of the output gap suggest that the economy returned to its long run productive potential, at C in Figure 35.10, in 1978. In the second period, 1979-1981, taxation rose and government spending fell during the downturn in the economy, although the money supply increased again. This difference in fiscal stance is a partial explanation of why the rise in unemployment was lower and the rise in inflation higher in the first period than in the second period. It can be argued that the shift to the right in the aggregate demand curve was greater in the mid-1970s than the early 1980s.

The result was that the economy took much longer to return to the point C on its LRAS curve in this second period. Treasury estimates of the output gap suggest this did not occur until 1986.

The period of stagflation between 1988 and 1990 was different from the two previous periods. This was caused, not by a supply side shock but by a demand side shock. The Conservative government was partly responsible for stoking up an unsustainable boom in 1986-88, called the 'Lawson boom' after Nigel Lawson, the Chancellor of the Exchequer at the time. When inflation began to rise, it reacted by raising interest rates from 7.5 per cent in May 1988 to 15 per cent in October 1989 and keeping them at those levels for nearly a year. This, together with a high value of the pound, produced a prolonged recession lasting through to the end of 1992 despite the fact that inflation peaked in the 3rd quarter of 1990. The economy did not return to production on the LRAS curve until 1997.

Oil crises have led to inflation.

In all three periods of stagflation, the long run aggregate supply curve was probably still shifting to the right. The productive potential of the economy was increasing despite the actual fall in GDP being recorded. However, some economists argue that these periods of stagflation destroyed some of that productive potential. Capital equipment became redundant through lack of demand and was scrapped. Workers became long term unemployed, deskilled and demotivated, some never to work again. On this argument, stagflation is responsible for slowing down the growth of the productive potential of the economy. So the long run aggregate supply curve shifts less quickly to the right, leading to permanently lower equilibrium output and a higher price level.

Figure 13 Stagflation caused by supply side shocks

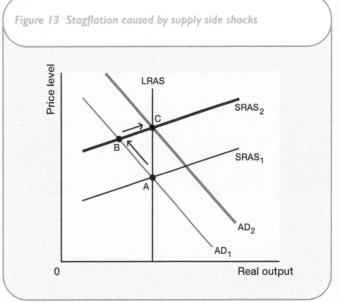

DataQuestion

The UK economy, 2005-06

Disappointing year for the economy

2005 has not been a boom year for the economy. Economic growth has been below trend whilst unemployment has very slightly risen. The housing market has been subdued, with average house price rises of a 'mere' 5 per cent, even if 5 per cent is arguably the right long term rate of growth of house prices. Consumers have not been increasing their spending as much as in previous years, hit by a variety of factors including higher interest rates, higher petrol prices and higher gas and electricity bills.

2005 could have been worse

At the same time, 2005 could have been much worse. Oil prices rising at times to over $60 a barrel, nearly twice the price of 12 months earlier, could have sparked off much higher inflation, as indeed it did in the 1970s. The same rising oil prices and the general steep rise in world commodity prices could have sparked a recession in the world wide economy, causing Britain's exports to slump and sending it too into a recession. Consumers could have taken real fright at deteriorating economic conditions and decided to cut back on their borrowing and increase their saving by considerably reducing their spending. The US economy, with its huge imbalances, could have suddenly gone into recession. It remains extremely vulnerable to overseas lenders which are financing the US current account deficit of over 5 per cent of GDP. If that finance dried up, the value of the dollar would plummet, US imports would shrink and some of those lost US imports would be UK exports.

Dangers for 2006

Dangers remain for 2006. The greatest danger is probably external, from a world recession. However, British consumers could cut back on their spending. The government is fortunately in the middle of a large expansion of public spending and has proved reluctant to increase its taxes too much to pay for it. So the government sector should provide a positive boost to GDP. With luck, it will be enough to keep the output gap close to zero and the economy on course.

1. Outline (a) the demand side factors and (b) the supply side factors that influenced the equilibrium level of national output in 2005.
2. Using a diagram, explain why the rise in real national output was low and 'below trend' in 2005.
3. Using a diagram, explain how a recession in the US economy could affect the equilibrium level of real output and the price level of the UK economy.
4. To what extent is it important that the output gap should be 'close to zero' and the economy is kept 'on course'?

27 Economic growth

Summary

1. Economic growth is the change in potential output of the economy shown by a shift to the right of the production possibility frontier. Economic growth is usually measured by the change in real national income.
2. Economic growth is caused by increases in the quantity or quality of land, labour and capital and by technological progress.

Economic growth

Economies change over time. Part of this change involves changes in productive capacity - the ability to produce goods and services. Increases in productive capacity are known as ECONOMIC GROWTH. Most economies today experience positive economic growth over time. For example, the UK economy is growing at around 2.5 per cent per annum. This means that its productive potential is doubling roughly every 25 years. The Chinese economy is growing at around 10 per cent per annum. This means its productive potential is doubling roughly every 7 years.

The productive potential of an economy can fall as well as rise. Recent wars in Africa, for example, have lead to negative economic growth for some countries. Equally, the collapse of communism in the early 1990s and the move to a market economy for countries like Russia or Poland led initially to a fall in productive potential because of the economic disruption caused.

The business cycle

It is not possible to measure the productive capacity of an economy directly because there is no way of producing a single monetary figure for the value of variables such as machinery, workers and technology. Instead, economists use changes in GDP, the value of output, as a proxy measure.

The problem with using GDP is that, in the short term, GDP fluctuates around the long term rate of growth. These fluctuations are known as the BUSINESS CYCLE or TRADE CYCLE or ECONOMIC CYCLE. All business cycles are slightly different. However, they tend to have four main phases. These are illustrated in Figure 1.

Peak or boom When the economy is in boom, GDP is growing particularly fast. Unemployment is likely to be low and spending high. The rate of growth of GDP is likely to be above its long term trend rate. There will be inflationary pressures due to expanding aggregate demand. Firms will increasing their investment to cope with demand.

Downturn In a downturn, the economy is slowing down. The rate of growth of GDP will be falling and unemployment will be rising. Consumer and investment spending will be slowing and inflationary pressures will be falling.

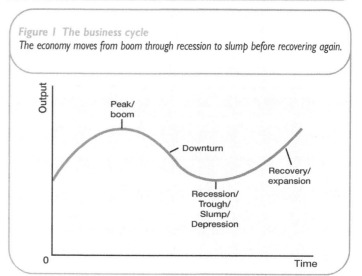

Figure 1 The business cycle
The economy moves from boom through recession to slump before recovering again.

Recession or trough or slump or depression At the bottom of the economic cycle, the rate of growth of GDP may be close to zero or may be negative. The deeper the recession, the larger will be the fall in the GDP and the longer the recession will last. In a recession, unemployment will be high and possibly still rising. Consumers and firms will be reluctant to take on debt because they fear they will not be able to repay it. Firms will be reluctant to invest in case they cannot sell the goods produced by the new investment. Inflation will be low and could even be negative.

Recovery or expansion In a recovery, the rate of growth of GDP begins to pick up again. Consumers and firms begin to regain confidence and spend more. Unemployment begins to fall.

In the UK, the government defines recession as where GDP falls in at least two successive quarters. On this definition, the last recession in the UK occurred in 1990-1991. Since then, the pattern of the trade cycle has followed the pattern set in the 1950s and 1960s. Recessions have been very mild. GDP has not fallen. Rather the rate of growth of GDP has dipped below its long term trend rate of growth. In a boom, the rate of growth of GDP has been slightly above the average long term rate of growth. When the economic cycle is very mild, the terms 'depression' and 'recovery' tend not be used. Economists and media commentators tend to talk about the economy going from recession to boom and back again to recession.

There are many different reasons why the short run rate of growth of GDP may fluctuate around its long term trend. But they can be classified into two main types.

- **Demand-side shocks** are shocks which affect aggregate demand. For example, there may be a sudden collapse in stock market prices which sends consumer confidence plummeting, or the central bank may raise interest rates sharply because inflation is getting too high, or the world economy may go into recession, hitting UK exports sharply and so sending the UK economy into recession.
- **Supply-side shocks** are shocks which affect aggregate supply. For example, a large rise in world commodity prices could raise the price level substantially in the UK, leading to lower spending and a recession. An outbreak of trade union militancy which saw large wage increases in the economy could again raise the price level substantially and send the economy into recession.

The output gap

The difference between the actual level of GDP and its estimated long term value at a point in time is known as the OUTPUT GAP. In Figure 2, the straight line is the trend rate of growth in GDP over a long period of time. It is assumed that this shows the level of GDP associated with the productive potential of the economy. The actual level of GDP varies around the trend growth line. This fluctuation is the business cycle. When the economy is in recession and there is high unemployment and deflation, the actual level of GDP will be below the trend line. A NEGATIVE OUTPUT GAP is then said to exist. In an inflationary boom, the actual level of GDP is likely to be above the trend line. A POSITIVE OUTPUT GAP then exists.
For the purposes of the International Baccalaureate, an inflationary gap is defined as occuring when there is a positive output gap, i.e. when the economy is operating at full employment and there is an increase in aggregate demand. A deflationary gap occurs when there is a negative output gap, i.e. aggregate demand is below the productive potential of the economy, or the long run aggregate supply level.

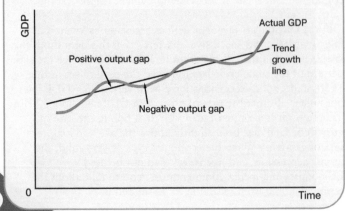

Figure 2 The output gap
The trend rate of growth of GDP approximates the growth in productive potential of the economy. When actual GDP falls below this or rises above it, there is said to be an output gap. When actual GDP growth falls below this, there is a negative output gap. When actual GDP growth rises above it, there is a positive output gap.

The production possibility frontier

Production possibility frontiers (PPFs) can be used to discuss economic growth. The PPF shows the maximum or **potential** output of an economy. When the economy grows, the PPF will move outward as in Figure 3. A movement from A to C would be classified as economic growth. However, there may be unemployment in the economy. With a PPF passing through C, a movement from B (where there is unemployment) to C (full employment) would be classified as ECONOMIC RECOVERY rather than economic growth. Hence, an increase in national income does not necessarily mean that there has been economic growth. In practice it is difficult to know exactly the location of an economy's PPF and therefore economists tend to treat all increases in GNP as economic growth.

Figure 3 can also be used to show the conflict between investment and consumption. One major source of economic growth is investment. All other things being equal, the greater the level of investment the higher will be the rate of growth in the future. However, increased production of investment goods can only be achieved by a reduction in the production of consumption goods if the economy is at full employment. So there is a trade off to be made between consumption now and consumption in the future. The lower the level of consumption today relative to the level of investment, the higher will be the level of consumption in the future.

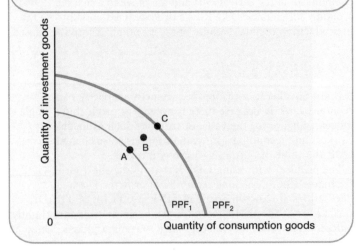

Figure 3 Production possibility frontiers
A movement from A to C would represent economic growth if there were a shift in the production possibility frontier from PPF₁ to PPF₂. A movement from B to C would represent economic recovery if the production possibility frontier was PPF₂.

The causes of economic growth

Fluctuations in the level of GDP around the trend rate of growth are caused by demand and supply side shocks. However, what explains why the productive potential of the economy increases over time?

National output can be increased if there is an increase in the quantity or quality of the inputs to the production process. Output can also be increased if existing inputs are used more efficiently. This can be expressed in terms of a **production function**:

Output = f (land, labour, capital, technical progress, efficiency)

The remainder of this unit will concentrate on the ways in which the quantity and quality of the factors of production can be increased and on what determines technical progress.

Land

Different countries possess different endowments of land. Land in economics is defined as all natural resources, not just land itself. Some countries, such as Saudi Arabia, have experienced large growth rates almost solely because they are so richly endowed. Without oil, Saudi Arabia today would almost certainly be a poor Third World country. Other countries have received windfalls. The UK, for instance, only started to exploit its oil and gas resources in the mid 1970s. However, most economists argue that the exploitation of raw materials is unlikely to be a significant source of growth in developed economies, although it can be vital in developing economies.

Labour

Increasing the **number** of workers in an economy should lead to economic growth. Increases in the labour force can result from three factors.

Changes in demography If more young people enter the workforce than leave it, then the size of the workforce will increase. In most western developed countries the population is relatively stable. Indeed, many countries are experiencing falls in the number of young people entering the workforce because of falls in the birth rate from the late 1960s onwards.

Increases in participation rates Nearly all men who wish to work are in the labour force. However, in most Western countries there exists a considerable pool of women who could be brought into the labour force if employment opportunities were present. In the UK, for instance, almost all of the increase in the labour force in the foreseeable future will result from women returning to or starting work.

Immigration A relatively easy way of increasing the labour force is to employ migrant labour. In the UK, for example, there have been large inward flows of migrant labour from Eastern Europe in recent years. It should be noted that increasing the size of the labour force may increase output but will not necessarily increase economic welfare. One reason is that increased income may have to be shared out amongst more people, causing little or no change in income per person. If women come back to work, they have to give up leisure time to do so. This lessens the increase in economic welfare which they experience.

Increasing the size of the labour force can increase output but increasing the quality of labour input is likely to be far more important in the long run. Labour is not **homogeneous** (i.e. it is not all the same). Workers can be made more productive by education and training. Increases in **human capital** are essential for a number of reasons.

- Workers need to be sufficiently educated to cope with the demands of the existing stock of capital. For instance, it is important for lorry drivers to be able to read, typists to spell and shop assistants to operate tills. These might seem very low grade skills but it requires a considerable educational input to get most of the population up to these elementary levels.
- Workers need to be flexible. On average in the UK, workers are likely to have to change job three times during their lifetime. Increasingly workers are being asked to change roles within existing jobs. Flexibility requires broad general education as well as in-depth knowledge of a particular task.
- Workers need to be able to contribute to change. It is easy to see that scientists and technologists are essential if inventions and new products are to be brought to the market. What is less obvious, but as important, is that every worker can contribute ideas to the improvement of techniques of production. An ability of all workers to take responsibility and solve problems will be increasingly important in the future.

Capital

The stock of capital in the economy needs to increase over time if economic growth is to be sustained. This means that there must be sustained investment in the economy. However, there is not necessarily a correlation between high investment and high growth. Some investment is not growth-related. For instance, investment in new housing or new hospitals is unlikely to create much wealth in the future. Investment can also be wasted if it takes place in industries which fail to sell products. For instance, investment in UK shipbuilding plants during the late 1970s and early 1980s provided a poor rate of return because the shipbuilding industry was in decline. Investment must therefore be targeted at growth industries.

Question 1

Figure 4 The ouput gap, UK

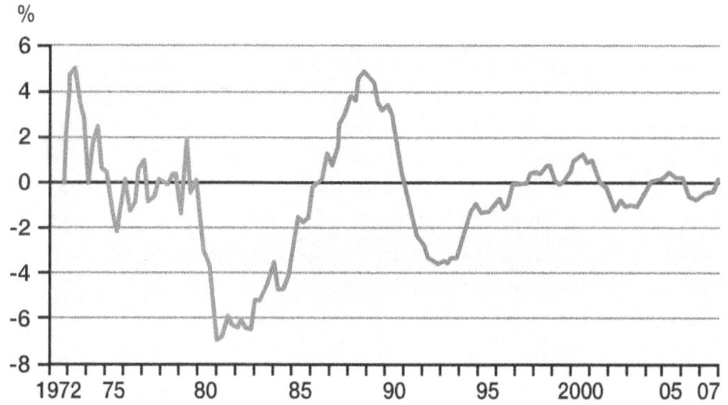

Source: adapted from HM Treasury, *Evidence on the UK economic cycle,* July 2005, Budget 2007 - The Economy

(a) Explain what is meant by an output gap, illustrating your answer by referring to 1981 and 1987.
(b) Using a production possibility frontier diagram, explain where the economy was in relation to its productive potential in (i) 2000 and (ii) 2005.
(c) The economy grew relatively fast between 1982 and 1987. To what extent was this economic recovery or economic growth?

'Garbage jobs' are holding back the Spanish economy. These are jobs which are short term, offer little security and give few benefits. Of the 900 000 jobs created in the Spanish economy last year, two thirds of them carried contracts of six months or less. Temporary contracts now cover more than 35 per cent of all jobs in Spain compared to an EU average of 12 per cent.

On the plus side, the widespread use of temporary contracts has helped Spain more than halve its official unemployment rate since the 1993 recession. There are now officially 60 per cent more people in work compared to 1993.

However, temporary contracts offer little, if any, training. The goal of young people with university degrees is to get a job with a permanent contract, such as a civil service post. This, economists fear, is discouraging young people from being entrepreneurial. Those with a permanent contract don't want to leave their jobs unless it is to take another one offering a permanent contract. This discourages labour mobility and labour flexibility. 'Garbage jobs' have ultimately led to Spain failing to improve its poor labour productivity record compared to the rest of Europe.

Source: adapted from the *Financial Times*, 21.10.2005.

(a) Explain why Spain has an unemployment problem compared to the rest of the Euro area and the USA.
(b) Explain three factors which might have caused Spain to grow less fast than it might otherwise have done in the 1990s and 2000s.

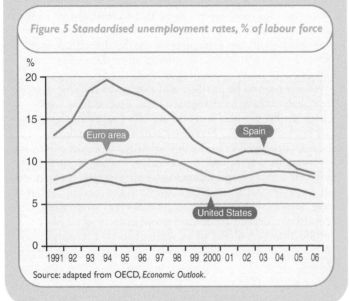

Figure 5 Standardised unemployment rates, % of labour force

Source: adapted from OECD, *Economic Outlook*.

Technological progress

Technological progress increases economic growth in two ways.

● It cuts the average cost of production of a product. For instance, a machine which performed the tasks of a simple scientific calculator was unavailable 100 years ago. 50 years ago, it needed a large room full of expensive equipment to do this. Today calculators are portable and available for a few pounds.

　　● It creates new products for the market. Without new products, consumers would be less likely to spend

increases in their income. Without extra spending, there would be less or no economic growth.

Efficiency

The way in which the factors of production are used together is vital for economic growth. Increased efficiency in the use of resources in itself will bring about rises in output.

In a market economy, competition should lead to greater efficiency. Firms which use more efficient production techniques will drive less efficient firms out of the market. Firms which develop new, better products will drive old products out of the market. So economic growth can come about because of government policies which promote competition and protect innovation. For example, policies such as privatisation, deregulation and control of monopolies should increase competition. Laws which protect patents and copyright will encourage innovation.

Markets promote efficiency but they can also fail. So government may have to step in to redress market failure. In the past, some have argued that market failure is so widespread that the government should own most, if not all, of industry. This socialist or communist view is mostly rejected today. The problem was that in communist countries like Russia, government failure became so great that it outweighed any benefits from the correction of market failure. However, in countries like France, Germany and Italy today, many still argue that the government should be highly interventionist. They argue that by owning key industries like electricity, gas and the postal service and providing subsidies to other key industries, the state can promote economic growth.

In Third World countries, many of the features of a functioning market economy may be missing. Resources are then combined inefficiently. For example, laws may not exist which protect property rights, or laws may exist but the state may take assets away from private citizens and businesses through corruption, bribery and a judiciary which doesn't uphold the law. If property rights are not protected, citizens and firms have little incentive to save and invest in the long term. Widescale bribery leads to resources being appropriated by a few individuals rather than being used in the most efficient manner across the economy. Another problem is that there may be no properly functioning capital markets. Farmers in rural areas, for example, may have no access to banks. They are then cut off from access to relatively cheap loans to expand their businesses. At worst, there may be civil war and a complete breakdown of government. Civil wars lead to negative growth as assets, both physical and human, are destroyed.

Four distinctions

Economic growth is typically measured by the rate of change of output or GDP. When measuring GDP, four important distinctions should be made.

● Economic growth is typically measured by the rise in the output of goods and services over time. Economic growth is changes in **real** GDP and not changes in **nominal** GDP which also includes increases in prices. Real GDP over time has to be measured using one year's prices. So for example, economic growth for 1988-2008 might be measured with all prices adjusted to 2006 prices.
● Real GDP is a proxy measure of the **volume** of goods and

services produced. It is equal to the quantity produced in an economy. The **value** of goods and services produced is volume times the average price. So a proxy measure of the volume of goods produced can be calculated by taking the nominal value of GDP and dividing it by the price level.

● **Total GDP** is the total amount of GDP produced in an economy. However, when comparing living standards, it is often more important to compare **GDP per capita** or total GDP divided by the size of the population. Similarly, growth in GDP per capita, which takes into account both change in GDP and the change in population, is often more useful when

comparing living standards than simply using growth in total GDP.

● Falling economic growth does not mean that the level of GDP itself is falling. China is currently growing at 10 per cent per annum. If its growth rate fell to 2 per cent per annum, its GDP would still be rising by 2 per cent each year. A falling rate of growth simply means that GDP is not rising as fast as before. So it is very important to distinguish between the **level** of GDP and the **rate of growth** of GDP. Only if the rate of growth of GDP became negative would GDP be falling.

memorize

Question 3

Figure 6 *Growth in investment and GDP in selected OECD countries, 1993-2006, annual average*

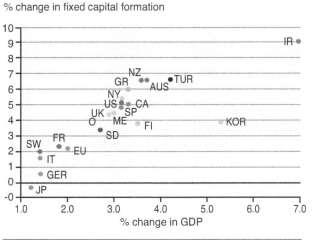

% change in fixed capital formation

Source: adapted from OECD, *Economic Outlook*.

- Aus - Australia
- Ca - Canada
- Fi - Finland
- Fr - France
- Ger - Germany
- Gr - Greece
- Ir - Ireland
- It - Italy
- Jp - Japan
- Kor - Korea
- Me - Mexico
- Nz - New Zealand
- Ny - Norway
- Sp - Spain
- Sd - Sweden
- Sw - Switzerland
- Tur - Turkey
- UK - United Kingdom
- US - United States
- EU - Euro area
- O - Total OECD

(a) What relationship would economic theory suggest exists between investment and economic growth?
(b) To what extent is this relationship shown by the data?

Key terms

Boom - period of time when the economy is growing strongly and is operating around its productive potential.
Business or economic or trade cycle - regular fluctuations in the level of economic activity around the productive potential of the economy. In business cycles, the economy veers from recession, when it is operating well below its productive potential, to booms when it is likely to be at or even above its productive potential.
Economic growth - growth in the productive potential of the economy. It is typically measured by growth in real GDP although this is only a proxy measure because actual GDP can be above or below the productive potential of the economy at a point in time.
Economic recovery - the movement back from where the economy is operating below its productive potential to a point where it is at its productive potential.
Output gap - the difference between the actual level of GDP and the productive potential of the economy. There is a **positive output gap** when actual GDP is above the productive potential of the economy and it is in boom. There is a **negative output gap** when actual GDP is below the productive potential of the economy.

Applied economics

Britain's growth rate

Worries about Britain's growth rate date back over a century. In Edwardian times, for example, it was not difficult to see the economic advance of Germany and France and compare it with the poor economic performance of the UK economy. Britain's poor growth performance persisted in the 1950s, 1960s and 1970s.

As Table 1 shows, the UK had the lowest average annual rate of growth between 1960 and 1979 of the seven largest industrial economies of the world (the **Group of Seven** or **G7**). By the 1980s and 1990s, however, the UK had ceased to be at the bottom of the growth league. In the 1990s, for the first time, the UK's average rate of

Table 1 *Average annual growth in GDP, G7 countries, 1960-2004*

	1960-67	1968-73	1974-79	1980-90	1991-2000	2001-06
						(%)
Canada	5.5	5.4	4.2	2.8	2.8	2.6
United States	4.5	3.2	2.4	3.3	3.3	2.5
United Kingdom	3.0	3.4	1.5	2.6	2.6	2.5
France	5.4	5.5	2.8	2.4	2.4	1.6
Japan	10.2	8.7	3.6	3.9	3.9	1.4
Germany	4.1	4.9	2.3	2.3	2.3	1.0
Italy	5.7	4.5	3.7	2.3	2.3	0.9
Average G7	5.0	4.4	2.7	2.8	2.8	1.8

Source: adapted from OECD, *Historical Statistics, Economic Outlook.*

growth was almost equal to the G7 average. In the 2000s, it was higher than the G7 average.

Table 1 would suggest that over the period 1960-1979, the best performing G7 countries were Japan and the European countries of Germany, France and Italy. Between 1991 and 2006, the position was reversed with the 'Anglo-Saxon' countries of the UK and the USA performing best. Note that Canada throughout the period 1960 to 2006 has performed better than or equal to the G7 average.

All economists agree that the causes of economic growth are complex and that there is no single easy answer to raising a country's trend rate of growth. So what might have caused the relatively poor economic performance of the UK before the 1980s and what might have happened since the 1980s to raise the UK's relative performance? Also, what might have caused countries such as France, Germany, Italy and Japan to performed relatively poorly over the period 1991-2006?

Labour

Education and training Most economists would agree that education and training is one of the key factors, if not the most important factor, in determining long run growth rates. For much of the 20th century, countries such as France and Germany were perceived by some to have better education systems than the UK. Whilst the UK could provide excellence in the education of its top 10 or 20 per cent to the age of 21, it lagged behind some continental countries and the USA in its education of the bottom 80 per cent. In the USA, where standards for children to the age of 18 tend to be fairly low, there is a widespread acceptance that the majority of post-18 year olds will stay on and do some form of college course. The USA still has the highest proportion of 18-24 year olds in full time education of any country in the world. Germany's system of technical and craft education has been seen as a major contributor to its economic success over the past 50 years. Japan has an education system which delivers high standards across the ability range.

In the UK, academic children going through to A levels and university degrees received an education which was as, good as, if not better than, their French, German or US peers. However, education for the rest

was arguably poor. In the 1960s and 1970s, governments put opportunity and equality at the top of their list of priorities. Comprehensive schools were introduced to give all children a better chance of success whilst the number of university places was considerably increased to give young people more access to higher education. It wasn't till the 1980s that much emphasis was put on the quality of education and lifting standards. The 1980s saw the introduction of the National Curriculum in schools, Ofsted inspections of schools and school league tables. In the 1990s, new national vocational qualifications (NVQs) were introduced, designed to provide qualifications for training in work. Their school or college based equivalent, GNVQs, were introduced to help those for whom academic A level and GCSE examinations were not suitable. The 1990s also saw the introduction of targets into education, for instance for achievement in National Curriculum tests. Targets were intended to raise standards in schools which performed poorly, and to give good schools an incentive to achieve even better results. In 1997, the Labour government under Tony Blair was elected which, for the first time, put education as a top priority in its manifesto. Since 1997, education has been specifically linked by government to the long term performance of the economy. Education spending has been raised as a proportion of GDP and a target of getting 50 per cent of the 18-21 year olds into some form of higher education has been set. It could be argued that the relative improvement of the British educational system compared to other G7 countries has played a part in helping the UK achieve relatively higher growth.

Catching up Why can China grow by 10 per cent per annum whilst the UK barely manages a quarter of that? One suggestion is that the high economic growth rate represents the gains from transferring workers from low productivity agriculture to higher productivity manufacturing and service industries. If a worker can produce £500 per year in output as an agricultural worker but £1 000 working in a factory, then the act of transferring that worker from agriculture to industry will raise the growth rate of the economy. This theory was popular in explaining why the UK performed badly relative to the rest of the EU in the 1950s and 1960s. In 1960-67, for instance, the average proportion of agricultural workers in the total civilian working population of the then Common Market was 18.1 per cent, but was only 4.2 per cent in the UK. By the 1990s, the proportion of workers in agriculture was less than 5 per cent in France and Germany and there was little scope for major transfers of labour out of the primary sector in northern Europe. Hence, this competitive advantage viz a viz the UK has disappeared. However, this theory can still explain why countries like China or Poland, with large amounts of labour in agriculture, can grow at rates several times that of EU countries.

Flexible labour markets In the 1990s, the UK government saw flexible labour markets as key to its **supply side reforms**. Labour markets are flexible when it is relatively easy for firms to hire and fire labour, and for workers to move between jobs. Inflexible labour markets create market failure, partly because they tend to lead to unemployment. There are many different aspects to creating flexible labour markets. One is education and training, discussed above. An educated workforce is more attractive to firms and helps workers to change jobs when the need arises. Another aspect is government rules and regulations about employment. Health and safety laws, maximum working hours, minimum wages, minimum holiday entitlements, redundancy regulations and maternity and paternity leave are all examples of government imposed rules which increase the cost of employment to firms and reduce the ability of firms to manage their workforces to suit their production needs.

It is argued that, in EU countries, firms have to comply with too many rules and regulations. They then become reluctant to take on workers, leading to high unemployment and lower growth. In contrast, the UK and the US have fewer regulations and this partly explains their higher growth rates in the 1990s and 2000s. Other aspects of flexible labour markets include pensions and housing. If workers are to move between jobs easily, they must carry with them pension rights. If they lose their pension rights every time they change job, they will be reluctant to move. Difficulty in obtaining housing discourages workers from moving between geographical areas. Part time working is important too. In flexible labour markets, workers should be able to choose how many hours they wish to work and how many jobs they have at any time. If work structures are such that part time working is discouraged, then the skills of many workers at home bringing up children are likely to go unutilised. Equally, there may not be enough full time work in the economy, but flexible labour markets should mean that workers could choose to build up **portfolios** of jobs, making several part time jobs equal to one full time one.

Taxes Another argument put forward is that taxes can have an important impact on growth levels. Before 1979, it could be argued that Britain's tax regime discouraged work, enterprise and investment. For example, the Labour government during 1974-1979 introduced a top marginal tax rate on earned income of 83 per cent. Average tax rates had also been rising since the 1950s as the size of the state expanded and government spending rose. The Conservative government elected in 1979 was committed to lowering the tax burden by lowering levels of government spending. By 1997, when it was defeated at the polls, it had succeeded in limiting government spending to around 40 per cent of GDP, up to 10 per cent less than many of its continental EU rivals. Since then, both the level of government spending as a proportion of GDP and taxation have risen. Increased public spending has

been necessary to fund increases in expenditure on health and education. Nevertheless, by 2007, the UK still had relatively low taxes compared to its main EU partners. These relatively low taxes since the 1990s can be argued to be a cause of the UK's higher economic growth.

Lower taxes help in a number of ways. Some economists argue that low taxes encourage workers with no job to enter the labour force, and those with jobs to work harder. This can lead to higher economic growth. Also, low taxes paid by firms on employing labour encourage firms to employ labour. In France and Germany, social security taxes paid by firms on the labour they employ are relatively high. This discourages them from employing labour, leading to high unemployment. This means that there are large unemployed resources which could act as a drag on long term growth. Equally, high taxes on labour and profits can discourage inward investment by foreign companies wanting to set up plants in a country. Inward investment doesn't just create jobs and wealth directly. It often acts as a competitive spur to domestic firms which have to compete with the new entrants. Improving efficiency and developing new products in response can raise growth rates.

Immigration In recent years, net migration, the difference between immigration and emigration, has been positive, averaging 200 000 per annum. Around 500 000 migrants per annum have been arriving in the UK, many of them young males and, since the EU was expanded in 2004, from Eastern Europe. This boost to the population has almost certainly increased the UK's rate of growth of GDP simply because there are now more workers in the population. Countries which attract and accept migrants, such as the USA and Canada, tend to grow faster simply because of the impact of migrants on output in the economy.

Capital

Table 2 shows that the UK has consistently devoted less of its GDP to investment than other G7 countries. Economic theory would suggest that investment - the addition to the physical capital stock of the country - is essential for economic growth. How can an economy

Table 2 *Gross fixed capital formation as a percentage of GDP*

Per cent

	1960-67	1968-73	1974-79	1980-90	1991-2000	2001-06
Canada	22.6	22.1	23.5	22.0	18.9	20.2
United States	18.1	18.4	18.8	19.1	17.9	18.6
United Kingdom	17.7	19.1	19.4	18.7	16.7	16.6
France	23.2	24.6	23.6	21.0	18.8	19.4
Japan	31.0	34.6	31.8	29.7	28.2	23.5
Germany	25.2	24.4	20.8	22.2	22.0	18.1
Italy	24.9	24.0	24.0	22.4	19.8	20.8

Source: adapted from OECD, *Historical Statistics*, United Nations Statistics Division.

increase its growth rate if it does not increase the amount it is setting aside to increase the productive potential of the economy? There is a number of possible explanations for why investment and growth rates may or may not be linked.

Quality, not quantity Some economists have argued that it is not the quantity of investment that is important but its direction. The two classic examples used for the UK are Concorde (the supersonic plane) and the nuclear power programme. Large sums of public money were poured into the development of Concorde and the nuclear power programme in the 1960s. Both proved uncommercial. In this view, increasing investment rates without there being the investment opportunities present in the economy would have little or no effect on growth rates. The money would simply be wasted. Moreover, how could investment be increased in an economy? The simplest way would be for government to spend more on investment, either through its own programmes, by investing directly in industry, or through subsidies. Free market economists would then argue that the government is a very poor judge of industries and projects which need further investment. The money would probably be squandered on today's equivalents of Concorde. Only if firms increase investment of their own accord in free markets can growth increase. Even this is no guarantee of success. In the late 1980s and early 1990s, Japanese industry increased its investment because of very low interest rates on borrowed money. In 1986, Japan spent 27.3 per cent of its GDP on investment. In 1990, this peaked at 32.2 per cent. Despite this, the Japanese economy spent much of the 1990s in recession, with an average growth rate of just 1.5 per cent. In retrospect, Japanese companies had clearly overinvested. There was far too much capacity for the levels of production required.

Short-termism In the USA and the UK, banks do not invest in companies. They lend to companies over fairly short time periods, typically up to five years, but many loans (e.g. overdrafts) are repayable on demand. Shares in companies are owned by shareholders, and these shares are traded on stock markets. Stock markets are driven by speculators who are not interested in where a company might be in five or ten years time. They are only interested in the size of the next dividend payment or the price of the share today. In contrast, in Germany and Japan banks own large proportions of industry through shareholdings. The banks are interested in the long term development of companies. Losses this year are less important if the long term future of a company is bright and secure. It is therefore argued that US and UK stock markets lead to short-termism. Firms will only invest if they can make a quick profit to satisfy shareholders who are only interested in the financial performance of the company over, say, 12 months. In Germany and Japan, firms can afford to make long term investment decisions even if these involve poorer short term performance, secure in the knowledge that their

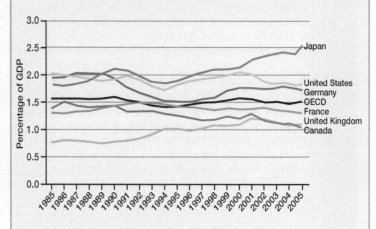

Figure 7 *Business R&D as a percentage of GDP*

Source: adapted from OECD, Main Science and Technology Indicators.

shareholders are interested in the long term future of the business.

Supporters of US style capitalism argue that long termism can mask poor investment decisions. When the Japanese economy went into a prolonged period of low or negative growth following the economic bubble of the late 1980s, Japanese companies often failed to take the necessary steps to restructure despite making substantial losses over a lengthy period of time. Without the pressures of shareholders wanting a fast return, they preferred to safeguard the interests of management and workers. This has contributed to the problems of Japanese industry. In France, Germany and Italy, long termism has not prevented them suffering lower economic growth rates than the USA. Indeed, the pressures of globalisation and the single market within the EU are making their firms more short termist. They are finding that their companies are facing the threat of takeover by US or UK companies. One way of fighting this is to increase short term profitability.

Lack of savings The USA and the UK have relatively low savings ratios. Given that over the long term exports roughly equal imports for a country, and the government budget deficit tends to fluctuate around a fixed proportion of GDP, then savings must roughly equal a constant proportion of investment. Higher savings will thus allow higher investment. In the UK, firms have large tax incentives to save through not distributing all their profits to shareholders. This retained profit could be increased through even lower taxation, or the government could increase its savings by moving to a budget surplus. Individuals could be persuaded to save more again through tax incentives.

Innovation The UK spends a relatively low proportion of its GDP on research and development (R&D). For most of the post-war period, an above average share of that R&D has been devoted to defence research. Hence, some economists argue that R&D spending in total needs to be increased for higher growth, and a larger proportion needs to be spent on civilian projects. The UK's poor R&D record is shown in Figure 7. Others argue that it is not so much the quantity that is important as the use to which R&D is put. It is often pointed out that the UK has a good international record in making discoveries and in inventions. However, too many of those have not been taken up by UK businesses. Instead, the ideas have gone overseas and been used by foreign firms as the bases for world-beating products. In this argument, UK firms have been very poor in the past at making a commercial success of R&D.

Catching up Catching up can apply to capital as well as to labour. For instance, a new DVD factory in China is likely to increase labour productivity (output per worker) far more than a new DVD factory in the UK. This is because the workers in China are more likely to have been employed in very low productivity jobs before than in Britain. So, countries like China can import foreign technologies and take huge leaps in productivity, which is then reflected in high economic growth rates. Some economists argue that, in the long run, all countries will arrive at roughly the same output per worker and grow at the same rate. This is because technology is internationally available. Countries can bring their capital stock up to the level of the most productive country in the world. Countries like the USA, however, which has grown at around 2.5 per cent per annum since the Second World War, can't take huge technological leaps like this. It has to create new technologies and new products to sustain its growth.

One argument put forward to explain the US economy's superior performance compared to European countries like France and Germany during the 1990s and 2000s is that its companies have invested much more heavily in IT (information technology). Not only has IT spending as a proportion of GDP been higher, but US companies have integrated IT into their operations much more deeply. The USA has therefore gained a technological advantage over other developed countries which has allowed it to sustain its growth rate whilst many other developed countries have fallen behind.

Privatisation and deregulation Capital may be tied up in relatively unproductive firms or industries. Releasing this capital can increase growth rates. The experience of the 1980s and 1990s in the UK has been that privatisation and deregulation are powerful ways of improving capital productivity. Nationalised industries, such as water, electricity, coal, gas and the railways were inefficient in the 1960s and 1970s. They employed too much capital and too much labour. Privatisation saw output per unit of capital and labour increase substantially as workforces were cut and assets sold off or closed down. The process was painful. In the coal industry, for instance, nearly 200 000 workers lost their jobs between 1980 and 2000. However, in a fast changing economy, failure to move resources between industries leads to inefficiency and slower growth.

Openness to imports One way of protecting domestic jobs is to erect protectionist barriers against imports. For instance, foreign goods can be kept out by imposing high taxes on imports (called **tariffs** or **customs duties**). It can be argued, though, that protectionism is likely to lead to lower long term economic growth. This is because domestic firms can become insulated from world best practice. There is reduced incentive to invest and innovate if more competitive goods from abroad are kept out of the domestic market.

France and Germany in the 1990s and 2000s have perhaps been more protectionist in their policies than the UK and the USA. Because France and Germany are part of the EU, there is a limit to the amount of protectionism that they can implement compared to other EU countries such as the UK. However, one example of protectionism was the failure of most EU countries to open up their service industries such as banking to foreign competition for much of the 1990s and early 2000s. Equally, countries like France and Germany failed to open up utility markets such as electricity, gas and telecommunications over the same period. Part of the superior performance of the UK and US economies over the period might be due to increased foreign competition in markets other than those traditionally exposed to trade.

Export-led growth Some Third World countries have grown particularly fast over the past 40 years. Their growth has tended to be fuelled by exports. Countries like South Korea, Taiwan and China have been highly successful in selling their goods into Western markets. As with low protectionist barriers to imports, successful exporting requires domestic firms to be competitive with the best firms around the world. This encourages efficiency and investment, both important in promoting economic growth. The UK has some world class industries such as financial services. However, for much of the past 40 years, its balance of payments on current account has been in deficit. This would suggest that growth in the UK has not particularly been export led.

Macroeconomic management

Some economists argue that recessions do not affect long term growth rates. Growth lost in a recession is made up in the boom which follows. Others argue that the fall in GDP in deep recessions may never be recouped in the subsequent upturn. This is because in a deep recession, labour can become de-skilled, leading to permanently higher unemployment. Capital can also be destroyed as firms cut costs, pulling down factories and throwing away equipment. The UK suffered deeper and longer recessions in the 1970s, 1980s and early 1990s than countries in Europe. This may help account for lower UK growth rates at the time. Equally, the higher growth rate in the UK in the 1990s and 2000s may be because the UK avoided a recession in the middle 1990s and early 2000s, which afflicted European countries.

DataQuestion — Ireland's economic miracle

Ireland has been one of Europe's success stories over the past 30 years. From being one of the European Union's poorest countries, it has now caught up and is among the richer nations of Europe.

Some experts trace Ireland's economic success back to the introduction of free secondary education in the 1960s. Cuts in taxes on businesses in the 1980s and cuts in top rates of income tax on earners provided a boost for business and enterprise. The 1980s also saw an increase in the labour force with the traditional net outflow of labour from Ireland reversing to become a net inflow. Today, an annual 30 000 more workers arrive in Ireland than leave to seek jobs abroad, attracted by a booming job market. Multinational companies were attracted to Ireland from the 1970s onwards by its educated, English speaking workforce and low business taxes. Jobs have been created in manufacturing and service industries, whilst jobs in low productivity agriculture have

been in decline. The enormous productivity gains from these trends have allowed Irish workers to see large pay rises over time without unit labour costs rising too much. Centralised wage agreements have allowed the government to introduce flexible working practices. In exchange for wage moderation, income tax was cut.

Typical of Ireland's success story is Galway. Digital Computers set up a mainframe computer factory in the city in 1971 and became an important employer in the area. Changing patterns of demand saw the factory close in 1994. Since then, Galway has reinvented itself and hosts one of the world's largest clusters of medical device manufacturing companies. Today there are 28 companies in the city employing 5 000 people. 15 of these are locally owned, many headed by former Digital Computers employees.

Source: adapted from the *Financial Times*, 27.5.2005.

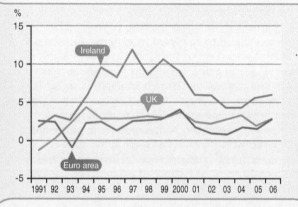

Figure 8 Economic growth: annual % change in GDP

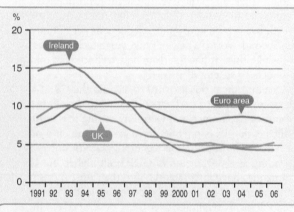

Figure 9 Unemployment: standardised measure %

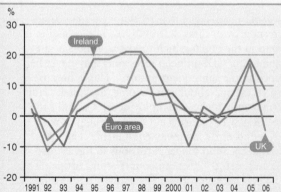

Figure 10 Investment: real gross private sector capital formation excluding housing: annual % change

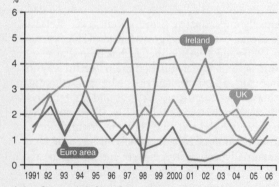

Figure 11 Growth in labour productivity: annual % change

Note: 'euro area' is the group of EU countries which have adopted the euro as their currency, including Germany, Italy, Spain, France and Ireland but excluding the UK.
Source: adapted from OECD, *Economic Outlook*.

1. (a) Explain what is meant by economic growth.
   (b) Compare the recent growth performance in Ireland with the UK and the whole euro area.

2. Discuss whether higher levels of capital investment can solely account for Ireland's superior economic performance since 1991.

28 Economic growth and welfare

Summary

1. National income is often used as the main indicator of the standard of living in an economy. A rise in GDP per head is used as an indication of economic growth and a rise in living standards.
2. However, there are many other important components of the standard of living, including political freedom, the social and cultural environment, freedom from fear of war and persecution, and the quality of the environment.
3. Economic growth over the past 100 years has transformed the living standards of people in the western world, enabling almost all to escape from absolute poverty.
4. Economic growth is likely to be the only way of removing people in the Third World from absolute poverty.
5. Economic growth has its costs in terms of unwelcome changes in the structure of society.
6. Some believe that future economic growth is unsustainable, partly because of growing pollution and partly because of the exploitation of non-renewable resources.

National income and economic welfare

National income is a measure of the income, output and expenditure of an economy. It is also often used as a measure of the **standard of living**. However, equating national income with living standards is very simplistic because there are many other factors which contribute to the economic welfare of individuals.

Political freedoms We tend to take civil liberties for granted in the UK. However, other governments in the world today are totalitarian regimes which rule through fear. In some countries, membership of an opposition party or membership of a trade union can mean death or imprisonment. The freedom to visit friends, to travel and to voice an opinion are likely to be more valuable than owning an extra television or being able to buy another dress.

The social and cultural environment In the UK, we take things such as education for granted. We have some of the world's finest museums and art galleries. We possess a cultural heritage which includes Shakespeare and Constable. The BBC is seen as one of the best broadcasting organisations throughout the world. However, we could all too easily live in a cultural desert where the main purpose of television programming might be to sell soap powders and make a profit. Alternatively, the arts could be used as political propaganda rather than exist in their own right.

Freedom from fear of violence If a person doesn't feel safe walking the streets or even at home, then no number of microwave ovens or videos will compensate for this loss. Equally, fears of war, arbitrary arrest, imprisonment or torture make material possessions seem relatively unimportant.

The working environment How long and hard people have to work is vital in evaluating standards of living. One reason why the average worker is far better off today than 100 years ago is because his or her working year is likely to be about half the number of hours of his or her Victorian counterpart's. Equally, the workplace is far safer today than 100 years ago. Industrial accidents were

Question 1

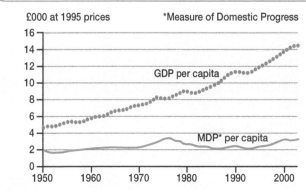

Figure 1 Comparison of MDP per capita vs GDP per capita

£000 at 1995 prices   *Measure of Domestic Progress

GDP per capita

MDP* per capita

Source: adapted from Office for National Statistics, Thomson Datastream, CML.

It's official. 1976 was the best on record for the quality of life in Britain, according to an index of economic, social and environmental progress published by the New Economics Foundation, a think-tank. Unlike the standard GDP figure, the measure of domestic progress (MDP) takes into account social and environmental costs, including the damage done by crime, the depletion of natural resources, and pollution such as emissions of greenhouse gases. Britain in the seventies, with less crime, less income inequality, a rise in the national capital stock because of a boom in public sector investment, and lower energy consumption because there were fewer cars and centrally-heated houses, was better-off than today.

Most alternative measures of quality of life seem to show that Britain in the past was better off than today. However, those old enough to remember 1976 might be surprised that this was the best year for Britain's overall affluence. For many, the mid-1970s with record inflation, rising unemployment, strikes and no home computers, mobile phones or DVDs was a rather grey and dismal period. The MDP only captures a very small number of the variables that might go to make up a standard of living index. So perhaps GDP is a better guide after all.

Source: adapted from the *Financial Times*, 16.3.2004.

(a) Why is GDP not the only measure of the standard of living of a country?
(b) What other factors might be included in a measure of the standard of living?
(c) What are the problems identified with the MDP as a measure of the standard of living?

then commonplace and workers received little or no compensation for serious injuries or even death.

The environment Environmental issues are currently at the forefront of people's consciousness. There is an understanding that production activities can damage the environment and that in future we may well have to stop consuming certain products if we are to safeguard the environment.

Benefits of growth

The rate of economic growth has accelerated historically. Even five hundred years ago, most people would have seen little change in incomes over their lifetimes. In Victorian England, the economy grew at about one per cent per annum. Over the past 60 years, the UK economy has grown at an average of 2.6 per cent per annum.

Table 1 Economic growth rate of £100 over time

Years	Growth rates				
	1%	2%	3%	5%	10%
0	£100	£100	£100	£100	£100
5	£105	£110	£116	£128	£161
10	£110	£122	£130	£163	£259
25	£128	£164	£203	£339	£1 084
50	£164	£269	£426	£1 147	£11 739
75	£211	£442	£891	£3 883	£127 189
100	£271	£724	£1 870	£13 150	£1 378 059

Growth at these rates since the end of the Second World War in 1945 has led to undreamt of prosperity for the citizens of the industrialised world. Consider Table 1. It shows by how much £100 will grow over time at different rates. At one per cent growth, income will roughly double over the lifetime of an individual. At 2 per cent, it will quadruple over a lifetime. At 3 per cent, it is doubling every twenty five years. At 5 per cent, it only takes about 14 years to double income. At 10 per cent, it only takes about 7 years to double income.

If recent growth rates are a guide to the future, average British workers in 30 years' time will earn in real terms twice what they are earning today. When they are in their seventies, they can expect workers to earn four times as much as their parents did when they were born.

These increases in income have led to the elimination of **absolute poverty** for most citizens in industrialised countries.

- Life expectancy has doubled over the past 300 years and infant mortality rates have plummeted.
- People have enough to eat and drink. What we eat and drink is nearly always fit for human consumption.
- Housing standards have improved immeasurably.
- Nearly everyone can read and write.

Future increases in income are generally desirable. Very few people would prefer to have less income rather than more income in the future (remember economics assumes that people have **infinite wants**). So economic growth has generally been considered to be highly desirable. Moreover, in 2005 only 16 per cent of the world's population lived in 'high income' countries such as the USA, the UK and Japan, with an average annual income per person of $32 500 at 2005 purchasing power parity prices. 36.5 per cent lived in 'low income' countries with an average yearly income of

The photographs show a modern kitchen and a kitchen at the start of the 20th century. To what extent do they show that economic growth has been desirable?

just $2 486, not even ten per cent of the average income of high income countries. Many who live in low and middle income countries suffer absolute poverty. It can be argued that the only way to eliminate malnutrition, disease, bad housing and illiteracy in these countries is for there to be real economic growth.

Arguments against growth

Despite the apparent benefits, the goal of economic growth is questioned by some economists and environmentalists.

The falsity of national income statistics One argument is that the increase in national income has been largely fictitious. Three hundred years ago much of the output of the economy was not traded. Women were not on the whole engaged in paid work. Much of the supposed increase in income has come from placing monetary values on what existed already. Much of the increase in income generated by the public sector of the economy comes not from increased production but from increased wages paid to public sector workers who produce the same amount of services. Whilst there is some truth in this, it cannot be denied that material living standards have increased immeasurably over the past three hundred years. People not only consume more goods and services, they have on average far more leisure time.

Negative externalities Another argument is that modern industrialised societies have created large negative **externalities**. For instance, some put forward the view that growth has created a large pool of migrant workers, wandering from job to job in different parts of the country. They become cut off from their roots, separated from their families. The result is alienation and loneliness, particularly of the old, and the collapse of traditional family values. Crime rates soar, divorce rates increase, stress related illnesses become commonplace and more and more has to be spent on picking up the pieces of a society which is no longer content with what it has.

Supporters of this view tend to look back to some past 'golden age', often agricultural, when people lived mainly in villages as parts of large extended families. However, historical evidence suggests that such a rural paradise never existed. Life for many was short and brutish. Drunkenness was always a problem. Family life was claustrophobic and did not allow for individuality. Most people were dead by the age when people today tend to divorce and remarry.

Growth is unsustainable Perhaps the most serious anti-growth argument is that growth is unsustainable. SUSTAINABLE GROWTH can be defined as growth in the productive potential of the economy today which does not lead to a fall in the productive potential of the economy for future generations. Consider again Table 1. If a country like the UK grew at an average 3 per cent per annum then in 25 years' time national income will be twice as large as it is today; in fifty years' time, when an 18 year old student will be retired, it will be over 4 times as large; in 75 years' time, when on current life expectancy figures that student would be dead, it will be nearly 9 times as large; and in 100 years' time it will be nearly 19 times as large. If the average wage in the UK today of a full time employee was £27 000 per annum, then in 100 years' time it will have risen to £800 000 per annum in real terms.

Each extra percent increase in national income is likely to use up **non-renewable resources** such as oil, coal and copper. In the late 1970s, the Club of Rome, a forecasting institute, produced a report called 'The Limits to Growth'. The report claimed that industrialised economies as we know them would collapse. They would be caught between a growth in pollution and a decline in the availability of scarce resources such as oil, coal and timber. Oil was projected to run out in the next century and coal by the year 2400. In the 1980s and 1990s, the world was gripped by reports that people were destroying the ozone layer and raising the world's temperature through the greenhouse effect. The planet cannot support growth rates of even 1 or 2 per cent per year. Growth must stop and the sooner the better.

Economic theory suggests that the future may not be as bleak as this picture makes out. In a market economy, growing scarcity of a resource, such as oil, results in a rise in price. Three things then happen. First, demand and therefore consumption falls - the price mechanism results in conservation. Second, it becomes profitable to explore for new supplies of the resource. Third, consumers switch to substitute products whilst producers are encouraged to find new replacement products. After the massive rise in oil prices in 1973-74, the world car makers roughly halved the fuel consumption per mile of the average car over a period of ten years through more efficient engines. Brazil developed cars which ran on fuel made from sugar. In recent years, oil companies have begun to mix biofuels with their traditional oil based fuels to sell at the pumps.

Governments too respond to pressures from scientists and the public. The activities of industry are far more regulated today in the western world than they were 30 years ago. Individual governments, for instance, have introduced strict controls on pollution emissions, regulated disposal of waste and sought to ration scarce resources like water or air through systems of tradable licences. Even more impressive has been the willingness of governments to sign international agreements designed to safeguard the environment. For instance, in 1987, 93 governments signed the Montreal Protocol to phase out production of CFC chemicals, a major contributor to the destruction of the ozone layer. Signatories to the 1997 Kyoto Protocol agreed to reduce greenhouse gas emissions by 5.2 per cent from 1990 levels between 2008-2012.

What is worrying, however, is that the market mechanism and governments are frequently slow to act. Governments and markets are not good at responding to pressures which might take decades to build up but only manifest themselves suddenly at the end of that time period. Some scientists have predicted that global warming is now already irreversible. If this is true, the problem that we now face is how to change society to cope with this. There is no clear consensus as to how we could reverse economic growth, consume less, and cope with the coming catastrophe, without creating an economic nightmare with mass starvation.

Increasing inequality Some economists have argued that economic growth is increasing inequalities in income and wealth. Karl Marx, the founder of communism in the 19th century, argued that workers would live on subsistence wages whilst all the benefits of economic growth would go to the owners of capital. It is commonly argued today that the benefits of globalisation are going mainly to the rich countries of the world and to multinational companies and very little is going to poor developing countries. The evidence is far more complex. Karl Marx has been proved wrong. Even those working on the minimum wage in the UK can consume far more goods and services than a prosperous artisan in the 19th century. As for individual economies, the picture is mixed. Average income inequalities between China and the USA are rapidly diminishing. With China growing at 10 per cent per annum and the USA at below 3 per cent, mathematically average income inequality must be falling. This doesn't mean to say that the average US citizen doesn't get more benefit in dollars than the average Chinese citizen from a growing world economy. A US citizen who gets 3 per cent of $40 000 will get more in absolute terms than a Chinese citizen who gets 10 per cent of $7 000. However, countries ranging from South Korea, Taiwan and Singapore to Ireland, Poland and Estonia have found that their high economic growth rates have either given them incomes equal to the rich nations of the world or rapidly reduced the gap between them and the rich world. In practice, whether growth leads to greater income inequality between countries and within countries is dependent partly on the chance outcomes of the market. However, it is also crucially dependent on government policy. Governments can, through provision of measures such as minimum wages, pensions, working tax credits, universal free education and health care, and tax regimes which make the rich pay a disproportionate amount of tax, ensure that the benefits of growth are widely distributed in society. As China has shown, the fastest way to relieve poverty and reduce the income differential between itself and the world's richest nation, the USA, is to grow at double digit rates per annum.

The anti-growth lobby One point to note is that supporters of the anti-growth lobby tend to be people who are relatively well off. Cutting their consumption by 25 per cent, or producing environmentally friendly alternative technologies, might not create too much hardship for them. However, leaving the mass of people in the Third World today at their present living standards would lead to great inequality. A small minority would continue to live below the absolute poverty line, facing the continual threat of malnutrition. A majority would not have access to services such as education and health care which people in the West take for granted. Not surprisingly, the anti-growth lobby is stronger in the West than in the Third World.

Key terms

Sustainable growth - growth in the productive potential of the economy today which does not lead to a fall in the productive potential of the economy for future generations.

Applied economics

The standard of living in the UK since 1900

GDP is often used as the major economic indicator of welfare. Table 2 shows that, on this basis, living standards in the UK rose considerably last century. Between 1900 and 1931 GDP rose 15 per cent and between 1900 and 2004 it rose 668 per cent. Population has increased too, but even when this has been taken into account, the rise in income per person is impressive.

It is possible to chart a multitude of other ways in which it can be shown that the standard of living of the British family has improved. For instance, 14.2 per cent of children in 1900 died before the age of 1. In 2007, the comparable figure was 0.5 per cent. In 1900, the vast majority of children left school at 12. Today all children stay on till the age of 16, whilst 53 per cent of 18 year olds are in full time or part time education or training. In 1900, few people were able to afford proper medical treatment when they fell ill. Today, everyone in the UK has access to the National Health Service.

Table 3 illustrates another way in which we are far better off today than a family at the turn of the century. It shows the weekly budget of a manual worker's family in a North Yorkshire iron town, estimated by Lady Bell in her book *At The Works*. The family lived off 7½ home-made loaves of 4lb (1.8kg) each thinly scraped with butter, 4lb (1.8kg) of meat and bacon, weak tea, a quart of milk and no vegetables worth mentioning. In 2005-06, whilst average consumption for five people of bread was only 3.5kg a week, tea 0.17kg and sugar 0.47kg, on the other hand meat consumption was 5.0kg, fresh potato consumption was 2.9kg, and butter, margarine, lard and other oils consumption was 0.92kg. Moreover, today's diet is far more varied and ample with fruit and vegetables apart from potatoes playing a major part. Malnutrition, not uncommon in 1900, is virtually unknown in the UK today.

The budget in Table 3 also says a great deal about the very restricted lifestyle of the average family in 1908. Then, a family would consider itself lucky if it could take a day trip to the seaside. In comparison, individuals took an estimated 44.2 million holidays abroad in 2005.

In 1908, houses were sparsely furnished. The main form of heating was open coal fires; central heating was virtually unknown. Very few houses were wired for electricity. Table 3 shows that the typical house was lighted by oil. All the electrical household gadgets we take for granted, from washing machines to vacuum cleaners to televisions, had not been invented. The 1lb of soap in the 1908 budget would have been used to clean clothes, sinks and floors. Soap powders, liquid detergents and floor cleaners were not available. 'Gold Dust' was the popular name for an exceptionally caustic form of shredded yellow soap notorious for its ability to flay the user's hands. Compare that with the numerous brands of mild soaps available today.

Workers worked long hours, six days a week with few holidays, whilst at home the housewife faced a life of drudgery with few labour-saving devices. Accidents were frequent and old age, unemployment and sickness were dreaded and even more so the workhouse, the final destination for those with no means to support themselves.

Ecologically, the smoke-stack industries of industrial areas such as London, the Black Country and Manchester created large scale pollution. The smogs which are found in many cities such as Mexico City and Los Angeles today were common occurrences in turn-of-the-century Britain. The urban environment was certainly not clean 100 years ago.

Socially and politically, women, who formed over half the population, were not emancipated. In 1900, they did not have the vote, their place was in the home, they were often regarded as biologically inferior to men, and they were debarred from almost all public positions of influence and authority. In many ways, the standard of living of women improved more than that of men during the 20th century because of the repressive attitude held towards women 100 years ago.

Overall, it would be very difficult to look back on 1900 and see it as some golden age. For the vast majority of those in Britain today, the start of the third millennium is a paradise in comparison. However, whilst there might be little absolute poverty today, it could be argued that there is considerable relative poverty. It could also be argued that the poorest today are probably still worse off than the top 5 per cent of income earners in 1900.

Table 2 GDP, GDP per head and population, 1901-2006

	GDP (£bn at 2002 prices)	Population (millions)	GDP per head (£ at 2002 prices)
1901	152.8	38.2	4 001
1911	176.1	42.1	4 172
1921	155.8	44.0	3 540
1931	188.4	46.0	4 096
1951	294.8	50.2	5 795
1961	383.0	52.7	7 253
1971	510.7	55.9	9 130
1981	599.0	56.4	10 629
1991	777.4	57.4	13 535
2001	1 027.9	59.1	17 388
2006	1 173.1	60.6	19 358

Note: GDP is at market prices.
Source: adapted from *Social Trends, Annual Abstract of Statistics*, Office for National Statistics.

Family budget in 1908
Income 18s 6d, family of five

	s.	d.
Rent	5	6
Coals	2	4
Insurance	0	7
Clothing	1	
Meat	1	0
14lb of flour		6
3½ lb of bread meal		5
1lb butter	0	4½
Half lb lard		1
1lb bacon	1	2½
4 lb sugar	0	9
Half lb tea	0	8
Yeast	0	9
Milk	0	1
1 box Globe polish	0	3
1lb soap	0	3
1 packet Gold Dust	0	3
3 oz tobacco	0	9
7lb potatoes	0	3
Onions	0	1
Matches	0	1
Lamp oil	0	2
Debt	0	3
Total	18	6

Table 3

DataQuestion Comparative living standards in the UK

Table 4 Income, prices and population

	1971	2006
GDP (£bn at current prices)	57.5	1 309.9
Retail Price Index (1971 = 100)	100	981
Population (millions)	55.9	60.6

Source: adapted from *Economic Trends, Annual Abstract of Statistics, Monthly Digest of Statistics*, Office for National Statistics.

Table 5 Population[1]

	Millions	
	1971	2006
Under 18	15.8	13.1
Adults not of pensionable age	31.0	36.1
Pensionable ages[1]	9.1	11.4
Total population	55.9	60.6

1 Pensionable age is 60+ for women and 65+ for men.

Source: adapted from *Annual Abstract of Statistics*, Office for National Statistics.

Table 6 Number of abortions, Great Britain

	1971-72	2005
Abortions	63 400	199 019

Source: adapted from *Social Trends*, Office for National Statistics.

Table 7 Households: by type of household and family

	1971 %	2006 %
One person		
Under state pension age	6	14
Over state pension age	12	14
One family households		
Couple no children	27	28
Couple with children	43	29
Lone parent household	7	10
Other	5	5
Total	100	100
All households (millions)	18.6	24.2

Source: adapted from *Social Trends*, Office for National Statistics.

Figure 2 Mortality: by sex and leading group of causes

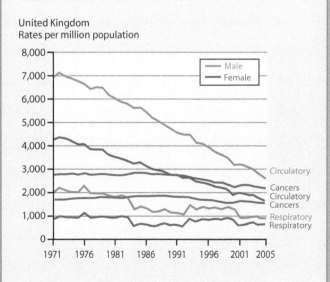

United Kingdom
Rates per million population

Source: adapted from *Social Trends*, Office for National Statistics.

Table 8 Percentage of households owning selected consumer durables

	1970-72	1981	2005-2006
Washing machine	65	78	95
Tumble dryer	0	23	58
Microwave	0	0	91
Dishwasher	0	4	35
Television	93	97	98
CD Player	0	0	88
Home computer	0	0	65
Video recorder	0	0	86
Telephone	35	75	92
Internet connection	0	0	55
Mobile phone	0	0	79

Source: adapted from *Social Trends*, *Family Spending*, Office for National Statistics.

Table 9 Education

	1970-71	2006
Ratio of pupils to teachers in state schools	22.60	17.0
Numbers in state nursery schools (millions)	0.05	0.15
Numbers in all schools (millions)	10.20	9.90
Numbers in higher education (millions)	0.62	2.49
Government spending on education as % of GDP	5.20	5.60

Source: adapted from *Social Trends*, *Annual Abstracts of Statistics*, Office for National Statistics.

Table 10 Employment and unemployment, UK, millions

	1971	2006
Employment		
Males		
full time	15.5	15.5
Females		
full time	9.0	13.3
Total unemployed[1]	0.75	0.96

1 Claimant count unemployed.

Source: adapted from *Economic and Labour Market Review*, Office for National Statistics.

Table 11 Real gross weekly earnings of selected workers, £ at 2006 prices

	1971	2005-06
Waiter/waitress	140	128
Caretaker	213	283
Bricklayer/mason	265	462
Carpenter/joiner	273	433
Nurse	140	431
Primary teacher	314	534
Solicitor	466	965
Medical practitioner	670	1 245

Source: adapted from *New Earnings Survey*, *Annual Survey of Hours and Earnings*, Office for National Statistics.

Table 12 Average daily flow of motor vehicles on motorways

		Thousands
	1971	2005
Vehicles on motorways	28.5	75.5

Source: adapted from *Transport Statistics*, Office for National Statistics.

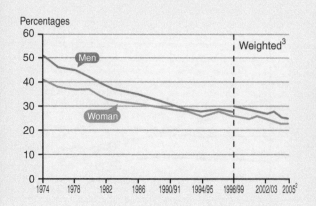

Figure 3 Prevalence of adult cigarette smoking: by sex

Note: weighted data after 1998/99 to compensate for non-response and to match known population distributions.
Source: adapted from *Social Trends*, Office for National Statistics.

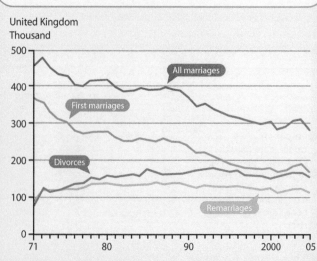

Figure 4 Marriages and divorces

Source: adapted from *Social Trends*, Office for National Statistics.

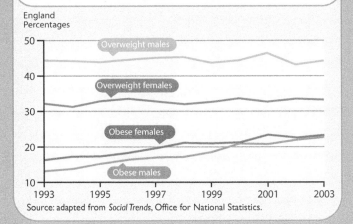

Figure 5 *Proportion of adults who are obese or overweight: by sex*

England
Percentages

Overweight males
Overweight females
Obese females
Obese males

Source: adapted from *Social Trends*, Office for National Statistics.

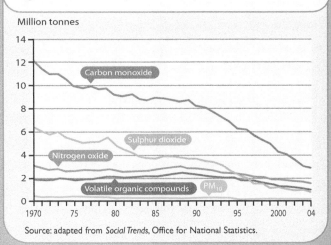

Figure 6 *Emissions of selected air pollutants*

Million tonnes

Carbon monoxide
Sulphur dioxide
Nitrogen oxide
Volatile organic compounds   PM$_{10}$

Source: adapted from *Social Trends*, Office for National Statistics.

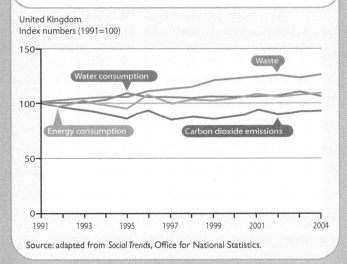

Figure 7 *Environmental impact of households*

United Kingdom
Index numbers (1991=100)

Waste
Water consumption
Energy consumption   Carbon dioxide emissions

Source: adapted from *Social Trends*, Office for National Statistics.

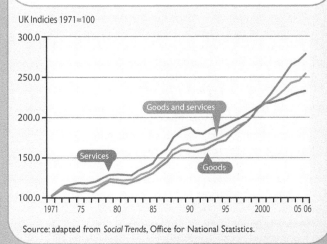

Figure 8 *Volume of domestic household expenditure on goods and services*

UK Indicies 1971=100

Goods and services
Services
Goods

Source: adapted from *Social Trends*, Office for National Statistics.

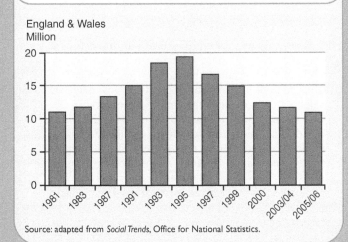

Figure 9 *British crime survey offences*

England & Wales
Million

Source: adapted from *Social Trends*, Office for National Statistics.

You have been asked to write a magazine article from an economic perspective comparing the early 1970s and 2006. The focus of the article is a discussion of whether living standards improved in the UK over the period. Construct the article as follows.

1. In your introduction, pick out a small number of key statistics which you feel point out the differences between the two periods.
2. In the main part of the article, compare and contrast the two periods, pointing out how living standards improved and also where it could be argued that the UK was worse off in 2006 than in the early 1970s.
3. In the conclusion, discuss whether rising GDP will be sufficient to ensure that the UK is better off in 2020 than in 2006.

Applied economics

New perspectives in economics

Economics is a discipline with a long history. Like other disciplines, it is constantly evolving. Some of the frontier work in economics today is being done developing and expanding existing theoretical models. However, some of the most exciting work today is in applying existing standard economic theory to novel situations. In 2005, an American economist, Steven Levitt, with a journalist, Stephen Dubner, published *Freakonomics: A Rogue Economist Explores the Hidden Side of Everything*, which went on to sell millions of copies worldwide. The book is made up of six chapters based on academic research done by Steven Levitt. It includes an investigation as to why almost all drug dealers earn low wages and quickly give up the occupation. It also looks at cheating by US teachers in terms of the grades they give their students and also why sumo wrestlers cheat. In the UK, Tim Harford, the 'Underground Economist', publishes a popular and easy to understand column each Saturday in the *Financial Times* on similar themes.

One of the key tools being used in this research is **data mining**. There is a considerable number of databases now available which can be interrogated. Equally, economists are creating their own databases for research purposes. By asking the right questions and formulating hypotheses, valid conclusions can be drawn.

Another key element of this new economics is linking economics with other social sciences. Over the past 50 years in the physical sciences, there has been an enormous growth for example in biochemistry and biophysics, the fusing together of biology, chemistry and physics at the borders of their disciplines. In economics, new fields of enquiry are being opened up by combining **sociology** or **psychology** with economic theory. In 2002 Daniel Kahneman, a psychologist and someone who claims to have never taken a single economics course, won the Nobel Prize in Economics for his work on **prospect theory**. Prospect theory describes decisions between alternatives that involve risk, such as buying a lottery ticket or taking out insurance. It has a base in psychology because it models how people actually behave rather than modelling how they ought to behave if they want to achieve certain outcomes. Linked to sociology and psychology is also a growing use of experiments in economics.

The economics of happiness

One branch of this new type of economics is called the ECONOMICS OF HAPPINESS or HAPPINESS ECONOMICS. One of the most often quoted comments

about economics is that it is the **dismal science**. This came from Thomas Carlyle writing in 1849: 'Not a 'gay science', I should say, like some we have heard of, no a dreary, desolate and, indeed, quite abject and distressing one; what we might call, by way of eminence, the dismal science.' Thomas Carlyle was a famous writer and social commentator of the time. He was contrasting some of the negative predictions of economics of his age with a 'gay science' which at the time referred to 'life-enhancing knowledge'.

The economics of happiness has some of its theoretical roots in the work being done in England in the time of Thomas Carlyle. Jeremy Bentham was a philosopher who put forward the theory of **utilitarianism**. This stated that human beings should act in a way that would cause 'the greatest happiness of the greatest number'. This was a philosophy which could guide the individual: should I spend this £500 on a holiday for myself or should I use it to pay for the tuition fees of my child at university? It was also a philosophy which could guide government policy: should the government increase taxes on high income earners to pay for extra spending on the health service, or should taxes and spending on health care stay the same?

An assumption of utilitarianism is that happiness can be measured in the same way that the weight of a loaf of bread can be measured. If happiness cannot be measured, then individuals, governments and other decision makers cannot make the calculations necessary to ensure 'the greatest happiness of the greatest number'. The whole theory then becomes useless as a basis for decision making. Following Bentham's death, the consensus view in neo-classical economics came to be that happiness could not be measured. Economics could say nothing about the happiness or value that one individual puts on consuming a good or taking a job compared to another individual.

Another criticism of utilitarianism was that happiness is not the only goal in life There are many other goals that human beings might have. They might prefer to be rich or famous rather than happy. Their goal might be to uphold the honour of the family. Status, power, possessions, control and sex are other possibilities. People's goals differ from culture to culture and it is arguably too simplistic to reduce everything to happiness.

The economics of happiness refutes these problems and argues that happiness can indeed be measured and that happiness should be seen as the most important goal of individuals whatever their culture.

- Surveys can validly be used to ask people about the extent to which they are happy. With a survey large enough to be statistically valid, survey results produce reliable evidence about states of happiness and satisfaction. Such survey methods have been used in psychology for decades. They are backed up by neuroscience. During the 1990s, it was discovered that happiness was associated with measurable electrical activity in the brain. This could be picked up by MRI scans. So it is possible to tell physiologically whether or not someone is telling the truth when they say they are happy.

- Looking across cultures, philosophies and religions, and using evidence from sociological and psychological studies, it is clear that happiness is a goal of human beings. It is true that happiness might be given different names such as well-being, satisfaction, fulfilment or utility. But for the economics of happiness, these different names are all pointing to the same goal. Happiness can then be argued to be the most important goal. If asked, 'why do I want to be wealthy or powerful?', most people would say 'because it leads to happiness'. Wealth, power or status are not ends in themselves. They are stepping stones to happiness. Think too of the reverse question: 'Is the goal of life to be unhappy?' Or 'Does it matter that people are unhappy?' Few people would argue that they wanted to be unhappy and that it didn't matter whether their relatives and friends and other people were happy or not.

GDP and happiness

Traditional economics states that the fundamental economic problem occurs because human wants are infinite but resources are only finite. Economic growth helps solve this problem because it allows more human wants to be satisfied. Economic growth leads to rising living standards and, by implication, greater happiness.

Economists have long recognised that the quantity of goods that consumers can buy is only one part of the measurement of the standard of living. In the unit 'Economic growth and welfare', it was explained that other factors such as the social and cultural environment and political freedom contribute to the standard of living. However, there is an implicit assumption that GDP remains one of the most important components of economic welfare.

Economists using psychological surveys, though, present a more complex picture. Using surveys from across the world (cross sectional surveys), they have found that happiness and income are positively related at low levels of income but higher levels of income are not associated with increases in happiness. The idea that increases in GDP do not lead to increases in happiness is called the **Easterlin Paradox**, after Richard Easterlin, an economist, who identified this problem in a 1974 research paper. One piece of evidence for this from research conducted is illustrated in Figure 1. Using UK survey data, in Figure 2, another piece of research suggests that life satisfaction in the UK has actually declined since the 1970s despite a more than 60 per cent

rise in GDP. All the survey evidence for the USA and Japan also concludes that there has been no increase in happiness in those countries over the last 50 years.

The conclusion from research is that an increase in consumption of material goods will improve well-being when basic needs are not being met, such as adequate food and shelter. But once these needs are being met, then increasing the quantity of goods consumed makes no difference to well-being. Having a new high-definition television, or a new car when you already have a reasonable, functioning TV and car doesn't increase your well-being in the long term.

Factors affecting happiness apart from GDP

There is a number of factors which have been identified which contribute to happiness from survey evidence.

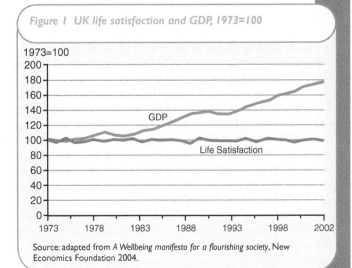

Figure 1 *UK life satisfaction and GDP, 1973=100*

Source: adapted from *A Wellbeing manifesto for a flourishing society*, New Economics Foundation 2004.

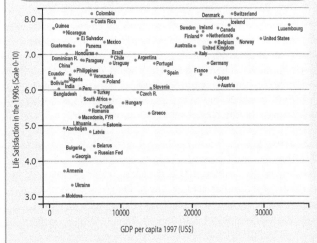

Figure 2 *An international comparison of the life satisfaction and GDP of nations*

Source: adapted from *A Wellbeing manifesto for a flourishing society*, New Economics Foundation 2004.

Relationships Friends and family have a very important role to play in happiness. In a 2007 research paper, the economist Nattavudh Powdthavee gave estimates of the monetary value of different types of relationships. As can be seen from Table 1, meeting friends and relatives just once or twice a month had a monetary value of £31 000 per year per capita. This should be compared with average real annual household income per capita of £9 800. Talking to neighbours on most days was worth £40 800 a year. Being married was worth £68 400. On the other hand, being divorced led to a negative monetary value of £21 600 per year. It is possible to dispute the exact size of these figures. However, the casual observer can see that individuals place a high value on relationships. Friendships are prized. Partners in a marriage give up well paid jobs for the sake of their marriage. Most divorced people seek to remarry. The high point of consumerism in today's Britain, Christmas, is one where people give gifts to each other and spend time together as families. Being alone, cut off from friends, family and even casual day to day encounters, is associated with low self-esteem, depression and mental illness.

Work Work provides income and satisfaction. However, research also shows that aspects of work depress happiness. Long commuting journeys, tight work deadlines, lack of control over how a job is done and housework have all shown up in surveys as being negatively correlated to happiness and well being. Overall, the survey evidence suggests that workers in high income countries would be happier if they had lower incomes but more leisure time. As for unemployment, in the same survey quoted in Table 1, it was calculated to have a negative happiness value of £66 400 per year.

Health Having good health has a very high monetary value in terms of happiness. In Table 1, the valuation put on excellent health is £303 000 per year. Surveys suggest that health and happiness are correlated. Figure 3 shows data which link happiness with blood pressure. Countries with above average incidence of high blood pressure are also those with the lowest happiness scores. Good psychological health leads to happiness. Mental ill health has large negative impacts on happiness. There is some evidence that mental health problems in rich countries have been increasing over time, possibly due to the increasing fragmentation of society and increased stress in the workplace.

Trust Some economists have investigated trends over time in civic issues. Trust in society of other individuals and of government has declined, as Table 2 shows. Civic participation has also declined. People are less likely to be involved in public groups such as trade unions, churches, scouts, charities or amateur football teams. The private space has expanded as the public space has diminished. Surveys suggest this is likely to have reduced

Table 1 Valuation of life events

		£ per year
Meet friends and relatives		
	Once or twice a month	31 000
	Once or twice a week	47 000
	On most days	62 400
Talk to neighbours		
	Once or twice a week	22 800
	On most days	40 800
Married		68 400
Living as a couple		57 800
Separated		-5 400
Divorced		-21 600
Unemployment		-66 400
Disabled		-61 000
Health: good		237 000
Health: excellent		303 000

Source: adapted from *Putting a price tag on Friends, Relatives and Neighbours: using Surveys of Life Satisfaction to Value Social Relationships*, Nattavudh Powdthavee 2007.

happiness. Partly this is because it limits the occasions when people meet together, form friendships, develop a positive image and give themselves a purpose in life. Civic participation also has positive externalities. When an amateur player turns up to a football practice, it benefits all the other members of the football team. Reducing civic participation reduces those positive externalities.

Table 2 Percentage who say 'most people can be trusted', Britain

	%
1959	56
1981	43
1995	31

Source: adapted from *What would make a happier society?*, Richard Layard 2003.

Relative income Although increasing absolute levels of GDP in rich countries seems to have no effect on happiness, there is a positive correlation in studies

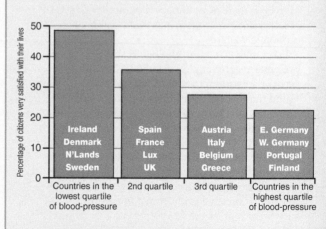

Figure 3 Blood pressure and happiness, survey evidence across 16 European countries

Percentage of citizens very satisfied with their lives

Ireland Denmark N'Lands Sweden	Spain France Lux UK	Austria Italy Belgium Greece	E. Germany W. Germany Portugal Finland
Countries in the lowest quartile of blood-pressure	2nd quartile	3rd quartile	Countries in the highest quartile of blood-pressure

Source: adapted from *Happiness, Health and Economics*, Andrew Oswald, 2007.

Table 3 Valuation of happiness: Hungary 1995

	Rise in happiness (index)
Income	
Family income rises by 50% relative to average income	1.0
Freedom	
Quality of government improves: living in Hungary compared to Belarus 1995	2.5
Religion	
Answering yes rather than no to 'God is important in my life'	2.0
Trust	
Answering yes rather than no to 'In general people can be trusted'	1.0
Morality	
Answering yes rather than no to 'Cheating on taxes is never justifiable'	1.0

Source: adapted from *What would make a happier society?*, Richard Layard 2003.

between relative income and happiness. Surveys across countries consistently show that those with above average incomes tend to have higher levels of happiness than those with below average incomes. For example, evidence suggests that if everyone today in the UK were to see an increase in their income by 50 per cent, on average there would be no increase in happiness or well-being. On the other hand, those receiving 30 per cent more than the average income today do report being happier than those receiving 30 per cent less than the average income. There are two suggested explanations for this.

One is that income is a symbol of social status. Psychologically, we are happier if we feel we have more status. This competitive streak is 'hard-wired' into our brains and comes from our biological roots as apes. The second explanation is that above average incomes are correlated with a number of other factors which are associated with happiness. For example, those on above average income tend to enjoy better health and live longer. They have more control over their work environment and are less likely to perform short repetitive tasks. They are less likely to be unemployed.

Other factors Good government contributes to happiness. Surveys suggest, for example, that happiness under the communist regimes of the former Soviet Union and Eastern Europe was low because of the repressive nature of these regimes. Table 3 gives an estimate for the relative happiness of Hungary in 1995, a former communist state but now a democracy, compared to Belarus, which was still effectively communist. Being religious is associated with happiness. It could be that being religious is correlated with going to a church or other place of worship and being with a community. So being religious helps relationships. Or it could be that religion gives a positive purpose to life. Being moral also seems to be associated with happiness. Table 3, for example, reports survey evidence that those answering 'yes' to the question 'Cheating on

taxes is never justifiable' are happier than those who say no.

Policy implications

Increasing economic growth has traditionally been assumed to lead to an increase in economic welfare, well-being and happiness. Research from the economics of happiness suggests that this is likely to be true at current low levels of world income. Increased GDP is likely to benefit citizens of India, China or South Africa. But increasing GDP in the rich countries of the world such as the UK or the USA is unlikely to be be associated with increased well-being. The implication is that policies designed to increase GDP whatever their other consequences should be abandoned. Instead, economic policy should be directed at improving those aspects of life which most increase levels of well-being or most reduce the risk of large falls in well-being. The economics of happiness is still relatively new and there is no agreed policy agenda amongst economists who support this theory. However, examples of the sort of policy being put forward including the following.

Relationships Relationships are very important to happiness. Traditional economics suggests that labour mobility associated with flexible labour markets is a source of economic growth. However, geographic mobility breaks up family and community relationships and reduces trust by people in others. Therefore there might be net gains to society if policies were adopted to reduce geographical mobility and encourage more stable

communities. Markets might be less efficient but people might be happier.

Work Paid work leads to many examples of loss of well-being which might be addressed by government policy. For example, lengthy commuting leads to a loss of well-being. Government policies to reduce the length of time of commuter journeys would therefore increase happiness. This could come about through improving transport links. Or it could come about through planning policies which encourage workers to live nearer their place of work. Interestingly, survey evidence suggests that when workers travel together with friends or colleagues, this reduces the loss of well-being caused by commuting. This is probably because of the positive impact on happiness of relationships. Encouraging car sharing, which would have positive environmental consequences, could therefore increase happiness because people travel together and because it might reduce journey times with reduced congestion. Another example of loss of well-being is the number of hours worked by employees. Neo-classical economics suggests that taxes on income should be reduced to increase incentives to work, but it might lead to greater happiness if incentives to work longer hours were reduced through higher taxes. Unemployment and job insecurity are other examples of situations which lead to a loss of well-being. Free market economists suggest that labour laws which increase job security and make it more difficult to make workers redundant reduce economic efficiency and increase unemployment. But a combination of laws which give greater job security with job creation schemes and intensive training, seen for example in Scandinavian countries, might lead to higher levels of happiness even if they are costly to the taxpayer.

Health UK health statistics show that levels of physical health are improving in most areas. Obesity, though, is growing at an alarming rate. Obesity is linked to increased risk of illness and also reduce quality of life. Therefore, the average level of happiness could be prevented from falling if the government made serious efforts to stem obesity. Mental health has been deteriorating over time. Yet mental health is an underfunded area of the National Health Service. Survey evidence suggests that only a quarter of people suffering from depression are being treated by the NHS. One in six of the population suffer from mental ill health such as depression, anxiety and serious phobias, 15 per cent of people will experience a major depression at some point in their lives, half of all people classified as disabled have a mental illness, and yet only 12 per cent of the NHS budget is devoted to mental health. Spending much more on mental health would increase happiness.

Economists are developing indices of happiness or well-being. These are composite indices taking a number of different variables and weighting them in order of importance similar to indices such as the UN's Human Development Index or the Index of Sustainable Economic Welfare. However, they are open to criticism about exactly what variables are included and what weightings are used. Unless a body like the United Nations produces a standardised formula, it is unlikely that a single common measure of happiness, similar to GDP for output and income, will become a target for national governments.

Key terms

The economics of happiness - investigates exactly what contributes to welfare and attempts to put values on some of these factors.

DataQuestion

Bhutan

Bhutan is one of the world's poorer countries. Situated in the Himalayas between India and China, it is a Buddhist kingdom. In 2005, average GDP measured in purchasing power parities was $5 620 and it was classified by the United Nations as a low income country.

Table 4 Selected development indicators 2005

	Bhutan	UK
GDP per capita, US$ at ppp	5 620	35 580
Life expectancy, males (2005)	62	76
Infant mortality rate (0-1 year) per 1000 live births	53	5
Tuberculosis prevalence, active 100 000 population	174	10
Percentage of population with access to improved drinking water	62	100
Percentage of the population with access to improved sanitation	70	100
Average annual rate of real GDP growth 2000-2005, percent	8	3
Energy consumption per capita oil equivalent (thousand kg), 2004	65	3 711
Internet users per 100 population	1	47

In 1972, the King of Bhutan, Jogme Singye Wangchuck, first used the term 'Gross National Happiness' to signify the direction he wanted Bhutan's economy to take. The term has never precisely been defined. However, it was an attempt to say that development was more than just increased in output as measured by the UN definition of GDP. True development was also about spiritual development, a concept which links to the country's Buddhist values.

In 1998, Bhutan's prime minister, Jigmi Thinkley identified four pillars of Gross National Happiness.
1. Sustainable and equitable socio-economic development is about improvement of physical, intellectual, social and economic health through services such as health, education, trade and commerce, road and bridge construction, employment, urban development and housing.
2. Conservation of the environment is about, for example, the law which states that the minimum tree cover in the kingdom must be 65 per cent of the land, and that hydropower projects should have minimal environmental impact.
3. Preservation and promotion of culture is about promoting Bhutanese religion, language and literature, art and architecture, performing arts, national dress, traditional etiquette, sport and recreation.
4. Good governance is moving Bhutan towards being a constitutional monarchy.

In a 2005 survey, 45 per cent of Bhutanese adults reported being very happy, 52 per cent reported being happy and only 3 per cent reported not being happy. In the USA, the comparable figures were 30 per cent very happy, 58 per cent pretty happy and 12 per cent not too happy.

A new study conducted by the University of Leicester compiled data from 178 countries and 100 global studies to map happiness across the world. Denmark came top with Switzerland 2nd, but surprisingly Bhutan was 8th. Despite having the highest average per capita GDP in the world, the USA only came 23rd whilst the UK came 41st. Most of Africa and the former Soviet republics scored worst. Burundi, Zimbabwe and the Democratic Republic of Congo were the world's least happy places. The report's author, Adrian White, said that countries with good access to healthcare and education came out on top.

Some people claim that shopping is therapeutic, but does buying things actually make people happier? In Bhutan, shopping is becoming a more regular experience especially for the urban young. There are now plenty of cheap clothes imported from a globalised marketplace available for sale. Fifty years ago, the economy was almost totally agrarian, based on subsistence agriculture where barter was the norm and money virtually unheard of. According to Kuenzang Roder, Bhutan's best known writer, people were poor but life's details had meaning. In 1998, Bhutan's king allowed in television and the Internet. This introduced a fever among the people for a different way of life and for new products. Now, at night, young people in Bhutan's capital take off their traditional dress and put on imported blue jeans to go dancing. 'The culture of fast clothes is coming in, and it's a very confusing kind of experience. Now shades of dissatisfaction with the traditional way of life are creeping in everywhere - from private living rooms to call-in radio talk shows.'

Source: adapted from en.wikipedia.org; World Bank, World Development Report; www.developments.org.uk; www.bhootan.org; news.independent.co.uk, *www.le.ac.uk*.

Figure 4   *Subjective well-being, by country 2005-2006*

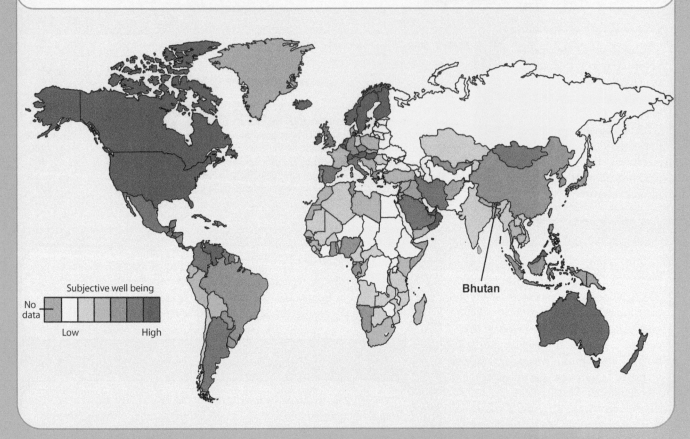

Subjective well being

No
data

Low   High

Bhutan

Source: adapted from en.wikipedia.org.

1. Explain the possible distinction between GDP and happiness, using Bhutan as an example.
2. Discuss whether the main aim of Bhutan's government should be to maximise growth in GDP.

Summary

1. Unemployment is a stock concept, measuring the number of people out of work at a point in time. Unemployment will increase if the number of workers losing jobs is greater than the number of people gaining jobs.
2. Four types of unemployment can be distinguished: frictional unemployment caused by workers taking time to move jobs; seasonal unemployment caused by some jobs only being available at certain times of the year structural unemployment caused by a failure of labour markets to respond to long term changes in the economy; and cyclical unemployment caused by a lack of aggregate demand in recessions.
3. The costs of unemployment include financial costs to the unemployed, to taxpayers and to local and national economies. They also include non-financial costs such as possible increased vandalism or increased suicides.

The measurement of unemployment

Unemployment, the number of people out of work, is measured at a point in time. It is a **stock concept**. However, the level of unemployment will change over time.

Millions of people seek jobs each year in the UK. Young people leave school, college or university seeking work. Former workers who have taken time out of the workforce, for instance to bring up children, seek to return to work. Workers who have lost their jobs, either because they have resigned or because they have been made redundant, search for new jobs.

Equally, millions of workers lose their jobs. They may retire, or leave work to look after children or they may resign or be made redundant from existing jobs.

Unemployment in an economy with a given labour force will rise if the number of workers gaining jobs is less than the number of people losing their jobs. In the first half of 2007, for instance, 1.2 million workers lost their jobs. However, the numbers gaining jobs were slightly higher per month than the numbers losing jobs. The result was a net fall in unemployment over the period. This flow of workers into or out of the stock of unemployed workers is summarised in Figure 1.

Unemployment will also increase if there is a rise in the number of people seeking work but the number of jobs in the economy remains static. During most years in the 1970s and 1980s, there was a rise in the number of school leavers entering the job market as well as more women wanting a job in the UK. It can be argued that at least some of the increase in unemployment in these two decades was a reflection of the inability of the UK economy to provided sufficient new jobs for those extra workers in the labour force.

Types of unemployment

Unemployment occurs for a variety of reasons. A number of different types of or reasons for unemployment can be distinguished.

Table 1 Unemployment flows, 2005-2007

	Thousands	
	Inflow	Outflow
2005 Q3	603.2	591.1
2005 Q4	624.7	591.2
2006 Q1	622.3	594.0
2006 Q2	617.3	603.3
2006 Q3	627.8	627.0
2006 Q4	624.3	644.7
2007 Q1	630.4	663.2
2007 Q2	611.7	649.9

Source: adapted from *Economic & Labour Market Review*, Office for National Statistics.

(a) In which quarters did unemployment: (i) increase; and (ii) decrease? Explain your answer.
(b) Explain whether unemployment was higher or lower in the 2005 3rd quarter than in 2007 2nd quarter.

Figure 1 Flow into and out of the stock of unemployed workers

An increase in unemployment

Workers leaving jobs → The labour market → Workers gaining jobs → The unemployed

A fall in unemployment

Workers leaving jobs → The labour market → Workers gaining jobs → The unemployed

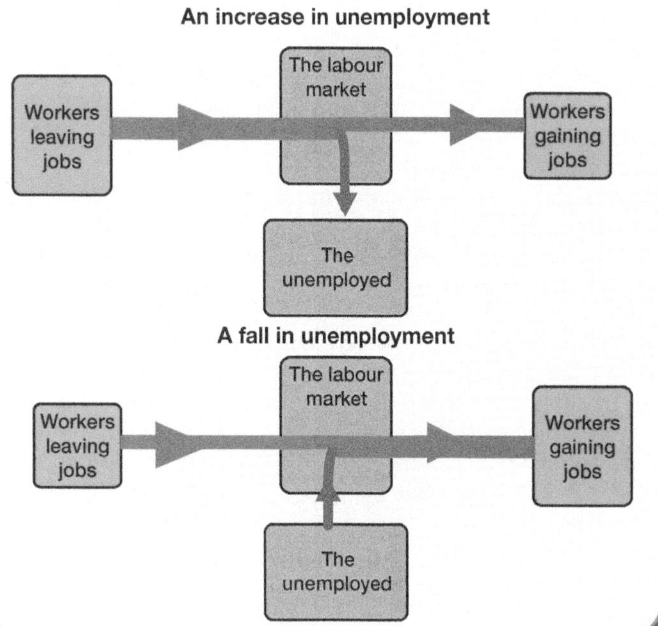

Frictional unemployment Most workers who lose their jobs move quickly into new ones. This short-term unemployment is called FRICTIONAL UNEMPLOYMENT. There will always be frictional unemployment in a free market economy and it is not regarded by most economists as a serious problem. The amount of time spent unemployed varies. The higher the level of unemployment benefits or redundancy pay, the longer workers will be able to afford to search for a good job without being forced into total poverty. Equally, the better the job information available to unemployed workers through newspapers, jobcentres, etc. the shorter the time workers should need to spend searching for jobs.

Seasonal unemployment Some workers, such as construction workers or workers in the tourist industry, tend to work on a seasonal basis. SEASONAL UNEMPLOYMENT tends to rise in winter when some of these workers will be laid off, whilst unemployment falls in summer when they are taken on again. There is little that can be done to prevent this pattern occurring in a market economy where the demand for labour varies through the year.

Structural unemployment Far more serious is the problem of STRUCTURAL UNEMPLOYMENT. This occurs when the demand for labour is less than its supply in an individual labour market in the economy. One example of structural unemployment is **regional unemployment**. Throughout the post-war period, the South of England has tended to be at full employment while regions such as Northern Ireland have consistently suffered unemployment. This has occurred because of a lack of mobility of factors of production between the regions. Another example is **sectoral unemployment**. The steel and shipbuilding industries in the UK declined sharply in the late 1970s and early 1980s leaving a considerable number of skilled workers unemployed. Unfortunately their skills were no longer needed in the economy and without retraining and possible relocation, they were unable to adapt to the changing demand. **Technological unemployment** is another example of structural unemployment. Groups of workers across industries may be put out of work by new technology. Again, without retraining and geographical mobility these workers may remain unemployed.

Cyclical or demand-deficient unemployment Economies tend to experience business cycles. These are movements from boom to recession over time. CYCLICAL or DEMAND-DEFICIENT UNEMPLOYMENT is unemployment which occurs when the economy is not in boom. It is when there is insufficient aggregate demand in the economy for all workers to get a job. In a recession, it is not just workers who are unemployed. Capital too is underutilised. So factories and offices can remain empty. Machinery and equipment can lie unused.

Cyclical unemployment is caused by a lack of demand in the economy. Frictional, seasonal and structural unemployment are caused by supply side factors. For example, if labour markets were more efficient, workers would move from job to job more quickly. So the time taken to get a new job would be shorter. In the case of frictional unemployment, an increase in the amount of information of jobs available to jobseekers would reduce the time they spent searching for a job. In the case of structural unemployment, making it easier to get cheap rented accommodation in areas of low unemployment would help workers in areas of higher unemployment to

Question 2

The economy is currently in recession and the following workers are unemployed. Explain under which type of unemployment their circumstances might be classified.

(a) Katie Morris is a 30 year old in Devon with a husband and two children. She works in the local hotel trade in the summer months on a casual basis but would like to work all the year round.
(b) John Penny, aged 22 and living in London, was made redundant a couple of weeks ago from a furniture store which closed down. He is currently seeking work in the retail sector.
(c) Manus O'Brien lives in Belfast in Northern Ireland. Aged 56, he last had a job 12 years ago working in a local factory.
(d) Clare Livingstone, aged 31, lost her job 6 months ago working as a surveyor for an estate agent in Guildford in the South East of England. She is currently looking for another surveyor's job but the local housing market is very depressed.
(e) Gavin Links, aged 40, has been out of work for 18 months. A former manager of a factory in the West Midlands, he is seeking a similar job within travelling distance of where he currently lives.

move. Better retraining of workers would also help reduce structural unemployment.

Using diagrams to illustrate unemployment

Unemployment can be illustrated using a variety of diagrams. Figure 2 shows a production possibility diagram. The economy is operating at its productive potential when it is somewhere on the production possibility frontier such as at point A. There are unemployed resources when the economy is operating within the frontier such as at point B.

Aggregate demand and supply analysis can be used to distinguish between demand side and supply side causes of

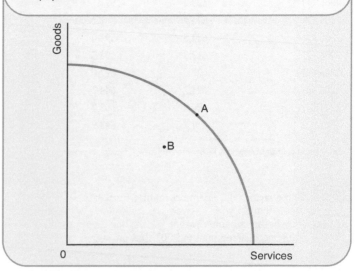

Figure 2 The production possibility frontier
At any point on the production possibility frontier, there is no unemployment due to a lack of demand. At point B, there is cyclical unemployment.

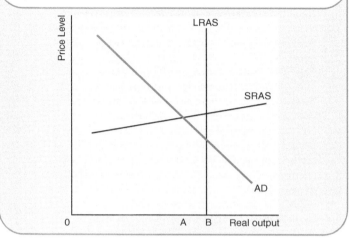

Figure 3 *Cyclical unemployment* The economy is in equilibrium in the short run at an output level of 0A. This is below the level of 0B, shown by the long run aggregate supply curve, where there would be no demand-deficient unemployment.

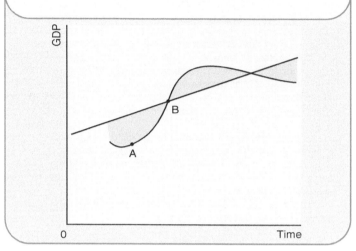

Figure 5 *Unemployment and the output gap* Cyclical unemployment occurs if the actual level of income is below its long run trend level, for example at A.

unemployment. In Figure 3, the economy is in short run equilibrium at an output level of 0A. However, what if the LRAS curve is to the right of this point? Then there must be cyclical or demand-deficient unemployment. The economy is in recession. Output at 0A does not represent the productive potential of the economy which is higher at 0B. However, if there is an increase in aggregate demand, shown in Figure 4 by the shift in the aggregate demand curve from AD_1 to AD_2, full employment can be restored.

The same point can be illustrated using the concept of the output gap. The trend growth of the economy is shown by the upward sloping straight line in Figure 5. At point A, there is a negative output gap and the economy is in recession. So there is cyclical unemployment. An increase in demand will move the economy to B and eliminate demand-deficient unemployment.

Supply side causes of unemployment include frictional, seasonal and structural unemployment. In Figure 4, there is likely to be some frictional, seasonal and structural unemployment at an output level of 0B. This is because the long

run aggregate supply curve is drawn on the assumption that there are limited resources and markets may work imperfectly. For example, some workers may be structurally unemployed because they do not have the right skills for the jobs on offer in the market. This lack of skills is taken into account when drawing the long run aggregate supply curve. If through training they acquire new skills and then get jobs, this leads to a rightward shift of the long run aggregate supply curve. A fall in frictional, seasonal and structural unemployment is shown by a rightward shift of the long run aggregate supply curve.

In Figure 5, the long run trend line of growth is drawn assuming the gradual shift to the right in the long run aggregate supply curve shown in Figure 4. If the long run trend rate of growth is 2.5 per cent, then in Figure 4, the LRAS curve is shifting to the right by 2.5 per cent per year on average. So the trend rate of growth assumes there will be supply side improvements to the economy over time. This may or may not include supply side improvements which reduce frictional, seasonal or structural unemployment. However, past evidence would suggest that existing structural unemployment tends to fall over time. Of course, there may be new supply side shocks which lead to new structural unemployment. If the long run trend rate of growth could be raised, say from 2.5 per cent to 3.0 per cent, there is a greater likelihood that structural unemployment will fall. A rise in the long run trend rate of growth would be shown by a shift upwards in the trend growth line in Figure 5.

The costs of unemployment

Long term unemployment is generally considered to be a great social evil. This is perhaps not surprising in view of the following costs of unemployment.

Costs to the unemployed and their dependants The people who are likely to lose the most from unemployment are the unemployed themselves. One obvious cost is the loss of income that could have been earned had the person been in a job. Offset against this is the value of any benefits that the worker might receive and any value placed on the extra leisure time which an unemployed person has at his or her disposal.

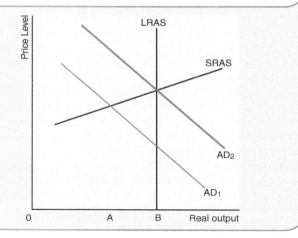

Figure 4 *Eliminating cyclical unemployment* The cyclical unemployment in the economy at the short run equilibrium of 0A can be eliminated by raising aggregate demand, shown by the shift in the aggregate demand curve from AD_1 to AD_2.

In a study of 6000 employed and unemployed workers, a team of academics found that the unemployed had poor psychological health. They were more likely to be depressed, less likely to mix with people in work and had little access to social support networks or to information about jobs. One of the team, Richard Lampard of Warwick University, concluded that unemployment directly increases the risk of marriage break-up, finding that the chances of the marriage of an unemployed person ending in the following year are 70 per cent higher than those of a person who has never been out of work.

The study also found that men in low-paid insecure jobs suffered almost the same level of psychological distress as those who were out of work altogether. It was found that there was a close correlation between perceived job security and psychological well-being. Women were found to be just as distressed by lack of paid work, but less affected by the prospect of an insecure low-paid job.

(a) What problems face the unemployed, according to the article?
(b) Why might these problems give rise to costs not just for the unemployed but also for society as a whole?

Key terms

Cyclical or demand-deficient unemployment - when there is insufficient demand in the economy for all workers who wish to work at current wage rates to obtain a job.
Frictional unemployment - when workers are unemployed for short lengths of time between jobs.
Seasonal unemployment - when workers are unemployed at certain times of the year, such as building workers or agricultural workers in winter.
Structural unemployment - when the pattern of demand and production changes leaving workers unemployed in labour markets where demand has shrunk. Examples of structural unemployment are regional unemployment, sectoral unemployment or technological unemployment.

For most unemployed it is likely that they will be net financial losers.

The costs to the unemployed, however, do not finish there. Evidence suggests that unemployed people and their families suffer in a number of other ways. One simple but very important problem for them is the stigma of being unemployed. Unemployment is often equated with failure both by the unemployed themselves and by society in general. Many feel degraded by the whole process of signing on, receiving benefit and not being able to support themselves or their families. Studies suggest that the unemployed suffer from a wide range of social problems including above average incidence of stress, marital breakdown, suicide, physical illness and mental instability, and that they have higher death rates.

For the short term unemployed, the costs are relatively low. Many will lose some earnings, although a few who receive large redundancy payments may benefit financially from having lost their job. The social and psychological costs are likely to be limited too.

However, the long term unemployed are likely to be major losers on all counts. The long term unemployed suffer one more cost. Evidence suggests that the longer the period out of work, the less likely it is that the unemployed person will find a job. There are two reasons for this. First, being out of work reduces the human capital of workers. They lose work skills and are not being trained in the latest developments in their occupation. Second, employers use length of time out of work as a crude way of sifting through applicants for a job. For an employer, unemployment is likely to mean that the applicant is, to some extent, deskilled. There is a fear that the unemployed worker will not be capable of doing the job after a spell of unemployment. It could show that the worker has personality problems and might be a disruptive employee. It could also be an indication that other employers have turned down the applicant for previous jobs and hence it would be rational to save time and not consider the applicant for this job. The long term unemployed are then in a catch-22

situation. They can't get a job unless they have recent employment experience. However, they can't get recent employment experience until they get a job.

Costs to local communities Costs to local communities are more difficult to establish. Some have suggested that unemployment, particularly amongst the young, leads to increased crime, violence on the streets and vandalism. Areas of high unemployment tend to become run down. Shops go out of business. Households have no spare money to look after their properties and their gardens. Increased vandalism further destroys the environment.

Costs to taxpayers The cost to the taxpayer is a heavy one. On the one hand, government has to pay out increased benefits. On the other hand, government loses revenue because these workers would have paid taxes if they had been employed. For instance, they would have paid income tax and National Insurance contributions on their earnings. They would also have paid more in VAT and excise duties because they would have been able to spend more. So taxpayers not only pay more taxes to cover for increased government spending but they also have to pay more because they have to make up the taxes that the unemployed would have paid if they had been in work.

Costs to the economy as a whole Taxpayers paying money to the unemployed is not a loss for the economy as a whole. It is a **transfer payment** which redistributes existing resources within the economy. The actual loss to the whole economy is two-fold. Firstly there is the loss of output which those workers now unemployed could have produced had they been in work. The economy could have produced more goods and services which would then have been available for consumption. Secondly there are the social costs such as increased violence and depression which are borne by the unemployed and the communities in which they live.

Applied economics

Measures of unemployment

In economic theory, the unemployed are defined as those without a job but who are seeking work at current wage rates. Measuring the number of unemployed in an economy, however, is more difficult than economic theory might suggest. There are two basic ways in which unemployment can be calculated.

● Government can undertake a survey of the population to identify the employed and the unemployed. The international standard for this method has been produced by the International Labour Organisation (ILO) and is the basis for the **Labour Force Survey (LFS)** conducted by the government in the UK. The Labour Force Survey generates monthly **LFS unemployment** statistics, sometimes called **ILO unemployment** statistics.

● The government can count all those who register as unemployed. In the UK, **claimant count** unemployment statistics are produced based on the numbers claiming benefit for being unemployed.

Unemployment is expressed in two ways. It can be stated as an absolute figure, as millions of workers, or it can be stated as a relative measure, as a percentage of the workforce, the **unemployment rate**. Expressing it in millions gives a clear indication of the numbers affected by unemployment. Expressing it as percentage is better when the number of workers in the economy is changing. For instance, using absolute figures to compare US unemployment with UK unemployment may not be helpful because there are about five times as many workers in the US as in the UK. Comparing it as a percentage allows a more meaningful comparison to be made. Equally, the size of the workforce is likely to change over time. In 1950 in the UK, there were

23.7 million in the labour force of which 0.4 million were unemployed on a claimant count basis. In 2007, there were 30.8 million in the labour force of which 1.7 million were unemployed on the ILO measure. Unemployment was much higher in 2007, but so too was the size of the workforce.

The claimant count

Until 1997, the main measure of UK unemployment was the claimant count. However, the claimant count figure had come under increasing criticism because it was felt to be open to government manipulation. In the 1980s and 1990s, the UK government introduced over 30 different changes to the way in which the claimant count was calculated, most of which served to reduce the numbers officially unemployed. Not only was the claimant count open to manipulation but it was also not an internationally recognised way of measuring unemployment. Hence, it could not be used to compare UK unemployment levels with those in other countries.

ILO (or LFS) unemployment

In 1998, the newly elected Labour government decided to make the ILO count the main measure of unemployment in the UK. ILO unemployment figures had been collected first on a biannual (once every two years) basis in 1973, and then annually from 1984. In 1993, it became a quarterly count and since 1997 has been monthly. The ILO count is taken from a wider survey of employment called the Labour Force Survey (LFS). 60 000 households, with over 100 000 adults, are surveyed. The questionnaire used covers household size and structure, accommodation details, basic demographic characteristics, such as age, sex, marital status and ethnic origin, and economic activity. To be counted as unemployed, an individual has to be without a paid job, be available to start a job within a fortnight and has either looked for work at some time in the previous four weeks or been waiting to start a job already obtained.

ILO unemployment compared to the claimant count

Figure 6 shows that ILO unemployment figures differ significantly from claimant count figures. ILO unemployment tends to be above claimant count unemployment in a recovery and boom situation, but roughly equal to it in a recession.

ILO unemployment is likely to be above the claimant count figure because the claimant count excludes a number of key groups of unemployed workers.

● Many female unemployed workers are actively looking

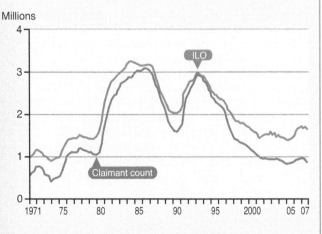

Figure 6 *ILO and claimant count measures of employment, seasonally adjusted*

Millions

Source: adapted from *Monthly Digest of Statistics*, Office for National Statistics.

for work (and are therefore included in ILO unemployment) but are not entitled to benefits for being unemployed. For instance, they might not have built up sufficient National Insurance contributions to qualify for unemployment benefit, a National Insurance benefit. They may also be living in a household where the husband or partner is earning too high a wage for them to qualify for means tested benefit.

● Older, particularly male, workers in their 50s and 60s may be collecting a pension from their previous employer or be supported financially by their spouse. They are therefore not entitled to benefits but may be actively seeking work.

● Workers are not entitled to register as unemployed with the DSS until they have been out of work for a number of weeks. However, anyone interviewed for the ILO count who is unemployed and is looking for work is counted as unemployed regardless of how long they have been unemployed.

The claimant count, however, may include some unemployed who would not be included in the ILO count. For instance, those working in the **hidden economy** may claim benefits for being unemployed but actually be in work, usually as a self employed worker.

Both the ILO and claimant counts could be argued to underestimate overall unemployment.

● They do not include part time workers who are actively seeking full time work, for instance.

● Those on government training and work schemes who would prefer to be in proper employment are not included. This particularly affects young workers.

● There are some out of work who are not actively seeking work or receiving benefits for being unemployed but who would take a job if offered.

Table 2 Employment and unemployment, UK, spring each year, seasonally adjusted, millions

	Total in employment Millions	ILO unemployed Spring each year (millions)
1989	26.7	2.1
1990	26.9	2.0
1991	26.4	2.4
1992	25.6	2.8
1993	25.3	3.0
1994	25.4	2.8
1995	25.7	2.5
1996	26.0	2.3
1997	26.4	2.0
1998	26.7	1.8
1999	27.1	1.8
2000	27.4	1.6
2001	27.7	1.4
2002	27.9	1.5
2003	28.2	1.5
2004	28.4	1.4
2005	28.7	1.4
2006	28.9	1.7
2007	29.0	1.7

Source: adapted from *Economic & Labour Market Review*, Office for National Statistics.

This mainly applies to women bringing up families. Table 2 illustrates this point. Between its peak in 1993 and 2007, ILO unemployment fell by 1.3 million whilst the total in employment increased by 3.8 million.

● Some unemployed workers have been taken off the unemployment registers by moving them onto sickness and disability benefits. As Figure 7 shows, numbers claiming sickness and disability benefits have risen from 0.7 million in 1979 to 2.4 million in 2006. Areas of the country with relatively high unemployment also have relatively high levels of sickness and disability benefit claimants. Some economists argue that all those on sickness and disability benefits should be included amongst the unemployed since all could work given the right working conditions.

However, both measures of unemployment could be argued to overestimate unemployment. Some of those out of work find it almost impossible to get a job. Those with physical and mental disabilities, some ex-criminals or some with no qualifications find the job market very difficult. Some economists would argue that these workers are unemployable and therefore should not be counted as unemployed. A minority of those working in the hidden economy may claim benefits and may declare on surveys that they are out of work and seeking work.

Figure 7 Jobless numbers on sickness and disability benefit; unemployment claimant count

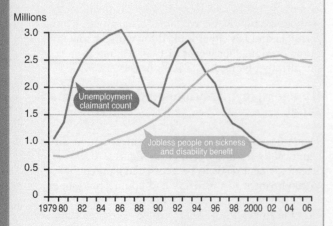

Source: adapted from *Annual Abstract of Statistics, Economic & Labour Market Trends*, Office for National Statistics.

DataQuestion

Unemployment in Wolverhampton

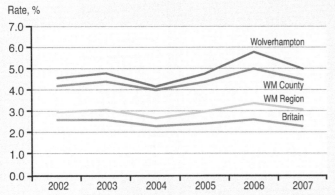

Figure 8 *Local (Wolverhampton), county (West Midlands County), regional (West Midlands Regional) and national (Britain) Unemployment Rates*

Source: adapted from Wolverhampton City Council, *Monthly Unemployment Briefing*, August 2007.

Forty jobs have gone at a Wolverhampton factory after its work was shifted to China, Germany and Bulgaria. Ideal Standard in Bushbury, which has been producing brass taps in the city for 105 years, says it makes business sense to move its manufacturing abroad. The company, which will shed another 30 jobs by the end of the month, is the second Wolverhampton factory this week to make redundancies while taking advantage of cheap labour in other countries. Turner Powertrain Systems revealed this week that it is cutting 75 jobs and considering farming work out to India.

Source: adapted from the *Express & Star*, 1.10.2005.

Table 3 Claimant count summary: August 2007

	Male		Female		Total	
	Number	Rate %	Number	Rate %	Number	Rate %
Wolverhampton	5 210	6.8	2 023	2.9	7 233	5.0
W'ton travel to work area	9 725	5.9	3 728	2.5	13 453	4.3
W Midlands County	52 798	6.4	18 699	2.5	71 497	4.5
W Midlands Region	74 381	4.3	27 812	1.8	102 193	3.1
Great Britain	596 231	3.2	230 063	1.4	832 294	2.3

Unemployment rate: unemployment as a % of the working age population.

Source: adapted from Wolverhampton City Council, *Monthly Unemployment Briefing*, August 2007.

Unemployment facts

The proportion of children living in households where no one holds a job is the highest in Europe. This is mainly due to the high number of workless lone-parent households and, as a result, half of all children living with one parent are in income poverty.

Those who are unemployed are more likely to have poor educational qualifications and have been in low paid jobs in the past than those currently in work.

Unemployed people are three times more likely than average to be victims of violent crime. Lone parents, who have above average rates of unemployment, are more than twice as likely as average to be burgled.

Over the past ten years, the chance of a household, where either the head of the household or the spouse is unemployed, having an income below 60 per cent of the average income for all households was between 70 and 80 per cent.

While the total number of jobs in the UK has been rising, the number of jobs in manufacturing, construction and other production industries has been falling.

Two fifths of those making a new claim for Jobseeker's Allowance were last claiming less than six months ago.

Spending on travel by households on low incomes is only one quarter that of households on average incomes.

Source: adapted from New Policy Institute at www.jrf.org.uk.

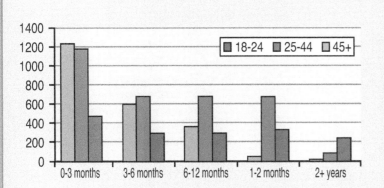

Figure 9 *Wolverhampton unemployment count: age and duration July 2007*

Source: adapted from Wolverhampton City Council, *Monthly Unemployment Briefing*, July 2007.

Table 4 Comparisons of selected social statistics

	Wolverhampton	West Midlands	England/GB
Perinatal mortality rate 2001[1], England	13.1	10.0	8.3
Life expectancy at birth 2001-2002, years, England			
Males	74.5	75.4	76
Females	80.1	80.3	80.6
% change in resident population, GB			
1984-1994	- 3.5	+ 1.5	+ 2.5
1994-2004	- 2.5	+ 1.6	+ 3.4
Qualifications, % of residents, 2006			
Degree, NVQ4 or above	18.0	23.9	27.4
No qualifications	25.1	17.5	13.8
Economically active, % of population of working age, 2006			
Males			
Employees	67.2	65.0	64.9
Self employed	7.9	12.2	13.2
Females			
Employees	57.5	62.9	64.3
Self employed	3.1	4.4	5.1
Economically inactive, % of population of working age, 2006			
Wanting a job	6.3	5.0	5.4
Not wanting a job	19.7	17.7	16.0
Job seekers allowance, claimants as % of population of working age, September 2007	4.9	3.0	2.2
Employee jobs, % of total, 2005			
Full-time	69.1	68.1	67.9
Part-time	30.9	31.9	32.1
of which			
Manufacturing	15.5	15.2	11.1
Services	79.6	78.8	82.9

1 Number of stillbirths and deaths under one week per thousand live births and stillbirths.

Source: adapted from *nomis, Official Labour Market Statistics*, Office for National Statistics; Wolverhampton City Council, *Statistics*.

One in seven of the working population are claiming incapacity benefit in some parts of Wolverhampton. In the worst-hit areas, 15 per cent of people are off work and claiming because of long-term illness or disability. Numbers vary widely between areas. Over 14 per cent are on incapacity benefit in parts of Bilston and Ettingshall. In affluent Wightwick and Penn, it is just 5 per cent. Wolverhampton South West MP Rob Marris said that 'some of that will be a hangover from our manufacturing heritage'. Wolverhampton North East MP Ken Purchase said: 'At the moment there are many people who could work but are not getting the right kind of support to do it and we have plans to help people back into work.' Nationally, there are 2.7 million people claiming at a cost of £12 billion a year.

Source: adapted from the *Express & Star*, 6.1.2006.

Figure 9 West Midlands Region, West Midlands County and Wolverhampton

1. Using the data, compare the employment and unemployment situation in Wolverhampton with the West Midlands and Great Britain.
2. Discuss the economic costs that might be created by the redundancies at Ideal Standard and Turner Powertrain Systems to (a) the individuals concerned and their families; (b) the local community in Wolverhampton; (c) taxpayers; (d) the UK economy.

31 Inflation

Summary

1. Inflation is a general sustained rise in the price level.
2. Inflation is measured by calculating the change in a weighted price index over time. In the UK, the two main measures are the Retail Price Index and the Consumer Price Index.
3. A price index only measures inflation for average households. It also cannot take into account changes in the quality and distribution of goods over time.
4. Inflation may be demand-pull or cost-push depending on whether it is caused by excessive demand or rising costs.
5. Inflation is generally considered to give rise to economic costs to society. These include shoe-leather and menu costs, psychological and political costs, and costs which arise from the redistribution of income in society. Some economists believe that inflation also results in higher unemployment and lower growth in the long term.
6. Deflation, falling prices, tends to lead to depressed demand in an economy.
7. Unanticipated inflation tends to give rise to higher economic costs than anticipated inflation.

The meaning of inflation

INFLATION is defined as a sustained general rise in prices. The opposite of inflation - DEFLATION - is a term which can have two meanings. Strictly speaking it is defined as a fall in the PRICE LEVEL. However, it can also be used to describe a slowdown in the rate of growth of output of the economy. This slowdown or recession is often associated with a fall in the **rate of inflation**. Before the Second World War, recessions were also associated with falls in prices and this is the reason why deflation has come to have these two meanings.

A general rise in prices may be quite moderate. CREEPING INFLATION would describe a situation where prices rose a few per cent on average each year. HYPER-INFLATION, on the other hand, describes a situation where inflation levels are very high. There is no exact figure at which inflation becomes hyper-inflation, but inflation of 100 or 200 per cent per annum would be deemed to be hyper-inflation by most economists.

Measuring inflation

The inflation rate is the change in average prices in an economy over a given period of time. The price level is measured in the form of an index. So if the price index were 100 today and 110 in one year's time, then the rate of inflation would be 10 per cent.

Calculating a price index is a complicated process. Prices of a representative range of goods and services (a **basket** of goods) need to be recorded on a regular basis. In the UK, there are two widely used measures of the price level: the RETAIL PRICE INDEX (RPI) and the CONSUMER PRICE INDEX (CPI). In theory, on the same day of the month, surveyors are sent out to record 110 000 prices for a variety of items. Prices are recorded in different areas of the country as well as in different types of retail outlets, such as corner shops and supermarkets. These results are averaged out to find the average price of goods and this figure is converted into **index number form**.

Changes in the price of food are more important than changes in the price of, say, tobacco. This is because a larger proportion of total household income is spent on food than on tobacco. Therefore the figures have to be **weighted** before the final index can be calculated. For instance, assume that there are only two goods in the economy, food and cars, as shown in Table 1. Households spend 75 per cent of their income on food and 25 per cent on cars. There is an increase in the price of food of 8 per cent and of cars of 4 per cent over one year. In a normal average calculation, the 8 per cent and the 4 per cent would be added together and the total divided by 2 to arrive at an average price increase of 6 per cent. However, this provides an inaccurate figure because spending on food is more

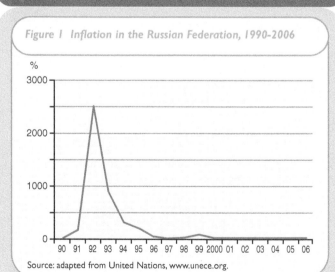

Table 2

Year	Weights			% annual increase in prices	
	Food	All other items	Total	Food	All other items
1	300	700	1 000	10	10
2	250	750	1 000	5	10
3	200	800	1 000	4	6
4	150	850	1 000	3	2
5	125	875	1 000	4	4
6	120	880	1 000	6	4
7	120	880	1 000	5	7
8	110	890	1 000	8	10

Table 2 shows the price index weights given to food and to all other items in each of eight years. It also shows the percentage annual increase in prices of those items.
(a) Calculate the rate of inflation (i.e. the percentage increase in prices) in each year 1 to 8.
(b) What would the price index in years 2-8 be if the price index were 100 in year 1?

Table 3 Index of Retail Prices

	Average annual percentage change						
	1977-81	1982-86	1987-91	1992-96	1997-2000	2001-04	2005-06
General index	13.4	5.5	6.5	2.7	2.8	1.9	3.0
Pensioner index, two person household	12.8	5.3	5.3	2.8	1.6	1.6	2.9

Source: adapted from *Economic Trends Annual Supplement*, Office for National Statistics.

(a) Explain why the change in the General Index of Retail Prices may differ from the change in the Pensioner Index.
(b) A two person pensioner household where the pensioners retired in 1976 receives pensions linked to the General Index of Retail Prices. In which years would it, on average, have seen (i) an increase and (ii) a decrease in its real purchasing power? Explain why this occurs.

important in the household budget than spending on cars. The figures have to be weighted. Food is given a weight of ¾ (or 0.75 or 750 out of 1 000) and cars a weight of ¼ (or 0.25 or 250 out of 1 000). The average increase in prices is 8 per cent multiplied by ¾ added to 4 per cent multiplied by ¼ (i.e. 6 per cent + 1 per cent). The weighted average is therefore 7 per cent. If the RPI were 100 at the start of the year, it would be 107 at the end of the year. In order to calculate a weighting, it is necessary to find out how money is spent. In the case of the Retail Price Index, the weighting is calculated from the results of the Expenditure and Food Survey. Each year, a few thousand households are asked to record their expenditure for one month. From these figures it is possible to calculate how the average household spends its money. (This average household, of course, does not exist except as a statistical entity.)

Table 1

Commodity	Proportion of total spending	Weight	Increase in price	Contribution to increase in RPI
Food	75%	750	8%	6%
Cars	25%	250	4%	1%
Total	100%	1 000		7%

The accuracy of price indices

It is important to realise that any price index is a weighted average. Different rates of inflation can be calculated by changing the weightings in the index. For instance, the Retail Price Index calculates the average price level for the average household in the UK. However, it is possible, again using data from the Expenditure and Food Survey,

to calculate price indices for pensioner households or one parent households. One major difference between these households and the average household is that they spend a larger proportion of their income on food. So a 10 per cent rise in the price of food compared to a 5 per cent rise in the price of all other items will result in a higher rate of inflation for pensioners and one parent households than for the average household. In fact each individual household will have a different rate of inflation. The Retail Price Index only measures an average rate of inflation for all households across the UK.

The household spending patterns upon which the index is based also change over time. For instance, food was a far more important component of the Retail Price Index 30 years ago than it is today because spending on food was then a higher proportion of total spending. The index cannot indicate changes in the quality of goods. Cars might increase in price because their specifications improve rather than because there has been an inflationary price rise. The weights for the Retail Price Index are changed annually to take account of changes in spending patterns. However, this does not get round the fact that the average 'basket' or 'bundle' of goods purchased in 1950 and upon which the RPI for 1950 was calculated was very different from the average bundle of goods purchased in 2008.

The causes of inflation

Inflation can be caused by two main factors: too much demand in the economy or rising costs.

Demand-pull inflation In the market for oil, a significant rise in demand for oil with no increase in supply will lead to a rise in the price of oil. The same occurs at a macroeconomic level. If aggregate or total demand rises and there is no increase in aggregate supply, then DEMAND-PULL INFLATION is likely to occur. Demand-pull inflation is caused by excessive demand in the economy. When there is too much demand, the price level, (or average level of prices in the economy) will rise. Excessive increases in aggregate demand in the UK can come about for a variety of reasons.
● Consumer spending may rise excessively. Interest rates could

Question 4

Pay settlements have risen sharply to a six year high. This has triggered concerns that wage demands will fuel inflation. In turn this could lead to workers stepping up their wage demands to offset the higher cost of living. Some analysts are pointing out that strong consumer demand could add to inflationary pressures. They point out that firms are now more willing to raise prices and widen their profit margins in response to growth in sales. On the other hand, labour productivity is also growing, offsetting the impact of wage increases on costs. There is also the likelihood that the Bank of England will raise interest rates if inflation threatens to go too high.

Source: adapted from the *Financial Times*, 2.2.2007.

(a) Explain two factors mentioned in the article which might be causing cost-push inflation.
(b) Explain one factor mentioned in the article which might be causing demand-pull inflation.
(c) Explain two factors mentioned in the article which might limit inflationary pressures.

be low and consumers are spending large amounts on their credit cards, or consumer confidence could be rising because house prices are rising.
- Firms may substantially increase their investment spending. Perhaps they are responding to large increases in demand from consumers and need extra capacity to satisfy that demand.
- The government might be increasing its spending substantially, or it could be cutting taxes.
- World demand for UK exports may be rising because of a boom in the world economy.

Cost-push inflation Inflation may also occur because of changes in the supply side of the economy. COST-PUSH INFLATION occurs because of rising costs. There are four major sources of increased costs.
- Wages and salaries account for about 70 per cent of national income and hence increases in wages are normally the single most important cause of increases in costs of production.
- Imports can rise in price. An increase in the price of finished manufactured imports, such as television sets or cars, will lead directly to an increase in the price level. An increase in the price of imported semi-manufactured goods and raw materials, used as component parts of domestically produced manufactured goods, will feed through indirectly via an increase in the price of domestically produced goods.
- Profits can be increased by firms when they raise price to improve profit margins. The more price inelastic the demand for their goods, the less will such behaviour result in a fall in demand for their products.
- Government can raise indirect tax rates or reduce subsidies, thus increasing prices.
Firms will try to pass on increases in their costs to customers. For example, if a firm gives a 5 per cent pay rise to its workers, and wages account for 80 per cent of its costs, then it will need to increase prices by 4 per cent (80 per cent of 5 per cent) to maintain its profit margins. Competition in the market may mean that it finds it difficult to pass on these price rises and maintain sales. However, if costs are rising over time, firms will have to increase their prices and this leads to inflation.

Sometimes, inflation may be primarily demand-pull in nature. In other time periods, it may be mainly cost-push. In a stable but growing economy with no demand-side or supply-side shocks, inflation is likely to be caused by a mix of the two factors.

The costs of inflation

A sustained rise in the price level is generally considered to be a problem. The higher the rate of inflation the greater the economic cost. There is a number of reasons why this is the case.

Shoe-leather costs If prices are stable, consumers and firms come to have some knowledge of what is a fair price for a product and which suppliers are likely to charge less than others. At times of rising prices, consumers and firms will be less clear about what is a reasonable price. This will lead to more 'shopping around' (wearing out your shoes), which in itself is a cost.

High rates of inflation are also likely to lead to households and firms holding less cash and more interest bearing deposits. Inflation erodes the value of cash, but since nominal interest rates tend to be higher than with stable prices, the opportunity cost of holding cash tends to be larger, the higher the rate of inflation. Households and firms are then forced to spend more time transferring money from one type of account to another or putting cash into an account to maximise the interest paid. This time is a cost.

Menu costs If there is inflation, restaurants have to change their menus to show increased prices. Similarly, shops have to change their price labels and firms have to calculate and issue new price lists. Even more costly are changes to fixed capital, such as vending machines and parking meters, to take account of price increases.

Psychological and political costs Price increases are deeply unpopular. People feel that they are worse off, even if their incomes rise by more than the rate of inflation. High rates of inflation, particularly if they are unexpected, disturb the distribution of income and wealth as we shall discuss below, and therefore profoundly affect the existing social order. Change and revolution in the past have often accompanied periods of high inflation.

Question 5

In 2005, the Index of Retail Prices rose by 2.8 per cent and in 2006 by 3.2 per cent. How might the following have been affected by the change?

(a) A pensioner on a fixed income.
(b) A bank deposit saver, given that the rate of interest on a bank deposit saving account was 2.0 per cent in 2005 and 2.5 per cent in 2006.
(c) A worker whose personal income tax allowance was £4895 between April 2005 and March 2006 and £5035 between April 2006 and March 2007.
(d) A mother with one child who received £17.00 in child benefit between April 2005 and March 2006 and £17.45 between April 2006 and March 2007.

Redistributional costs Inflation can redistribute income and wealth between households, firms and the state. This redistribution can occur in a variety of ways. For instance, anybody on a fixed income will suffer. In the UK, many pensioners have received fixed pensions from private company pension schemes which are not adjusted for inflation. If prices double over a five year period, their real income will halve. Any group of workers which fails to be able to negotiate pay increases at least in line with inflation will suffer falls in its real income too.

If **real** interest rates fall as a result of inflation, there will be a transfer of resources from borrowers to lenders. With interest rates at 10 per cent and inflation rates at 20 per cent, a saver will lose 10 per cent of the real value of saving each year whilst a borrower will see a 10 per cent real reduction in the value of debt per annum.

Taxes and government spending may not change in line with inflation. For instance, if the Chancellor fails to increase excise duties on alcohol and tobacco each year in line with inflation, real government revenue will fall whilst drinkers and smokers will be better off in real terms assuming their incomes have risen at least by as much as inflation. Similarly, if the Chancellor fails to increase personal income tax **allowances** (the amount which a worker can earn 'tax free') in line with inflation, then the burden of tax will increase, transferring resources from the taxpayer to the government.

Unemployment and growth Some economists, mainly monetarists, have claimed that inflation creates unemployment and lowers growth. Inflation increases costs of production and creates uncertainty. This lowers the profitability of investment and makes businessmen less willing to take the risk associated with any investment project. Lower investment results in less long term employment and long term growth.

There is also a balance of payments effect. If inflation rises faster in the UK than in other countries, and the value of the pound does not change on foreign currency markets, then exports will become less competitive and imports more competitive. The result will be a loss of jobs in the domestic economy and lower growth.

The costs of deflation

Over the past fifty years, the main problem that countries have faced is high rates of inflation. However, there can also be problems associated with deflation, falling price levels. Between 1995 and 2007, Japan experienced falling prices which averaged 0.1 per cent per year and reached 0.9 per cent in 2002. This might seem insignificant but it had a serious impact on the Japanese economy. Falling prices were caused mainly by a lack of demand in the economy. However, they also caused demand

to be depressed.

With falling prices, consumer confidence tends to be low. Consumers are concerned about the future and know that if they don't buy today, they might be able to buy at a cheaper price tomorrow. A lack of consumer confidence then feeds into a lack of business confidence and lower investment. Although interest rates tend to be very low with deflation, the real cost of borrowing is higher. If prices fall by, say, 1 per cent, then the real cost of borrowing is the actual or nominal interest rate plus 1 per cent.

The depressing effect on demand of deflation is the key reason why economists suggest that the ideal rate of change of the price level is a positive 1 or 2 per cent. Very low inflation means that the costs of higher inflation are avoided. At the same time, very mild inflation tends to be associated with economic growth and increasing prosperity.

Anticipated and unanticipated inflation

Some inflation is **unanticipated**; households, firms and government are uncertain what the rate of inflation will be in the future. When planning, they therefore have to estimate as best they can the expected rate of inflation. It is unlikely that they will guess correctly and hence their plans will be to some extent frustrated. On the other hand, inflation may be **anticipated**. Inflation may be a constant 5 per cent per year and therefore households, firms and government are able to build this figure into their plans.

Unanticipated inflation imposes far greater costs than anticipated inflation. If inflation is anticipated, economic agents can take steps to mitigate the effects of inflation. One way of doing this is through INDEXATION. This is where economic variables like wages or taxes are increased in line with inflation. For instance, a union might negotiate a wage agreement with an employer for staged increases over a year of 2 per cent plus the change in the Retail Price Index. The annual changes in social security benefits in the UK are linked to the Retail Price Index. Economists are divided about whether indexation provides a solution to the problem of inflation. On the one hand, it reduces many of the costs of inflation although some costs such as shoe leather costs and menu costs remain. On the other hand, it reduces pressure on government to tackle the problem of inflation directly. Indexation eases the pain of inflation but is not a cure for it.

Moreover, indexation may hinder government attempts to reduce inflation because indexation builds in further cost increases, such as wage increases, which reflect past changes in prices. If a government wants to get inflation down to 2 per cent a year, and inflation has just been 10 per cent, it will not be helped in achieving its target if workers are all awarded at least 10 per cent wage increases because of indexation agreements.

Key terms

Consumer Price Index (CPI) - a measure of the price level used across the European Union and used by the Bank of England to measure inflation against its target.

Cost-push inflation - inflation caused by increases in the costs of production in the economy.

Creeping inflation - small rises in the price level over a long period of time.

Deflation - a fall in the price level.

Demand-pull inflation - inflation which is caused by excess demand in the economy.

Headline rate of inflation - the increase in consumer prices including all housing costs. This is the RPI in the UK.

Hyper-inflation - large increases in the price level.

Indexation - adjusting the value of economic variables such as wages or the rate of interest in line with inflation.

Inflation - a general rise in prices.

Price level - the average price of goods and services in the economy.

Retail Price Index (RPI) - a measure of the price level which has been calculated in the UK for over 60 years and is used in a variety of contexts such as by the government to index welfare benefits.

Underlying rate of inflation - the RPIX, the increase in consumer prices excluding changes in mortgage costs, or the RPIY, which also excludes indirect taxes.

Applied economics

The Retail Price Index (RPI)

Measures of inflation

In the UK, there is a wide variety of different measures of inflation. The two most commonly used are the Retail Price Index (RPI) and the Consumer Price Index (CPI).

The Retail Price Index is the traditional measure of the price level in the UK. Apart from informing economists and economics agents such as government or firms of the rate of inflation, it is also used for the indexation of pensions, state benefits and index-linked gilts (a form of long term government borrowing). Trade unions and firms may use the RPI in wage agreements and property companies may use it for calculating increases in leases (rents) on property. Utility regulators, which set prices for firms in industries such as telecommunications and water, may impose restrictions on price increases, or set price falls in terms of the RPI.

There are different measures of the RPI.

- The RPI itself measures the average price of the typical 'basket of goods' bought by the average household. It therefore measures average consumer prices.
- The RPIX excludes mortgage payments from the RPI calculation. This allows policy makers to see how prices are changed without including what can be a volatile and distorting element of the RPI, particularly when house prices are rising particularly fast or are falling.
- The RPIY excludes both mortgage payments and indirect taxes. When a government increases taxes on, say, cigarettes or petrol, these would be included in the RPI. By excluding them, policy makers are able to see how prices in the wider economy are changing. The RPIX and the RPIY are sometimes referred to as

the UNDERLYING RATE OF INFLATION, whilst the RPI is called the HEADLINE RATE OF INFLATION. The RPI is the headline rate because it is the measure which tends to be quoted in newspapers and on television and radio. The RPIX and the RPIY are underlying rates because they give a more reliable measure of trends in inflation over time.

The Consumer Price Index (CPI)

The CPI is a more recent measure of the price level and inflation. It is a measure which was developed by the European Union to be used across all countries in the EU. Before the introduction of the CPI, every country had a slightly different way of measuring the price level. The CPI in the UK before 2003 was called the Harmonised Index of Consumer Prices (HICP), 'harmonised' because it was a common measure across the EU. The CPI has only been calculated in the UK since January 1996, with estimates going back to 1988, and so this limits its use in making historical judgments about inflation. It has been used by the Bank of England to measure inflation against its target since 2003, and is therefore now the key indicator for monetary policy, replacing the RPI. However, the RPI is still widely used in other contexts. The two measures will continue to be used side by side in the future and there are no plans to phase out the calculation of the RPI.

Comparing the RPI and CPI

There is a variety of differences between the calculations of the CPI and the RPI. One important difference is that the CPI excludes a number of items relating to housing, whereas these are included in the RPI. Excluded from the CPI are council tax, mortgage interest payments, house depreciation, buildings insurance, and estate agents' and conveyancing fees. Another important difference is that the CPI uses a different way of calculating the mean value compared to the RPI. The CPI uses a geometric mean whereas the RPI uses an arithmetic mean.

Figure 2 shows how annual measures of the RPI, RPIX, RPIY and the CPI have differed since 1989. The CPI tends to be below the RPI for two reasons. One is that for most of the period 1989-2006 housing costs rose at a faster rate than other items. Since the CPI excludes many housing costs, it has tended to be lower. Second, using a geometric mean, as with the CPI, mathematically always produces a lower number than using an arithmetic mean, as with the RPI. On average, this mathematical difference has been 0.5 per cent of inflation over the period 1996-2006.

Calculating the RPI and CPI

The RPI and the CPI are calculated from the same data which is collected through monthly surveys. Two types of survey are carried out.

Prices are recorded in around 150 different areas of the UK. These locations are chosen through a random sampling method and around 30 are changed each year. 110 000 prices are collected per month of a typical 'basket of goods' bought by consumers. Around 650 items are included in the basket. Over time, what is included in the basket is changed to reflect changes in consumer spending. For example, rabbits were taken out of the index in 1955, whilst condoms were added in 1989 and credit card charges and DVD players in 2007.

In addition, a further 10 000 prices are collected centrally each month for items where local sampling would be inappropriate. Prices of goods in catalogues, utility (gas, electricity and telephone) prices, internet prices, road tolls, and mortgage interest payments are examples.

The typical basket of goods is constructed from another survey, the Expenditure and Food Survey. This survey asks around 7000 respondent households a year selected at random to keep diaries of what they spend over a fortnight. A spending pattern for the average family can then be worked out. The RPI and CPI are weighted to reflect the importance of different expenditures within the total. So the price of gas carries more weight in the index than the price of processed fruit because households spend more on gas. Figure 3 shows how weights have changed between 1962 and 2007. The proportion spent on food in the average budget has been declining over time as incomes have risen (food has a very low positive income elasticity of demand). Travel and leisure and housing and household expenditure, on the other hand, have been rising.

The CPI is based on the average basket of goods bought by all households. The RPI excludes high income households, defined as the top 4 per cent by income of households, and pensioner households which derive at least three quarters of their total income from state pensions and benefits. These two types of household are considered to have atypical spending patterns and so would distort the overall average.

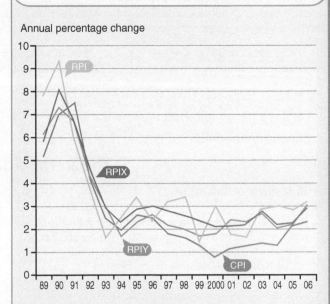

Figure 2 Inflation rates

Source: adapted from *Economic & Labour Market Review*, Office for National Statistics.

Figure 3 Changes in the basket of goods used to calculate the RPI, 1962-2007

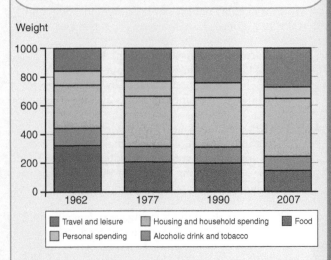

Source: adapted from *Monthly Digest of Statistics*, Office for National Statistics.

DataQuestion

Inflation

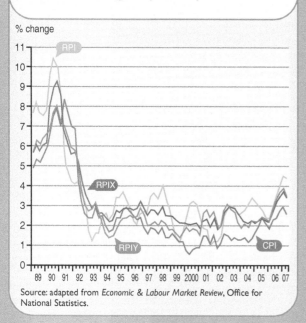

Figure 4 *Different measures of inflation, CPI, RPI, RPIX, RPIY; % change on previous year*

Source: adapted from *Economic & Labour Market Review*, Office for National Statistics.

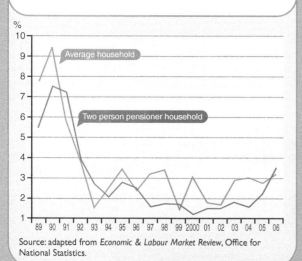

Figure 5 *RPI inflation for different households*

Source: adapted from *Economic & Labour Market Review*, Office for National Statistics.

1. What is meant by 'inflation'?
2. Explain different ways in which inflation might be measured.
3. How might each of the following have been affected by inflation: (a) a UK pensioner, still alive today, who retired in 1989 with a company pension which remained the same and a state pension which increased in line with changes in the RPI; (b) UK 'techno-geek' who was 16 in 1989, and who loves everything from computers to mobile phones to cars; (c) a Brazilian food shopper in the early 1990s?

The RPI/CPI

What exactly does the RPI or CPI measure? Each year, items are added to the basket of goods used in the calculation of the index and each year items are removed. You won't find corsets, rabbits or men's cardigans in the RPI index any more but you will find DVDs, mobile phone handsets and frozen chicken nuggets. What's more, when the same item stays in the index, its specification may well change. This isn't true for potatoes, but it is true for, say, cameras. Forty years ago, few cameras had a built in flash. Today, even the cheapest cameras come with flash as a standard feature. Forty years ago, cars didn't come with air conditioning as standard but many do today. As for computers, whose specifications become more powerful by the year and month, how can the RPI/CPI hope to reflect such changes?

Does it matter that the basket of goods is constantly changing? The simple answer is yes. By changing the composition of the index, statisticians are not measuring the change in price of a fixed and unchanging basket of goods. Instead, they are attempting to measure changes in prices of how we spend our money. Presumably, we now buy, say, trousers rather than corsets, chicken rather than rabbits, or replica football team shirts rather than cardigans, because we prefer to do so. The amount of satisfaction to be gained from consuming some items rather than others is greater. So changes represent an increase in our living standards, the equivalent of a falling cost of living. As for increases in quality in goods, a failure to take these into account means that we overestimate the price paid for goods over time. When a software company puts additional features into a new computer game, but sells it for the same price as old computer games without these features, prices have effectively fallen but the RPI/CPI won't pick this up.

Inflation in Brazil

Before the conquest of hyper-inflation in Brazil in 1994, both Brazilian retailers and shoppers behaved in ways which seem strange today. Workers would be paid either at the end of the week or the end of the month. With prices going up every day, consumers would rush out with their pay packets and spend as much as they could afford. So retailers became used to sharp peaks in spending at the end of each week and a very large peak at the end of the month. There was little shopping around by consumers because they found it so difficult to keep up with changing prices. They had little or no idea what was a good price and what was expensive on any single shopping expedition. As for retailers, they often made their profit not from sales but from getting free credit. They would receive goods on credit, sell them immediately, but only have to pay in 30 or 60 days time. In the meantime, they could put the money in the bank and earn interest linked to the rate of inflation. In a good month, with inflation of say, 100 per cent, they could double their money.

Summary

1. The balance of payments accounts are split into two parts. The current account records payments for the exports and imports of goods and services. The capital account records saving, investment and speculative flows of money.
2. The current account is split into two parts: trade in visibles and trade in invisibles.
3. The balance of payments accounts must always balance. However, component parts of the accounts may be positive or negative. If there is a surplus on the current account, then outflows on the capital account must be greater than inflows.
4. A current account surplus is often seen as a sign of a healthy economy, whilst a current account deficit is seen as a cause for worry. But current account deficits are not necessarily bad as they may be a sign of borrowing which could finance expansion.
5. A current account deficit is most unlikely to be financed by government. The balance of payments deficit and the government deficit are two completely different entities.

The balance of payments

The BALANCE OF PAYMENTS ACCOUNT is a record of all financial dealings over a period of time between economic agents of one country and all other countries. Balance of payments accounts can be split into two components:

- the CURRENT ACCOUNT where payments for the purchase and sale of goods and services are recorded;
- the CAPITAL and FINANCIAL ACCOUNTS where flows of money associated with saving, investment, speculation and currency stabilisation are recorded.

Flows of money into the country are given a positive (+) sign on the accounts. Flows of money out of the country are given a negative (-) sign.

The current account

The current account on the balance of payments is itself split into **several** components.

Trade in goods Trade in goods is often called trade in VISIBLES. This is trade in raw materials such as copper and oil, semi-manufactured goods such as car components and finished manufactured goods such as cars and DVD players. Visible exports are goods which are sold to foreigners. Goods leave the country, whilst payment for these goods goes in the opposite direction. Hence visible exports of, say, cars result in an **inward** flow of money and are recorded with a positive sign on the balance of payments account. Visible imports are goods which are bought by domestic residents from foreigners. Goods come into the country whilst money **flows out**. Hence visible imports of, say, wheat are given a minus sign on the balance of payments. The difference between visible exports and visible imports is known as the BALANCE OF TRADE.

Trade in services A wide variety of services is traded internationally, including financial services such as banking and insurance, transport services such as shipping and air travel, and tourism. Trade in services is an example of trade in INVISIBLES. These are intangible services. Exports of invisibles are bought by foreigners. So an American tourist paying for a stay in a London hotel is an invisible export. So too is a Chinese company buying insurance in the City of London or a Taiwanese company hiring a UK owned ship. With invisibles, money flows into the UK, as it would if a French company bought a machine manufactured in the UK, a visible export for the UK. Hence, on the official UK balance of payments accounts, invisible service exports are called export credits in services. Imports of services for the UK are services which are bought from foreigners. A holiday taken by a UK national in Spain would be an invisible import for the UK. So too would be a UK firm hiring a private jet from a German company. With invisible imports, money flows abroad. Hence they are called debits on the official UK balance of payments accounts.

Income and current transfers Not all flows of money result from trade in goods and services. **Income** results from the loan of factors of production abroad. For the UK, most of this income is generated from interest, profits and dividends on assets owned abroad. Equally, interest, profits and dividends on UK assets owned by foreigners have to be paid out. For some countries, their main income comes from the repatriation of earnings from national workers in foreign countries. For example, a Pakistani national may work in Kuwait and send back income to support his family in Pakistan. Current transfers are a range mainly of government transfers to and from overseas organisations such as the European Union. Income and current transfers are examples of invisibles along with trade in services.

The CURRENT BALANCE is the difference between exports and total imports. It can also be calculated by adding the balance of trade in goods with that of services, income and current transfers.

Current account deficits and surpluses

The balance of payments account shows all the inflows of money to and the outflows of money from a country. Inflows must equal outflows overall and therefore the balance of payments must always balance. This is no different from a household. All the money going out from a household in spending or saving over a period of time must equal money coming in from earnings, borrowings or running down of savings. If a household spends £60 going out for a meal, the money must have come from somewhere.

However, there can be surpluses or deficits on particular parts of the account. Using the example of the household again, it can spend more than it earns if it borrows money. The same is true of a national economy. It can spend more on goods and services than it earns if it borrows money from overseas. So it can have a CURRENT ACCOUNT DEFICIT, where exports are less than imports, by running a surplus on its capital account. Equally, it can run a CURRENT ACCOUNT SURPLUS, exporting more than it imports, by running a deficit on its capital and financial account. A deficit on the capital account for the UK means that it invests more abroad than foreigners invest in the UK.

Often, the media talk about a 'balance of payments deficit'. Strictly speaking, there can never be a balance of payments deficit because the balance of payments must always balance, i.e. it must always be zero. What the media are, in fact, referring to is either a balance of trade deficit or a current account deficit. Similarly, the term 'trade gap' is a term used in the media, usually to mean a deficit on the balance of trade in goods.

Causes of changes in the current account balance

The current account balance will change over time. It may move from surplus to deficit, for example, or a deficit may get larger. To explain why this occurs, we need to distinguish between the factors which affect trade in goods and services and those which affect income and current transfers.

Trade in goods and services Goods and services sold to foreigners are exports. Goods and services bought by domestic consumers, firms and government from overseas are imports. Exports and imports change over time for a variety of reasons.
- The exchange rate may change. A rise in the exchange rate will tend to increase imports and reduce exports. A fall in the exchange rate will tend to reduce imports and increase exports.
- The price in national currencies of goods and services may change. For example, an increase in labour productivity (output per worker) will reduce costs of production and so should lead to a fall in the price of the product, all other things being equal. An increase in domestic inflation will push up a variety of costs to firms. For example, workers are likely to demand higher wages to compensate them for the impact of higher inflation. So firm's prices are likely to rise, making them less competitive against foreign suppliers, all other things being equal.
- Many goods and services are non-homogenous. This means the product of one firm is different from that of another firm. It may be the quality of the product, its design, its functions and features, its aesthetic appearance or after-sales service that differ. For example, a Mars Bar is different from a Twix although both are chocolate bars. A beach holiday in Benidorm in Spain is different from a walking holiday in the Alps even though both are holidays. Exporters can gain a competitive advantage by improving their product and making it better than products from other firms.
- Aggregate demand may change in the domestic economy or in the world economy. A world recession, for example, will hit UK exports. A UK recession will lead to lower imports as consumers and firms buy fewer goods and services. In contrast, a world boom should raise UK exports. A boom in the UK is likely to see a rise in imports.

Income and current transfers The relative importance of income and current transfers differs from country to country. For some Third World countries, the repatriation of earnings of people working abroad is very important. Curbs on migrant workers in host countries can then hit those earnings hard. The UK records a large surplus on the profit and interest on assets owned abroad. A world recession which hits the profits made by foreign firms partly or wholly owned by UK investors will reduce this surplus. An improvement in the investment strategies of foreigners investing in UK assets could lead to a deterioration in the surplus.

When is a current account deficit or surplus a problem?

Current account deficits are generally seen as undesirable and a sign of economic weakness. Conversely, current account surpluses are usually seen as signs of the economic strength of a country. This, though, is a very crude way of analysing the balance of payments. One reason why this is crude is because the size of the current account surplus or deficit is important in deciding its significance. Using the analogy of the household again, if the income of a household is £100 000 per year and its spending over the year is £100 010, it has overspent. However, overspending by £10 on an income of £100 000 in one year is of almost no significance. On the other hand, take a household living solely from state benefits. If income is £100 per week, and spending is £110, then this household is likely to be in serious trouble. Unless it has substantial savings to draw on, overspending £10 each week on an income of £100 will soon become unsustainable. Where will the £10 per week come from? If it is from borrowing, then the money must eventually be repaid, eating into a very low income.

This is also the case for a national economy. If the country runs a current account deficit year after year, but this current account deficit is very small in relation to national income over time, then it is of little significance economically. Equally, if a country runs a large deficit over a short period of time, but then follows this with a large surplus over the next period, then it is relatively unimportant. Only if the current account deficit or surplus is large in relation to income and is sustained over a period of time does it really matter.

The Czech Republic, since 1990, has been relatively successful in making the transition from being a command economy, where the state dominated every economic decision, to a market economy, where markets are used to allocate a significant proportion of an economy's resources. Over the period 1994-2008, average economic growth in the Euro area (the EU countries which have adopted the euro including France, Germany and Italy) was an estimated 2.2 per cent, two thirds that of the Czech Republic.

Inevitably, in opening itself up to other markets, it has sucked in significant levels of imports. Czech consumers have bought cheaper and better quality goods from other countries, whilst Czech businesses have imported raw materials and capital goods from abroad.

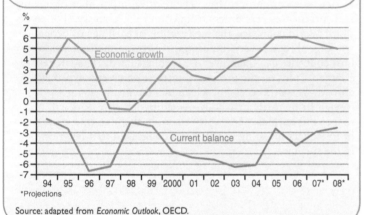

Figure 1 *Czech Republic: economic growth (%) and current account balance as a % of GDP*

*Projections

Source: adapted from *Economic Outlook*, OECD.

(a) Use the data to explain why the Czech Republic has been a success story in the 1990s and 2000s.
(b) Discuss whether its large current account deficits. throughout the period are a problem for the Czech Republic.

Large sustained current account deficits

Large sustained current account deficits are usually considered undesirable because they become unsustainable. Deficits on the current account may occur because the government of a country spends excessively on foreign goods and services. Or it could be private firms and individuals which are spending too much, importing far more than they are exporting. Whether it is government or the private sector, the current account deficit has to be financed. Either the level of borrowings abroad is increased, or there is a net run down in savings and investments held abroad. Governments and firms can borrow abroad so long as foreign lenders think that they can repay the loans with interest in the future. But if the current account deficit is large and sustained, there usually comes a point when lenders think that the borrowers may **default** on their loans (i.e. not pay them). Lenders then stop lending. At this point, the country is in serious difficulties.

Countries like Poland, Brazil and Uganda in the 1980s, and Thailand and South Korea in the 1990s, have all faced this **credit crunch**, the point at which foreign lenders refuse to lend any more. They are then forced to return their current account to equilibrium. This means cutting down on imports, or exporting more goods which previously might have been sold on the domestic market. Citizens therefore have fewer goods available to them and their consumption and standard of living falls.

If the economy is fundamentally strong, the adjustment will be painful but relatively short, lasting just a few years perhaps. For countries which have very weak economies, the credit crunch can have a negative impact for decades. In sub-Saharan Africa, the credit crunch which occurred in the early 1980s led to Western banks and other agencies refusing to lend significant sums for the next 20 years. This crippled the economies of certain countries and deprived them of foreign funds which could have helped them to grow.

However, large sustained current account deficits may be beneficial to an economy. It depends on its rate of **economic growth**. If an economy is growing at 3 per cent per annum, but is running a large current account deficit of 5 per cent of GDP per annum, then it will run into problems. Its foreign debt as a percentage of GDP is likely to grow over time. However, if the economy is growing at 10 per cent per annum, and there is a current account deficit of 5 per cent of GDP, accumulated foreign debt as a percentage of GDP is likely to fall. Although foreign debt in absolute terms will be growing, the income of the country available to repay it will be growing even faster. Countries like the USA in the nineteenth century, and South Korea and Malaysia in the late part of the twentieth century, have all run significant current account deficits over a period of time, but they have tended to benefit from this because the money has been used to strengthen their growth potential. Even so, both South Korea and Malaysia were caught up in a credit crunch in the late 1990s when foreign lenders judged that too much had been lent to East Asian economies. High levels of foreign borrowing carry risks for countries even when their economies are highly successful on measures of national economic performance such as economic growth, unemployment and inflation.

Large sustained current account surpluses

Some countries run large sustained current account surpluses. One reason for this is that the government of the country keeps its exchange rate artificially low. China, for example, currently adopts such a policy. The advantage is that a low exchange rate encourages exports but makes imports less competitive. Strong exports help create jobs and boost economic growth. Another possible advantage of exporting more than importing is that a country can increase its net foreign wealth. This is a strategy being pursued by some Middle Eastern oil exporting countries such as Saudi Arabia and Kuwait. It has the benefit that the economy then should receive ever increasing amounts of income from that wealth, which can be used to buy more foreign goods and services than would otherwise be the case. This is like a household which consistently saves money. In the long term, it can use the interest on that saving to buy more goods than it would otherwise have been able to afford.

A sustained current account surplus may also make sense if there are long term structural changes occurring. Japan ran large current account surpluses during the last quarter of the twentieth century, consequently building up its net wealth that of the USA. The benefit of a large reduction in the Chinese surplus to any single country, even to the USA, the largest economy in the world, will be relatively small.

Government deficits and balance of payments deficits

One common mistake is to assume that any current account deficit is paid for by the government. Another common mistake is to assume that government borrowing is the same as the current account deficit. The current account is made up of billions of individual transactions. Each one is financed in a different way. So a UK firm importing machinery will use different finance from a family taking a holiday in France. A Chinese firm buying specialist car parts from a UK company will finance this in a different way from a German firm buying insurance from a broker at Lloyds of London. If a current account deficit has been caused mainly by excessive government spending, then the government is likely to have borrowed at least some of the money from abroad. However, a current account deficit may be caused mainly by private consumers and firms buying too many imports and borrowing the money from abroad to pay for them. The relationship between the current account deficit, private sector borrowing and government borrowing is therefore complex and depends upon individual circumstances.

Governments may choose to attempt to correct current account deficits or surpluses. They have a variety of ways in which they could attempt this, which have various advantages and disadvantages. These are discussed later in this book. However, governments may choose to do nothing and allow free market forces to correct any imbalances. The last time the UK government and the Bank of England attempted to influence directly the current account was in the 1970s.

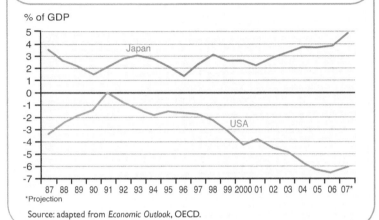

Figure 2 Japan and the USA: current account balances as a percentage of GDP

% of GDP

*Projection

Source: adapted from *Economic Outlook*, OECD.

(a) Compare the current account balance of the USA with that of Japan during the late 1980s, 1990s and 2000s.
(b) Discuss the possible benefits and costs to Japan of running a persistent current account surplus.

overseas. However, in the first half of the twenty first century, the structure of the Japanese population will change dramatically. From having very few pensioners in proportion to workers, the population will age significantly and there will be a high proportion of pensioners to workers. It could well be that Japan will run down its wealth overseas to pay for the goods and services consumed by non-productive pensioners. Japan could therefore move from having sustained current account surpluses to current account deficits.

Large sustained current account surpluses have their disadvantages though. First, they reduce what is available for consumption now. If the surplus were eliminated, resources used for exports could be diverted to produce goods for domestic consumption. Or the country could increase imports, again increasing the amount available for consumption.

Second, sustained current account surpluses cause friction between countries. If China has a current account surplus, the rest of the world must have a deficit. If China is a net lender, building up wealth overseas, the rest of the world must be a net borrower, building up debts overseas. Countries which attempt to reduce their current account deficits can only be successful if other countries reduce their current account surpluses. On a microeconomic level, trade unions and firms in deficit countries often accuse firms in surplus countries of 'poaching' jobs. If China reduced its trade surplus by reducing exports to the United States, then firms in the United States might be able to fill the gap created by expanding their output.

In practice, the benefits to one country of another country reducing its surplus are likely to be small. If China's exports fall, US producers are just as likely to find that other countries like South Korea or the UK fill the market gap. When the USA has a large current account deficit and China a large surplus, a reduction in the Chinese surplus will improve the current account positions of many countries around the world, not just

Key terms

Balance of payments account - a record of all financial dealings over a period of time between economic agents of one country and all other countries.
Balance of trade - visible exports minus visible imports.
Capital and financial accounts - that part of the balance of payments account where flows of savings, investment and currency are recorded.
Current account - that part of the balance of payments account where payments for the purchase and sale of goods and services are recorded.
Current balance - the difference between total exports (visible and invisible) and total imports. It can also be calculated by adding the balance of trade to the balance on invisible trade.
Current account deficit or surplus - a deficit exists when imports are greater than exports; a surplus exists when exports are greater than imports.
Invisibles - trade in services, transfers of income and other payments or receipts.
Visibles - trade in goods.

Applied economics

The UK current account

The parts of the current account

The Office for National Statistics divides the UK current account into four parts, shown in Table 1.

- Trade in goods. Exports of goods minus imports of goods is equal to the balance of trade in goods.
- Trade in services. The main services traded are transport (such as shipping or air transport), travel and tourism, insurance and other financial services, and royalties and licence fees.
- Income. Some countries, such as Pakistan or Egypt, earn substantial amounts from the repatriation of income from nationals working abroad. For the UK, such income is relatively unimportant. Nearly all income in the UK balance of payments accounts relates to UK investments abroad and to foreign investments in the UK (investment income).
- Current transfers. Most current transfers relate to the UK's membership of the European Union. The UK has to pay part of its tax revenues to the EU, but in return receives payments such as agricultural subsidies or regional grants.

Visibles in the account are the trade in goods. Invisibles are the trade in services, income and current transfers. In terms of relative size, invisibles outweigh visibles. The most important invisible is not trade in services but income. Current transfers are relatively insignificant. The UK's current balance is therefore crucially dependent not just on trade in goods and services, but also on income from foreign investments. Comparing this to a household, it is as if the financial soundness of the household is dependent not just on wage earnings and spending, but also very much on interest and dividends on savings and also on payments of interest on loans.

The current account over time

Since the Second World War, there has been a number of consistent trends on the UK current account.

- The balance of trade in goods has been negative, as can be seen from Figure 3. Visible exports have tended to be less than visible imports.
- The overall balance on trade in services, income and current transfers has been positive. Invisible credits have been greater than invisible debits.
- Breaking down invisibles, the balance of trade in services has nearly always been positive - more services have been sold abroad than have been bought from abroad. The balance on income has usually been positive too. Income brought into the country by UK people living abroad and income earned from investments abroad have been greater than income leaving the country. However, the balance on income fluctuates much more from year to year than the balance of trade in services. Current transfers since the 1960s have always been negative.

Since joining the EU in 1973, most of the negative balance is due to the UK paying more into EU coffers than receiving in grants.

The size of the current account balances

In the 1950s and 1960s, the current account posed a major problem for the UK. At the time, the value of the pound was fixed against other currencies. In years when the current account went into deficit, currency speculators tended to sell pounds sterling in the hope that the government would be forced to devalue the pound, i.e. make it less valuable against other currencies. Quite small current account deficits as a percentage of GDP, as in 1960 or in 1964, thus presented large problems for the government of the day.

From the 1970s, the pound was allowed to float, changing its value from minute to minute on the foreign exchange markets. Figure 4 shows that there were two periods when the UK's current account position could have become unsustainable in the long term. In 1973-75 the UK, along with most Western countries, suffered a severe economic shock from a rise in commodity prices, particularly oil prices. Following the Yom Kippur war of October 1973 between Egypt and Israel, the members of OPEC chose to restrict supply of oil to the west and as a result its price quadrupled. Import prices rose sharply and the current account approached 4 per cent of GDP in 1974. The UK government was forced to

Table 1 The current balance, 2006 (£m)

Trade in goods		
Export of goods	245 105	
Import of goods	328 736	
Balance on trade in goods		- 83 631
Trade in services		
Export of services	124 586	
Import of services	95 392	
Balance of trade in services		29 194
Balance on trade in goods and services		- 54 437
Income		
Credits	241 350	
Debits	222 795	
Balance		18 555
Current transfers		
Credits	16 165	
Debits	28 064	
Balance		- 11 899
Current balance		- 47 781

Source: adapted from *The Pink Book*, United Kingdom Balance of Payments, Office for National Statistics.

react by cutting domestic spending, which in turn reduced demand for imports. In 1986-89, there was another sharp deterioration in the current account due to the 'Lawson boom', named after the then Chancellor, Nigel Lawson. Fast increases in domestic spending led to sharp increases in imports.

Since the late 1980s, the current account has been consistently in deficit within a range of 0.2 per cent of GDP to 4 per cent of GDP. It could be argued that this should pose long term problems for the UK. If the UK is consistently spending more than it is earning abroad, this will lead to a long term build-up of debt. Just as households who consistently borrow more and more money should get into financial difficulties, so too should a country.

There are two reasons which might explain why the UK has not encountered problems relating to its persistent current account deficits in the 1990s and 2000s. One is that the deficits are manageable given the economy's average growth rate of between 2.5 and 3.0 per cent over the period. For a household, so long as income is rising faster than debt, there should be no debt problem. Certainly, the financial markets have not shown any particular concern about the UK's current account deficits. Foreign lenders have not refused to lend UK borrowers any more money as they did, for example, to countries such as Mexico, South Korea or Poland when they had debt crises over the past 30 years.

The other reason is that the current account deficit is not the main determinant of the net debt owed by UK citizens, businesses and government to foreigners. The main determinant is changing asset values, such as stock market prices in New York or bond prices in Frankfurt. Since 1997 the net debt of the UK, the difference between what UK households, businesses and government own abroad and what they owe to foreigners, has varied from plus 49 per cent of GDP to minus 150 per cent. Such huge swings are accounted for not by current account deficits but by changes in asset values.

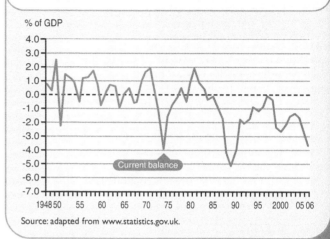

Figure 4 The current balance as a percentage of GDP

Source: adapted from www.statistics.gov.uk.

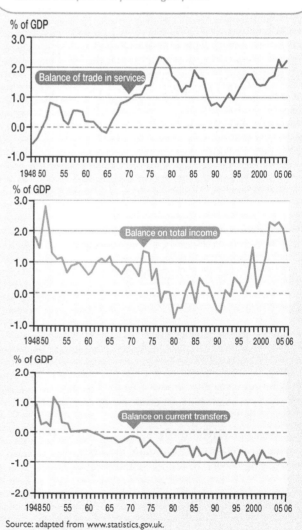

Figure 5 Balances of trade in services, total income and current transfers as a percentage of GDP

Source: adapted from www.statistics.gov.uk.

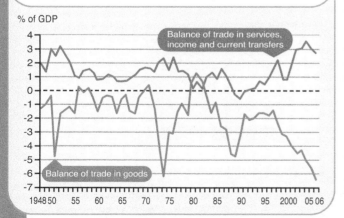

Figure 3 The balance of trade in goods, and the balance of trade in services, income and current transfers, as a percentage of GDP

DataQuestion

The trade gap

Trade gap at an all time high

The trade gap has reached an all time record. Never before has the UK seen such a large deficit in our trade in goods. In 2006 it reached 6.4 per cent of GDP. The last time it approached that level was in 1974 when the economy was in crisis due to a result of overspending by government, crippling strike action by workers and the first international oil crisis. The trade gap in goods far outweighs the surpluses the UK earned last year on its invisibles. Our overall current account deficit recorded in 2006 was 3.7 per cent of GDP.

The mystery of our investment income

Strange things are happening abroad. According to the latest statistics for 2006, the UK earned a net 1.5 per cent of GDP on its net foreign assets. What that means is that the UK earned 1.5 per cent more on the foreign assets owned by UK householders, businesses and government than foreigners earned on UK assets that they owned. However, the statistics also show that the value of foreign assets owned by the UK is less than the value of UK assets owned by foreigners. UK households, businesses and government in 2006 owed to foreigners 10 per cent more than the value of the UK's assets they owned abroad. With these sorts of figures, we ought to be paying out more than we receive. Obviously, UK investors are better at making a return on their overseas assets than foreign investors in the UK.

1. Describe the changes in the balance of trade and total investment income shown in the data.
2. What might be the implications for the current account balance of the changes shown in the data?
3. Discuss the extent to which the deterioration in the 'trade gap' in 2006 might have been of economic significance.

Figure 6 Record trade deficit for the UK

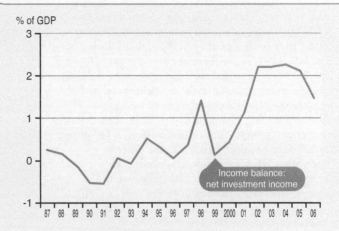

Figure 7 Income balance: net investment income as a percentage of GDP

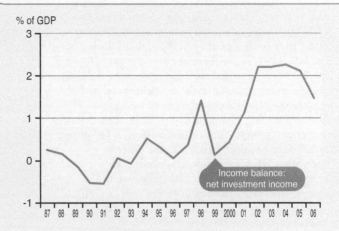

Figure 8 UK net international assets as a percentage of GDP

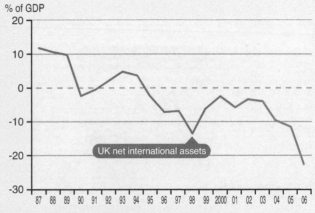

Source: adapted from www.statistics.gov.uk.

Summary

1. Fiscal policy, the manipulation of government spending, taxation and borrowing, affects aggregate demand. It can also affect the pattern of economic activity.
2. The effect on aggregate demand of a change in government spending or taxation is increased because of the multiplier effect.
3. Classical economists argue that fiscal policy cannot, in the long term, affect the level of output. Hence, it cannot influence unemployment, but can raise inflation.
4. Keynesian economists argue that fiscal policy can affect both output and prices. Hence, fiscal policy can be used to influence both inflation and unemployment.
5. Fiscal policy cannot, as a demand side policy, influence long term economic growth, but it can be used to help an economy out of a recession or reduce demand pressures in a boom.
6. Fiscal policy, through its effect on aggregate demand, can influence imports and the current balance.

Fiscal policy

The UK government has been responsible for between 40 and 50 per cent of national expenditure over the past 20 years. The main areas of public spending are the National Health Service, defence, education and roads. In addition, the government is responsible for transferring large sums of money round the economy through its spending on social security and National Insurance benefits. All of this is financed mainly through taxes, such as income tax and VAT.

In the post-war era, governments have rarely balanced their budgets (i.e. they have rarely planned to match their expenditure with their receipts). In most years, they have run BUDGET DEFICITS, spending more than they receive. As a result, in most years governments have had to borrow money. In the UK, the borrowing of the public sector (central government, local government and other state bodies such as nationalised industries) over a period of time is called the PUBLIC SECTOR NET CASH REQUIREMENT (PSNCR). In three fiscal periods, between 1969-70, 1988-91 and 1999-2001, the UK government received more revenue than it spent. The normal budget deficit was turned into a BUDGET SURPLUS. There is then a negative PSNCR. A budget surplus allows the government to pay off part of its accumulated debt. This debt, called the NATIONAL DEBT, dates back to the founding of the Bank of England in 1694.

The government has to make decisions about how much to spend, tax and borrow. It also has to decide on the composition of its spending and taxation. Should it spend more on education and less on defence? Should it cut income tax by raising excise duties? These decisions about spending, taxes and borrowing are called the FISCAL POLICY of the government.

There are two key dates in the year for fiscal policy. One is the day of the BUDGET which occurs in March. In the Budget, the Chancellor gives a forecast of government spending and taxation in the coming financial year. Changes in taxation are also announced. The other key date occurs in November or December with the Chancellor's **Pre-Budget Report** and **Comprehensive Spending Review**. In this report, the Chancellor gives another forecast of government spending and taxation and announces the government's spending plans for the year. The financial year in the UK starts on 6 April and runs until 5 April the following year.

Aggregate demand

Government spending and taxation changes have an effect on

aggregate demand. A rise in government spending, with the price level constant, will increase aggregate demand, pushing the AD curve to the right as in Figure 2.

Equally, a cut in taxes will affect aggregate demand. A cut in taxes on income, such as income tax and National Insurance contributions, will lead to a rise in the disposable income of households. This in turn will lead to a rise in consumption expenditure and hence to a rise in aggregate demand. This rise,

Question 1

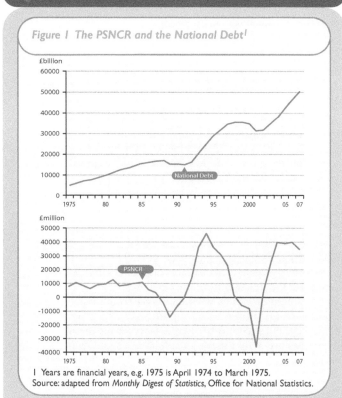

Figure 1 The PSNCR and the National Debt[1]

1 Years are financial years, e.g. 1975 is April 1974 to March 1975.
Source: adapted from *Monthly Digest of Statistics*, Office for National Statistics.

(a) (i) What is meant by the PSNCR? (ii) In which years did the government have a budget surplus?
(b) Using examples from the data, explain the link between the PSNCR and the National Debt.
(c) If a government wanted to pay off its National Debt over a number of years, how could it achieve this?

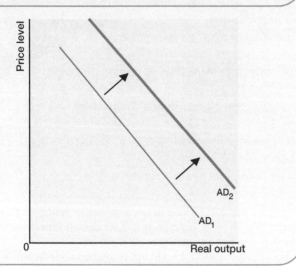

Figure 2 Changes in aggregate demand
A cut in taxes will lead to a shift to the right in the aggregate demand curve from AD_1 to AD_2 as will a rise in government spending.

Question 2

Explain the probable effect the following would have on aggregate demand, all other things being equal:
(a) a rise in income tax rates;
(b) a cut in council tax rates;
(c) a cut in spending on education;
(d) a rise in VAT rates combined with an increase in spending on the NHS.

because the price level is assumed to remain constant, will shift the AD curve to the right, as in Figure 2.

An increase in government spending or a fall in taxes which increases the budget deficit or reduces the budget surplus is known as EXPANSIONARY FISCAL POLICY. Fiscal policy is said to **loosen** as a result. In contrast, a higher budget surplus or lower deficit will lead to a **tightening** of the fiscal stance.

The multiplier

A rise in government spending (G) will not just increase aggregate demand by the value of the increase in G. There will be a multiple increase in aggregate demand. This **multiplier effect** will be larger the smaller the leakages from the circular flow.

In a modern economy, where leakages from savings, taxes and imports are a relatively high proportion of national income, multiplier values tend to be small. However, Keynesian economists argue that they can still have a significant effect on output in the economy if the economy is below full employment.

The output gap

Changes in government spending and taxation have an impact on the size of the output gap. In Figure 3, the actual path of GDP over time is shown by the red line. Between time period 2 and 3, the economy is going through a downturn or recession with actual GDP below its trend level. There is a negative output gap. Between time period 1 and 2, the

economy is in boom, with GDP above its trend level. There is a positive output gap. Through its fiscal policy, however, the government can reduce the impact of the cycle, shown by the blue line. By increasing spending relative to taxation and adopting an expansionary fiscal policy, it can bring the actual level of GDP up closer to the trend level between time periods 2 and 3. By cutting its spending relative to taxation and adopting a tighter fiscal stance, it can bring the actual level of GDP down closer to the trend level between time periods 1 and 2.

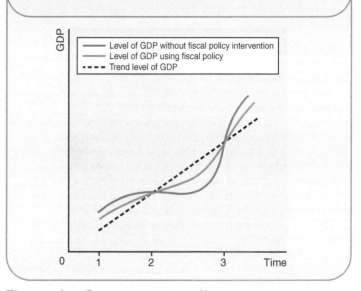

Figure 3 Fiscal policy and the output gap
Through adjusting its level of spending and taxation, governments can bring the actual level of GDP closer to its trend level. When there is a negative output gap, governments should spend more and tax less. When there is a positive output gap, governments should spend less and tax more.

The goals of government policy

The government has four major macroeconomic policy goals. These are to achieve full employment with little or no inflation in a high growth economy with an external balance (current account) equilibrium. Fiscal policy affects each of these variables through its impact on aggregate demand.

Fiscal policy can be used to achieve a wide variety of objectives. For example, it can be used to improve standards of health care through increased spending on the health service of a country. It can be used to make incomes less unequal by taxing the wealthier and giving benefits to the less well off. However, when it is used to influence directly the level of aggregate demand it becomes an example of a DEMAND SIDE POLICY or a policy of DEMAND MANAGEMENT. Whether governments deliberately use fiscal policy to influence aggregate demand or not, changes in the balance between government spending and taxation have an effect on the four key objectives of government policy: inflation, unemployment, the rate of economic growth and the balance of payments.

Inflation An increase in government spending or a fall in taxes which leads to a higher budget deficit or lower budget surplus will have a tendency to be inflationary. A higher budget deficit or lower budget surplus leads to an increase in aggregate demand. In Figure 4, this is shown by a shift in the aggregate demand curve to the right. This in turn leads to an increase in

increase in aggregate demand will lead to increasing inflation. The nearer the level of full employment at OD, the greater will be the rise in inflation from a given rise in government spending or fall in taxes.

Unemployment A greater budget deficit or a lower budget surplus will tend to reduce the level of unemployment, at least in the short term. A greater budget deficit will lead to an increase in aggregate demand which, as shown in Figure 4, will lead to a higher equilibrium level of output. The higher the level of output the lower is likely to be the level of unemployment.

As with inflation, there is a variety of factors which determines the extent to which unemployment will fall. The smaller the change in government spending and taxation, the less impact it will have on aggregate demand and the labour market. If the long run aggregate supply schedule is vertical, then increases in aggregate demand can only lead to higher inflation and they will have no impact on the level of output and unemployment. In the

Question 5

The Labour government which took office in February 1974 barely had a majority in Parliament and therefore was unwilling to increase taxes and cut public expenditure to tackle soaring inflation and a large balance of payments deficit. In November 1974, another general election took place and this time the Labour government secured a workable majority. In the 1975 Budget, it cut planned public expenditure and increased taxes, both by over £1 000 million. Further cuts in public expenditure were announced in 1976. The budget deficit fell from £10 161 million in 1975 to £8 899 million in 1976 and to £5 419 million in 1977. However, the government relaxed its fiscal stance in 1978, and the budget deficit increased to £8 340 million.

(a) What is meant by 'the multiplier'?
(b) Explain, using the concept of the multiplier, the likely effect that the change in fiscal policy between 1974 and 1976 had on national income.
(c) Using a diagram, discuss the impact that the change in the government's fiscal stance in 1978 is likely to have had on prices and output.

the price level from P_1 to P_2. So inflation increases.

The extent to which there is an increase in inflation depends on a number of factors. One is the size of the change in government spending or taxation. If the change in the budget deficit or surplus is very small, it will have little impact on the price level. Another factor is the shape of the aggregate supply curve. The short run aggregate supply curve is likely to be relatively shallow and so an increase in aggregate demand is likely to have a relatively small impact on prices. In the long term, however, the aggregate supply curve could vary from being horizontal to vertical. Classical economists argue that the long run aggregate supply curve (LRAS) is vertical. So, in Figure 5, an increase in aggregate demand has a relatively large effect on inflation. In contrast, the Keynesian view suggests that the LRAS curve is L shaped. In Figure 6, where the LRAS curve is horizontal, the economy has high levels of unemployment. Any increase in aggregate demand to AD_2 will have no impact on prices. If the level of output rises beyond OB, however, an

Figure 5 The long run classical view

In the long run, classical economists argue that expansionary fiscal policy has no effect on equilibrium output and therefore cannot reduce unemployment. However, it will lead to a higher level of prices.

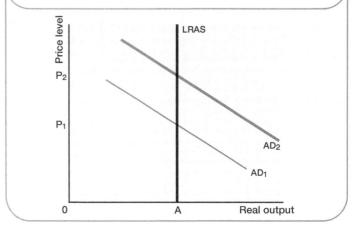

Figure 4 Fiscal policy and aggregate demand

A rise in government spending or a cut in taxes will shift the aggregate demand curve to the right from AD_1 to AD_2. In the short run this will be inflationary because the equilibrium price level will rise from P_1 to P_2, but equilibrium output will expand from Q_1 to Q_2.

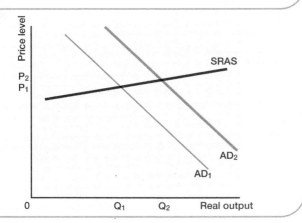

Figure 6 The Keynesian view

The effectiveness of fiscal policy depends upon how close the economy is to full employment. At output levels below OB, expansionary fiscal policy can increase output and reduce unemployment without increasing inflation. Between OB and OD, expansionary fiscal policy will increase both output and inflation. At full employment, OD, expansionary fiscal policy will result only in extra inflation.

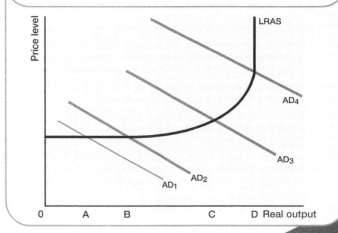

classical model, shown in Figure 5, the economy is in equilibrium at output 0A. An increase in the budget deficit might push the level of output beyond 0A in the short term because the SRAS is upward sloping, but in the long term it will revert to 0A. Hence, in the classical model, demand side fiscal policy cannot be used to alter unemployment levels in the long term. In a Keynesian model, this is also true if the economy is at full employment, at 0D in Figure 6. But at output levels below this, expansionary fiscal policy will lead to higher output and lower unemployment. If output is below 0B, expansionary fiscal policy can bring about a fall in unemployment without any increase in inflation.

Economic growth Expansionary fiscal policy is unlikely to affect the long term growth rate of an economy. This is because economic growth is caused by supply side factors such as investment, education and technology. However, expansionary fiscal policy is likely, in the short term, to increase GDP. As Figure 4 shows, in the short term an increase in aggregate demand will lead to higher output. Keynesian economists argue that expansionary fiscal policy is an appropriate policy to use if the economy is in recession below full employment. So in Figure 6, expansionary fiscal policy could be used to shift the aggregate demand curve from, say, AD_3 to AD_4. This would then return the economy to operating at full capacity on its production possibility frontier. Fiscal policy which pushes the aggregate demand curve beyond AD_4 would lead to no extra growth in output, but would be highly inflationary. In this situation, the economy would be OVER-HEATING. Classical economists argue that fiscal policy cannot be used to change real output in the long term because the long run aggregate supply curve is vertical. Shifting aggregate demand as in Figure 5 has no effect on output.

The balance of payments Expansionary fiscal policy leads to an increase in aggregate demand. This means that domestic consumers and firms will have more income and so will increase their spending on imports. Hence, the current account (exports minus imports) position will deteriorate. Tighter fiscal policy, on the other hand, will reduce domestic demand and hence demand for imports will fall. The current account position should then improve. There may be other less important influences on exports and imports. For instance, if domestic demand falls because of tighter fiscal policy, then domestic firms may increase their efforts to find markets for their goods by looking overseas.

Question 4

Explain, using diagrams, the likely impact of the following on unemployment, inflation, economic growth and the current balance.
(a) The large rises in government spending on health and education between 2003 and 2007 which were not totally matched by increases in taxation.
(b) The virtual freezing of government spending in the early 1980s at a time when tax revenues were rising.

Equally, a fall in aggregate demand due to tighter fiscal policy should moderate the rate of inflation. British goods will be lower priced than they would otherwise have been. Hence, they will be more competitive against imports and foreigners will find British exports more keenly priced. This should lower imports and raise exports, improving the current account position.

Trade offs

Changing aggregate demand has different effects on key macroeconomic variables. The government may not be able to achieve improvements in one without bringing about a deterioration in the other, at least in the short term.
- Expanding the economy to bring it out of recession and reduce unemployment is likely to lead to higher inflation.
- Tightening fiscal policy to reduce inflation is likely to lead to higher unemployment and lower levels of GDP.
- Contracting the domestic economy by tightening fiscal policy to improve the current account situation will also lead to lower inflation, but will increase unemployment.

A rise in demand could lead to changes in income distribution and damage to the environment due to higher production levels. Fiscal policy therefore needs to be used in conjunction with other policies if the government is to steer the economy towards lower inflation and unemployment, higher growth and a current account equilibrium.

Affecting the pattern of economic activity

Fiscal policy can be used to influence **macroeconomic** variables

Key terms

Budget - a statement of the spending and income plans of an individual, firm or government. The Budget is the yearly statement on government spending and taxation plans in the UK.
Budget deficit - a deficit which arises because government spending is greater than its receipts. Government therefore has to borrow money to finance the difference.
Budget surplus - a government surplus arising from government spending being less than its receipts. Government can use the difference to repay part of the National Debt.
Demand side policies or demand management - government use of fiscal and other policies to manipulate the level of aggregate demand in the economy.

Expansionary fiscal policy - fiscal policy used to increase aggregate demand.
Fiscal policy - decisions about spending, taxes and borrowing of the government.
National Debt - the accumulated borrowings of government.
Over-heating - the economy over-heats if aggregate demand is increased when the economy is already at its full productive potential. The result is increases in inflation with little or no increase in output.
Public Sector Net Cash Requirement (PSNCR) - the official name given to the difference between government spending and its receipts in the UK.

such as the level of demand in the economy. However, it can also be used to influence the **distribution of income**. Through taxes and spending, income can be redistributed in general from those who are better off to those who are worse off. At a **microeconomic level**, fiscal policy is used to influence the pattern of economic activity.

- By providing goods and services directly, the government influences the level of provision of goods such as public and merit goods. If left to free market forces, these goods would either be underprovided or not provided at all.

- Through public spending and taxes, the government influences the pattern of economic activity in the private sector. For example, taxes on cigarettes discourage their consumption. Charges on waste disposal reduce the amount of waste going to land fill sites. Subsidies to firms taking on unemployed workers encourage them to employ workers who otherwise might not get a job. Building a new motorway in Scotland might attract more industry to Scotland at the expense of the South East of England.

Applied economics

A history of fiscal policy

1950-1975

During the period 1950-75, fiscal policy was probably the most important way in which governments manipulated aggregate demand. During the 1950s, governments learnt to use the 'fiscal levers' with more and more confidence. In a recession, such as in 1958, the government would cut taxes to stimulate spending in the economy. This might also be accompanied by public spending increases, although it was recognised that these would take longer to multiply through the economy than tax cuts. In a boom, when the economy was over-heating, as in 1960, the government would increase taxes and possibly cut public spending.

Borrowing in the economy was mainly controlled through direct controls on banks and building societies, specifying who was allowed to borrow money, or through controls on hire purchase, the most common way of financing the purchase of consumer durables.

In the 1960s, governments began to recognise some of the limitations of fiscal policy. The Labour government of 1964-66 experimented briefly with a National Plan, an attempt to model the economy in terms of the inputs and outputs of each industry. This plan was then to be used to help the government identify where particular industries were failing or creating 'bottlenecks' and might need further investment. This supply side experiment was abandoned as the economy faced yet another sterling crisis, which ultimately ended in the pound being devalued in 1967. Another policy used from 1966 was an incomes policy - government limits on the pay rises that could be given to workers. This supply side measure was designed to lower inflation whilst allowing the economy to grow and enjoy low rates of unemployment.

The last bout of traditional Keynesian demand management came in 1972-73 when the government cut taxes and increased public spending to put the economy into boom. This boom, called the Barber boom (after Anthony Barber, the then Chancellor of the Exchequer), ended disastrously as inflation spun out of control, fuelled by the oil price increases of 1973-74.

1975-1997

The mid-1970s saw a wholesale disillusionment with

traditional Keynesian demand management techniques. A classical model of the economy became increasingly accepted as the model for governments to work with. In 1976, the Labour Prime Minister of the day, Jim Callaghan, in addressing his party conference, stated that: 'We used to think that you could just spend your way out of a recession, and increase employment by cutting taxes and boosting government spending. I tell you in all candour that that option no longer exists, and that in so far as it ever did exist, it worked by injecting inflation into the economy.'

The view was taken that cutting taxes produced only a temporary increase in aggregate demand. Unemployment would fall and growth would rise. However, as in the Barber boom, the medium term consequences would be a rise in the inflation rate. To reduce inflation, the government would have to tighten its fiscal stance by raising taxes. Aggregate demand would fall and the economy would return to its equilibrium position but at a higher level of prices and of inflation.

From 1979, when Margaret Thatcher won her first general election, fiscal policy was used for two separate purposes. First, it was used for micro-economic objectives as part of supply side policy for the government. For instance, income tax was cut to increase incentives to work. Second, it was used to ensure that monetary targets were met. In particular, it was felt that changes in the PSNCR (known as the PSBR at the time), such as might come about if taxes were cut, would have no effect on aggregate demand if the money for the tax cuts was genuinely borrowed from the non-bank sector. For instance, if the government cut taxes by £1 and financed this by borrowing from the non-bank sector, then there could be no increase in aggregate demand. The taxpayer would have £1 extra to spend but the lender to the government would have £1 less to spend. On this view, increases in the PSNCR completely **crowd-out** other expenditure in the economy resulting in no increase in aggregate demand. They could only work in a Keynesian manner if the increase in the PSNCR was financed through printing the money (the government has the unique power in the economy to print money) and thus increasing the money supply.

During the period of the Lawson boom (1986-89, named after Nigel Lawson, the then Chancellor) and the following recession (1990-92), the government allowed public spending and taxes to change in line with output and employment. Therefore, in the boom, the government allowed a large budget surplus to emerge. In the recession, the PSNCR was allowed to grow and by 1993 had reached over 5 per cent of GDP. In 1994-95, the government used active fiscal policy to cut this large deficit, increasing tax rates and introducing new taxes, whilst keeping a tight rein on public spending. On Keynesian assumptions, this put a brake on aggregate demand as it increased during the recovery. On classical assumptions, the tax increases had no effect on aggregate demand because the accompanying cuts in government borrowing released resources for the private sector to borrow and spend. One of the main reasons why the government felt it was so important to reduce the PSNCR was because of concerns that otherwise the National Debt would grow out of control.

Since 1997

In 1997, a Labour government under Tony Blair was elected. Tony Blair was succeeded as Prime Minister in 2007 by his Chancellor, Gordon Brown. Like previous governments since the mid- 1970s, the two post 1997 Labour administrations did not believe that fiscal policy should be used to manage aggregate demand. Demand management was left to the Bank of England through its operation of **monetary policy**. Instead, fiscal policy was used to achieve a number of objectives such as:

- expanding health and education: government spending was increased to finance an expansion of the provision of merit goods such as health and education;
- lessening income inequality: taxes and government spending were used to make the distribution of income less unequal;
- supply side reforms: rates of tax and government spending programmes were used to improve the performance of the supply side of the economy;
- maintaining the possibility of joining the European Monetary Union: one of the criteria for joining was that the UK should have stable public finances, with annual government borrowing at less than 3 per cent

of GDP. Note that the way in which the British government measures its annual borrowing and its National Debt is different from the measures used by the EU. The British government measure is more flattering to UK public finances than the EU measure.

There was a recognition that changes in government spending and taxation could play a positive role in the trade cycle. In a recession, when the output gap was negative, government spending would increase because of increased welfare benefits to the unemployed. Tax revenues would also fall because households and businesses would have less income and be spending less. Higher government spending and lower tax revenues would increase aggregate demand from what it would otherwise have been and help pull the economy out of recession. Equally, in a boom, when the output gap was positive, government would be raising large amounts of extra tax whilst its spending on welfare benefits would fall. This would dampen growth in aggregate demand, helping to prevent the economy from overheating.

The government was also concerned that the National Debt should not increase substantially as a proportion of national income. In 1998, the government therefore announced two new 'fiscal rules'.

- The **golden rule** stated that government would only borrow money to invest over the whole period of a trade cycle. It could increase borrowing to finance current expenditure such as welfare payments or wages in a recession, but this would have to be matched by repayments of debt in a boom. Therefore, government spending and taxation could help reduce the size of the fluctuation experienced in a trade cycle by influencing aggregate demand. However, over the whole cycle, net borrowing for this purpose would be zero. The government is allowed, however, to be a net borrower to finance its capital expenditure (i.e. investment), such as the building of new motorways or new hospitals.
- The **public debt rule** stated that the ratio of public debt to national income would be held at a 'stable and prudent' level over the trade cycle at less than 40 per cent of GDP.

Figures 10 and 11 in the data question show the extent to which the government achieved those objectives up to 2007.

DataQuestion   The pre-budget report: October 2007

In his October 2007 Pre-Budget Report, the Chancellor announced a number of changes to both government spending and taxation. For example, there would be additional spending by 2010-11 of £14.5 billion on education, £900 million on science and £3.6 billion on transport.

Overall, he predicted that total government expenditure in

2008-09 would increase by £28.2 billion compared to the estimated amounts for 2007-08. Tax and other receipts would rise by £30 billion compared to the estimated outturn for 2007-08. Public sector borrowing would therefore hardly change compared to the previous year's outturn.

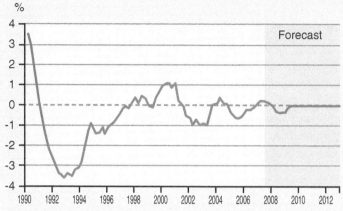

Figure 7 The output gap

Source: adapted from *2007 Pre-Budget Report and Comprehensive Spending Review: the economy and public finances - supplementary charts and tables*, HM Treasury.

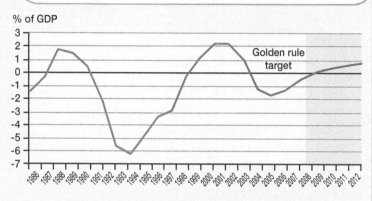

Figure 10 Surplus/deficit on government current budget as a percentage of GDP

Source: adapted from *2007 Pre-Budget Report and Comprehensive Spending Review: the economy and public finances- supplementary charts and tables*, HM Treasury.

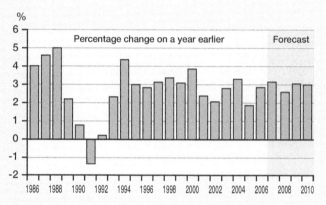

Figure 8 Growth in GDP

Source: adapted from *2007 Pre-Budget Report and Comprehensive Spending Review*, HM Treasury.

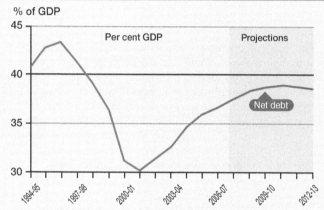

Figure 11 National debt as percentage of GDP

Source: adapted from *2007 Pre-Budget Report and Comprehensive Spending Review: the economy and public finances- supplementary charts and tables*, HM Treasury.

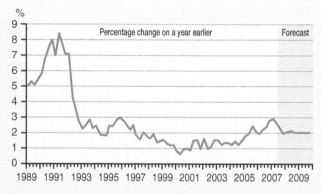

Figure 9 Inflation (annual % change in CPI)

Source: adapted from *2007 Pre-Budget Report and Comprehensive Spending Review*, HM Treasury.

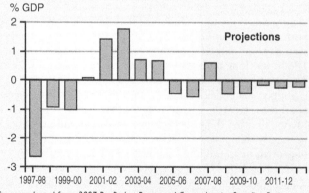

Figure 12 Estimated impact of changes in fiscal policy on GDP

Source: adapted from *2007 Pre-Budget Report and Comprehensive Spending Review*, HM Treasury.

1. Explain how the Chancellor proposed to change government spending, taxation and government borrowing in his 2007 Pre-Budget Report.
2. Figure 12 shows how changes in government spending and taxation in one year affected GDP in that year. To what extent did the changes in fiscal policy over the period 1997-2007 help smooth out the effects of the trade cycle?
3. 'The changes in total government spending, taxation and government borrowing in the 2007 Pre-Budget Report will have no impact on GDP, unemployment and inflation.' Evaluate this statement.
4. To what extent were the Chancellor's plans announced in October 2007 in accordance with his 'fiscal rules'?

Summary

1. Supply side policies are designed to increase the average rate of growth of the economy. They may also help reduce inflation and unemployment and improve the current account position.
2. Some economists, called supply side economists, believe that governments should not intervene in the workings of the free market. The government's role, they argue, is to remove restrictions to the operations of individual markets. Keynesian economists believe that governments need to intervene on the supply side to correct market failure.
3. Aggregate supply in the economy can be increased if government intervenes to ensure that labour markets operate more efficiently and if there is an increase in human capital over time.
4. Governments need to encourage firms to invest and take risks if aggregate supply is to increase.
5. Privatisation, deregulation and increased competition can increase aggregate supply.
6. Regional policy and inner city policy can also increase aggregate supply.

Supply side policies

The long run aggregate supply curve shows the productive potential of the economy. At any point in time there is only so much that an economy can produce. Over time, the productive potential of the economy will, hopefully, grow. This can be shown by a shift outwards in the production possibility frontier or by a shift to the right in the long run aggregate supply curve.

SUPPLY SIDE POLICIES are government policies designed to increase the rate of economic growth. They act broadly across the whole economy. They may also act specifically in certain markets to remove BOTTLENECKS which prevent the whole economy from growing faster.

Figure 1 illustrates economic growth. A shift to the right in the LRAS curve increases output from 0A to 0B. In the UK and the USA, the trend rate of growth for most of the second half of the twentieth century has been around 2.5 per cent. However, average economic growth has been higher in the first half of the first decade of the 2000s and some economists claim that better supply side policies might have lifted the trend rate of growth for both of these economies. In contrast, the Japanese economy has seen its trend rate of growth fall decade by decade since the 1960s. So long term growth rates are not necessarily a constant. They can be influenced by factors such as government policy.

Supply side policies can also affect other economic variables apart from growth. Figure 1 shows that a shift to the right in the LRAS, all other things being equal, leads to a fall in the price level. So supply side policies which succeed in increasing the trend rate of growth of an economy can help to moderate inflation.

Supply side policies also affect unemployment. Economies are constantly changing, with new industries growing and old industries dying. Over time, new technology allows more to be produced with fewer workers. If the economy does not grow fast enough, more workers can lose their jobs in a year than new jobs are created. Unemployment therefore grows. In contrast, fast economic growth is likely to see more new jobs being created than old jobs are lost and so unemployment falls. Faster economic growth in the UK and the US in the second half of the 1990s has been associated in both countries with falling unemployment. There comes a time, as in the UK in the 1950s, when the economy is at full employment and everyone who wants a job is able to get one. Supply side policies can then play a crucial role in ensuring that inflation does

not become a problem. They can help keep growth in aggregate supply equal to growth in aggregate demand.

Supply side policies affect the current account too. Increasing aggregate supply allows more goods and services to be available for export and reduces the need to import goods. In practice, effective supply side policies increase the competitiveness of domestic industry in relation to foreign industry. Domestic goods become cheaper or better quality or are of a higher specification than foreign goods. Hence exports rise compared to imports.

Different approaches

Economists agree that government can affect the supply side of the economy. However, they disagree about how this should be done.

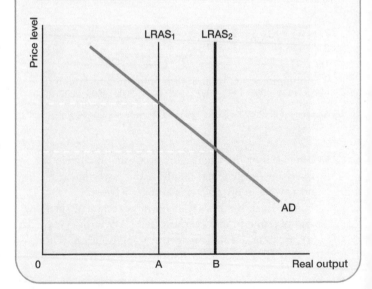

Figure 1 Supply side policies
Effective supply side policies push the long run aggregate supply curve to the right. This increases economic growth and reduces inflationary pressures. It may also bring about a reduction in unemployment and lead to higher exports and lower imports.

Supply side economists Supply side economists tend to be associated with free market economics. They believe that free markets promote economic efficiency and that government intervention in the economy is likely to impair economic efficiency. Government still has a vital role to play in the economy, according to these economists. Government is responsible for creating the environment in which free markets can work. This means eliminating the barriers which exist to the perfect working of markets. SUPPLY SIDE ECONOMICS therefore tends to be the study of how government can intervene using **market orientated** policies.

Interventionist economists Some economists believe that free markets often fail to maximise economic efficiency in the economy. Governments therefore have to correct **market failure**. This means intervening in free markets to change the outcome from that which it would otherwise have been.

In the rest of this unit, we will consider these two types of supply side policy - market orientated policies and interventionist policies.

Labour market policies

The level of aggregate supply is determined in part by the quantity of labour supplied to the market and the productivity of that labour. For instance, all other things being equal, an economy with 10 million workers will produce less than an economy with 20 million workers. Equally, an economy where workers have little **human capital** will have a lower output than one where there are high levels of human capital. Free market economists argue that there is a number of ways in which the quantity and quality of labour are restricted because markets are not allowed to work freely.

Trade unions The purpose of a trade union is to organise workers into one bargaining unit. The trade union then becomes a monopsonist, a sole seller of labour, and prevents workers from competing amongst themselves in the job market. Economic theory predicts that if trade unions raise wage rates for their members, then employment and output will be lower in otherwise competitive markets. So free market economists argue that government must intervene to curb the power of trade unions, for instance by reducing their ability to strike.

State welfare benefits Workers are unlikely to take low paid jobs if state benefits are a little below or equal to the pay being offered. Hence, state benefits reduce the level of aggregate supply because more workers remain unemployed. Free market economists argue that the solution is to cut state unemployment benefits to encourage workers to take on low paid jobs. An alternative approach is to give benefits or tax credits to those who take on low paid jobs. For there to be a positive incentive to work, the benefit plus pay must be greater than the benefits the worker would have received had he been out of work.

Minimum wages If there is a minimum wage which is set above the market clearing wage, then unemployment will be created. Minimum wages prevent some workers who would be prepared to work for lower pay from getting jobs. Hence aggregate supply is lowered. Free market economists tend to argue that minimum wages should be abolished.

Marginal tax rates High marginal rates of tax (the rate of tax on the last £1 earned or spent) discourage economic activity. A tax on cigarettes leads to fewer cigarettes being bought. A tax on work (income tax) leads to people working less. A tax on profits (corporation tax) is a disincentive to firms to make profits. Lowering certain taxes will therefore raise the level of economic activity and increase aggregate supply.

Supply side economists believe that the supply of labour is relatively elastic. A reduction in marginal tax rates on income will lead to a significant increase in 'work'. This could mean individuals working longer hours, being more willing to accept promotion, being more geographically mobile, or simply being prepared to join the workforce.

Work is, arguably, an inferior good, whilst leisure, its alternative, is a normal good. The higher an individual's income, the less willing he or she is to work. So a cut in marginal tax rates will have a negative income effect at the margin (i.e. the worker will be less willing to work). However, a cut in marginal tax rates will have a positive substitution effect because the relative price of work to leisure has changed in favour of work (i.e. the worker will be more willing to work).

Supply side economists believe that the substitution effect of a tax cut is more important than the income effect and hence tax cuts increase incentives to work. If cutting marginal income tax rates encourages people to work harder and earn more, then in theory it could be that tax revenues will increase following a tax cut. For instance, if 10 workers, each earning £10 000 a year, pay an average 25 per cent tax, then total tax revenue is £25 000 (10 x £10 000 x 0.25). If a cut in the tax rate to 20 per cent were to make each worker work harder and increase earnings to, say, £15 000, tax revenues would increase to £30 000 (10 x £3 000). This is an example of the LAFFER

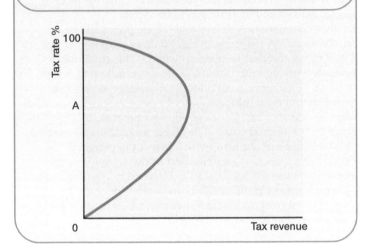

Figure 2 *The Laffer curve*
As tax rates increase, economic activity is discouraged and hence the rate of growth of tax revenues falls. Above 0A, an increase in tax rates so discourages economic activity that tax revenues fall.

CURVE effect, named after Professor Arthur Laffer who popularised the idea in the late 1970s. Figure 2 shows a Laffer curve, which plots tax revenues against tax rates. As tax rates increase, the rate of growth of tax revenue falls because of the disincentive effects of the tax. 0A shows the maximum revenue position of the tax. At tax rates above 0A, an increase in the tax rate so discourages economic activity that tax revenues fall.

Poverty and unemployment traps The combination of marginal rates of income tax and withdrawal of benefits can lead to poverty and unemployment traps. The POVERTY or EARNINGS TRAP occurs when a low income working individual or household earns more, for example by gaining promotion, getting a better paid job or working more hours, but the net gain is little or even negative. It occurs because as income increases, welfare benefits are withdrawn. Equally, the individual or household might start to pay tax. For example, if an individual loses 50p in benefits when earning an extra £1, and then pays income tax and National Insurance contributions at 30 per cent, then the net gain from earning the extra £1 is only 20p (£1 - 50p - 30p). The effective marginal rate of tax here is 80 per cent. If the benefit loss were 90p in the pound, the individual would be 20p worse off. The effective marginal rate of tax here would be 120 per cent. The poverty trap is a major disincentive for those working and receiving benefits to work harder or increase their skills. The UNEMPLOYMENT TRAP occurs when an individual is little better off or is even worse off getting a job than staying unemployed because of loss of benefits and taxation. The unemployment trap, where it occurs, is a major disincentive for the unemployed to find work. One solution to both kinds of trap is to lower welfare benefits but this increases poverty. The other solution is to reduce taxes on income and the rate of welfare benefit withdrawal as incomes increase. This is a more expensive solution for the government and the taxpayer.

Taxes on labour Firms will not take on workers if their total wage cost is too high. Part of the total cost is the wages of workers. However, many countries tax firms for employing labour, often by imposing employer contributions to state

social security funds. In the UK, for instance, employers have to pay National Insurance employers' contributions. The higher the tax, the fewer workers will be employed and hence the lower will be the level of aggregate supply.

Reducing the cost of changing jobs In a modern fast-changing economy, workers are likely to be changing jobs on a relatively frequent basis. Some workers will even become **portfolio workers,** having a mix of part-time jobs at any one time rather than a single full time job. If the labour market is such that workers find it difficult to get new jobs when they are made redundant, then unemployment will rise and aggregate supply will fall. So the government must ensure that **barriers to mobility** between jobs are as low as possible. One important barrier to mobility can be pensions. If pension rights are typically provided by individual employers, then a worker who is frequently moving from employer to employer will lose out. Hence, governments should give workers the opportunity to provide for their own pension which they can take with them from job to job. Another problem in the UK has been a lack of geographical mobility due to rigidities in the housing market. If house prices in the south of England are much higher than in the north, then workers will be discouraged from moving from north to south. Equally, if workers are unable to rent houses at an affordable rent in an area, then low paid workers will not be able to move into that area to take up jobs.

Education and training Increasing the level of human capital of workers is vital if economies are to develop. Increased levels of

In a recent report on the UK economy, the OECD (Organisation for Economic Co-operation and Development) highlighted weaknesses in the UK education and training system that were hindering its growth performance. It was particularly critical of educational provision for less academic students. It said that 'much more could still be done to improve basic literacy and numeracy, thus providing a strong foundation for continued learning'. It also argued that 'continuously improving the relevance and quality of vocational programmes is as important as it is to expand their provision'.

It was worried that the tax and benefits system might discourage individuals from acquiring intermediate skills. It pointed out that, whilst gross earnings of workers with intermediate skills were significantly higher than those of low skilled workers, net income was little different if those workers had children because of tax credits that low skilled, low pay workers can claim. For 16-18 year olds, pilot schemes which have paid teenagers to stay in education appear to have boosted engagement in continued learning. But an alternative might be to increase the very light taxation faced by teenagers taking a job at 16.

Source: adapted from OECD, *Economic Survey of the United Kingdom 2005.*

(a) Using a diagram, explain why the quality of the labour force is so important for the long term growth of the UK economy.
(b) Suggest why improving 'basic literacy and numeracy' might be important for increase the long term human capital stock of the economy.
(c) Explain why taxes and benefits might be a disincentive to acquire skills in the UK.

education and training will raise the marginal revenue product of workers (i.e. will raise the value of output of workers). This in turn will shift the aggregate supply curve to the right. The value of human capital in the economy is one of the most important determinants of the level of aggregate supply.

The capital market

Increasing the capital stock of the country, such as its factories, offices and roads, will push the aggregate supply curve to the right. According to classical economists, the government has a key role to play in this.

Profitability Firms invest in order to make a profit. The higher the rate of profit, the more investment will take place. Hence, government must create an environment in which firms can make profits for their owners. One way of doing this is by reducing taxes on company profits. Another is to reduce inheritance tax which might be paid by a small business owner when passing on his or her business to a family relative. Another is to reduce taxes on employing workers. Reducing the amount of government red tape, like planning permissions, can also help reduce costs and increase profitability.

Allocating scarce capital resources The government is in a poor position to decide how to allocate resources. It should leave this as much as possible to the private sector. Hence, state owned companies should be **privatised** wherever possible. Government should offer only limited taxpayers' money to subsidise industry. The government should stay well clear of trying to 'back winning companies'.

Increasing the range of sources of capital available to firms Firms can be constrained in their growth if they are unable to gain access to financial capital like bank loans or share capital. Government should therefore encourage the private sector to provide financial capital, particularly to small businesses. They may, for instance, offer tax incentives to individuals putting up share capital for a business.

The goods market

Inefficient production will lead to a lower level of aggregate supply. For instance, if UK car workers produce 50 per cent fewer cars per worker with the same equipment as German workers, then the level of aggregate supply in the UK can obviously be increased if UK labour productivity is raised. The government has a key role to play in increasing efficiency.

Free market economists argue that the most important way of securing increased efficiency is through encouraging **competition**. If firms know that they will go out of business if they do not become efficient, then they have a powerful incentive to become efficient producers. The government can increase competition in the market in a number of ways.

Encouraging free trade Fierce foreign competition results in a domestic industry which has to be efficient in order to survive. The government should therefore liberalise trade, removing tariffs (taxes) and other barriers to imports.

Encouraging small businesses Small businesses can operate in markets where there are no large businesses. Competition here

is intense. However, small businesses can operate in markets where there are very large firms. Small businesses then force larger firms to remain cost competitive. Otherwise the larger firms will lose market share.

Privatisation Privatising firms, and in the process creating competition between newly created firms, eliminates the distortions created by the operation of public sector monopolies.

Deregulation Removing rules about who can compete in markets will encourage competition.

Interventionist approaches

Interventionist economists would tend to take a different approach to government policy and aggregate supply. They would tend to focus on issues of where free markets fail. For instance, they would agree with free market economists that a key aspect of government policy must be to increase education and training. However, whereas free market economists would argue that training should be left to individual companies or groups of companies in a local area, interventionist economists would argue that training is best organised by government. The state should, for instance, impose levies on firms to finance state organised training placements and schemes.

With regard to investment in physical capital, free market economists would argue that profit should direct the level and pattern of investment. Interventionist economists would argue that if investment is insufficient in the economy, then the government should intervene and, for instance, use taxes to set up state owned companies or subsidise investment by private industry.

In the 1950s and 1960s in the UK, the main supply side problem was that of regional inequality with the north of England, Scotland and Northern Ireland experiencing higher

Question 3

Britain's offshore industry has reacted angrily to the UK Chancellor's decision to impose an extra 10 per cent tax on profits from North Sea oil fields. It will raise an estimated £6.5 billion in revenue for the government over the next three years. The UK Offshore Operators Association said that: 'It is almost beyond comprehension that the government has failed to grasp the vulnerability of the industry's future in the UK. His move could not come at a worse time. North Sea activity has recovered remarkably since 2002 when it was last hit by a punitive tax charge.' It went on to say that: 'It will deter investment in new fields and make older fields less attractive for increased recovery. Moreover, the impact will be felt significantly by smaller oil and gas producers. The unexpected tax hit on the industry in 2002 led to a major slump in investor confidence in the North Sea. Exploration and development activity fell to record lows as investment left the North Sea for other less challenging parts of the globe with lower costs.'

Source: adapted from Press Release, United Kingdom Offshore Operators Association, December 2005.

(a) Explain the link between company taxes and North Sea oil exploration and development.
(b) What impact might the 10 per cent extra tax on North Sea oil profits have on long run aggregate supply?

unemployment rates than the south and the Midlands. The interventionist policy response was a mixture of offering incentives to firms investing in high unemployment regions and making it difficult for firms to expand in low unemployment regions.

Supply side policies and aggregate demand

Supply side policies can have an impact on aggregate demand. For example, any supply side policy which results in higher government spending or lower taxes will increase or reduce aggregate demand directly through changes in levels of spending. However, supply side policies can also have indirect effects. Supply side policies which succeed in reducing unemployment, for example, might lead to a rise in consumer confidence. In turn, this will encourage households to borrow more money and so raise aggregate demand. Hence, supply side policies can sometimes lead to both increases and decreases in an economic variable. For example, supply side policies which succeed in increasing investment will in the long term shift the aggregate supply curve to the right reducing inflationary pressures. But the increase in investment in the short term will increase aggregate demand, increasing inflationary pressures.

Question 4

Scientific innovation, knowledge transfer, skills enhancement and transport improvements are main elements of the £100 million spending plan, unveiled today, which is intended to kick-start the north of England's economy.

The Northern Way business plan is an attempt by three northern regional development agencies to tackle the north-south divide in economic performance. The Northern Way has put the output gap between north and south at £30 billion. It calculated this by comparing the Gross Value Added per capita of the three northern regions with the all-England average in the five years 1999-2003.

The £100 million will fund a variety of initiatives to improve the competitiveness of the three regions. For example, £15 million will be spent funding centres of excellence in leadership, innovation and the skills for sustainable communities. £12 million will produce some small but significant transport improvements and develop the case for a new approach to transport investment in the North. £3 million will help establish a new £6.5 million National Industrial Biotechnology Facility in the Tees Valley.

Source: adapted from the *Financial Times* 20.6.2005; Press Release, The Northern Way, 20.6.2005.

Using examples from the passage, explain how assistance from the government might increase aggregate supply.

Key terms

Bottleneck - a supply side constraint in a particular market in an economy which prevents higher growth for the whole economy.
Laffer curve - a curve which shows that at low levels of taxation, tax revenues will increase if tax rates are increased; however, if tax rates are high, then a further rise in rates will reduce total tax revenues because of the disincentive effects of the increase in tax.
Poverty or earnings trap - occurs when an individual is little better off or even worse off when gaining an increase in wages because of the combined effect of increased tax and benefit withdrawal.
Supply side economics - the study of how changes in aggregate supply will affect variables such as national income; in particular, how government microeconomic policy might change aggregate supply through individual markets.
Supply side policies - government policies designed to increase the productive potential of the economy and push the long run aggregate supply curve to the right.
Unemployment trap - occurs when an individual is little better off or even worse off when getting a job after being unemployed because of the combined effect of increased tax and benefit withdrawal.

Applied economics

Supply side policies in the UK

Since 1979, the government has been committed to implementing supply side policies aimed at improving the workings of free markets. A wide range of measures have been introduced which are described below.

The labour market

Trade union power In the 1960s and 1970s, there was a fierce debate about trade union power. It was widely recognised that trade unions, which at their membership peak in 1979 represented half of all UK workers, had considerable power in the workplace at the time. In 1979, the Conservative party under Margaret Thatcher was elected into office with a manifesto pledge to reduce trade union power and make UK industry more flexible and competitive. A number of Acts were passed which effectively made secondary picketing illegal and firms gained the power to sue trade unions involved for damages. Industrial action called by a union now had to be approved by a secret ballot of its membership. Secret ballots were also made compulsory for elections of trade union leaders. Closed shops, places of work where employers agreed that all workers should be trade union members, became more difficult to maintain and enforce. The government also took an extremely hard line with strikes in the public sector, refusing to give in to union demands. The breaking of strikes, such as the miners' strike of 1983-85, increased the confidence of private employers to resist trade union demands. By the mid-1990s, with the loss of over one quarter of their members since 1979, trade unions had become marginalised in many places of work and considerably weakened in others.

The election of a Labour government in 1997 did not reverse this position. In 1999, it passed the Employee Relations Act 1999 which forced employers to recognise the negotiating rights of trade unions if a majority of workers in the workplace voted in favour. However, whilst this might increase union membership in the long term, it is unlikely in itself to greatly increase union power.

Wage bargaining Supply side economists view collective bargaining as an inflexible way of rewarding workers. They advocate individual pay bargaining with payment systems based on bonuses and performance related pay. By reducing the power of trade unions, the government in the 1980s and early 1990s went some way to breaking collective bargaining. It encouraged employers to move away from national pay bargaining to local pay bargaining. In the public sector, it attempted to move away from national pay agreements to local ones. The Labour government elected in 1997 was more sympathetic to trade unions but made it clear it would not reverse most of the trade union reforms of the 1980s and early 1990s. However, the 1999 Employee Relations Act increased the ability of trade unions to force recognition by employers of their negotiating rights. At the same time, the signing of the Social Chapter influenced some larger firms to set up works councils which involve trade unions. The government is also supporting greater social partnerships between businesses and unions which may also encourage collective bargaining.

State welfare benefits Supply side economists tend to argue that welfare benefits can be a major disincentive to work. The benefit system needs to avoid creating **poverty traps** (where an increase in wages leads to a fall in income for a worker after tax has been paid and benefits withdrawn) and **unemployment traps** (where unemployed workers find that they can receive a higher income from remaining unemployed than by taking low paid jobs). In the 1980s, one solution to this was to cut the real value of benefits for low income households. It was made more difficult to collect unemployment benefits and the unemployed

came under much greater pressure to accept jobs that were offered or take up places on training schemes. The Labour government elected in 1997 was committed both to reducing poverty and unemployment. Its main initiative to get round both the unemployment and poverty traps was the Working Families Tax Credit, introduced in 1999, and replaced by the Child Tax Credit and the Working Tax Credit in 2003. These increased the take home pay of low income earners by giving them benefits paid through their earnings. Even so, effective marginal rates of tax for some low paid can still be far more than the 40 per cent top rate of income tax paid by high income earners. With regard to unemployment, some economists argue that much of the fall in unemployment in the 1990s and 2000s occurred simply because the long term unemployed were shifted onto disability and incapacity benefits. In the early 2000s, the government made some attempt to make it more difficult to claim these benefits and to get some of those already on these benefits onto training schemes or into work. By 2008, however, success had been very limited.

Social legislation Legislation protecting the rights of workers goes back to the nineteenth century when curbs were placed on the employment of children and of women. Over time, workers have gained more and more rights. For example, workers are protected by law from the moment they apply for a job to the time they leave. Holiday entitlements, maternity and paternity leave, sickness, disability, training, health and safety and discrimination are all covered by legislation. In 1997, the UK signed the Social Chapter of the Maastricht Treaty 1992, which gave Brussels the right to introduce regulations covering conditions of employment in the UK. Businesses tend to view regulations as 'red tape' which impairs their competitiveness. However, most other European countries, such as France and Germany, have more onerous regulations and view the UK as being relatively lightly regulated.

Training and education Education and training are recognised by the government as keystones of its supply side policies. Whilst the education of the top 20 or 30 per cent of the population by ability has traditionally been, by international standards, excellent, the education of the rest of the population has tended to be at best mediocre and at worst poor. Since the 1980s, the government has attempted to address these problems in a variety of ways. One has been to take central control of the curriculum in schools, for example through the National Curriculum established in the 1980s and more recently through numeracy and literacy initiatives. Another has been to set targets for schools and colleges for student attainment. Another has been through inspection of schools and colleges, such as the work of Ofsted. The idea of competition between schools, and a much greater variety of schools which parents may choose for their children, has been experimented with and remains a central plank of government policy. Successive governments have encouraged more students to stay on in education to 18 and 21. Today training in the UK is the responsibility of a variety of bodies including Regional Development Agencies, Learning and Skills Councils and the Small Business Service.

Much work has been done on providing vocational routes through education, although reform of the vocational framework begun in the 1980s has produced mixed results. This has arguably meant that the educational pathway for less academic students remains poorer than in many of our industrial competitors. Training in the workplace has also come in for continued criticism and lifelong training for workers in the UK, particularly those with low skills, continues to be criticised by international organisations like the OECD.

Marginal tax rates Marginal income tax rates by 1979 were very high. The standard rate of income tax was 33 per cent whilst the highest rate on earned income was 83 per cent. The incoming Conservative government made it a priority to cut these and within ten years the highest marginal income tax rate was 40 per cent, where it has remained since. Income tax cuts were designed in part to increase incentives to work. Incentives to accumulate wealth were given by cuts in both inheritance tax and capital gains tax rates. Employers too have gained with Employers National Insurance contributions falling. The UK has continued to have almost the lowest social security taxes on

employers and employees in Europe.

Help to businesses

If aggregate supply is to increase, the private sector needs to expand. Hence, according to supply side economists, the government needs to create an environment in which business can flourish.

Small businesses Small businesses are important in the economy because they provide new jobs and can become the big businesses of tomorrow. Conservative governments between 1979 and 1997 placed particular importance on the development of an 'enterprise culture' and laid the groundwork for many of the policies which are in operation today. Existing small businesses are helped through reduced rates on taxes on profits (corporation tax) and tax allowances for investment. They may be eligible for short term loans in circumstances when a commercial bank would refuse to lend to them. Advice is available from the Small Business Service. Regulation ('red tape') is often less for small businesses than large businesses. However, the burden of regulation on small businesses is often heavier because they have fewer resources and less expertise to deal with the regulations with which they have to comply. New small businesses can get a variety of help from grants and loans for training.

Innovation and research Since 1997, the government has been keen to promote innovation and research. Tax allowances have traditionally been available to businesses spending on innovation and research. However, there is a variety of programmes which enable some businesses to gain grants for research and development (R&D), and to set up knowledge transfer networks between industry and an academic establishment.

Goods markets

It is argued that competition increases both productive and allocative efficiency. Markets should therefore be made as competitive as possible. Encouraging competition was central to government policy after 1979.

Deregulation and privatisation In the 1980s, the government introduced policies to privatise state owned companies and deregulate markets. Nearly all state owned companies were privatised by the end of the 1990s including British Telecom and the gas industry. Central government departments and local authorities were encouraged to offer such services as waste collection or cleaning to tender rather than employing staff directly to provide the service. Many controls were abolished, such as legal restrictions on pub opening hours and Sunday trading. Since 2000, the government has further increased the involvement of the private sector in providing public sector services. For example, 2004 saw the opening of the UK's first private toll motorway. In the NHS, the government is contracting out operations to private sector health companies. Many new buildings, such as schools and hospitals, are being built and operated by the private sector and the Private Finance Initiative (PFI). The private sector companies are then leasing back the facilities to the state sector for its use. In 2006, the postal letter service was opened up for the first time to serious competition.

Encouragement of international free trade Fierce foreign competition results in a domestic industry which has to be efficient in order to survive. Since 1979, governments have tended to advocate policies of free trade on most issues. For instance, they have been more willing than most other European governments to see greater free trade in agriculture. The UK has also been one of the most welcoming to foreign companies wanting to set up in the UK.

Regional and industrial policy

Before 1979, the main focus of supply side policies was regional and industrial policy. Regional policy aimed to help poorer regions of the UK to attract businesses and create jobs. Industrial policy aimed to help industries which were undergoing difficult trading conditions, such as textiles, shipbuilding, the motor manufacturing industry, coal mining and steel. Since 1999, each region of the UK had a Regional Development Agency (RDA) working to create jobs and improve the competitiveness of the region. The most high profile work of the nine RDAs has been giving grants to incoming foreign companies wanting to set up large showcase manufacturing plants. However, most of their spending is spread amongst a wide range of initiatives, from grants to small start up businesses, to promoting training of workers, to encouraging infrastructure developments such as new roads or airports.

DataQuestion

Supply side economics

France, unlike the UK or the USA, tends to be mistrustful of free market supply side economics. In the 2007 presidential elections, the different candidates put forward a range of policies which were interventionist rather than free market in nature. The Socialist candidate, for example, Ségolène Royal proposed a sharp rise in the level of the minimum wage, an extension of the law to more workers giving them a right to work a basic 35 hour week, and giving state-funding for young people to get their first job. The cap which limits taxes paid by individuals on their income and wealth to 60 per cent would be abolished, increasing taxes for very high income earners and wealthy individuals. Firms that paid large amounts of their profit to shareholders in dividends would pay higher taxes on profits than firms which retained profit to invest back in the company. Aid given to companies which set up in high unemployment areas would have to be repaid if they subsequently moved the jobs created abroad.

Nicholas Sarkozy, the right wing candidate who won the election, was slightly more free market in his approach. He proposed cutting the limit on taxes on income and wealth paid by individuals from 60 per cent to 50 per cent. Firms would not have to pay any employer taxes on overtime pay given to workers who worked more than the 35 hour week. There would be a more flexible contract of employment for employees which would give employers more rights to sack them. Unemployment benefits would be cut if an unemployed person turned down two job offers. Taxes would be cut for private investment in start up companies. Taxes on company profits would be cut to the European average. However, companies which gave increases in dividends which were much higher than the increases they gave to workers in wages would be taxed more heavily on their profits.

Source: adapted from the *Financial Times*, 30.3.2007.

1. Explain how any four of the measures proposed by the two candidates might increase economic growth of the French economy.

2. Discuss whether Ségolène Royal's policies were more interventionist than those of Nicholas Sarkozy.

Summary

1. Governments can influence the economy through the use of monetary policy – the control of monetary variables such as the rate of interest, the money supply and the volume of credit.
2. Changing interest rates can change the level of aggregate demand through its effect on consumer durables, the housing market, household wealth, saving, investment, exports and imports.
3. A rise in interest rates is likely to reduce inflationary pressures, but lead to lower growth in output and have an adverse effect on unemployment. Exports are likely to fall, but the impact on imports is uncertain and so the overall impact on the current account is likely to vary from economy to economy.
4. The use of monetary policy gives rise to a variety of trade offs such as greater inflation or greater unemployment.

Money and the rate of interest

Government can, to some extent, control the rate of interest and the amount of money circulating in the economy. They can also affect the amount of borrowing or credit available from financial institutions like banks and building societies. MONETARY POLICY is the manipulation of these monetary variables to achieve government objectives.

The RATE OF INTEREST is the price of money. This is because lenders expect to receive interest if money is supplied for loans to money markets. Equally, if money is demanded for loans from money markets, borrowers expect to have to pay interest on the loans.

At various times in the past, governments have used credit controls, such as restrictions on the amount that can be borrowed on a mortgage or on hire purchase, as the main instrument of monetary policy. Equally, some governments have attempted directly to control the supply of money, the amount of money available for spending and borrowing in the economy. In recent years, the rate of interest has been the key instrument of monetary policy. For instance, both the Bank of England and the Federal Reserve Bank, the central bank of the USA, have used interest rates to achieve their policy objectives.

Aggregate demand

The rate of interest affects the economy through its influence on aggregate demand (AD). The higher the rate of interest, the lower the level of aggregate demand. There is a variety of ways in which interest rates affect the AD curve.

Consumer durables Many consumers buy consumer durables such as furniture, kitchen equipment and cars on credit. The higher the rate of interest, the greater the monthly repayments will have to be for any given sum borrowed. Hence, high interest rates lead to lower sales of durable goods and hence lower consumption expenditure.

The housing market Houses too are typically bought using a mortgage. The lower the rate of interest, the lower the mortgage repayments on a given sum borrowed. This makes houses more affordable. It might encourage people to buy their first house or to move house, either trading up to a more expensive house or trading down to a smaller property. There are three ways in which this increases aggregate demand. First, an increase in demand for all types of housing leads to an increase in the number of new houses being built. New housing is classified as investment in national income accounts. Increased investment leads to increased aggregate demand. Second, moving house stimulates the purchase of consumer durables such as furniture, carpets and kitchens. This increases consumption. Third, moving house may release money which can be spent. A person trading down to a cheaper house will see a release of equity tied up in their home. Those trading up may borrow more than they need for the house purchase and this may be used to buy furniture or perhaps even a new car.

Wealth effects A fall in rates of interest may increase asset prices. For instance, falling interest rates may lead to an increase in demand for housing, which in turn pushes up the price of houses. If house prices rise, all homeowners are better off because their houses have increased in value. This may encourage them to increase their spending. Equally, a fall in interest rates will raise the price of government bonds. Governments issue bonds to finance their borrowing. They are sold to individuals, assurance companies, pension funds and others who receive interest on the money they have loaned to government. Like shares, bonds can go up and down in value. Rises in the price of bonds held by individuals or businesses will increase their financial wealth, which again may have a positive impact on consumer expenditure.

Saving Higher interest rates make saving more attractive compared to spending. The higher the interest rate, the greater the reward for deferring spending to the future and reducing spending now. This may lead to a fall in aggregate demand at the present time.

Investment The lower the rate of interest, the more investment projects become profitable. Hence the higher the level of investment and aggregate demand. Equally, a rise in consumption which leads to a rise in income will lead, in turn, to a rise in investment. Firms will need to invest to supply the extra goods and services being demanded by consumers.

The exchange rate A fall in the interest rate is likely to lead to a fall in the value of the domestic currency (its exchange rate). A fall in the value of the pound means that foreigners can now get more pounds for each unit of their currency. However, UK residents have to pay more pounds to get the same number of US dollars or Japanese yen. This in turn means that goods priced in pounds become cheaper for foreigners to buy, whilst foreign goods become more expensive for British firms to buy. Cheaper

Question 1

Retailers are calling for a further cut in interest rates today after a survey showed another month of weak sales. According to the British Retail Consortium (BRC) survey published today, like-for-like sales, excluding the effect of new stores, were running below last year's levels for a fifth consecutive month. Kevin Hawkins, the BRCs director-general, said: 'Any growth came from heavy discounting, which is not sustainable. The underlying position is still weak and unlikely to improve unless and until there are further cuts in interest rates.' His call was echoed by Geoff Cooper, chief executive officer of Travis Perkins, the builders' merchant and owner of Wickes, which reported falling sales yesterday. 'We don't see consumer confidence or the housing market picking up for the rest of the year', he said.

Source: adapted from the *Financial Times*, 6.9.2005.

(a) Why did (i) Kevin Hawkins and (ii) Geoff Cooper want a cut in interest rates?

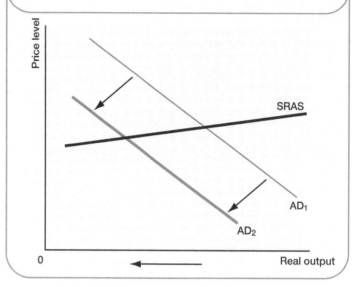

Figure 1 A rise in interest rates

A rise in interest rates shifts the aggregate demand curve left from AD_1 to AD_2. This leads to a fall in the price level.

British goods should lead to higher exports as foreigners take advantage of lower prices. In contrast, more expensive foreign goods should lead to fewer imports as British buyers find foreign goods less price competitive. Greater export levels and fewer imports will boost aggregate demand.

Policy objectives

The government has four key macroeconomic policy objectives - to control inflation and unemployment, to maintain a current account equilibrium and to secure high economic growth. Interest rate policy can affect all of these.

Inflation Interest rate policy today is used mainly to control inflation. Figure 1 shows a shift to the left in the aggregate demand curve caused by a rise in interest rates. This leads to a lower equilibrium price level.

Higher interest rates in practice rarely lead to the falling prices shown in Figure 1. This is because in modern economies aggregate demand tends to increase over time irrespective of government policy. For instance, most workers get pay rises each year, which increases aggregate demand. Profits of companies tend to increase which allows higher dividends to be paid to shareholders. A shift to the right in the aggregate demand curve from AD_1 to AD_2 caused by the annual round of pay rises is shown in Figure 2. This leads to a rise in the price level. If the government then increases interest rates, aggregate demand shifts back to the left to AD_3. Prices are then higher than at the start of the year with AD_1 but are not as high as they would otherwise have been. Interest rates have thus moderated the increase in the price level, i.e. they have moderated the inflation rate.

A loosening of monetary policy by lowering interest rates shifts the aggregate demand curve to the right and leads to a higher equilibrium level of prices. Looser monetary policy tends therefore to be inflationary.

Unemployment Tightening monetary policy by raising interest rates will tend to lead to a fall in equilibrium output, as shown in Figure 1. Lower output is likely to be associated with lower levels of employment and hence unemployment is likely to rise. Loosening monetary policy by allowing interest rates to fall, on the other hand, is likely to lead to lower unemployment.

The long run policy implications could be different, though. According to classical economists, the long run aggregate supply curve is vertical. Changing the level of interest rates will therefore have no impact on either output or unemployment in the long run. In Figure 3, a fall in interest rates pushes the aggregate demand curve to the right but real output remains at 0A. However, there is an increase in the price level. For classical economists, then, any fall in unemployment in the short term caused by a loosening of monetary policy will not be sustained in the long term. Unemployment will revert to its original level.

For Keynesian economists, the impact of loosening monetary policy depends upon how near the economy is to full

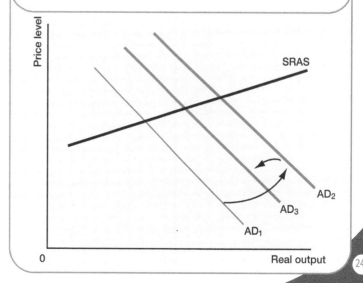

Figure 2 A rise in interest rates with increasing aggregate demand

Aggregate demand tends to increase over time. Raising interest rates moderates the increase. Instead of shifting to AD_2, the aggregate demand curve only shifts to AD_3. Inflation is thus lower than it would otherwise have been.

In its Minutes for August 2005, the Monetary Policy Committee of the Bank of England explained why it had cut interest rates by 0.25 per cent. Part of the reason was a 'gentle labour market loosening since the turn of the year'. The total number of hours worked per week and the employment rate had fallen whilst unemployment had risen a little. Growth in average earnings of workers had 'eased a little since the start of the year'.

Inflation in prices of inputs to the service sector had 'eased'. In contrast, inflation in prices of inputs to the manufacturing sector were running at their highest level since 1986, due mainly to large increases in oil prices. Despite this bad news from manufacturing, price inflation of goods and services produced by both manufacturing and service industries (output inflation) had 'eased further'.

Source: adapted from Bank of England, Monetary Policy Committee Minutes, August 2005.

(a) Explain the links between inflation (as measured by the RPI or CPI) and (i) wage increases; (ii) costs of materials and other inputs to firms.
(b) Why does an easing of wage increases and material cost increases allow the Bank of England to change interest rates?

employment. In Figure 4, the nearer the economy is to 0A, the full employment level of output, the less impact falling interest rates will have on output and unemployment and the more they will have on inflation.

Economic growth Economic growth is a long run phenomenon. Shifting the aggregate demand curve is unlikely to have an impact on the position of the long run supply curve. The only possible link is if lower interest rates encourage investment which in turn increases the capital stock of the economy and its productive potential. Monetary policy can, however, be used to influence booms and recessions. In a boom, tighter monetary policy will reduce aggregate demand and thus lower the

increase in short run output. In a recession, looser monetary policy may increase aggregate demand and hence increase equilibrium output. Some economists argue that severe recessions depress the long run trend rate of growth. Physical and human capital are destroyed and the economy starts its recovery from a lower level than would otherwise be the case. These economists would argue that keeping the output gap low throughout the trade cycle leads to a higher long term growth rate than if the output gap is large in successive cycles. Monetary policy can play a part in keeping the economy near to its long run trend rate of growth.

The current balance In the 1950s and 1960s, the UK government used monetary policy to influence the current balance. Higher interest rates lead to lower aggregate demand. This reduces the amount of imports purchased and hence improves the current account position. On the other hand, higher interest rates should also raise the value of the currency.

The Bank of England yesterday cut official interest rates by 0.25 per cent for the fourth time since September, citing a 'continuous slowdown' in the UK economy. Ciàran Barr, senior UK economist at Deutsche Bank in London, said: 'We feel there is more to come. January's data are expected to be on the soft side, with the killer statistic being the first fall in gross domestic product since the second quarter of 1992.' Kate Barker, the Confederation of British Industry's chief economic adviser, said further rate cuts would be needed to ward off an outright recession. 'With continued weak global trends restraining prices in many sectors, inflation pressure is minimal', Ms Barker said.

Source: adapted from the *Financial Times*, 8.1.1999.

(a) Explain what was happening to the UK economy in late 1998.
(b) How might the 0.25 per cent cut in interest rates have affected (i) output and (ii) inflation?

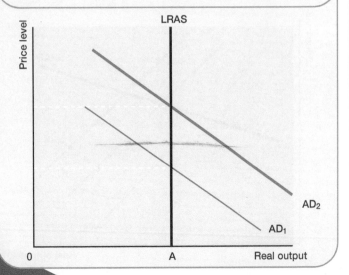

Figure 3 *Interest rates and the classical long run aggregate supply curve*
If the long run aggregate supply curve is vertical, changing interest rates will have no effect on either output or unemployment.

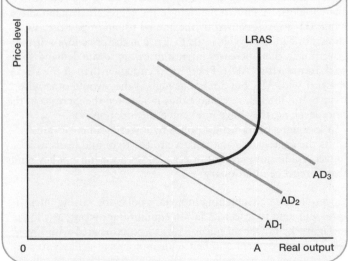

Figure 4 *Interest rates and the Keynesian long run aggregate supply curve*
The nearer to full employment at OA, the less impact a fall in interest rates will have on output and employment and the more on inflation.

Key terms

Bank base rate - the interest rate which a bank sets to determine its borrowing and lending rates. It offers interest rates below its base rate to customers who deposit funds with it, whilst charging interest rates above base rate to borrowers.

Central bank - the financial institution in a country or group of countries typically responsible for the printing and issuing of notes and coins, setting short term interest rates, managing the country's gold and currency reserves and issuing government debt.

Instrument of policy - an economic variable, such as the rate of interest, income tax rates or government spending on education,

which is used to achieve a target of government policy.

Monetary policy - the attempt by government or a central bank to manipulate the money supply, the supply of credit, interest rates or any other monetary variables, to achieve the fulfilment of policy goals such as price stability.

Rate of interest - the price of money, determined by the demand and supply of funds in a money market where there are borrowers and lenders.

Target of policy - an economic goal which the government wishes to achieve, such as low unemployment or high growth.

A higher value of the pound will make it more difficult for UK firms to export and easier for foreign firms to sell imports to the UK. This will lead to a worsening of the current account position. Which effect is the larger varies from economy to economy and depends upon how sensitive imports are to falls in domestic income (i.e. the value of income elasticity of demand for imports). It also depends upon how sensitive exchange rates are to changes in interest rates and the sensitivity of exports and imports to changes in exchange rates (i.e. the values of price elasticity of demand for exports and imports).

Trade offs

The use of monetary policy, like other government policies such as fiscal policy, can have trade offs between objectives.

- A rise in interest rates in the short term might reduce inflation, but, because of the fall in aggregate demand, it might increase unemployment and reduce the rate of growth of GDP. The fall in aggregate demand or spending in the economy is also likely to lead to a fall in imports, spending on foreign goods. Hence a rise in interest rates might lead to an improvement in the current account position in the balance of payments.

- A fall in interest rates has the converse effect. It might reduce unemployment and stimulate growth in GDP. However, it is likely to lead to a rise in the inflation rate and a deterioration in the current account on the balance of payments.

Changes in interest rates can also impact on other government policy objectives.

- Consistently high interest rates may lead to a high value of the exchange rate and low investment. Both of these may damage the economy's international competitiveness.

- Interest rate changes can affect the distribution of income in a variety of ways. For example, higher interest rates should benefit savers at the expense of borrowers. Given that pensioners are significant savers and young workers are significant borrowers, higher interest rates will result in a redistribution of income from young workers to pensioners.

Monetary policy may also conflict with other types of policy. For example, fiscal policy may be expansionary at a time when the Bank of England is tightening monetary policy by raising interest rates. The government may be pursuing supply side policies to raise investment when interest rates are being raised to reduce inflation.

Applied economics

The functions of the central bank in the UK

Since 1997, monetary policy in the UK has been controlled by the Bank of England. This is the CENTRAL BANK of the UK. Central banks tend to have a number of functions.

- They are responsible for the issue of notes and coins. These are sold to the banking system which in turn passes them on to customers as they withdraw cash from their accounts.

- They supervise the financial system, often in conjunction with other bodies specifically set up to regulate distinct parts of the financial system.

- They manage a country's gold and currency reserves. These can be used to influence the level of the exchange rate.

- They act as bankers to the government, usually managing the National Debt of the country. They arrange for the issue of new loans to cover current borrowing by a government.

- They act as bankers to the banking system. Usually, they act as lender of last resort. If a bank gets into short term difficulties, not able to raise enough cash to meet demands from its customers, the central bank will supply cash to the banking system to relieve this liquidity shortage.

Targets and instruments

Although the Bank of England is independent of the UK government, its activities are still broadly controlled by government. With regard to monetary policy, the government sets the Bank a TARGET for inflation which it has to achieve. This target was initially set at maintaining inflation, as measured by the RPIX, within a range of 1 to 4 per cent and subsequently modified to 2.5 per cent plus or minus 1 per cent per annum. Today the target is 2.0 per cent plus or minus 1 per cent as measured by the CPI. The Bank of England, therefore, has not been given any targets concerning the other three main macroeconomic policy objectives of government - unemployment, growth and the current account. These are influenced by other policies such as fiscal policy and supply side policies.

Since the mid-1980s, the Bank of England has chosen the rate of interest as its main INSTRUMENT of monetary policy. Each month, it announces whether or not it will change bank base rates. In the 1950s and 1960s, controls on credit (the borrowing of money) were significant instruments of monetary policy as well. In the 1970s and early 1980s, the emphasis shifted to the control of the money supply, the total stock of money in the economy. However, these proved unsatisfactory in an open economy like the UK, where it was increasingly easy for borrowers to gain access to funds abroad and where there was increasing competition between financial institutions.

Bank base rates

BANK BASE RATE is the rate of interest around which the main UK banks fix their lending and borrowing rates. Customers who lend money (i.e. deposit money) with a bank will get a rate of interest less than the base rate. Customers who borrow money will be charged a rate higher than base rate. The difference or spread between borrowing and lending rates is used by the bank to pay its operating costs and provide it with a profit. Each bank can in theory fix its own base rate. However, competitive pressure means that all banks have the same base rate. If one bank had a higher base rate, it would attract more deposits from other banks but would lose customers who wanted to borrow money. It could easily end up with far too much on deposit and too little being lent out. The reverse would be true if a bank set its base rate below that of other banks.

The Bank of England controls base rates through its day to day provision of money to the banking system. In practice, banks in the UK can't decide to have a different base rate from the rate of interest set by the Bank of England, which is technically called the **repo rate**.

Bank base rates are short term rates of interest. They influence other interest rates in other money markets. For instance, building societies are likely to change their interest rates if bank base rates change. If they don't, they face customers moving their business to banks who might offer more competitive deposit or borrowing rates. However, many customers only use banks or only use building societies. Many would not switch their savings from one to the other if a small difference in interest rates appeared, so sometimes building societies will not change their interest rates if the Bank of England changes bank base rates by, say, one quarter of a per cent. There are many other money markets which are even less linked to bank base rates. Credit card rates, for instance, don't tend to change if bank base rates change by 1 or 2 per cent. Long term interest rates may also not be affected by changes in short term rates of interest. Therefore, the Bank of England only has very imperfect control of all the different money markets in the UK.

Factors affecting the decision to change interest rates

The decision whether to change interest rates in any one month is taken by the Monetary Policy Committee (MPC). This is a group of 9 people. Five are from the Bank of England, including the Governor of the Bank of England. The other four are independent outside experts, mainly professional economists. Inflation is the Bank of England's only target. Therefore, the Monetary Policy Committee considers evidence about whether inflationary pressure is increasing, decreasing or remaining stable at the time. If it believes that inflationary pressure is increasing, it is likely to raise interest rates to reduce aggregate demand. If inflationary pressure is weak, it can cut interest rates to boost aggregate demand and allow unemployment to be reduced and output to increase. In coming to any decision, it looks at a wide range of economic indicators.

For instance, it will consider the rate of increase in average earnings. If wages are rising at a faster rate than before, this could be an indication that labour is becoming scarcer in supply. The same could then also be true of goods and services. Equally, faster rising wages could feed through into higher costs for firms. They would then be forced to pass on these costs to customers and so this would be inflationary.

Another indicator is house prices. If house prices are rising fast, it is an indicator that households have money to spend which could spill over into higher demand for goods and services. Higher house prices also add to household wealth and could encourage them to borrow more, which would increase aggregate demand.

The exchange rate is important too. If the exchange rate is falling, it will make British exports more competitive and imports less competitive. This will increase aggregate demand. A rising exchange rate, on the other hand, will tend to reduce aggregate demand.

The output gap is another significant indicator. This measures the difference between the actual level of output and what economists estimate is the potential level of output of the economy. If all factors of production are fully utilised, any increase in aggregate demand will lead to higher inflation.

Problems facing the Monetary Policy Committee

One of the problems facing the Monetary Policy Committee is that economic data for one month is unreliable. If the statisticians say that average earnings increased 0.564 per cent last month, it is almost certain that this is not totally accurate. Therefore the members of the MPC have to make judgments about how plausible are the statistics presented to them.

Another problem is that economists don't agree about exactly how the economy works. Some economists might attach more importance, for instance, to an increase in wage inflation than others. All economists accept that the real world is so complicated that it is often difficult to capture it and

portray it in economic theories and models. Finally, the data is often contradictory. Some indicators will suggest an increase in inflationary pressures whilst others will show a decrease. It is less common for most of the economic data to be pointing in the same direction. This is especially a problem if the Committee is being successful at controlling inflation over a period of time. Then, the output gap is likely to be around zero, with economic resources fully utilised. It is unlikely that one month's figures will show any clear trend. This is very different from a situation where there is, say, a large negative output gap, showing the economy operating at well below its productive potential and with high unemployment. Then it is likely to be clear that interest rates could be cut without inflation moving above its target level. Equally, if there is a large positive output gap, the situation is unsustainable in the long term and increased inflation is almost inevitable. Then it is clear that interest rates must rise to choke off demand.

DataQuestion — Will the Bank of England cut interest rates today?

The Monetary Policy Committee, meeting today, will have to decide whether to change interest rates. Industry and retailers want to see interest rates cut. They are complaining of a lack of spending in the economy. On the other hand, the Monetary Policy Committee might feel that inflationary pressures are still too strong to justify a cut in interest rates.

Figure 5 Current CPI inflation projection based on interest rates at 5.75 per cent

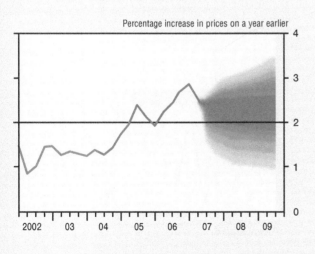

Source: adapted from Bank of England, *Inflation Report*, August 2007.

Figure 6 Bank base rate (%)

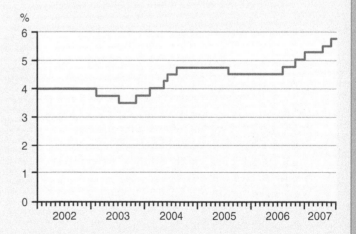

Source: adapted from *Economic & Labour Market Review*, Office for National Statistics.

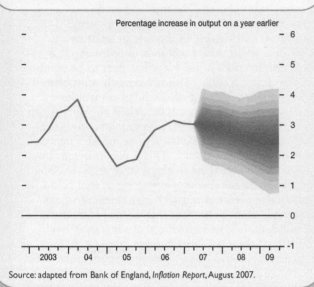

Figure 7 Current projection of real GDP growth based on constant interest rates at 5.75 per cent

Percentage increase in output on a year earlier

Source: adapted from Bank of England, *Inflation Report*, August 2007.

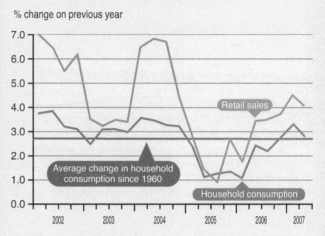

Figure 8 Real household consumption, real retail sales, percentage change on a year earlier

% change on previous year

Retail sales

Average change in household consumption since 1960

Household consumption

Source: adapted from *Economic & Labour Market Review*, Office for National Statistics.

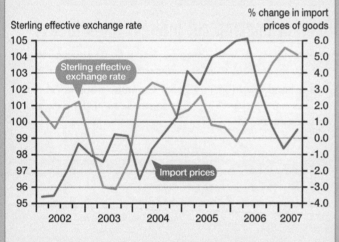

Figure 9 Import prices of goods, percentage change on a year earlier; Sterling effective exchange rate 2000=100

Sterling effective exchange rate

% change in import prices of goods

Sterling effective exchange rate

Import prices

Source: adapted from *Economic & Labour Market Review*, Office for National Statistics.

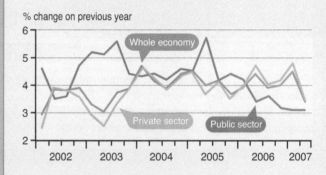

Figure 10 Average earnings growth, including bonuses, percentage change on a year earlier

% change on previous year

Whole economy

Private sector

Public sector

Source: adapted from *Economic & Labour Market Review*, Office for National Statistics.

1. Outline the trends in inflation between 2002 and 2007.
2. Explain the link between changing interest rates and inflation. Illustrate your answer by looking at the period 2002 to 2007 shown in the data.
3. Assess whether the Bank of England should have raised interest rates, cut them or left the same in August 2007.
4. Why might the Monetary Policy Committee find it difficult to decide whether or not to change interest rates in any one month?

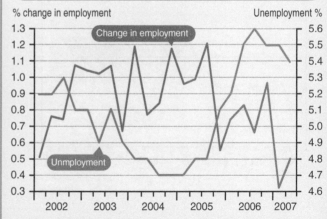

Figure 11 Employment, percentage change on previous year; unemployment rate (ILO), per cent

% change in employment

Unemployment %

Change in employment

Unmployment

Source: adapted from *Economic & Labour Market Review*, Office for National Statistics.

Summary

1. The value of a currency in a floating exchange rate system is determined by the forces of demand and supply.
2. Governments can influence the value of their currency by changing interest rates and by intervening directly on the foreign exchange markets using their gold and foreign currency reserves.
3. A rise in the value of a currency is likely to reduce exports but increase imports. A fall in the value of a currency is likely to increase exports but reduce imports.
4. Raising the exchange rate is likely to benefit inflation but will tend to reduce output, increase unemployment and lead to a deterioration in the current account. A fall in the exchange rate is likely to increase both inflation and output, reduce unemployment and lead to an improvement in the current account.

Exchange rate systems

The value of currencies like the US dollar, the Japanese yen and Britain's currency, the pound sterling, is determined by the foreign currency markets. At any point in time, there are buyers in the market for a currency and there are sellers. The forces of demand and supply then determine the price of the currency.

This system of determining exchange rates is known as a **free or floating exchange rate system**. There have been and still are other types of system. For instance, the value of the pound was fixed against the US dollar between 1946 and 1971. The Bank of England guaranteed to exchange pounds for US dollars at a **fixed exchange rate**. This is an example of a fixed exchange rate system. Before 1914, the world's major currencies were fixed in value in relation to gold. In Europe, before the euro became the official currency of the eurozone, each separate currency was fixed against each other at a specific rate. The value of the French franc could not change against the German deutschmark. Today, the euro itself is allowed to float against other currencies and so its value is determined within a floating exchange rate system.

This unit will consider exchange rate policy within a floating exchange rate system. This is the situation that faces the government in the UK and the European Central Bank which controls the euro today.

Influencing the exchange rate

Exchange rate policy tends to be administered by the **central bank** of a country which controls exchange rates and its gold and foreign currency reserves. It is important to understand that some governments, through their central banks, choose to allow free market forces to determine the exchange rate of their currency. For example, the UK government and Bank of England do not attempt to influence the value of the pound. Other central banks, like the Bank of Japan or the People's Bank of China, have an active policy of manipulating exchange rates. Central banks with an active exchange rate policy can influence the value of their currency in two main ways.

Interest rates Increasing domestic interest rates is likely to increase the value of the currency. This is because higher interest rates in, say, the UK makes depositing money in London more attractive. Savings are attracted into the UK from overseas, whilst UK firms and institutions are less attracted to sending their savings to New York, Tokyo or Paris. Hence the demand

for pounds is likely to increase, shown by a shift to the right in the demand curve for pounds, whilst the supply decreases, shown by a shift to the left in the supply curve. This results in a new higher equilibrium price.

Use of gold and foreign currency reserves Central banks have traditionally kept gold and foreign currency reserves. These are holdings of gold and foreign currencies which can be used to alter the value of a currency. If the Bank of England wanted to increase the value of the pound, it would sell some of its foreign currency reserves in exchange for pounds. This would increase the demand for the pound and hence raise its price. If it wanted to reduce the value of the pound, it would sell pounds for foreign currency, increasing supply and hence reducing the equilibrium price.

The ability of governments to influence the exchange rate is limited when the currency is floating. Almost all flows of money across the foreign exchanges are speculative and don't relate to the purchase of actual exports or imports. These flows of HOT MONEY are generated by individual speculators, hedge funds and banks attempting to make a profit by dealing in foreign exchange. They are so large that a country's foreign currency reserves could be used up within days trying to support a value of the exchange rate which the markets believed was too high. Equally, interest rate differentials between countries have to be substantial to have a significant impact on the value of the currency. Even so, governments can and do intervene to nudge exchange rates in directions which they believe desirable.

How exchange rate movements affect the economy

Exchange rate movements mainly affect the real economy through their effects on exports and imports. A rise or APPRECIATION in the exchange rate will tend to make exports more expensive to foreigners but imports cheaper to domestic customers. A fall or DEPRECIATION in the exchange rate will have the reverse effect, making exports cheaper and imports more expensive.

To understand why, consider a good priced at £100 which is being sold for export to the US by a UK firm. If the exchange rate is £1=$1, the US customer will have to pay $100. If the value of the pound rises to £1=$2, then the US customer will have to pay $200 for it. At the new higher

The pound rose yesterday to its highest level against the dollar since Black Wednesday, the day in September 1992 when the pound was forced out of the Exchange Rate Mechanism. One factor was a report by the Organisation for Economic Co-operation and Development (OECD) which said that the Bank of England would need to increase its interest rates to control inflation. Another factor was reports that Asian central banks have been shifting their foreign exchange rate holdings out of dollars into other currencies such as the pound. Central banks in Japan, China and South Korea in recent years have been selling their own domestic currencies in exchange for US dollars in an attempt to weaken the value of their own currencies.

Source: adapted from the *Financial Times*, 2.12.2004.

(a) Explain why a rise in domestic interest rates by the Bank of England might affect the exchange rate value of the pound.
(b) Explain why the sale of South Korean Won or Japanese Yen by the South Korean and Japanese central banks for US dollars might affect the value of the Won or the Yen.

exchange rate, the US customer has to pay more dollars to acquire the same number of pounds as before.

Similarly, consider a good priced at $100 in the US. If the exchange rate is £1=$1, then it will cost a UK customer £100. If the exchange rate rises to £1=$2, the cost to the UK customer will fall to £50.

A rise in the value of the pound will make UK firms less price competitive internationally. British exporters will find their orders falling as foreign customers switch to other, cheaper sources. In domestic markets, British firms will find that foreign imports are undercutting their prices and gaining market share. Exactly how much EXPORT and IMPORT VOLUMES, the number of goods sold, will change depends upon their price elasticity of demand. If the price elasticity of demand for exports is elastic, with a value of, say, 2, then a 10 per cent rise in the price of exports to foreigners will result in a 20 per cent fall in export volumes.

Firms may, however, adopt a different response to an appreciation or depreciation of the currency. They may choose to keep prices to customers in their currency the same. For instance, with the good priced at £100 which is sold to the USA, the British firm could decide to keep the price at $100 when the exchange rate appreciates from £1=$1 to £1=$2. What this means is that the British exporter would then only receive £50 for the good. The British firm would not lose market share as a result, but it would see its profit margins fall. There are two reasons why an exporter might be prepared to accept a lower price for the product in domestic currency terms. First, it may think that the foreign currency movement is temporary. For marketing reasons, it does not want to be constantly changing its foreign currency price every time there is a small change in the exchange rate. Second, it may have been earning **abnormal profit** previously, a higher level of profit than the minimum needed to keep the firm supplying the good.

If firms keep their prices to customers the same in their currencies, then export and import volumes will remain unchanged. However, profitability will have changed. If a currency appreciates in value, exporters will be forced to cut their prices in their own currency to maintain prices in foreign currencies. Their profitability will decline and

it will become less attractive to export. Export values will fall too because, although volumes have remained the same, prices in domestic currency terms will have fallen. As for imports, foreign firms importing to the UK that choose to keep their sterling prices the same will see their profits rise. This will give them a greater incentive to sell into the UK. They might choose, for instance, to advertise more aggressively. Import volumes are therefore likely to rise, increasing import values as a result.

A third alternative is that firms may choose to change their export and import prices but not by as much as the change in the exchange rate. For instance, assume that the value of the pound rises 10 per cent against the US dollar. A UK exporting firm may choose to absorb 6 per cent of the rise by reducing the pound sterling price by 6 per cent and passing on the remaining 4 per cent by raising the dollar price. Profit margins fall and there could be some loss of market share because US customers now face higher prices. However, this might be better for the firm than either cutting its sterling price by 10 per cent, eating into its profit margins, or raising US dollar prices by 10 per cent and risking losing substantial market share.

Which type of strategy a firm chooses to use to some extent depends upon the industry in which it operates. For commodity products, like steel, wheat or copper, firms are likely to have little control over their market. They will be forced to pass on price rises or falls to customers as exchange rates change. Firms which can control their markets, like car manufacturers, tend to leave prices unaltered as exchange rates change.

The macroeconomic impact of changes in exchange rates

Changes in exchange rates can affect the performance of an economy.

British cheese manufacturers, like most exporters to the USA, are suffering from the recent large rise in the value of the pound against the dollar. It has risen from $1.56 to the pound in November 2002 to $1.79 in December 2003.

Neal's Yard Dairy, a UK seller of high quality cheese, is partially protected because its US customers are less price sensitive than many. Its dollar prices have risen by an average 10 per cent over the past year. 'People go into a shop and spend the same amount on cheese. If the prices have increased, then they buy less', said Jason Hinds, sales manager of Neal's Yard. Exporters of non-niche, commodity cheeses are in for tougher times. Customers buy these purely on price. Stephen Jones, managing director of Summerdale International, a cheese export agency in Taunton, said its global sales could drop from £3m to £2m next year. UK exporters are relieved, though, that they are not in the euro area. The euro has appreciated far more against the US dollar than the pound. Jason Hinds said: 'Our products in the US look cheap compared to cheeses from France or Italy.

Source: adapted from the *Financial Times*, 6.1.2004.

(a) Explain the impact that the rise in the value of the pound against the dollar in 2003 had on UK cheese exporters.
(b) Why might the rise in the value of the euro against the dollar have given British cheese exporters a competitive advantage?

Inflation A rise in the exchange rate is likely to moderate inflation for two reasons. First, a higher exchange rate will tend to lead to a fall in import prices, which then feeds through to lower domestic prices. As explained above, some importers will choose to keep their foreign currency prices the same in order to increase their profit margins. However, other importers will cut their foreign currency prices. The extent to which a rise in the exchange rate leads to a fall in domestic prices depends upon what proportion of importers choose to cut prices.

Second, a higher exchange rate will lead to a fall in aggregate demand. Exports will fall and imports will rise as explained above. The fall in aggregate demand then leads to a fall in inflation. The extent to which aggregate demand falls depends upon the price elasticity of demand for exports and imports.

The higher the price elasticities, the greater will be the change in export and import volumes to changes in prices brought about by the exchange rate movement.

The reverse occurs when there is a depreciation of the exchange rate. Import prices will tend to rise, feeding through to higher domestic inflation. Aggregate demand will rise as exports become more price competitive and imports less price competitive. As a result, inflation will tend to increase.

Economic growth A change in the exchange rate may have an impact on long term growth rates. A higher exchange rate which discourages exports and encourages imports may lead to lower domestic investment, and vice versa for a lower exchange rate. However, the main impact of a changing exchange rate will be felt on short run output. A rise in the exchange rate will dampen output in the short term because exports fall and imports rise, leading to a fall in aggregate demand. A fall in the exchange rate will lead to rising exports and falling imports, raising aggregate demand and thus equilibrium output.

Unemployment A rise in the exchange rate will tend to increase unemployment. This is because an exchange rate rise will tend to lower aggregate demand and thus equilibrium output. A fall in the exchange rate will tend to reduce unemployment. Changes in unemployment will be felt unequally in different sectors of the economy. In those industries which export a significant proportion of output, or where imports are important, there will tend to be larger changes in employment and unemployment as a result of exchange rate changes. In industries, particularly some service industries, where little is exported or imported, changes in the exchange rate will have little effect on employment and unemployment.

The current balance A rise in the exchange rate is likely to lead to a deterioration in the current balance. A rise in the exchange rate will lead to lower exports as they become less price competitive. The volume of imports is likely to rise leading to higher import values. So the current account position (exports minus imports) is likely to deteriorate. On the other hand, a fall in the exchange rate is likely to lead to an improvement in the current balance. Exports are likely to rise, but imports fall.

Question 3

In 2003 and 2004, the Japanese central bank spent an estimated £150bn buying up US dollars with Japanese yen to depress the value of the yen against the dollar. This was part of a much longer period of intervention in foreign currency markets going back to 1991, all designed to lower the yen:US$ exchange rate. The Japanese economy in the early 2000s was in a weak state having spent much of the previous decade either in recession or experiencing low growth. The Japanese central bank wanted to support the recovery of the Japanese economy with a low exchange rate.

However, since March 2004 intervention has stopped. One possible reason is that the Japanese central bank has become concerned about the recent boom in commodity prices. Japan is a major importer of commodities such as oil, having few natural resources itself. The lower the value of the yen, the higher the cost of imported commodities for Japanese manufacturers. Imported inflation poses a threat both to the competitiveness and profitability of Japanese companies and to the economy as a whole.

Figure 1 *Japan, annual percentage growth in export volumes and GDP; $ oil prices and $ index of all other primary commodities*

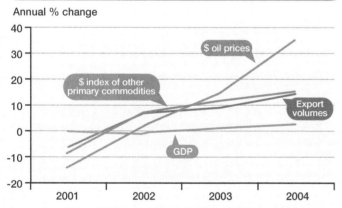

Annual % change

Source: adapted from OECD, *Economic Outlook*; *The Times*, 29.3.2004; www.dailyfx.com, May 2005.

(a) Explain how Japan's central bank used its intervention in foreign currency markets as an instrument of policy to improve the performance of the Japanese economy.
(b) Using Figure 1, discuss the extent to which this intervention was successful in achieving its aims.

Key terms

Appreciation or depreciation of a currency - a rise or fall in the value of a currency when the currency is floating and market forces determine its value.
Export and import volumes - the number of exports and imports. In statistics, they are usually expressed in index number form. They can be calculated by dividing the value of total exports or imports by their average price.
Hot money - short term, speculative flows of money across foreign exchanges, made in order to make a profit on the difference between the buying and selling price of the currency.

Applied economics

UK government policy

Since September 1992, the UK government has chosen not to use the exchange rate as an instrument of policy. Instead, it has allowed the pound to float freely on the foreign exchange markets. So it has not used either interest rates or its foreign currency reserves to affect the price of sterling.

This policy has been very much influenced by the experience during the period 1990-92. In 1990, the Conservative government with John Major as Chancellor of the Exchequer decided to join the Exchange Rate Mechanism (ERM) of the European Monetary Union (EMU). This was a mechanism designed to stabilise the value of European exchange rates prior to the creation of a single currency, the euro. Any single ERM currency was fixed in value against other currencies within the ERM within a band. For instance, the French franc was fixed against the German deutschmark within a 2.5 per cent band. So the French franc could appreciate or depreciate in value against the deutschmark but within very narrow limits.

The British government's main economic concern since 1988 had been combating inflation, which had risen from 4 per cent in 1987 to 10 per cent in 1990. It decided to enter the ERM at a high value for the pound. This put pressure on import prices and prevented a future fall in the exchange rate from reigniting inflation. Between 1990 and September 1992, it used its foreign currency reserves to keep the value of the pound within its band against other European currencies. More importantly, it was forced

to keep interest rates high. By 1991, inflation was falling rapidly but the economy was in a deep recession. The government wanted to ease monetary policy by cutting interest rates, but was prevented from cutting them as much as they wanted because high interest rates were needed to keep the value of the pound high. In September 1992, the pound came under fierce selling pressure. Despite the government using an estimated £30 billion in foreign currency reserves buying up pounds to keep its value within its band, speculation continued against the pound. On Black Wednesday, September 15, the government was forced to abandon its membership of the ERM. The pound rapidly fell 15 per cent in value.

This illustrates the problem that governments face when attempting to defend a value for the currency. Speculative flows of money are so large that it can be difficult for a government to prevent the markets from driving the currency up or down in value.

Since 1992, the UK government has chosen not to defend any particular value of the pound. However, the United Kingdom periodically reviews whether or not to join the single European currency. If it does join, it will have to peg the pound against the euro and it, together with the European Central Bank, will have to defend that value for a period of time. Under current arrangements the pound would eventually be abolished and the euro would become the UK's currency. Once the pound has disappeared, exchange rate policy will no longer be the responsibility of the UK government. It will pass to the European Central Bank.

DataQuestion

The value of the pound

In October 1990, the British government fixed the value of the pound against a basket of European currencies which would eventually become the euro. It fixed the pound at a deliberately high value because it wanted to reduce inflation within the economy. The high value of the pound meant that exports became less competitive whilst imports became more competitive. However, less than two years later, in September 1992, the government was forced to take the UK out of the Exchange Rate Mechanism (ERM). Free market forces now determined the value of the pound, pushing it quickly down by over 15 per cent.

In 1996, free market forces pushed up the average value of the pound again, and it eventually reached a high in

2000. The 30 per cent rise from its low in 1996 to its high in 2000 severely limited export growth, whilst imports rose substantially. The value of the pound then eased from its 2000 high.

These movements of the effective exchange rate, the average value of the pound against other currencies, masked individual movements. For example, whilst the average value of the pound fell between 2000 and 2003, the value of the pound against the dollar rose significantly. This meant that whilst UK exporters in general benefited from currency movements over this period, UK exporters to the US suffered.

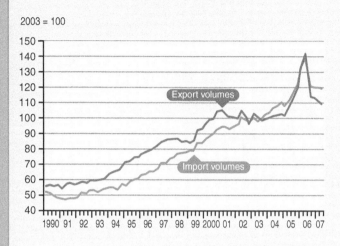

Figure 2 Export and import volumes, trade in goods, seasonally adjusted, 2003=100

2003 = 100

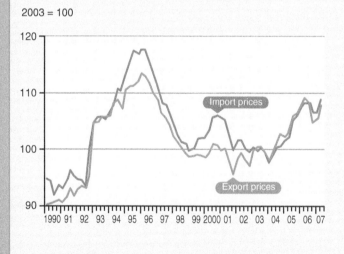

Figure 3 Export and import prices, trade in goods, not seasonally adjusted, 2003=100

2003 = 100

Source: adapted from *Economic & Labour Market Review,* Office for National Statistics.

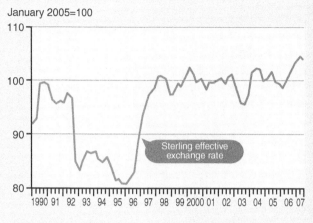

Figure 4 Selected exchange rates

January 2005=100

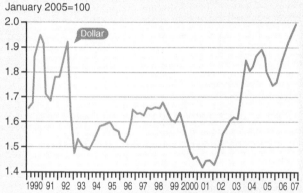

January 2005=100

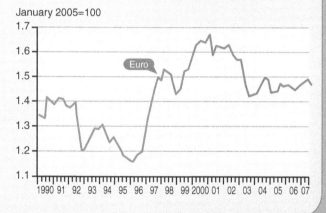

January 2005=100

1. Using the data in Figure 4, describe briefly what happened to the value of the pound between 1990 and 2007. Support your description with statistics.
2. Explain how the fall in the effective exchange rate of the pound between 1992 and 1996 might have affected (a) export and import volumes; (b) average export and import prices; (c) the profitability of UK exporting firms.
3. What impact on the economic performance of the UK might the fall in the value of the pound against the euro have had between 2000 and 2007?

37 Free market and mixed economies IB I

Summary

1. The function of any economic system is to resolve the basic economic problem.
2. In a free market economy, resources are allocated through the spending decisions of millions of different consumers and producers.
3. Resource allocation occurs through the market mechanism. The market determines what is to be produced, how it is to be produced and for whom production is to take place.
4. Government must exist to supply public goods, maintain a sound currency, provide a legal framework within which markets can operate, and prevent the creation of monopolies in markets.
5. Free markets necessarily involve inequalities in society because incentives are needed to make markets work.
6. Free markets provide choice and there are incentives to innovate and for economies to grow.
7. In a mixed economy, a significant amount of resources are allocated both by government through the planning mechanism, and by the private sector through the market mechanism.
8. The degree of mixing is a controversial issue. Some economists believe that too much government spending reduces incentives and lowers economic growth, whilst others argue that governments must prevent large inequalities arising in society and that high taxation does not necessarily lead to low growth.

Economic systems

The function of an economy is to resolve the basic **economic problem** - resources are scarce but wants are infinite. Resources therefore need to be allocated. This allocation has three dimensions:

- **what** is to be produced;
- **how** is it to be produced;
- **for whom** it is to be produced.

An ECONOMIC SYSTEM is a complex network of individuals, organisations and institutions and their social and legal interrelationships. The function of an economic system is to resolve the basic economic problem. Within an economic system there will be various 'actors'.

- Individuals. They are consumers and producers. They may own factors of production which they supply for production purposes.
- Groups. Firms, trade unions, political parties, families and charities are just some of the groups which might exist in an economic system.
- Government. Government might range from a group of elders in a village, to a local authority, to a national or international parliament. One key role of government is to exercise power. It establishes or influences the relationships between groups, for instance through the passing of laws.

Relationships between groups can be regulated by law. In many cases, however, they are regulated by custom - traditional ways of organisation which are accepted by participants within the economic system.

Free market economies

A FREE MARKET ECONOMY (also called a FREE ENTERPRISE ECONOMY or a CAPITALIST ECONOMY or a MARKET ECONOMY) is an economic system which resolves the basic economic problem mainly through the market mechanism. There is a number of key characteristics of the system.

The main actors The four main types of actors within the system are consumers, producers, owners of private property (land and capital) and government.

Motivation In a pure free market economy, consumers, producers and property owners are assumed to be motivated by pure self-interest. Their decisions are based upon private gain. Consumers aim to maximise their individual welfare or utility. Producers aim to maximise profit. The owners of the factors of production aim to maximise their wages, rents, interest and profits.

Government on the other hand is assumed to be motivated by considerations of the good of the community and not by self-interest. It seeks to maximise social welfare.

Private ownership Nearly all factors of production within the economy are owned mainly by private individuals and organisations. Government has a duty to uphold the rights of citizens to own property. This it does mainly through the legal system.

Free enterprise Owners of the factors of production as well as producers of goods and services have the right to buy and sell what they own through the market mechanism. Government places few limits on what can be bought and sold. Workers can work for whom they want. Homeowners can sell their houses if they so wish. People are free to set up their own businesses. Consumers are free to use their money to buy whatever is offered for sale. Producers are free to sell whatever they wish to sell.

Competition Competition will exist if economic units are free to allocate their resources as they wish. Producers will have to compete for the spending 'votes' of consumers. Workers will have to compete for the spending 'votes' of their employers. Those wishing to borrow money will have to compete with everyone else who wishes to borrow.

Decentralised decision making Because individual economic agents are free to choose how they wish to allocate resources, decision making within a market economy is decentralised.

Bargain hunters were out in force yesterday as a growing number of retailers opened their doors on Boxing Day, heralding the start of the sales season. At Selfridges in Oxford Street, the store rang up 5 000 transactions between 9.00 a.m. and 10. a.m., with designer handbags being the first five items rung through the tills.

Germans are flocking to have their loved ones cremated in the Czech Republic. Hearses from as far away as Berlin are carrying German corpses over the border where cremation services are offered for less than a third of German prices.

Novartis, the Swiss drug company, has developed Coartem, the first artemisinin combination therapy (ACT) to tackle malaria. ACTs are the most effective treatment for the disease. Sales of Coartem are low, though, because at $2.50 per adult treatment, it is still 10-20 times more expensive than other malaria drugs.

Source: adapted from the *Financial Times*, 27.12.2005.

(a) Explain, using the data to illustrate your answer, how resources are allocated in a market economy.

There is no single body which allocates resources within the economy. Rather, the allocation of resources is the result of countless decisions by individual economic agents. This is Adam Smith's **invisible hand** of the market. He argued that although economic actors pursued their own self interest, the result would be an allocation of resources in the economy which would be in the interests of society as a whole.

The market mechanism

Any type of economic system must be capable of allocating resources. In particular, it must be able to provide a mechanism for deciding **what, how** and **for whom** production will take place. How are resources allocated under a market mechanism?

What is to be produced? In a pure free market, it is the consumer which determines the allocation of resources. Consumers are **sovereign**. Each consumer has a certain amount of money to spend and each £1 is like a spending vote. Consumers cast their spending votes when they purchase goods and services. Firms receive these spending votes and this in turn enables them to buy the factors of production needed to produce goods and services. How firms cast their spending votes on

factors of production in turn will determine how much income each individual consumer has to spend. What happens if consumers want to change the composition of the bundle of goods that they are currently buying? Say, for instance, they decide they want to buy more clothes but buy fewer package holidays. The increase in demand for clothes initially will increase the price of clothes. Clothing manufacturers will consequently earn abnormal profit, profit over and above what is normal in the industry. They will respond to this by increasing production of clothes. New firms too will set themselves up, attracted by the high profit levels. Supply will thus expand as will the degree of competition in the industry. This will force down prices to a level where clothing manufacturers are making a high enough profit to stop some going out of business, but a low enough profit to prevent new suppliers from being attracted into the industry. In the package holiday business, the fall in demand will result in a price war. Profitability will fall. Some firms may even make losses. As a result, firms will scale back the number of holidays offered and some firms may even go bankrupt. This will continue until package holiday firms once again can earn a sufficiently high level of profit to prevent firms leaving the industry.

Changes in the goods market will then be reflected in the factor markets. Demand for workers, buildings, machines, raw materials etc. will rise in the clothing industry, but fall in the package holiday industry. There will thus be a transfer of resources from one industry to the other.

Notice the key role of profits in this mechanism. Profits act as a signal for what is to be produced. If firms are earning abnormal profits, it is a signal that consumers wish to buy more of a product. If firms are earning insufficient profits or even losses, it must be a signal that consumers wish to see a fall in production in that industry.

How is it to be produced? Producers are in competition with each other. All other things being equal, consumers will buy from the producer which offers the lowest price. So producers must produce at lowest cost if they are to survive in the market place. This then determines how goods are produced. Firms will adopt the lowest cost technique of production. Hence, free markets result in **productive efficiency**.

For whom? Consumers spend money. The amount of money they can spend is determined by their wealth and by their income. In a free market economy, this is determined by ownership of the factors of production. Workers receive income from sale of their labour, owners of land receive rents, etc. Those with high incomes and wealth are therefore able to buy large amounts of goods and services. Those with low incomes and little wealth can only buy a few goods and services. In a market economy, the wealthy gain a disproportionate share of what is produced. The poor receive relatively little.

The role of government in a free market economy

Government has a number of key roles in a free market economy.
- Some goods will not be provided by the market mechanism. Examples are defence, the judiciary and the police force. These are known as **public goods**. The government therefore has to provide these

and raise taxes to pay for them.

- The government is responsible for the issue of money and for the maintenance of its value. In a market economy, the government has a duty to maintain stable prices.

- The government needs to ensure an adequate legal framework for the allocation and enforcement of property rights. It is pointless having a system based upon individual self-interest if citizens are unable to defend what they have gained. For instance, owners of private property need to be protected from the possibility of theft. There need to be laws about contracts of purchase and sale. It must be illegal willfully to destroy other people's property.

- It is equally important that property rights of any value are allocated to an economic unit in society. If they are not, they will treated as a **free good** (a good unlimited in supply) and over-consumed. The atmosphere is one example of an economic resource which in the past has been owned by no one. Producers and consumers have polluted the atmosphere. This would not be important if it weren't for the fact that we now recognise that such pollution can have an adverse impact upon economic units. At worst, it is predicted that the greenhouse effect and the destruction of the ozone layer will wipe out most life on this planet. Contrast this with the care that people show with their own private property.

- Markets may malfunction for other reasons. In particular, firms or trade unions may seek to gain control over individual markets. Governments therefore need to have powers to break up monopolies, prevent practices which restrict free trade and control the activities of trade unions.

The role of government is vital in a market economy. Without government, there would be anarchy. However, in a free market economy, the presumption is that government should intervene as little as possible. Government regulation should be the minimum necessary to secure the orderly working of the market economy. Government spending should be confined to the provision of public goods.

An evaluation of free market economies

Choice In a rich free enterprise economy, consumers will be faced with a wide range of choice. Firms will compete with each other either on price if a good is homogeneous, or on a wider range of factors such as quality if the good is non-homogeneous. However, choice is not available to all. Those with high incomes will have a great deal of choice. Those on low incomes will have little. It matters little to low income families, for instance, if there are 100 types of luxury car on the market, or if it is possible to take cruises on even more luxurious liners. In a planned economy, consumers may find it impossible to spend all their income because goods which are priced within the reach of everyone are not in the shops. In a free enterprise economy, there may be plenty of goods in the shops, but they may be out of the price range of the poorest in society.

Quality and innovation One advantage claimed of a free market economy is that there are strong incentives built into the system to innovate and produce high quality goods. Companies which fail to do both are likely to be

In 1993, Nigel Lawson, a former Chancellor of the Exchequer, gave a speech at the British Association's annual conference. In the speech, he said: 'Throughout the western world ... capitalism has appeared to be in the ascendant and socialism in retreat.' One reason for this was that: 'the rational decisions needed to make a modern economy even halfway efficient can be taken only by a multiplicity of decision-makers armed with the knowledge provided by a myriad of market prices.' A key characteristic of the system is self interest. 'A regard for one's self-interest is a prominent feature in the make-up of almost all mankind. It is not the only feature, but it is a uniquely powerful one. The characteristic of market capitalism is not that it alone is based on the idea of channelling self-interest for the greater good - not that there is anything wrong with that. It is rather that it is a unique mechanism for doing so directly, with the least interposition of government.'

Capitalism also possesses key moral features. 'The family, which looms large in the scheme of market capitalism, is not only the foundation of a stable society, but an important bulwark against tyranny - as is of course the institution of private property, the more widely spread the better. Another key feature of market capitalism is the private sector, non-monopolistic firm. Capitalism is sometimes portrayed as an unattractive competitive jungle, where the values of co-operation are lost in a free-for-all. What this overlooks is that the private sector firm itself provides a model of effective co-operation.'

As for inequality, 'absolute equality, even in the sense in which it is theoretically attainable, must of necessity lead to misery. If there is to be no greater reward for work or saving or effort of any kind than is meted out to those who decline to work or save or make any effort, then remarkably little work, saving or effort will be undertaken. If two people are working at the same job, with equal skill, and one chooses to work overtime while the other does not, failure to pay the former more would be seen as not merely self-defeating but grossly inequitable.' Government has an important role to play here. 'Just as the sensible successful businessman who seeks to help those less fortunate will do so not by changing the way he runs his business but by applying part of his personal wealth to philanthropy, so the wise government will best help the poor not by interfering with the market but by creating a well-designed social security safety net alongside it.'

(a) Identify from the passage the main characteristics of a market economy.
(b) Why, according to Nigel Lawson, does the pursuit of self interest and the existence of inequality in society lead to greater efficiency in the economy?

driven out of business by more efficient firms. However, this assumes that there is consumer sovereignty in the market. In practice, markets tend to be oligopolistic in structure, dominated by a few large producers which manipulate the market through advertising and other forms of marketing in order to exploit the consumer. So whilst choice and innovation are greater than under planned systems, the advantages of free market economies may not be as great as it might at first seem.

Economic growth In a free market economy, there may be considerable dynamism. However, some free market economies have grown at a considerably faster rate than other free market economies. Many mixed economies too have grown at comparable if not higher rates to the USA. So free markets are not necessarily the key to high economic growth.

Distribution of income and wealth In a pure free market economy, resources are allocated to those with spending power. Individuals with no source of income can pay the ultimate penalty for their economic failure - they die, perhaps from starvation or cold or disease. This fear of economic failure and its price is a major incentive within the free market system for people to take jobs, however poorly paid. One problem with this mechanism is that there are many groups in society who are likely to have little or no income through no fault of their own. The handicapped, orphaned or abandoned children and old people are examples. Free market economists point out that there is a mechanism by which such people can find support - charity. Individuals who earn money can give freely to charities which then provide for the needs of the least well off in society, or individuals can look after their aged relatives, their neighbours and their children within the local neighbourhood community. In practice, it is unlikely that individuals would give enough to charities, or that the better off would provide accommodation for tramps in their homes to fulfil this role. In a free market economy, there is no link whatsoever between need and the allocation of resources. The unemployed can starve, the sick can die for lack of medical treatment, and the homeless can freeze to death on the streets. Income is allocated to those with wealth, whether it is physical, financial or human wealth.

Risk Individuals take great care to reduce the economic risk which lies at the heart of any free market economy. They can overcome the problem of risk by insuring themselves. They take out health insurance. They buy life insurance contracts which pay out to dependants if they should die. Unemployment and sickness can also be insured against. To cope with the problem of old age, individuals ensure that they have pension contracts. However, only a percentage of the population have enough foresight or the income to insure themselves adequately. This then means that many in a free market economy become poor, perhaps unable to support themselves, or die through lack of medical attention.

Planned economies

In a free market economy, economic decision making is decentralised. Millions of economic agents individually make decisions about how resources are allocated. In contrast, in a COMMAND ECONOMY (or PLANNED ECONOMY or CENTRALLY PLANNED ECONOMY) resources are allocated

by government through a planning process. In a pure planned economy, every item is allocated through rationing from education and health to clothes and food. For example, individuals may be allocated a flat in which to dwell, a school to which to send their children and a bread ration which has to be collected from their local bread store. Workers are told where to work by the state and planners decide how production is to take place. In practice, there are always parts of the economy which are not rigidly controlled in this way. Equally, black markets where goods and services are traded illegally are a feature of all planned economies.

The first command economy was created in the Soviet Union (the Soviet Union was dissolved in 1990 to form Russia and a number of other countries such as the Ukraine) in the 1920s and 1930s. China and countries in Eastern Europe became command economies in the 1950s. A number of Third World countries such as Vietnam and Cuba also adopted planning models. Today there are relatively few command economies. North Korea and Cuba are two remaining examples.

Most former planned economies transformed themselves into mixed economies in the 1990s and early 2000s. This is because it became clear that planned economies were performing far less well than other types of economy. Incomes over time were rising less fast in planned economies. Citizens also resented the lack of freedom which is part of any planned economy.

Mixed economies

A MIXED ECONOMY, as the name implies, is a mixture of a planned economy and a free enterprise economy. In practice, no **pure** planned economies or free enterprise economies exist in the

---

Question 3

There are signs of change in communist North Korea. In the capital, Pyongyang, some women are sporting fake Burberry check coats and carrying handbags bearing Ralph Lauren's Polo logo. Sofas are sold on street corners for about $80, about 40 months average salary. Even in the countryside, there are signs of trade. Women sit with drinks and snacks laid out on cardboard boxes, whilst a shoe repairman lounges in the sun. In 2002, the regime introduced economic reforms which liberalised some prices and wages.

However, the reforms have mainly been stifled by the regime's desire to control information and economic independence. In 2005, the government reinstituted the public distribution system for staple foods. With famine never very far away, and the country reliant upon foreign food aid, Pyongyang residents are lucky to receive all their rations. However the rations don't just consist of rice alone. When food is short, heavier foods such as corn and potatoes make up the weight. Food is also available on the black market for those who can afford to pay. In the provinces people receive only 50 to 70 per cent of their rations. However they, unlike city dwellers, have more opportunities to make up the short fall by growing their own food in private gardens.

Source: adapted from the *Financial Times*, 18.4.2007.

(a) Explain the link between 'food rations' and a centrally planned economy like North Korea.
(b) Why does the existence of black markets in North Korea suggest that the planning system is not working effectively?

world. What we call free enterprise economies are economies where most resources are allocated by the market mechanism. What are called planned economies are economies where most resources are allocated by the planning process. Mixed economies are economies where the balance between allocation by the market mechanism and allocation by the planning process is much more equal.

Characteristics of mixed economies

A mixed economy possesses a number of characteristics.

The main actors The four main types of actor within the system are consumers, producers, factor owners and government.

Motivation In the private sector of the economy, consumers, producers and factor owners are assumed to be motivated by pure self-interest. The public sector, however, is motivated by considerations of the 'good' of the community.

Ownership The factors of production are partly owned by private individuals and organisations, but the state also owns a significant proportion.

Competition In the private sector of the economy there is competition. In the state sector, however, resources will be allocated through the planning mechanism. This implies that consumers are offered a choice of goods and services within the private sector of the economy but little or no choice within the public sector.

Government Government has a number of important functions. One is to regulate the economic activities of the private sector of the economy. It needs, for instance, to ensure that competition exists and that property laws are upheld. Another function is to provide not just public goods but also **merit goods**, like education and health care. These may be provided directly by the state, or provision may be contracted out to private firms but still paid for out of tax revenues. The state may also choose to own key sectors of the economy, such as the railways, postal services and electricity industries. Many of these will be **natural monopolies**.

The degree of mixing

There is considerable controversy about the degree of mixing that should take place in a mixed economy. In 2007, 54.1 per cent of GDP was accounted for by public spending in Sweden compared to 44.7 per cent in Germany, 44.9 per cent in the UK and 36.9 per cent in the free market economy of the USA.

In Sweden, there is much greater government spending per capita than, say, in the USA. This means that in Sweden compared to the USA all citizens have access to medical care free at the point of consumption, there are generous state pensions, automatic retraining for those made unemployed and free child care for all working mothers. However, there is a cost. Taxes in Sweden are much higher than in the USA. The fundamental issues concern the following.
- To what extent should the state ensure that all its citizens enjoy a minimum standard of living? For instance, should the

state provide insurance for those who become unemployed? Should it in effect guarantee them a job by training longer term unemployed workers until they succeed in obtaining work? Do citizens have a right to free medical care?
- To what extent should there be inequalities in society? The degree of inequality in an economy like Sweden is far less than in the USA. Inequality in the UK increased in the 1980s as both taxes and government spending were cut as a proportion of GDP. Inequality decreased when this trend was reversed in the 1990s and 2000s.
- To what extent should citizens be free to choose how to spend their money? In Sweden, the effective tax burden is approximately 55 per cent, leaving little more than 45 per cent of income for individuals and companies to choose how to spend. In Sweden, free child care for mothers is provided whether an individual wants it or not.
- To what extent are incentives needed to ensure continued high growth? Until the late 1980s, the top rate of income tax in Sweden was 72 per cent, with the ordinary worker paying between 40 and 50 per cent. Tax reforms in the late 1980s switched the burden of tax from income tax, reducing it to 30 per cent for 85 per cent of workers, but extending the 30 per cent VAT rate to a much wider range of goods and services. The top marginal rate of income tax at 60 per cent in 2007 was still much higher, though, than the 35 per cent in the USA. Supply side economists would argue that higher rates of tax discourage incentives to work and take risks and that this will lead to lower economic growth.
- To what extent is government an efficient provider of goods and services compared to the private sector?

Mixed economies can be judged on the above issues. They could also be evaluated according to their environmental impact. Mixed economies have a better record on the environment than command economies or, arguably, most free market economies. Indeed, the Scandinavian mixed economies are in the forefront of implementing measures to protect the environment from industrial activity.

Key terms

Command or planned economy - an economic system where government, through a planning process, allocates resources in society.
Economic system - a complex network of individuals, organisations and institutions and their social and legal interrelationships.
Free market economy, or free enterprise economy or capitalist economy or market economy - an economic system which resolves the basic economic problem through the market mechanism.
Mixed economy - an economy where both the free market mechanism and the government planning process allocate significant proportions of total resources.

Applied economics

The UK - a free market economy?

In 1979, before the radical government of Margaret Thatcher took power, the UK was quite clearly a mixed economy. Many of the leading industries in the country, such as gas, electricity, telecommunications and the railways were in state control. The government was spending about 45 per cent of the country's income, a very similar proportion to other mixed economies such as France and West Germany. Education and health were both provided by the state along with a wide variety of services from libraries to parks to roads. There was widespread control of the labour market, with minimum wages in many industries and conditions of employment of workers regulated by law.

The changes implemented in the 1980s transformed the shape of the UK economy. The privatisation programme led to large amounts of state assets being sold off to the private sector. The list was long but included car companies (the Rover Group and Jaguar), steel firms (British Steel), energy companies (British Petroleum, British Gas, the electricity companies, British Coal), water companies (the water boards) and telecommunications (BT). The role of the state was cut as public spending programmes axed services. Where the government felt that it could not privatise the service, it attempted to introduce competition into the public sector. For instance, private firms were encouraged to bid for public sector contracts. In the health service, a competitive internal market was established.

Moreover, a wide range of reforms was instituted to reduce regulation and imperfections in markets. In the labour market, trade unions lost the power to act as monopoly suppliers of labour. Rules and regulations in various financial markets were removed to encourage greater competition. In the bus industry, firms were allowed to compete freely on national and local routes.

The spirit of 'Thatcherism' was to release the energies of entrepreneurs in society, to encourage people to work hard and take risks. The successful had to be rewarded and hence marginal rates of income tax were cut, particularly for high earners. On the other hand, those who avoided work should be penalised and hence benefits such as unemployment benefit were cut. The result was an increase in inequality in society.

Arguably, the aim of the Thatcher revolution was to transform the UK's mixed economy into a free market economy. The reforms were not deep enough to achieve this. Health, for instance, continued to be provided by the state unlike, say, in the USA. Welfare benefits were also much more generous than in the USA. On the other hand, a divide had been created

between the 'social model' welfare states of Continental Europe and the 'Anglo-Saxon' model of the UK which was becoming more like that of the USA.

When a Labour government was elected in 1997, it stated that it did not intend to raise the proportion of national income spent by the state in the long term. Government spending was tightly controlled with the result that large budget surpluses emerged. However, the government had already stated that improving education was a priority which necessitated increases in spending. It also came under increasing pressure from the electorate to improve the National Health Service. In 2000, the government announced that it would raise its health spending as a percentage of GDP to the average for the EU by 2008. This meant taking spending on health from 6.8 per cent of GDP in 2000 (of which 1 per cent was spending on private health care) to a possible 8 or 9 per cent by 2008.

Large increases in spending on health and education have, in part, helped push up government spending as a percentage of GDP from a low of 37.5 per cent in 2000 to an estimated 45 per cent in 2008, as can be seen in Figure 1. (Note that the percentages in Figure 1 are ones calculated by the OECD, the international forecasting organisation, and that the UK government calculates its government spending as a percentage of GDP in a different way which gives a different outcome). This was still below the eurozone average but considerably above that of the USA. As such, the UK remains a mixed economy with far more similarities to other EU mixed economies than to the more free market USA.

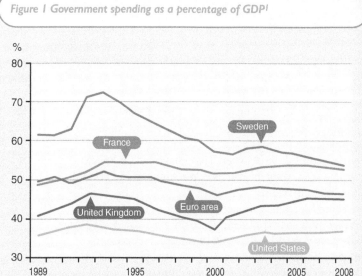

Figure 1 Government spending as a percentage of GDP[1]

1 Figures for 2007 and 2008 were estimates.
Source: adapted from OECD, Economic Outlook.

DataQuestion

The US economy

Table I Income distribution and purchasing power parity estimates of GNP

	Date of estimate of income distribution	% share of national income							PPP estimates of GNP per capita US$, 2006
		Lowest 10%	Lowest 20%	Second quintile	Third quintile	Fourth quintile	Highest 20%	Highest 10%	
United States	2000	1.9	5.4	10.7	15.7	22.4	45.8	29.9	44 260
UK	1999	2.1	6.1	11.4	16.0	22.5	44.0	28.5	35 580
Germany	2000	2.8	8.5	13.7	17.8	23.1	36.9	22.1	31 830
France	1995	3.2	7.2	12.6	17.2	22.8	40.2	25.1	33 740
Sweden	2000	3.6	9.1	14.0	17.6	22.7	36.6	22.2	35 070

Source: adapted from the World Bank, *World Development Indicators*.

Face of America that destroys its Land of Free myth

Until a year ago, my image of the United States was of a wealthy, classless, melting-pot society whose values were embodied in the tough, free-thinking rebel usually portrayed by John Wayne. That image took a knock during seven days in Arkansas last summer and crumbled this week in Texas.

There is certainly money. In Houston, mirror-glass skyscrapers soar confidently over immaculate parks. In its fabulously wealthy River Oaks suburb, colonnaded million-dollar mansions exceed the dreams of avarice. However, look again and you see another face of America. Shacks and shanty settlements strung out along the highways. Second-hand cars at a half or even a third

of British prices. Wal-Mart supermarkets where a pair of jeans costs a fiver.

At first, it strikes you as a land of bargains. Then you talk to ordinary Americans and realise that the prices match the wages and the wages, in many cases, are desperately low. One of our coach drivers earned a wretched £4 500 a year - below the official poverty level. The average American family of four earns barely £10 000 and to reach that level, both partners invariably work. In the Land of the Free there is no free lunch. If you can work, you do.

If that sounds fine in theory, what it means in practice is that both our coach drivers in Houston were women, one middle-aged, the other well into her 60s. It means that a woman hotel executive I met in Brownsville returned to work two weeks after giving birth and thought her employers generous for paying her salary during her absence. It means that employees accept two weeks' annual holiday as the norm. It means that a word like 'welfare' which has a friendly, benevolent ring to European ears, is regarded in the States as the work of the devil. Welfare and free health care would sap the American spirit, so the story goes.

The education system is a problem too for Americans. America has recognised the appalling state of its educational system and is making much of its latest drive to improve schools and recruit better teachers. However, there is little talk of producing educated people for their own sake. The motivation, as always, is hard cash and the need to be more competitive against the better-educated Japanese and Europeans. The campaign for better schools seems to overlook the most important

Table 2 Annual average real growth of GDP

						Annual growth in real GDP, %	
	Canada	UK	USA	France	Japan	Germany	Italy
1960-2007	3.8	2.5	3.0	3.1	4.9	2.7	3.1
1960-67	5.5	3.0	4.5	5.4	10.2	4.1	5.7
1968-73	5.4	3.4	3.2	5.5	8.7	4.9	4.5
1974-79	4.2	1.5	2.4	2.8	3.6	2.3	3.7
1980-89	3.1	2.4	2.5	2.2	4.0	1.8	2.4
1990-99	2.4	2.1	3.0	1.7	1.7	2.2	1.5
2000-07	2.9	2.7	2.6	1.9	1.8	1.6	1.4

Source: adapted from OECD, *Historical Statistics, Economic Outlook.*

They call it the Land of the Free yet small-town sheriffs and corporate bosses hold powers that feudal lords would have envied. They boast their classlessness yet have created a society far more formal and unmixed than our own. And they still foster the belief that any backwoods kid can make it to president, blithely ignoring the fact that every president in living memory has been very wealthy indeed. You can still make your way to the top in America but it means climbing over rather more backs than Britons might find comfortable.

The woman hotel executive in Brownsville epitomised the thrusting, go-getting face that America likes to project. Back at work a fortnight after childbirth and every inch the liberated ambitious female. How does she do it? Simple. She has a live-in Mexican maid on £25 a week and God knows how she looks her in the eyes on pay day.

Source: *Express and Star.*

point, that a good education produces thoughtful, innovative people who are prepared to break the mould and try something new. Maybe that is deliberate. For in its present state of intellectual awareness, America is happy to swallow myths that we Europeans laughed out years ago.

1. Using the USA as an example, explain how resources are allocated in a free market economy.
2. (a) To what extent are incomes unequal in the USA?
   (b) Are inequalities in income desirable in a free market economy?
3. Discuss what might be the advantages and disadvantages to an individual of migrating to work in the USA from the UK.

Study skills

When you start your AS/A Level course, you should try to evaluate whether or not your study and organisational skills are effective. For instance:

- are you always present and on time for classes or lectures?
- do you always hand work in on time?
- is work done to the best of your ability?
- do you work in a suitable environment?
- do you leave time to plan and evaluate your work?
- do you participate in all learning activities in a way which helps you to learn?
- do you listen to advice and act on constructive comments about your work?

Having good study skills does not necessarily mean that work is done well in advance, or that the room where you work at home is tidy. Some students are very organised in what might at first seem chaotic situations. For instance, they might always write their essays close to the time they have to be handed in. Or their study room might look an incredible mess. However, if you work best under pressure of deadlines, and you know what is where in the mess of your room, then it could be argued that in fact you are an organised student!

In class

The core of your study is likely to take place in the classroom or lecture room. Not only will you spend a considerable proportion of your studying time in class, but what you do in the classroom and the instructions you receive there will influence what you do outside. Effective classroom skills are therefore essential. They include the following.

Attending classes regularly and on time Good organisational skills involve attending all lessons unless there are serious reasons for absence. They also involve arranging doctor's and dentist's appointments, driving lessons or holidays outside class time so that work is not missed.

Always being attentive It is important to be attentive at all times and engage in the activities being presented. Participation in class also helps other students to learn.

Making clear and concise notes during lessons Notes can act as a record of what has been said. Taking notes whilst the teacher/lecturer is talking is a form of active learning. It can help some students to focus on what is being said and identify what they don't understand. For other students, though, note taking can get in the way of understanding what the teacher or lecturer is saying. They may prefer to read handouts or notes given out by the teacher or lecturer. You have to decide what is best for you.

Asking questions of the teacher or lecturer It is unlikely that all students will understand everything that goes on in a lesson. Asking questions helps to fill in these gaps. It is also very important to keep you focussed on the lesson. If you are thinking about what you do and don't understand, you will inevitably be participating in that lesson.

Formulating questions is also important for developing oral skills, which will be essential in the world outside of school or college.

Participating in classroom discussions Classroom discussions enable you to practice important key learning skills. Some students find they want to contribute more than others. Remember though that in a discussion, listening is as important as talking. All participants must respect the contributions of others. There must be a balance between communication and listening.

Preparing for the next lesson Many schools and colleges issue their students with homework diaries, or encourage them to buy one. They are a useful tool for planning and organising work. They help you to remember what you have to do and structure your out of class activities.

Planning outside the class

Planning is an essential part of good study skills. By keeping a diary, for instance, students can see at a glance what needs to be done and when. They can then mentally allocate time slots for completion of the work. For work which is not structured by the teacher or lecturer, such as coursework or revision, students need to construct a plan. Typically, this will show dates and the work to be done on or by a particular date. It may also show times during the day when work is to be done. Some students find it helpful to discipline themselves by the clock. So they plan to start, say, revision at 9.00 each morning, have a ten minute break each hour on the hour, break for lunch at 1.00, etc.

It may also be helpful to construct precise plans for day to day work outside the classroom. When you start on your AS/A level course, for instance, it might be useful to plan meticulously when you are going to complete work during the first month. This will ensure that work gets done and you have set out on your course with good work habits. Hopefully, you will then be able to relax your planning because you will have got into a sound routine for completing work.

Planning tends to increase in importance:
- the longer the task to be completed:
- the less structure is given by your school or college for its completion.

Organising time

Every student has different preferences about organising time. Some of the key issues are as follows.

Time during the week You have to decide when you want to complete your work during the week. There are likely to be conflicting claims on your time. For instance, you may have a part time job which takes priority at certain times of the week. You may have family or social commitments. You may decide that you will never work on Friday or Saturday nights (except in emergencies!). There are no right or wrong times to study. However, it is essential to build in enough time during the week to study. AS/A level examinations have been developed on the assumption that you are studying full time for 1 to 2 years.

Time during the day Some people work best in the morning, some in the afternoon and some at night. You should know whether you are a 'morning person' or otherwise. Try to work at times of day when you are most likely to learn effectively.

Breaks Breaks are essential to maintain concentration. How frequent and how long your breaks need to be varies from one individual to another. You need to find out what works best for you. Try to be as disciplined as possible in your approach to breaks. It is all too easy for the break to extend itself over the whole period when you planned to work. Get to know what is most likely to stop you from getting back to work. For instance, if you start watching television during your break, do you find that you only go back to work at the end of the programme?

Variety Some students like variety in what they do. So during an hour's work session, they may do a little on three pieces of work. Others find that they cannot cope with such short blocks of time and would rather concentrate on just one piece of work. Longer pieces of work, such as essays or coursework, may need to be broken down and completed in several different work sessions anyway.

Networking and resources

It is important that students make use of all the resources that are available to them. Here are some suggestions about how to find help when completing work.

The textbook Using a textbook effectively will help students to achieve the highest possible marks for their work. Remember that the textbook is there to help you understand a topic. The relevant section should be read before you attempt a piece of work and you are likely to want to refer to the textbook as you write. You may wish to consult a number of textbooks if, for example, you do not understand a particular area in one book.

The library Schools and colleges will have libraries, perhaps even in the classroom or lecture room, of books and other materials which can be borrowed. Reading around a topic is an essential part of preparing any work such as an essay. Libraries will also hopefully carry daily quality newspapers. Economics is about the real world. AS/A level Economics students should be aware of the major economic issues of the day and be able to discuss them.

The Internet The Internet can be very useful in the learning process. It is most perhaps useful when students are able to use the same site repeatedly. They know what is on the site and how to navigate around it. There may be more difficulties, however, when searching for general information. This requires skill in using search engines to find appropriate sites which can often take time. The Internet is likely to be very useful to students working on their own in Economics when researching coursework.

Ask the teacher/lecturer Make full use of your teacher or lecturer as a resource. If you are stuck on a piece of homework, for instance, ask the teacher or lecturer to help you out. If you frequently need help, it is a good idea to start the homework

well in advance of the date it needs to be handed in, so that you can contact the teacher or lecturer.

Network with fellow students Students may find networking with friends helpful. If they have a problem, they can call a friend or see them in school or college. Students who prefer to work in this way should be aware of which students in their teaching group are most likely to give helpful advice. Networking is a valuable tool in the learning process both to the person who receives the help and the person who gives it.

Parents, business people, etc. Parents, family members, friends or contacts in the business community may all be sources of help in different situations and for different pieces of work.

The work environment

Your work environment needs to be chosen to maximise learning. Students often work either in a library or study area, or at home in their own room. What is there about these work places which makes them effective?

Availability Your work place should be available to you when you want to study. If you like to complete as much work as possible at school or college, and work hard between time-tabled lessons, then the library might be an excellent environment for you. You may prefer to complete homework in your own home. Your bedroom may be the only place where you are guaranteed that you can work uninterrupted. Not only must a place be available but so too must the resources. If you are undertaking research, for instance, you may have to work in a library or at a computer terminal.

Music, television and noise Some students find it easy to concentrate in the midst of chaos. They like distractions and find it easier to work if they know they can also listen to music, stroke the dog or have a conversation. Many students find distractions impossible to cope with. To work effectively, they need relative peace and quiet. They might or might not like background music.

Alone or in groups Some students find that working in a group is ineffective. One person may start talking about a non-work issue and work is then never resumed. They therefore prefer to work alone. However, other students who can avoid such distractions find working in groups highly effective. It means they can instantly network with others when they have a problem.

Furniture Furniture can be very important in studying. Some students prefer to read in an armchair and write at a desk. You may find it easier to create work spaces where particular types of work can be done. Make sure that the chair you sit in is comfortable and doesn't give you back problems.

Lighting Experiment with lighting to reduce eye strain. If you find studying makes you tired very quickly, one reason might be inadequate lighting. You can also use lighting to create a mood which encourages you to study.

Movement Your work environment should allow you to move around if you wish. When trying to memorise something, for instance, some students may prefer to walk around, whereas others may prefer to sit.

Preparing for tests and examinations

Different students prepare effectively for tests or examinations in a variety of different ways. You have to find out what is most effective for you. Different methods may also be useful in different circumstances. For instance, you may want to spend most time memorising information for an essay-based examination, but for a multiple-choice examination you may want to spend most time practising past questions.

Written notes   Many students use notes in their revision. Notes are useful records of what has been learned either because the student has made them and therefore hopefully can understand them, or because they have been given by the teacher or lecturer and show what material is likely to occur in the examination.

Good note taking is a skilled art. Notes are meant to be a precis, a shortening of what, for instance, might be found in a textbook. So it is important to develop a style of writing notes which does shorten material.
- Miss out common words like 'the' and 'a' which do not affect the meaning.
- Abbreviate words. For example, write 'gov' for 'government', 'C' for consumption, or 'P' for price.

Notes should be clearly laid out using headings and subheadings. Ideally, headings and subheadings should be colour coded to make them easier to skim read. The headings should provide a story in themselves which prompts you to remember the material contained underneath each heading. Highlight key terms within the notes. Star, circle or underline important points.

Some students like to work from notes written on A4 paper. Other students like to transfer notes onto small cards where there is less on each card. Whichever method you use, make sure that the notes are logically ordered and can be referred to instantly.

When memorising material from notes, some students find it helpful to think of the layout of individual pages. This then prompts memory recall of what is on the page.

The textbook   Some students dislike revising from notes and prefer to use a textbook. They may find it easier, for instance, to read printed material rather than their own handwriting. They may want to use material collected together rather than a series of handouts or loose pages. Also, notes may be incomplete in places.

Some students rely on both notes and textbooks for revision. Revising from a textbook involves the same skills as revising from notes. The textbook will have chapter or unit headings, and headings and subheadings within these. These provide the skeleton on which the detail should be hung.

Pictures and visual presentations   Some students find pictures particularly helpful when revising. Examples of commonly used visual presentations include mind maps, flow charts and family trees, which are illustrated in Figures 1 to 3. These illustrations summarise the main points in unit 4, The Demand Curve, of this book. Visual presentations work through helping the

student see a topic laid out. Places on the page can be visualised and connections clearly identified.

Oral methods   Some students like to be 'tested' by another person on a topic to see if they have learnt the material. Repeating words or phrases can be helpful. So too can devising word associations and mnemonics. A word association is linking one word with another. For instance, you may be particularly interested in football, and decide to remember the main components of aggregate demand (consumption, investment, government spending and exports minus imports) by assigning each term to the name of a football club. Remember the football clubs and you remember the components. Alternatively, you may make up a mnemonic, a rhyme or phrase usually associated with the first letter of each word. For instance, you could have Clobber In Gap Extremely Important OR Chelsea In Goal Excitement Incident for consumption, investment, government spending, exports and imports.

Active learning   Some students find it difficult just to sit and memorise material. They need to be doing something to help them remember.
- One way is to construct a set of notes, or a mind map. Once written out, the notes may be of little use, but it is in the doing that the learning has taken place.
- You may want to practice past examination questions. Multiple choice question papers, for instance, are best revised for in this way. If you practice essay questions, it is often more useful to spend scarce time writing out essay plans for a wide variety of questions than answering a few essays in detail.
- You may use published materials which give short answer questions on a topic such as 'Define economies of scale', or 'List the costs of unemployment'.
- Some students practice past homework tasks which they have been set and then compare their results with their first marked attempt.

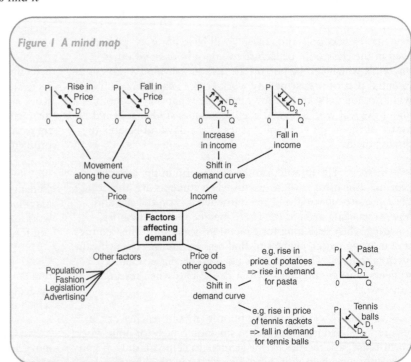

Figure I   A mind map

Figure 2 *Flow charts*

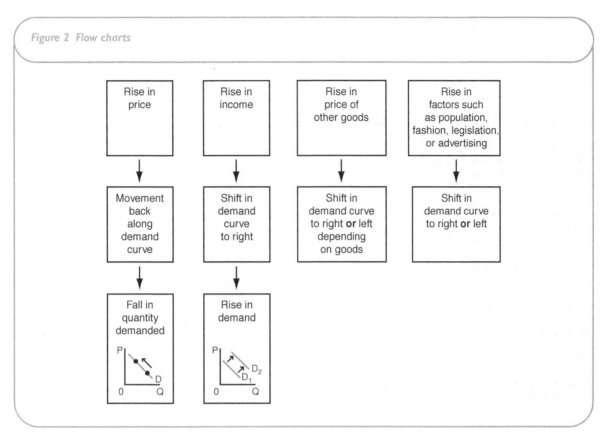

Figure 3 *A family tree*

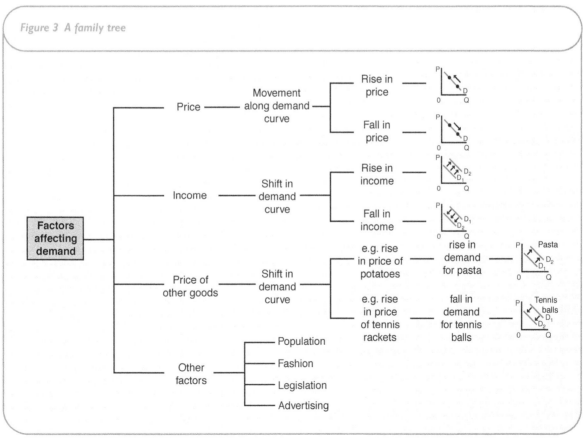

Assessment criteria

Specifications are drawn up and papers are set to test a range of assessment criteria. These are qualities and skills which a candidate must demonstrate to the examiners to gain marks in any form of assessment. In Economics at AS/A level, these assessment criteria are grouped into four areas.

Demonstration of knowledge and understanding of the specified subject content **Knowledge and understanding** requires candidates to show that they can recognise economic concepts and terms and be able to define or explain them. For instance, *Explain what is meant by economies of scale* asks for a definition of economies of scale (knowledge) and a good answer is likely to give examples to demonstrate clear understanding of the term. Knowledge and understanding are also present when economic theories are used. For instance, knowledge is required when drawing a demand and supply diagram. Has the candidate correctly identified the axes? Is the demand curve downward sloping? Is the supply curve upward sloping? Is the candidate using proper conventions by clearly labelling the axes and the demand and supply curves? Another example would be the link between interest rates and inflation. Does a candidate show knowledge of the chain of causality between a change in interest rates, a change in aggregate demand and a change in the equilibrium price level of the economy?

Application of knowledge and critical understanding to economic problems and issues arising from both familiar and unfamiliar situations Knowledge is essential for any economist, but the knowledge must be **applied** to economic problems to be of use. For instance, being able to define economies of scale is of little use if economies of scale at work in motor vehicle manufacturing cannot be recognised. Application is the skill of being able to use knowledge in a wide variety of contexts. Some of these contexts will be familiar. For instance, you might have studied leisure industries during your course and in the examination a question is set on economies of scale in leisure industries. The context may, however, be unfamiliar. For instance, you may have studied the environment as part your course. In the examination, a question on pollution permits in the USA may be set. Pollution permits is part of expected knowledge and understanding but the USA may be an unfamiliar context. Another example of application would be using mathematical formulae to work out answers to problems. Calculating a value for price elasticity of demand is application.

Analyse economic problems and issues **Analysis** is the process of breaking down information into relevant parts and then using this to understand a problem or issue. A simple piece of analysis, for instance, would be to identify a trend from a set of unemployment figures on a graph. The graph might be accompanied by a passage which contains information about why unemployment might be falling. The skill of analysis is needed to link the trend with its causes. Analysis would also be required if a candidate were asked to identify possible government policies to tackle unemployment. The candidate might have to select which policies from a list might be appropriate and justify why these policies might be effective.

Evaluate economic arguments and evidence, making informed judgements **Evaluation** requires candidates to make conclusions and argue which courses of action might be most appropriate in a situation. If a government wanted to reduce unemployment today, which would be the most effective policies for it to pursue? If global warming is to be stopped, what are the most important actions which consumers and firms must take? It is relatively easy to make a simple judgement. At this level, though, examiners expect candidates to be able to justify their answers. It is this justification which tends to carry most marks. To do this, candidates must weigh up the evidence presented to them and judge which is important and which is not. They must consider whether the information presented is reliable and whether or not it is complete enough to come to a decision. If it is not, what other information is required to come to a definitive conclusion? Candidates must also distinguish between fact and opinion.

Candidates are also assessed in Economics AS/A level on the **quality of written communication**. Candidates must:
- select and use a form and style of writing appropriate to purpose and complex subject matter. For instance, candidates must be able to write an essay, or a short answer to a question;
- organise relevant information clearly and coherently, using specialist vocabulary when appropriate. So candidates must, for instance, be able to write in paragraphs and they must be able to use terms like price elasticity or the current balance when these are required;
- ensure writing is legible, and spelling, grammar and punctuation are accurate, so that meaning is clear. Candidates must therefore write clearly, construct proper sentences and spell correctly.

Command, directive or key words

Questions typically start off with command or key words. These words indicate which skills are required when answering the question. It is important for candidates to respond in an appropriate manner. For instance, if candidates are asked to evaluate a problem, but only show knowledge and understanding, then they will lose most of the marks for that question. Command words can be grouped according to what skills will be required in an answer.

Knowledge and understanding

- Define - to give the exact meaning of a term or concept using words or mathematical symbols whose meaning is already understood by the reader, e.g. *Define what is meant by economies of scale.*
- Describe - to give an account of something, e.g. *Describe the costs of inflation.*
- Give - to state or say, e.g. *Give two examples of goods in which Saudi Arabia has a comparative advantage in production.*

- How - to present an account of something, e.g. *How does the government raise taxes?*
- Identify - to single out from other information, e.g. *Identify three factors which cause inflation.*
- Illustrate - to use examples to explain a point, e.g. *Illustrate the way in which monopolists keep out competitors from their markets.*
- List - to state in the briefest form, e.g. *List three factors which affect the demand for a product.*
- Outline - to give a short description of the main aspects or features, e.g. *Outline the arguments used by Greenpeace against genetically modified (GM) crops.*
- State - to give or say, e.g. *State three factors which affect elasticity of supply.*
- Summarise - to bring out the main points from a more complex set of data, e.g. *Summarise the main arguments in favour of government intervention.*
- What - to clarify a point, e.g. *What are the main characteristics of a perfectly competitive industry?*

Application

- Apply - use knowledge of economics to understand a situation, issue or problem, e.g. *Apply the theory of perfect competition to the market for potatoes.*
- Calculate - use mathematics to work out an answer, e.g. *Calculate the price elasticity of demand if price increases from £3 to £4.*
- Distinguish between - identify the characteristics which make two or more ideas, concepts, issues, etc. different, e.g. *Distinguish between price elasticity of demand and income elasticity of demand.*
- Explain - making clear. It is often useful to define terms and give examples in an explanation, e.g. *Explain how prices are determined in a free market.*
- Suggest - give possible reasons or ideas. These must be plausible but not necessarily correct. 'Suggest' may require candidates to analyse a problem and not just apply economic problems, e.g. *Suggest reasons why the firm did not put up its prices.*

Analysis

- Analyse - to break down into constituent parts in order to be able to understand an issue or problem. Analysis involves recognising what is important, and relating to knowledge and understanding of economics where necessary, e.g. *Analyse the reasons for the firm investing in new machinery.*
- Compare and contrast - to show the similarities and differences between two or more ideas or problems, e.g. *Compare and contrast the performance of the UK and Chinese economies over the past ten years.*
- Examine - to break down an issue or problem to understand it, e.g. *Examine the problems facing the UK economy today.*
- Investigate - to look for evidence to explain and analyse, e.g. *Investigate why the government chose to cut interest rates in May.*

Evaluation

- Assess - to analyse an economic issue or problem and then to weigh up the relative importance of different strands, e.g. *Assess the impact of high interest rates*

on the UK economy.
- Comment on - invites the candidate to make their judgements based upon evidence which they have presented, e.g. *Comment on why the Bank of England thought it necessary to raise interest rates in June.*
- Critically analyse - to analyse an issue or problem and then to weigh up the relative importance of part of this analysis, e.g. *Critically analyse the problems facing the industry today.*
- Do you think - invites candidates to put forward their own opinions about an issue or problem. However, the marks will always be awarded for the quality of the arguments put forward and not for any individual opinions, e.g. *Do you think the government should have allowed the motorway to be built?*
- Discuss - to compare a number of possible views about an issue or problem and to weigh up their relative importance. A conclusion is essential, e.g. *Discuss the advantages and disadvantages of fixing rents in the housing market.*
- Evaluate - like discuss, to compare a number of possible views about an issue or problem and weigh up their relative importance. A final judgement is essential, e.g. *Evaluate the policies available to government to reduce unemployment.*
- To what extent - invites candidates to explain and analyse and then to comment upon the relative importance of arguments, e.g. *To what extent should the government rely upon interest rates to control inflation?*

Levels of response

Questions which test the higher order skills of analysis and evaluation are likely to be marked using a levels of response mark scheme. Rather than giving candidates a mark or several marks for a point made or an argument developed within an answer, the answer is marked holistically (as a whole). It is then compared to descriptions of what answers might look like in terms of the skills displayed. The answer is then put within a level. This level will have a range of marks which the examiner can award depending upon whether it is a good answer within that level or not.

For instance, a levels mark scheme might have three levels and 12 marks are awarded. The level descriptors are as follows.

Level 1

One or more reasons given, but little development of points. The answer lacks coherence and there is no valid analysis or evaluation. 1-3 marks

Level 2

Several reasons given with reasonable analysis. Arguments are expressed with some confidence and coherence. Evaluation, though, is weakly supported by evidence. 4-8 marks

Level 3

A good coverage of the main reasons. Sound analysis with clear links between the issues raised. Arguments for and against have been evaluated and a conclusion reached. 9-12 marks

Mark schemes are available from the awarding bodies. You should become familiar with the levels of response mark schemes used by examiners on the papers you will sit. To gain a mark in the highest level, candidates typically have to give evidence of all four main skills of knowledge, application, analysis and evaluation.

Multiple choice questions

Some awarding bodies use multiple choice questions as a form of assessment. They are used mainly to test lower order skills of knowledge and application. They are also a convenient way of testing breadth. A data response question or an essay is likely to cover only one topic. If there is choice, candidates may be encouraged only to revise part of the course in the hope that they will still be able to answer a full set of questions. A multiple choice test covers the whole course and therefore penalises candidates who are selective in their revision.

Success at multiple choice questions involves being thoroughly familiar with the basics of economics. It also requires skill in answering multiple choice questions, just as essays requires essay writing skills. Practice on questions is therefore very important. Using past question papers from the awarding body can also be very helpful. Not only will it help you familiarise yourself with the style of multiple choice question being used, but past questions may be reused on new papers.

There are two ways in which candidates are likely to get to a correct answer on a multiple choice question.
- Knowing the correct answer.
- Eliminating the wrong answers.

Candidates should make full use of the laws of probability. If the correct answer is not obvious, but two out of four responses can be eliminated, the chances of getting the answer right are improved from 1 in 4 for guessing to 1 in 2. Taken over a whole paper, a strategy of eliminating wrong answers can significantly improve marks.

Some multiple choice tests require candidates not just to give an answer from A to D but also to justify their answers. The written explanation should be short and to the point.

In an examination, do not spend more than the allotted time on any single question but pass over it. For instance, if there are 30 questions to be answered in 30 minutes, there is on average just 1 minute per question. Don't spend 10 minutes working out question 5. Come back at the end to the questions which you have missed out. If you have nearly run out of time, always make sure that there is an answer to every question. You will then have some chance rather than no chance to gain marks. Some candidates prefer to draw a line through incorrect responses (i.e. wrong answers) within a question and visibly isolate the correct answer.

Data response questions

Data response questions are used to test a candidate's ability to apply their knowledge and understanding to familiar or unfamiliar data. They usually also require candidates to display skills of analysis and evaluation as well.

The data presented may be verbal or in numerical form, or a mixture of both. Candidates often find data in verbal form easier to understand and interpret. However, in practice, examiners construct questions so that there is little or no difference in outcome in marks between questions which contain mainly verbal data and those which contain mainly numerical data.

Some awarding bodies only use real data, such as

newspaper extracts or statistics from government sources. Others also use hypothetical or imaginary data - data which has been made up by the examiner. In some areas of Economics, it is difficult to obtain real data. Exact figures for price elasticity of demand is one example. Therefore some examiners prefer to use imaginary data for questions.

There is a number of ways in which candidates can improve their performance on data response questions in examinations.
- Read through the material thoroughly.
- Use highlighter pens to mark what you think are important words or passages.
- Highlight the key words in a question.
- Think carefully about what each question is asking of you. In particular, think about the skills you are required to display in a question.
- If there are any numerical calculations, show all your workings carefully. You may get marks for the workings even if you fail to get the final answer correct.
- Have a clear understanding of how long each answer should be. For instance, assume there are 60 marks overall, with the first two questions being awarded 5 marks each, the third question carrying 10 marks, the fourth carrying 15 marks and the last 25 marks. The first question should be roughly one fifth the length of the last question and should take only $5/60$ of the time to complete. Many candidates write too much on questions which carry few marks and too little on questions which carry many marks.
- Be aware of what economic concepts and theories the question is testing.
- Some candidates find it helpful to prepare plans for longer answers.
- Make sure you don't run out of time. It is usually better to abandon one part and move onto the next if you are running out of time rather than attempting to create the perfect answer on that part.
- Last parts of data response questions may expect candidates to write for around 20 minutes. These questions then become small essays and the techniques for writing essays outlined below need to be applied to them.

Sometimes, it is appropriate to use a diagram in a data response question. Some questions, in fact, specifically ask for a diagram to be drawn. There are some easy rules to remember when drawing diagrams.
- Examiners will expect to see standard diagrams which are found in any Economics textbook.
- When drawing diagrams, make sure they are large enough to be read.
- Diagrams are easier to read and look much better if they are drawn with a ruler where appropriate.
- Always label the axes and the lines or curves.
- Always refer to and explain the diagram in your written answer.

Essays

Essays are often used to test higher order skills of analysis and evaluation, although there are likely to be marks for knowledge and application in the mark scheme too. Typically, candidates are expected to write for 35 to 45 minutes on an essay title which is likely to be split into two separate but linked parts. Essay writing is a skill which needs to be practised and learnt. It requires putting together (or **synthesising**) a number of ideas to form one complete answer. Essays are likely to be marked using levels of response mark schemes.

Candidates can improve their essay writing skills if they can learn the following techniques.

- Before you start writing, have a clear understanding of what the question is asking. In particular, identify the skills which will be required from you to write a successful essay by looking at the command words. Identify too the areas of economics of relevance to the essay. Some candidates also find it useful to highlight the key words in an essay title to focus them on what the question is asking. For instance, take the following question: *Evaluate the policies which a government might adopt to deal with the problem of youth unemployment.* The key words here are *Evaluate*, *government policies* and *youth unemployment*. Evaluate means that you will have to compare the effectiveness of different types of government policy. You will be expected to argue that some might be more useful than others in order to gain the maximum number of marks. Government policies to deal with unemployment is the main area of economic knowledge. However, especially important is the word *youth*. Your answer must focus on *youth* unemployment if it is to get the higher marks.
- Some candidates find it useful to write out an **essay plan**. This is a brief synopsis of what you will write. It allows you to jot points down and to see how they can be organised to form a coherent whole. Often candidates start their answer and add points to their plan as they go along because writing triggers their memories. This is good practice, but always check that your new points will not unbalance the structure of your answer. Adding new material after you have written your conclusion, for instance, may gain you extra marks but it is unlikely to help you get the highest marks.
- Paragraph your essay properly. Remember that a paragraph should contain material on one idea or one group of ideas. A useful technique to use is to see a paragraph as an opening sentence which makes a point, and the rest of the paragraph as an explanation or elaboration of that point.
- Include diagrams wherever they are appropriate. Advice about the effective use of diagrams is given above.
- Write a concluding paragraph. This is especially important if you are answering an evaluation question. The conclusion gives you the opportunity to draw your points together and to weigh up the arguments put forward.
- With two part questions, ensure that you have allocated your time effectively between the two parts. Don't spend too much time on the first half of the question. It is particularly important to work out how long to spend on each part if the two parts carry very unequal mark weighting.
- Essays are continuous pieces of prose. They should not include bullet points, lists, subheadings, etc.
- Spot the story. Many essay questions are set because they cover a topical issue. Recognising what this topical issue is should help you decide what to stress in your essay. Knowledge of the issue will also give you additional material to introduce into the essay.
- Adapt your material to suit what is required. Don't write out an answer to an essay question you have already answered in class and memorised and which is similar to the essay question set. Equally, don't write 'everything I know about' one or two key words in the essay title. For instance, answering a question about the costs of inflation by writing at length about the causes of inflation is likely to be an inappropriate answer.
- Remember there are likely to be marks for quality of language in the mark scheme. Write in a simple and clear style and pay attention to your spelling.

Coursework

You may be required to write a piece of coursework. You are likely to be given extensive help in doing this by your teacher or lecturer.

Planning One key issue in coursework for the student is time management. Coursework is likely to be carried out over a period of time. It is important that deadlines are not missed because they are weeks or months ahead before the coursework is due to be handed in. It is also important that all work is not left to the end when there may not be enough time to complete it. Planning is therefore very important. Your teacher or lecturer is likely to help you in this, setting goals and helping you to complete the coursework well within the time limit required.

Following specification instructions The examination specification will give detailed instructions about how topics should be chosen, how the coursework should be written up and how marks will be awarded. You should always keep a copy of this with your work. Awarding bodies also publish specification support materials for teachers and lecturers. These too will contain information about coursework which should be made available to you. High marks are usually gained by following what examiners have told candidates to do.

Choice of topic Your first task will be to decide upon a topic to research. This should be an investigation into an economic problem or issue. The choice of topic is vital for two reasons. First, the student must be able to obtain primary and/or secondary data on the topic. Secondary data is data and information which have already been collected by someone else. It is likely to be the main source if not the sole source of data for the investigation. It might, for instance, include newspaper articles, government statistics, or material from web sites on the Internet. Primary data is data which have been collected directly by the student and do not come from another source. The results of a questionnaire conducted by the student would be an example. Primary data may not be available for the chosen topic. Primary data may also be of poor quality, for example from a poorly conducted survey. So primary data should only be included when it is reliable and relevant to the chosen topic.

Choice of topic is also important because it will determine whether the candidate can display all the skills required by the examination. This will include both analysis and evaluation. The key is to phrase the coursework title as a problem or issue. 'Is the package tour industry an oligopoly?' may not be a suitable title. It does not give candidates sufficient scope to display skills of evaluation. A title which asked whether the UK or EU competition authorities should allow a merger which is currently being proposed between package tour companies is a more suitable title. Candidates will be able to explore the issue, including commenting on the oligopolistic nature of the package tour industry. They will then have to use this analysis to evaluate a policy decision. This is precisely what economists working for the competition authorities would, of course, also be doing.

Collecting information Collecting information is likely to take time although the Internet is now increasingly reducing this. For example, a newspaper search may have taken a number of sessions in a library but may now be carried out in the session using a search engine and a site. Gathering statistical information from government publications such as *Social Trends* and converting it into a form which is useful in your chosen assignment may take longer. However, the Internet may be equally time consuming. You may have to sift through large amounts of irrelevant information to find something of value.

If you undertake any primary research, you should have a clear understanding of the techniques you are using and what makes them valid as evidence. For instance, if you construct a questionnaire, you should be aware of the issues involved in setting appropriate questions. You should also understand the size and nature of the sample needed to give valid results. Data are likely to be collected from the following sources:

- books, including textbooks;
- newspapers;
- magazines;
- specialist trade journals;
- advertising literature;
- government statistical publications including *Monthly Digest of Statistics, Economic and Labour Market Review, Annual Abstract of Statistics, Social Trends, Regional Trends, Environmental Statistics* and *Transport Statistics*;
- websites on the Internet.

When collecting information, seek the help of others where possible. For instance, if you use a library, ask the librarian for help in finding material. If you use the Internet, make sure that you understand how best to use a search engine.

Collecting information is time consuming and challenging. Don't underestimate the difficulty of this part of the task.

Structuring the report The awarding body will give clear guidance on how the report should be laid out and what should be included. For instance, awarding bodies may recommend that there should be:

- a contents page;
- an introduction outlining the economic issue or problem to be investigated, framed in the form of either an hypothesis to be tested or a question requiring further investigation;
- a brief outline of economic concepts and theories relevant to the issue or problem, in some cases involving reference to existing literature;
- a brief outline of the technique(s) to be used to collect the relevant data;
- a presentation of the findings related to the hypothesis or the question posed;
- an evaluation of the findings and method of research, with recommendations where appropriate;
- a bibliography of sources.

When writing your report, remember that you are writing about economic theory and presenting the evidence you have collected to arrive at a set of conclusions. It is important to avoid writing everything you can find from textbooks about certain economic theories, or forgetting that the purpose of collecting evidence is to evaluate problems or issues.

Report writing

Students may be required to write a report. The style of a report is different from that of an essay.

- It should begin with a section showing who the report is for, who has written it, the date it was written and the title. If the report is written under examination conditions, this may all be omitted.
- It should be broken down into a number of sections. Each section should address a particular issue. A heading should start each section to help the reader see the structure of the report. In most reports, sections are numbered in sequence.
- A section may be broken down into sub-sections, each with their own headings and their own numbers. For instance, section 3 of the report may have two sub-sections, 3.1 and 3.2.
- The report must be written in complete sentences and not in note form. However, unlike in an essay, it is acceptable to use bullet points to further structure the report.
- Use diagrams wherever appropriate. Diagrams must be part of the argument used in the report. It is important that the reader understands why they have been included.

A report will require you to draw conclusions and make judgements, i.e. show that you can evaluate an issue or problem. The evaluation can be presented at the end of the report, or it can be included in each section of the report. If it is included in each section, a conclusion or summary still needs to be written at the end to bring together what has been said earlier.

The report should also highlight missing information that would have been useful or, perhaps, was essential, to come to reasoned conclusions or recommendations. The reliability or accuracy of the information provided could also be questioned.

If the report is written in examination conditions, as with a data response question, take time at the start to read through the data given. Highlight key ideas or data. It may not be necessary to understand all the data before you start writing as this may waste important time which may be needed to write the report. However, it is important to understand what is required of you before you start writing.

Constructing a plan is essential. A report is a complex piece of writing. Identify the main headings of your report and jot down the main points which you are likely to include under each heading. You may add to your plan as you write your report if you think of new points. In an examination, you are unlikely to have the time to write a number of drafts of the report. However, outside the examination room, it would be useful to produce several drafts.

A

Absolute poverty
and economic growth 196
Accelerator coefficient 153
Accelerator theory of investment 153
defined 153, 154
Activity rates
and economic growth 187
Ad valorem taxes
defined 78, 81
and incidence of tax 79
Advertising
and upward sloping demand
curves 74
Affordability index
and housing 290-38
Aggregate
defined 161, 165
Aggregate demand 161-168
defined 161, 165
and equilibrium output 177-183
and fiscal policy 231-236
and supply side policies 242
Aggregate demand curve
defined 161, 165
derivation of 161-162
movements along 161-162
shifts in 162-163, 164-165
Aggregate output 177-183
Aggregate supply curve 169-175
defined 169, 173
long run 170-173
short run 169-170
and economic growth 171
and equilibrium output 177-183
(See also Supply side policies)
Agriculture
and economic growth 190
and elasticity 114
and price stabilisation 112-120
(See also Common Agricultural
Policy)
Aims of economic policy
(see Goals of government)
Air pollution 102
Alienation
and the division of labour 11
All other things being equal
(See Ceteris paribus)
Allocation of resources
and the basic economic problem 2-5
and free market economies 258-261
and markets 12
and mixed economies 262
and planned economies 261
through the market mechanism 84-86
Allocative efficiency
defined 91, 93
and agriculture 93-94
(See also Efficiency)
Allowance, tax 220
Alternative or appropriate technology
197

Ando, Albert 146
Animal spirits
and investment schedule 153
Anticipated inflation 220
Appreciation of currency 253-254
defined 253, 255
(See also Exchange rates)
Appropriate or alternative technology
197
Assured tenancy 31
Assymetric information
defined 92, 93
Average propensity to consume
143-144, 146, 147-148
defined 143, 147
value of 144, 146, 147-148
Average propensity to save 145, 150
defined 145, 147

B

Balance of payments 224-230
deficit 225-227
and fiscal policy 234, 235-236
and inflation 220
and monetary policy 249
and policy goals 131-132, 234, 235-236
and trade offs 234
(See also Balance of trade,
Current account on the balance
of payments, Gold and foreign
currency reserves, Invisible
trade, Visible trade)
Balance of payments accounts 213-230
defined 224, 227
current account 224-227
capital account 224
of UK 224-230
Balance of trade
defined 224, 227
Balance on invisible trade
defined 224, 227
Bank base rate
defined 249, 250
(See also Bank of England,
Central Bank, Monetary Policy,
Rate of interest)
Bank of England
functions of 249
and exchange rates 249
and lender of last resort 249
and monetary policy 249-250
and National Debt 231
(See also Central bank,
Monetary policy)
Barber, Anthony 235
Barber boom 235
Barter 12
Base period
defined 18, 20
Base rates
(see Bank base rate, Rate of interest)
Basic economic problem 2-5

defined 2, 5
and economic systems 129
and what, how and for whom 10
Basket (see Effective exchange rate,
Retail Price Index)
Benefits (see Private benefits, Social
benefits, Unemployment benefits,
Welfare benefits)
Bentham, Jeremy 202
Bhutan 207
Bio-fuels 128
Black economy (see Hidden economy)
Black market
defined 138, 140
and price controls 113
Black Wednesday 256
Boom 185
(See also Barber boom, Lawson
boom, Trade cycle)
Bottlenecks
defined 238, 242
Budget, government 158, 231
defined 231, 234
UK annual 231
and data 17
Budget deficit 158, 231
defined 231, 234
(See also Public Sector Net Cash
Requirement)
Budget surplus 158, 231
defined 231, 234
(See also Public Sector Net Cash
Requirement)
Buffer stock scheme 114-116
defined 115, 116
Business cycle (see Trade cycle)
Buy-to-let 43

C

Callaghan, James 235
Canada
growth rates 189
investment 191, 192
Capital
circulating 11, 14
defined 11, 14
equity (see Shares)
fixed 11, 14
working 11, 14
(See also Factor mobility, Human
capital, Investment, Physical
capital)
Capital and financial account on
the balance of payments
defined 224, 227
Capital consumption (see Depreciation)
Capital gains tax 244
Capital goods 152
Capital markets 241
Capital-output ratio
defined 153, 154
and accelerator theory 153

Capital productivity
defined 11, 14
(See also Productivity)
Capital stock
and investment 151
Capitalist economies
(see Free market economies)
Carbon emissions trading 126-127
(see also Pollution permits)
Carbon offsetting 126
Carlyle, Thomas 202
Cartels
and supply 41
(See also Organisation for
Petroleum Exporting Countries)
Central bank 249-251
defined 249
independence of 249
and exchange rate policy 256
and inflation 249-251
and monetary policy 249-251
(See also Bank of England)
Central government (see Government)
Central planning
(see Command economies)
Centrally planned economies
(see Command economies)
Ceteris paribus
defined 26, 27
and demand 30
and price determination 46
CFCs 197
Child tax credit 243
China 9, 197
Choice
defined 2, 5
public choice theory 123-124
and free market economies 260
and mixed economies 262
as part of the basic economic
problem 1-2
Cinema market 23
Circular flow of income 135-136
defined 135, 140
and multiplier 163-164
and national income measurement
135
and transfer payments 137
(See also Injections, Withdrawals)
Circulating capital
defined 11, 14
Claimant count unemployment 213-214
and data 17
Classical economics
and aggregate demand 164-165
and equilibrium output 178-182
and long run aggregate supply
172-173
Closed economy
defined 135, 140
Closed shop 242
Cocoa 44

Collective bargaining 243
Command economies
defined 261, 262
Common Agricultural Policy (CAP)
28-29, 93-94, 117-120
and economic efficiency 93-94
and government failure 123
and intervention price 117-120
and market distortions 109, 123
and mountains 114
as buffer stock scheme 113-114,
117-120
Competition
and efficiency 92
and free market economies 258
and mixed economies 262
and supply side economics 241, 244
Competitive demand
defined 53-54, 55
Complements
defined 53, 55
and cross elasticity of demand 67
and price determination 53
Composite demand
defined 54, 55
Compulsory competitive tendering
(see Competitive tendering)
Congestion charging 51, 81-82
Conservation
(see Environment, Externalities)
Constant prices
defined 18, 20
Consumer behaviour, theories of 12-13
Consumer durables
(see Durable goods)
Consumer expenditure
(see Consumption)
Consumer surplus 34, 48-49
defined 34
Consumers
and objectives 12-13
and resource allocation 84-86
Consumption 143-150
defined 143, 147
determinants of 143-146, 147-150
patterns of 143, 147
and aggregate demand curve 161-162
Consumption externalities 98
defined 98, 101
(See also Externalities)
Consumption function 143-146, 147-150
defined 143, 147
and composition of households 145
and credit 145, 149-150
and disposable income 143, 147
and expectations 145, 150
and inflation 144, 149, 218-219
and the rate of interest 144, 146,
149-150, 218-219
and UK 147-150
and wealth 144, 146, 148-149
Controlled experiment 24

Consumer Price Index 217-218,
221-222, 223
defined 217, 221
Corporation tax 244
Cost-push inflation 219
defined 219, 221
Council housing 35, 43
CPI (see Consumer Price Index)
Credit
and consumption 145, 149-150
Credit crunch 226
Creeping inflation
defined 217, 221
Cross elasticity of demand 66-67
defined 66, 68
and food 69-70
Cross-price elasticity of demand
(see Cross elasticity of demand)
Crowding out 235
Currencies (see Exchange rates)
Current account on the balance of
payment 224-230
defined 224, 227
deficit 130, 225-227, 225-227
surplus 130, 225-227
and exchange rates 255
and fiscal policy 234-236
and monetary policy 248-249
and policy goals 234, 235-236, 249
(See also Protectionism)
Current account deficit 130, 225-227
defined 225, 227
Current account surplus 130, 225-227
defined 225, 227
Current balance 130, 224-229
defined 225, 227
as policy goal 234, 249
(See also Balance of trade,
Invisible balance, Visible trade)
Current prices
defined 18, 20
Current transfers 95, 224, 225, 228, 229
Customs duties
vs excise duties 74
(See also Tariffs)
Cycles (see Trade cycle)
Cyclical unemployment
defined 210, 212
Czech Republic 134

D Data 17-23
collection 17-18
interpretation of 19-20
presentation of 19-20
reliability 17-18
use of 17-18
and hypotheses 17-18
Deadweight or welfare loss 98,
Decoupling 118
Default 226

Deflation
    defined 217, 221
    costs of 220
Demand 30-38
    aggregate (see Aggregate demand)
    composite 54-55
    defined 30, 34
    derived 54-55
    desired 48
    determinants of 30-33
    effective 30
    excess 45
    fall in 31
    increase in 31
    joint 53, 55
    planned 48
    and price determination 45-52
        (See also Aggregate demand,
        Competitive demand, Cross
        elasticity of demand, Demand
        curve, Derived demand,
        Economic rent, Exchange rates,
        Income elasticity of demand,
        Individual demand curve,
        Market demand curve, Price
        elasticity of demand)
Demand curve 30-38
    aggregate (see Aggregate demand
        curve)
    defined 30, 34
    elasticity along 60-62
    individual 33-34
    market 33-34
    movements along 31,
    shifts 31
    upward sloping 73, 74
    and Giffen goods 73
    and incidence of tax 80-81
    and price determination 45-52
Demand deficient unemployment
    (see Cyclical unemployment)
Demand for capital (see Capital,
    Marginal efficiency of capital)
Demand management 232-234,
    defined 232, 234
    (See also Fiscal policy)
Demand pull inflation 218-219
    defined 218, 220
Demand side policy 232-236
    defined 232, 234
Demand-side shock 186
Demerit good 107
    defined 107, 110
Demography (see Population)
Depreciation (as capital consumption)
    and investment 151
    and national income measurement
        137
Depreciation (of currency) 253-255
    defined 253, 255
        (See also Devaluation, Exchange
        rates)

Depression 129, 185
    defined 129, 132
        (See also Great Depression, Trade
        cycle)
Deregulation
    and economic growth 193
    and supply side policies 241, 244-245
Derived demand
    defined 54, 55
Desired demand 48
Desired supply 48
Disequilibrium model 26
    (See also Equilibrium)
Dismal science 202
Disposable income
    defined 143, 147
    and consumption function 143, 147
Distribution of income
    and consumption 146
    and free market economies 261
    and market failure 93
    and mixed economies 262
    and national income 139
    and pattern of economic activity 235
    and policy goals 131-132
    and savings 146
        (See also Redistribution of income)
Division of labour
    defined 11, 14
    and increased productivity 11
Domestic economy
    defined 161, 165
Downturn 185
    (See also Trade cycle)
Dubner, Stephen 202
Durable goods 143, 144, 246
    defined 143, 147
Dynamic efficiency 90
    defined 90, 93
Dynamic model
    defined 26, 27

E **Earnings** (see Wages)
    UK change in 40
Earnings trap
    defined 240, 242
Easterlin, Richard 203
Easterlin paradox 203
Economic activity
    pattern 234-235
Economic cycle (see Trade cycle)
Economic efficiency
    (see Allocative efficiency, Efficiency)
Economic goods
    defined 2, 5
    and scarcity 2
Economic growth 129-130, 185-194
    causes 186-193
    defined 185, 189
    vs recovery 186
    and aggregate supply curve 171-172

    and current account deficits 226
    and education 4, 187, 190
    and exchange rates 255
    and fiscal policy 234, 235-236
    and global warming 103
    and inflation 220
    and happiness 203-206
    and living standards 195-201
    and monetary policy 248-249
    and production possibility frontier
        4, 186
    and supply side economics 238-245
    and welfare 195-201
    as policy goal 131-132, 234, 248-249
        (See also Short-termism, Supply
        side policies)
Economic models (see Models)
Economic performance 129, 226
Economic problem
    (see Basic economic problem)
Economic recovery
    defined 186, 189
    (See also Trade cycle)
Economic systems 129, 258
    defined 258, 262
    and basic economic problem 10
        (See also Free market economies,
        Mixed economies and command
        economies)
Economic welfare (see Utility)
Economics
    definition of 2, 10
Economics of happiness 202-208
    defined 202, 206
Economies
    countries (see individual countries,
        e.g. Japan)
    functions of 10-14
    types
    (see Free market economies, Mixed
        economies, command economies)
Education
    and externalities 96
    and growth 171, 187, 190
    and human capital 190
    and long run supply curve 171
    and supply side policies 241, 243-244
    as merit good 107
Effective demand
    defined 30, 34
Efficiency 90-95
    defined 90, 93
    vs equity 93
    and basic economic problem 3
    and competition 92
    and economic growth 188
    and imperfect competition 92
    and information 92-93
    and merit goods 108, 109
    and production possibility frontier
        3, 4
    and public goods 108, 109

(See also Allocative efficiency,
Dynamic efficiency, Productive
efficiency, Static efficiency)
Elasticity of demand 59-71
and devaluation 254
and greenhouse gas emissions 102-104
(See also Cross elasticity of demand,
Income elasticity of demand,
Price elasticity of demand)
Elasticity of supply 67-68
(See also Price elasticity of supply)
Emission Trading Scheme 126-127
Employee Relations Act 242, 243
Endowment of factors
and growth 187
**Enquiry into the Nature and Causes
of the Wealth of Nations** 11, 84
Enterprise culture 244
Entrepreneur 11
Entrepreneurship
defined 11, 14
nature of 11
price of 84
Environment 96-105
and CAP 120
and economic growth 197
and government failure 125-128
and government policy 98-101, 125-128
and petrol 82
and macroeconomic policy goals
131-132
and pollution permits 100-101, 126-127
and road transport 81-82
and taxes 81-82, 100
(See also Carbon emissions
trading, Carbon offsetting, CFCs,
Externalities, Global warming,
Landfill taxes, Property rights,
Regulation, Renewable energy
certificates, Subsidies)
Environmental Protection Act 99
Equal Pay Act 1970 215
Equilibrium
defined 26, 27
stable 26, 48
unstable 26
Equilibrium model 26
Equilibrium output 177-183
long run 178-182
short run 177-178
Equilibrium price
defined 41, 45
and taxes and subsidies 78
Equity (fairness)
and government 107-108
and public and merit goods 107-108
and privatisation 4360
ESA 136
European Central Bank 256
European System of Accounts 136
European Union (EU)
and protectionism 193

(See also Common Agricultural
Policy)
Ex ante demand and supply 48
Ex post demand and supply 48
Excess demand
defined 45, 49
and minimum prices 114
(See also Demand-pull inflation,
Positive output gap)
Excess supply
defined 45, 49
Exchange
and the division of labour 12
Exchange Rate Mechanism (ERM) 256
Exchange rate systems 253
Exchange rates 253-257
defined 86
equilibrium 86
and depreciation and appreciation
253-254
and government policy 253, 254-
255, 256
and living standards 140
and monetary policy 246-247, 249
and the rate of interest 246-247,
249, 253, 256
(See also Effective exchange rate)
Excise duties and incidence of tax
78-81
Exogenous variables
and price determination 80
Expansion
and trade cycle 185
Expansionary fiscal policy 232
defined 232, 234
(See also Fiscal policy)
Expectations
and consumption 145, 150
and investment 152-153
Expenditure
and circular flow of income 135
and measurement of national
income 135-140
and price elasticity of demand 68
Expenditure and Food Survey 218, 222
Experiments 24
Export volumes 240
defined 254, 255
Exports 130
defined 224, 227
determinants of 159, 225
and aggregate demand 162, 163, 164
and depreciation 253-254
and exchange rates 159, 253-256
and injections 136
External benefit
defined 96, 101
(See also Externalities)
External cost
defined 96, 101
Externalities 96-105
defined 96, 101

in consumption 98
in production 97-98
internalising 100
negative 96
positive 96
and consumer sovereignty 116-117
and demerit goods 107
and economic growth 197
and government policy 99-101
and market failure 92
and national income 139
and taxes 100
Externalities in consumption 98
defined 98, 101
(See also Externalities)
Externalities in production 97-98
defined 97, 101
(See also Externalities)

F **Factor endowments**
and economic growth 187
Factor incomes
(see Profit, Rate of interest, Rent, Wages)
Factor mobility
barriers to 93, 240
and labour market failure 93, 240
Factors of production
defined 10, 14
and production 10-11
and resource allocation 84
(See also Capital, Factor mobility,
Labour, Land, Profit, Wages)
Fairness (see Equity)
Financial account on the balance of
payments 224
defined 224, 227
Financial economies of scale 276
Firms
aims of 13
and resource allocation 84-86
Fiscal policy 231-237
defined 231, 234
expansionary 232
UK history 235-236
loosening of 232
tightening 232
(See also Government spending,
Public Sector Net Cash
Requirement, Taxes)
Fixed capital
defined 11, 14
Fixed capital formation
(see Gross fixed capital formation)
Flexible labour market 187, 190-191
Flow
and national income 139
and saving 146
Food
consumption of 72
and cross elasticity of demand 69-70
and estimated price elasticity 69

and income elasticity 75
and inferior goods 75
Forecasting models 137
Foreign currency reserves 253, 256
Foreign exchange (see Exchange rates)
France
and control of companies 294
and growth rates 189
and investment 191, 192
Free enterprise economies
(see Free market economies)
Free exchange rate system
(see Floating exchange rate system)
Free goods
defined 2, 5
and free market economies 260
and opportunity cost 2
and property rights
and scarcity 2
Free market economies 258-261
defined 258, 262
Free market forces
defined 48, 49
Free markets
and resource allocation 84-86
(See also Free Market economies,
Markets, Supply side economics,
Supply side policies)
Free rider problem 106-107
defined 106, 110
Free trade
and economic growth 193
and supply side policies 241, 245
Frictional unemployment
defined 210, 212
Friedman, Milton 146
Full capacity
defined 171, 173
Full employment
and long run aggregate supply
curve 171, 179
and production possibility frontier
3-4, 171, 186

G7 189
GDP (see Gross domestic product)
General models
defined 26, 27
and price determination 53
**General Theory of Employment,
Interest and Money, The** 163
General theory of the second best
(see Second best, general theory of)
Geographical mobility (see Factor
mobility, North-South divide)
Germany
and current account 132-133
and growth rates 132-133, 189
and inflation 132-133
and investment 191, 192
and unemployment 132-133

Giffen, Sir Robert 73
Giffen goods
defined 73, 74,
and income and substitution effects 73
and price consumption curve 73
Global warming 102-104, 197
Globalisation
and specialisation 11
Glut 45
GNI (see Gross National Income)
Goals of firms 13
Goals of government 234, 235-236,
247-249, 254
Gold and foreign currency reserves
(see Foreign currency reserves)
Golden Rule 236
Goods (see Economic goods, Free
goods, Giffen goods, Inferior
goods, Luxuries, Merit goods,
Normal goods, Public goods,
Visible trade)
Goods market 84
Government
and free market economies 258,
259-260
and goals 234, 235-236, 247-249, 254
and mixed economies 262
and objectives 13
and planned economies 261
and resource allocation 86
(See also Budget deficits,
Government expenditure, Local
government, National Debt,
Public Sector Net Cash
Requirement, Regulation, Taxes)
Government borrowing
(see Bank of England, Public Sector
Net Cash Requirement)
Government debt (see National Debt)
Government failure 122-128
defined 122, 125
and CAP 119
**Government macro-economic
objectives** 131-132, 234, 235-236,
247-249, 254
Government policy
(see Policy goals, Policy instruments)
Government spending
reasons for 158
and aggregate demand 162, 163, 164
and fiscal policy 231-235
and injections 136
and merit goods 107
and public goods 106
and transfer payments 137, 162
Graph
presenting data 19-20
Great Depression
Green belt policies 43, 58
Greenhouse effect
(see Global Warming)
Grey goods 354

Gross domestic product (GDP)
defined 137, 140
and happiness 203-206
(See also Economic growth)
Gross fixed capital formation (GFCF)
UK 154-156
and GDP 137
(See also Investment)
Gross National Happiness 207
Gross national income (GNI)
defined 137, 140
Gross value added (GVA) 137
Growth of economy
(see Economic growth)
GVA 137

Happiness economics 202-208
defined 202, 206
Harford, Tim 202
Headline rate of inflation
defined 221
Health
and happiness 204, 206
HICP 221
Hidden hand 84
Hidden economy (see Black economy)
Homogeneous goods
and comparative advantage
91, 92
Horizontal summing
and demand 33-34
and supply 307
Hot money
defined 253, 255
Households
and consumption 145
House prices 35-36, 290
and aggregate demand 246
Housing 35-38, 43-44, 57-58
council 43
owner occupied 35, 43-44
rented 35,43
and aggregate demand 246
and consumption 144, 148
and government policy 44, 57-58
and Green Belt policies 43, 58
and interest rates 246
and mobility of labour 438-439
and new housing 43-44, 393-394
and planning restrictions 43, 57-58
and population 37, 58
and rent controls 35, 290
Housing Associations 35, 43
Human capital or wealth
defined 10, 14
and economic growth 187
and investment 151
and national income 139
and supply side policies 241, 243
and unemployment 212
Human Development Index (HDI)
206

Hyperbola
  and price elasticity of demand
    61-62
Hyperinflation 130, 217
  defined 217, 221
Hypothesis 24
  and economic data 17

I **ILO unemployment** 213-214
Immigration
Immobility (see Factor immobility)
Imperfect competition
  and efficiency 92
  and market failure 92
Import volumes
  defined 254, 255
Imported inflation
  (See Cost-push inflation)
Imports 130, 224
  defined 224, 227
  determinants of 159, 225
  and aggregate demand 162, 163
  and depreciation 253-254
  and exchange rates 253-256
  and withdrawals 136
    (See also Balance of payments,
    Balance of trade, Current
    balance, Marginal propensity to
    import)
Imputed costs
  defined 271, 279
Incentive function 85
Incentives 191, 239, 244
Incidence of taxation 78-83
  defined 79, 81
Income
  and balance of payments 224, 225,
    228, 229, 230
  and demand 30-31
    (See also Circular flow of
    income, Disposable income,
    Distribution of income,
    Equilibrium income,
    National income, Permanent
    income, Redistribution of
    income, Transitory income)
Income distribution
  (see Distribution of income)
Income effect
  defined 73, 74
  and normal, inferior and Giffen
    goods 73
  and supply of labour 239-240
Income elasticity of demand 66
  defined 66, 68
  calculation of 66
  and food 75
  and normal, inferior and Giffen
    goods 72-73
Income redistribution
  (see Redistribution of income)

Increasing returns to scale
  defined 268, 269
Independent schools 38
Index linking (see Indexation)
Index numbers 18-19, 217-218
  defined 18, 20
  (See also Retail Price Index)
**Index of Sustainable Economic
  Welfare** 206
Index of the terms of trade
  (see Terms of trade)
Indexation 220
  defined 220, 221
Indicative planning
Indirect cost (see Fixed costs)
Indirect tax
  and inflation 221
  and price 78-83
    (See also Excise duties, Value
    Added Tax)
Individual demand curve
  defined 33-34
Individual supply curve
  defined 41, 42
Industrial policy 245
Industrial relations (see Trade unions)
Industry supply curve
  (see Market supply curve)
Inefficiency
  (see Efficiency, Market failure)
Inelastic demand
  defined 60, 63
  price 60-63
  cross 67
  income 66
  and expenditure 68
    (See also Price elasticity of demand)
Inelastic supply 67
Inequality
  and economic growth 197
  and market failure 93
  (see Distribution of income, Equity)
Inferior goods 30, 72-73
  defined 72, 74
  work as 239-240
  and food 75
  and income elasticity 72-73
  and income and substitution effects
    73, 239-240
  and Giffen goods 73
  and labour 239-240
Infinite wants (see Wants)
Inflation 130, 217-223
  anticipated 220
  causes of 218-219
  costs of 218-219
  creeping 217
  defined 217, 221
  headline rate 221
  hyperinflation 130, 217
  measurement of 217-218
  unanticipated 220

underlying 221
  and aggregate output 177-183
  and the Consumer Price Index
    217-218, 221-222, 223
  and consumption 144, 149
  and economic growth 220
  and the exchange rate 255
  and exchange rate systems 255
  and fiscal policy 232-233, 235-236
  and investment 220
  and monetary policy 247, 249-251
  and policy goals 131-132, 234,
    235-236, 247, 255
  and the Retail Price Index 217-218,
    221-222, 223
  and unemployment 220
    (See also Cost-push inflation,
    Demand-pull inflation, Imported
    inflation)
Information
  and government failure 122
Information failure 92
Inheritance tax 244
Injections to circular flow 135-136, 164
  defined 135, 140
Innovation
  and economic growth 192
  and free market economies 260
  and supply side policies 244
Interest (see Rate of interest)
Interest rates (see Rate of interest)
Internalising externalities 99, 100
International competitiveness 94
International Labour Organisation (ILO)
  213
**International Natural Rubber
  Organisation (INRO)** 121
International trade (see Trade)
Intervention price 115, 117-118
Interventionist policies 239, 241-242
Inventories (see Stocks)
Inventory cycle
  defined 517, 518
Investment 151-157
  defined 151, 154
  accelerator model of 153
  marginal efficiency of capital
    theory of 151-151
  net 151
  planned 151-152
  public sector 151
  replacement 153
  UK 154-157
  and aggregate demand curve 162-163
  and aggregate output 181
  and economic growth 187, 189,
    191-192
  and human capital 151
  and injections 136
  and interest rates 246
  and long run aggregate supply 171
  as gross fixed capital formation 154

Investment grants 245
Investment multiplier (see Multiplier)
Investment schedule 151-154
  (See also Marginal efficiency of
  capital curve)
Invisible balance
  defined 224, 227
Invisible credits and debits 224
Invisible hand 84
Invisible trade
  defined 224, 227
Ireland 134, 194
Italy
  growth rates 189

J Japan
    behaviour of firms 294-295
    current account 132-133
    growth rates 132-133, 189
    inflation 132-133
    investment 191, 192
    unemployment 132-133
  Job satisfaction 408
  Joint demand
    defined 53, 55
    and price determination 53
  Joint supply
    defined 55
  just-in-time
    and long run aggregate supply 171

K Kahneman, Daniel 202
  Keynes, John Maynard
    and animal spirits 153
    and consumption function 146
    and multiplier 163
  Keynesian economics
    aggregate demand curve 164-165
    aggregate supply curve 170-173
    consumption function 146, 147
    equilibrium output 179-181
    saving 146
  Keynesian multiplier (see Multiplier)
  Keynesian unemployment
    (see Cyclical unemployment)
  Kyoto Protocol 197
  (See also Global warming)

L Labour 10, 14
    and growth 187, 190-191
    and specialisation 11
    as factor of production 10
  Labour Force Survey 213
  Labour market
    equilibrium 419, 420, 421, 422
    imperfectly competitive 421-422
    perfectly competitive 420-421
    segmented 439
    and aggregate supply 172-173,

239-241, 242-244
Labour market clearing
  classical view 172-173
  Keynesian view of 172-173
Labour mobility (see Factor mobility)
Labour market flexibility 187, 190-191
Labour productivity 11
  defined 11, 14
  (See also Productivity)
Laffer, Arthur 240
Laffer curve 239-240
  defined 239, 242
Land
  defined 10, 14
  and growth 187
Landfill tax 125-126
Laws
  defined 24, 27
Lawson, Nigel 236
Lawson boom 148, 150, 166, 236
Leakage
  defined 136, 140
  and multiplier 164
Learning and Skills Councils 244
Leisure
  activities 7-8
  markets 14
  and cinema market 23
  and objectives of economic actors
    14-15
  and opportunity cost 243
Lender of last resort 249
Levitt, Steven 202
LFS 213
Life-cycle hypothesis of consumption
  146
Living standards
  (see Standard of living)
Local authority housing 43
Long run aggregate supply curve
  170-173
  defined 170, 173
  classical 172-173
  Keynesian 172-173
  shifts in 171-172
  and equilibrium output 178-182
LRAS curve
  (see Long run aggregate supply curve)
Luxuries
  and income elasticity of demand 63
  and price elasticity of demand for
    73-74

M Maastricht Treaty 243
  Macroeconomic model 26
  Macroeconomics 26
    defined 129, 132
  Major, John 166
  Mansholt Plan 117
  Manufacturing sector
    defined 12, 14

Margin
  defined 4, 5
  and decision making 13
Marginal benefit
  and efficiency 97
    (See also Externalities, Private
    benefits, Private costs)
Marginal cost
  and externalities 97
    (See also Externalities, Private
    costs, Social costs)
Marginal efficiency of capital 151-152
  defined 151, 154
Marginal efficiency of capital curve
  explained 152-154
  shifts in 153-154
Marginal private benefit
  defined 98, 101
Marginal private cost
  defined 97-8, 101
Marginal private cost and benefit
  curves 97-98
Marginal propensity to consume
  defined 143, 147
  and multiplier 164
Marginal propensity to save
  defined 145, 147
Marginal social benefit 97-98
  defined 98, 101
Marginal social cost 97-98
  defined 98, 101
Marginal social cost and benefit
  curves 97-98
Marginal tax rates 191, 239, 244
Market
  defined 12, 14
Market clearing 45-49
  (See also Labour market clearing)
Market clearing price
  defined 45, 49
Market demand curve
  defined 27, 28
Market economies
  (see Free market economies)
Market failure 92
  defined 92, 93
  types of 92
  and externalities 96-101
  and government 99-101, 122-125
  and missing markets 92
  and prices 112
  and public choice theory 123-125
  and public and merit goods 106-107
Market forces
  and economic growth 197
Market orientated policies 239
Market prices
  and equilibrium price 45
Market stabilisation 112-121
Market supply curve
  defined 41, 42

Marshall, Alfred
and Giffen goods 73
Maximising behaviour 86
Maximum prices 112-113
Menu costs of inflation 219
Merit goods 107
defined 107, 110
and market failure 92, 107
and mixed economies 262
and prices 112
Microeconomic model 26
Microeconomics 26
defined 129, 132
Miners' strike (1984-85) 242
Minimum prices 113-114
and EU 113-114
Minimum wage legislation
and supply side economics 239
Missing markets 92
Mixed economies 261-262
defined 261, 262
Mobility of land, labour and capital
(see Factor mobility)
Models 25-26
defined 25,27
Modigliani, Franco 146
Monetary accommodation 183
Monetary policy 246-252
defined 246, 249
UK monetary policy 249-251
and aggregate demand 246-247
and control of inflation 247
and policy objectives 247-249
(See also Rate of interest)
Monetary Policy Committee (MPC)
250-251
Monetary targets 250
Money
and barter 12
and exchange 12
Montreal protocol 197
Mortgage 36-38
Motivation
and work 6
Movement along the demand curve 31
Movement along the supply curve 39
Multiplier
defined 164, 165
and fiscal policy 232
Multiplier effect 163-164
defined 163, 165
and aggregate demand 164-165

N National Curriculum 243
National Debt 231, 249
defined 231, 234
National economic performance
(see Economic performance)
National expenditure
measurement of 135
and the circular flow of income 135

(See also Aggregate demand,
National income)
National income
defined 135, 140
comparison between countries 139
comparison over time 139
measurement of 135-139
statistics, accuracy of 137-138, 196
statistics, use of 137-138
and the circular flow of income 135
and living standards 139-143,196
(For changes in national income,
see Economic growth)
National Insurance contributions
(NICs) 240, 244
National output (see Output)
National Plan 235
National Vocational Qualifications
(NVQs) 190
Necessities
and income elasticity of demand
73-74
and price elasticity of demand 63
Needs
defined 2, 5
and wants 2
Negative externality
defined 96, 101
and demerit goods 107
and prices 112
(See also Externalities)
Negative output gap
defined 186, 189
and fiscal policy 232
Neo-classical economists
and supply side economics 238-239
Net investment 151
Net invisibles
(see Balance on invisible trade)
Net national income 137
Nimby 57
Nominal GDP 188-189
Nominal values
defined 18, 20
Non-durable goods 143, 144
defined 143, 147
Non-excludability 106
Non-human wealth 139
(See also Physical capital)
Non-pure public goods
defined 107, 110
Non-renewable resources
defined 10, 14
and economic growth 197
Non-rivalry 106
Non-sustainable resources 10,14
Normal goods 30-31, 72
defined 72, 74
and food 75
and income and substitution effects 73
and work 239
Normative economics 24, 28

defined 24, 27
Normative statements
defined 24, 27
North Sea oil
and growth 187
Nuclear power 127-128

O Objectives of firms
(see Goals of firms)
Occupational mobility
(see Factor mobility)
Oil
elasticity of demand for 64-65
markets for 16
North Sea 187
UK industry 16
(See also Oil crises, OPEC)
Oil crises
as supply side shock 174-175
OPEC (Organisation for Petroleum
Exporting Countries)
and price elasticity of demand for
oil 64-65
and supply side shocks 174
as cartel 41
Open economy
defined 135, 140,
Opportunity cost
defined 2, 5
and allocation of resources 13
and basic economic problem 2-8
and comparative advantage 90
and investment 152
and leisure 6
and work 6
Organisation for Petroleum Exporting
countries (see OPEC)
Other things being equal
(see Ceteris paribus)
Output
and the circular flow 130
and national income measurement
135-139
Output gap 186, 515
defined 186, 189
negative 186
positive 186
and fiscal policy 232
and unemployment 211
Own-price elasticity of demand
(see Price elasticity of demand)
Owner occupation (see Housing)
Overheating
defined 234
Over-specialisation 11

P Paradox of value 34
Partial model
defined 26, 27
and price determination 53

Participation rate (see Activity rates)
Peak
    trade cycle 185
Pensions 483-485
    and labour mobility 240
    and opportunity cost 6
    and supply side policies 240
Perfectly or infinitely elastic and
    inelastic demand 60-61
    and tax revenues 80-81
Perfectly or infinitely inelastic
    demand and tax revenue 80-81
Perfectly elastic or inelastic supply 67
    and tax revenues 80-81
Permanent income
    defined 146, 147
Permanent income hypothesis 146
Permits
    pollution 100-101
Personal pensions 240
Personal savings ratio
    (see Average propensity to save)
Phillips curve 132
Physical capital
    and economic growth 191
    and investment 151
    and Third World 681
Picketing 242
Planned demand and supply 48
Policy goals 131-132, 234, 235-236,
    247-249, 254
Policy instruments
    (see Instrument of policy)
Pollution
    and externalities 96-101
    and free goods and scarcity 2
    and property rights 99-100,
        (See also Environment,
        Externalities)
Pollution permits 100-101
Population
    and consumption 145
    and demand 32
    and economic growth 187
    and housing 37
    and living standards 139
Pork barrel politics 13, 128
Portfolio worker 191, 240
Positive economics 24, 28
    defined 24, 27
Positive externality
    defined 96, 101
    and merit goods 107
    and prices 112
    (See also Externalities)
Positive statements
    defined 24, 27
Poverty trap 240, 242,
    defined 240, 243
Powdthavee, Nattavudh 204
PPPs (See Purchasing power parities)
Pre-Budget Report 231

Price equilibrium 45
Price ceilings 112-113
Price determination 45-52
    and complements 53
    and composite demand 54-55
    and derived demand 54
    and joint supply 55
    and substitutes 53-54
Price elasticity of demand 59-65
    defined 59, 63
    calculation 59-60
    determinants of 62-63
    elastic 60-62
    graphical presentation of 60-62
    inelastic 60-62
    infinitely or perfectly elastic 60-62
    infinitely or perfectly inelastic 60-62
    unitary elasticity 60-61
    and devaluation 254
    and food 69
    and incidence of tax 80-81
    and manufactures 112
    and total expenditure or revenue 68
Price elasticity of supply 67-68
    defined 67, 68
    calculation of 67
    determinants of 67-68
    and commodities 112
    and incidence of tax 80-81
    and manufactures 112
Price index (see Retail Price Index)
Price leadership
    defined 345, 346
Price level
    defined 217, 221
        (See also Aggregate demand
        curve, Inflation)
Price stabilisation 112-120
Price taker 236
Prices
    constant vs current 18
    and the allocation of resources 84-86
        (See also Maximum prices and
        Minimum prices)
Primary commodities
    cocoa 44
    copper 52
    milk 54
    nickel 47
    rubber 121
    tin 116
    wool 44
    and buffer stock schemes 114-116
    and price stabilisation 114-116
        (See also Oil, OPEC)
Primary sector
    defined 11, 14
Private benefits
    defined 96, 101
    (See also Externalities)
Private costs
    defined 96, 101

    (See also Externalities)
Private Finance Initiative (PFI) 245
Private goods
    defined 106, 110
Privatisation
    and economic growth 193
    and supply side policies 241, 244-245
Producer surplus 42, 48-49
    defined 42
Production externalities 97-98
    defined 97, 101
    (See also Externalities)
Production possibility boundary or
    Production possibility curve
    (see Production possibility frontier)
Production possibility frontier
    defined 3, 5
    and basic economic problem 3-5
    and economic growth 4, 186
    and efficiency 3, 4, 91
Productive capacity 185
Productive efficiency 90-91
    defined 90, 93
    and production possibility frontier 91
    and public and merit goods 109
    and supply 40
Productive potential of an economy
    and economic growth 3-4, 185, 186
    and long run aggregate supply
        curve 171
    and the production possibility
        frontier 3-4, 186
Productivity
    defined 11, 14
    and the division of labour 11
    and economic growth 193
    and education and training 190
    and national income 138
    and privatised industry 381
    and the production possibility
        frontier 4
Profit
    defined 13, 14
    and the allocation of resources 84-86
    and investment 152, 154, 156
    and objectives of firms 13
    and supply 39, 41
    and supply side policies 242
Property rights
    and pollution 99-100,101
Prospect theory 202
Protectionism
    and agriculture 94
    and economic growth 193
PSNCR (see Public Sector Net Cash
    Requirement)
Public choice theory 123-125
    defined 123,125
Public expenditure
    (see Government spending)
Public goods 106
    defined 106, 110

and free rider problem 106-107
and market failure 92, 106
Public Sector Net Cash Requirement
(PSNCR)
defined 231, 234
and balance of payment deficits 227
and demand management 235-236,
(See also Budget deficit)
Public spending
(see Government spending)
Purchasing power parities
defined 139, 140
and comparison of national income 139

Q Quasi-public goods
defined 107, 110
and transport 501
Quotas
and CAP 118
(See also Protectionism)

R Rate of interest
defined 246, 249
determination 85
determined by Bank of England 249
real 220
and aggregate demand 246-247, 248
and consumption 144, 146, 149-150
and economic growth 248-249
and the exchange rate 246-247, 249,
253, 256
and inflation 247, 249-251
and monetary policy 246-252
and unemployment 247
Rationality
and basic economic problem 3
and public spending 107
Rationing function 85
Real GDP 188-189
Real multiplier (see Multiplier)
Real rate of interest 220
Real values
defined 18, 20
Realised demand 48
Realised supply 48
Recession
defined 129, 132
and economic growth 185
and inflation 217
and output gap 186
(See also Cyclical
unemployment, Trade cycle)
Recovery 185, 514
(See also Trade cycle)
Rectangular hyperbola
and unitary elasticity 61-62
Red tape 243, 244,
Redistribution of income
and consumption 146
and inflation 220

(See also Distribution of income)
Reflation (see Recovery)
Regional Development Agencies 244, 245
Regional policy 245
Regional unemployment 210
(See also Structural unemployment)
Regulation
and externalities 98-99,101
and pollution 98-99,101
and public and merit goods 108,
109, 110
Renewable Energy Certificates 127
Renewable resources
defined 10, 14
Rent controls 35, 290, 112-113
Rented housing (see Housing)
Repo rate 250
Research and Development (R&D)
and economic growth 192
Reserves (see Gold and foreign
currency reserves)
Resource allocation (see Allocation of
resources)
Resources
renewable vs non-renewable 10
and basic economic problem 2-5
and economic growth 197
(See also Land)
Retail Price Index (RPI)
construction of 18
RPIX 221, 222
RPIY 221, 222
and measurement of inflation
217-218, 221-222, 223
Retained profit
defined 152, 154
and investment 152, 154, 156
Retirement 6
(see also Pensions)
Revenue
and elasticity 68
and tax 79
Risk
and entrepreneurship 11
RPI (see Retail Price Index)
RPIX 198, 199
RPIY 198, 199

S Salaries (see Wages)
Sampling 17
Satisfaction (see Utility)
Saving
defined 143, 147
determinants 145-146
and growth 192
and interest rates 246
and withdrawals 136
Savings
vs saving 146
Savings function
defined 145, 147

Savings ratio
(see Average propensity to save)
Scarce resources
defined 1, 5
and basic economic problem 1, 10
Scientific method
defined 24, 27
and economic data 17
Seasonal unemployment
defined 210, 212
Secondary picketing 242
Secondary sector
defined 12, 14
(See also Manufacturing industry)
Secret ballot 242
Sectoral unemployment 210
(See also Structural unemployment)
Sectors of industry 12
(See also Primary sector, Secondary
sector, Tertiary sector)
Service industry (see Tertiary sector)
Set aside 118
Shares
upward sloping demand curve for 74
and consumption 144, 148
Shift in the demand curve
defined 31, 34
Shift in the supply curve 40-41
Shoe leather costs of inflation 219
Short run aggregate supply curve 169-170
defined 169, 173
assumptions behind 170
shifts in 170
Short-termism 124, 192
Shortages 45
Signalling function 85-86
Simplification
and model building 26
Slumpflation (see Stagflation)
Small Business Service 243, 244
Small businesses
and supply side policies 241, 244
Smith, Adam
and the division of labour 11
and free markets 84,
and paradox of value 34
SNA 136
Snob appeal
and upward sloping demand
curves 74
Social benefits
defined 96, 101
(See also Externalities)
Social Charter 243
Social costs
defined 96, 101
and unemployment 212
Social housing 43
Social security taxes 244
Social science 24
Social security benefits
(see Welfare benefits)

Specialisation 11, 12
    defined 11, 14
    and increased productivity 11
    and long run aggregate supply 171
    (See also Division of labour)
Specific tax
    defined 78, 81
    and incidence of tax 78-81
Speculative goods
    and upward sloping demand curve 74
Spillover effect (see Externalities)
SRAS curve (see Short run aggregate
    supply curve)
Stable equilibrium price 48
Stagflation
    in UK 182-183
Stakeholders
    defined 13, 14
Standard of living
    and economic growth 195-201
    and happiness 203-206
    and national income 139-143
State benefits (see Welfare benefits)
Static efficiency 90
    defined 90, 93
Static model
    defined 26, 27
Stock (vs flows)
    and saving 146
    and unemployment 209
    and wealth 139
Stocks (physical)
    as working capital 11
Strikes 242
Structural unemployment
    defined 210, 212
Subsidies
    defined 78, 81
    and price determination 79, 81
    and public and merit goods 108, 109
    (See also Common Agricultural
    Policy)
Subsistence economy 138
Substitutes
    defined 53, 55
    and cross elasticity of demand 67
    and determination of price 53-54
    and determination of price elasticity
    of demand 58-59
    and determination of elasticity of
    supply 68
Substitution effect
    defined 73, 74
    and Giffen, inferior and normal
    goods 73
    and supply of labour 239-240
Superior goods (see Luxuries)
Supply curve 39-42
    defined 39, 42
    horizontal summing 41
    individual 41
    joint 55

market 41
    movements along 39
    shifts in 40, 45-47
    and indirect taxes and subsidies 78-81
    and price determination 45-52
    (See also Aggregate supply curve)
Supply of goods 39-44
    defined 39, 42
    desired 48
    determinants of 39-41
    fall in 39, 40
    joint 55
    planned 48
    and price determination 45-52
        (See also Excess supply, Price
        elasticity of supply)
Supply of labour
    and supply side economics 239
Supply of money (see Money supply)
Supply side economics 239
    defined 239, 242
    and growth theory 190-191
    and unemployment 238
Supply side policies 238-245
    defined 238, 242
    and aggregate demand 242
    and economic growth 190-191
Supply side shocks 170, 186
    defined 170, 173
    (See also Oil, Aggregate supply curve)
Survey
    and economic data 17
Sustainable development 197
Sustainable growth
    defined 197, 198
Sustainable resources
    defined 10, 14
System of National Accounts 136

T   **Tables**
    presenting data 19
Targets
    defined 249
    and exchange rate policy 254
    and monetary policy 250
Tax allowance 220
Tax, incidence 78-81
    defined 78, 81
Tax rates
    marginal 191, 239, 244
    and incentives to work 191, 239, 244
Tax revenues
    and the incidence of tax 79, 80-81
    and inflation 220
    and unemployment 215
Taxes
    ad valorem 78-81
    indirect 78-81
    specific 78-81
    unit 78-81
    and economic growth 191

    and environment 81-82,100, 101
    and externalities 100
    and fiscal policy 231-235
    and happiness 206
    and hidden economy 138
    and inflation 220
    and investment 241
    and supply side policies 239-240,
        241, 244
    and unemployment 212
    and withdrawals 136
Technical efficiency 90-91
    defined 90, 93
Technical progress
    and growth 186, 192-193
    and investment 152
    and living standards 139
    and production possibility frontier 4
Technological unemployment 210
    (See also Structural unemployment)
Technology
    appropriate 197
    and complements 53
    and housing 43-44
    and investment 152
    and long run aggregate supply
        curve 171
    and long run costs 278
    and the production function 266
    and supply 40
    and the very long run 266
Tertiary sector
    defined 12, 14
    (See also Service industry)
Thatcher, Margaret 165, 235
Theory 24-25
    defined 24, 27
    and data 17
Theory of the second best
    (see Second best, general theory of)
Time
    and price elasticity of demand 63
    and elasticity of demand for labour 403
    and elasticity of supply 68
Total expenditure
    and elasticity 68
Tourism
    and destinations for UK residents
        76-77
    and UK employment 21-22
    and UK spending on 21
Trade
    and money and exchange 12
Trade cycle 185-186
    defined 185, 189
Trade deficit
    (see Balance of payments, Balance
    of trade, Current account on the
    balance of payments)
Trade gap 225
Tradable permits
    (see Pollution permits)

Trade-offs
and government policy 132, 234, 249

Trade surplus
(see Balance of payments, Balance of trade, Current account on the balance of payments)

Trade unions
and market failure 92
and supply side policies 239, 242-243

Trade weighted exchange rate index
(see Effective exchange rate)

Training
and externalities 96
and economic growth 190
and merit good 107
and supply side policies 241, 243-244

Transfer payments
defined 137, 140
and government spending 162
and national income accounts 137
and unemployment benefits 212

Transformation curve
(see Production possibility frontier)

Trend rate of growth
and long run aggregate supply 170-171
Trough 185

U **Unanticipated inflation** 220
Uncertainty (see Risk)
Underemployment 685
Underlying rate of inflation 221, 339
defined 221

Undistributed profit
(see Retained profit)

Unemployment 130, 209-216,
claimant 213-214
costs 211-212
ILO unemployment 213-214
measurement 209, 213-214
types 209-211
and exchange rates 255
and fiscal policy 234-236
and inflation 220
and monetary policy 247-248
and policy goals 131-132, 234, 235-236, 248-249
and production possibility frontiers 4, 186, 210

Unemployment benefit
and incentives to work 239, 243,
and measurement of unemployment 213

Unemployment trap 240, 243
defined 240, 242

Unit tax 78-81
defined 78, 81

Unitary elasticity 60-61
defined 60, 63

United States
balance of payments 132-133

growth rates 132-133, 191
inflation rates 132-133
investment 191, 192
unemployment 132-133

Unstable equilibrium 48
Utilitarianism 202
Utility
defined 13, 14
maximisation 86

V **Value Added Tax** (VAT)
and the incidence of tax 78-81

Veblen goods 74
Velocity of circulation of money
579-583, 600
defined 579, 583

Visible exports 224
Visible imports 224
Visible trade
defined 224, 227
(See also Balance of trade)

W **Wages, wage rates, pay and earnings**
and aggregate supply 170-173
(See also Minimum wage)

Wants
defined 2, 5
and basic economic problem 2, 10

Wealth
monetary or financial 144
physical 144
v. national income 139
and consumption 144, 146, 149-150
and monetary policy 246
(See also Capital, Human capital, Physical capital)

Wealth of Nations, The
(See Smith, Adam)

Weighted index 217-218, 222
(See also Retail Price Index)

Welfare benefits
and supply side policies 239, 243,
and transfer payments 137

Withdrawal
defined 136, 140
and multiplier 164

Work
and happiness 204, 206
and inferior goods 239
and motivation 6
and opportunity cost 6-7

Working capital
defined 11, 14

Working tax credit 243